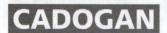

South of France

Cadogan Guides
West End House, 11 Hills Place, London W1R 1AH, UK
e-mail:guides@cadogan.demon.co.uk

The Globe Pequot Press
6 Business Park Road, PO Box 833, Old Saybrook, Connecticut
06475–0833

Copyright © Dana Facaros and Michael Pauls 1992, 1994, 1997,
1999
Illustrations © Pauline Pears 1992, 1994, 1996

Updated by Mark Igoe 1999
Additional updating: Jacqueline Chnéour and Linda McQueen

Book and cover design by Animage
Maps © Cadogan Guides, drawn by Map Creation Ltd

Editor: Dominique Shead
Series editor: Linda McQueen
Editorial director: Vicki Ingle

Proofreading: Susannah Wight
Indexing: Caroline Wilding
Production: Book Production Services

A catalogue record for this book is available from the British Library
ISBN 1-86011-908-5

The author and publishers have made every effort to ensure the accuracy of the information in this book at
the time of going to press. However they cannot accept any responsibility for any loss, injury or
inconvenience resulting from the use of information contained in this guide.

Printed in Great Britain by Cambridge University Press

Promenade des Anglais.

Acknowledgements

The authors would like to thank Yves and Marie Roland-Gosselin in Ganges. Thanks also to Eric and Gordon at Sardine Research in Sète; and to Mark Igoe for updating this edition, apart from the French Riviera chapter which was updated by Jacqueline Chnéour and Linda McQueen.

The publishers would like to thank Susannah Wight for proofreading and Caroline Wilding for indexing.

About the Authors

Dana Facaros and Michael Pauls have written over 20 books for Cadogan Guides including four on France. They live in southwest Ireland with their two children and seven cats.

About the Updater

Mark Igoe has been travel writing for twenty years and visiting France for thirty. On this occasion he was ably assisted by Dr Peter Carnell, accomplished geophysicist, archaeologist, arcane phone number finder and upside-down map reader.

Please help us to keep this guide up to date

We have done our best to ensure that the information in this guide is correct at the time of going to press. But places and facilities are constantly changing, and standards and prices in hotels and restaurants fluctuate. We would be delighted to receive any comments concerning existing entries or omissions, as well as suggestions for new features. All contributors will be acknowledged in the next edition, and authors of the best letters will receive a copy of the Cadogan Guide of their choice.

Contents

Art and Architecture

Topics

The French Riviera: Menton to Cannes

The Côte d'Azur: l'Esterel to Bandol

Introduction

'Our nights are
more beautiful
than your days,'
Racine boasted to
his Parisian friends,
writing home from Uzès in the Gard. The nights are indeed thrilling, dry and
clear and boiling with stars. After dawn, the southern sun quickens landscapes of sculpted hills and purple mountains, cypresses and lavender.
Vincent Van Gogh, who saw more clearly into the heart of this extravagant
world than anyone else, painted those landscapes, and especially those
cypresses, as if they were moving and alive, with a lyrical and passionate
intensity. Come to the hills around St-Rémy when the mistral is up, and you
will see nature imitating art.

We outsiders have had an on-again off-again love affair with the south of
France ever since the Romans colonized it and spent their decline lounging
around their heated pools. Even the medieval popes and cardinals in
Avignon succumbed to its worldly temptations, its wines and the scents of its
maquis, its roses and violets, the droning hum of the cicadas. The popes'
court painters, some of the greatest artists of the 14th century, lent their
radiant Madonnas something of the voluptuous Mediterranean light and
colour that would one day inspire Van Gogh, Cézanne, Renoir, Matisse and
the Fauves, painters whose works have changed the way our eyes see not
only the south of France, but the rest of our world as well.

These days, our world has decided on Provence as its possible paradise.
Millions of people come here every year, hoping to catch a glimpse of it,
wishing it didn't have so many second homes, holiday flats, trinket shops
and traffic jams. To see the region at its best the delicate question of *when* to
go becomes as important as where; in August, the worst month, even the
dullest town on the coast of Provence can be as frantic as the monkey-pit in a
zoo. One reason why we've included Languedoc-Roussillon, the 'other',

western half of Mediterranean France, is not only for its own considerable and undeservedly little-known merits, but because much more of it is unspoiled. Within this larger territory, extending from the Alps to the Pyrenees, there's something for every taste: relics and monuments of a past that goes back a million years; medieval villages, some all but abandoned Brigadoons and others immaculately restored; world-class collections of art; mountain wildernesses and national parks; lively music and theatre festivals; ski resorts and wine roads; casinos and nightclubs; superb markets and restaurants that rival Paris' finest. Of course you can simply do as the Romans did and lounge around the pool, idly dreaming about what's for lunch. No wonder that Pope Gregory XI, who returned the papacy to Rome in 1377, took one look at the Eternal City and immediately decided to pack his bags to return to the comforts and delights of Avignon. Much to the relief of the Italians, he died before he could go.

A Guide to the Guide

Never think that this nebulous Anglo-Saxon concept 'the South of France' has any definite boundaries. Every writer who has ever covered the subject draws the line where he or she sees fit, and we must do the same. We definitely think we've given you the best of it, pushing as far into such inland regions as the Provençal Alps if there is something worth the trip. The real innovation is that this book covers the entire French Mediterranean coast, offering a surprising alternative to overcrowded Provence—Languedoc and Roussillon.

For convenience's sake, the contents of this book follow a fairly strict east to west order, beginning on the Italian frontier with the eastern section of the Côte d'Azur. This is **The French Riviera**, with dramatic corniche roads and outrageous fleshpots like Monaco and Cannes, as well as great museums of modern art, music festivals, and superb restaurants; here too is Nice, one of the most delightful cities in France. **The Côte d'Azur** covers the western Côte d'Azur: the blood-red cliffs of the Esterel and the chestnut forests of the Maures, the lovely Iles d'Hyères, the navy city of Toulon and France's beach-blanket Babylon, St-Tropez. To the west, in **Metropolitan Provence**, lies Marseille, the metropolis of Provence, set in a coastline of dramatic cliffs and fjord-like *calanques*; here too is staid and elegant Aix-en-Provence, and the lovely countryside around Cézanne's Mont Ste-Victoire.

The Provençal Alps follows the same east–west course, but takes the inland route through the maritime Alps and their secret valleys, difficult of access but worth the trouble for the scenery—Mercantour National Park and the Grand Canyon of the Verdon—and for the art in their medieval chapels. Next (**Northern Provence: the Vaucluse**) comes the heartland of Provence: the Lubéron and Mont Ventoux, and pockets of exquisite villages full of artists and refugees from the coast. From here we descend the Rhône, beginning in **Down the Rhône: Orange to Beaucaire** with Orange and its Roman theatre, through lively Avignon, the medieval city of the popes, and through the celebrated vineyards of Châteauneuf-du-Pape and Tavel, France's finest rosé. As the Rhône continues south (**Down the Rhône: the Alpilles, Crau and Camargue**) it passes some of the south's most curious natural features: the jagged

Alpilles, the rock-strewn plain of the Crau, and the marshlands of the Camargue, where Provençal cowboys herd wild bulls and horses. Roman Provence is well represented in St-Rémy and Arles, and the Middle Ages come to life in St-Gilles and Aigues-Mortes.

West of the Rhône lies Languedoc, with all the interest of Provence and only the fraction of the tourists—except perhaps at the magnificent Pont du Gard, one of the three most visited sights in France. This is covered in **Nîmes, the Gard and Montpellier**, along with the art town of Uzès, Nîmes with its famous Roman monuments, and dynamic Montpellier, a university city that rivals Paris in its enthusiasm for culture and technology. **The Hérault** introduces the biggest wine-producing region of France, with rural delights equal to those of Provence—little wine regions like the Minervois, and the serendipitous tree-lined Canal du Midi. Its coast offers long miles of open beaches and the pretty resort town of Agde, founded by the ancient Greeks.

The next *département* is the Aude, (**Narbonne, Carcassonne and the Corbières**); here you'll find the surprising city of Narbonne, with its magnificent cathedral; Carcassonne, the biggest and best-preserved medieval fortress city in Europe; and scores of spectacular castles hanging over the lonely landscapes of the Corbières. Last but not least, there are the Catalans in **Roussillon**: sweet wines, medieval art, Pyrenean valleys and the delicious Côte Vermeille on the Spanish border.

Travel

Before You Go

A little preparation will help you get much more out of your holiday in the south of France. Check the calendar of events (*see* pp.16–18) to help you decide where you want to be and when, and book accommodation early. If you plan to base yourself in one area, write ahead to the local tourist offices listed in the text for complete lists of self-catering accommodation, hotels, and campsites in their areas, or else contact one of the many companies in the UK or USA (see pp.31–2). For more general information and a complete list of tour operators, get in touch with a French Government Tourist Office:

UK: 178 Piccadilly, London W1V OAL, ✆ (0891) 244 123.

Ireland: 10 Suffolk St, Dublin 1, ✆ (1) 679 0813, ✉ (1) 874 7424.

Australia: Level 22, 25 Bligh St, Sydney, NSW 2000, ✆ (02) 9231 5898.

USA: 444 Madison Avenue, New York, NY 10022, ✆ (900) 990 0040, ✉ (212) 838 7855; 676 N. Michigan Ave, Chicago, IL 60611, ✆ (312) 751 7800, ✉ (312) 357 6339; 9454 Wilshire Blvd, Suite 715, Beverly Hills, CA 90212, ✆ (310) 271 6665, ✉ (310) 276 2835. Nationwide information ✆ freephone (900) 990 0040.

Canada: 1 1981 Ave McGill College, No. 490, Montreal, Quebec H3A 2W9, ✆ (514) 288 4264, ✉ (514) 845 4868; 30 St Patrick St, Suite 700, Toronto M5T 3A3, ✆ (416) 593 4723, ✉ (416) 979 7587.

Getting There

By Air

The main international airports in the south of France are at Nice, Marseille, Montpellier and Toulouse. Thanks to deregulation and the disintegration of state monopolies, prices are becoming more competitive; shop around and book ahead, especially in the summer and during the Easter holidays, to ensure a seat and save money. Check with your travel agent or your major Sunday newspaper for bargains or packages. There are a number of charters from London to Nice, but from most other points of departure—the rest of the UK, Ireland, North America, Australia, etc.—it's often cheaper to fly to Paris and from there catch a cheap flight or train to the south: Air France's air-rail France Vacance pass may be your best deal. Air France, London, ✆ (0181) 742 6600, has a daily service to Toulouse from London Heathrow, to Nice in association with British Midland and serves Marseille via Paris. British Airways ✆ (0345) 222111, serves Nice with four flights a day from Heathrow; Marseille with three flights a day from Gatwick; Montpellier daily from Gatwick; and Toulouse three times daily from Gatwick. There is a BA reservations number in France on ✆ 0802 802 902.

British Midland, ✆ (0345) 554554, has two flights a day to Nice fom London Heathrow, or East Midlands Airport with excursion fares from £139 return, while new no-frills airline Easyjet, ✆ (0990) 292929, also flies daily to Nice, from Luton and Liverpool airports, with fares starting as low as £39 single if you book well in advance. Ryanair, ✆ (0541) 569 569, now flies from Stansted to Carcassonne, return fares at present £93 but with frequent specials. All services may be less frequent in winter.

There are domestic flights on Air France from Orly Airport in Paris to Marseille and Toulouse (every half hour), Nice (every hour) and less frequently Nîmes, Perpignan, Toulouse and Montpellier; sizeable discounts exist if you fly in low 'blue' periods (in the UK, contact Nouvelles Frontières, 2/3 Woodstock St, London W1R 1HE, ☎ (0171) 620 2233). Students who equip themselves with the relevant ID cards are eligible for considerable reductions, not only on flights, but on trains and admission fees to museums, concerts, and more. Agencies specializing in student and youth travel can help in applying for the cards: try STA, ☎ (0171) 361 6161, and Campus Travel, ☎ (0171) 730 3402, in London or branches throughout the UK; STA, ☎ (03) 347 4711, in Australia; STA, ☎ (800) 777 0112, in the US; CUTS, ☎ (416) 979 2406 in Canada.

By Train

Air prices and airport hassles make France's highspeed TGVs (*trains à grande vitesse*) a very attractive alternative. TGVs shoot along at the average of 170mph when they're not breaking world records, and the journey from Paris' Gare de Lyon to Marseille takes only 4 hours and 44 minutes; to Avignon 3 hours and 45 minutes; to Montpellier 5 hours; to Nice 7 hours. Costs are only minimally higher on a TGV. Some weekday departures require a supplement (30–40F); all require a seat reservation (20F), which you can make when you buy your ticket or at the station before departure. Another pleasant if slower way of getting there is by overnight sleeper after dinner in Paris, although beware: robberies in the compartments at night have been known to occur. People under 26 are eligible for a 30% discount on fares (*see* the travel agencies above) and there are other discounts if you're 60 or over available from major travel agents.

If you plan some long train journeys, look into the variety of rail passes: France's national railway, the SNCF, offers foreign travellers France Railpass that gives you either four days (they don't have to be consecutive) of unlimited travel in a 15-day period, or nine days of travel within 30 days. It includes extras like a day's free travel in Paris (from the airport, the Métro, etc.), TGV supplements (except the seat reservation), and discounts on car rentals and Channel crossings. Get it before you leave from travel agents or SNCF offices: at 179 Piccadilly, London W1, 'The Rail Shop', ☎ (0990) 300003 for bookings. For other possible passes and discounts once you arrive in France, *see* below (p.5). For simple information SNCF has created a new organization Rail Europe, whereby you pay for the pleasure of asking for train times; it costs 50p a minute at all times, ☎ (0990) 848848. This handles bookings for all services including Eurostar and Motor Rail, and acts for other continental railway companies. In the USA contact 610 Fifth Ave, New York, NY 10020, ☎ (212) 582 2816 (or ☎ (800) 848 7245). Other alternatives include the well-known Inter-Rail pass for European residents (of at least 6 months) under the age of 26, which offers a month's unlimited travel in Europe and 50% reductions on Channel ferries, and various Eurail passes for non-Europeans, valid for 15 days to three months.

By Coach

Unless you land a bargain plane ticket, the cheapest way to get from London to the south of France is by National Express Eurolines coach ☎ (0990) 80 80 80; tickets available from any National Express office. There are two journeys a week: to Aix and Marseille (19 hours); to Avignon (19 hours approximately) and to Toulouse (22 hours).

A car entering France must have its registration and insurance papers. If you're coming from the UK or Ireland, the dip of the headlights must be adjusted to the right. Carrying a warning triangle is mandatory, and this should be placed 50m behind the car if you have a breakdown. Drivers with a valid licence from an EU country, Canada, the USA or Australia no longer need an international licence. If you're driving down from the UK, you can either go through or around Paris, a task best tackled on either side of the rush hour, or take the A26 via Rheims and Troyes. The various autoroutes will get you south the fastest but be prepared to pay some 500F in tolls; the N7 south of Paris takes much longer, but costs nothing and offers great scenery.

A fairly comfortable but costly option is to put your car on the train. Motorail accommodation is compulsory, in a 4-berth (1st class) or 6-berth (2nd class) carriage. Linen is provided, along with washing facilities. Compartments are not segregated by sex. Services run from both Boulogne and Dieppe to Avignon and Fréjus/St-Raphaël, and from Boulogne to Nice and also to Narbonne.

Taking Le Shuttle is the most convenient way to travel by car to France. It takes only half an hour from Folkestone to Calais on the train while remaining in your car, although you can get up to stretch your legs. Shuttles through the Channel Tunnel in low season cost £169 return, rising to £199 return at peak times. If you travel at night (10pm–6am) the cost drops to £149 return. The price is per car less than 6.5m in length, driver and all passengers; for information and bookings, call ✆ (0990) 353535.

If you prefer the bracing sea air, you've plenty of choice, although changes and mergers may be on the horizon. Short ferry crossings currently include Dover–Calais with P&O ✆ (0990) 980 980, SeaFrance ✆ (0990) 711711, and Stena ✆ (0990) 707070, or by Hoverspeed, ✆ (0990) 240241, which offers the fastest crossing at 35 minutes. Stena also operates Newhaven–Dieppe, P&O has crossings from Portsmouth to Cherbourg and Le Havre, and Brittany Ferries, ✆ (0990) 360360, operates between Plymouth and Roscoff in Brittany. Prices vary considerably according to season and demand so it pays to shop around for the best deal.

If you plan to hire a car, look into air and holiday package deals as well as combination 'Train and Auto' rates to save money, or consider leasing a car if you mean to stay three weeks or more. Prices vary widely from firm to firm, and beware the small print about service charges and taxes: three firms to try in the US are France Auto Vacances, ✆ (800) 234 1426, Europe by Car Inc, ✆ (800) 223 1516 or Renault, ✆ (800) 221 1052.

Entry Formalities

Passports and Visas

Holders of EU, US and Canadian passports do not need a visa to enter France for stays of up to three months, but everyone else still does. Apply at your nearest French Consulate: the most convenient visa is the *visa de circulation*, allowing for multiple stays of three months over a three-year period. If you intend to stay longer, the law says you need a *carte de séjour*, a requirement EU citizens can easily get around as passports are rarely stamped. Usually non-EU citizens can as well, but the creeping rise of xenophobic legislation in France as a sop to the extreme right wing National Front—which has its powerbase in the south—suggests that non-EU citizens had best apply for an extended visa before leaving home, a complicated procedure requiring proof of income, etc. You can't get a *carte de séjour* without the visa, and obtaining it is a trial run in the *ennuis* you'll undergo in applying for a *carte de séjour* at your local *mairie*.

Health and Travel Insurance

Citizens of the EU who bring along their E-111 forms are entitled to the same health services as French citizens. This means paying up front for medical care and prescriptions, of which costs 75–80% are reimbursed a week to ten days later. As an alternative, consider a travel insurance policy, covering theft and losses and offering 100% medical refund; check to see if it covers your extra expenses in case you get bogged down in airport or train strikes. Beware that accidents resulting from sports are rarely covered by ordinary insurance. Canadians may or may not be covered in France by their provincial health coverage; Americans and others should check their individual policies.

Getting Around

By Train

Nationwide information number, © 08 36 35 35 35 (3.35F a minute).

The SNCF runs a decent and efficient network of trains through the major cities of the south, with an added service called the *Métrazur* that links all the resorts of the Côte d'Azur from Menton to St-Raphaël as often as every half hour in the peak summer season. There are two narrow-gauge trains worth taking for their mountain scenery: the Nice to Digne *Train des Pignes* operated by the Chemin de Fer de Provence (French rail passes are valid, other passes are granted a 50% discount) and the SNCF's *Le Petit Train Jaune* from Villefranche-de-Conflent to Latour-de-Carol in the Pyrenees, with bus connections at either end to Perpignan and Andorra.

Prices have recently gone up but are still reasonable. If you plan on making only a few long hauls the France Railpass (*see* above) will save you money. Other possible discounts hinge on the exact time of your departure. The SNCF has divided the year into blue (off-peak) and white (peak) periods, based on demand: white periods run from Friday noon to midnight Saturday, and from Sunday 3pm to Monday 10am and during holidays (all stations give out little calendars). If you depart in a Période Bleue with a return ticket and travel over 1000km you'll get a 25% discount (Billet Séjour). Couples are eligible for a free Carte Couple which entitles one to pay half-fare when travelling together if they depart during a blue period. Anyone over 60 can purchase a Carte Vermeil (270F) valid for a year, offering 50% off blue period departures, 20% off white period, and 30% off train journeys from France to 20 countries in Europe; a Carte Vermeil limited to four departures is 143F. There is also a 12–25 card which offers 50% reductions on blue period and TGV classes AD and BD and a 25% reduction on white period and TGV classes AP and BP. Anyone can save money by buying a second-class ticket at least a week in advance (Découverte), the only condition being that you must use it at the designated time on the designated train, with no chance for reimbursement if you miss it.

Tickets must be stamped in the little orange machines by the entrance to the lines that say *Compostez votre billet* (this puts the date on the ticket, to keep you from using the same one over and over again). Any time you interrupt a journey until another day, you have to re-compost your ticket. Long-distance trains (*Trains Corail*) have snack trolleys and bar/cafeteria cars; some have play areas for small children. Nearly every station has large computerized lockers (*consigne automatique*) which take about half an hour to puzzle out the first time you use them, so plan accordingly; also note that any recent terrorist activity in France tends to close them down across the board.

By Bus

Do not count on seeing any part of rural France by public transport. The bus network is barely adequate between major cities and towns (places often already well served by rail) and rotten in rural areas, where the one bus a day fits the school schedule, leaving at the crack of dawn and returning in the afternoon; more remote villages are linked to civilization only once a week or not at all. Buses are run either by the SNCF (replacing discontinued rail routes) or private firms. Rail passes are valid on SNCF lines and they generally coincide with trains. Private bus firms, especially when they have a monopoly, tend to be a bit more expensive than trains; some towns have a *gare routière* (coach station), usually near the train station, though many lines start from any place that catches their fancy.

By Car

Unless you plan to stick to the major cities or the coast, a car is regrettably the only way to see most of Provence and Languedoc. This too has its drawbacks: expensive petrol and car hire rates, and an accident rate double that of the UK (and much higher than the US). The vaunted French logic and clarity breaks down completely on the asphalt. Be careful; in Carcassonne, for example, there is an intersection where traffic converges from five directions, regulated by a signal that gives the green light simultaneously to three of them. Never expect any French driver to be aware of the possibility of a collision.

Roads are generally excellently maintained, but anything of less status than a departmental route (D-road) may be uncomfortably narrow. Mountain roads are reasonable except in the vertical department of Alpes-Maritimes, where they inevitably follow old mule tracks. Shrines to St Eloi, patron of muleteers, are common here, and a quick prayer is a wise precaution. Conditions vary widely; in rural Languedoc you may catch up on your sleep while you drive; traffic in the Côte d'Azur, the 'California of Europe', can be diabolically Californian and parking a nightmare. Many towns now have pricey guarded car parks underneath their very heart, spectacularly so in Nice, and even in smaller towns such as Vence. Everywhere else, the blue 'P' signs will infallibly direct you to a village or town's already full car park. Watch out for the tiny signs that indicate which streets are meant for pedestrians only (with complicated schedules in even tinier print); and for Byzantine street parking rules (which would take pages to explain—do as the natives do, and especially be careful about village centres on market days).

Unless sweetened in an air or holiday package deal, car hire in France is an expensive proposition (350–400F a day, without mileage for the cheapest cars; *see* p.4). Petrol (*essence*) at the time of writing is 6F a litre for unleaded, 6.40F a litre leaded, 4.50 for diesel (*gasoil*), but varies considerably, with motorways always dearer. Petrol stations keep shop hours (most close Sunday and/or Monday) and are rare in rural areas, so consider your fuel supply while planning any forays into the mountains—especially if you use unleaded. If you come across a garage with petrol-pump attendants, they will expect a tip for oil, windscreen-cleaning or air.

Speed limits are 130km/80mph on the autoroutes (toll motorways); 110km/69mph on dual carriageways (divided highways); 90km/55mph on other roads; 50km/30mph in an 'urbanized area'—as soon as you pass a white sign with a town's name on it and until you pass another sign with the town's name barred. Fines for speeding, payable on the spot, begin at

1300F and can be astronomical if you fail the breathalyser. If you wind up in an accident, the procedure is to fill out and sign a *constat amiable*. If your French isn't sufficient to deal with this, hold off until you find someone to translate for you so you don't accidentally incriminate yourself. If you have a breakdown and are a member of a motoring club affiliated with the Touring Club de France, ring the latter; if not, ring the police. The French have one delightfully civilized custom of the road; if oncoming drivers unaccountably flash their headlights at you, it means that the *gendarmes* are lurking just up the way.

Always give priority to the right (*priorité à droite*) at any intersection—anywhere, unless you're on a motorway or on a road with a yellow diamond 'priority route' sign. This French anachronism is a major cause of accidents; most people only follow the rule when they're feeling generous. When you (inevitably) get lost in a town or city, the *toutes directions* or *autres directions* signs are like Get Out of Jail Free cards.

By Boat

The major towns, as well as the islands, along the Côte d'Azur are linked by regular boat services. These come in handy especially in the summer when travelling by road is hot purgatory. Most are included in the text; just look for signs near the port for the Gare Maritime. In Languedoc, *see* the 'Getting Around' sections for Narbonne and Béziers for cruises and boat rentals on the Canal du Midi and the lagoons.

Yacht, motorboat and sailing-boat charters are big business, especially along the Riviera. Companies and individual owners hire them out by the hour or day, or in the case of yachts, by the week or fortnight. Average cost per week for a 16m yacht that sleeps six, including food, drink and all expenses is 90,000F—about what six people would pay for a week in a luxury hotel. If things are slow you may dicker the price down. Contact individual tourist offices for lists of firms or try Camper & Nicholsons, 25 Bruton Street, London W1X 7DB, ✆ (0171) 629 2769, website www.cnconnect.com. Books on sailing in the area include Reeds' Mediterranean Navigator (Thomas Reed Publications) and South France Pilot by Robin Brandon (Imray Laurie); these and other nautical books and maps in English may be found at Le Silmar, 10 Rue Jean Braco, 06310 Beaulieu-sur-Mer, ✆ 04 93 01 36 71. For canal-boats, *see* 'Special Interest Holidays', below.

By Bicycle

Cycling spells more pain than pleasure in most French minds, and one of the hazards of driving in the Alps and Pyrenees is suddenly coming upon bands of cyclists pumping up the kinds of inclines that most people require escalators for. If you mean to cycle in the summer, start early and stop early to avoid heatstroke. French drivers, not always courteous to fellow motorists, usually give cyclists a wide berth; and yet on any given summer day, half the patients in a French hospital are from accidents on two-wheeled transport. Consider a helmet. Also beware that bike thefts are fairly common, especially along the Côte d'Azur, so make sure your insurance covers your bike—or the one you hire.

Getting your own bike to France is fairly easy: Air France and British Airways carry them free from Britain. From the US or Australia most airlines will carry them as long as they're boxed and are included in your total baggage weight. In all cases, telephone ahead. Certain French trains (called Autotrains, with a bicycle symbol in the timetable) carry bikes for free; otherwise you have to send it as registered luggage, and pay a 40F fee, with delivery guaranteed within five days. You can hire bikes of varying quality (most of them 10-speed) at most SNCF stations and in major towns. The advantage of hiring from a station means that you can drop it off at another, as long as you specify where when you hire it. Rates run at around 50F a day, with a deposit of 300–400F or credit card number. Private firms hire mountain-bikes (*VTTs* in French) and racing bikes.

On Foot

A network of long-distance paths or *Grandes Randonnées*, GRs for short (marked by distinctive red and white signs), take in some of the most beautiful scenery in the south of France. Each GR is described in a Topoguide, with maps and details about camping sites, refuges, and so on, available in area bookshops or from the Comité National des Sentiers de Grande Randonnée, 8 Ave Marceau, 75008 Paris, ☎ 01 47 23 62 32. An English translation covering several GRs in the region, *Walks in Provence*, is available from Stanfords, Long Acre, London WC2. Otherwise, the best maps for local excursions, based on ordnance surveys, are put out by the Institut Géographique National (1:50,000 or 1:100,000), available in most French bookshops.

There are 5000km of marked paths in the Alpes Maritimes alone. Of special interest are: GR 5 from Nice to Aspremont, the Gorges de la Vésubie and St-Dalmas-Valdeblore; GR 52 from Menton up to Sospel, the Vallée des Merveilles to St-Dalmas-Valdeblore; GR 52a and GR 5 through Mercantour National Park, both of which are open only from the end of June to the beginning of October. GR 51, nicknamed 'the balcony of the Côte d'Azur', from Castellar (near Menton) takes in the Esterel and Maures before ending at Bormes-les-Mimosas.

In Provence, GR 9 begins in St-Tropez and crosses over the region's most famous mountains: Ste-Baume, Ste-Victoire, the Lubéron and Ventoux. GR 4 crosses the Dentelles de Montmirail and Mont Ventoux en route to Grasse, GR 6 crosses much of the area in this book, from the Alps through the Vaucluse and Alpilles, to Beaucaire and the Pont du Gard before veering north up the river Gard on to its final destination by the Atlantic. GR 42 descends the west bank of the Rhône from near Bagnols-sur-Cèze to Beaucaire.

The Pyrenees are magnificent walking country, and the ideal way to take in the beauties of the Corbières and famous citadels of the Cathars from Padern, Peyrepertuse and Puilaurens to Montségur is by way of Le Sentier Cathare (described in French in Louis Salavy's *Le Sentier Cathare*), well marked and endowed with places to eat and stay en route. The Geocentre Map of Southern France with index is a good guide to walks in the region. Other walks in the mountains are covered in the excellent book *Randonnées Pyrénéennes* by J. L. Sarret.

Special-interest Holidays

There are a number of ways to combine a holiday with study or a special interest. For information, contact the French Centre on ☎ (0171) 792 0337 or the Cultural Services of the French Embassy: 22 Wilton Crescent, London SW1, ☎ (0171) 235 8080, or at 972 Fifth Ave, New York, NY 10021, ☎ (212) 439 1400. French universities are easy to enter if you're already enrolled in a similar institution at home; tuition fees are nominal but room and board are up to you. The Cultural Services can send a prospectus and tell you what paperwork is required.

in France

Alliance Française, 2 Rue Paris, 06000 Nice, ☎ 04 93 62 67 66, ✆ 04 93 85 28 06: (closed between Christmas and New Year for 1 week) French classes on all levels. Courses last a month but they can and will tailor to your needs.

Neige et Merveilles, Castérino, 06430 St-Dalmas-de-Tende, ✆ 04 93 04 88 58: offers pony-trekking and guided walks for school groups.

Atelier du Safranier, 2 bis Rue du Cannet, 06600 Vieil Antibes, ✆ 04 93 34 53 72: year-round courses in painting, engraving, lithography, etc., and watercolour classes on a boat.

L'Ecole du Moulin, Restaurant L'Amandier, Mougins 06250, ✆ 04 93 90 11 90: year-round Cuisine du Soleil cookery courses lasting a week under the auspices of Roger Vergé Inc.

Institut de Paléontologie Humaine, 1 Rue René Panhard, 75013 Paris, ✆ 01 43 31 62 91, 🖷 01 43 31 22 79: palaeontology students or fans can spend a minimum of 15 or 30 days excavating caves in southeast France (address your letter to M. Henry de Lumley).

Centre Etudes Linguistiques d'Avignon, 16 Rue Sainte Catherine, ✆ 04 90 86 04 33, 🖷 04 90 85 92 01: for French courses at all levels.

Direction des Antiquités Préhistoriques et Historiques of each *département* has summer openings for volunteers who are invited to assist at archaeological digs. Write to them in early spring. The address in Provence, 21–23 Blvd du Roy René, 13617 Aix-en-Provence; in Languedoc, 5 bis Rue de la Salle l'Evêque, 24000 Montpellier.

Maeva, 92 Route de la Reine, 92100 Boulogne-Billancourt ✆ 01 46 99 53 53, 🖷 01 41 22 10 46: self-catering apartments, hotels and other accomodation with sports such as skiing.

Vedel, 30 Rue Pierre Euzeby, 13200, Arles, ✆/🖷 04 90 49 69 20, e-mail act.vedel@provnet.fr : courses in Provençal cuisine from a meal to a week, including trips to the Camargue, a winery and the hills to pick herbs. Courses in French, English and Japanese.

from the UK

Allez France, 27 West St, Storrington, West Sussex RH20 4DZ, ✆ (01903) 748 100 🖷 (01903) 745044: city breaks in Nice, wine tours, gastronomic holidays, short breaks in Antibes, Juan-les-Pins and Gorges du Verdon.

Andante, Grange Cottage, Winterbourne Dauntsey, Salisbury, Wiltshire SP4 6ER, ✆ (01980) 610 555, 🖷 (01980) 610 002, e-mail andante.travel@virgin.net. Archaeological and historical study tours, including artists on the Côte d'Azur.

Cirrus Travel Ltd, Waterford House, Erfstadt Court, Wokingham, Berks RG40 2YF, ✆ (0118) 936 2300, 🖷 (0990) 134714, website www.glider.co.uk, e-mail glider@cirrrus.uk.com. First-class coach travel aboard 'The Glider'.

CV Travel, 43 Cadogan Street, London SW3 2PR, ✆ (0171) 581 0851, 🖷 (0171) 584 5229. Country-house accommodation and tailor-made holidays.

Euro Academy, 77a George Street, Croydon CR0 1LD, ✆ (0181) 686 2363, 🖷 (0181) 8850, French language courses with activities or sports options in Nice.

Alternative Travel Group, 69–71 Banbury Road, Oxford OX2 6PE, ✆ (01865) 515678, 🖷 (01865) 310299: walking and cycling holidays in Provence; wine tours.

Arblaster & Clarke, Clarke House, Farnham Road, West Liss GU33 6JQ, ✆ (01730) 895 353, 🖷 (01730) 892 888: expert-escorted wine tours of major wine regions.

Artscape Painting Holidays, 7 Clifftown Parade, Southend-on-Sea, Essex SS1 1DP, ✆ (01702) 435 990: painting courses in Provence.

Belle France, 15 East St, Rye, East Sussex, TN3 5 3Z, ✆ (01892) 890 885, 🖷 (01892) 223 666: walking holidays in Provence; cycling holidays in Provence and the Camargue.

Headwater Holidays, 146 London Road, Northwich CW9 5HH, ✆ (01606) 48699, 🖷 (01606) 48761: cycling for 10 or 6 nights; walking in the Gorges du Verdon.

Hoseasons Holidays, Sunway House, Lowestoft NR32 2LW, ✆ (01502) 500 555, 🖷 (01502) 500 532, e-mail mail@hoseasons.co.uk: canal tours of the Camargue, with a base at Beaucaire; canal tours of the Midi.

InnTravel, Hovingham, York YO6 4JZ, ✆ (01653) 628811: walking and cycling holidays.

J. M. B. Travel Consultants Limited, 'Rushwick', Worcester WR2 5SN, ✆ 01905 425628, 🖷 01905 420219: opera and music festivals in the south of France.

LSG Theme Holidays, 201 Main Street, Thornton LE67 1AH, ✆ (01509) 231 713 or (01509) 239 857 (24 hrs): a French company offering painting and language courses; cultural discovery; photography; cooking; horseriding in Provence; rambling in Languedoc.

Martin Randall, 10 Barley Mow Passage, London W4 4PH, ✆ (0181) 742 3355, 🖷 (0181) 742 1066: lecturer-accompanied cultural tours of Provence.

Plantagenet Tours, 85 The Grove, Moordown, Bournemouth BH9 2TY, ✆/🖷 (01202) 521895: cultural tours, including 'The Provence Tour'.

Sherpa Expeditions, 131a Heston Rd, Hounslow, Middlesex TW5 0RD, ✆ (0181) 577 2717, 🖷 (0181) 572 9788: walking treks in Provence, the Cerdagne, and Languedoc.

Susi Madron's Cycling for Softies, 2 and 4 Birch Polygon, Rusholme, Manchester M14 5HX, ✆ (0161) 248 8282, 🖷 (0161) 248 5140: easy cycling in Provence and the Camargue.

Waymark Holidays, 44 Windsor Road, Slough SL1 2EJ, ✆ (01753) 516 477, 🖷 (01753) 517 016: walking tours, centre-based in Provence and Languedoc-Roussillon.

from the USA

A Touch of France, 660 King George Road, Fords, NJ 008863, ✆ (908) 738 4772, 🖷 (908) 738 4722: specialist tours focusing on all aspects of French culture.

Abercrombie & Kent, 1520 Kensington Road, Oakbrook, IL 60521, ✆ (630) 954 2944, 🖷 (630) 954 3324: rail tours on the Côte d'Azur.

Adventure Center, 1311 63rd Street, Suite 200, Emeryville, CA 94608, ✆ (510) 654 1879, 🖷 (510) 654 4200: walking and camping in Provence.

Baumeler Tours, 10 Grand Avenue, Rockville Centre, NY 11570, ✆ (516) 766 6160: cycling in Provence.

Dailey-Thorp Travel, 330 West 58th Street, New York, NY 10019, ✆ (212) 307 1555, 🖷 (212) 974 1420: music and opera tours.

Horizons, 108 North Main St, Sunderland, MA 01375, ✆ (301) 855 6573: New England crafts programme in Venasque: painting, fabric printing and photography.

Int'l Curtain Call, 3313 Patricia Avenue, Los Angeles, CA 90064, ✆ (310) 204 4934, 🖷 (310) 204 4935: opera and music tours, e.g. Paris–Avignon–Aix-en-Provence–Cannes.

Le Boat Inc., 215 Union Street, Hackensack, NJ 07601, ✆ (201) 342 1838, 🖷 (201) 342 7498: crewed motor or sailing yacht and bareboats from Côte d'Azur ports.

Progressive Travels Inc., 224 West Galer, Suite C, Seattle, WA 98119, ✆ (206) 285 1987, 🖷 (206) 285 1988: luxury and standard cycling and walking tours in Provence.

Practical A–Z

Provence and Languedoc have a basically Mediterranean climate, one wafted by winds that give it a special character. The most notorious is the mistral (from the Provençal *mistrau*, or master) supposedly sent by northerners jealous of the south's climate—rushing down the Rhône and gusting east as far as Toulon and west to Narbonne, sparing the hot-house of the Côte d'Azur. On average the mistral blows 100 to 150 days a year, nearly always in multiples of three, except when it begins at night. It is responsible for the dryness in the air and soil (hence its nickname, *mangio fango*, or mud-eater). Houses in its line of fire are built *pointes en avant*, at an angle, the north side blank and in the shade, protected by cypresses, while on the south side plane trees protect the house from the strong sun. It blows so hard that it can drive people mad: an old law in Provence acquitted a murderer if it could be proved that he killed his victim while the mistral was blowing. But the mistral has its good points: it blows away harmful miasmas and pollution from the Rhône and makes the stars radiantly clear, as alive as in Van Gogh's painting, *Starry Night*.

Besides the Master, there are twenty-two other winds, most importantly: the east wind, or *levant*, or southeasterly 'Greek' wind which brings the much desired rain; the *pounent*, or west wind; and the suffocatingly hot sirocco from Africa. The region from the Spanish border to Montpellier is occasionally bulldozed by the *tramontane*, the 'Catalan wind' from the northwest.

Rainfall varies widely across the south. The Pyrenees get more rain than most places on this planet—over two metres a year (Prats de Mollo, with 838mm in 16 hours, holds the local record) while the Camargue barely gets 500mm a year, the least rainfall in France. In the average year, it rains as much in Nice (750mm per year) as Brest and more in Marseille than Paris. In the heart of Provence it rains much less frequently—not at all in the summer, and violently in spring and autumn (up to 135mm in an hour)—hence the *restanques* or terraces carved in the hills by the farmers to prevent erosion.

Each season has its pros and cons. In January all the tourists are in the Alps or Pyrenees; in February the mimosa and almonds bloom on the Côte d'Azur. In April and May you can sit outside at restaurants and swim, and within an hour's drive ski at Auron or Isola 2000. By June, the mistral slows down and the resorts begin to fill up; walking is safe in the highest mountains. July and August are bad months, when everything is crowded, temperatures and prices soar (Perpignan has the highest average summer temperatures in France) and tempers flare, but it's also the season of the great festivals in Avignon, Aix, Juan-les-Pins and Nice.

Once French school holidays end in early September, prices and crowds decrease with the temperature. In October the weather is traditionally mild on the coast, although torrential downpours and floods are not unknown; the first snows fall in the Pyrenees and Alps. November is another bad month; it rains and many museums, hotels, and restaurants close down. December brings Christmas holiday tourists and the first skiers.

average temperature chart in °C (°F)

	Jan	Feb	Mar	April	May	June	July	Aug	Sept	Oct	Nov	Dec
Nice	11(52)	12(54)	14(56)	17(62)	20(69)	22(72)	24(75)	26(79)	25(77)	20(69)	16(61)	13(55)
Avignon	7(44)	7(44)	11(52)	15(59)	17(62)	21(70)	23(73)	25(77)	23(73)	16(61)	10(50)	8(45)

Perpignan

12(54) 12(54) 13(55) 17(62) 20(69) 23(73) 28(82) 28(82) 26(79) 20(69) 16(61) 14(56)

Font-Romeu

−2(28) −2(28) 1(34) 4(39) 7(44) 10(50) 14(56) 15(59) 11(52) 7(44) 2(36) 0(32)

Consulates

UK   Nice: 11 Rue Paradis, ☏ 04 93 82 32 04; Marseille: 24 Ave du Prado, 6e, ☏ 04 91 15 72 10

USA   Nice: 31 Rue Maréchal Joffre, ☏ 04 93 88 89 55 or 04 9388 82 61; Marseille: 12 Blvd Paul Peytral, 6e, near the Préfecture, ☏ 04 91 54 92 00

Canada Paris: Avenue Montaigne, 8e, ☏ 01 44 43 29 00

Ireland Antibes: Villa les Chênes Verts, 152 Blvd Kennedy, ☏ 04 93 61 50 63

Crime and the Police

Everyone in Marseille seemed most dishonest. They all tried to swindle me, mostly with complete success.

Evelyn Waugh

There is a fair chance that you will be had in the south of France, though probably not in Marseille; thieves and pickpockets go for the flashier fish on the Côte d'Azur. Road pirates prey on motorists blocked in traffic, train pirates prowl the overnight compartments looking for handbags and cameras, car bandits just love the ripe pickings in cars parked in isolated scenic areas or tourist car parks (they go for expensive or rental cars; the latter discernable by their number plates, as most are registered in department 51). In the cities, beware the bands of gypsy children, who push sheets of cardboard in the faces of their victims to distract them as they go through their pockets. Although violence is rare, the moral of the story is to leave anything you'd really miss at home, carry travellers' cheques and insure your property, especially if you're driving. Report thefts to the nearest *gendarmerie*, not a pleasant task but the reward is the bit of paper you need for an insurance claim. If your passport is stolen, contact the police and your nearest consulate for emergency travel documents. Carry photocopies of your passport, driver's licence, etc.; it makes it easier when reporting a loss. By law, the police in France can stop anyone anywhere and demand an ID; in practice, they only tend to do it to harass minorities, the homeless, and scruffy hippy types. If they really don't like the look of you they can salt you away for a long time without any reason.

The drug situation is the same in France as anywhere in the West: soft and hard drugs are widely available, and the police only make an issue of victimless crime when it suits them (your being a foreigner just may rouse them to action). Smuggling any amount of marijuana into the country can mean a prison term, and there's not much your consulate can or will do about it.

Disabled Travellers

When it comes to providing access for all, France is not exactly in the vanguard of nations; many Americans who come over are appalled. But things are beginning to change, especially in newer buildings. Access and facilities in 90 towns in France are covered in *Touristes Quand Même! Promenades en France pour les voyageurs handicapés*, a booklet usually available in the tourist offices of large cities, or contact the Comité National Français de Liaison pour la

Réadaptation des Handicapés, 236B Rue Tolbiac, 75013 Paris, © 01 53 80 66 66. Hotels with facilities for the handicapped are listed in Michelin's *Red Guide to France*; a new book *Gîtes accessibles aux personnes handicapées* (45F), published by Gîtes de France, lists self-catering accommodation possibilities (*see* below, p.31, for their address).

Other useful addresses: **RADAR** (The Royal Association for Disability and Rehabilitation), 250 City Road, London, © (0171) 250 3222; Minicom © (0171) 637 5315. **Mobility International USA**, PO Box 3551, Eugene, OR 97403, USA, © (541) 343 1284. Both cover all aspects of travel information.

Environment

'Come to the Côte d'Azur for a change of pollution,' they say. Constantly threatened by frequent oil spills, a suffocating algae mistakenly released into the sea at the Oceanographic Institute of Monte Carlo, too many cars and too many people, the well-named 'California of Europe', from Marseille to Menton, may be the first place in southern Europe to achieve total ecological breakdown.

As elsewhere in the Mediterranean, a sad litany of forest fires heads the television news in summer. Especially in Provence, most of the herbs and trees are xerophytes, able to thrive in dry hot conditions on poor rocky soils. Most forests are pine—Aleppo pines in limestone, maritime pines in the Maures and Esterel. Here they often close roads in summer to decrease the chance of fires. Most are caused by twits with matches (you'll be more careful, won't you?), though many fires are deliberately instigated by speculators who burn off protected forests to build more holiday villas and suchlike. Fires often lead to erosion and flooding, though the local governments now do a good job of re-forestation. The weird wasteland of Blausasc, in a valley north of Nice (caused by greedy logging in the 1800s), shows what Provence would soon look like if they didn't.

The most spectacular environmental non-issue continues to be the overbuilding of the Côte d'Azur. The damage is done; one of the most exceptional parts of the Mediterranean coast has been thoroughly, thoughtlessly, irreparably ruined. Since the war there has simply been too much money involved for governments to act responsibly; most of the buildings you'll see were put up illegally—but there they are. Though this is changing—a politically connected developer near St-Tropez was recently forced to demolish an illegal, half-built project—local governments continue to promote industrial and tourist growth in areas where there is absolutely no room to grow. Paris bureaucrats are as responsible as local politicians; in public transport, for example, they insist on pushing a new TGV route around the coast, bringing down even more people instead of improving local transport that might cut down on the ferocious traffic they already have. The new route is a monster, cutting across scores of scenic areas and wine regions; citizen groups in the south fought it tooth and nail but the 'biggest construction site in Europe' is well underway.

Other enemies of the Midi include: the army, which has commandeered enormous sections of wilderness (Plan de Canjuers and parts of the Crau, Ile du Levant, Roussillon's Plateau d'Opoul) and regularly blows them to smithereens in manoeuvres and target practice; the nuclear industry, with France's nuclear research centre at Cadarache and most of its nuclear missiles hidden away on the Plateau de Vaucluse; the *chancre coloré*, a fungus that, like phylloxera, came from the US (on wooden crates during the Second World War) and now threatens the lovely plane trees of Provence; and finally the truly villainous national electric company, EDF, which once tried to flood the Grand Canyon du Verdon. The one genuine contemporary ecological disaster is the Etang de Berre, now entirely surrounded by the industrial and suburban sprawl of Marseille, a ghastly horror of power pylons, pollution and speculative development. Here too the EDF is involved; heated water, pumped from their giant power plant into the lagoon, is killing off the few remaining fish. Local groups are fighting hard to make them stop.

In August, ecological dysfunction reaches its apogee on the sands of St-Tropez's crowded beaches, laced with trash, condoms, and human excrement. But there's another side to the story—over a hundred miles of clean, underpopulated beaches in Languedoc and Roussillon, and a mountainous hinterland from the Italian border to the Spanish that is still mostly pristine and delightful. Nature lovers can find everything they desire, and much that is new and strange—as long as they avoid the Côte d'Azur.

Festivals

The south of France offers everything from the Cannes Film Festival to the village fête, with a pilgrimage or religious procession, bumper cars, a *pétanque* tournament, a feast (anything from sardines to cassoulet to paella) and an all-night dance, sometimes to a local band but often a travelling troupe playing 'Hot Music' or some other electrified cacophony. Bullfights (*see* p.27) play a part in many *fêtes* or *ferias* from Spain to the Rhône. A *bravade* (as in St-Tropez) entails pistol or musket-shots; a *corso* is a parade with carts or floats. St John's Day (24 June) is a big favourite and often features bonfires and fireworks.

At Catalan *festas* you're bound to see the national dance, the *sardana*, a complex, circular dance that alternates 16 long steps with 8 short ones, properly accompanied by a *cobla*, a band of a dozen instruments, some unique to Catalunya. In the southern Rhône valley people still like to celebrate with a *farandole*, a dance in 6/8 time with held hands or a handkerchief, which may be as old as the ancient Greeks. One-man musical accompaniment is provided by a little three-holed flute called a *galoubet* played with left hand, and a *tambourin*, a drum played with the right. Both *farandoles* and flamenco enliven the proceedings of the 24 May pilgrimage at Saintes-Maries-de-la-Mer, by far the best attended of all popular festivities in the south.

Overleaf is a calendar of events. Note that dates change every year; for complete listings and precise dates of events, pick up a copy of the annual lists, available in most tourist offices.

Food and Drink

...and south of Valence, Provincia Romana, the Roman Provence, lies beneath the sun. There there is no more any evil, for there the apple will not flourish and the Brussels sprout will not grow at all.

Ford Madox Ford, *Provence*

Eating is a pleasure in the south, where seafood, herbs, fruit and vegetables are often within plucking distance of the kitchen and table. The high quality of these fresh native ingredients demands minimal preparation—Provençal cooking is perhaps the least fussy of any regional French cuisine, and as an added plus neatly fits the modern definition of a healthy diet. For not only is the south a Brussels sprout-free zone, but the artery-hardening delights of the north— the rich creamy sauces, butter, cheese and egg dishes, mega-calorie desserts—are rare birds in the land of olives, fresh vegetables, apricots and almonds.

Calendar of Events

January

Sunday nearest the 17th	*Fête de St-Marcel*, folkdancing and singing at **Barjols**; every four years (next 2002) Barjols does an ox roast as well
27	*Fête de Ste-Dévote*, **Monaco**
End of month	**Monte Carlo** rally

February

2	*Fête des Chandelles*, **Marseille**
3	Festival of olives and late golden Servan grapes, **Valbonne**
First week	International Circus Festival, **Monaco**; *Fête des Oursins*, sea-urchin festival at **Carry-le-Rouet**
10 days at Carnival	*Fête du Citron*, **Menton**; *Feria du Carnaval*, at **Nîmes**
Carnival	**Nice** has the most famous festivities in France; during the school break in **Prats-de-Mollo**, traditional celebrations
Ash Wednesday	*Les Pailhasses* at **Cournonterral**, a 14th-century parade of boys in straw and turkey feathers, who try to squirt wine on passers-by
10	*Corso du Mimosa*, **Bormes-les-Mimosas**
End of month	*Fête de l'Ours*, ancient bear festival in **Arles-sur-Tech**

March

25	*Festin es Courgourdons*, folklore and dried sculpted gourds, and folklore, **Nice**
Sunday before Palm Sun	Traditional Carnival at **Limoux**

April

Throughout month	International tennis tournaments, **Monaco** and **Nice**
Maundy Thursday/ Good Friday	*Procession de La Sanch*, in **Perpiganan**, **Collioure**, and **Arles-sur-Tech**; Procession of the Dead Christ, **Roquebrune-Cap-Martin**
Good Friday–Easter	Bullfights in **Arles**
Easter	Flower and sweets fair, **Villefranche-de-Conflent**
25	Winegrowers' festival and blessing of the vines, **Châteauneuf-du-Pape**; *Fête de St-Marc*, **Villeneuve-lez-Avignon**
Last Sunday	*Fête des Gardians*, traditional rodeo in **Arles**

May

Third week after Easter	*Bravade St-François*, **Fréjus**
Second week	**Cannes** Film Festival
Second weekend	*Fête de la Rose*, **Grasse**
Sunday after the 15th	*Fête de St-Gens*, costumes, pistol shots, etc., at **Monteaux**
16–17	*Bravade de St-Torpes*, **St-Tropez**
Third Sunday	Cherry Festival, **Le Luc-en-Provence**
Ascension weekend	Festival of ochre and colour, **Roussillon**; **Monaco** International Grand Prix
24–25	Gypsy pilgrimage at **Saintes-Maries-de-la-Mer**
Late May–mid-July	International music festival, **Toulon**
10 days at Pentecost	Bullfights at **Nîmes**; *Cavalcade*, music festival at **Apt**

June

June–September	Music events in the Arènes, **Nîmes**; *Mirondela dels Arts*, with folklore, crafts, concerts, etc., at **Pézenas**
Throughout month	*Festival de la Danse et de l'Image*, **Toulon**
Early June	*Printemps des Comédiens*, theatre festival in **Montpellier**
1	*Cérémonie du St-Vinage*, **Boulbon**
15	*Bravade des Espagnols*, **St-Tropez**
Last half of June	Jazz and chamber music, in **Aix**; *Nuits Musicales*, music festival in **Uzès**
Corpus Christi	*Procession dai limaça*, **Gorbio**
Sunday before St John's	*Fête de St-Eloi*, blessing of the mules at **Arles-sur-Tech**
23–24	*Fête de St-Jean*, with processions, **Entrevaux**; with bonfires, dancing, and fireworks in **Perpignan**, **Céret** and **Villefranche-de-Conflent**
Sunday after the 24th	*Fête Provençal*, with blessings of animals, in **Allauch** (near Marseille)
Late June–early July	*Festival International de Danse*, in **Montpellier**

July

Last Saturday	Folklore festival of St Jean, **Les Baux**; *Fête de la Tradition*, **Arles**
Last Sunday	*Fête de la Tarasque*, **Tarascon**
July–August	International Fireworks Festival, **Monaco**; Festival of Early Music, **Entrevaux**; *Nuits de l'Empéri*, theatre festival in **Salon**; modern music festival, **St-Paul-de-Vence**; Festival of Dance, Music and Theatre, **Vaison-la-Romaine**; *Nuits de la Citadelle*, music and theatre at **Sisteron**; Côtes du Roussillon wine festival, **Perpignan**; *Rencontres Internationales d'Eté à la Chartreuse*, concerts, dance and theatre at **Villeneuve-lez-Avignon**; *Joutes nautiques*, **Agde**
Throughout month	International Music Festival, **Vence**; music festival, **Carcassonne**; *Rencontres Internationales de la Photographie*, **Arles**; *Festival de la Côte Languedocienne*, with concerts in **Béziers**; *Festival de la Sorgue*, music, theatre and dance at **Fontaine-de-Vaucluse** and around
4–14	*Festival Américain*, **Cannes**
First Sunday	*Fête de St-Eloi*, bullfights and a decorated cart pulled by 40 horses in **Châteaurenard**
First two weeks	Dance Festival, **Aix**; International Folklore Festival, **Marseille**
Second Sunday	*Fête de St-Pierre*, with water jousts, etc., **Cap d'Antibes**
Mid-July	Jazz festivals in **Nice** and **Toulon**; *Corso de nuit* for Notre-Dame-de-Santé, **Carpentras**; *Soirées Musicales*, **St-Maximin-la-Ste-Baume**; film festival, **La Ciotat**
14	Fireworks in many places for Bastille Day; **Avignon** and **Carcassonne** put on excellent shows
Last three weeks	Music Festival, **Aix**; *Festival de Radio France*, classical music and jazz in **Montpellier**
Mid-July–mid-Aug	International Theatre Festival, **Avignon**; Festival Pablo Casals, **Prades**; *Festival Passion*, operettas, ballet, and music at **Carpentras**
21–22	*Fête de Ste-Madeleine*, **St-Maximin-la-Ste-Baume**
Last two weeks	International Jazz Festival, **Juan-les-Pins**; music festival, **Orange**; fête in **Martigues**, with theatre, seafood, music and dancing; music festival,

	Béziers; *Festival de la Mer*, **Sète**; *Rencontres cinématographiques*, meet film directors at **Prades**
Last Sunday	Donkey races and village fête, **Lacoste**
30	*Festa Major*, processions and distribution of Ste-Tombe's water, **Arles-sur-Tech**
End July	Folklore Festival and *Batailles des Fleurs*, **Nice**

August

All month	Chamber Music Festival, **Menton**; Music and Dance Festival, **Arles**; *Tournoise de joutes*, nautical jousts at **Sète**, culminating around the 25th
First two weeks	*Médiévales*, jousts and medieval crafts and costumes, **Carcassonne**; Music and Theatre festival, **Gordes**
First Tuesday	*Journées du Terroir*, flea markets and bullfights, **Sommières**
First Sunday	Lavender Festival, **Digne**; *Fête de la Madeleine*, with parade of flowered carts, **Châteaurenard**; Jasmine festival, **Grasse**
5	Passion procession, **Roquebrune**
9 and 11	*Fête de St-Laurent*, with bullfights, at **Eygalières**
14–18	*Feria* at **Collioure**, with fireworks
15	Village *fête* and operettas, **Le Thor**; *Feria* in **Béziers** with fireworks, parades, and fountains of wine
Third week	*Provençal festival* with processions, *bravades* and drama, **Séguret**
First Sunday after 20th	*Fête du Traou*, dancing and *polenta* feasts at **Tende**
Second last Sunday	*Festival International de Sardanes*, Catalan dance festival, **Céret**
Third week	Provençal wine festival, **Séguret**
End of August	Bullfights at **Béziers**; *Fête de St-Louis*, with historical re-enactment, at **Aigues-Mortes**
29–29	*Fête de Notre-Dame-de-Grace*, **Maillane**

September

First week	*Fête de Musique in Catalogne*, **Elne**
First Sunday	*Festin des baguettes*, **Peille**
8	Village *fête* and pilgrimage to Notre-Dame-des-Fontaines, **Brigue**
Mid-month	*Festival du Cinéma Méditerranéen*, **Montpellier**
Third week	*Feria des Vendanges*, bullfights at **Nîmes**
Last week–first week Oct	*Nioulargue*, yacht race in **St-Tropez**

October

Mid-October	*Fête-Votive*, with Provençal bullfights, at **Aigues-Mortes**
22	*Fête de Ste-Marie-Jacobé*, **Saintes-Maries-de-la-Mer**
Third Sunday	*Fête du Vin Nouveau*, **Béziers**

November

Last Friday	*Foire St-Siffrein*, with truffle market, **Carpentras**
Last Sunday	*Foire des Santons*, until Epiphany, at **Marseille**

December

All month	Festival of Italian Cinema, **Nice**; Music festival, **Marseille**
24	Provençal midnight mass at **Ste-Baume**, **Séguret** and **Fontvieille**, with shepherds at **Allauch** (near Marseille); midnight mass in the Arènes at **Nîmes**; *Fête des Bergers* and midnight mass, **Les Baux**; torchlight and wake, **Séguret**

Some of the most celebrated restaurants in the world grace the south of France, but there are plenty of stinkers, too. The most tolerable are humble in their mediocrity (Languedoc is full of these) while others are oily with pretensions, staffed by folks posing as Grand Dukes and Duchesses fallen on hard times, whose exalted airs are somehow supposed to make their clients feel better about paying an obscene amount of money for the eight *petits pois à la graisse de yak* that the chef has so beautifully arranged on a plate. These places never last more than a year or two, but may just be in business as you happen by.

Just as intimidating for the hungry traveller are France's much ballyhooed gourmet bibles, whose annual awarding or removing of a star here, a chef's hat there, grade food the way a French teacher grades a *dictée* in school. Woe to the chef who leaves a lump in the sauce when those incognito pedants of the perfect palate are dining, and whose guillotine pens will ruthlessly chop off percentage points from the restaurant's final score. The less attention you pay them, the more you'll enjoy your dinner.

Restaurant Basics

Restaurants generally serve between 12 noon and 2pm and in the evening from 7 to 10pm, with later summer hours; *brasseries* in the cities generally stay open continuously. Most post menus outside the door so you know what to expect and offer a choice of set-price menus; if prices aren't listed, you can bet it's not because they're a bargain. If you summon up the appetite to eat the biggest meal of the day at noon, you'll spend a lot less money, as many restaurants offer special lunch menus—an economical way to experience some of the finer gourmet temples. Some of these offer a set-price gourmet *menu dégustation*—a selection of chef's specialities, which can be a great treat. At the humbler end of the scale, bars and brasseries often serve a simple *plat du jour* (daily special) and the no-choice *formule*, which is more often than not steak and *frites*. Eating *à la carte* anywhere will always be more expensive, in many cases twice as much.

Menus sometimes include the house wine (*vin compris*). If you choose a better wine anywhere, expect a scandalous mark-up; the French wouldn't dream of a meal without wine, and the arrangement is a simple device to make food prices seem lower. If service is included it will say *service compris* or s.c., if not *service non compris* or s.n.c.

French restaurants, especially the cheaper ones, presume everyone has the appetite of Gargantua. A full meal consists of: an apéritif (*pastis*, the national drink of the south, is famous for its hunger-inducing qualities), hors d'oeuvres or a starter (typically, soup, paté, or *charcuterie*), an *entrée* (usually fish, or an omelette), a main course (usually meat, poultry, game or offal, *garni* with vegetables, rice or potatoes), often followed by a green salad (to 'lighten' the stomach), then cheese, dessert, coffee, chocolates and *mignardises* (or petit-fours) and perhaps a *digestif* to round things off. Most people only devour the whole whack on Sunday afternoons, and at other times condense this feast to a starter, *entrée* or main course, and cheese or dessert. Vegetarians will have a hard time in France, especially if they don't eat fish or eggs, but most establishments will try to accommodate them somehow.

When looking for a restaurant, homing in on the one place crowded with locals is as sound a policy in France as anywhere. Don't overlook hotel restaurants, some of which are absolutely top notch even if a certain red book refuses on some obscure principle to give them more than two stars. To avoid disappointment, call ahead in the morning to reserve a table, especially at the smarter restaurants, and especially in the summer. One thing you'll soon notice is that there's a wide choice of ethnic restaurants, mostly North African (a favourite for their economical couscous—spicy meat and vegetables served with a side dish of *harisa*, a hot red pepper sauce on a bed of steamed semolina); Asian (usually Vietnamese, sometimes Chinese, Cambodian, or Thai); and Italian, the latter sometimes combined with a pizzeria, although beware, quality very much depends on geographical proximity to Italy, i.e. the pasta and pizza are superb in Nice, tolerably good in Marseille, and often a pasty mess in Languedoc.

Don't expect to find many ethnic restaurants outside the Côte and the big cities; country cooking is French only (though often very inventive). But in the cosmopolitan centres, you'll find not only foreign cuisine, but specialities from all over France. There are Breton *crêperies* or *galetteries* (with whole-wheat pancakes), restaurants from Alsace serving *choucroute* (sauerkraut and sausage), Périgord restaurants featuring *foie gras* and truffles, Lyonnaise *haute cuisine* and *les fast foods* offering *basse cuisine* of chips, hot dogs, and cheese sandwiches.

There are still a few traditional French restaurants that would meet the approval of Auguste Escoffier, the legendary chef (and a native of Provence); quite a few serve regional specialities (*see* below) and many feature *nouvelle cuisine*, which isn't so *nouvelle* any more, and has come under attack by devoted foodies for its expense (only the finest, freshest and rarest ingredients are used), portions (minute compared to usual restaurant helpings, because the object is to feel good, not full), and sheer quackery. For *nouvelle cuisine* is a subtle art, to emphasize the natural flavour and goodness of a carrot by contrasting or complementing it with other flavours and scents; disappointments are inevitable when a chef is more concerned with appearance than taste, or takes a walk on the wild side, combining oysters, kiwis and cashews or some other abomination. But *nouvelle cuisine* has had a strong influence on attitudes towards food in France, and it's hard to imagine anyone going back to smothering everything in a *béchamel* sauce.

The Cuisine of Provence and the Côte d'Azur

Thanks to the trail-blazing work of writers and chefs like Elizabeth David and Roger Vergé, Provençal cooking no longer sends the average Anglo-Saxon into paroxysms of garlic paranoia as it did a hundred years ago. Many traditional dishes actually presage *nouvelle cuisine*, and their success hangs on the quality of the ingredients and fragrant olive oil, like the well-known *ratatouille*—aubergines (eggplant), tomatoes, garlic and courgettes (zucchini) cooked separately to preserve their individual flavour, before being mixed together in olive oil—or *bagna cauda*, a dish of the southern Alps, consisting of raw vegetables dipped in a hot fondue of garlic, anchovies and olive oil.

A favourite hors d'oeuvre is *tapenade*, a purée of olives, anchovies, olive oil and capers served on toast. The best known starter must be *salade niçoise*, interpreted in a hundred different ways even in Nice, but in general containing most of the following: tomatoes, cucumbers, hard-boiled eggs, black olives, onions, anchovies, artichokes, green peppers, croutons, green beans, and sometimes tuna and even potatoes. In Nice pasta dishes come in all sorts of shapes, but the favourites are *ravioli* and *gnocchi* (potato dumplings), two forms served throughout Italy and invented here when Nice was still *Nizza* (the city has many other special dishes: *see* pp.98–9). Another dish that tastes best in the summer, *soupe au pistou*, is a thick minestrone served with a fresh basil, garlic, and pine-nut sauce similar to Italian *pesto*.

Aïoli, a mayonnaise made from garlic, olive oil, lemon juice and egg yolks, served with codfish, snails, potatoes or soup, is for many the essence of Provence; Mistral even named his nationalist Provençal magazine after it. In the same spirit Marseille named its magazine *Bouillabaisse*, for its world-famous soup of five to twelve kinds of Mediterranean fish, flavoured with saffron; the fish is removed and served with *aïoli* or *rouille*, a sauce of fresh red chilli peppers crushed with garlic, olive oil, and the soup broth. Because good saffron costs money and the fish, especially the gruesome *racasse* (scorpion fish) are rare, a proper *bouillabaisse* will cost at least 200F.

A less expensive but delicious alternative is *bourride*, a soup made from white-fleshed fish served with *aïoli*, or down a gastronomical notch is *baudroie*, a fish soup with vegetables and garlic. A very different kettle of fish is the indigestible Niçoise favourite, *estocaficada*, salt cod (and salt cod guts) stewed with tomatoes, olives, garlic, and eau-de-vie. Less adventurous yet an absolutely delicious dish is *loup aux fenouille*, sea bass grilled over fennel stalks.

Lamb is the most common meat dish; real Provençal lamb (becoming increasingly rare) grazes on herbs and on special salt-marsh grasses from the Camargue and Crau. Beef usually comes in the form of a *daube*, slowly stewed in red wine and often served with ravioli. A Provençal cook's prize possession is the *daube* pan, which is never washed, but wiped clean and baked to form a crust that flavours all subsequent stews. Rabbit, or *lapin à la provençale*, is simmered in white wine with garlic, mustard, tomatoes and herbs. The more daunting *pieds et paquets* are tripe packages stuffed with garlic, onions and salt pork, traditionally (although rarely in practice) served with calf's or sheep's trotters. Also look for *capoun fassum*, cabbage stuffed with sausage and rice, and *artichauts à la barigoule*, artichokes filled with pork and mushrooms.

Purely vegetable dishes, besides ratatouille, include *tian*, a casserole of rice, spring vegetables and grated cheese baked in the oven; *tourta de blea*, a sweet-savoury Swiss chard pie; stuffed courgette (zucchini) flowers; grilled tomatoes with garlic and breadcrumbs (*à la provençale*); and *mesclum*, a salad of dandelion and other green leaves. There aren't many Provençal cheeses: *banon*, nutty discs made from goat, sheep, or cow's milk, wrapped in chestnut leaves, is perhaps the best known; *poivre d'Ain* is banon flavoured with savoury; thyme and bay add a nuance to creamy sheep's milk *tomme arlésienne*.

Specialities of Languedoc-Roussillon

In France's 'culinary desert', as the region of Languedoc-Roussillon is unkindly known, they have the expression *manjar fòrça estofat* (to eat lots of stew), describing a masochist or someone who suffers martyrdom without complaint. What more can you say about a region that goes into raptures over *cassoulet*—beans, pork, *confits* and sausage stewed in goose fat? It is quite possible, as the Languedociens claim, that theirs is a subtle and complex cuisine—but at home; you can't confirm it from the restaurants. A poor and introverted region for 700 years, Languedoc does not much go out for dinner, and only recently has tourism been an influence on the few restaurants available.

Stay away from the dreary-looking places in the towns; some of these offer cuisine on the level of the average London sandwich bar. But out in the villages, in a growing number of new hotel-restaurants with younger owners, and in scores of *fermes-auberges*, you'll find something more to your liking, an honest, earthy cuisine entirely based on traditional local ingredients: game dishes, rabbit, pigeon, morels and *cèpes*, *foie gras*, occasionally truffles, Corbières wine and, in western Languedoc, plenty of duck, usually in the form of a *confit* (cooked and preserved in its own fat—much better than it sounds). The eternal bean stew cassoulet (*see* Castelnaudary) is still the king of the Languedocien table, along with regional variations like the *fricassée* of Limoux; the queen, ever since the Middle Ages, has been *brandade de morue*, salt cod purée with garlic, olive oil and milk. Fresh seafood, though simply prepared, is always good along the coast; there are plenty of mussels and oysters, raised in the coastal lagoons.

Some Languedocien basics have relatives in Provence. *Aïoli* (or *aïllade*) is a favourite sauce, and seafood dishes like *bouillabaisse* are similar, although here you may find ham and leeks involved. Sète is famous for its delicious *bourride*; then there's *bourboulhade*, a kind of poor man's *bouillabaisse* made of salt cod and garlic, or yet another B-soup, *boullinade*, a thicker fish soup with Banyuls wine. Sète, the seafood capital of Languedoc, also specializes in *seiches farcies*, cuttlefish stuffed with the meat of its tentacles mixed with sausage, and *langouste à la sètoise*, crawfish with cognac, tomatoes, and garlic. *Escargots*, or snails, come at you in all directions, with anchovies, as in Nîmes, or grilled (*cargolade*), or even in *bouillabaisse*. Land dishes you may encounter include *mourtayrol*, a delicious chicken *pot-au-feu* flavoured with saffron, and *rouzoles*, crêpes filled with ham and bacon. When the cheese platter comes around, it may have *pelardons*, the favourite goat's cheese from the Cévennes.

The Catalans in Roussillon have many sterling qualities, but display only the most modest ones in their restaurants. The totem fish of the *département* is the little anchovy of Collioure, which hardy souls from Spain to Marseille pulverize with garlic, onion, basil and oil to make *anchoïade*, a favourite apéritif spread on raw celery or toast. A popular starter is *gambas à la planxa*, prawns grilled and served on a plank, or anchovies with strips of red pepper, which is better than it sounds. Main courses include *roussillonnade*, a dish of *bolet* mushrooms and sausages grilled over a pine-cone fire, and *boles de Picolat*, Catalan meatballs with mushrooms cooked in sauce. And the classic dessert is *crème catalane*, a caramel-covered trifle flavoured with anis and cinnamon. Courses ranging from a day to a week on the region's cooking are available at Arles (*see* p.9).

Markets, Picnic Food and Snacks

The food markets in the south of France are justly celebrated for the colour and perfumes of their produce and flowers. They are fun to visit, and become even more interesting if you're cooking or gathering the ingredients for a picnic. In the larger cities food markets take place every day, while smaller towns and villages have markets on one day a week (we've listed all the ones we know in the text), which double as a social occasion for the locals. Most markets finish around noon.

Other good sources for picnic food are the *charcuteries* or *traiteurs*, both of which sell prepared dishes sold by weight in cartons or tubs. You can also find counters at larger super-markets. Cities are snack-food wonderlands, with outdoor counters selling pastries, crêpes, pizza slices, *frites*, *croque-monsieurs* (toasted ham and cheese sandwiches) and a wide variety of sandwiches made from *baguettes* (long thin loaves of bread).

Drink

You can order any kind of drink at any bar or café—except cocktails, unless it has a certain cosmopolitan savoir-faire or stays open into the night. Cafés are also a home from home, places to read the papers, play cards, meet friends, and just unwind, sit back, and watch the world go by. You can spend hours over one coffee and no one will try to hurry you along. Prices are listed on the *Tarif des Consommations*: note they are progressively more expensive depending on whether you're served at the bar (*comptoir*), at a table (*la salle*) or outside (*la terrasse*). French coffee is strong and black, but lacklustre next to the aromatic brews of Italy or Spain (you'll notice an improvement in the coffee near their respective frontiers). If you order *un café* you'll get a small black *express*; if you want milk, order *un crème*. If you want more than a few drops of caffeine, ask them to make it *grand*. For decaffeinated, the word is *déca*. Some bars offer *cappuccinos*, but again they're only really good near the Italian border; in the summer try a *frappé* (iced coffee). The French only order *café au lait* (a small coffee topped off with lots of hot milk) when they stop in for breakfast, and if what your hotel offers is expensive or boring, consider joining them. There are baskets of croissants and pastries, and some bars will make you a *baguette* with butter, jam or honey. If you want to go native, try the Frenchman's Breakfast of Champions: a *pastis* or two, and five non-filter *Gauloises*. *Chocolat chaud* (hot chocolate) is usually good; if you order *thé* (tea), you'll get an ordinary bag. An *infusion* is a herbal tea—*camomile*, *menthe* (mint), *tilleul* (lime or linden blossom), or *verveine* (verbena). These are kind to the all-precious *foie*, or liver, after you've over-indulged at the table.

Mineral water (*eau minérale*) can be addictive, and comes either sparkling (*gazeuse* or *pétillante*) or still (*non-gazeuse* or *plate*). If you feel run down, *Badoit* has lots of peppy magnesium in it—it's the current trendy favourite, even though Perrier comes from Languedoc. The usual international corporate soft drinks are available, and all kinds of bottled fruit juices (*jus de fruits*). Some bars also do fresh lemon and orange juices (*citron pressé* or *orange pressée*). The French are also fond of fruit syrups—red *grenadine* and ghastly green *diabolo menthe*.

Beer (*bière*) in most bars and cafés is run-of-the-mill big brands from Alsace, Germany, and Belgium. Draft (*à la pression*) is cheaper than bottled beer. Nearly all resorts have bars or pubs offering wider selections of drafts, lagers and bottles.

The strong spirit of the Midi comes in a liquid form called *pastis*, first made popular in Marseille as a plague remedy; its name comes from the Latin *passe-sitis*, or thirst quencher. A pale yellow 90% nectar flavoured with anis, vanilla and cinnamon, pastis is drunk as an apéritif before lunch and in rounds after work. The three major brands, *Ricard*, *Pernod* and *Pastis 51*, all taste slightly different; most people drink their '*pastaga*' with lots of water and ice (*glaçons*), which makes it almost palatable. A thimble-sized *pastis* is a *momie*; mixed with grenadine it becomes a *tomate*; with *orgeat* (almond and orange flower syrup) it's a *mauresque*, and a *perroquet* is with mint.

Other popular apéritifs come from Languedoc-Roussillon, including *Byrrh* 'from the world's largest barrel', a sweet wine mixed with quinine and orange peel, similar to *Dubonnet*. Spirits include the familiar Cognac and Armagnac brandies, liqueurs and *digestifs* made from walnuts, cherries, pears and herbs (these are a speciality of the Alps), and fiery *marc*, the grape spirit that is the same as Italian *grappa* (but usually better).

wine

One of the pleasures of travelling in France is drinking great wines for a fraction of what you pay at home, and discovering new ones you've never seen in your local shop. The south holds a special place in the saga of French wines, with a tradition dating back to the Greeks, who are said to have introduced an essential Côtes-du-Rhône grape variety called *syrah*, originally grown in Shiraz, Persia. Nurtured in the Dark and Middle Ages by popes and kings, the vine-yards of Provence and Languedoc-Roussillon still produce most of France's wine—certainly most of its plonk, graded only by its alcohol content. Some of Provence's best-known wines grow in the ancient places near the coast, especially its quartet of tiny AOC districts *Bellet,*

Bandol, Cassis and *Palette*. But the best-known wines of the region come from the Rhône valley, under the general heading of *Côtes-du-Rhône*, including *Châteauneuf-du-Pape*, *Gigondas*, the famous rosé *Tavel*, and the sweet muscat apéritif wine, *Beaumes-de-Venise*. Elsewhere, winemakers have made great strides in boosting quality in the past 30 years, recognized in new AOC districts. Even greater strides have been made in Languedoc-Roussillon, the rising star on the French wine charts. Corbières, the fourth AOC district in France, and Minervois are only the two best known, while seldom-exported delights like *La Clape* and *Faugères* await the wine explorer. Languedoc is also the home of *Blanquette de Limoux*, the world's oldest sparkling wine, *Banyuls*, France's answer to port, and *Rivesaltes*, a sweet muscat good Catalans drink all the livelong day.

'If rules inhibit your enjoyment of wines, there should be no rules,' Alexis Lichine wrote in the 1950s, and it still holds true today. The innocent drinker has to put up with even more words and snootery than the beleaguered eater. Confronting a wine list makes a lot of people nervous, while an oily, obsequious *sommelier* can ruin their entire meal. Note that restaurants make a good portion of their income from marking up wines to triple or quadruple the retail price. Save money by buying it direct from the producers, or *vignerons*. In the text we've included a few addresses for each wine to get you started.

If a wine is labelled AOC (*Appellation d'Origine Contrôlée*) it means that the wine comes from a certain defined area and is made from certain varieties of grapes, guaranteeing a standard of quality. *Cru* on the label means vintage; a *grand cru* is a great, noble vintage. Down the list in the vinous hierarchy are those labelled VDQS (*Vin de Qualité Supérieure*), followed by *Vin de Pays* (guaranteed at least to originate in a certain region), with *Vin Ordinaire* (or *Vin de Table*) at the bottom, which may not send you to seventh heaven but is usually drinkable and cheap. In a restaurant if you order a *rouge* (red) or *blanc* (white) or *rosé* (pink), this is what you'll get, either by the glass (*un verre*), by the quarter-litre (*un pichet*) or bottle (*une bouteille*). *Brut* is very dry, *sec* dry, *demi-sec* and *moelleux* are sweetish, *doux* sweet, and *méthode champenoise*, sparkling.

If you're buying direct from the producer (or a wine co-operative, or *syndicat*, a group of producers), you'll be offered glasses to taste, each wine older than the previous one until you are feeling quite jolly and ready to buy the oldest (and most expensive) vintage. On the other hand, some sell loose wine à la petrol pump, *en vrac*; many *caves* even sell the little plastic barrels to put it in.

Health and Emergencies

Local hospitals are the place to go in an emergency (*urgence*). If you need an ambulance (SAMU), dial © 15; police and ambulance, © 17; fire, © 18. Doctors take turns going on duty at night and on holidays even in rural areas: ring one to listen to the recorded message to find out what to do. To be on the safe side, always carry a phone card (*see* telephones, below). If it's not an emergency, pharmacists are trained to administer first aid, and dispense free advice for minor problems. In rural areas there is always someone on duty if you ring the bell; in cities *pharmacies are* open on a rotating basis and addresses are posted in their windows and in the local newspaper. Doctors will give you a brown and white *feuille de soins* with your prescription; take both to the pharmacy and keep the *feuille* for insurance purposes at home. British subjects who are hospitalized and can produce their E-111 forms (*see* p.5) will be billed later at home for 20% of the costs that French social insurance doesn't cover.

Money and Banks

The franc (abbreviated with an F) consists of 100 centimes. Banknotes come in denominations of 500, 200, 100, 50 and 20F; coins in 20, 10, 5, 2 and 1F, and 50, 20, 10, and 5 centimes. You can bring in as much currency as you like, but by law are only allowed to take out 5000F in cash. Travellers' cheques or Eurocheques are the safest way of carrying money; if you have a four digit PIN number your credit cards will be accepted nearly everywhere—VISA (*Carte Bleue* in French) is the most widely recognized—and will allow you to draw up to 2000F at a time from automatic cash dispensers. If you plan to spend a lot of time in rural areas, where banks are few and far between, you may want to opt for International Giro Cheques, exchangeable at any post office.

Banks are generally open from 8.30am–12.30pm and 1.30–4pm; they close on Sunday, and most close either on Saturday or Monday as well. Exchange rates vary, and nearly all take a commission of varying proportions. *Bureaux de change* that do nothing but exchange money (and exchanges in hotels and train stations) usually have the worst rates or take out the heftiest commissions, so be careful. It's always a good bet to purchase some francs before you go, especially if you arrive during the weekend.

You will now find your bills submitted in Euros as well as francs. Don't let this worry you; the Euro does not become the currency of cash before 2002. However in 1999 it is possible for residents of the EMU member countries to hold Euro bank accounts and some companies and organizations in Euroland will be trading in them this year. SNCF is one for instance: if you want to buy a train ticket direct from them, and you hold a Euro account, you could pay in Euros. Since Ireland is the only English-speaking EMU member at the moment, it pays to be Irish.

Opening Hours, Museums and National Holidays

While many shops and supermarkets in Marseille, Nice and other large cities are now open continuously Tuesday–Saturday from 9 or 10am to 7 or 7.30pm, businesses in smaller towns still close down for lunch from 12 or 12.30pm to 2 or 3pm, or in the summer 4pm in the afternoon. There are local exceptions, but nearly everything shuts down on Mondays, except for grocers and *supermarchés* that open in the afternoon. In many towns Sunday morning is a big shopping period. Markets (daily in the cities, weekly in villages) are usually open mornings only, although clothes, flea and antique markets run into the afternoon.

Most museums close for lunch as well, and often all day on Mondays or Tuesdays, and sometimes for all of November or the entire winter. Hours change with the season: longer summer hours begin in May or June and last until the end of September—usually. Some change their hours every darn month. We've done our best to include them in the text, but don't sue us if they're not exactly right. Most close on national holidays and give discounts if you have a student ID card, or are an EU citizen under 18 or over 65 years old; most charge admissions ranging from 10–30F. Churches are usually open all day, or closed all day and only open for mass. Sometimes notes on the door direct you to the *mairie* or priest's house (*presbytère*) where you can pick up the key. There are often admission fees for cloisters, crypts and special chapels. On French **national holidays**, banks, shops, and businesses close; some museums do, but most restaurants stay open. They are: January 1, Easter Sunday, Easter Monday, May 1, May 8 (VE Day), Ascension Day, Pentecost and the following Monday, July 14 (Bastille

Day), August 15 (Assumption of the BVM), November 1 (All Saints'), November 11 (First World War Armistice), and Christmas Day.

Post Offices and Telephones

Known as the PTT or *Bureaux de Poste*, easily discernible by a blue bird on a yellow background, **post offices** are open in the cities Mon–Fri 8am–7pm, and Saturdays 8am until noon. In villages offices may not open until 9am, break for lunch, and close at 4.30 or 5pm. You can receive letters *poste restante* at any of them; the postal codes in this book should help your mail get there in a timely fashion. To collect it, bring some ID. You can purchase stamps in tobacconists as well as post offices.

Nearly all **public telephones** have switched over from coins to *télécartes*, which you can purchase at any post office or newsstand for 40F for 50 *unités* or 96F for 120 *unités*. The French have eliminated area codes, giving everyone a ten-digit telephone number. If **ringing France from abroad**, the international dialling code is 33, and drop the first '0' of the number. For **international calls from France** dial 00, wait for the change in the dial tone, then dial the country code (UK 44; US and Canada 1; Ireland 353; Australia 61; New Zealand 64), and then the local code (minus the 0 for UK numbers) and number. The easiest way to reverse the charges is to spend a few francs ringing the number you want to call and giving them your number in France, which is always posted in the box; alternatively ring your national operator and tell him or her that you want to call reverse charges (for the UK dial 00 33 44; for the US 00 33 11). For directory enquiries, dial 12, or try your luck on the free, inefficient Minitel electronic directory in every post office.

Racism

Unfortunately in the south of France the forces of bigotry and reaction are strong enough to make racism a serious concern. We've heard some horror stories, especially about Marseille, Nice, Toulon and Roussillon, where campsites and restaurants suddenly have no places if the colour of your skin doesn't suit the proprietor; the bouncers at clubs will inevitably say it's really the cut of your hair or trousers they find offensive. If any place recommended in this book is guilty of such behaviour, please write and let us know; we will not only remove it in the next edition, but forward your letter to the regional tourist office and relevant authorities in Paris.

Shopping

Some Provençal villages have more boutiques than year-round residents but their wares are rarely compelling. Traditional handicrafts have all but died out, and attempts to revive them have resulted in little model houses and *santons*, terracotta Christmas crib figures dressed in 18th-century Provençal costumes, usually as artful as the concrete studies of the Seven Dwarfs sold at your neighbourhood garden centre. Every town east of the Rhône has at least one boutique specializing in Provençal skirts, bags, pillows and scarves, printed in intense colours (madder red, sunflower yellow, pine green) with floral, paisley or geometric designs. Block-print fabrics were first made in Provence after Louis XIV, wanting to protect the French silk industry, banned the import of popular Indian prints. Clever entrepreneurs in the papal-owned Comtat Venaissin responded by producing cheap imitations still known today as *indiennes*. The same shops usually sell the other essential bric-à-brac of the south—dried lavender potpourris, sachets of *herbes de Provence* (nothing but thyme and bay leaves), perfumed soaps.

Big name French and Italian designers and purveyors of luxury goods have boutiques at Cannes, Monaco and Nice. Moustiers, Vallauris and Biot have hand-made ceramics, and in Provence at least a million artists wait to sell you their works. Fontaine-de-Vaucluse has a traditional paper and stationery industry; Cogolin specializes in pipes and saxophone-reeds; Grasse sells perfumes and essential oils.

The sweet of tooth will find western Provence heaven. Nearly every town has its own speciality: candied fruits in Apt, the chocolates and *calissons* (marzipan candies shaped like little boats) of Aix, *berlingots* (mint-flavoured caramels) in Carpentras, *nougats* in Vence, *marrons glacés* in Collobrières, and orange-flavoured chocolates called *papalines* in Avignon.

Sport and Leisure Activities

bullfights

The Roman amphitheatres at Nîmes and Arles had hardly been restored in the early 1800s when they once again became venues for *tauromachie*. Attempts to abolish the sport in the 1900s fell flat when the poet Frédéric Mistral, the self-appointed watchdog of all things Provençal, intervened; and if anything, bullfights are now more popular than ever.

However, the most traditional bullfights in Provence and Languedoc are not bloody. The *courses provençales* (or *courses libres*) can be traced back to the bull games described by Heliodorus in ancient Thessaly. Played by daring young men dressed in white called *razeteurs*, the sport demands grace, daring and dexterity, especially in leaping over the barriers before a charging bull. The object is to remove a round cockade from between the horns of the bull (or cow) by cutting its ribbons with a blunt razor comb—a sport far more dangerous to the human players than the animals. The animals used for the *courses provençales* are the small, lithe, high-horned breed from the Camargue; good sporty ones retire with fat pensions.

You will see three other types of bullfight advertised: the *corrida*, or traditional Spanish bull-fight, where the bull is put to death. The bullfighters are usually Spanish as well, and the major festivals, or *ferias*, bring some of the top *toreros* to France, although beware that the already expensive tickets tend to be snapped up by touts. A *novillada*, pitting younger bulls against apprentice *toreros* (*novilleros*) is less expensive, but much more likely to be a butchery void of *arte*. In a *corrida portuguaise* the bullfighter (*rejoneador*) fights from horseback, but doesn't kill the bull.

pétanque

Like pastis and olive oil, *pétanque* is one of the essential ingredients of the Midi, and even the smallest village has a rough, hard court under the plane trees for its practitioners—nearly all male, although women are welcome to join in. Similar to *boules*, the special rules of *pétanque* were according to tradition developed in La Ciotat (*see* p.166). The object is to get your metal ball closest to the marker (*bouchon* or *cochonnet*). Tournaments are frequent and well attended.

rugby union

Rugby is the national sport of Languedoc and the southwest, and the cradle of most of the players on the national team (although movements to change one of the Five Nations from France to Occitania have so far fallen flat). Although the best teams lately have been Toulouse, Agen and Bordeaux, you can still see fiery matches in Béziers, longtime champions (the town has three rugby schools), and Carcassonne. Nice and Toulon also have impressive sides. In some places they play 'Cathar rugby'—13 to a side instead of 15.

skiing

Ideally, if the weather ever decides to settle down, you can do as in California: ski in the morning and bake on the beach in the afternoon. The biggest resorts in the Alpes Maritimes are Isola 2000, Auron and Valberg and, closest to Nice, Gréolières-les-Neiges. On the Mediterranean end of the Pyrenees, there's Font-Romeu, although snowfall has been just as unreliable there in recent years. Hence package deals going from abroad are practically non-existent. For the Alpes Maritimes, contact the Comité Régional de Tourisme Provence Alpes Côte d'Azur, C.M.C.I., 2 rue Henri Barbusse, 13241 Marseille, © 04 91 56 23 63.

water sports and beaches

In 1763, the consumptive English writer and doctor, Tobias 'Smellfungus' Smollett tried something for his health that shocked the doctors in Nice: he went bathing in the sea. Most extraordinary of all, it made him feel better, and he recommended that people follow his example, though it would be difficult for women 'unless they laid aside all regards to decorum'—as they so often do in the most fashionable resorts. There are scores of fine, sandy beaches along the coast, although *not* on the Riviera east of Juan-les-Pins. Anyone who arrives with any ideas about access to the sea being a natural God-given right will be appalled to learn that paying concessions occupy most of the Provençal shore; free, quiet beaches require more effort (the Calanques west of Cassis, the coves below the Esterel and the Maures, the Hyères islands).

Languedoc-Roussillon is a completely different story: less glamour, but more miles of free sandy beaches than anywhere in the western Mediterranean, stretching into the horizon on either side of its scores of small resorts—until you reach the rocky Côte Vermeille at any rate. Areas are always set aside for *les naturistes*, or nudists: Cap d'Agde and the Ile du Levant are two of Europe's biggest nudist resorts.

Every town on the coast hires out equipment for water sports, often for hefty prices. Juan-les-Pins claims to have invented water skiing. Experienced windsurfers head for Brutal Beach off Cap Sicié, west of Toulon. The best diving is off Ile Port-Cros National Park (for a list of diving clubs, contact the Fédération Française d'Etudes et de Sports Sous-Marins, 24 Quai de Rive Neuve, 13007 Marseille, © 04 91 33 99 31, ✆ 04 91 54 77 43).

If you're genuinely jaded and have a weakness for medical-psychobabble, you can even indulge in *thalassothérapie* to help make you thin, fit, stress-free, or even turn you into a laid-back non-smoker.

Tourist Information

Every city and town, and most villages, have a tourist information office, usually called a *Syndicat d'Initiative* or an *Office de Tourisme*. In smaller villages this service is provided by the town hall (*mairie*). They distribute free maps and town plans, hotel, camping, and self-catering accommodation lists for their area, and can inform you on sporting events, leisure activities, wine estates open for visits, and festivals. Addresses and telephone numbers are listed in the text, and if you write to them they'll post you their booklets to help you plan your holiday before you leave.

Hotels

In the south of France you can find some of the most splendid hotels in Europe and some genuine scruffy fleabags of dubious clientele, with the majority of establishments falling somewhere between. Like most countries in Europe, the tourist authorities grade them by their facilities (not by charm or location) with stars from four (or four with an L for luxury—a bit confusing, so in the text luxury places are given five stars) to one, and there are even some cheap but adequate places undignified by any stars at all.

We would have liked to put the exact prices in the text, but almost every establishment has a wide range of rooms and prices—a very useful and logical way of doing things, once you're used to it. In some hotels, every single room has its own personality and the difference in quality and price can be enormous; a large room with antique furniture, a television or a balcony over the sea and a complete bathroom will cost much more than a poky back room in the same hotel, with a window overlooking a car park, no antiques, and the WC down the hall. Some proprietors will drag out a sort of menu for you to choose the level of price and facilities you would like. Most two-star hotel rooms have their own showers and WCs; most one stars offer rooms with or without. The following guide will give you an idea of what prices to expect. Côte d'Azur hotels will be near the top of the range, while Languedoc hotels tend to be near the bottom.

Note: all prices listed here and elsewhere in this book are for a double room.

★★★★	400–2300F
★★★	240–700F
★★	150–500F
★	130–300F

Hotels with **no stars** are not necessarily dives; their owners probably never bothered filling out a form for the tourist authorities. Their prices are usually the same as one-star places.

Standards vary so widely that it's impossible to be more precise, but we can add a few more generalizations. **Single rooms** are relatively rare, and usually two-thirds the price of a double, and rarely will a hotelier give you a discount if only doubles are available (again, because each room has its own price); on the other hand, if there are three or four of you, **triples or quads** or adding extra beds to a double room is usually cheaper than staying in two rooms. Flowered wallpaper, usually beige, comes in all rooms with no extra charge—it's an essential part of the French experience. **Breakfast** (usually coffee, a croissant, bread and jam for 30F or 40F) is nearly always optional: you'll do as well for less in a bar. As usual rates rise in the busy season (holidays and summer, and in the winter around ski resorts), when many hotels with restaurants will require that you take **half-board** (*demi-pension*—breakfast and a set lunch or dinner). Many hotel restaurants are superb and described in the text, and non-residents are welcome. At worst the food will be boring, and it can be monotonous eating in the same place every night when there are so many tempting restaurants around. In the off-season board requirements vanish into thin air.

Your holiday will be much sweeter if you **book ahead**, especially anywhere near the Côte d'Azur from May to October. The few reasonably priced rooms are snapped up very early across the board. In Provence and Languedoc, July and August are the only really impossible months; otherwise it usually isn't too difficult to find something. Phoning a day or two ahead is always a good policy, although beware that hotels will only confirm a room with the receipt of a cheque covering the first night (although many now take a credit card number). Tourist offices have complete lists of accommodation in their given areas or even *département*, which come in handy during the peak season; many will even call around and book a room for you on the spot for free or a nominal fee.

Chain hotels (Sofitel, Formula One, etc.) are in most cities, but always dreary and geared to the business traveller more than the tourist, so you won't find them in this book. Don't confuse chains with the various **umbrella organizations** like *Logis et Auberges de France*, *Relais de Silence*, or the prestigious *Relais et Châteaux* which promote and guarantee the quality of independently owned hotels and their restaurants. Many are recommended in the text. Larger tourist offices usually stock their booklets, or you can pick them up before you leave from the French National Tourist Office. If you plan to do a lot of driving, you may want to pick the English translation of the French truckers' bible, *Les Routiers*, an annual guide with maps listing reasonably priced lodgings and food along the highways and byways of France (£8.99, Routiers Limited, 25 Vanston Place, London SW6 1AZ).

Bed and breakfast: In rural areas, there are plenty of opportunities for a stay in a private home or farm. *Chambres d'hôtes*, in the tourist office brochures, are listed separately from hotels with the various *gîtes* (*see* below). Some are connected to restaurants, others to wine estates or a château; prices tend to be moderate to inexpensive. Also try B & B France, PO Box 66, Bell Street, Henley-on-Thames, Oxon RG9 1XS, ℭ (01491) 578803, ℯ 410806, e-mai bookings@bedbreck.demon.co.uk (catalogue £5.50); or in France, 6 Rue d'Europe, 95470 Fosses, ℭ 01 34 68 83 15 (catalogue 50F).

Youth Hostels, Gîtes d'Etape, and Refuges

Most cities and resort areas have youth hostels (*Auberges de Jeunesse*) which offer simple dormitory accommodation and breakfast to people of any age for around 40–70F a night. Most offer kitchen facilities as well, or inexpensive meals. They are the best deal going for people travelling on their own; for people travelling together a one-star hotel can be just as cheap. Another down-side is that many are in the most ungodly locations—in the suburbs where the last bus goes by at 7pm, or miles from any transport at all in the country. In the summer the only way to be sure of a room is to arrive early in the day. Most require a Youth Hostels Association membership card, which you can usually purchase on the spot, although regulations say you should buy them in your home country (UK: from YHA, 14 Southampton Street, London WC2; USA: from AYH, P.O. Box 37613, Washington DC 20013; Canada: from CHA, 1600 James Maysmyth Dr, 6th floor, Gloucester, Ottawa, Ont K1B 5N4; Australia: from AYHA, 60 Mary St, Surrey Hills, Sydney, New South Wales 2010). Another option in cities is the single-sex dormitories for young workers (*Foyers de Jeunes Travailleurs et de Jeunes Travailleuses*) which will rent out individual rooms if any are available, for slightly more than a youth hostel.

A *gîte d'étape* is a simple shelter with bunk beds and a rudimentary kitchen set up by a village along GR walking paths or a scenic bike route. Again, lists are available for each *département*; the detailed maps listed under 'On Foot', *see* p.8, mark them as well. In the mountains similar rough shelters along the GR paths are called *refuges*, most of them open summer only. Both charge around 40F or 50F a night.

Camping

Camping is a very popular way to travel, especially among the French themselves, and there's at least one campsite in every town, often an inexpensive, no-frills place run by the town itself (*camping municipal*). Other campsites are graded with stars like hotels from four to one: at the top of the line you can expect lots of trees and grass, hot showers, a pool or beach, sports facilities, and a grocer's, bar and/or restaurant, and on the coast, prices rather similar to one-star hotels (although these, of course, never have all the extras). But beware that July and August are terrible months to camp on the Côte d'Azur, when sites become so overcrowded (St-Tropez is notorious) that the authorities have begun to worry about health problems. You'll find more *lebensraum* in Languedoc and off the coast. If you want to camp outside official sites, it's imperative to ask permission from the landowner first, or risk a furious farmer, his dog and perhaps even the police.

Tourist offices have complete lists of campsites in their regions, or if you plan to move around a lot pick up a *Guide Officiel Camping/Caravanning,* available in French bookshops. A number of UK holiday firms book camping holidays and offer discounts on Channel ferries: Canvas Holidays, ✆ (01383) 644 000; Eurocamp Travel, ✆ (01565) 62 62 62; Keycamp Holidays, ✆ (0181) 395 4000.

Gîtes de France and Other Self-catering Accommodation

The south of France offers a vast range of self-catering: inexpensive farm cottages, history-laden châteaux with gourmet frills, sprawling villas on the Riviera, flats in modern beach resorts or even on board canal boats. The *Fédération Nationale des Gîtes de France* is a French government service offering inexpensive accommodation by the week in rural areas. Lists with photos arranged by *département* are available from the Maison des Gîtes de France, 35 Rue de Godot de Mauroy, 75439 Paris Cedex 09, or in the UK from the official rep: **Gîtes de France**, 178 Piccadilly, London W1V 9DB, ✆ (0171) 493 3480. If you want to stay in châteaux, request the *Chambres d'Hôtes et Gîtes de Prestige*. Prices range from 1000F to 2000F a week. Other options are advertised in the Sunday papers or contact one of the firms listed below. The accommodation they offer will nearly always be more comfortable and costly than a *gîte*, but the discounts holiday firms can offer on the ferries, plane tickets, or car rental can make up for the price difference.

in the UK

Allez France, 27 West Street, Storrington, West Sussex RH20 4DZ, ✆ (01903) 742 345: wide variety of accommodation from cottages to châteaux.

Angel Travel, 34 High Street, Borough Green, Sevenoaks TN15 8BJ, ✆ (01732) 884 109: villas, *gîtes* and flats in Provence, Côte d'Azur and Languedoc.

The Apartment Service, 5–6 Francis Grove, London SW19 4DT, ✆ (0181) 944 1444, 🖷 (0181) 944 6744, e-mail res@apartment.co.uk. Selected apartment accommodation in cities for long or short stays.

Belvedere Holiday Apartments, 5 Bartholomews, Brighton BN1 1HG, ✆ (01273) 323 404: studio flats and apartments along the coast from Menton to Cap d'Agde.

Bowhills, Mayhill Farm, Swanmore, Southampton SO32 2QW, ✆ (01489) 877627: luxury villas, farmhouses, mostly with pools.

Brittany Ferries, The Brittany Centre, Wharf Road, Portsmouth PO2 8RU, ✆ (01705) 827701: *gîtes*.

Crystal Holidays, Crystal House, Arlington Road, Surbiton KT6 6BW, ✆ (0181) 241 4000: villas in Languedoc-Roussillon and the Côte.

Destination Provence, Amberwood House, Coxwold, York Y06 4AA, ✆(01765) 609091, ✆ (01765) 690091: villas and flats in Provence.

Dominique's Villas, 13 Park House, 140 Battersea Park Road, London SW11 4NB, ✆ (0171) 738 8772, ✆ (0171) 498 6014: large villas and châteaux with pools in Provence and the Côte.

French Life Holidays, 26 Church Street, Horsforth, Leeds LS18 5LG, ✆ (01532) 390 077: apartments and *gîtes* in the south of France.

French Villa Centre, 175 Selsdon Park Road, South Croydon CR2 8JJ, ✆ (0181) 651 1231: *gîtes*, *villages de vacances*, and coastal villas in the Var and Vaucluse.

InnTravel, Hovingham, York YO6 4JZ, ✆ (01653) 628811: apartments with pools.

International Chapters, 102 St John's Wood Terrace, London NW8 6PL, ✆ (0171) 722 9560: farmhouses, *châteaux*, and villas in Provence and the Côte.

LSG Theme Holidays, 201 Main Street, Thornton, Coalville LE67 1AH, ✆ (01509) 231713: seaside *gîtes*.

Meon Villas, Meon House, College Street, Petersfield GU32 3JN, ✆ (01730) 268411, ✆ (01730) 230 399: villas with pools.

Palmer and Parker Villa Holidays, The Beacon, Penn HP10 8ND, ✆ (01494) 815 411: upmarket villas with pool.

Unicorn Holidays, 2 Place Farm, Wheathampstead AL4 8SB, ✆ (01582) 834400: fly-drive and tailor-made holidays to châteaux-hotels.

Westbury Travel, 1 Belmont, Lansdown Road, Bath BA1 5DZ, ✆ (01372) 826699: apartments, villas, and *gîtes* inland and by the sea.

Vacances en Campagne, Bignor, Pulborough, West Sussex RH20 1QD, ✆ (01798) 869433: farmhouses, villas and *gîtes*.

VFB Holidays, Normandy House, High Street, Cheltenham GL50 3FB, ✆ (01242) 240310: from rustic *gîtes* to luxurious farmhouses.

in the USA

At Home Abroad, 405 East 56th St, New York, NY 10022, ✆ (212) 421 9165: *châteaux* and farmhouses, Provence and the Côte.

Hideaways International, P.O. Box 1464, Littleton, MA 01460, ✆ (423) 947 2322: farmhouses and *châteaux*.

Hometours International, Inc., P.O. Box 11503, Knoxville, TN 37937 ✆ (423) 690 8484: bed and breakfast, apartments, villas and travel service.

Overseas Connections, 211 E. 43rd St, New York, NY 10023, ✆ (212) 681 0983: villas and apartments in Provence and the Côte d'Azur.

RAVE (Rent-a-Vacation-Everywhere), 135 Meigs St, Rochester, NY 14604, ✆ (716) 256 0760: villas and apartments in Provence and on the Riviera.

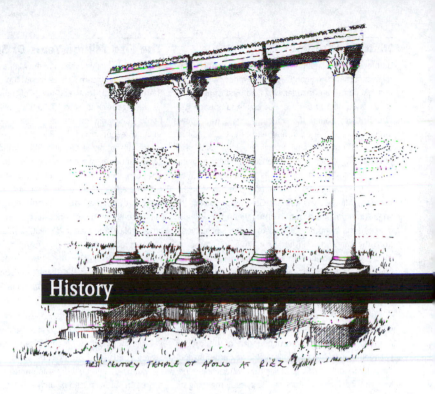

First century temple of Apollo at Riez

History

Historical Outline

Before starting, a little political geography might help to relieve some major confusions. In France, almost all regional names are maddeningly fluid. First of all, there is Provence, which has never had any fixed boundaries. The Romans called the southern coast their dear 'province', one of their first and most delectable conquests outside Italy. Specifically, this was the province of *Gallia Narbonnensis*, stretching from Toulouse to Geneva, though its rich heartland was always the coastal area from Narbonne to Marseille. In the early Middle Ages, ancient Gaul was evolving its linguistic north-south distinction between the *langue d'oc* and the *langue d'oeil* (two words for saying 'yes', from the Latin *hoc* and *hoc ille*). 'Provence' came to mean the *oc* domain, the southern third of what is now France, from the Dordogne to Lyon; both troubadour poets and noblemen's secretaries enjoyed making a connection with the classical civilization that built the Pont du Gard, the arch of Orange and the amphitheatres of Nîmes and Arles.

At the same time, the political boundary of the Rhône, between lands subject to the Holy Roman Emperors and those claimed by the kings of France, was redefining the terminology. 'Provence' took on the political meaning of the semi-independent county east of the Rhône, while the rest, as far as Toulouse and Aquitaine, was grabbed by force by the French in the 13th century and took the name of Languedoc. Provence held out longer, until its union with the French crown in 1486. Today, southern regionalists call the entire Midi Occitania (a word only invented in the 17th century).

Roussillon, the modern *département* of Pyrenées-Orientales, followed an entirely different history; part of the Catalan nation since the 10th century, it was an essential part of the County of Barcelona and later the Catalan Kingdom of Aragon, until the French annexed it in 1559.

Under the *ancien régime*, under the Revolution and all the regimes that followed it, these areas were smothered, politically and culturally, by imperialist France. The turning of the tide has come only in our own time, with the election of the 1981 Socialist government, and the beginnings of regional autonomy. The five *départements* east of the Rhône are now the artificially designed region of Provence-Côte d'Azur; those to the west (along with Lozère, in the Cévennes), are in Languedoc-Roussillon, still cut off from its traditional capital, Toulouse, by the intent of the Paris planners.

The First Million Years Or So

The first inhabitants, with all of the Midi to choose from, not surprisingly seem to have picked the Côte d'Azur for their residence. Tools and traces of habitation around Monaco go back as far as 1,000,000 BC. The first identifiable personality on the stage, however, is 'Tautavel Man'; a recent remarkable find in the small Roussillon village of that name has unearthed hundreds of thousands of bones of a people who rate among the very first Europeans yet discovered—at least 450,000 BC, and perhaps as old as 680,000. Someone may have been around through all the millennia that followed, but evidence is rare; more bones have been found in caves around Nice, from about 200,000 BC. Neanderthal Man turns up about 60,000 BC (at Ganges, in the Hérault, and other places). The first evidence of the Neanderthalers' nemesis, that quarrelsome and unlovable species *Homo Sapiens*, appears some 20,000 years later.

Neolithic civilization arrived as early as 3500 BC, and endured throughout the region for the next 2000 years. People knew agriculture and raised sheep, traded for scarce goods (obsidian from the islands around Sicily, for example), and built dry-stone houses; one of these has been reconstructed by archaeologists at Cambous, in the Hérault. The Neolithic era left few important monuments here: an impressive but little-known temple complex at Castellet, near Arles, and some large dolmens in the Minervois, the northern Hérault, and the Massif des Maures. Of succeeding ages we know more about technology than culture and changes in population: the use of copper began about 2000 BC, iron *c.* 800 BC. In both cases the region was one of the last parts of the Mediterranean basin to catch on.

By now, at least, the inhabitants have a name, even if it is a questionable one applied by later Greek and Roman writers: the Ligurians on the east coast and the Iberians in the west. There is plenty of room for confusion here; culturally and racially there may have been little difference between the two. From about 800 BC, they begin building their first settled villages, today called by the Latin name *oppidum*, a word you will see often in the south; it even survives in village names, such as Oppèdette in Provence. An *oppidum* is a small, fortified village, usually on a hilltop, built around a religious sanctuary or trading centre. Already, more advanced outsiders were coming to make deals with the natives: the Phoenicians, Etruscans and, most importantly, the Greeks.

A major event of this same era was the arrival of the Celts, Indo-European cousins of the Ligurians and Iberians from the north. Beginning in coastal Languedoc in the 8th century BC, they gradually spread their conquests eastwards until the 4th century at the expense of the Ligurians. At the same time, Greek merchant activity was turning into full-scale colonization. The Ionian city-states of Asia Minor had become over-populated, agriculturally exhausted and politically precarious, and their citizens sought to reproduce them in new lands. The first was *Massalia*—Marseille, *c.* 600 BC. Soon Massalia was founding colonies of its own: Nice, Hyères and Agde were among the most important. Greek influence over the indigenous peoples was strong from the start; as with everywhere else they went, they brought the vine (wild stocks were already present, but the Celts hadn't worked out what to do with them) and the olive, and also their art. The Celts loved Greek vases, and had metals and other raw materials to offer in return. Increased trade turned some of the native *oppida* into genuine cities, such as Ensérune, near Béziers, and Arles.

Roman Provincia

From the start, the Greeks were natural allies of the young city of Rome—if only because they had common enemies. Besides the strong Etruscan federation, occupying the lands in between the two, there were their trade rivals, the Phoenicians (later Carthaginians) and occasionally the Celts and Ligurians. As Rome gobbled up Etruria and the rest of Italy, the area became of increasing importance; a fact Hannibal demonstrated when he marched his armies along the coast towards Italy in 218 BC, with the full support of the Celts (historians still argue over how and where he got the elephants across the Rhône).

When the Romans took control of Spain in the Second Punic War (206), the coasts of what they called Gaul became a logical next step. In 125, Roman troops saved Marseille from a Celtic attack. This time, though, they had come to stay. The reorganization of the new province—'Provincia'—was quick and methodical. Domitius Ahenobarbus, the vanquisher of the Celts, began the great Italy-Spain highway that bears his name, the Via Domitia, in 121. New cities were founded, most importantly Aix (122) and Narbonne (118), which became the capital of what was now officially called *Gallia Narbonensis*. Dozens of other new foundations followed over the next century, many of them planned colonies with land grants for veterans of the legions. The Celts were not through yet, though. Two northern tribes, the Cimbri and Teutones, mounted a serious invasion of Gaul and Italy in 115. They raided those areas continuously until 102, when they were destroyed by a Roman army under Marius near Mte-Ste-Victoire, near Aix. Marius, later populist dictator in Rome, became a folk hero and the subject of Provençal legends ever after. Celtic-Ligurian resistance continued intermittently until 14 BC; the great monument at La Turbie, on the border of Gaul, commemorates the defeat of the last hold-outs in the Alps.

The downfall of Marseille, still the metropolis of Provence and still thoroughly Greek in culture and sympathies, came in 49 BC. Always famed for its careful diplomacy, the city made the fatal mistake of supporting Pompey over Julius Caesar in the Roman civil wars. A vengeful Caesar crippled its trade and stripped it of nearly all its colonies and dependencies. Thereafter, the influence of Marseille gave way to newer, more Romanized towns: Aix, Narbonne, Nîmes, Arles, Fréjus.

Throughout all this, Provence had been easily assimilated into the Roman economy, supplying food and raw materials for the insatiable metropolis. With Caesar's conquest of the rest of Gaul, the Rhône trade route (which had always managed to bring down a little Baltic amber and tin from Cornwall) became a busy river highway and military route. Under the good government and peace bestowed by Augustus (27 BC–14 AD) and his successors, Provence blossomed into an opulence never before seen. The cities, especially those of the Rhône valley, acquired theatres, amphitheatres for the games, aqueducts, bridges and temples. Provence participated in the political and cultural life of the Empire, even contributing one of the better emperors, Antoninus Pius (from Nîmes, 138–161 AD), only obscure because his reign was so peaceful and prosperous.

Large areas of Roman towns have been excavated at Glanum and Vaison-la-Romaine, and both have turned up a preponderance of wealthy villas. This is the dark side of Roman Provence; from the beginning of Roman rule, wealthy Romans were able to grab up much of the land, forming large estates and exploiting the indigenous population. This trend was magnified in the decadent, totalitarian and economically chaotic late Empire, when, throughout Roman territory, the few remaining free farmers were forced to sell themselves into virtual serfdom to escape crushing taxation. After 200 AD, in fact, everything was going wrong so that trade and the cities stagnated while art and culture decayed; the first of the barbarian raids took place and brought Germans into Provence in the 250s, when they destroyed Glanum.

Constantine, while yet Emperor of only the western half of the empire (312–323), often resided at Arles and favoured that city; his baths there were probably the last big Roman building project in Provence. His pro-Christian policy gave the cult its first real influence in Gaul, at least in the cities; under his auspices, the first state-sponsored Church council was held at Arles in 314. Before that Christianity does not seem to have made much of an impression (later, to make up for it elaborate mythologies were constructed to place Mary Magdalene and other early saints in Provence after the Crucifixion; cf. the towns of Stes-Maries-de-la-Mer and St-Maximin-la-Ste-Baume).

600 Years of Uninvited Guests

French historians always blame the barbarian invaders of the 5th century for destroying the cities of Provence—as if Teutonic warriors enjoyed pulling down temple colonnades on their days off. In fact, few armies passed through Provence; the Visigoths, in the early 400s, were the most notable. Though government collapsed in chaos, business went on much as usual, with the Roman landowners (and their new German colleagues) gradually making their transition to feudal nobles. Arles, untouched by the troubles, became the most important city of the west, and briefly the capital, under Constantius III in 412. The weakness of the central power brought some long-due upheavals in the countryside, with guerrilla bands and vigilante justice against the landlords. The old and new rulers soon found common cause. For a while, a clique of a hundred of the biggest landowners took over administration in Gaul, even declaring one of their own as 'emperor' in Arles (455), with the support of the Visigoths.

The Visigoths soon tired of such games, and assumed total control in 476, the year the Western Empire formally expired. They had to share it, however, with the Ostrogoths, who had established a strong kingdom in Italy and seized all of Provence east of the Rhône—the beginnings of a political boundary that would last in various forms for a thousand years. When the Eastern Empire under Justinian invaded Italy, the Franks were able to snatch the Ostrogoths' half (535). They were never able to hold it effectively, and the area gradually slipped into virtual independence.

The Visigoths kept their part, a distant zone of their Spanish kingdom, until the Arab invasion of the early 700s rolled over the Pyrenees. In 719 the Arabs took Narbonne. The next two centuries are as wonderfully confused as anything in prehistory. There is the legend of the great Spanish Caliph Abd ar-Rahman, defeated in battle and leaving a treasure buried somewhere in the Alpilles. And a document survives, in which the bishops of Agde are rebuked by the Pope for minting coins with the image of Muhammad. Charles Martel, the celebrated Frankish generalissimo who stopped the Arab wave at Poitiers, made an expedition to the southern coast in 737–39, brutally sacking Agde, Marseille, Avignon and Aix. His mission was hardly a religious crusade—rather taking advantage of the Visigothic defeat to increase Frankish hegemony in the south; the cities of Provence are recorded as petitioning the Arabs at Cordoba to help them keep the nasty Franks out.

The Arabs couldn't help; the climate was too eccentric and the pickings too slim for them to mount a serious effort in Gaul. The nascent Franks gained control everywhere, and the entire coast was absorbed by Charlemagne's father, Pépin the Short, in 759. Under Charlemagne (768–814), Occitania seems to have shared little in the Carolingian revival of trade and culture, and after the break-up of the empire (at the Treaty of Verdun in 843) its misery was complete. The 9th- and 10th-century invasions were the real Dark Age in many parts of Europe. Provence suffered constant and destructive raids by the Normans, the Arabs again, who held the Massif des Maures and St-Tropez until the 970s, and even the Hungarians, who sacked what was left of Nîmes in 924.

The Beginnings of the Middle Ages

Even in this sorry period, the foundations were being laid for recovery. Monastic reformers in Charlemagne's time, men such as Benedict of Aniane (in the Hérault) helped start a huge expansion of Church institutions. The Abbey of St-Victor in Marseille took the lead in this, founding hundreds of new monasteries around Occitania; hard-working monks reclaimed land from forests and swamps—later they sat back and enjoyed the rents, while always keeping up the holy work of education and copying books. Pilgrimages became an important activity, especially to Arles (St-Trophime) and St-Guilhem, near Aniane; getting a sleepy and locally-bound society moving again and providing an impetus to trade.

The Treaty of Verdun (see above) had confirmed the Rhône as a boundary, and politically Provence and Languedoc went their separate ways. The Kingdom of

Provence (or 'Kingdom of Arles'), proclaimed by a great-grandson of Charlemagne in 879, was little more than a façade for a feudal anarchy. Though the Kingdom was united with the Kingdom of Burgundy in 949, and formally passed to the Holy Roman Empire in 1032, the tapestry of battling barons and shifting local alliances continued without effective interference from the overlords. Across the Rhône it was much the same; Frankish control was almost non-existent, and the biggest power in Languedoc was that of the County of Toulouse.

The most important result of the Carolingian collapse was the birth of a new nation in the eastern Pyrenees—Catalunya. The Catalans, who spoke a language closely related to the Occitan of Languedoc and Provence, coalesced around the County of the Cerdagne, deep in the mountains. In the 10th century this dynasty became Counts of Barcelona, and expanded its control into what is now Roussillon.

Occitan and Catalan Medieval Civilization

As elsewhere in Europe, the year 1000 is the rough milestone for the sudden and spectacular development of the medieval world. Towns and villages found the money and energy to build impressive new churches. The end of the foreign raiders made the seas safe for merchants, from Genoa, Pisa and Barcelona mostly, but also a few from Marseille. New cities were founded, notably Montpellier, in 985. In 1002, the first written document in Occitan appears. The great pilgrimage to Santiago de Compostela, in Spain, made what was left of the old Roman roads into busy highways once more; along the main southern route the first of the medieval trade fairs appeared, at the new town of St-Gilles-du-Gard.

Things were on the upswing throughout the 11th century, and the trend was given another boost by the Crusades, which began in 1095. With increased prosperity and contact with a wider world, better manners and the rudiments of personal hygiene were not slow to follow. Feudal anarchy began to look quite genteel—maintaining a delicate balance of power, with feudal ties and blood relations keeping the political appetites of rulers from ever really getting out of hand. From the more civilized east, and from nearby Muslim Spain, came new ideas, new technologies and a taste for luxury and art. As an indication of how far Occitania had come, there are the troubadours (*see* pp.57–8), with modern Europe's first lyric poetry. Almost every court of

the south was refined enough to welcome and patronize them.

The growing cities began to assert themselves in the 12th century, often achieving a substantial independence in *communes* governed by consuls: Avignon in 1129, Arles in 1132, Perpignan and Nîmes in 1198. In the countryside, successive waves of monastic reform spawned a huge number of new institutions: first the movement led from Cluny, in the 11th century, and in the 12th the Cistercians, who started a score of important monasteries. Efficiently exploiting the lands bequeathed by noblemen made them rich, and also did much to improve the agricultural economy all round.

Probably the richest corner of the south was the Catalan Pyrenees; substantial iron deposits, and the most advanced methods of smelting them, provided the capital for a Catalan trading empire based in Barcelona and Perpignan. From then on Catalunya's rise was dramatic. By 1125 the Counts of Barcelona controlled much of Provence south of the Durance; in 1137 they became Kings of Aragon, which included much of western Spain as well as Roussillon. Besides its wealth, Catalunya was characterized by its unique constitution, recognizing the interests of the new middle class as well as nobles, and writing down elaborate codes of rights called *fueros* as a check on royal absolutism.

The other leading power in the region, Toulouse, contended with the Catalans for Provence while being overlords of all Languedoc, excepting Carcassonne and Béziers, ruled by the Trencavel family, and Narbonne, with its independent Viscounts.

The Cathars and the Rape of Languedoc

It was a great age for culture, producing not only the troubadours but an impressive display of Romanesque architecture, and original schools of sculpture in Roussillon and at Arles. Perhaps the most remarkable phenomenon of the times was a widespread religious tolerance, shared by rulers, the common people and even many among the clergy. A long and fruitful exposure to the culture of Muslim Spain, as well as the presence of a large Jewish community, an important element in the towns since Roman times, must have helped. Still, such goodwill is hard to account for in medieval Europe. Like the troubadour poetry it is an indication of just how advanced Occitan society was, at its height in the 12th century.

Unfortunately, this tolerance was also to bring about the fall of the Occitan nation. Religious dissenters of various persuasions sprang up everywhere. Most of the new sects soon died out, and are little known today—like the extremist 'Petrobrusians' of St-Gilles, who didn't fancy churches, sacraments, relics or priests, and who even had their doubts about the crucifixion of Jesus.

One sect, however, made startling inroads into every sector of society in 11th- and 12th-century Languedoc—the Cathars, or Albigensians. This Manichaean doctrine (see pp.54–5), obsessed with Good and Evil, had in its upright simplicity a powerful attraction for industrious townspeople and peasants. In many ways it was the very picture of 17th-century English Puritanism, though without any of the Puritans' noxious belligerence towards the less perfect; this kept it in good standing with the worldly nobility, and also allowed Cathar and Catholic villagers to live peacefully side by side.

The Cathars were never a majority in any part of the south; in most places they never made up more than 10% of the population. They might have passed on as only a curious footnote to history, had they not provided the excuse for the biggest and most flagrant land grab of the Middle Ages. The 'Albigensian Crusade', arranged after the 1208 murder of a papal legate, was a cynical marriage of convenience between two old piratical enemies, the papacy and the crown of France. One wanted the religious competition stifled, the other sought to assert its old Carolingian claim to the lands of the Counts of Toulouse. Diplomacy forced King Philip Augustus to disclaim any part in the affair, but nevertheless a big army of knights from the Ile-de-France went south in 1209 to burn some heretics and snatch what they might. Their leader made the difference: too smart, too brutal and too lucky, the sort of devil that changes history—Simon de Montfort. His vicious massacres at Béziers, where the Catholic population tried to defend the heretics and were incinerated along with them inside the churches, and his taking of the impregnable fortress town of Carcassonne put the fear of God into the southerners; Montfort won battle after battle and took every town he attacked, save only Beaucaire.

In a last attempt to save their fortunes, Count Raymond VI of Toulouse and King Peter II of Aragon combined to meet the northerners. With an overwhelmingly superior force, they blundered their way to crushing defeat at the Battle of Muret in 1213. Montfort soon claimed the titles of Count of Toulouse and Viscount of Carcassonne and Béziers for himself. The Languedociens continued to resist until after his death in 1218; six years later, again under the pretence of a 'crusade', King Louis VIII took the matter in his own hands. Coming south with another army he forced the annexation of all eastern Languedoc and Carcassonne, the fortress key to the Midi, in 1229. The remainder of the century saw the inexorable consolidation of French power; the building or rebuilding of gigantic fortifications, as at Carcassonne and Peyrepertuse, begun by St Louis (King Louis IX, 1226–70), and the new port of Aigues-Mortes, used by Louis as base for his two Crusades (1249 and 1270).

Four centuries after the fall of the Carolingian Empire, the French once again had their foothold in the south. Languedoc was through, its distinctive culture quickly snuffed out. If Montfort's men had been Paris' shock troops, the occupying force would be made up of French bureaucrats and monks. The monks took charge of many village churches, replacing parish priests to keep an eye on the population. The Inquisition arrived to take care of the heretics—and of course anyone the northerners found politically suspect, or whose property they coveted. The last Cathar stronghold, the Château de Quéribus, fell to royal troops in 1255. The troubadours found less and less around them worthy of a song. One of the most famous, Folquet de Marseille, had already gone over to the side of France and bigotry. As a zealous convert and becoming Bishop of Toulouse, he was an extremely ferocious oppressor of the few surviving Cathars.

The Turn of Provence

Provence was still free, enjoying a prosperous era under its Catalan counts though still troubled by incessant feudal struggles, waged by such local powers as the seigneurs of Les Baux and Forcalquier. Count Raymond Berenger V (1209–45) was usually strong enough to keep them in check; under him Provence did very well, and developed a constitutional government on the Catalan model. Provence managed temporarily to avert French aggression in a roundabout way. In 1246, Raymond Berenger's daughter and heir married Charles of Anjou—St Louis' brother. The ambitious Angevin used Provence as a springboard to create a Mediterranean empire that at its height, in the 1280s, included southern Italy and parts of Greece.

The city of Avignon and its hinterlands, the Comtat Venaissin, loyal possessions of Toulouse, had suffered greatly at the hands of Louis VIII after the Albigensian Crusade. In 1274 Charles and Louis arranged to give the Comtat to the Papacy—its discreetly delayed share of the Albigensian booty. In 1309 Pope Clement V, fleeing anarchy in Rome, installed himself at Carpentras in the Comtat. Politically, the popes found Provence a convenient new home and decided to stay—the 'Babylonian Captivity' (as jealous Italians called it) that would last over a century. They soon moved to Avignon, purchasing the city in 1348 and conducting a worldly court that seemed a Babylon indeed to many.

The late 14th century brought hard times to Provence: first the Black Death in 1348, and then political instability under the hapless Queen Jeanne (1343–82). Once more the Seigneurs of Les Baux and their imitators raged over the land, with bands of unscrupulous mercenaries (the *Grandes Compagnies*) to help them ravage town and country. The Popes returned to Rome in 1377; they kept control of Avignon and the Comtat, though French-supported Antipopes held Avignon as late as 1403. After 1434, peace had returned and Provence was ruled by Good King René (Count of Provence, and only 'king' from his claim to Sicily, in which the Angevins had been replaced by the Aragonese after the 'Sicilian Vespers' revolution of 1282). The 'Good' is equally spurious. René was open-handed to courtiers, and a patron of artists, but his futile dream of recapturing Sicily and Naples led him to wring the last penny out of everyone else.

René's successor, Charles III, lasted only a year and died without an heir (1481), bequeathing Provence to the French crown. It was intended to be a union of equals, maintaining Provençal liberties and institutions. As such, the Provençal Estates-General ratified the agreement. The French immediately went back on their word, attempting to govern through royal commissioners, but their attempts to swallow Provence whole had to wait. Louis XI and Charles XII needed a peaceful Provence as a bridge for their invasions of Italy; the region paid for this, with two destructive invasions in the 1520s and 30s by France's arch-enemy Charles V, Holy Roman Emperor and King of Spain. This era also saw a landmark in the cultural effacement of Occitania, the 1539 Edict of Villars-Cotterets that decreed French as the official language throughout the kingdom.

The Wars of Religion

Meanwhile, a big dose of the new Protestant heresy was floating down the Rhône from Calvin's Geneva. The Occitans received it more than warmly, and soon there were large Protestant communities in all the towns. Though this seems a repeat of the Cathar story, the geographical distribution is fascinating—the old Cathar areas (like the Aude), now were loyally Catholic, while the orthodox regions of the 1300s now came out strongly for the dissenters; in eastern Languedoc (the Hérault and Gard) they attracted about half the population. Tolerance was still out of fashion, and the opening round of a pointless half-century of religious wars came with the 1542 massacres in the Lubéron mountains. The perpetrator was the *Parlement* in Aix (pre-Revolution *parlements* were not parliaments, but powerful judicial bodies appointed by and responsible to the King); the victims mostly Waldensians (Vaudois), pre-Reformation heretics who had migrated to Provence before the union with France, to escape oppression there.

In the open warfare that followed across the south, there were massacres and atrocities enough on both sides. Protestants distinguished themselves by the wholesale destruction of churches and their art (as at St-Gilles); churches were often converted into fortresses, as can be seen throughout Languedoc. Henry IV's 1598 Edict of Nantes acknowledged Protestant control of certain areas (Nîmes, Montpellier, Uzès, Gignac, Clermont-l'Hérault, Aigues-Mortes, Sommières, Orange, Lourmarin). The French monarchy had been weakened by the wars, but as soon as it recovered new measures were introduced to keep the south in line. Under Cardinal Richelieu in the 1630s, the laws and traditions of local autonomy were swept away; after 1639 the Etats-Généraux of Provence was not allowed to meet until the eve of the Revolution. As insurance, scores of feudal castles (such as Beaucaire and Les Baux) were demolished to eliminate possible points of resistance.

Louis XIV's revocation of the Edict in 1685 caused more troubles. Thousands of Protestants, the south's most productive citizens, simply left; most of the community in Orange went off to colonize new lands in Prussia. Louis' long and oppressive reign continued the impoverishment of the south, despite well-intentioned economic measures by his brilliant minister Colbert: starting new manufactures (Villeneuvette, near Clermont l'Hérault); founding the port of Sète; and helping Paul Riquet build the Canal du Midi. In the 18th century, things picked up considerably in Languedoc, with the beginnings of an important textile industry—usually promoted by the remaining Protestants: silk around Nîmes and parts of Provence (where farmers gave up their bedrooms to raise the delicate silkworms in them), and linen and cotton goods in Montpellier,

Carcassonne and Orange. It was a great start, though unfortunately the English and their machines would come along to ruin Languedoc's cloth trade after 1800.

In Provence, the century told a miserable tale; economic stagnation, deforestation of mountain areas that have still not been entirely repaired today, and plagues: the biggest, in 1720, carried off almost half the population of Marseille. The one bright spot was the growing naval town of Toulon.

The Partitions of Catalunya

Roussillon had followed a quite different history, though the result was the same. Under Jaume I the Conqueror (1213–76), Aragon reached the height of its merchant empire, while keeping the French at bay along the castle-strewn Roussillon–Languedoc border. Before his death, Jaume decided to divide the kingdom between his two sons, leading to the brief but exotic interlude of the 'Kingdom of Majorca' and a brief golden age for Perpignan, its capital. The French tried to take advantage of the split, again shamelessly proclaiming a 'crusade' against the piously orthodox Catalans (the pope, who wanted the Aragonese out of Italy, had given his approval), but they were thrown back across the border in 1285.

Aragon was reunited in 1344, but its troubles were just beginning. After the Black Death in 1348, recessions and political strife led to a long and disastrous decline in Catalan commerce. The union of Aragon and Castile to form the Kingdom of Spain in 1492 was a disaster for the Catalans, meaning the introduction of the Inquisition, the gradual destruction of the *fueros* and a total ruin of their commerce. The long series of wars between France and Spain resulted in the ceding of Roussillon to France in 1659. Immediately, that province suffered systematic and heavy-handed Frenchification, leading to revolts in the mountain valleys that were violently suppressed. The southern angle of France's mystic hexagon was now substantially complete; Provence, Languedoc and Roussillon would continue to be treated as conquered provinces until 1981.

The Joys of Being French

> There has never been a north-south discussion, on territory currently French, except in terms of kicks in the ass: invasions, police raids, financial extortion and the squeezing of brains into the form of the Hexagon.
>
> Yves Roquette, National Secretary of the Institut d'Etudes Occitanes

The French Revolution was largely a Parisian affair, though southerners often played important roles (the Abbé de Sieyes and Mirabeau), while bourgeois delegates from the manufacturing towns fought along with the Girondins in the National Assembly for a respectable, liberal republic. Unfortunately, the winning Jacobin ideology was more centralist and more dedicated to destroying any taint of regional difference than the *ancien régime* had ever dreamed of being. Whatever was left of local rights and privileges was soon decreed out of existence, and when the Revolution divided France into homogenous departments in 1790, terms like 'Provence' and 'Languedoc' ceased to have any real political meaning.

In 1792 volunteers from Marseille had brought the *Marseillaise* to Paris, while local mobs wrecked and looted hundreds of southern churches and châteaux. Soon, however, the betrayed south became violently counter-revolutionary. Incidents occurred like the one in the village of Bédoin, near Carpentras, in 1793; when someone cut down the 'liberty tree', French soldiers burned the town and shot 63 villagers to 'set an example'. The Catalans raised regiments of volunteers against the Revolution. The royalists and the English occupied Toulon after a popular revolt, and were only dislodged by the brilliant tactics of a young commander named Bonaparte in 1793.

The south managed little enthusiasm for Napoleon or his wars. The Emperor called the Provençaux cowards, goading them by saying that theirs was the only part of France that never gave him a decent regiment. Today the tourist offices promote the 'Route Napoléonienne', where Napoleon passed through from Elba in 1815 to start the Hundred Days—but at the time he had to sneak along those roads in an Austrian uniform, to protect himself from the Provençaux.

After Waterloo, the restored monarchy started off with a grisly White Terror in Nîmes and elsewhere. After the Revolution of 1830, the 'July Monarchy' of King Louis Philippe brought significant changes. The old industrious, Protestant strain of the south finally got its chance with a Protestant Prime Minister from Nîmes, François Guizot (1840–48); his liberal policies and his slogan—*enrichissez-vous!*—opened an age where there would be a little Protestant in every Frenchman. Guizot's countrymen were rapidly demanding more; radicalism and anti-clericalism (except in the lower Rhône and Vaucluse) increased throughout the century. Southerners supported the Revolution of 1848 and the Second Republic, and many areas, especially in the

Provençal Alps, put up armed resistance to Louis Napoleon's 1851 coup. Under the Second Empire (1852–70), France picked up yet another territory: Nice and its hinterlands (now the *département* of Alpes-Maritimes), with a mixed population of Provençaux and Italians. This was the price exacted by Napoleon III in 1860 for French aid to Vittorio Emanuele II in Italy's War of Independence.

Oppression and Resistance

The second half of the century saw the beginnings of a national revival in Occitania. In Provence it was all cultural and apolitical: a linguistic and literary revival bound up with Nobel Prize-winning poet Frédéric Mistral and the cultural group called the *Félibrige* (see pp.55–6), founded in 1854. In Languedoc it was all political and unconcerned with culture, focusing on the first of modern France's agricultural movements. Markets since the 1800s had encouraged Languedoc to become one vast vineyard. Phylloxera hit in 1875, but the quick recovery favoured the biggest producers who could afford the new American stocks. A huge wine boom in the 1880s was followed by an even huger bust; with competition from Algeria and Italy, prices by 1904 dropped to one-third of their 1890 levels. In 1907 the farmers went on the warpath, led by a charismatic café-keeper from the Aude named Marcellin Albert. Monster meetings in Narbonne and Montpellier attracted over 100,000 each; Paris sent troops to occupy the region, but some of the conscript regiments came close to mutiny. Finallly Albert was tricked into calling off a general strike by leftist Prime Minister Clemenceau. The movement dwindled, but farmers devoted their attention to building a strong cooperative system and keeping the political pressure on by more orthodox means; French politics would never be quite the same.

To counter these advances, the post-1870 Third Republic pursued French cultural oppression to its wildest extremes. History was re-written to make Occitania and Roussillon seem eternal parts of the 'French nation.' The Occitan languages were lyingly derided as mere *patois*, bastard 'dialects' of French; children were punished for speaking their own language in school, a practice that lasted until the 1970s. Roussillon was not even permitted political participation—the government and parties arranged to have outsiders stand for its seats in the National Assembly.

After 1910, economic factors conspired to defeat both the political and cultural aspirations of the Midi; rural depopulation, caused by the breakup of the pre-industrial agricultural society, drained the life out of the villages—and decreased the percentage of people who spoke the native languages. The First World War decimated a generation—go into any village church in the south and look at the war memorial plaques; from a total population of a few hundred, you'll see maybe 30 names of villagers who died for the 'Glory of France'. By 1950, most villages had lost at least half their population; some died out altogether.

After the French débâcle of 1940, the south found itself under the Vichy government. German occupation came in November 1942, after the American landings in North Africa, provoking the scuttling of the French fleet in Toulon to keep it out of German hands. After 1942, the Resistance was active and effective in the Provençal Alps, the Vaucluse and the Catalan Pyrenees—not to mention Marseille, where the Germans felt constrained to blow up the entire Vieux Port area. Liberation began two months after D-Day, in August 1944. American and French troops hit the beaches around St Tropez, and in a remarkably successful (and little-noticed) operation they had most of Provence liberated in two weeks. In the rugged mountains behind Nice, some bypassed German outposts held out until the end of the war.

The California of Europe

The post-war era was all sweetness and ice-cream and reinforced concrete, a series of increasingly passionless snapshots: the Côte d'Azur become a myth of the masses—Grace Kelly with Cary Grant in *To Catch a Thief*, later with Rainier the Third in *Monaco*; socialist Languedoc farmers on a demonstration, wondering why someone couldn't sell all the goddamned wine they grow; grey and effective political machine bosses like Gaston Deferre of Marseille (socialist), or Jacques Médecin of Nice (gastronome-fascist); Paris bureaucrats expounding the glories of the Durance hydro-electric scheme, meant to make Provence the Ruhr Valley of Tomorrow.

The changes have in fact been momentous. The overdeveloped, ever more schizophrenic Côte d'Azur has become the heart of Provence—the tail that wags the dog. Besides its resorts it has the likes of IBM and the techno-paradise of Sophia-Antipolis. Above all, the self-proclaimed 'California of Europe' has money, and will acquire more; in two or three decades it will be the first province in centuries to start telling Paris where to get off. Meanwhile, the increasingly posh Vaucluse has the highest rural crime and suicide rates in France.

Those Languedoc farmers have learned their lesson; they make less wine, and much better. Their region, which stopped losing population about 1955, is changing fast. A typically French planning effort of 1968 has made its coastline into a growing tourist region, with new resorts like Cap d'Agde and La Grande Motte. Montpellier, under its dynamic mayor Georges Frêche, strives to become the futuristic metropolis of the Midi; jealous Nîmes bestirs itself to keep pace.

The greatest political event has been the election of the Socialist Mitterrand government in 1981, followed by the creation of regional governments across France. Though their powers and budgets are extremely limited, this represents a major turning point, the first reversal of a thousand years of increasing Parisian centralism. Its lasting effects will not be known for decades, perhaps centuries; already the revival of Occitan language and culture is resuming; indicators include such things as new school courses in the language, and some towns and villages changing the street signs to Languedocien, Provençal or Catalan. Roussillon is just beginning to feel the great upsurge of Catalan culture that began after the restoration of democracy in Spain.

Politics, quiet in most of the south, can still be primeval in Provence. Jean-Marie Le Pen and his tawdry pack of bigots find their biggest following here, riding a wave of resentment against immigrants that Le Pen himself has done more than anyone else to create (200,000 North Africans have arrived since 1945—but this is a Provençal tradition; there were anti-Italian pogroms in Marseille, Aigues-Mortes and other towns in the 1890s). Lately Le Pen's National Front has been scaring the daylights out of the French political class by winning control of four Provençal cities: first Toulon and Orange, lately the gruesome Marseille suburbs of Marignane and Vitrolles. At the time of writing, Le Pen is primed for a serious assault on the regional council in the next elections. Although support for the National Front remains high in the south, the party's failure to reach any understanding with the centre right in the last national elections may represent the high-water mark of its success.

Provence's poisonous political malaise isn't just about immigrants. Many National Front voters are former Socialists, disgusted by the massive corruption that Socialist politicians enjoyed during the Mitterrand years. In France's tightly-controlled political system, where the established parties collaborate closely to monopolize power and exclude grass-roots challenges, a vote for Le Pen is the only kind of protest vote available. With a persona that is part teddy bear, part comic-opera generalissimo, Le Pen is easy to underestimate. But he has proved extremely able not only at making racism seem respectable, but also in tapping the frustrations of people who feel powerless and oppressed by an utterly sleazy and intellectually bankrupt political class.

Art and Architecture

VAUCLUSE
CHURCH IN LACOSTE

Great art and architecture in the south of France neatly coincides with its three periods of prosperity: the Roman, the Middle Ages, and the mid-19th and early 20th centuries, when railways opened up the coast not only to aristocrats, but to artists as well.

Prehistoric

Some of the very first art in Europe was made by Palaeolithic residents of the Riviera, who made the lumpy fertility goddesses, sea-shell bonnets and necklaces displayed in the prehistory museums of **Monaco**, **Nice** and **Menton**. Their Neolithic descendants left few but tantalizing traces of their passing: dolmens and a few menhirs (especially in the Hérault and Gard) and a tomb-temple complex at **Castellet** near Arles. **Cambous**, north of Montpellier, has a reconstructed communal Neolithic house, with low walls and a thatched roof that resembles the traditional cowboy dwellings (*cabanes des gardians*) in the Camargue. The first shepherds may well have put up the drystone, corbel-roofed huts called *bories*, rebuilt countless times and still a feature of the landscape (most notably in the 18th-century '*village des bories*' outside **Gordes**).

In the Iron Age (1800–1500 BC), the Ligurians or their predecessors covered the Alpine **Vallée des Merveilles** under Mont Bégo with extraordinary rock incisions of warriors, bulls, masked figures and inexplicable symbols. In a similar style are the statue-steles—menhirs with faces—found in Tuscany and Corsica as well as around **Nîmes** (in the Musée de la Préhistoire) and at **St-Pons** in the Espinouse mountains of Hérault.

Celto-Ligurian: 8th–3rd Centuries BC

The arrival of the Celts around 800 BC coincided with an increase in trade; Greek, Etruscan and Celtic influences can be seen in the artefacts of this age (as at the **Oppidum of Ensérune** near Béziers). The local Celts had talent for jewellery and ironwork and sculpture—and the habit of decapitating enemies and carving stone images of warriors clutching their heads. Look for them in the archaeology museum in **Nîmes**, in the Musée Granet in **Aix**, the Musée d'Archéologie Méditerranée in **Marseille** and in the Lapidary Museum of **Avignon**.

Gallo-Roman: 3rd Century BC–4th Century AD

Archaeologically the Greeks are the big disappointment of Provence—the only remains of their towns are bits of wall at **Marseille** and at **St-Blaise** on the Etang de Berre. But what the Romans left behind in their beloved *Provincia* makes up for the Greek: the **Pont du Gard**; the theatre of **Orange**, with the only intact stage building in the West; the Maison Carrée and amphitheatre at **Nîmes**; the amphitheatre and cryptoporticus in **Arles**; the elegant 'Antiques' of **St-Rémy**; the Pont Flavien at **St-Chamas**; the trophy at **La Turbie**; the excavated towns at **Vaison-la-Romaine** and **Glanum** (St-Rémy).

Thanks to the Celts, Provence was the one province of the western Roman empire that developed a definite style of its own, characterized by vigorous, barbaric reliefs emboldened by deeply incised outlines. Battle scenes were the most popular subject, or shields and trophies arranged in the exotic, uncouth style you see on the triumphal arches of **Orange** and **Carpentras**, or in the new Musée Archéologique in **Arles**, which also has an excellent collection of models of the ancient towns and monuments of Provence. Roman landowners lived in two-storey stone houses, with their farm buildings forming an enclosed rectangular courtyard known as a *mansio*, the ancestor of the modern Provençal farmhouse, the *mas*; two large ones have been excavated in Les Lecques by **Bandol**.

Early Christian and Dark Ages: 5th–10th Centuries

Very few places in France had the resources to create any art at all during this period; the meagre attempts were nearly always rebuilt later. The oldest Christian relics are a remarkable sarcophagus from the 2nd century in **Brignoles**, and other sarcophagi from the next century in the crypt of St-Victor in **Marseille** and in the Musée Archéologique at **Arles**, both close to Roman pagan models. Octagonal baptistries from the 5th and 6th centuries survive in **Fréjus**, **Aix**, **Riez** and **Six-Fours-les-Plages**, which also has an 8th-century Syrian-style church. Many crypts are really the foundations of original Dark Age churches, and fragments of Merovingian-era reliefs will often be found set in a later church's wall.

Romanesque: 11th–14th Centuries

When good times returned in the 11th century, people began to build again, inspired by the ancient buildings they saw around them. There is not only a great stylistic continuity from Roman to Romanesque (rounded arches, barrel vaults, rounded apses), but also in the vigorous Celtic-inspired decoration of Roman Provence.

The south has four distinct varieties of Romanesque: Provençal, Lombard, Languedocien, and Catalan, although the terms must be applied loosely; the enduring charm of Romanesque is in its very lack of restrictions and codes, giving architects the freedom to improvise and solve problems in highly original and sophisticated ways. Although parish and monastic churches were usually in the basilican form (invented for Roman law courts, and used in Rome's first churches), masons also created extremely esoteric works, often built as funeral chapels in pre-Christian holy sites: see **Montmajour**, or the even odder seven-sided church at **Rieux Minervois** and a triangular one at **Planès** in the Pyrenees.

Of the four styles, the Provençal is the most austere and heaviest, characterized by simple floor plans, thick-set proportions, few if any windows, minimal if any decoration, and façades that are often blank. Churches that could double as fortresses were built along the pirate-plagued coast in the 11th and 12th century: St-Honorat in the **Iles-Lérins**, the basalt parish church at **Agde**, and the church of **Stes-Maries-de-la-Mer** are striking examples. In the mid-12th-century, the Cistercians founded three important new abbeys in a sombre and austere style, the 'Three Sisters': **Le Thoronet**, **Sénanque**, and **Silvacane**. An octagonal dome at the transept crossing is a common feature of more elaborate churches, especially **Avignon** cathedral, the Ancienne-Major in **Marseille**, **Vaison-la-Romaine**, **Le Thor** and **Carpentras** (the ruined original). The finest of the few paintings that survive from this epoque is the 13th-century fresco cycle at the Tour Ferrande, in **Pernes-Les-Fontaines**. **Ganagobie** has the only floor mosaics from the period, as well as some very good sculpture.

In general, churches in the Rhône valley are more ornate, thanks to a talented group of sculptors known as the School of Arles. The wealth of ruins inspired them to adapt Roman forms and decorations to the new religion, complete with triumphal arches, gabled pediments, and Corinthian columns. The saints on the façade of St-Trophime in **Arles** seem direct descendants of Gallo-Roman warriors. Arlésien artists also created the remarkable façade of **St-Gilles du Gard**, portraying the New Testament—the true dogma in stone for all to see, perhaps meant as a refutation of the Cathar and other current heresies. Yet other Romanesque sculpture in the area, as at **Vaison-la-Romaine**, seems nothing but heretical.

As you move west into Languedoc, Romanesque becomes more decorative and fanciful, befitting the land of troubadours (**St-Martin-de-Londres** and the frescoed **Chapelle de Centeilles** in the Minervois).

abbey de Sénanque

Even when the austere Cistercians built here, as at **Fontfroide**, the mood is much less sombre. Itinerant Lombard masons in the 12th century built Italian Romanesque churches, characterized by blind arcading and bands of decorative stonework, especially around the apse (as at **St-Guilhem-le-Désert**). The Lombard campanile, pierced with patterns of windows, was adapted by the Catalans, especially in the Pyrenees (**Elne**). But **Uzès** has something even rarer in its Tour Fenestrelle: a round, arcaded six-storey campanile, typical of Byzantine Italy.

Along with the Arles craftsmen, the Catalans produced the finest medieval sculpture in the south, with the school of sculptors at the magnificent 11th-century abbey of **St-Michel-de-Cuxa**. Their work is characterized by precise and fanciful detail, arabesques and floral patterns, supremely elegant without the classicizing of the Arles school; more of their best sculpture may be seen at **Serrabonne** and **Elne**, the most beautiful cloister in the Midi.

Catalunya also produced the vigorous and original Master of Cabestany, who in the early 12th century even went to Tuscany to teach the Italians how to sculpt. His best works in France are the tympanum at **Cabestany**, at **St-Papoul**, near Castelnaudary, and in a pair of capitals at **Rieux Minervois**. Catalans could paint, too; there are rare medieval frescoes at **St-Martin-de-Fenollar**, south of Perpignan.

Although examples of medieval palaces still stand in **Brignoles**, **St-Gilles**, and **Villemagne** in the Hérault, the greatest secular architecture of the period is military, often done with surprising originality. The vertiginous castle of **Peyrepertuse** is only the most enormous example of the scores of imposing works around the Languedoc and Roussillon border—one of the very best regions in Europe for castles. St Louis built the walls and towers of **Carcassonne** in a romantic fairy-tale style that has few equals, while the king's other project, **Aigues-Mortes** (1270s), is a grid-planned, square and functional modern town encased in a perfect set of walls.

Gothic and Early Renaissance: 14th and 15th Centuries

Though Gothic elements first appeared in Provence in 1150 (the façade of St-Victor in Marseille) and in Languedoc around 1250 in the Abbaye St-Martin-du-Vignogoul, ogival vaulting and pointy arches belonged to a foreign, northern style that failed to touch southern hearts.

Builders stuck to their Romanesque guns longer than anyone in France, and when Gothic made its final triumph it was usually a pale reflection of the soaring cathedrals of the Ile-de-France. The exceptions were built by northerners after the French conquest: the cathedrals of **Béziers**, **Carcassonne** and especially **Narbonne**, an unfinished, spectacular work that is the third-tallest Gothic church in France.

Gothic also found a home in **Avignon**, when the 14th-century popes summoned architects from the north to design the flamboyant Papal Palace, St-Pierre, the Convent des Célestines and St-Didier (other isolated examples are the **Abbaye de Valmagne** near Sète, the basilica of **St-Maximin-la-Ste-Baume**, and **Clermont-l'Hérault**). The Catalans, as ever marching to a different drummer, developed their own brand of Gothic, where width and strength counted more than height. The master of the genre, Guillermo Sagrera, designed **Perpignan**'s cathedral and the complex vaulting in its Salle Capitulaire.

Painting in the south of France took a giant leap forward when the papal court in Avignon attracted some of Italy's finest *trecento* artists, especially Simone Martini of Siena and Matteo Giovanetti of Viterbo, whose frescoes inspired the graceful fairy-tale style known as International Gothic (*see* **Avignon** and its Petit Palais museum).

A new local style developed from International Gothic, and from the precise style of the Flemish painters favoured by the last popes: the early 15th-century *School of Avignon*. The school's greatest masters were from the north: the exquisite Enguerrand Quarton (*c.* 1415–66) from Laon (**Villeneuve-lez-Avignon**), and Nicolas Froment (Cathedral, **Aix**); also see Aix's church of the Madeleine and the Petit Palais museum in **Avignon**. King René, the great patron of the artists, built himself a fine chivalric castle in **Tarascon** and had a hand in the evolution of French sculpture when he invited the Italian Renaissance master Francesco Laurana to Provence (*see* artists' directory, below).

At the same time the *School of Nice*, led by the prolific Ludovico Brea, produced scores of altarpieces typical of northern Italian provincial styles—charming and luminous, if a good hundred years behind the Renaissance revolution going on in Tuscany. The Brea gang had some stiff competition in the early 15th century from a pair of little known Piedmontese painters, Giovanni Canavesio and Giovanni Baleison, who would be much better known had they left their charming pastel fresco cycles in less remote churches (**Notre-Dame-des-Fontaines** in the Roya Valley, and others in the nearby valleys of the Vésubie and Tinée).

High Renaissance: Late 15th and 16th Centuries

Despite its promising start, subjugation by the French and the Wars of Religion made the Renaissance a non-event in Occitania. The few buildings of the day are imitative, mostly of the heavy, classicizing Roman style, as in the palace of the Cardinal Legate in **Avignon**. The best Renaissance building, the once delightful **Château La Tour d'Aigue** in the Lubéron, is only a burnt-out shell, although you can get a hint of its former glory in the elegant château in nearby **Lourmarin**. **Narbonne** has some exquisite Flemish Renaissance tapestries. Locally, the best work of this period is minute—in the carved wooden doors and choir stalls in **Vence**, **Bar-sur-Loup** and **Fréjus**.

The Age of Bad Taste: 17th–18th Centuries

The French prefer to call this their *époque classique* and even in the poor, benighted south admittedly many fine things were done. Towns laid out elegant squares, fountains and promenades (**Pernes-les-Fontaines, Aix, Barjols**); trees were planted on a grand scale, on market squares, along the Canal du Midi, and on the roads, especially in the western Aude, crossed with 18th-century avenues of plane trees. **Montpellier** and **Moustiers** have collections from their thriving faïence industries of the day (as does **Narbonne**'s art museum and **Marseille**'s Musée Cantini). Southerners went ape for organs, gargantuan works sheathed in ornate carved wood. The mother of them all is in **Narbonne** Cathedral; others adorn the churches in **Béziers** and **Uzès**.

But nearly everything else is all wrong. People took the lovely churches left to them by their ancestors and tricked them out like cat-houses in pink and purple and tinkered so much with the architecture that it's often difficult to tell the real age of anything. Aix, the capital of Provence and self-proclaimed arbiter of taste, knocked over its magnificently preserved Roman mausoleum and medieval palace of the counts of Provence just

before the Revolution. The 17th- and 18th-century *hôtels particuliers* of **Aix**, **Pézenas**, **Uzès** and **Montpellier**, while lending a distinctive urbanity and ostentation to these cities, are rarely first-rate works of architecture in their own right, but rather eclectic jumbles with touches from Gothic, Renaissance, and Baroque style-books.

The one great sculptor and architect the south produced in the period, Pierre Puget, suffered the usual fate of a prophet in his own land, although he did manage one great project: the Vieille Charité, in **Marseille**. In painting, the south produced two virtuoso court painters, Hyacinthe Rigaud and Fragonard, whose portrayals of happily spoiled, rosy-cheeked aristocrats hide the side of their personalities that provoked the Revolution. The most sincere paintings of the age are the naive ex votos in many churches (some of the best are from sailors, as at Notre-Dame-de-la-Garde in **Marseille**, in Notre-Dame-de-Bon-Port at **Cap d'Antibes**, and Notre-Dames-des-Auzils, near **Gruissan**).

One architect who (unlike Puget) never lacked for work was Louis XIV's Maréchal Sébastien Vauban, whose forts and fortress-towns crop up everywhere; **Villefranche-de-Conflent** is a perfectly preserved example of 17th-century urban design. The next generation after Vauban produced the streamlined, modern Baroque fortresses near the Spanish border in the region around **Collioure**.

The best Baroque churches in the region are Italian: St-Michel in **Menton** and the Chapelle de la Miséricorde in **Nice**.

France's Little Ice Age: Late 18th–mid-19th Centuries

If the last era lacked vision, taste in the neoclassical/Napoleonic era had all the charm of embalming fluid. The Revolution destroyed more than it built; the wanton devastation of the region's greatest Romanesque art (begun in the Wars of Religion) was a loss matched only by the mania for selling it off in the early 20th century to the Americans. The greatest monuments of the Napoleonic era include the cold, funereal Musée Masséna in **Nice** and the paintings in many museums (especially the Musée Granet, in **Aix**) by David, Ingres, and Hubert Robert, the latter of whom specialized in scenes of melancholy Roman ruins in Provence and Italy, capturing the taste of the day (it was also a great age for cemeteries).

For the first time, however, there was a reaction to purposeful destruction of the past. Ruskin's contemporary, Viollet-le-Duc (1814–79), restored architecture, rather than just wrote about it (the walls of **Carcassonne** and **Avignon**, and the archbishop's palace of **Narbonne**). Thanks to the Suez Canal, **Marseille** suddenly had money to burn and tried to revive the past in its own way, with monstrous neo-Byzantine basilicas and the overripe Baroque Palais Longchamp.

Revolutions in Seeing: 1850–1939

A lady once came to look at Matisse's paintings and was horrified to see a woman with a green face. 'Wouldn't it be horrible to see a woman walking down the street with a green face?' she asked him. 'It certainly would!' Matisse agreed. 'Thank God it's only a painting!'

In the 1850 Paris Salon, hanging amongst the stilted historical, religious, and mythological academic paintings were three large canvases of everyday, contemporary scenes by Gustave Courbet. Today it's hard to imagine how audacious his contemporaries found Courbet's new style, which came to be called Realism—almost as if it took the invention of photography by Louis Daguerre (1837) to make the eye see what was 'really' there. 'Do what you see, what you want, what you feel,' was Courbet's proto-hippy advice to his pupils. One thing he felt like doing was painting in the south of France, where his art revelled in the bright colour and light (especially his *Bonjour, Monsieur Courbet* of 1854 in **Montpellier**'s Musée Fabre). Courbet's visit was a major influence on the 19th-century painters of Provence, especially Paul Guigou and Frédéric Bazille, who painted Realist subjects drenched in southern sunlight.

In the 1860s, as physicists discovered that colour derives from light, not from form, the Impressionists made it their goal to strip Courbet's new found visual reality of all subjectivity and to simply record on canvas the atmosphere, light, and colour the eye saw, all according to the latest scientific theories. Although many of the great Impressionists spent time in the south, only the sensuous Renoir moved down permanently, and then only on doctor's orders (to **Cagnes-sur-Mer**, in 1895).The crucial role the south

was to play in modern art dates from the 1880s, thanks to two artists most closely associated with Provence today, Vincent Van Gogh and Paul Cézanne.

Van Gogh, one of the greatest innovators in the history of painting, was self taught. Influenced at first by the Impressionists and Japanese prints he saw in Paris, his move to sunny Arles in 1888 thoroughly revolutionized his work: he responded to the heightened colour and light of Provence on such an intense, personal level that colour came less and less to represent form (as it did for the Impressionists), but instead took on a symbolic value; colour became the only medium Van Gogh found powerful enough to express his extraordinary moods and visions.

This revolutionary independence of colour from form was taken to an extreme by a group of painters that the critic Louis Vauxcelles nicknamed the **Fauves** ('wild beasts') for the violence of their colours. The Fauves used colour to interpret, rather than describe, moods and rhythms to the detriment of perspective and detail and even recognizable subject matter. As a movement the Fauves lasted from 1904 until 1908, but in those few years revolutionized centuries of European art. 'Fauve painting is not everything,' Matisse explained. 'But it is the foundation of everything.'

Nearly all the Fauves—André Derain, Matisse, Maurice Vlaminck, Raoul Dufy, Kees Van Dongen—painted in St-Tropez as guests of the hospitable painter Paul Signac, and at La Ciotat, Cassis, L'Estaque and Collioure. The results paved the way for Expressionism, Cubism, and Abstraction—avenues few of the Fauvists themselves ever explored. For after 1908 the collective new vision these young men had shared in the south of France vanished as if they had awoken from a mass hypnosis; all went their separate ways, leaving others to carry their ideas on to their logical conclusions (best collections are in the Musée de l'Annonciade in **St-Tropez** and the Musée d'Art at **Bagnols-sur-Cèze**).

Cézanne's innovations were as important as Van Gogh's, although his response to Provence was analytical rather than emotional, perhaps because he was born in the south. Loosely associated with the Impressionists in the 1860s and '70s, Cézanne stood apart; his interest was not so much in depicting what he saw, but in the contradiction between the eye and mind, between the permanence of nature and the ephemeral qualities of light and movement. 'Nature is always the same, but none of it lasts beyond what we perceive,' he wrote, and by the 1880s he had undertaken his stated task of 'making Impressionism solid and enduring, like the art of the museums', exploring underlying volumes, planes and structure, not through perspective, but through amazingly subtle variations of colour.

In 1908, Georges Braque and Raoul Dufy went to paint together at L'Estaque in homage to Cézanne. The beginnings of the prismatic splitting of forms are in their respective works, and when the same critic Vauxcelles saw Braque's paintings, he came up with a new name for the new art: **Cubism**. In 1912 Braque and Picasso worked together in Sorgues, near Avignon, and produced canvases that verge on abstraction. Matisse, one of the Fauves who settled permanently in Provence, kept apart from subsequent schools, and was the most outstanding among hundreds of artists who now flocked to the south.

Even Picasso, another lone genius who moved permanently to Provence after the Second World War and to whom modesty was a stranger, acknowledged Matisse as his equal, and in many ways his master. And one of the great art debates of the 20th century has been who is the greater artist and innovator of the two, Picasso being considered by many to have the upper hand.

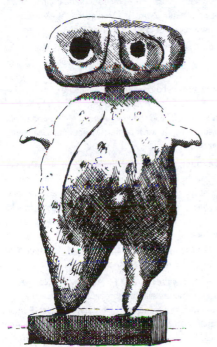

In architecture, this was the opulent age of the Côte d'Azur's Belle Epoque confections, its Russian Orthodox cathedrals, grand hotels, villas and casinos, all done in a lavish, imaginative holiday spirit that often trod lightheartedly over contemporary rules of good taste and decorum.

Only a few buildings survive, which, along with old photographs, give a hint of what **Nice**, **Cannes**, **Monaco** and **Menton** looked like at the turn of the century. The Moorish, Bengali, Norman, Tuscan and troubadour follies that went up (nearly all built by extravagant foreigners) caused outrage when they were built and are sorely missed now that all but a handful have been demolished.

Post-war

After the war, artists from many lands continued to pour into the hill villages of Provence: Picasso, Bonnard, Léger, Chagall, Nicholas de Staël, Max Ernst, André Masson and Vasarély to name only the most prominent. The 1960s saw a reaction to the often precious art world in the 'second' School of Nice, led by often provocative multi-media iconoclasts like César, Arman and Ben, all displayed in a spanking new contemporary art museum in **Nice**, one of several giant projects built by the ambitious mayors of the south. None has been more ambitious than Georges Frêche, the human dynamo who runs **Montpellier** and chose Ricardo Bofill to create the neo-neoclassical residential quarter called Antigone. The single most influential post-war building in the south has been Le Corbusier's *Unité d'Habitation* in **Marseille** (1952); if you don't care for warmed-over Bauhaus on stilts, there's the futuristic planned resort of **La Grande Motte** in Languedoc, begun in 1968 as the first post-modernist building ensemble in the south. The most artful, delightful building in recent years is the Catalan architect José-Luis Sert's Fondation Maeght, in **St-Paul-de-Vence**.

In **Nîmes**, Sir Norman Foster's glass and steel Carré d'Art was beset by criticism when it opened in May 1993, but his influence has led to a new impetus in architectural expansion in the south. New developments are planned in Nîmes, Montpellier, Aix-en-Provence and Marseille. The south, it seems, is no longer the architectural backwater it once was: indeed, as Jean Bousquet, mayor of Nîmes declares, its cities will soon rival Paris in the race to be a metropolis for the 21st century.

Artists' Directory

Bazille, Frédéric (1841–70). A native of Montpellier, who linked up with Monet in Paris in 1862 and with him was the first to paint the human figure and even nudes out of doors, inspired by the spontaneity of photography. His career was cut short in the Franco-Prussian war of 1870 (Musée Fabre, **Montpellier**).

Bonnard, Pierre (1867–1947). Although his early career is closely associated with the Nabis (a group of painters who rejected naturalism and natural colour), Bonnard changed gear in 1900 to become one of the 20th century's chief Impressionists, painting colour-saturated landscapes and domestic scenes, after 1939 around his villa in Le Cannet, near Cannes (**Bagnols-sur-Cèze**, Musée de l'Annonciade, **St-Tropez**).

Braque, Georges (1882–1963). One of Cubism's founding fathers, Braque worked so closely with Picasso (in Céret in 1911, in Borgues in 1912, and elsewhere) that their early works are practically indistinguishable (Musée de l'Annonciade, **St-Tropez**).

Brea, Ludovico (active 1475–1544). Leader of the International Gothic Nice School, influenced by the Renaissance in his later career; although commissioned to do hieratic medieval-style subjects, his precise line and beautiful sense of light and shadow stand out—still, to call him the 'Fra Angelico of Provence' like some French critics is going too far. He invented a shade of wine-red French artists still call *rouge brea* (Franciscan church in Cimiez, **Nice**; Palais Carnolès, **Menton**; **Lucéram**, and **Monaco** cathedral).

Canavesio, Giovanni (c. 1425–1500). Of Piedmont, collaborated with **Giovanni Baleison** to paint the finest Renaissance frescoes in Provence; the style is typical of North Italian early Renaissance, colourful and precise, without much of the intellectuality of Tuscan painting (**Notre-Dame-des-Fontaines**, near La Brigue, retables at **Lucéram** and many chapels in the Valleys of the Vésubie and Tinée).

Cézanne, Paul (1839–1906). Born and died in Aix-en-Provence, where fellow schoolmate Emile Zola was his best friend, until Zola published his autobiographical *L'Oeuvre* that thinly disguised Cézanne as the failed painter Lantier. Cézanne's painting went through several distinct periods: a sombre romantic stage (1861–71); an Impressionistic manner, inspired by Pisarro (1872–82); a period of synthesis (1883–95), combining elements of Impressionism with an interest in volume, surface planes, and the desire to represent perspective by colour only; and lastly, his lyric period (1896–1906), where singing rhythms of colour and form are intellectually supported by the basic tenets of Cubism, splitting the planes and volumes into prisms, expressing the tension between seeing and knowing (Musée Granet, **Aix**).

Chagall, Marc (1887–1985). Highly individualistic and spiritual painter and illustrator who drew many themes from Jewish-Russian folklore and the Old Testament; he spent his last years in Vence (Musée National Message Biblique Marc Chagall, **Nice**; Maeght Foundation, **St-Paul-de-Vence**).

Cocteau, Jean (1889–1963). Writer, surrealist film director, and illustrator, who painted pastel mural decorations in a number of chapels and town halls in the south (Mairie and Museum, in **Menton**; Chapelle de St-Pierre, **Villefranche-sur-Mer**).

Corot, Jean Baptiste Camille (1796–1875). Landscape painter of ineffable charm, made the typical French sojourn in Rome to discover the calm and tranquillity of classical landscapes; in his smaller, spontaneous sketches and private portraits his modern techniques make him a precursor of the Impressionists; painted with Ziem in Martigues (Musée Calvet, **Avignon**; Musée des Beaux-Arts, **Marseille**).

Courbet, Gustave (1819–77). High prince of the 19th-century Realist school, and a keen student of luminosity in nature. His journey to Montpellier in 1854 brought about a considerable lightening of his palette; his seascapes are awash in atmosphere, and his studies of skies, light, and shadows inspired Monet and Bazille (Musée Fabre, **Montpellier**; Musée des Beaux-Arts, **Marseille**).

Daumier, Honoré (1808–79). Born in Marseille, began his career risking jail terms as a political caricaturist for a magazine. But Daumier was also a highly original pre-Expressionist painter in the Goya mould, best known for his hypnotic, violently lit scenes based on the inherent tragedy of the human condition—a precursor of Toulouse-Lautrec, Degas, and Picasso (Musée des Beaux-Arts, **Marseille**).

David, Jacques-Louis (1748–1825). Napoleon's favourite neoclassical painter, as cold and perfect as ice, portrayed the Frenchies of his day in kitsch-Roman heroic attitudes and costumes (Musée Granet, **Aix**; Musée Fabre, **Montpellier**; Musée Calvet, **Avignon**).

Delacroix, Eugène (1798–1863). Had little truck with the neoclassicism of David, and instead based his art on the chromatics and lighting of Constable. 'In painting, all is reflection,' he said; many of his landscapes and North African watercolours presaged Impressionism (Musée Fabre, **Montpellier**).

Derain, André (1880–1954). Along with Vlaminck, key Fauvist painter of extraordinary innovation and originality, who took Fauvism and Expressionism to the limit before the First World War (Musée de l'Annonciade, **St-Tropez**).

Dufy, Raoul (1877–1953). Dufy's most original and energetic painting was as a Fauve. After a brief flirtation with Cubism with Georges Braque in L'Estaque (*see* Musée Cantini, **Marseille**), his style took on its characteristic graphic quality, and he spent much of his remaining life in Nice, painting pleasing lightweight decorative interiors (Musée Dufy, **Nice**).

Fragonard, Jean Honoré (1732–1806). Native of Grasse and student of Boucher, Fragonard painted frivolous rococo scenes in anaemic pastels but with a verve and erotic wit that found favour with France's spiritually bankrupt nobility, who longed to escape into his canvases (Villa-Musée Fragonard, **Grasse**).

Granet, François Marius (1775–1849). Native of Aix and a pupil of David; although his canvases are run-of-the-mill academic, his watercolours and sketches reveal a poetic observation of nature that became the hallmark of the Provençal school (Musée Granet, **Aix**; Musée d'Art et d'Histoire, **Grasse**).

Guigou, Paul (1834–71). Landscape painter born in Villars, in the Vaucluse. Influenced by Corot's landscapes, Guigou sought out the most arid parts of Provence, especially the banks of the Durance, for his subjects, illuminating them with scintillating light and colour. Unable to make a living in the south, he took teaching jobs in the north, where he died at age 37, just as his career began to take off (Musée des Beaux-Arts, **Marseille**; Musée Granet, **Aix**).

Ingres, Jean Auguste Dominique (1780–1867). As the most important neoclassical pupil of David, Ingres was acclaimed the master of official academic art, where he was capable of producing enormous mythological howlers. However, in his more appealing intimate subjects, especially his female nudes, he distorted proportions to achieve a sinuous eroticism and line that inspired Picasso, among other artists (Musée Granet, **Aix**; Musée Fabre, **Montpellier**).

Laurana, Francesco (*c.* 1430–1502). Itinerant Istrian sculptor trained in Tuscany, best known for his precocious geometrical softening of features and forms, especially in his portrait busts (St-Didier, **Avignon**; Ancienne-Major, **Marseille**).

Léger, Fernand (1881–1955). Went from an early figurative manner to Cubism. Wounded in the First World War, Léger attempted to create an art that interpreted the experiences of ordinary people in war, work and play, culminating in his paintings of colourful, geometric highly-stylized figures of workers and factories. Léger also worked in many media especially mosaics and ceramics (Musée National Fernand Léger, **Biot**; Fondation Maeght, **St-Paul-de-Vence**).

Maillol, Aristide (1861–1944). Sculptor from Banyuls who spent much of his career in Paris, though he never forgot his hometown, returning each summer to model female nudes on the pulchritude of the local nymphets (Hôtel de Ville, **Perpignan**, war memorials and museum in **Banyuls**; Musée de l'Annonciade, **St-Tropez**).

Matisse, Henri (1869–1954). A trip to the south in the 1890s converted Matisse to the vivid colours that are a hallmark of his work. After he became one of the leading Fauves, the hot colours of the south continued to saturate his ever sensuous, serene, and boldly drawn works, qualities apparent even in the paper cut-outs of his last bedridden years. After 1917 he settled in Nice (Musée Matisse, **Nice**; Chapel of the Rosary, **Vence**; Musée de l'Annonciade, **St-Tropez**).

Monticelli, Adolphe (1824–86). A native of Marseille, a student of Ziem and one of Van Gogh's great inspirations. Obsessed with light ('*La lumière, c'est le ténor*,' he claimed), he conveyed its effects with pure unmixed colour applied with hard brushes; subjects dissolve into strokes and blobs of paint (Musée des Beaux-Arts and Musée Cantini, **Marseille**).

Picasso, Pablo (1881–1973). Born in Málaga, Spain, the 20th century's most endlessly inventive artist is especially celebrated for his mastery of line and his great expressive power. In 1948 Picasso abandoned Paris and moved to Provence, settling first in Vallauris, then Cannes, and finally at Mougins, where he died. Living in Provence heightened the Mediterranean and pagan aspects of his extraordinarily wide-ranging work; he also loved to attend the bullfights at Arles (Musée Picasso, **Antibes**; castle chapel at **Vallauris**; Musée Réattu, **Arles**; Musée d'Art Moderne, **Chéret**).

Puget, Pierre (1620–94). Baroque sculptor, painter and architect who began his career painting ships' figureheads before he went on to study in Rome under Bernini. Unappreciated at home, he spent much of his time sculpting enormous saints in Genoa (Vieille Charité and Musée des Beaux-Arts, all in his native **Marseille**; also the *Atlantes* of **Toulon**'s old Hôtel de Ville).

Renoir, Pierre-Auguste (1841–1919). Was as joyful as Van Gogh was tormented. Renoir combined Impressionism with the traditional 'gallant' themes of Fragonard, updated to the 19th century: pretty girls, dances, fêtes, children, nudes, bathers, pastorals. Racked by rheumatism, he spent his last years in Cagnes, painting warm voluptuous nudes and landscapes (Musée Renoir, **Cagnes-sur-Mer**).

Rigaud, Hyacinthe (1659–1743). Born in Perpignan, painter of sumptuous royal portraits, in great demand for his ability to make his subjects look lofty yet amiable as well as for his accurate depiction of their swell get-ups (museums in **Perpignan**, **Narbonne** and **Aix**).

Seurat, Georges (1859–91). Theorist and founder of neo-impressionism, with his technique of *pointillisme* (juxtaposing dots of pure colour to achieve a greater luminosity); although he was highly influential, none of his followers could match his precision and vision (Musée de l'Annonciade, **St-Tropez**).

Signac, Paul (1863–1935). Georges Seurat's most faithful follower down the path of *pointillisme*, the science of reducing a scene into dots of colour. When Seurat died, Signac left Paris and discovered St-Tropez in 1892, where influenced by the Fauves he gradually abandoned his dots for a freer style (Musée de l'Annonciade, **St-Tropez**).

Van Dongen, Kees (1877–1968). A Fauve painter of verve and elegance, who after Fauvism became the chief chronicler of Riviera society and mores of the 1920s and '30s (Musée Chervet, **Nice**; Musée de l'Annonciade, **St-Tropez**).

Van Gogh, Vincent (1853–90). Along with Cézanne, is most responsible for the images the outside world has of Provence—an unforgettable visionary, brilliantly-hued land, palpitating with energy. Coming from the cold, wet climes of the Netherlands and Paris, Van Gogh sought in the south 'a different light, in the belief that to look at nature under a clearer sky could give us a better idea of the way the Japanese see and draw; finally, I seek a stronger sun'. Instead he found in the landscapes an underlying violence, tragedy and madness, which he painted with an intense lyricism that has never been equalled, in a 'research into the infinite' that ended with suicide. He sold but one painting in his short life, and ironically only one of the 800 or so canvases he painted around Arles remains in the south of France today: in the Fondation Angladon-Dubrujeaud, in **Avignon**.

Van Loo, Carle (1705–65). Native of Nice and younger brother of the less successful Jean-Baptiste van Loo, Carle was a rococo painter in the 'grand style' and a keen rival of Boucher, painting hunt scenes, religious paintings, and designing Gobelin tapestries for the kings of France and Savoy (Ste-Marthe, **Tarascon**; Musée Jules Chéret, **Nice**).

Vernet, Claude Joseph (1714–89). Born in Avignon, a landscape painter best known for his many seascapes and ports; one of the first French painters interested in the play of light and water, if in a picturesque manner (Musée Calvet, **Avignon**; Musée des Beaux-Arts, **Marseille**).

Vuillard, Edouard (1868–1940). Like his good friend Bonnard, Vuillard began as a Nabi and later became better known for his Impressionistic, intimate, domestic scenes (Musée de l'Annonciade, **St-Tropez**).

Ziem, Félix (1821–1911). Started off illuminating canvases with a sense of light audacious for the period. Having found a successful formula, he repeated himself from then on. Much admired by Van Gogh, Ziem's favourite subjects were Venice and Martigues, where he founded an art colony with Jean Baptiste Corot (Musée Ziem, **Martigues**; Musée Jules Chéret, **Nice**).

Topics

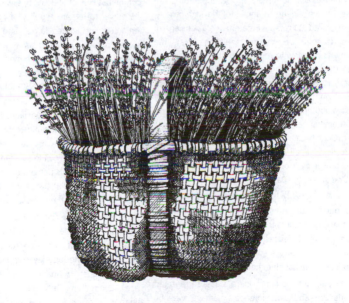

The Cathars

. . . because we are not of this world, and this world is nought of ours, give us to understand that which Thou understandest, and to love that which Thou lovest.

Cathar prayer

Dualism, as the philosophers call it, has always been with us. The Greek Gnostics saw Good and Evil as contending, independent forces that existed forever. Good resided somewhere beyond the stars; evil was here and now—in fact creation itself was evil, the work not of God but of a fallen spirit, identifiable with Satan. Our duty on earth was to seek purity by refusing to have anything to do with it. In the 3rd century AD, a Persian holy man named Mani took up the same theme and made quite a splash; his teachings spread gradually back into the West, where the earliest Church councils strongly condemned them as the 'Manichaean Heresy'. Among other places, the Manichaeans had been active in southern Gaul.

Always present in the Byzantine Empire, Manichaean ideas hit the Balkans in the 9th century; the 'Bogomil' or 'Bulgar' dualists reached a wide following, leaving hundreds of oddly carved crosses as monuments. From there, the idea spread rapidly throughout Europe. The new sect appears in the chronicles of the 11th century, variously called Bulgars or Patarenes, Albigensians or Cathars (from a Greek word meaning pure). The Church was not slow to respond. In Italy and northern France the heretics were massacred and burned; in England, apparently, they were only branded with hot irons. In worldly and open Occitania, however, they gained a foothold and kept it. The new faith was popular among peasants, townspeople and even many nobles; Occitan Catharism was organized into a proper church at a council at St-Felix-de-Caraman in 1167, presided over by a prelate named Nicetas, or Nikita, from Dragovici in the Balkans.

The Cathars probably believed that their faith was a return to the virtue and simplicity of the early Church. Their teaching encouraged complete separation with the Devil's world; feudal oaths, for example, were forbidden, and believers solved differences between themselves by arbitration rather than go to law.

Some features were quite modern. Cathars promoted vegetarianism and non-violence; marriage was by simple agreement, not a sacrament—enhancing the freedom and status of women by doing away with the old Roman paternalist tradition and laws. Two other points made Catharism especially attractive to an increasingly modern society. It had a much more mature attitude towards money and capitalism than the Roman church—no condemnation of loans as usury, and no church tithes. This earned it support in the growing cities; like the later Protestants, many Cathars were involved in the textile trades. Cathar simplicity and its lack of a big church organization made a very favourable contrast with the bloated, bullying and thoroughly corrupt machinery of the Church of Rome.

Best of all, Catharism had a very forgiving attitude towards sinners. If creation itself was the Devil's work, how could we not err? Cathars were divided into two levels: the mass of simple believers, upon whom the religion was a light yoke indeed—no mass and few ceremonies, no money-grubbing, easy absolution—and the few *perfecti*, those who had received the sacrament called the *consolament*, and were thenceforth required to lead a totally ascetic life devoted to faith and prayer. Most Cathars conveniently took the *consolament* on their deathbeds.

Catharism was a strong and growing force when the Albigensian Crusade began in 1209; the papacy, the behaviour of which has always been a strong argument for the basic tenet of dualism, saw enough of a threat to its power to require a policy of genocide. The terror, enforced by French arms and overseen by the Dominicans and Cistercians, was vicious and successful. Its climax came in 1244, with the fall of the Cathar holy-of-holies, the temple fortress at Montségur in the Pyrenees (*département* of Ariège). Cathars who survived the mass exterminations were hunted down ruthlessly by the new Inquisition; Guillaume Bélibaste, the last of the *perfecti*, was burned at Villerouge-Termenès in the Aude in 1321. Nevertheless, doctrines are always more difficult to kill than human beings, and Catharism survived its persecutors in a number of forms, especially in its influence on the later southern Protestants, and on the Catholic Jansenists of the 1600s.

There are practising Cathars today; if you want to seek them out, the village of Arques, in the Aude, might be a good place to start, or else consult the worthy books (in French) of a modern-day sympathizer named René Nelli. There are probably fewer actual Cathars than books about them. Catharism did have a strong esoteric tinge to it, reserved for the *perfecti*. In the past few decades, this angle has been explored in every sort of work, from the serious to the pathetically inane, speculating on various 'treasures', real or metaphysical, that the last *perfecti* may have hidden, or connecting the sect with other favourite occult themes: the Templars (who in fact were their enemies), the Holy Grail (said to have been kept at Montségur), the Illuminati and Rosicrucians of the 15th century and onwards, or the body and possible descendants of Jesus Christ (*see* Rennes-le-Château, pp.442–3).

Nelli and other authors have some provocative things to say about the greatest and most mysterious of all the Arthurian epics, Wolfram von Eschenbach's *Parzifal*—they see the poem as a sweeping Cathar allegory, confirming Montségur as the Grail castle, and identifying Parzifal with the Cathars' protector, Raymond Trencavel of Carcassonne. Trencavel's chroniclers also have an uncanny habit of comparing the Viscount to Christ, especially after his betrayal and death at the hands of Simon de Montfort; his dynasty, like that of the Counts of Toulouse, was quite a vortex for this sort of weirdness.

The weirdest of all modern Europe's occultist sects, the Nazis, were obsessed with the Cathars and the legends that have grown up around them. After their occupation of the south in 1942, they sealed off all the important Cathar sites and cave refuges in the Pyrenees, and Nazi high-priest Alfred Rosenberg sent teams of archaeologists to dig them up amidst the utmost secrecy. In 1944, not long before liberation, a group of local Cathars sneaked up to Montségur for an observance to commemorate the 700th anniversary of their forebears' last stand. A small German plane, with a pilot and one passenger, appeared and circled the castle. The Cathars, expecting the police, watched in amazement as the plane, by means of skywriting equipment, traced a strange, eight-branched cross over their heads, and then disappeared beyond the horizon.

Mistral and the Félibrige

The attitude of the French was best expressed by Paul Morand's speech upon being admitted to the Académie Française: 'To write in French is to see flowing the waters of a mountain stream, next to which all languages are muddy rivers; it is to live in a crystal palace.' To someone like Morand, master of *pointu* or 'proper' French with all its mushy slushy vowel sounds, one of the muddiest rivers was *langue d'Oc*. Its demise became a priority in the 19th century; after subjugating the south politically and religiously, Paris decided to finish off the job linguistically and decreed French the sole legal language in the schools, military, government, and press.

One of the strategies of the *Franchimands* (as the southerners call French speakers) was to divide and conquer: *langue d'Oc*, claimed the central Frenchifyers, was actually thousands of dialects and could never constitute a language. Even the southerners admit to seven 'grand dialects' of Occitan, three of which fall into the confines of this book: the Dauphinois of the Alpine valleys, Provençal, and Languedocien, the descendant of the troubadours' language. But it was in Provence that the reaction to the *Franchimands'* linguistic imperialism took its most curious form—in a sentimental, artificially contrived literary movement called the Félibrige.

According to legend, the idea for the Félibres was 'born of a mother's tear' when the mother of the poet Joseph Roumanille wept because she couldn't understand the French verses of her son. Not long after, on 21 May 1854, at the Château de Font Ségugne near Avignon, Roumanille, Frédéric Mistral and five other poets proclaimed the formation of a literary school to 'safeguard indefinitely for Provence its language, its colour, its easy liberty, its national honour, and its fine level of intelligence, for such as it is, we like Provence'. It was the 24-year-old Mistral who came up with the name for the school when he quoted a folk rhyme on the Seven Sorrows of Mary from his native village Maillane: *li sètt felibre de la Lèi*—the seven doctors or sages of the law. As 21 May (the day when the sun is in the constellation of the Pleiades, or seven sisters) was the feast day of Santo Estello, the seven-pointed star of the Cathars was adopted as one of the Félibres' symbols. In later years, after Mistral's epic *Miréio* gave the movement its lustre, 21 May would be celebrated with a Grand Félibre Banquet when all the fifty members or *Majoraux* and their leader, the *capoulié* (Mistral, naturally) would pass around the *Coupo Santo*, the Félibres' Holy Grail.

The Félibres' greatest moment came in 1904, when Mistral won the Nobel Prize for literature, the only writer in a minority language ever to be awarded a Nobel Prize. Thanks to him and the other Félibres Provence became conscious and proud of its separate identity; the richness of the language charmed even foreigners like Ezra Pound, who wrote and translated Provençal. But in spite of these successes, the Félibrige best serves as a lesson on how *not* to revive a language. Today only a few people in their eighties in remote areas still use Provençal as a daily tool, a sorry record compared to the subsequent revivals of Irish, Catalan, Basque, Welsh, and, most successful of all, Hebrew.

Where did the Félibres go wrong? Not for lack of trying: unlike the courtly troubadours, they purposely wrote in a simple style to appeal to the *paysans*. Slipshod grammar and spelling were codified in Mistral's labour of love, the *Trésor du Félibrige* (a work accused by some of passing off the rustic dialect of Maillane as the last word in Provençal). But the Félibres' biggest mistake was confusing language and time, associating Provençal with folklore and the past, and shunning the necessary political fight with Paris in a romantic illusion that their poetry was powerful enough to revive a dying tongue. Mistral's powerful, mystical evocation of western Provence (the real hero of all his epics) was more of a swansong to a dying culture, not the foundation for a Renaissance of a new troubadour movement.

For nearly everything Mistral celebrated in his poetry was undergoing a sea change—Italians, Corsicans, and Spaniards were moving in by the thousands, and helping to build new roads and railroads, while old farming practices, rural customs, traditions, and even villages were rapidly being abandoned. Mistral for all his art, energy, charm and influence could not turn the clock back. He had the unique honour of attending the unveiling of his own statue in Arles—a melancholy recognition that he was dead in his own lifetime.

Hocus Pocus Popes

Filling the lifeless shell of the papal palace in Avignon with the lost trappings of the medieval popes is not an easy task for the imagination. And the more you learn, the harder it gets, for besides all the harlots, speculators, gluttons, and cheats that Petrarch railed against, there seems to have been a shocking amount of voodoo. Accusations of sorcery had already sullied the name of one Occitan pope, Sylvester II (Gerbert of the Auvergne), who reigned from 999–1003 after studying in the Islamic schools in Toledo, where he acquired a prophetic bronze head that advised him in sticky moments. Even today, his tombstone in St John Lateran sweats and rattles before the death of each pope.

In 1309, the French pope Clement V moved the papacy from Rome to Avignon, then died from eating a plate of ground emeralds (prescribed by his doctor for a stomach ache). He was succeeded by John XXII, a native of Cahors, who owed his election to a magic knife that enchanted the conclave of cardinals. This John was also a famous alchemist, and he filled the papal treasury with gold, while King Philip V gave him a pair of *languiers*, or amulets shaped like serpents' tongues, encrusted with gems that changed colour on contact with poison. They served the pope in good stead, as plenty of rivals in the Church were trying to do him in. The most notable culprits were Clement V's doctor, caught manufacturing a diabolical homunculus, and Hughes Geraud, Bishop of Cahors, who confessed in 1317 that he had tried to assassinate the pope 'by poison and by sorcery with wax images, ashes of spiders and toads, the gall of a pig, and the like substances'. John XXII ordered him burnt at the stake.

The next pope, Benedict XII, spent hundreds of thousands of florins on a new palace, and still had enough gold and precious stones left over to top up his treasury—thanks, it is said, to an elderly woman residing in Avignon's ghetto, who told him where to find the 'treasure of the Jews' buried under her hovel. And in the bitter end, just before the Anti-pope Benedict XIII was forced to flee Avignon, he sealed up a secret room in the palace with a cache of solid gold statues, confiding the secret to his friend, the Venetian ambassador. They were never found, although in Mistral's epic *Poème du Rhône* three Venetian ladies who inherited the secret come to the palace and remove the flagstones that cover up the secret room—only to discover a bottomless abyss.

Occitans, Catalans and Related Species

The place is Verdun, the date AD 843, and a fellow named Lothair is about to balls up European history for good. The three contentious grandsons of Charlemagne, unable to peaceably manage the Carolingian Empire, were deciding how to carve it up between them. The resulting Treaty of Verdun would be a linguistic landmark—one of the first documents issued in two new-fangled languages, later called French and German. It would also determine the future map of Europe. Lothair's two brothers were more sensible; Louis took the east, the future Germany, and Charles the Bald got the western half, most of what is now France. Lothair must have thought he was the clever one. Besides the imperial title (of dubious value) and the imperial capital, Aachen, he took away the richest lands of the Empire: northern Italy, Provence, Lorraine and Burgundy, along with Switzerland and the Low Countries.

If Lothair had considered what he would be leaving to his descendants, he might have noticed that this random collection of territories could never be held together for long. If he had had any sense of historical necessity, he might have said: 'You two can keep all the northern bits; just let me have what we Franks know as Aquitania, the land that folks in a thousand years are going to call southern France and Catalunya.' It would have made sense even then, a more coherent possession both culturally and politically. In the later Middle Ages, it would have seemed the obvious choice. This is Western Europe's nation that never was.

The nation would have been called Provence, most likely, as that was the name in the later Middle Ages for the Occitan-speaking lands that stretched from the Atlantic to the Alps. Its capital would probably have been Toulouse. Instead, after the speedy collapse of Lothair's and his brothers' kingdoms, the Occitan-speaking peoples south of the Loire and their Catalan cousins got centuries of a balanced feudal anarchy with no real overlord. Real power became fatally divided between two ambitious rivals, the County of Toulouse, and the new Catalan County of Barcelona, later the Kingdom of Aragon.

The Occitans didn't mind; the relative freedom gave them the chance to create their open, advanced civilization of poetry and tolerance, a March crocus heralding the blossoming of medieval Europe. The Catalans learned to sail and trade, and built themselves a maritime empire in the Mediterranean. Unfortunately, their lack of cooperation doomed the former to a brutal French military conquest, followed by the near-extinction of their language and culture. The Catalans, at least those south of the Pyrenees, would later suffer the same fate at the hands of Spain.

The great castles of Languedoc and Roussillon—Quéribus, Carcassonne, Salses and the rest—are the gravestones of the Lost Nation, the sites of defeats that marked its gradual, inexorable assimilation by the power of Paris and the north. Today, if you visit them in the off season the only other car in the car park will be likely to have a white Spanish tag with a 'B' for Barcelona. You may see the inscrutable Catalans—culturally much more alive than the poor Languedociens—picnicking in the snow at Peyrepertuse in December, or at Salses furtively taking voluminous notes on the guided tour. Catalans abroad, even when encumbered by children and small dogs, often have the raffish air of spies or infiltrating *provocateurs*; it's part of their charm. Here, they're on a real mission, piecing together the memorials and cultural survivals of a forgotten world—forgotten by everyone else, maybe, but a dream that the Catalans and France's Occitanian malcontents will never let die.

Troubadours

Lyric poetry in the modern Western world was born around the year 1095 with the rhymes of Count William (1071–1127), grandfather of Eleanor of Aquitaine. William wrote in the courtly language of Old Provençal (or Occitan) although his subject matter was hardly courtly ('Do you know how many times I screwed them? / One hundred and eighty-eight to be precise; / so much so that I almost broke my girth and harness…'). A descendant of the royal house of Aragon, William had Spanish-Arab blood in his lusty veins and had battled against the Moors in Spain on several occasions; but at the same time he found inspiration (for his form, if not his content) from a civilization that was centuries ahead of Christian Europe in culture.

The word *troubadour* may be derived from the Arabic root for lutenist (trb), and the ideal of courtly love makes its first appearance in the writings of the spiritual Islamic Sufis. The Sufis believed that true understanding could not be expressed in doctrines, but could be suggested obliquely in poetry and fables. Much of what they wrote was love poetry addressed to an ideal if unkind and irrational Muse, whom the poet hopes will reward his merit and devotion with enlightenment and inspiration. Christians who encountered this poetry in the Crusades converted this ideal Muse into the Virgin, giving birth to the great 12th-century cult of Mary. But in Occitania this mystic strain was reinterpreted in a more worldly fashion by troubadours, whose muses became flesh and blood women, although these darlings were equally unattainable in the literary conventions of courtly love. The lady in question could only be addressed by a pseudonym. She had to be married to someone else. The poet's hopeless suit to her hinged, not on his rank, but on his virtue and worthiness. The greatest novelty of all was that this love had to go unrequited.

Art songs of courtly love were known as *cansos*, and rarely translate well, as their merit was in the poet's skill in inventing new forms in his rhyming schemes, metres, melodies, and images. But the troubadours wrote many other songs as well, called *sirventes*, which followed established forms but took for their subjects politics, war, miserly patrons, and even satires on courtly love itself.

The golden age of the troubadours began in the 1150s, when the feudal lords of Occitania warred amongst each other with so little success that behind the sound and fury the land enjoyed a rare political stability. Courts indulged in new luxuries and the arts flourished, and troubadours found ready audiences, travelling from castle to castle. One of their great patrons was En Barral, Viscount of Marseille, who was especially fond of the reputedly mad but charming Peire Vidal. Vidal not only wrote of his love for En Barral's beautiful wife, but in a famous incident even went beyond the bounds of convention by stealing a kiss from her while she slept (her husband, who thought it was funny, had to plead with her to forgive him). Vidal travelled widely, especially after the death of En Barral in 1192, and wrote a rare nostalgic poem for the homeland of his lady fair:

> With each breath I draw in the air
> I feel coming from Provence;
> I so love everything from there
> that when people speak well of it,
> I listen smiling, and with each
> word ask for a hundred more,
> so much does the hearing please me.

(trans. by Anthony Bonner, in
Songs of the Troubadours)

Up Your Nose

If nothing else, Provence and Languedoc will make you more aware of that sense we only remember when something stinks. The perfumeries of Grasse will correct this 'scentual' ignorance with a hundred different potions; every *village perché* has shops overflowing with scented soaps, pot-pourris and bundles of *herbes de Provence*; every kitchen emits intoxicating scents of garlic and thyme; every cellar wants you to breathe in the bouquets of its wines. And when you begin to almost crave the more usual French smells of *Gauloise* butts, *pipi* and *pommes frites*, you discover that this nasal obsession is not only profitable to some, but healthy for all.

Aromathérapie, a name coined in the 1920s for the method of natural healing through fragrances, is taken very seriously in the land where one word *sentir* does double duty for 'feel' and 'smell'. French medical students study it, and its prescriptions are covered by the national social security. For as an aromatherapist will tell you, smells play games with your psyche; the nose is hooked up not only to primitive drives like sex and hunger, but also to your emotions and memory. The consequences can be monumental. Just the scent of a madeleine cake dipped in tea was enough to set Proust off to write *Remembrance of Things Past*.

Aromatherapy is really just a fashionable name for old medicine. The Romans had a saying *Cur moriatur homo, cui salvia crescit in horto?* (Why should he die, who grows sage in his garden?) about a herb still heralded for its youth-giving properties. Essential oils distilled from plants were the secret of Egyptian healing and embalming, and were so powerful that there was a bullish market in 17th-century Europe for mummies, which were boiled down to make medicine.

Essential oils are created by the sun and the most useful aromatic plants grow in hot and dry climates—as in the south of France, the spiritual heartland of aromatherapy. Lavender, the totem plant of the Midi, has been in high demand for its mellow soothing qualities ever since the Romans used it to scent their baths (hence its name from the Latin *lavare*, to wash). Up until the 1900s, nearly every farm in Provence had a small lavender distillery, and you can still find a few kicking about today. Most precious of all is the oil of *lavande fine*, a species that grows only above 3000 feet on the sunny side of the Alps; 150 pounds of flowers are needed for every pound of oil.

For centuries in Provence, shepherds were regarded as magicians for their plant cures, involving considerable mumbo-jumbo about picking their herbs in certain places and certain times—and indeed, modern analysis has shown that the chemical composition of a herb like thyme varies widely, depending on where it grows and when it's picked. When the sun is in Leo, shepherds make *millepertuis*, or red oil (a sovereign anaesthetic and remedy for burns and wounds) by soaking the flowers of St John's wort in a mixture of white wine and olive oil that has been exposed to the hottest sun. After three days, they boil the wine off, and let the flowers distill for another month; the oil is then sealed into tiny bottles, good for one dose each, to maintain the oil's healing properties.

Still awaiting a fashionable revival are other traditional Provençal cures: baked ground magpie brains for epilepsy, marmot fat for rheumatism, dried fox testicles rubbed on the chest for uterine disease and mouse excrement for bedwetting.

Eze

The French Riviera: Menton to Cannes

A calcined, scalped, rasped, scraped, flayed, broiled, powdered,
leprous, blotched, mangy, grimy, parboiled, country, without trees,
water, grass, fields—with blank, beastly, senseless olives and orange-
trees like a mad cabbage gone indigestible.

Swinburne

Just west of Italy begins that 20km swathe of Mediterranean
hyperbole that represents the favourite mental image
of the French Riviera, where the landscapes are at
their most vertical and oranges and lemons
ripen against a backdrop of snow-topped

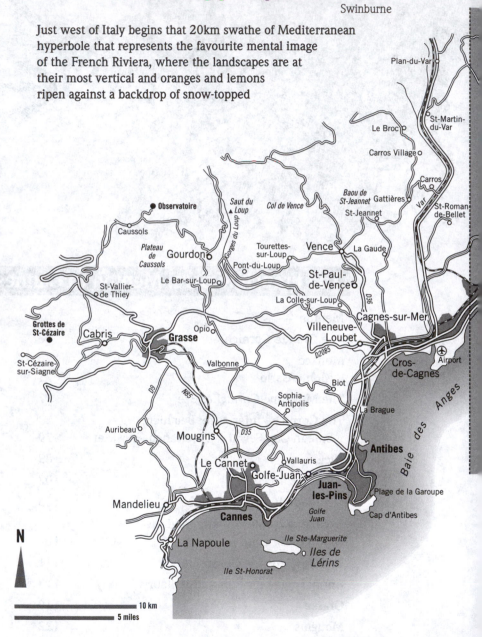

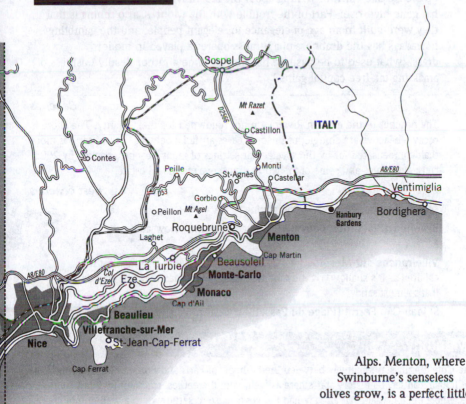

Alps. Menton, where Swinburne's senseless olives grow, is a perfect little sun-trap, rivalled only by Beaulieu a bit further along, the only place in France where bananas ripen naturally. Superb villas and gardens, that once belonged to dukes and kings, are scattered along the shore of St-Jean-Cap-Ferrat, Roquebrune, and Cap Martin. High in the mountains hang spectacular medieval villages and La Turbie, the trophy erected by the Romans to celebrate their final victory over the indomitable Ligurian tribes who until then had effectively kept the Empire from the sweet delights of Provence.

Although first tamed by the Romans, this easternmost and tastiest morsel of the Côte d'Azur long remained a world apart, ruled until the mid-19th century by the Grimaldis of Monaco, and noted above all for its lemons and poverty. Bad feelings with the French over Napoleon brought the first English and Russians, with their titles and weak lungs, to winter here, in spite of the difficult roads. They built hotels, villas and casinos in the grand, fulsome rococo spa style of the period, and to this day the spirit lingers, a slightly musty violet perfume in a semi-tropical climate. Ian Fleming summed up the bygone spirit in writing about the fate of Monaco, where high class has gone high rise: 'Part of the trouble with the Monte-Carlo rooms is that they were built in an age of elegance for elegant people, and the gambling nowadays has the drabness of a Strauss operetta played in modern dress...what used to be pastime has now become a rather deadly business of amassing tax-free capital gains.'

Beaches

The beaches of the eastern Riviera are not renowned for their beauty. The shore is rocky—beaches are shingle, or in some cases artificial pebble. Lack of sand is more than compensated for by the spectacular settings of many beaches, backed by 200m cliffs, palm trees and some of the world's most expensive real estate.

best beaches

Monaco: chic and sharp; safe swimming.

Beaulieu (Plage des Fourmis): backed by palms, view across to Cap Ferrat.

Villefranche-sur-Mer: the trendiest beach in the region, also the best for children as it's shallow, right by the train station, and has very fine shingle that's almost sand.

St-Jean-Cap-Ferrat (Plage du Passable): views to Villefranche.

Menton

The Côte d'Azur starts halfway between the fleshpots of Paris and Rome at Menton, right on the Italian frontier. Its history starts here as well, with the earliest traces of Riviera humans—folk who a million years ago already had the good sense to settle where a wall of mountains, still crowned with snow in April, blocks out the cold so that lemons can blossom all year.

Despite this early start, the Menton area wasn't inhabited again until the 10th century, when settlers clustered around the Annonciade hill, where they felt safe from Saracen pirates. The town first belonged to the Counts of Ventimiglia—little better than pirates themselves—then briefly joined Provence before it was sold to Charles Grimaldi of Monaco in 1346. The Grimaldis became rich from taxing Menton's citrus fruit up to 1848, when the town and its neighbour Roquebrune declared their independence. Unlike most of the revolts in Europe that fateful year, this puny one succeeded, and the Free Towns of Menton and Roquebrune endured until 1860, when the people voted to unite with France, and Charles III of Monaco sold his claim on the towns to Napoleon III for four million gold francs. The following year a Dr J. Henry Bennet wrote *Mentone and the Riviera as a Winter Climate*, a book that soon attracted a community of 5000 Brits, led by Queen Victoria herself in 1883. In the Second World War, the Germans wrecked Menton's port, and, when they were chased out, lobbed bombs on to it from the Italian side of the border. The damage wasn't repaired until 1956.

Nattering nabobs of negativism claim Menton has a poor beach (true) and as much atmosphere as your grandmother's antimacassar, where 30 per cent of the population are retirees (the highest percentage in France) and most of the rest are poodles. On the other hand,

Menton is one of the prettiest towns on the coast, magnificently situated, low on craft shops but high on relaxation compared to the hard-edged glamour-pusses to the west.

Getting Around

By train: The *Métrazur* trains that run between St-Raphaël and Ventimiglia, and all others running between Nice and Italy, stop in Menton (Menton-Centre), Rue de la Gare. There's also a stop—Menton-Garavan—behind the port.

By bus: Buses depart from the Esplanade du Careï, between the two avenues north of the train station, every half-hour to Nice, by way of Roquebrune-Cap-Martin and Monte-Carlo. Others will take you to Ventimiglia. There are three buses daily to Castillon and Sospel, while Transports Breuleux, ✆ 04 93 35 73 51, in Rue Masséna (near the station), have similar daily services to Ste-Agnès, Gorbio, and Castellar. All local Menton bus-lines pass by Esplanade du Careï.

Tourist Information

Palais de l'Europe, 8 Ave Boyer, ✆ 04 92 41 76 76, ✉ 04 92 41 76 78; also at the coach station, on the Esplanade du Careï, ✆ 04 93 28 43 27. **Post office:** ✆ 04 93 28 64 84, on the corner of Cours George V and Rue Edouard VII.

market days

Daily, opposite the Cocteau Museum, in a pretty building with ceramic decorations; flea market on Friday.

Jean Cocteau, Love, and Lemons

Menton is squeezed between the mountains and a pair of shingle-beached bays: on the Italian side, the **Baie de Garavan**, where villas and gardens overlook the yacht harbour, while the **Baie du Soleil** (the Roman *Pacis Sinus* or Gulf of Peace) stretches 3km west to Cap Martin. In between these two bays stands a little 17th-century harbour bastion that Jean Cocteau converted into the **Musée Cocteau**, ✆ 04 93 57 72 30 (*open 10–12 and 2–6; adm*), to hold his playful series of *Animaux Fantastiques*, a tapestry of *Judith et Holopherne*, while the happier love affairs of the Mentonnais are portrayed in the *Innamorati* series, also on display.

This theme of Menton's lovers was first explored by Cocteau in his decorations for the 1957 **Salle des Mariages**, ✆ 04 92 10 50 00, (*open 8.30–12.30 and 1.30–5; closed Sat and Sun*), in the **Hôtel de Ville**, five minutes' walk away in Rue de la République. A lemon-picker weds a fisherman amid rather discouraging mythological allusions: on the right wall there's a wedding-party in Saracen costume, referring to the Mentonnais' Saracen blood, although amongst the company we see the bride's frowning mother, the groom's jilted girlfriend and her armed brother. The other wall shows Orpheus turning back to see if his beloved Eurydice is following him out of hell, condemning her to return there forever; while on the ceiling Love, Poetry (mounted on Pegasus) and Science (juggling planets) look on. Love was also a favourite theme of the original Riviera inhabitants, who carved the little Cro-Magnon Venuses now housed in the **Musée de la Préhistoire Régionale**, Rue Loredan Larchey, ✆ 04 93 35 84 64 (*open 10–12 and 2–6, closed Tues; adm free*). Dioramas recreate the area's cave interiors from that time, but the star exhibit is the 30,000-year-old skull of Menton Man (found just over the

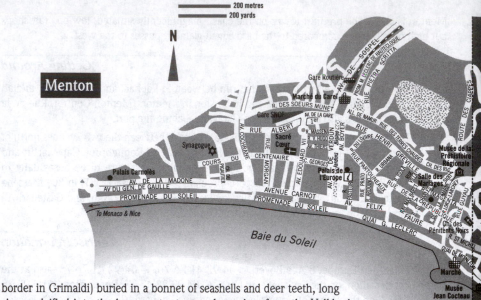

200 metres
200 yards

N

Baie du Soleil

border in Grimaldi) buried in a bonnet of seashells and deer teeth, long since calcified into the bone; note, too, rock carvings from the Vallée des Merveilles, high above Menton in the Roya valley of the Alpes-Maritimes.

The 1909 **Palais d'Europe** was once the casino, but is now an exhibition hall (*closed Tues*) and the tourist office. In front of it is the exotic **Jardins Biovès**, the most tidied, kempt, combed and swept bit of green space you're ever likely to come across, where the elderly sit in sunshine in beige and grey to match their poodles, glumly watching life pass them by. Here the fantastical lemon-studded floats of Menton's *Fête du Citron* are parked at carnival time. A kilometre west, the summer home of the princes of Monaco, the **Palais Carnolès** (1717), is now an art museum, the **Musée des Beaux-Arts Palais Carnolès**, 3 Ave de la Madone, © 04 93 35 49 71, bus 3 (*open 10–12 and 2–6, closed Tues*). It holds a Byzantine-inspired *Virgin and Child* from 13th-century Tuscany, Ludovico Brea's luminous *Madonna and Child with St Francis*, and all the previous winners from Menton's very own Biennale of painting, some of which are so awful you can only wonder what the losers were like. Other works were donated by the English landscape and portrait artist Graham Sutherland, who lived part of every year in Menton from 1947 until he died in 1980.

The Vieille Ville, and the Gardens of Garavan

The tall, narrow 17th-century houses of Menton's Vieille Ville are reminiscent of the old quarter of Genoa, knitted together by anti-earthquake arches that span stepped lanes named after old pirate captains and saints. It's hard to believe that the quiet main street, **Rue Longue** (the Roman Via Julia Augusta), was, until the 19th century, the main route between France and Italy. According to legend, the lady at the Palais Princier (at No.123) received a secret nocturnal visit from Casanova, who crept in through the sewers.

From Rue Longue a ramp leads up to the *parvis* of the ice-cream-coloured church of **St-Michel** (1675), and its equally charming Baroque neighbour, the **Chapelle des Pénitents Blancs**, headquarters of one of the old Riviera's many religious confraternities (*see* **Nice**). The *parvis* itself has a pebble mosaic of the Grimaldi arms, used as the setting for Menton's megastar chamber music festival in August. The Montée du Souvenir leads to the top of the Vieille Ville, where the citadel was replaced in the 19th century by the romantic, panoramic **Cimetière du Vieux Château**, curiously unmarked on the tourist map, but just a quick steep haul up from those sitting out their last years below. Guy de Maupassant called it the most aristocratic cemetery

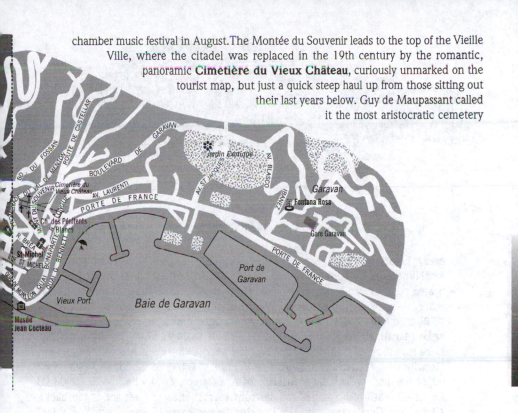

in Europe—the venerable names inscribed on the hierachical array of ornate tombs and little pavilions include William Webb-Ellis, the 'inventor of rugby'. Many were consumptives in their teens and twenties who, like Aubrey Beardsley, only came to Menton to die.

From the cemetery, Boulevard de Garavan leads into the neighbourhood where this dead élite would reside if they were alive today, and to the **Jardin Exotique**, ✆ 04 93 35 86 72, planted with 700 species from around the world (*open 10–12.30 and 3–6 summer, 10–12.30 and 2–5 winter; adm*). One road off the boulevard, Ave Blasco-Ibañez, was named after the author of *The Four Horsemen of the Apocalypse* (1867–1928) who lived here in the **Villa Fontana Rosa** and decorated his garden with colourful *azulejo* tiles from his native Valencia (*guided tours only, ✆ 04 92 10 33 66*). **Villa Isola Bella**, on the other side of the Garavan station, was the home of another victim of tuberculosis, Katherine Mansfield (1888–1923); although ailing she was happy here, and fictionalized her experiences in a number of short stories.

Menton ✉ *06500*   ***Where to Stay***

All but one of Menton's old grand hotels have been converted into flats, and no sparkling new ones have risen to take up the slack. If you've got the readies, the last *grande dame* is the ★★★★**Hôtel des Ambassadeurs**, 3 Rue Partouneaux, ✆ 04 93 28 75 75, ✉ 04 93 35 62 32: gracious, spacious, pink and balconied, and slap bang in the middle of town. There's nearly

Menton

every luxury you'd expect for the price, but no pool. *Open all year*. The ★★★**Napoléon**, 29 Porte de France, ℘ 04 93 35 89 50, 🖂 04 93 35 49 22, has a heated pool covered in the winter and soundproofed, air-conditioned rooms. *Closed mid-Nov–mid-Dec*. The ★★★**Royal Westminster**, 1510 Promenade du Soleil, ℘ 04 93 28 69 69, 🖂 04 92 10 12 30, has quiet, elegant rooms with sea views. The popular ★★**Le Magali**, 10 Rue Villarey, ℘ 04 93 35 73 78, 🖂 04 93 57 05 04, fills up quickly, so be sure to reserve a room with a balcony overlooking the garden. *Open all year*. Elsewhere try ★★**Claridge's**, 39 Ave de Verdun, ℘ 04 93 35 72 53, 🖂 04 93 35 42 90, or the more welcoming ★★**Bristol**, 24 Ave Carnot, ℘ 04 93 57 54 32, 🖂 04 93 28 12 62, with high ceilings and seafront rooms (cheaper ones are at the back). *Closed Nov*. Good bargains include **Pension Beauregard**, 10 Rue Albert Iᵉʳ, ℘ 04 93 28 63 63, 🖂 04 93 28 63 79, below the station, a sweet place with a quiet garden. *Closed Nov*. Menton's **youth hostel** is just above town on the Plateau St-Michel, ℘ 04 93 35 93 14, 🖂 04 93 35 93 07.

Eating Out

For posh nosh, there's **La Veranda** at the Ambassadeurs (*see* above). Otherwise Menton is gastronomically a humble place. All along Rue St Michel masses of restaurants vie for your attention with tempting displays of hot pastries and baguettes spilling out into the street at lunchtime that somehow miss the mark. At No.23 try the tasty Moroccan dishes at **Darkoum**, ℘ 04 93 35 44 88 (*menus at 90 and 130F*). Between the market and the sea, opposite the Musée Cocteau in the bright blue **Le Nautic**, ℘ 04 93 35 78 74, at 27 Quai de Monléon, serves up every possible fish dish, including *bouillabaisse*. *Closed Mon*. Tucked away off the main street, at 5 Rue Piéta, is the **Crêperie St-Michel**, ℘ 04 93 28 44 64, whose alarmingly brisk service and odd mixture of decoration (on the mantelpice a sailing ship, a pair of men's shoes, a painting of a Red Indian chief and a photo of Eric Cantona) make it a good lunch stop if you've a bus to catch. Up at Monti, on the Rte de Sospel, the panoramic **Pierrot-Pierrette**, ℘ 04 93 35 79 76 (*140–180F*), complements the views with delicious fresh blue trout. *Closed Mon, and most of Jan*.

Menton isn't exactly a hopping place, but just in case check the Menton page in *Nice-Matin* or the glossy brochure published by the tourist office every three months. The young grumble that there's nothing to do, and head west to Monaco for nightlife; **Le Casino** with its disco **Le Brummell** (both ✆ 04 92 10 16 16) are disdained as tourist ghettos. Classical music concerts take place in the church of **St-Michel**, especially in August during the **chamber music festival**. If you've brought the kids there's mini-golf, go-karting etc. at **Koaland**, 5 Ave de la Madone, ✆ 04 92 10 00 40. Once in a while an undubbed film is shown on one of the three screens at the air conditioned **Eden**, 11 Rue de la République, ✆ 04 92 10 13 52.

North of Menton

Four narrow mountain valleys converge at Menton, the villages hanging over their slopes, linked by bus from Menton and to each other by mule-tracks. Above the easternmost valley is **Castellar** (7km from Menton), laid out on a grid plan in 1435 to replace the original 1258 village, built by the counts of Ventimiglia high on a rocky peg. An hour's hike will take you to the ghostly ruins of old Castellar; or take the less strenuous walk up the Sospel road as far as the waterfall at the **Gourg de l'Oura**. Up the second valley, the Val du Careï, the medieval monastery of **L'Annonciade** (5.5km from Menton) has gone through countless transformations over the years; best of all are its grand views and its ex votos dating back to the 1600s, including an unusual one—a piece of a zeppelin. Further up the Val du Careï, amid the viaducts of the old Menton–Sospel railway, you can wander through the scented **Forêt de Monti**, then up to **Castillon**, awaft with the scent of fresh concrete and artisan shops, well into its third incarnation as 'the most beautiful new village in France' after being flattened by an earthquake in 1887 and bombed in 1944.

From Menton the narrow, winding D22 noodles up to **Ste-Agnès**, at 650m the loftiest village on the entire coast. There are 3 buses a day from Menton, or drive up, passing under and over the mighty viaducts of the A8, which look as insubstantial as spider's legs once you reach Ste-Agnès. The village was founded in the 900s, they say, by a Saracen who fell in love with a local girl and converted to Christianity for her sake. It certainly looks old enough—a crazy quilt of vaulted passageways and tiny squares that have unfortunately succumbed to trinket-shopitis. When you can't look at another smirking *santon*, head up Rue Longue for a view that stretches to Corsica on a clear day. On foot, a path descends from Ste-Agnès to Menton in two hours, or better still, take the one-hour shortcut called the *Balcon de la Côte d'Azur* to **Gorbio** (from Menton it's 8km). Gorbio is just as picturesquely medieval as Ste-Agnès but has somehow been spared the trinkets. The best time to visit is at *Fête Dieu* (Corpus Christi) in June, for the medieval *Procession dai limaça* when the village lanes are lit by thousands of flickering lamps made from snail shells filled with olive oil, set in beds of sand.

A Dip into Italy

Just over the border, in the village of Grimaldi, the beachside **Balzi Rossi** (red caves) were the centre of a sophisticated Neanderthal society that flourished *c.* 100,000 to 40,000 BC and produced some of Europe's first art, displayed in the **Museo Preistorico** (*museum and caves open 9–1 and 2.30–7.30, closed Mon; adm*). The town of **Ventimiglia** has a large **market** every Friday. Outside Ventimiglia at Mortola Inferiore, you can visit the extraordinary

Hanbury Gardens, a botanical paradise of acclimatized plants from around the world, founded in 1867 by Sir Thomas Hanbury. *Open 10–4, closed Wed; adm.* If you plan to go deeper into Italy, you can save thousands of lire by filling up with petrol in Menton; if you plan to feast on an excellent Italian meal, it's only 12km to Bordighera and the lovely art nouveau La Via Romana, Via Romana 57, ✆ (0184) 26 66 81.

✉ *06500*   ***Where to Stay and Eating Out***

★**Les Alpes** has the monopoly in **Castellar**, on Place Clemenceau, ✆ 04 93 35 82 83, ✆ 04 93 28 24 95, with tidy little rooms and good food. *Open all year.* Or go upmarket in **Castillon** at the ★★★**Bergerie**, ✆ 04 93 04 00 39, ✆ 04 93 28 02 91, with rustic but very comfortable rooms and more elaborate food. **Ste-Agnès** has the most in the way of accommodation up here: **Saint-Yves**, ✆ 04 93 35 91 45, ✆ 04 93 35 65 85, for sweet dreams, dreamy views and most notably, courtesy; or, from April to November, ★**La Vieille Auberge**, ✆ 04 93 35 92 02, is just before the entrance to the village, with a delightful garden. Full board is mandatory, but if you're not staying you can still stop by for a gargantuan feast. *Closed Wed, Jan.* There's another warm welcome and good dining at **Le Logis Sarrasin** ✆ 04 93 35 86 89 (*menus start at 85F*), offering 6 courses, including delicious *raviolis maison*. *Closed Mon and mid-Oct–mid-Nov.*

Menton to Nice: the Three Corniches

When most people hear 'Riviera', they mentally picture this 20km stretch of coast, where mighty mountains plummet drunkenly into the sea, and hairpinning *corniche* roads zigzag on ledges over vertiginous drops; where continental hormones go into overdrive as film stars in dark glasses race sporty convertibles down to 'Monte' to gamble their residuals away. A lot of that holds true, although the only racing that really happens is the Monaco Grand Prix. Traffic is nearly always slow and heavy—a fact that doesn't prevent some would-be James Bonds from contributing to an appalling accident rate. The worst traffic jams inch along the lowest road, the **Corniche Inférieure** (N98) through the seaside resorts; most of the frequent buses that ply the coast use this road, which runs parallel to the railway. To relieve the traffic, already choking in the 1920s, the most dramatic of the roads, the **Moyenne Corniche** (N7) was drilled through the rock and hung sheerly through the hills—which makes it the favourite for car chase scenes. Higher up, along the route of the Roman Via Aurelia (also called Via Julia Appia), Napoleon built the **Grande Corniche** (D2564) with the most panoramic views of all.

The Grande Corniche

Roquebrune-Cap-Martin

Nearly every potential building site in the lush mountain shore between Menton and Monaco is occupied by Roquebrune-Cap-Martin—from old Roquebrune just beside the Grande Corniche down to the exclusive garden cape of Cap Martin. Purchased by the Grimaldis in 1355 for 1000 florins, Roquebrune (like Menton) later revolted against Monaco and became a free town until joining France in 1861. The medieval village is all steep, winding, arcaded streets and over-restored houses, culminating at the top in the **Château** (*open winter 10–12 and 2–5; summer till 7; closed Fri in Nov and Dec*), with the oldest surviving *donjon* in France, erected in the 10th century by the counts of Ventimiglia against the Saracen threat. In the 1400s, Lambert of Monaco built much of what stands today; in 1911, Sir William Ingram purchased the castle, planted the mock medieval *tour anglaise* by the gate, and donated it all to the town in 1921. The antique-furnished rooms in the 11ft-thick walls are surprisingly poky—most people have bathrooms bigger than this lordling's reception hall. But the view from the top floor is huge enough for any ego. The castle guards lived below in picturesque **Rue Moncollet**, carved out of the living rock; another street under the castle, Rue du Château, leads to Rue de la Fontaine and Chemin de St-Roch and a remarkable contemporary of the castle: a **1000-year-old olive tree** measuring 33ft in circumference.

In 1467, as plague decimated the coastal population, the Roquebrunois vowed to the Virgin that if they were spared they would, in thanksgiving, annually re-enact tableaux of the Passion. The Virgin apparently thought it was a good deal, and the villagers have faithfully kept their side of the pact every year on 5 August. The best of the 500 roles involved in the colourful processions are jealously 'owned' by the oldest families, who pass them down to their descendants like heirlooms.

Cap Martin

In the 1890s a pair of empresses, Eugénie of France (widow of Napoleon III) and Elisabeth ('Sissi') of Austria, made Roquebrune's little peninsula of Cap Martin an aristocratic enclave, 'whispering of old kings come here to dine or die', as F. Scott Fitzgerald wrote. Churchill did the dining and Yeats, King Nikola of Montenegro and Le Corbusier the dying, the latter succumbing to a heart attack in 1965 while swimming off the white rocks beside what is now **Promenade Le Corbusier**—a lovely walk around the cape, past villas immersed in luxuriant pines, olives, cypresses and mimosas. Corby had been staying in one of the villas, one of the most beautiful on the Côte d'Azur, built in 1929 by furniture designer Eileen Gray; the story goes that he loved the house so much that he got a wealthy friend to buy it at auction, helping him defeat the higher bids of Aristotle Onassis by dragging the auctioneer off at a crucial moment.

Another spectacular path leads in an hour and a half from Cap Martin to Monte-Carlo Beach. If you walk it, look back towards the Cap to see the ruined tower of the long-gone convent of St-Martin. When it was built, the men of Roquebrune had vowed to protect the nuns from pirates, and one night in the late 1300s the tower's bell sounded the alarm; the Roquebrunois piled out of bed and ran down the hill to defend the good sisters, who laughingly confessed that they were just testing the bell's efficiency. A few nights later, pirates really did appear, and although the nuns rang like mad, their defenders only rolled over in bed. Next morning in the smouldering ruins, the older nuns were found with their throats slit, while the prettier ones were carted off to the slave markets of Barbary.

✉ *06190*

Where to Stay and Eating Out

Affordable hotels are scarce along the **Corniches**, but if money's no object there's the ★★★★**Vista Palace**, ✆ 04 92 10 40 00, 📠 04 93 35 18 94, the ultimate in luxury, hanging on a 305m cliff on the Grande Corniche, with a God's-eye view over Monaco; also a heated pool, squash, gym, and sauna. *Closed mid-Nov–mid-Mar.* Down on the poor sinners' level, the ★★**Westminster**, 14 Ave L.-Laurens, ✆ 04 93 35 00 68, 📠 04 93 28 88 50, has a pretty garden terrace near the junction of the lower two Corniches. *Closed mid-Nov–mid-Feb.*

Near **Roquebrune's** castle, in a former sheepfold cut into the rock, **Au Grand Inquisiteur**, 18 Rue du Château, ℂ/ 04 93 35 05 37 (*menus at 148F and 218F*) offers well-prepared Provençal dishes like *fleurs de courgette farcies. Closed Mon and Tues lunchtime, and Nov–Dec.* A cheaper troglodyte choice, **La Grotte**, Place des Deux-Frères, ℂ/ 04 93 35 00 04, also has tables outside at the entrance to the Vieille Ville in Roquebrune, and offers a 55F *plat du jour* and bargain menus. The owner of the cheese shop opposite runs **Les Tables du Berger**, 4 Rue V.H.-Carnolès, ℂ 04 93 57 40 60 (*menus 75F–260F*), a *restaurant gastronomique. Closed Sun eve, Mon.*

Monaco

Big time tax-dodgers agree: it's hard to beat Monaco for comfort and convenience when the time comes to snuggle down with your piggy chips. Unlike most other tax havens, the Principality is not an island, so you can purr over to France or Italy in the Lamborghini in only a few minutes. The grub is good, you can safely flaunt your jewels, and there's enough culture to keep you from feeling a total Philistine; the homeless and other riff-raff who might trouble your conscience are kept at bay. Security, understandably, is the prime concern: closed-circuit cameras spy over every corner, every traffic signal records every passing car. In emergencies, the whole Principality can be closed off in a few minutes. Rainier III, chairman of the board of Monaco Inc., will probably go down in history as the Principality's greatest benefactor. Through landfill and burrowing he has added a fifth to his realm and on it built more (but certainly not better) than any of his predecessors, creating a Lilliputian Manhattan. To obtain one of the precious resident's permits, you have to own or rent a flat in one of these grey towers and watch your ass. Residents who still choose to work, the Luciano Pavarottis and Claudia Schiffers, are hardly ever home. Money is the main topic of conversation no matter where you go in this perfectly sanitized bolthole on the Med, where a calendar of car races, circuses, fireworks, First Division football and opera puts a glittering mask over its ghoulish, acquisitive face.

History Starts with a Stinker

Seven hundred years ago, in 1297, an ambitious member of Genoa's Guelph party named Francesco Grimaldi the Spiteful dressed up like a friar and knocked at the door of the Ghibelline fortress at Monaco, asking for hospitality. The soldiers sleepily admitted him; the phoney friar pulled a knife from his robe, killed the soldiers, and let in his men. Although Francesco was the first Grimaldi to get into Monaco, the family only became lords of their rock when they purchased it outright from Genoa in 1308. They were once rulers of a mini-empire including Antibes and Menton, but the ambitions of others have reduced the Grimaldis' sovereign Ruritania to a sea-hugging 194 hectares (slightly larger than half of Central Park) under the looming mountain, Tête de Chien. Here Rainier III presides as the living representative of the oldest ruling family in Europe, and Europe's last constitutional autocrat.

For centuries the Grimaldis' main income came from a tax levied on Menton's lemons and olives, and when Menton revolted in 1848 they faced bankruptcy; Monaco was the poorest state in all Europe. In desperation, Prince Charles III looked for inspiration to the Duke of Baden-Baden, whose casino lured Europe's big-spending aristocrats every summer. Monaco, Charles decided, would be the winter Baden-Baden, and he founded the *Société des Bains de Mer* (SBM) to operate a casino and tourist industry, with the Principality as the chief shareholder. The casino was built on a rock that the prince named Monte-Carlo after himself, and he hired François Blanc, the talented French manager of the Homburg Baden casino, to create a gambling city to order, 10 per cent of all profits going to the crown. Blanc was one of the most successful financiers of the day, and he proved his worth. He loaned the French government nearly 5 million francs for the completion of Napoleon III's centrepiece, the Paris Opera, and in return assured that the French built a new railway from Nice in 1868. With transport to bring in the punters, the money poured by the bushel; in 1870 the coffers were so full that Charles abolished direct taxation in Monaco, a state of affairs that endures to this day.

But gone are those fond days when the Monégasques could live entirely off the folly of others. France and Italy legalized gaming in 1933, ending the Principality's monopoly; the proportion of its revenue that Monaco gleans from the tables has declined from 95 per cent to a mere 4 per cent. In the dark, bankrupt 1950s Rainier III gave his little realm a fairy-tale cachet by wedding an incandescent American film actress named Grace Kelly, bringing in a much needed injection of socialites and their fat bankrolls. Since then, the Prince and the omnipresent SBM have found new ways to keep Monaco's 5000 subjects and 30,000 residents from paying income tax, especially in 'offshore' banking (some 40 do business here), in the media (Télé and Radio Monte-Carlo), in 'business tourism' (there's a new ultra-modern congress hall) and tourism tourism, with no little interest fuelled by the media's scrutiny of the sadly tarnished fairytale lives of princesses Caroline and Stéphanie.

Getting Around

There are no customs formalities; you can just drive into Monaco along the **Corniche Inférieure**, or take the **helicopter** from Nice airport if you're in a hurry (7mins), or a **bus or taxi** (45mins). The Monaco/Monte-Carlo **railway** station is in Ave Prince-Pierre, © 93 10 60 15; **buses** every 30mins between Menton and Nice stop at several points along the Corniche. Small as it is, Monaco is divided into several towns: Monte-Carlo to the east, Fontvieille by the port, Monaco-Ville on the rock, and La Condamine below, and there's a **public bus network** to save you some legwork. More importantly, **free public lifts and escalators** operate between its tiers of streets.

Tourist Information

24 Boulevard des Moulins, Monte-Carlo, © 92 16 61 16, ✆ 92 16 60 00, e-mail magto.ny@ix.netcom.com., website www.monaco.mc/usa/

Note: In Monaco, if the telephone number has only 8 digits, you must dial © 00 377 before calling, even from France. If the number has 10 digits, it operates like a French number.

Monte-Carlo

Set back in the sculpture-filled gardens of Place du Casino rises the most famous building on the whole Côte d'Azur: the 1878 **Casino de Monte-Carlo**, © 377 92 16 23 00, a fascinating piece of Old World kitsch known in its heyday as the 'cathedral of hell'. Anyone over 21 with a passport can visit. One-armed bandits, American roulette, craps and blackjack tables click and clatter away just as in Las Vegas or Atlantic City. For 100F you can get into the *salons privés* (open from 3pm)—quieter, more intense—where oily croupiers, under gilt, over-the-top rococo ceilings, accept limitless bets on roulette and *chemin de fer*. In the Pink Salon Bar, where naked cigar-chomping nymphs float on the ceiling, Charles Deville Wells celebrated his three-day gambling spree in 1891 that turned $400 into $40,000 and inspired the popular tune *The Man who Broke the Bank at Monte-Carlo*. Whatever you do, don't miss the thrill of flushing one of the Casino's loos.

The casino's bijou opera-theatre, the **Salle Garnier** (*open only for performances*), was designed by Charles Garnier, his part of the payback for François Blanc's loan that completed his even more elaborate Paris Opera. Inaugurated by Sarah Bernhardt in 1879 and backed by pots of SBM money, it became one of the most exciting in Europe, commissioning operas from composers like Saint-Saëns and Massenet, and after 1911, ballets from the Ballets Russes de Monte-Carlo. Since the war it's gone bland and mostly serves as an excuse for residents to put on the dog. But in the old days its gods—Diaghilev, Nijinsky, Stravinsky, and set designers Picasso, Derain and Cocteau—held court among the dukes and flukes in the café of SBM's frothy **Hôtel de Paris**, next to the casino. Or as Katherine Mansfield put it: 'the famous Café de Paris with *real* devils with tails under their aprons cursing each other as they hand out the drinks. There at those tables sit the damned.'

If smug displays of wealth give you the misanthropic jitters, you can take comfort in the porcelain, metal, wood, and plastic people in the **Musée National de Monaco, Automates et Poupées d'Autrefois**, 17 Ave Princesse-Grace, ℰ 93 30 91 26 (*open daily Easter–Sept, 10–6.30; other times 10–12.15 and 2.30–6.30; adm*), in a pretty villa also designed by Charles Garnier. Jolliest among them is an enormous 18th-century Neapolitan *presepio* or Christmas crib, with 250 figurines from Virgin to sausage-vendor; a smaller room holds a Josephine Baker automaton in a grass skirt and Princess Caroline's Barbie and Ken. Further along Ave Princesse-Grace, you can unfray your nerves for free with a dose of Côte d'Azur Shintoism at the **Jardin Japonais** (*open daily, 9–nightfall*). Further east are beaches of imported sand, resort hotels, and that élite summertime rendezvous, the **Monte-Carlo Sporting Club**.

La Condamine and Fontvieille

The natural amphitheatre of La Condamine, the port quarter between Monte-Carlo and Monaco-Ville, has suffered the most from the speculators, their big cement brutes dwarfing the 11th-century votive chapel dedicated to Monaco's patron saint, **Ste-Dévote**. After her martyrdom in Corsica in 305, Dévote's body was put in a boat that sailed by itself, guided by a dove that flew out of her mouth, to Monaco (still known then as *Portus Herculis Monoeci*, after Hercules). In the 11th century some relic pirates snatched her bones, only to be foiled when the Monégasques set their boat on fire—an event re-enacted every 26 January amid the armada of yachts.

From Place Ste-Dévote Rue Grimaldi leads west to Place du Canton and the **Jardin Animalier**, ℰ 93 25 18 31 (*open daily 10–12 and 2–5*), used to acclimatize animals imported from the tropics. Or there's the Prince's very own **Collection de Voitures Anciennes**, ℰ 92 05 28 56 (*open 10–6, closed Nov*); and the **Musée Naval**, ℰ 377 92 05 28 48 (*hours as above*). More unusual are the prickly contents of another garden near the Moyenne Corniche, the **Jardin Exotique**, ℰ 93 30 33 65, where 7000 succulents planted in 1933 range from the absurd to the obscene (*bus 2, open 9–7, until 6 in the winter; adm*). The same ticket admits you to the adjacent **Grottes de l'Observatoire**, one of the few places in Provence inhabited in the Palaeolithic era, and curiously, the only cave in Europe that gets warmer instead of cooler as you descend into its maw. Here too is the **Musée d'Anthropologie Préhistorique**, with bones of reindeer, mammoths and hippopotami, along with some from early editions of humankind.

To the south, between the sea and the ultra-modern **Stade Louis II** © 92 05 40 11 (where AS Monaco regularly punish the rest of the French football league), stretches **Fontvieille Park** where the charming **Princess Grace Rose Garden** is a memorial to Monaco's beloved princess, film actress, and daughter of an Irish-American brick magnate in Philadelphia—the very same Kelly who supplied Ignatz mouse with ammo in George Herriman's classic comic strip *Krazy Kat*.

Up on the Rock: Monaco-Ville

In 1860 the principality of Monaco consisted of 2000 people living in this old Italian town, clinging spectacularly to a promontory 300m above the sea; they never dreamt it would turn into a shopping centre for Prince Rainier ashtrays or Princess Grace dolls. As scrubbed and cute as any town in Legoland, it offers devilries that in comparison make the casino seem like an honest proposition: the **Historial des Princes de Monaco**, Rue Basse (waxworks running the gamut from Francesco the Spiteful to Caroline and Stéphanie); the **Multi-vision Monte-Carlo Story**, on Rue Emile-de-Loth; the **Musée du Vieux Monaco**, and a **Musée des Souvenirs Napoléonien**, in the Place du Palais, with over 1000 items connected to the little Corsican including 'garments and toys belonging to the King of Rome!'—his ill-fated son. From June to October you can yawn your way through the plush **Palais Princier** itself, which, with its 19th-century 'medieval towers', is built around the Genoese fortress of 1215 (note the Grimaldi coat-of-arms, featuring a dagger-wielding monk). At other times when Rainier's at home you'll have to be content with the rooty-toot-toot 11.55am **Changing of the Monégasque Guard**.

Here, too, is Monaco's unattractive **Cathedral**, built in 1875 at the expense of a Romanesque chapel. From the chapel it inherited two lovely retables by Ludovico Brea from the early 1500s: *La Pietà* (over the sacristy door) and the grand *St-Nicolas* with 18 panels in the ambulatory. The more recent princes of Monaco are buried here, including Princess Grace, whose simple tomb inscribed GRATIA PATRICIA PRINCIPIS RAINIERII III UXOR is often bedecked with nosegays from admirers, all waiting for the miracle that will sway the Vatican to beatify her.

Monaco's most compelling attraction is nearby: the **Musée Océanographique de Monaco** in Ave St-Martin, © 93 15 36 00 (*open July and Aug 9am–8pm, 7pm rest of summer, Nov to Feb 10–6; adm*), founded in 1910 by Prince Albert Ier, who sank all of his casino profits into a passion for deep-sea exploration. To house the treasures he accumulated in his 24 voyages, he built this museum in a cliff, filling it with instruments, shells, whale skeletons, and on the ground floor a fascinating aquarium where 90 tanks hold some of the most surreal fish ever netted from the briny deep, including a mesmerizing cylindrical tank where thousands of identical fish swim in an endless circling herd. The rest of the building is taken up with research laboratories until recently headed by Jacques Cousteau, that specialize in the study of ocean pollution and radioactivity. You can park directly underneath (even the car parks in Monaco are so clean you can hear your tyres squeak), and get a lift straight up into the museum. Besides the aforementioned path east to Cap Martin, there's a path beginning at Fontvieille's Plage Marquet that heads west along the crashing sea to the train station at **Cap d'Ail** (Cape Garlic). A third trail begins on the D53 in **Beausoleil**, Monaco's French suburb, and ascends to the top of **Mont des Mules** in half an hour; an orientation table at the belvedere points out the sights, spread out like a map below.

Sports and Activities

Thanks to the SBM, there's always something to do in Monaco: a mountain-top 18-hole golf course high above the town at La Turbie, tennis and every imaginable water sport (but no free beaches), deep-sea tuna-fishing and cruises, helicopter tours of the coast. In January there's the **Monte-Carlo Rally**—the first one in 1902 occasioned the world's first tarmac road, designed to keep the spectators from being sprayed with dust. In April you can watch the tennis championship; the second week of May sees the famous **Monte-Carlo Grand Prix** (when even the pavements charge a hefty admission price).

Monaco ✉ 98030, ℭ (00 377–) — *Where to Stay*

Monte-Carlo

Monaco's hotels have nearly as many stars as the Milky Way, so if you'd like one of the few more reasonably priced rooms in the summer, you can't reserve early enough. Tycoons can check in at the palatial ★★★★★**Hôtel de Paris,** Place du Casino, ℭ 92 16 30 00, ✆ 92 16 38 49 (*1800–4800F*), opened in 1865 by the SBM for gambling czars and duchesses, or the beautiful Belle Epoque ★★★★★**Hermitage,** ℭ 92 16 40 00, ✆ 92 16 38 52, perched high on its rock in Square Beaumarchais. For a third of the price, and a view of the sea, the top choice is the old ★★★**Balmoral,** ℭ 93 50 62 37, ✆ 93 15 08 69, 12 Ave de la Costa.

Monaco-Ville

The new air-conditioned ★★★**Abela,** 23 Ave des Papalins, ℭ 92 05 90 00, ✆ 92 05 91 67, has a pool, garden, and sea view. Cheaper choices are all here, too: the modern, air-conditioned ★★**Terminus,** 9 Ave Prince-Pierre, ℭ 92 05 63 00, ✆ 92 05 20 10, ★★**De France,** 6 Rue de la Turbie (near the station), ℭ 93 30 24 64. *Closed Dec.* ★★**Helvetia,** 1 bis Rue Grimaldi, ℭ 93 30 21 71, ✆ 92 16 70 51; ★**Cosmopolite,** 4 Rue de la Turbie, ℭ 93 30 16 95, ✆ 93 30 23 05, all of which are adequate even if they don't bubble over with charm. The **Centre de la Jeunesse Princesse-Stéphanie,** 24 Ave Prince-Pierre, ℭ 93 50 83 20, ✆ 93 25 29 82, is close to the station, and fills up early each day in summer.

ℭ (00 377–) — *Eating Out*

In Monte-Carlo, those who make it big at the tables, or have simply made it big at life in general, dine in the incredible golden setting of the **Louis XV Alain Ducasse,** in the Hôtel de Paris, ℭ 92 16 30 01. This was a favourite of Edward VII as Prince of Wales, who once while dining here with his mistress was served a crêpe smothered in kirsch, curaçao and maraschino that its 14-year-old maker, Henri Charpentier (who went on to fame as a chef in America), accidentally set alight, only to discover that the accidental flambéing improved it a hundredfold. The Prince himself suggested that they name the new dessert after his companion, hence *crêpes Suzette*. Under Alain Ducasse, the youngest chef ever to earn three Michelin stars, the cuisine is once again kingly—made from the finest and freshest ingredients Italy and France can offer, as sumptuous and spectacular as the setting (*menus 840F and 950F, 480F lunch*). *Closed Tues and Wed*. The dining room of the Hermitage's **Belle Epoque**, © 92 16 40 01 (*menu at 450F*), is a riotous pink and silver period piece, and a historical monument to boot; the food (*salade de homard bleu à l'huile de crustacés sur une bataille de salsifis au fumet de truffes*, etc.) cooked by new chef, Joel Garrault, is equally classic. Just below the Hermitage, **Le St Benoît**, 10 ter Ave de la Costa (enter the car park and take the lift up), © 93 25 02 34 (*168–235F*), offers superb seafood to go with the views from the terrace, high above the port. *Closed Mon; July and Aug open Mon eve*. Gourmets on a diet can take solace at **L'Hirondelle**, 2 Av Monte-Carlo, © 92 16 49 47 (*menu 295F*), where lovely fresh and light dishes taste as good as they look, accompanied by swallow-eye views over the sea. *Closed eves*.

For rich duck dishes straight out of the Dordogne try **Le Périgordin**, 5 Rue des Oliviers, © 93 30 06 02 (*menus from 58–170F*). *Closed Sat lunch and Sun, and a fortnight in Aug*. Another good choice is **Tony**, near the palace, 6 Rue Comte Félix-Gastaldi, © 93 30 81 37, with generous menus from 95–180F. To brush shoulders with Crown Prince Albert and Boris Becker over a pizza go to **Le Texan**, 4 Rue Suffren Reymond, © 93 30 34 54, just up from the port, and its vivacious, rowdy, Tex-Mex atmosphere (*one of the best value places for beer in the Principality, 80–200F*).

Entertainment and Nightlife

Nightlife in Monaco is a glitzy, bejewelled fashion parade catered for by the omnipresent SBM at the **Monte-Carlo Sporting Club**, Ave Princesse-Grace, with its summer discotheque, Las Vegas-style floor shows, dancing, restaurants, and casino, or the similar offerings at **SBM/Loews Monte-Carlo**, 12 Ave des Spélugues, or at the American Bar at the Hôtel de Paris. Entrance is free but the drinks require a small bank loan at Monte-Carlo's number one dance club, the fantastical **Jimmy'Z**, 26 Ave Princesse-Grace, © 92 16 22 77, favourite of U2, Sting and rich old men. Young people from all along the coast drive to **Le Stars n' Bars**, 6 Quai Antoine 1er, © 93 50 95 95. *Open from 10pm*. Beer-drinking in a Brit-run imitation pub takes place at **Flashman's**, 7 Ave Princesse-Alice, © 93 30 09 03, which remains open to the wee hours.

In January the opera, theatre and ballet season begins (© 92 16 22 99 for info); in February an excellent **Circus Festival**; and in July/August a spectacular **Fireworks Festival** and concerts at the palace. The open air **Cinéma d'été**, © 93 25 86 80, 26 Ave Princesse-Grace, shows a different film in its original language every evening at 9.30, from June–Sept, or there's the 3-screen **Cinéma Le Sporting** in the Place du Casino.

North of Monaco

From Monaco, the D53 ascends to the Grande Corniche, a road the Romans called Via Julia Augusta, built to link up the Urbs to its conquests in Gaul and Spain. Several hard campaigns had to be fought (25–14 BC) before the fierce Ligurians finally let the road builders through, and in 6 BC the Roman Senate voted to erect a mighty commemorative monument known as the Trophy of the Alps (the Romans called it *Tropea Augusti* or 'Augustus's Trophy') at the base of Mont Agel. The views are precipitous, and you can escape the crowds by venturing even further inland to Peille and Peillon, two of the most beautiful villages on the Côte d'Azur.

Getting Around

There are four **buses** daily from Nice to La Turbie that continue up to Peille, but never on Sundays; and six each day from Monaco. Both Peillon and Peille have train stations, but they lie several steep kilometres below their respective villages.

Tourist Information

Peillon ✉ 06440: also at the Mairie, ✆ 04 93 79 91 04, ✇ 04 93 79 87 65.

Peille ✉ 06440: also at the Mairie, ✆ 04 93 91 71 71, ✇ 04 93 91 71 78.

La Turbie and its Trophy

Though hemmed in by upstart mini-villas and second homes, La Turbie (a corruption of *Tropea*) still retains its old typical core of narrow vaulted alleys, built back in the days when it merited a mention by Dante in *The Divine Comedy*; see the relevant immortal lines proudly engraved on the tower. La Turbie also has an elliptical 18th-century church, **St-Michel-Archange**, with a sumptuous Baroque interior of marble and agate and paintings that are attributed to, or by the schools of, Raphael, Veronese, Rembrandt, Ludovico Brea, Murillo and Ribera—not bad for a village of 2000 or so souls!

The old Via Julia Augusta (Rue Comte-de-Cessole) passes through town on its way to the **Trophy of the Alps**. This monument originally stood 147ft high, supporting a 20ft statue of Augustus; on its wall were listed the 44 conquered Ligurian tribes, and stairs throughout allowed passers-by to enjoy the view. When St Honorat saw the local people worshipping this marvel in the 4th century, he vandalized it; in the Dark Ages it was converted into a fort; Louis XIV ordered it to be blown up in 1705, and the stone was quarried to build St-Michel-Archange. The still formidable pile of rubble that remained in the 1930s was resurrected to 114ft and its inscription replaced thanks to a rich American's patronage, Edward Tuck. The only other such trophy to survive in situ is in Romania, although the base of an even older one has recently been found at Le Perthus (*see* p.474); a small **museum**, ✆ 04 93 41 10 11, on the site has models and drawings (*open summer 9–7, winter 9–12 and 2–5; adm*).

Peillon and Peille

The two villages are tiny and lovely; balanced atop adjacent hilltops, both require a wearying climb to reach. But Peille and Peillon aren't quite the Tweedledee and Tweedledum of the Côte. **Peillon**, most easily reached on the D53 from Nice, is a bit more posh, complete with a foyer—a cobbled square with a pretty fountain at the village entrance. Inside are peaceful medieval stairs and arches, and a restored Baroque parish church, but Peillon's big attraction is right at the entrance: the **Chapelle des Pénitents Blancs** (*ring the tourist office to arrange a visit*) adorned with a slightly faded cycle of Renaissance frescoes on the *Passion of Christ*, by the charming Giovanni Canavesio (*c.* 1485), who would certainly be better known had he painted anything outside the valleys of the Maritime Alps. From Peillon, there are trails that lead to steep but delightful countryside rambles.

One of those walks follows the Roman road in two hours to **Peille**, further up the D53. More isolated, Peille has more character, and its very own dialect, called *Pelhasc*. There's an ensemble of medieval streets like Peillon's and a church begun in the 12th century. Once, during a drought, Peille asked for help from a shepherd (in Provence shepherds often moonlight as sorcerers), and he made it rain on condition that the lord of this castle give him his daughter to wed—an event remembered in a *fête* on the first Sunday in September. The Church may frown at such goings-on, but Peille often had its own ideas on religion, preferring twice in the Middle Ages to be excommunicated rather than pay the bishop's tithes.

Where to Stay and Eating Out

La Turbie ✉ 06320

Stay and eat at the **★★Le Napoléon**, 7 Ave de la Victoire, ✆ 04 93 41 00 54, ✆ 04 93 41 28 93. *Open all year.* Ask for a room on the top floor, with views of the Trophy (*300–400F; good food, too, with menus from 75F*). The only other option is **★Cesare**, 16 Ave Albert 1er, ✆ 04 93 41 16 08. *Closed Nov.*

Peillon ✉ 06440

★★★Auberge de la Madone, ✆ 04 93 79 91 17, ✆ 04 93 79 99 36 (*rooms 450F–920F, menus at 140, 250 and 300F*), has comfortable rooms with traditional Provençal decor and views over the valley. Dine out on its terrace among the olives on seasonal dishes like *tourte d'herbes fines, pétales de foie gras, voilée à la vinaigrette de figue. Closed 20 Oct–20 Dec.*

Peille ✉ 06440

★Belvédère, ✆ 04 93 79 90 45 (*menus from 90F*), the only hotel in the village, has five simple rooms with grand mountain views but write ahead to book one. The restaurant does good ravioli and other Niçois dishes. The atmosphere is so uptight though, even the most good-natured soul might rebel. *Closed mid-Nov–mid-Dec.*

The Moyenne Corniche: Eze

Between Monaco and Nice, the main reason for taking the middle road has long been the extraordinary village of Eze, the most perched, perhaps, of any *village perché* in France, squeezed on to a cone of a hill 430m over the sea. It barely avoided being poached as well as perched in a catastrophic fire in 1986 that ravaged the pine forest that once surrounded it. Now the poaching is done on tourists; nearly every other house is a shop.

Tourist Information

Eze ✉ 05360: Place Général de Gaulle, ✆ 04 93 41 26 00, ✆ 04 93 41 26 00.

Eze

Eze, they say, is named after a temple the Phoenicians built on this hill to Isis. It then passed to the Romans, to the Saracens, and so on, although rarely did Eze change hands by force: even if an enemy penetrated its 14th-century gate and walls, the tight little maze of stairs and alleys would confuse the attackers, the better to ambush them or spill boiling oil on their heads. If the intruders got so far as to assault what remains of the castle these days—429m above sea level—they would run into the needles of the South American cacti in the **Jardin Exotique**, ✆ 04 93 41 10 30 (*open July and Aug 9–7; rest of year 9–12 and 2–5; adm*), a spiky paradise created on municipal initiative in 1949 by *ingénieur agronome* Jean Gastauld. Eze's other non-commercial attraction, the **Chapelle des Pénitents Blancs**, contains a 13th-century Catalan crucifix, the *Christ of the Black Death* (typical of medieval Catalan art, the sculptor emphasized Christ's divine nature, and he smiles, even on the Cross). Here too is a 14th-century *Madone des Forêts*, where baby Jesus, rather unusually, holds a pine-cone.

A scenic path descending to Eze-Bord-de-Mer is called the **Sentier Frédéric-Nietzsche** after the philosopher. Nietzsche, however, walked up instead of down, an arduous trek that made his head spin and inspired the third part of his *Thus Spake Zarathustra*.

Eze ✉ 06360   ***Where to Stay and Eating Out***

Eze-Grande Corniche

A road links the three Corniches at Eze, and there are hotels on each level. For four-star treatment, go to ★★★★**Les Terrasses d'Eze**, Rte de la Turbie, ✆ 04 92 41 55 55, ✆ 04 92 41 55 10, huge (80 rooms), expensive and '*ultra-moderne*', complete with sauna and a room for '*musculation*'. ★★**L'Hermitage**, 2km from the village at Col d'Eze on the Grande Corniche, ✆ 04 93 41 00 68, ✆ 04 93 41 24 05 (*starting at 200F, menus from 95F*), offers priceless views, but mundane food to go with its mundane rooms. *Closed Dec–15 Feb. Hotel closed 15 Oct–15 Feb.* From the hotel a footpath leads along the ancient *Voie Aurélienne* on to Mont Leuze, with breathtaking views over the Alps and down to the Mediterranean.

Eze-Moyenne Corniche

In Eze, along the Moyenne Corniche two luxurious inns have only a handful of rooms but superb kitchens: the ★★★★**Château Eza**, Rue de la Pise, ✆ 04 93 41 12 24, ✆ 04 93 41 16 64 (*menus from 250F*), is actually a collection of medieval houses linked together to form an eagle's nest, all sharing an extraordinary terrace, with Niçois and other Provençal specialities to match. *Closed Nov–Mar.* In a medieval castle rebuilt in the 1920s, the Relais & Châteaux ★★★★**La Chèvre d'Or**, Rue du Barri, ✆ 04 92 10 66 66, ✆ 04 93 41 06 72 (*rooms 1200–3800F*), has a small park, a pool, and more ravishing views; its restaurant serves refined, light versions of the French classics, accompanied by one of the Riviera's best wine cellars. *Closed Dec–Mar.* More modest choices in Eze include ★★**Le Golf**, Place de la Colette, ✆ 04 93 41 18 50, ✆ 04 93 41 29 93, and ★★**Auberge des Deux Corniches**, ✆/✆ 04 93 41 19 54. *Closed Nov–Dec.* Turbot or *filet de bœuf aux cèpes* go down nicely at **Le Troubadour**, 4 Rue du Brec, ✆ 04 93 41 19 03 (*lunch menu 125F, others 170F*), and the price is nice too. *Closed Sun, lunch Mon.* Head to the summit of the rock, **Le Nid d'Aigle**, Rue du Château, ✆ 04 93 41 19 08 (*130F menu and carte*), next door to the Jardin Exotique, for lofty fish (*daurade au pistou*, salmon). *Closed Wed.*

Eze-Bord-de-Mer

Set in a 4-acre park, the luxurious Riviera dream ★★★★**Le Cap Estel**, ✆ 04 93 01 50 44, ✆ 04 93 01 55 20, built by a Russian princess, has a heated pool. *Closed*

Oct–Mar. Or try the family-run **★★Eric Rivot**, © 04 93 01 51 46, @ 04 93 01 58 40 (*menus from 120F*), with rooms starting at 280F and gourmet dining.

The Corniche Inférieure

To the west of Eze-Bord-de-Mer another wooded promontory, Cap Ferrat, protrudes into the sea to form today's most fashionable address on the Côte d'Azur. The fascinating, wildly eclectic Villa Ephrussi de Rothschild and gardens crown the summit of Cap Ferrat, while the awful Leopold II, King of the Belgians, Otto Preminger and Somerset Maugham had sanctuaries by the sea. To the east, the peninsula and steep mountain backdrop keep Beaulieu so sheltered that it shares with Menton the distinction of being the hottest town in France, while to the west the Corniche skirts the top of the fine old village of Villefranche-sur-Mer, with a port deep enough for battleships—grey tokens from the grey world beyond the Riviera.

Getting Around

The most amusing way to visit is by way of the Côte d'Azur's equivalent of Hollywood's 'See the Homes of the Stars' bus tours: a 'train' starts on the quay at Villefranche and chugs around the promontory with a guide calling out, in French and abominable English, the names of the famous who live(d) in the villas.

Tourist Information

Beaulieu ✉ 06310: Place Clemenceau, © 04 93 01 02 21, @ 04 93 01 44 04.
St-Jean-Cap-Ferrat ✉ 06230: 59 Ave Semaria, © 04 93 76 08 90, @ 04 93 76 16 67.
Villefranche-sur-Mer ✉ 06230: Jardin François-Binon, © 04 93 01 73 68, @ 04 93 76 63 65, e-mail villefranche_sur_mer@riviera.fr.

market days

 Beaulieu: Mon–Sat. **Villefranche**: craft market, Tues morning, Place de la Paix; fruit, veg and flowers, Mon–Sat mornings, flea market, Sun, Place de la Paix; clothes, Sat morning, Place de L'Octroi.

Beaulieu

'*O qual bel luogo!*' exclaimed Napoleon in his Corsican mother tongue, and the bland name stuck to this lush banana-growing town overlooking the Baie des Fourmis, 'the Bay of Ants', which is so called for the black boulders in the sea. Beaulieu admits to a mere four days of frost a year and calls its steamy easternmost suburb La Petite Afrique, while most of its affluent population are trying to imitate Gustave Eiffel, who retired here and lived to be 90. Beaulieu's vintage casino has been renovated after four years of dilapidation, and is back to its former sparkling grandeur. The *thés dansants* held in **La Rotonde** are a further retro attraction, but the *real* magnet is a place so retro that even Socrates would feel at home there: the **Villa Kerylos**, © 04 93 01 01 44 (*open daily July–Aug 10–7, Sept–Oct 10.30–12.30 and 2–6 ; Dec–Feb weekdays 2–6 only, weekends 10.30–12.30 and 2–6; adm; bus stop Hôtel Métropole then a 5min walk*), a striking reproduction of a wealthy 5th-century BC Athenian's abode, furnishings, and garden, built in 1908 by archaeologist Théodore Reinach. Reinach spared no expense on the marbles, ivories, bronzes, mosaic and fresco reproductions to help his genuine antiquities feel at home; glass windows, plumbing and a hidden piano are the only modern anachronisms. And here, on a shore that reminded him of the Aegean, this ultimate philhellene lived himself like an Athenian, holding symposia, exercising and bathing with his male buddies, and keeping the womenfolk well out of the way.

St-Jean-Cap-Ferrat

Another retro-repro fantasy, the **Villa Ephrussi de Rothschild**, © 04 93 01 33 09 (*a 10min walk from the Corniche Inférieure, or catch the St-Jean bus which passes its entrance; open daily Feb–Oct 10–6, July and Aug 10–7; Nov–Jan weekends only 10–6; adm exp*), crowns the narrow isthmus of bucolic Cap Ferrat, enjoying spectacular views over both the Baie des Fourmis and the harbour of Villefranche. The flamboyant Béatrice de Rothschild, who never went anywhere without her trunk of fifty wigs and greeted guests to her parties dressed as Marie-Antoinette, was a compulsive art collector and lover of the 18th century, and, after marrying the banker Baron Ephrussi, had this Italianate villa specially built to house her treasures—a Venetian rococo room was designed for Béatrice's Tiepolo ceiling, while other rooms set off her Renaissance furniture, Florentine bridal chests, paintings by Boucher, rare Chinese screens and furniture, Flemish and Beauvais tapestries, Sèvres and Meissen porcelain, Louis-Quinze and Louis-Seize furniture, a covered Andalusian patio (a favourite location shot for James Bond and other films), a hidden bathroom and a collection of porcelain vases that ladies of yore discreetly slipped under their skirts when nature called. To create the equally eclectic gardens, the isthmus was given a crew cut, and terraced into different levels, all linked together by little pathways and stone steps. There's a French garden with a copy of the *Amour* fountain from the Petit Trianon; a Florentine garden, with a white marble ephebe; a Spanish garden, with papyrus, dates and pomegranates; also Exotic, Japanese, English and Provençal gardens, and a lapidary garden decorated with Romanesque capitals, arches, and gargoyles. For all the trouble she took to build this glorious pile, Béatrice actually spent very little time here, preferring her villa in Monte-Carlo as it was closer to the gambling tables. In the summer you can take luncheon, tea and cakes in the elegant, circular, former *salon d'hiver.*

Cap Ferrat, with its lush greenery, secret villas and little azure coves is ripe territory for strolls or swims—there are a dozen small beaches, albeit of fine gravel. **Plage de Passable** along Chemin du Roy, west of Villa Ephrussi, is popular with families and scuba divers. The 'Roy' in question was bad old King Leopold II of the Belgians, whose ruthless exploitation of the Congo (see Conrad's *Heart of Darkness*) helped to pay for his luxurious life here, where he took a swim every day with his beard neatly folded into a rubber whisker-protector and his valet ironed his newspapers. The villa (Les Cèdres) is now more democratically used for a delightful **zoo**, © 04 93 76 07 60 (*open daily 9.30–7 summer, 9.30–5.30 winter*).

If you have fortitude you can climb up and up the steep stairway for the tremendous view from the **Phare**, the lighthouse at the south tip of the promontory, near the Sun Beach swimming pool, © 04 93 76 08 36, (*open 9–12 and 3–6 summer; otherwise 3–4*); if you need fortitude, you can find a *pastis* in the former-fishing-now-yacht-port of **St-Jean-Cap-Ferrat**. Jean Cocteau painted the village's *Salle des Mariages*, but with hardly the same vigour as in Menton. A walking path circles around the dew-claw of land south of the port called **Pointe St-Hospice** where, in the 6th century, the Niçois saint Hospice had a hermitage (now marked by a 19th-century chapel). With one arm chained to the wall, Hospice lived off algae brought to him by pious souls, and uttered dire prophesies about barbarian invasions that came true, recorded by the Merovingian historian, Gregory of Tours. Modern-day invasions take place at nearby **Plage de Paloma**, favourite of Italian day-trippers and millionaire pensioners, and

Plage des Fosses. Another path, the **Promenade Maurice Rouvier** leads from St-Jean's beach to Beaulieu, passing **Villa Scoglietto** and its sea-defying garden, where Charlie Chaplin spent his summer holidays, and actor David Niven lived the last years of his life.

Villefranche-sur-Mer

In the 14th century, the deep, wooded bay between Cap Ferrat and Nice was a duty-free port, hence Villefranche's name. It became an important military port for the Savoys in the 18th century, a period that saw Villefranche take on the appearance it has today: tall, brightly coloured piled-up houses, narrow lanes and stairs, some so overhung with houses that they're actually tunnels like **Rue Obscure**, 'a good place for a knifing' as William Sansom described it, although it came in handy as a bomb shelter in the last war. The streets open up to the wide quay, given over to bars and restaurants, and a fine shingle and sand beach with a shallow slope and calm bay that's ideal for children. The charm of the place, and the presence of so many brawny sailors from around the world on shore-leave, made Villefranche a popular intello-gay resort in the 1920s, with Jean Cocteau weaving his personal mythologies with opium, 'fluids' and his friends in the little Hotel Welcome.

Villefranche's fishermen once stored their nets in the portside Romanesque **Chapelle St-Pierre**, Quai Courbet, © 04 93 76 90 70 (*open 9.30–12 and 2–5 winter, later in summer; adm*), and in 1957, as a gift to them, Cocteau frescoed it in 'ghosts of colours' with scenes from the Life of St Peter (walking on the water with an angel's help, which astounds the fish but makes Christ smile), plus images of the fishergirls of Villefranche, the gypsies at Saintes-Maries-de-la-Mer, and angels from Cocteau's private heaven. The Duke of Savoy's **Citadelle St-Elme** has been put back to work as the Hôtel de Ville with a few more paintings by Jean Cocteau (upstairs) and three free museums: the **Musée Volti**, © 04 93 76 33 27, with sculptures of women by a native of Villefranche and follower of Maillol; the **Musée Goetz Boumeester**, © 04 93 76 33 44, with works by Henri Goetz and his wife Christine Boumeester, and the **Collection Roux**, with ceramic figurines inspired by the medieval and Renaissance manuscripts (*all open June–Sept 10–12 and 3–7; Oct–May 10–12 and 2–5, closed Sun am, Tues and Nov*).

Where to Stay and Eating Out

Beaulieu-sur-Mer ✉ 06310

In the 1870s, when the fabulously wealthy James Gordon Bennett, owner of the *New York Herald* and the man who sent Stanley to find Livingstone, was booted out of New York society for his scandalous behaviour, he came to the Riviera and ran the Paris edition of his newspaper from ★★★★**La Réserve**, 5 Blvd Général-Leclerc, © 04 93 01 00 01, 🖷 04 93 01 28 99 (*menus 300–420F*), now one of the most exclusive hotels on the Riviera and, if a touch old-fashioned, offering its guests grand sea views, a beach and marina, heated pool and more delights, including an elegant neo-Renaissance restaurant. *Open mid-Mar–mid-Oct, then 23 Dec–10 Jan.*

Its gorgeous *fin-de-siècle* Italianate neighbour, ★★★★**Métropole**, 15 Blvd Maréchal Leclerc, © 04 93 01 00 08, 🖷 04 93 01 18 51 (*menus 400–500F*), boasts a fine seaside garden, heated seawater swimming pool, a more relaxed atmosphere, and exquisite dining. *Closed late Oct–Christmas.* Near the station, the modern

★★★**Artemis**, 3 Blvd Maréchal-Joffre, ✆ 04 93 01 12 15, ✉ 04 93 01 27 46, has rooms with balconies and access to a pool at the back; on the same street at No.29, ★★**Le Havre Bleu**, ✆ 04 93 01 01 40, ✉ 04 93 01 29 92, is an attractive hotel, with pleasant rooms, many with terraces.

The small, simple ★**Sélect**, 1 Place Général-de-Gaulle, ✆ 04 93 01 05 42, ✉ 04 93 01 34 30, near the station is convenient, yet impersonal; try the ★**Riviera** and its pretty wrought-iron balconies just up from the Basse Corniche on 6 Rue Paul-Doumer, ✆ 04 93 01 04 92, ✉ 04 93 01 19 31. Wood-fired pizzas and delicious pasta abound round the corner on Blvd Maréchal-Leclerc at **Le Catalan**, ✆ 04 93 01 02 78 (*à la carte*). *Closed Sun.*

St-Jean-Cap-Ferrat ✉ 06230

Even though its villas are the most exclusive on the Riviera, Cap Ferrat has hotels in all price ranges, beginning with one of the most beautiful small hotels on the entire Côte: a charming, voluptuous Italian villa, overlooking the pleasure port, ★★★★**Voile d'Or**, ✆ 04 93 01 13 13, ✉ 04 93 76 11 17 (*menus 270–360F*). Once owned by film director Michael Powell, who inherited it from his father (and sold it because no one ever paid their bar bills), the Voile d'Or is an ideal first or second honeymoon hotel, with a laid-back atmosphere, a garden hanging over the port, a heated pool, and rooms with every luxury a hotel could need. Its equally exceptional restaurant is favoured by the yachting set. *Closed Nov–Easter.*

At the very fashionable Belle Epoque ★★★★**Grand Hôtel du Cap Ferrat**, Blvd Général de Gaulle, ✆ 04 93 76 31 00, ✉ 04 93 01 23 07 (*menus 420 and 490F*), the already luxurious rooms have been restored in a more airy, comfortable Riviera style, all set in acres of gardens, lawns, and palms. A funicular railway lowers guests down to an Olympic-size seawater swimming pool just over the Mediterranean. The restaurant, on a terrace shaded by parasol pines, serves delicious meals decidedly unhealthy for your wallet. *Closed Jan.*

More down-to-earth choices include ★★★**Brise-Marine**, Ave Jean-Mermoz, ✆ 04 93 76 04 36, ✉ 04 93 76 11 49, with a garden, terrace, and large rooms, half with sea views; or ★★**Clair Logis**, near the centre of the Cap on 12 Ave Centrale, ✆ 04 93 76 04 57,✉ 04 93 76 11 85, a villa set in an enclosed garden. The one star option, ★**La Bastide**, 3 Ave Albert 1ᵉʳ, ✆ 04 93 76 06 78, ✉ 04 93 76 19 10, is not luxurious but has a pricey restaurant. *Closed Nov.*

Around the Port de Plaisance you'll find several nautically named beaneries, **Le Pirate**, ✆ 04 93 76 12 97; **Le Sloop**, ✆ 04 93 01 48 63 (excellent 155F menu); and **Skipper**, ✆ 04 93 76 01 00 (best for fish on its well known 95F menu). For a *frisson* of south coast *hauteur* with your cuisine, **Le Provençal** on Place Clemenceau, ✆ 04 93 76 03 97, ✉ 04 93 76 05 39, has only *à la carte*, where you can try delicacies like *fouillis d'asperges aux langoustines au jus de café* (*menus 190F, 350F and 490F*).

Villefranche-sur-Mer ✉ 06230

Just beside the port, the legendary ★★★**Welcome**, Quai Amiral-Courbet, ✆ 04 93 76 27 62, ✉ 04 93 76 27 66, is ideally situated, and all its finely decorated rooms are air-conditioned; those on the 5th floor are ravishing. *Closed mid-Nov–mid-Dec, half-board in season.* Or try the unpretentious, family-run ****Provençal**, 4 Ave du Maréchal-Joffre, © 04 93 01 71 42, ⊕ 04 93 76 96 00. *Closed Nov– Christmas.*

As you walk downhill towards the sea from the Corniche, in a quiet square, you pass the **Belle Epoque**, which serves daily lunch specials for 60F on a large covered terrace. For dinner, **Le Carpaccio**, Plage des Marinières, © 04 93 01 72 97 (count 300F *à la carte* for fish or crustaceans) has long been a favourite of the Rolls-Royce crowd from Monaco, yet remains affordable for a night-time splurge or a pizza. *Closed Tues.* In the old town, **La Grignotière,** 3 Rue du Poilu, © 04 93 76 79 83 (*menus 89–149F*), serves local Niçois specialities. *Closed Wed.*

Nice

Other places may be fun,
But when all is said and done,
It's so much nicer in Nice.

Sandy Wilson, *The Boyfriend*

The funny thing is, it's true. Agreeably named and superbly set on nothing less than the Bay of Angels, Nice has a gleam and sparkle in its eye like no other city in France: only a sourpuss could resist its lively old town squeezed between promontory and sea, its markets blazing with colour, the glittering tiled domes and creamy pâtisserie 19th-century hotels and villas, the immaculate, exotic gardens, and the famous voluptuous curve of the beach and the palm-lined Promenade des Anglais. It is the one town on the Côte that doesn't seem to need tourists, the one that stays open through the winter. You could go for the food alone, a seductive mix of the best of France and Italy; you haven't really had ravioli until you tuck into a plate in Nice, where it was invented.

The capital of the *département* of Alpes-Maritimes and France's fifth largest town (pop.400,000), Nice is the Hexagon's most visited city after Paris. The English have been coming for well over 200 years, back when 'Nizza la Bella' still belonged to Savoy, and Russian Tsarinas and Grand Dukes fleeing winter's blasts weren't far behind. The presence of so many rich, idle foreigners who stayed for months at a time formed a large part of the city's character: corruption, reactionary politics and organized crime are part of the famous *salade niçoise*, along with a high density of apricot poodles and frown-faced poodle ladies. But Nice also has a university, big culture (21 museums and counting), the brilliant light that Matisse loved and a genuine identity as a city—rough, affable and informal.

History

Nice was a hot-spot even 400,000 years ago, when hunters who tracked mammoths and learnt how to make fires to grill their prey frequented the caves of Terra Amata. The Ligurians, around 1000 BC, were the first to move in permanently, constructing their *oppida* at the mouth of the Paillon river, and on the hill overlooking the valley. Greeks from Marseille founded a commercial colony near the seaside *oppidum* that they named Nikaïa after an obscure military victory, or perhaps after the nymph Nikaia. Beset by Ligurian pirates, the

Nikaïans asked the Romans for aid. The Romans duly came, and stayed, but preferred to live near the hilltop *oppidum*, because it was closer to the Via Julia Augusta. They named this town *Cemenelum* (modern Cimiez), and made it the capital of the province of *Alpes Maritimae*. By the 3rd century AD *Cemenelum* had 20,000 inhabitants, all quickly going soft amid swimming pools and central heating.

But, by the 6th century, luxury-loving *Cemenelum* had collapsed with the rest of the Roman empire while Greek Nikaïa struggled on and regrouped itself in the 10th century around a cathedral. By the 1340s, with a population of 13,000, Nice was the third city in Provence after Marseille and Arles. The city's coat of arms had an eagle's head on it, and it looked to the right, to France. The Black Death and civil wars of the period soon cut it down to size, and in 1388 the city's leaders voted to hitch their wagon to a brighter star than Louis d'Anjou, and pledged allegiance to Amadeus VII, Count of Savoy. The eagle was redrawn to look left, towards Italy.

The Savoys fortified Nice and it grew rich trading with Italy. It had its own little Renaissance, thanks to Ludovico Brea and the other members of the mid 15th-century Ecole Niçoise— Antoine and François Brea, Jean Mirailhet, and Jacques Durandi—noted for their uncluttered, simple compositions and firm sense of line. The 17th century saw the first expansion of Nice outside its medieval walls, and in 1696 and 1705 came the first of several French interludes that interrupted Savoy rule—interludes that Louis XIV took advantage of to blow up the city's fortifications.

Cold Brits, and Absorption into the Mystic Hexagon

Although relations remained sour with France, the Savoys became firm allies with the English, and by 1755 the first trickle of milords began to discover the sunny charms of a Riviera winter. Doctor and novelist Tobias Smollett spent a year in Nice in 1763, and in his singularly grouchy *Travels through France and Italy* (1766) did what Peter Mayle has since done for Provence: made the Côte, because of, or in spite of, its quaint local characters, irresistible to the British. Even though it took at least two weeks to reach Nice from Calais, by 1787 there were enough Brits wintering here to support a casino (then a fashionable Venetian novelty), an English theatre, estate agent, and newspaper.

In 1830, when a frost killed all the orange trees, the English community raised funds to give the unemployed a job: building a seafront promenade along the Baie des Anges known to this day as the Promenade des Anglais. Part of its purpose was to keep English girls away from the riff-raff, or more particularly the Niçois—the British brought with their money attitudes so arrogant that as early as the 1780s, sensitive locals left town each winter to avoid being humiliated by their visitors.

In 1860, as Napoleon III's reward for promising to help Vittorio Emanuele II of Savoy create the future kingdom of Italy, a secret treaty was signed ceding Nice and Savoy to France. To keep up appearances, a plebiscite was held. Vittorio Emanuele encouraged his subjects to vote for French union, but even more encouraging was the presence of the French army marching through Nice, and French agents bullying the majority Italian-speaking population. The final result (24,449 pro-France to 160 against) stinks even to this day. But the railway arrived shortly thereafter, and Nice settled down to its chosen vocation as the winter haven for Europe's élite. Sumptuous neo-Moorish-Gothic-Baroque follies were built to house some

20,000 wintering Britons and Russians by 1890; 20 years later the numbers of foreigners had increased to over 150,000. Queen Victoria preferred the suburb of Cimiez; her haemophiliac son, Prince Leopold, introduced croquet to Nice before dying after slipping on the marble floor in the casino. The city even made an early bid to become the Hollywood of France, when the Victorine film studios were founded in 1911 and purchased in 1925 by Rex Ingram, who brought in a constant parade of big stars and writers. During the war, Marcel Carné used them to film *Les Visiteurs du Soir* and *Les Enfants du Paradis*.

Nice Today

Since the 1930s, many of Nice's hotels and villas have been converted into furnished flats while the concrete mixers of destiny march further and further west and up the valleys. The Victorine studios are still there, but plagued by noise from jets landing in Nice airport, they are used mostly for television commercials. Rents in the city are astronomical and property values are rivalled today in France only by Paris and Cannes; wealthy, politically conservative retirees help support an equally right-wing *rentier* population. All this money floating about has attracted the corruption and underworld activities of the *milieu*, previously associated only with Marseille.

For decades Nice was ruled as the personal fiefdom of the right-wing Médecin family, who pretend to be related to the Medici, although it doesn't look as if their dynasty will endure quite as long. Jean Médecin reigned from 1928 until 1965, and was succeeded by his flamboyant son Jacques, cook, crook and anti-Semite hoster of a National Front congress no other city would have, the man who twinned Nice with Cape Town when apartheid was still on the books. Jacques Médecin had an edifice-complex nearly the size of Mitterrand's in Paris, filling Nice with huge new public complexes, and his cronies had their fingers in all kinds of pies, most spectacularly Albert Spaggiari, who had got hold of the plans of Nice's sewer system in order to steal 46 million francs from the Société Générale, and was captured by the police only to escape the courtroom by jumping out of the window on to a waiting motorcycle and making a clean getaway. In 1990 the slow, grinding wheels of French justice began to catch up with Médecin, when it was discovered, among other things, that money for the Nice Opera was being diverted into the mayor's bank account. He took to his heels and hid out in Punta del Este, Uruguay, until 1995 when he was extradited to France, where he died in 1998. His sister Geneviève barely defeated the National Front candidate in local government elections, and took his old seat on the Conseil Général of the Alpes-Maritimes *département*; his successor as mayor of Nice, Honoré Bailet, had some troubles of his own, especially in the form of a son-in-law, accused of murdering a local restaurant owner.

Getting There and Around

By air: Nice's large, modern Aéroport Nice-Côte d'Azur is the second busiest in France, served by a wide variety of flights from around the world. Taxis into town are expensive. Buses run every 20 mins between the airport and coach station, ✆ 04 93 85 61 81, while bus 23 provides links with the train station every 30mins. The bus ticket to town includes free bus travel on any bus for the rest of the day, and after 10pm the yellow airport bus will detour to the train station if you ask the driver, or else stops in Place Masséna where the night buses depart. Flights to or from Paris go through Aérogare 2; all others go through Aérogare 1. Airline numbers include Air France, ✆ 0802 802 802; British Airways, ✆ 04 93 21 47 01/08 02 80 29 02 (direct no.); Delta ✆ 08 00 35 40 80.

VIEUX NICE

200 metres
200 yards

Place Garibaldi

Villa Arson

BOULEVARD DE GORBELLA

AVE DU REY

BOULEVARD DE CESSOLE

R. CASSINI

Gare Routière

JEAN JAURÈS

BLD. AUGUSTE RAYNAUD

AVENUE BORRIGLIONE

St-François
R. DE ST-FRANÇOIS
R. DU GOLF

FAURE
SUNBUS
FELIX

Place Centrale

Palais Lascaris

Place Masséna

Cathédrale Ste-Réparate

R. DE LA PRÉFECTURE

R. ROSSETTI
R. DU
GESU
R. DE L'OPÉRA

Eglise Ste-Rita

BOULEVARD

Palais de Justice

COURS
SALEYA

Place Général de Gaulle

R. ST. F. DE PAULE

Opéra

Hôtel de Ville

AVE MALAUSSENA

Musée Dufy

Tour Bellanda

QUAI DES ÉTATS-UNIS

Château

BLD. JOSEPH GARNIER

Chemin de Fer de Provence

R. CLÉMENT

RUE VERNIER

Opéra Plage

Castel Plage

Musée Naval

BOULEVARD GAMBETTA

Gare Nice Ville

AVENUE THIERS

Basilique Notre-Dame

AVE GEORGES CLEMENCEAU

AVE DU MARÉCHAL FOCH

Cathédrale Russe

AVE JEAN MÉDECIN

RUE ROSSINI

AUTOROUTE URBAINE SUD

R. DE CHATEAUNEUF

BOULEVARD VICTOR HUGO

BOULEVARD GAMBETTA

Jardin d'Alsace-Lorraine

RUE DU MARÉCHAL JOFFRE

BLD. FRANÇOIS GROSSO

AVE DES FLEURS

RUE DE LA BUFFA

Place MASSÉNA
R. DE LA LIBERTÉ

Eglise Anglicane

Musée des Beaux-Arts

RUE DE FRANCE

Musée Masséna

Casino Ruhl

Hôtel Negresco

PROMENADE DES ANGLAIS

RUE DE FRANCE

Florida Plage
Voilier Plage
Forum Plage
Neptune Plage
Blue Plage
Sporting Plage
Lido Plage
Ruhl Plage
Gallen Plage

VOIE RAPIDE

PROMENADE DES ANGLAIS

Bambou Plage

Baie

Musée d'Art Naïf Anatole Jakovsky

des Anges

Régence Plage
Miami Plage

To Airport

By train: Nice's train station, ✆ 08 36 35 35 35, is in Ave Thiers, not far from the centre of town, and has a handy left-luggage facility. Besides *Métrazur* trains between Ventimiglia and St-Raphaël, Nice has frequent connections to Marseille and its TGV to Paris (6hrs).

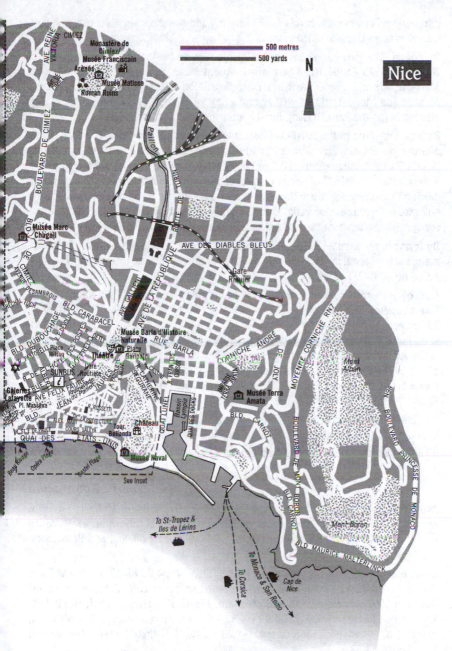

Nice

500 metres
500 yards

N

CIMIEZ
AVE REINE VICTORIA
Monastère de Cimiez/ Musée Franciscain
Arènes
Musée Matisse
Roman Ruins
BOULEVARD DE CIMIEZ
Paillon
ROUTE DE TURIN
Musée Marc Chagall
AVE DE CIMIEZ
AVENUE DES AMBROIS
AVE DES DIABLES BLEUS
BLD CARABACEL
BLD. DUBOUCHAGE
MARCHAL FOCH
BLD.
PASTORELLI
R. DE FRANCE
AVE FÉLIX FAURE
AVE GAMBETTA
AVE DE LA RÉPUBLIQUE
Gare Riquier
Musée Barla d'Histoire Naturalle
RUE BARLA
Théâtre
Place Garibaldi
Gare Routière
R. CASSINI
R. CATHERINE SÉGURANE
CORNICHE ANDRÉ DE JOLY
MOYENNE CORNICHE RN7
Mont Alban
RN9
SUNBUS
i
Galeries Lafayette
JEAN
MÉDECIN
PL. Masséna
R. DE PAUL
BLD.
ROSSETTI
DE LA PRÉFECTURE
COURS SALEYA
QUAI LUNEL
Bassin Lympia
QUAI DES DOCKS
Musée Terra Amata
BLD. CARNOT
BOULEVARD DE MONT BORON
BLD. CARNOT
BOULEVARD PRINCESSE DE MONACO
Tour Bellanda
Château
Musée Naval
QUAI DES ÉTATS-UNIS
Beau Rivage
Opéra Plage
Castel Plage
See Inset
To St-Tropez & Iles de Lérins
To Corsica
To Monaco & San Remo
Cap de Nice
Mont Boron
BLD MAURICE MAETERLINCK

The Gare du Sud, 4 bis Rue Alfred-Binet, ✆ 04 93 82 10 17, is served by the little *Train des Pignes* (so called for the pine-cones that the crew used to stop to collect for pine-nuts). You can take an excursion on this train to Provençal towns high up the Var valley—Entrevaux (*see* p.216), Annot (p.218) and St-André (p.218) are a cool and refreshing relief when the beaches are blistering and the shopping malls pall, and you can go as far as Digne for 218F return.

By coach: The *gare routière* is on the Promenade du Paillon, on the edge of Vieux Nice, ✆ 04 93 85 61 81. There are frequent buses to Grasse, Vence, Cannes, Marseille, Aix-en-Provence, Avignon, Brignoles, St-Raphaël, Le Muy, Cagnes, Antibes, Menton and Monte-Carlo, as well as one a day for Plan-du-Var, Puget-Théniers and Entrevaux (on the route to Gap). Bus 17 links the coach and train stations.

By bus: Buses run by the SUNBUS Company are more than nice. Pick up a free *Guide Horaire du Réseau Bus* with maps and schedules at the tourist office or from SUNBUS's information centre, 10 Ave Félix-Faure, ✆ 04 93 16 52 10. Several tourist tickets, called 'Nice by Bus', are available, offering limitless rides for one, five or seven days and including one trip to the airport; they save money if you make three or more bus trips a day. Buses stop early, around 9pm, and are replaced by four 'Noctambus' services, all leaving from Place Masséna. For **taxis**, call ✆ 04 93 13 78 78.

By ferry: In the summer FERRYTERRANEE has frequent sailings to Corsica. For information and reservations contact them at Gare Maritime, Quai du Commerce, ✆ 04 93 13 66 66, 🖷 04 93 13 66 81.

Car, bicycle and scooter hire: Among the cheapest car hire places is **Azur Rent-a-Car**, opposite the station on Ave Thiers, ✆ 04 93 88 69 69, 🖷 04 93 88 43 36, or at 25 Promenade des Anglais, ✆ 04 93 87 87 37, 🖷 04 93 87 95 55, or just by the aiport at 61 Route de Grenoble, ✆ 04 93 18 82 22, 🖷 04 93 18 98 68. International car hire giants **Avis**, are at 2 Ave des Phocéens at the end of Blvd Jean-Jaurès, ✆ 04 93 80 63 52, 🖷 04 93 87 32 92, or at the airport, ✆ 04 93 21 42 78, 🖷 04 93 21 44 53, and **Hertz** are at the airport, ✆ 04 93 21 36 72, 🖷 04 93 21 42 73 and 12 Ave de Suède, ✆ 04 93 87 11 87, 🖷 04 93 87 86 13, offer more expensive options.

For bike/moped/scooter hire, a few options include **Cycles Arnaud**, 4 Place Grimaldi, ✆ 04 93 87 88 55; or **Nicea Location Rent**, 9 Ave Thiers and 12 Rue de Belgique, ✆ 04 93 82 42 71, 🖷 04 93 87 76 36; or **Loca Sports**, 2 Rue Boissy d'Anglas, ✆ 04 93 13 94 29, 🖷 04 93 13 85 08.

Tourist Information

Ave Thiers, next to the train station, ✆ 04 93 87 07 07, 🖷 04 93 16 85 16, website www.nice-coteazur.org. Other offices include Terminal 1 at the airport ✆ 04 93 21 44 11, 🖷 04 93 21 44 50; near the airport, ✆ 04 93 83 32 64, and at 5 Promenade des Anglais, ✆ 04 92 14 48 00.

Main post office: near the station at 21 Ave Thiers, ✆ 04 93 82 65 00, and at Place Wilson, ✆ 04 93 13 64 10, with *poste-restante*. **Internet café**: 2 rue St-Siagre, off Ave Jean-Médecin, closed Sun and Mon am. **Medical**: Casualty ward, Hôpital St-Roch, 5 Rue Pierre-Devoluy, ✆ 04 92 03 33 75. All-night pharmacy, 7 Rue Masséna, ✆ 04 93 87 78 94. Nice-Médecins, ✆ 04 93 52 42 42 (24hrs). 24-hour dentistry on ✆ 04 93 76 53 53.

A 3- or 7-day **Artpass** can be obtained for 70F/140F from any museum ticket desk or the tourist office, or FNAC bookshop. On the first Sunday of every month, all museums in Nice are free.

Vin de Bellet: Only 1200 hectolitres are produced each year, and most of it never gets much further than the cellars of the Riviera's top restaurants. Pick up a bottle of your own by ringing ahead and following the Route de Bellet north of Rue de France (parallel to the Promenade des Anglais) to St-Roman-de-Bellet and the 18th-century **Château de Bellet** (✆ 04 93 37 81 57), or the **Château de Crémat**, just south of the *autoroute* A8, off Ave Durandi (✆ 04 92 15 12 15).

Vieux Nice

Dismissed as a dangerous slum in the 1970s, Nice's Vieille Ville, a piquant quarter east of Place Masséna, is busy becoming the trendiest part of Nice, brimful of cafés, bistros, night-clubs, designer boutiques and galleries. And the population, once poor and ethnically mixed, is now more than half French and upwardly mobile. But the shock of the new is mitigated by the tenacity of the Vieille Ville's old-grandmotherly underwear; paint and stationery shops, and no-name working-men's bars, have so far refused to budge. Picasso liked to walk here because it reminded him of the funky Barrì Chino in Barcelona.

'Vieux' in Vieux Nice means Genoese seaside Baroque—tall, steep *palazzi*, many with opulent 17th- and 18th-century portals and windows, turning the narrow streets and steps below into chasms that suddenly open up into tiny squares, each with its chapel. To this day the old Niçois are among the most religious people on the coast, and still join the confraternities of Penitents: lay organizations dedicated to public demonstrations of penitence, founded in Italy in the 14th century during the great Franciscan and Dominican revivals. Of the city's original seven confraternities, four still survive, all of which reside in this neighbourhood.

At its eastern end, the Vieille Ville is closed by **Colline du Château**, the ancient acropolis of Nikaïa and site of the 10th- to 12th-century town and cathedral. Of the latter, a few ruins remain—the Savoyards demolished it to make way for their citadel, which was in turn blown up by Louis XIV. You can walk up the steps, take a mini-train (*30F*) from the Promenade des Anglais which gives you a little tour through the flower market and around the Vieille Ville on the way, or pay a few *sous* to take the lift at the east end of the Quai des Etats-Unis near **Tour Bellanda** (where Berlioz composed his *King Lear Overture*) and the little **Musée Naval** (*open 10–12 and 2–5, summer 2–7, closed Mon, Tues, holidays and mid-Nov–mid-Dec; adm*), with ships' models. Among the gardens at the top of the hill are two cemeteries, one Jewish and one grandiose Italian, where you can find the tombs of Garibaldi's mum and Mercedes Jellinek, who gained immortality in 1902 when her father chose her name for a new line of Daimlers.

If you descend by way of the east flank of the hill, down Montée Eberlé and Rue Catherine-Ségurane (where Nietzsche lived between 1883 and 1888), you'll end up in the yellow, arcaded, 18th-century **Place Garibaldi**, named after its glowering statue of the hero of Italy's unification, who was born near the port in 1806. The Blue Penitents (all Penitents are named by the colour of their hooded robes) have their neoclassical chapel of **St-Sépulcre** on this square, while just around the corner, facing the esplanade on 60 bis Blvd Risso, is the **Musée Barla d'Histoire Naturelle** (*open 10–12 and 2–6, closed Tues, holidays, and mid-Aug–mid-Sept; temporarily closed, call ✆ 04 93 55 15 24*), where you can ponder, among other things, a 19th-century collection of 7000 painted plaster mushrooms.

South of Place Garibaldi off Rue Neuve is the city's oldest parish church, **St-Martin-St-Auguste**, where a monk named Martin Luther said a mass during his momentous pilgrimage to Rome. The interior was baroqued in the 17th century; its treasures include a fine *Pietà* (*c.* 1500) by a follower of Ludovico Brea, and a photocopy of Garibaldi's baptismal certificate. Further south, Rue Pairolière leads into 'Babazouck', the curious nickname for the heart of Vieux Nice, and **Place St-François**, where a pungent fish market takes place every morning except Monday. Continuing south, the **Chapelle de la Croix** in Rue de la Croix is the headquarters of the Pénitents Blancs, the oldest confraternity (founded in 1306) and the most popular, perhaps because they were still into public self-flagellation in the 1750s.

A block to the west, at 15 Rue Droite, the **Palais Lascaris** (*open 10–12 and 2–6, closed Mon, holidays and Nov; adm*) is a grand 1648 Genoese-style mansion. The ground floor contains a reconstructed pharmacy of 1738; the first floor or *piano nobile*, where guests would be received, is saturated with elaborate Genoese 'quadratura' (architectural *trompe-l'œil*) frescoes, Flemish tapestries, ornate woodwork, and a 1578 Italian precursor of the pianoforte. The next floor is devoted to popular traditions, furnishings, and manufacturing. Contemporary exhibitions take place at the corner of Rue Droite and Rue de la Loge, at the **Galerie Municipale Renoir** (*open 10.30–1 and 2–6, closed Mon and Sun*).

Take Rue Rossetti west to the cafés of pretty Place Rossetti, dominated by Nice's 17th-century **Cathédrale Ste-Réparate**, crowned with a joyful dome and lantern of glazed tiles in emerald bands. The uncorrupted body of Réparate, a 15-year-old virgin martyred in Caesarea in the 300s, arrived in Nice in a boat of flowers towed by a pair of angels (hence Baie des Anges). This same Réparate was the first patron saint of Florence before the city adopted intermediaries with greater heavenly clout, and here, too, in Nice, the young virgin is currently losing a popularity contest with St Rita of Cascia, whose cult has already usurped the 17th-century **Eglise Saint-Giaume**, at 1 Rue de la Poissonnerie. Here, her altar gets nearly all the business, possibly because her speciality is unhappy middle-aged housewives—Rita herself was burdened in the 14th century with a rotten husband, ungrateful children, and a smelly sore on her forehead that just wouldn't heal.

Rita's compatriot, Paganini, who died nearby in 1840 at 23 Rue de la Préfecture, had his share of troubles too, but most of them were posthumous. Ste-Réparate's bishop was convinced that the sounds Paganini made on his violin could only have been produced by the devil incarnate (the maestro liked to startle the neighbours by making it howl like a tomcat) and refused him a Christian burial. He even wanted to toss Paganini's body into the Paillon. In the end, however, the dead fiddler was shunted to Cannes and then to Genoa and Parma, where he was finally buried in 1896.

Cours Saleya

After the dark lanes of Vieux Nice, the sun pops back into the sky over Cours Saleya, an elongated little gem of urban planning, where bars and restaurants line up along the famous outdoor market, overflowing with flowers and sumptuous food displays worthy of the Riviera's gourmet vortex. The Cours is closed at one end by the 17th-century Ancien Sénat and **St-Suaire**, home of the Red Penitents, who assisted pilgrims. But the principal focal point of the Cours is the Black Penitents' **Chapelle de la Miséricorde**, designed in 1740 by Bernardo Vittone, a disciple of Turin's extraordinary Baroque architects Guarino Guarini and Juvarra. Inside (unfortunately locked except for special tours: ask at the tourist office), it's all virtuoso Baroque geometry, a gold and stucco confection with vertiginous *trompe-l'œil* paintings in the vault. A fine early Renaissance *Polyptique de la Miséricorde* (1430) by Jean Mirailhet hangs in the sacristy, painted for the confraternity, whose mission was to assure the dead a dignified burial.

A double row of one-storey buildings separates Cours Saleya from the Quai des Etats-Unis, where you'll find a pair of little museums (*both open Tues–Sat 10–12 and 2–6, Sun 2–6; adm*): the **Musée Alexis et Gustav-Adolf Mossa** at 59 Quai des Etats-Unis, featuring landscapes by Alexis, a native of Nice, and the exquisitely drawn mytho-morbid Symbolist works of his son Gustav-Adolf Mossa (1883–1971), who painted between 1903 and 1917 and then just stopped. At No.77 the **Musée Dufy** has a large collection of paintings by a much cheerier soul who spent his latter years in Nice, producing colourful 'café-society' art. Far more compelling are the handful of Dufy's early Fauve works, especially the remarkable 1908 *Bateaux à l'Estaque*, a Cubist painting predating Cubism itself, although Dufy, like many of the Fauves, never followed the direction he mapped out for others.

The Port, Terra Amata, and Hilltop Follies

To the east, Quai des Etats-Unis circles around the wind-punched hill of the Château, where it's known as Quai Rauba-Capéu ('hat thief') before it meets placid **Bassin Lympia**, the departure point for ferries to Corsica. Among the 18th-century buildings overlooking the port is the **Musée de Terra Amata**, 25 Blvd Carnot (*buses 1, 9, 10, from Nice Central; open 10–12 and 2–6, closed Mon and holidays*), built into the cave holding one of the world's oldest 'households', a pebble-walled wind-shelter built by hunters 400 millennia ago. A fascinating set of models, bones and tools helps evoke life in Nice at the dawn of time. Nor had things changed radically 200,000 years later, judging by the palaeolithic relics left in the nearby **Grotte du Lazaret** (*phone © 04 93 26 59 19 to arrange a visit; you need to be a scholar, or in a group of at least 10 people, although there are also some open days every year*).

Boulevard Carnot (the Corniche Inférieure) continues east past some extravagant Belle Epoque villas, culminating in eccentricity in the pink, turreted **Château de l'Anglais**. Built in 1858 by Colonel Robert Smith, a military engineer in India, the result weds English Perpendicular with mock-Mogul Palace to produce one of the best follies on the Riviera. Behind this rise the forested slopes of **Mont Boron**; off Route Forestière du Mont Boron, the magnificent **Sentier Bellevue**, meanders to the top, capped by a fort of 1880.

A far more delightful piece of military architecture, **Fort Alban**, is just off the Moyenne Corniche, above the youth hostel (take bus 14 to Chemin du Fort, or if you're driving, turn right off Rte Forestière du Mont Boron, on to Chemin du Fort du Mont Alban). Built in 1570, it bristles with four toy turrets roofed with glazed Niçois tiles. To the north, off the Grande Corniche, is an elegant **Observatoire**, Blvd Bischoffsheim, © 04 92 00 30 11, designed in part by Charles Garnier with a dome by Gustave Eiffel (*open Saturdays at 3; adm; bus 74 from Blvd Pierre-Sola*).

Up the Paillon

In the old days Nice's laundresses plied their trade in the torrential waters of the Paillon, and were scrubbing away in 1543, when Ottoman pirates, under the dread admiral Barbarossa, attacked. Hearing the racket on the walls, an exceptionally beefy laundress named Catherine Ségurane rushed to the highest tower, and with her hollering, enthusiasm and skilful wielding

Place Massena, Nice

of her washerwoman's paddle galvanized the defence. When she saw that Nice was about to fall, in spite of her best efforts, she climbed a ladder, bent over and dropped her drawers. The historians write that the Turks took one look at the biggest backside they had every seen and, fearing further revelations, retreated in complete confusion, and raised anchor.

The often dangerous Paillon was canalized and began to vanish under the pavements in the 1830s, and now secretly gushes or trickles below some of Nice's proudest showcases and gardens. Nearest the sea, Jardin Albert Ier is the site of the open-air **Théâtre de Verdure**, while upstream, as it were, vast **Place Masséna** is generously endowed with flower-beds and benches for Nice's sun-loving retirees. Further up, the Promenade du Paillon is dominated by the hanging gardens of the bus station/multi-storey car park, a mini-Babylon with an unsavoury reputation for small-time vice—vice that pales in the face of ex-mayor Jacques Médecin's pair of dreadnoughts looming beyond.

The first of these, reached by sets of Aztec temple steps, is Nice's answer to the Pompidou Centre in Paris: the 282-million-franc **Théâtre de Nice**, ✆ 04 93 80 52 60, and the marble-coated **Musée d'Art Moderne et d'Art Contemporain** (*open 11–6 exc Tues and hols; 11–10pm Fri; adm*). Inauspiciously inaugurated in June 1990, as the public revelations of Médecin's sins and fury over his anti-Semitism reached a pitch, the ceremony was boycotted by the Niçois art community, who convinced culture minister Jack Lang to stay away as well. If you overlook the fact that the roof was already leaking four months after it was finished, or that the museum had to be closed for major repairs in December 1991 when large cracks were discovered in its foundations, the building—four concrete towers, linked by glass walkways that seem to smile and frown and afford pleasant views over the city—is an admirable setting for the works of Christo, Niki de Saint-Phalle, Warhol, Dine, Oldenburg, Rauschenberg, and other influential figures of the 1960s and '70s. The primary focus is on the artists of the 'Second Nice school': Yves Klein, Martial Rayasse, César, Arman, Ben, and Swiss-born Jean Tinguely, whose New Realist concoctions of plastic consumer junk, broken machinery, musical intruments and exploding suicide machines spoof not only society, but also the artificial, rarefied and wordy world of contemporary art.

The view up the Paillon is blocked by Médecin's 1985 congress and art centre and *cinémathèque* called **Acropolis**, 1 Esplanade Kennedy, ✆ 04 93 92 83 00, a gruesome megalithic bunker of concrete slabs and smoked glass. No design could be more diametrically opposed (stylistically and philosophically) to the acropolis in Athens, and the mass of guitars in Arman's *Music Power* at the entrance hardly redeems it. Beyond this are more mastodons: a *Palais des Expositions* and a *Palais des Sports*.

West of Place Masséna and the Promenade des Anglais

The Paillon neatly divides Vieux Nice from the boom city of 19th-century tourism, full of ornate, debonair apartments and hotels. Important streets fan out from Place Masséna and the adjacent Jardin Albert Ier: Nice's main shopping street, **Ave Jean-Médecin**, leads up to the train station; **Rue Masséna**, the centre of a lively pedestrian-only restaurant and shopping zone; and the fabled, palm-lined **Promenade des Anglais**, still aglitter through the fumes of the traffic, which is usually as strangled as poor Isadora Duncan was when her scarf caught in the wheel of her Bugatti here in 1927. The long pebble beach is crowded day and night in the summer, when parties spontaneously erupt among the many illegal but tolerated campers.

Visitors from the opposite end of the economic spectrum check into the fabled Belle Epoque **Hôtel Negresco** (No.37), vintage 1906, although they no longer roll snake eyes in the 1929 **Palais de la Méditerranée**, a masterpiece of French Art Deco built by Frank Jay Gould. In 1960 it was the most profitable casino in France; by 1979 it was bankrupt, thanks to the machinations of Jacques Médecin and his cronies who favoured the rival **Casino Ruhl**. The Ruhl reopened next to the Negresco in spring 1995, in spite of the unsolved case of the disappearance and presumed murder of Agnès Le Roux, daughter of Renée Le Roux, at the time the main owner of the Palais de la Méditerranée. Five months before disappearing in 1977 Agnès had secretly sold her share in the family business to Jean-Dominique Fratoni, owner of the Ruhl and a man with mafia and Médecin links. Meanwhile the Palais de la Méditerranée was destined for the wrecking-ball, but the speculators gave in to the protests at the last minute, on the condition that the building had all its original innards removed like an Egyptian mummy. Another gem clinging tenaciously to the Promenade among the new buildings is at No.139, a flowery Art Nouveau-style villa of 1910 built by a Finnish engineer.

Next to the Negresco is the garden of the **Palais Masséna** (*open daily except Mon 10–12 and 2–6*). Built in the Empire style in 1901 for Prince Victor Masséna, the grandson of Napoleon's marshal, it was left to Nice on the condition that it become a *musée d'art et d'histoire*. At the entrance, a solemn statue of Napoleon tarted up in a toga sets the tone for the ground-floor salons—heavy and pompous and stylistically co-ordinated from ceiling stucco to chair leg. The atmosphere lightens upstairs with a pair of fine retables from the 1450s by Jacques Durandi, panels from a polyptych attributed to Ludovico Brea, ceramics and armour. The top floor displays statues of the Ten Incarnations of Vishnu, Spanish earrings, views of Nice, and rooms dedicated to hometown boys Garibaldi and the cruel and wicked Marshal Masséna, the military genius Napoleon called '*l'enfant gâté de la victoire*' whose appetite for atrocities was matched only by his greedy plundering. Then there's the obligatory Napoleana: a billiard-ball from St Helena and Josephine's bed, with a big 'N' on the coverlet.

Fine and Naïf Arts, and a Russian Cathedral

From the Masséna museum, a brisk ten-minute walk or bus 22 (get off at the foot of Rue Bassenetts and walk 100m up the path) leads to the handsome 1880 villa built by a Ukranian princess, enlarged by an American millionaire, and now home of the **Musée des Beaux Arts**, 33 Ave des Baumettes (*open 10–12 and 2–6, closed Mon; adm*). With the Matisses, Chagalls and Dufys in Nice's other museums, the Musée des Beaux Arts is left with 'old masters of the 19th century'—a euphemism for tired, flabby academic paintings and portraits of Madame this and Madame that, a *Portrait of an Old Man* by Fragonard and works by Carle Van Loo, a native of Nice. But there are a few meatier paintings: a 1615 *David* attributed to Tanzio da

Varallo, a Lombard follower of Caravaggio; a self-portrait by Russian aristocrat Marie Bashkirtseff; and a roomful of her contemporary Kees Van Dongen, including his entertaining 1927 *Tango of the Archangel*, which perhaps more than any painting evokes the Roaring Twenties on the Riviera—even the archangel, in his dinner-jacket, is wearing high-heels. One room is devoted to Félix Ziem, and another to the Belle Epoque's favourite lithographist, Jules Chéret, who introduced colour posters to France in 1866, most of them decorated with dancing doll-women caught in swirling pastel tornadoes of silly *putti*.

To the west, the perfume magnate Coty built the pink Château de Ste-Hélène, a building now used as the **Musée d'Art Naïf Anatole Jakovsky**, Ave Val-Marie, bus 6, 9, 10, 12, 23, 24, 34, stop *Fabron* (*open 10–12 and 2–6, closed Tues; adm*). The museum is formed around 600 paintings spanning the 17th to the 20th centuries, donated by Jakovsky, a tireless promoter of naïve art. The Yugoslavs are especially well represented, with an enthusiasm for the genre that perhaps in some way counterbalances the unsolvable, nightmarish imbroglio of their politics.

Two new commercial attractions have sprouted at the western end of Nice: one is the **Musée des Trains Miniatures** (*open daily from 9.30*); and near the airport you may already have noticed the mega-greenhouse of **Parc Floral Phœnix**, 405 Promenade des Anglais; bus 9, 10, 23, 24, 26 (*open every day 9–7, 9–5 in winter*), a Disneyland for botanists or garden lovers: its diamond dome supports 2500 different plants in 7 different tropical climates. The Park Floral also hosts the new white marble **Musée des Arts Asiatiques**, 'a swan that floats on the water of a peaceful lake', ✆ 04 92 29 37 00 (*open May–Oct, Wed–Mon, 10–6, Oct–April 10–7; closed Tues*). Chinese jade and bronze and Japanese lacquer and ceramics lead into Cambodian sculpture and Indian textiles; the up-to-the-minute multimedia displays and exhibitions with a spiritual theme make an original collection in an original and beautiful building.

In 1865, the young Tsarevich Nicholas was brought to Nice, and, like so many consumptives who arrived in search of health, he found the grim reaper instead. The luxurious villa where he died was demolished to construct a mortuary chapel and the great **Cathédrale Orthodoxe Russe St-Nicolas** (or **Eglise Russe**), located a few blocks from the west of the train station at 17 Blvd du Tzarévitch, just off Blvd Gambetta (bus 5, 7, 15, *open daily except Sun am, 9–12 and 2.30–6 in summer, 5 in winter; no shorts or sleeveless shirts; adm*). Paid for by Tsar Nicolas II and completed only five years before the Bolshevik Revolution, its five onion domes shine with a colourful coating of glazed Niçois tiles; inside are lavish frescoes, woodwork and icons.

Cimiez: Chagall, Matisse, and Roman Ruins

On the low hills west of the Paillon, where wealthy Romans lived the good life in *Cemenelum*, modern Niçois do the same in Cimiez, a luxurious 19th-century suburb dotted with the grand hotels of yesteryear. Bus 15 from the Gare SNCF will take you to the main attractions, beginning with the **Musée National Message Biblique Marc Chagall**, at the foot of Cimiez hill on Ave du Docteur Ménard, west of Blvd de Cimiez, ✆ 04 93 53 87 20 (*open Oct–June 10–5, July–Sept 10–6, closed Tues; adm*). Opened in 1971, the airy, specially designed building incorporates stained-glass windows and mosaics by Chagall while 17 canvases on Old Testament subjects glow on the walls, especially the red series of the *Song of Songs*. There are often temporary exhibits on Jewish art and studies, and a suitably biblical garden of olives and cypresses.

Cimiez owed much of its original cachet to Queen Victoria, and she's gratefully remembered with a statue in front of her favourite lodging, the Hôtel Excelsior Regina Palace on Ave Regina, off Ave Reine-Victoria. After the Second World War, the same hotel became headquarters for Henri Matisse, who died here in 1954, leaving the city a priceless collection of his works, displayed in the **Musée Matisse**, an exquisite late 17th-century Genoese villa in the olive-studded Parc des Arènes (*take bus 15, 17 or 22 from the Promenade des Anglais or Ave Jean-Médecin; open April–Sept 10–6, Oct–Mar 10–5, closed Tues and some holidays; adm*). It contains all the bronzes Matisse ever made, and other works of every period—from one of his first oil-paintings, done in 1890, to his paper cut-outs of the 1950s; among the best known works are *Nature Morte aux Grenades*, *Rococo Armchair*, designs for the chapel in Vence (*see* p.108), illustrations made for Joyce's *Ulysses*, and the world's largest collection of his drawings.

Adjacent to the Matisse Museum is the new **Musée Archéologique** (*open April–Sept 10–12 and 2–6; Oct–Mar 10–1 and 2–5, closed Mon and some holidays; adm*), entered through the excavations of *Cemenelum*. These include the baths, with a marble summer pool, and the amphitheatre, with seating for 4000 (unusually small for a population of 20,000, but perhaps the Romans here were too couth for gladiators). The museum houses vases, coins, statues, jewels, and models of what Cimiez looked like 2000 years ago.

From the archaeology museum it's a short walk across the Jardin Public to the Franciscan **Musée Franciscain, Eglise et Monastère de Cimiez** (*guided tours; open 10–12 and 3–6, closed Sun and holidays*). The Franciscans have been here since the 1500s, but their church was heavily restored in 1850, although it still has two beautiful altarpieces by Ludovico Brea: the *Vierge de Piété* and a *Crucifixion* on a gold background, together with other less explicable 17th-century paintings in the cloister that some scholars think may have alchemical meanings. There's a museum documenting Franciscan life in Nice from the 13th–18th centuries, including both documents and art. Dufy and Matisse are buried in the adjacent cemetery, and there are fine views over the valley of the Paillon.

The Ministry of Culture sponsors the activities in the 18th-century **Villa Arson**, 20 Ave Stephen-Liégeard, ✆ 04 92 07 73 73 (*open summer 1–7, winter 1–6; closed Mon*)—not headquarters for a pyromaniac club, but a centre for contemporary art, with students, studios for working artists, exhibitions, a library and a café.

Festivals

Nice is famous for its **carnival** in the two weeks before Lent, first mentioned in the 13th century. It died out in the early 1800s, and subsequent attempts to revive it to amuse the tourists only succeeded in 1873, when the painters Alexis and Gustav-Adolf Mossa took over the show. They initiated a burlesque royal cortège to escort the figure of King Carnival, *Sa Majesté Carnaval*, down Ave Jean-Médecin, accompanied by comical *grosses têtes*—masqueraders with giant papier-mâché heads. During the subsequent parades, dances and battles of flowers and sweets, King Carnival reigns from Place Masséna, only to be immolated on the night of Mardi Gras to the explosive barrage of fireworks. As mayor, Jacques Médecin was a big supporter of the carnival, much to the annoyance of many residents, especially since it cost more money to put on than it brought in, and was generally agreed to be a commercial rip-off; future carnivals will, it seems, be on a smaller scale. The second and third weeks of July see the excellent

Festival de Jazz in the Jardin Public de Cimiez; from the end of July to the beginning of August there are the **Festival International du Folklore** and more *Bataille des Fleurs*, and in September there's the **Fête de la Vigne**. The Comité des Fêtes handles all festival information at 5 Promenade des Anglais, ✆ 04 93 87 16 28.

Shopping

Vieux Nice is the most attractive place to shop, for art, cheap clothes and glorious food at the outdoor markets and local shops. In Cours Saleya, the morning **food and flower market** (daily 6am–5.30pm exc Mon, Sun pm only), with a wonderful array of herbs and every fruit you can imagine crystallized and glowing, is replaced on Monday by old books, clothes, and bric-à-brac; arts and crafts appear on Wednesday afternoon, and paintings on Sunday afternoons. At Place St-François is the **fish market** (every morning exc Monday) and many Niçois gourmets swear that the **olives and olive oil** from Nicolas Alziari, 14 Rue St-François-de-Paule, is the best in the world, though the Maison de l'Olive, 18 Rue Pairolière, also has a tempting display. The pedestrian zone around Place Masséna has scores of designer **clothes** shops and cheap boutiques, plus the wonderful pâtisserie Vogade right on the square, while in Ave Jean-Médecin you'll find Nice's biggest **department store**, Galeries Lafayette, and Marks & Spencer, as well as Nice Etoile, a centre with useful shops like the **bookshop** FNAC (which sells tickets to concerts and other events); and, up near Ave Thiers, Phox, which sells the cheapest camera film in Nice. The new **perfumery** chain Sephora, in Ave Jean-Médecin near Nice Etoile, sells its own range of stylish black-packaged toiletries in single scents like rosemary, caramel, honeysuckle or clementine, as well as the largest range of lipsticks aand perfumes possible to fit in one space.

For **antiques**, try the shops around Rue Antoine-Gauthier (by the port) or the antique market, Village Ségurane, at 28 Rue Catherine-Ségurane, daily exc Sun. For *santons* try La Couquetou, 8 Rue St-François-de-Paule, Au Cœur de Nice, 11 Rue Mascoïnat, or Les Poupées Yolande, Rue A.-Gauthier. **Provençal fabrics** can be found at Sainte Réparate Provence, 1 Rue Ste-Réparate, ✆ 04 93 13 03 14, and Les Olivades, 7 Rue de la Boucherie, and perfume oils for 15F a phial at La Maison de la Lavande, Rue St-Gaétan. Papeterie Rontani, 5 Rue Alexandre-Mari, ✆ 04 93 62 32 43, an old-fashioned, wood-floored shop, sells delicious paper of every sort, and maps a-plenty.

Sports and Activities

Many of the **paying beaches** along the Baie des Anges offer some kind of sport, including parascending, volleyball, jet-skiing and even bouncy castles. The beaches are expensive, but Galion charges by the half-day instead of stinging you for the full fee even if you only want a few hours' escape from the pebbles and local teenagers hogging the water's edge. Various companies around the port offer **diving** and **snorkelling**, including Nausicaa, 12 Ave Gustavin, ✆ 04 93 89 04 13, and L'Odyssée, 14 Quai des Docks, ✆ 04 93 89 42 44. The **Golf de Nice**, ✆ 04 93 29 82 00, open 9–7.30, is at 698 Route de Grenoble. To find out about **skiing** in the mountains behind the coast, visit the Comité Régional Côte d'Azur, 39 Rue Pastorelli, ✆ 04 93 80 65 77.

Nice is packed with hotels of all categories, and in the summer most are just as tightly packed inside. If you arrive without a reservation, the tourist office next to the station will book rooms for 10F. Get there by 10am in the summer, or risk joining the nightly slumber parties on the beach or in front of the station, where you'll encounter giant cockroaches from hell. Come instead in the off season, when many of the best hotels offer the kind of rates the French would call *très intéressant.*

expensive

Nice has luxury grand hotels galore, but for panache none can top the fabulous green-domed ★★★★**Negresco**, 37 Promenade des Anglais, ℰ 04 93 16 64 00, ◉ 04 93 88 35 68. A national historic monument, it was designed for Romanian hotelier Henri Negresco (who started his career as a gypsy violinist) by Edouard Niermans, architect of the Moulin Rouge and the Folies Bergères. The one hotel in Nice where a Grand Duke would still feel at home, and the last independent luxury hotel on the coast, its 150 chambers and apartments have all been redecorated with Edwardian furnishings and paintings by the likes of Picasso and Léger. Don't miss the *salon royal*, lit by a Baccarat chandelier made for the Tsar.

If hobnobbing with the rich and famous in the Negresco is out, there's the elegant Art Deco ★★★★**Beau Rivage**, 24 Rue St-François-de-Paule, ℰ 04 93 80 80 70, ◉ 04 93 80 55 77, on a pedestrian street in Vieux Nice overlooking the sea and Beau Rivage beach; Matisse spent two years here and Chekhov, during his stay, wrote *The Seagull*. The rooms are as luminous and beautiful as a Matisse and there's direct access to the beach. Or you can choose the modern comforts, roof-top pool, sauna, and many other amenities of the artsy, stylish ★★★★**Elysée Palace**, 59 Promenade des Anglais, ℰ 04 93 86 06 06, ◉ 04 93 44 50 40, with a façade dominated by an enormous bronze silhouette of a woman.

moderate

Best among the tri-star choices is the idiosyncratic ★★★**Windsor**, 11 Rue Dalpozzo (behind the Negresco), ℰ 04 93 88 59 35, ◉ 04 93 88 94 57, in the midst of a tropical garden, featuring a pool, an English-style pub, a Turkish hammam, a Thai sitting room and dreamy frescoes in the rooms. Another choice with character, ★★★**Vendôme**, in the centre of town at 26 Rue Pastorelli, ℰ 04 93 62 00 77, ◉ 04 93 13 40 78, has prettily renovated, air-conditioned rooms, a superb stairway, and a garden. More reasonable but still stylish choices include the handsome ★★**Nouvel Hôtel**, 19 bis Blvd Victor-Hugo, ℰ 04 93 87 15 00, ◉ 04 93 16 00 67, Belle Epoque in style, and ★★**Comté de Nice**, 29 Rue de Dijon, ℰ 04 93 88 94 56, ◉ 04 93 87 67 40, a pink confection with its own statue outside in a quiet little street off Ave Malausséna.

In quiet Cimiez, ★★**Le Floride** has lost some of its former charm, but is still an attractive old villa with a shady garden at 52 Blvd de Cimiez, and each blue room has a colour TV and bath ℰ 04 93 53 11 02, ◉ 04 93 81 57 46 (the restaurant now only serves lunch).

For long-term stays, there are three comfortable apartment-hotels just off the Promenade des Anglais, run by the Citadines group: **Nice Fleurs**, 17 Ave des Fleurs, ✆ 04 92 15 51 51, 📠 04 92 15 51 00; **Nice Buffa**, 21 Rue Meyerbeer, ✆ 04 93 16 54 54 , 📠 04 93 16 18 32; and **Promenade**, 3–5 Blvd F.-Grosso, ✆ 04 93 37 26 26, 📠 04 93 44 93 88.

inexpensive

There are plenty of cheaper choices; perhaps the one most likely to bring happiness is the 11-room **Porte Bonheur**, with its little garden at 146 Ave St-Lambert, ✆ 04 93 84 66 10, undignified even by a star but the only cheap hotel (bed only) in this list to be featured on French TV for its charm. Double rooms are 165F plus, but book well in advance to get one (*it's north of the station near the interesting 1930s church of Ste-Jeanne d'Arc, bus 1, 2, 22, 24 to Ave Borriglione*). A stone's throw from the station the friendly ★**La Belle Meunière**, 21 Ave Durante, ✆ 04 93 88 66 15, is a long-time favourite of budget travellers in Nice—it even has parking and a little garden for breakfast. *Closed 15 Nov–15 Feb.* In Vieux Nice, near the coach station, ★**Picardy**, 10 Blvd Jean-Jaurès, ✆ 04 93 85 75 51, has nice soundproof rooms of 170F plus in a family pension atmosphere.

The **Auberge de Jeunesse** is 4km east of town (*bus 14, stop: L'Auberge*) on Rte Forestière du Mont-Alban, ✆ 04 93 89 23 64, but beware that the last bus leaves at 7pm. Even further afield is Cimiez's **Clairvallon Relais International de la Jeunesse**, 26 Ave Scudéri, ✆ 04 93 81 27 63, 📠 04 93 53 35 88 (*bus 15, 17 or 22*), although it has the added plus of a pool. There are dormitory rooms in the **Espace Magnan**, west of the centre at 31 Rue Louis-de-Coppet (*bus 3, 9, 10, 12, 22 stop: Rosa Bonheur*), ✆ 04 93 86 28 75, 📠 04 93 44 93 22; or individual ones in the university residence halls at **Les Collinettes** during July and August, 3 Ave Robert-Schumann, ✆ 04 93 97 06 64 (*bus 14 or 17, stop: Châteauneuf*). Apply to the Auberge de Jeunesse to get a room here.

Eating Out

Although now a solidly French-speaking corner of the Hexagon, Nice's cuisine still has a heavy Ligurian accent, with a fondness for seafood, olive oil and tiny black olives, chick peas, fresh basil, and pine-nuts. A typical first course consists of pasta (ravioli filled with seafood or artichoke hearts, or served with a delectable walnut sauce), *gnocchi* or, in the winter, *soupe au pistou*, a hearty soup of courgettes (zucchini), tomatoes, beans, potatoes, onions and vermicelli, served with *pistou*, a sauce based on basil, pine-nuts, and garlic. Another Niçois favourite is *bourride*, a fish soup served with *aïoli* that many prefer to the more elaborate Marseille *bouillabaisse*, and teeny-tiny fish called *poutines*, by law only caught between Beaulieu and Cagnes, and which local cooks fry in omelettes or pile on top of pasta.

Another popular first course is the world-famous *salade niçoise*, which even in Nice is made in as many 'true and genuine' ways as *bouillabaisse* in Marseille—with quartered tomatoes, capers, black olives, spring onions, anchovies or tuna, green beans, and with or without hard-boiled eggs and potatoes. Main courses are often from the sea: grilled fish with herbs or, more of an acquired taste, *estocaficada*, wine-dried cods and guts, stewed in *eau-de-vie*, with potatoes, garlic, onions, and peppers. Favourite side dishes include *ratatouille* (another famous dish of Niçois origin) or boiled Swiss chard (*blette*) in vinaigrette. Snacks include chickpea *socca*, *pan-bagnat*, and stuffed vegetables or courgette flowers (*farcies*).

expensive

Gastronomic Nice is dominated by the Belle Epoque magnificence of the **Chantecler**, 37 Promenade des Anglais, ✆ 04 93 16 64 00, ✆ 04 93 88 35 68 (*lunch menus from 395F including wine*), the restaurant snuggling into the opulent arms of the Negresco. Here, chef Alain Llorca, successor to Dominique Le Stanc, has succeeded in seducing the Niçois with his own fabulous versions of Chantecler favourites like sea bass served with tomatoes and pesto, roast pigeon with foie gras ravioli and desserts like the exotic liquorice-flavoured meringue with raspberry sorbet. *Closed mid-Nov–mid-Dec.* **Don Camillo**, 5 Rue des Ponchettes, ✆ 04 93 85 67 95, ✆ 04 93 13 97 43 (*250–350F*), was opened by a former pupil of Maximin and Paul Ducasse, already celebrated for its homemade ravioli filled with Swiss chard *en daube* and fabulous desserts.

moderate

The best restaurant-hunting territory is Vieux Nice and, especially for fresh fish, around the port. **Atmosphère**, 36 Cours Saleya, ✆ 04 93 62 32 50 (*menus from 100F to 350F*), enjoys a privileged spot and offers good but hardly exceptional seafood, not always served with a smile, and the **Bœuf Saleya** is similar but with slightly better prices and good mussels in season. Elsewhere, **Brasserie Flo**, 4 Rue Sacha-Guitry, ✆ 04 93 13 38 38 (*last orders 12.30am, menus from 106F*), offers oysters and fish for late-night theatre crowds.

inexpensive

Less expensive choices abound. One of the best is up in Cimiez: **Auberge de Théo**, 52 Ave Cap de Croix, ✆ 04 93 81 26 19 (*90–180F*), where you'll find genuine Italian pizzas, salads with *mesclun* (Nice's special mixed salad), and Venetian *tiramisù* for dessert. *Closed Mon*. Best place to try near the station is **Voyageur Nissart**, 19 Rue Alsace-Lorraine, between the station and Ave Jean-Médecin, ✆ 04 93 82 19 60, which has two wide-ranging 65–95F menus.

For snacks and somewhere to sit, Vieux Nice's **René Socca**, 2 Rue Miralheti, ✆ 04 93 92 05 73, offers *socca*, *pissaladière*, pizza by the slice and much more, which you can down with a beer or wine at the bar across the street, *closed Mon and Nov*; **Denis le Niçois 'La Véritable Socca'**, 4 Rue St-François, ✆ 04 93 13 98 23, has entertaining service and cheap *beignets*, and opposite is a Brazilan and Tunisian restaurant with huge beef steaks if you need something more substantial than a stuffed courgette. Try **Cave Ricord**, 2 Rue Neuve, near Place Garibaldi, ✆ 04 93 85 30 87, a funny old-fashioned wine bar with *socca*, pizza, and *pan-bagnats* and other inexpensive dishes serving a slightly too touristy crowd; or the popular **La Taverne de L'Opéra**, 10 Rue St-François-de-Paule, ✆ 04 93 85 72 68 (*65–140F*), with excellent *socca* and other delights, plus jazz on summer Friday nights. On the corner of Avenue Félix-Faure and Place Masséna is a very central chain restaurant, **Hippopotamus**, that fills up reassuringly with locals at lunchtime; it serves several set menus at between 50F and 100F, with a lunchtime special of *plat du jour* and coffee at 49.50F. For Italian, try the small and cheap **Spaghettissimo**, 3 Cours Saleya, ✆ 04 93 80 95 07 (*120–150F*). For *choucroute* and couscous, there's **Le St-Germain**, 10 Rue Clément Roassal, ✆ 04 93 82 12 99. Little **Pasta Basta** in Rue de la Préfecture looks ordinary but offers *bruschetta*, salads and salmon *agnolotti* with rich tomato sauce cheaper than anywhere in trendy Cours Saleya.

For an exclusive afternoon tea, try the elegant **Pâtisserie Cappa**, 7–9 Place Garibaldi in Vieux Nice, ✆ 04 93 62 30 83. In Place Rossetti, it's hard to beat the variety of ice-cream at **Fenocchio**: lavender cream, jasmine sorbet and the bitterest chocolate imaginable make a heavenly combination.

Entertainment and Nightlife

You can find out what's happening in Nice in the daily *Nice-Matin*, though it's not much good for anything else except lining the canary's cage. Other sources covering the entire Côte are *7 jours/7 nuits*, distributed free in the tourist offices, or the *Semaine des Spectacles*, which appears Wednesdays in the news-stands, or Radio Riviera, the coast's English-language station broadcast out of Monaco at 106.3 and 106.5. Local news, hours of religious services in English and more are in the monthly English-language *Blue Coast Magazine*, a new, glossy look at life on the Riviera, distributed in newsagents and English bookshops. If you need a **babysitter**, try the babysitting service at 54 Blvd René-Cassin, ✆ 04 93 21 62 01.

The movie-goer in Nice is spoilt for choice: there's the **Pathé Nice**, 54 Av J.-Médecin, ✆ 08 36 68 22 88; **Pathé Masséna**, with the same phone number as Pathé Nice, and just down the road; **UGC Variétés**, 7 Blvd Victor-Hugo, ✆ 04 93 87 74 97; or for films in their original language at the **UEC Rialto**, 4 Rue de Rivoli, one block from the Negresco, ✆ 08 36 68 00 41; **Mercury**, 16 Place Garibaldi, ✆ 08 36 68 81 06; and **Cinémathèque de Nice**, 3 Esplanade Kennedy, ✆ 04 93 04 06 66. The Belle Epoque **Opéra de Nice**, 4–6 Rue St-François-de-Paule, information ✆ 04 93 13 98 53, reservations ✆ 04 92 17 40 40, puts on operas, concerts and recitals at various locations including the **Acropolis** (1 Esplanade Kennedy), the **Théâtre de Nice** (Esplanade des Victoires), and the **Théâtre de Verdure** (on the Promenade des Anglais). Classical music concerts are organized by **La Fondation Sophia-Antipolis à l'Hôtel Westminster**, 27 Promenade des Anglais, ✆ 04 93 88 29 44, free at the **Fondation Kosma**, at the Conservatoire de Nice, 24 Blvd de Cimiez, ✆ 04 92 26 72 20, and at the **Musée Chagall** (*Sept–May*), and also **Musée des Beaux-Arts**, 33 Ave des Baumettes, ✆ 04 93 62 18 12 (*once a month, Oct–May; adm*). Music, from ancient to avant-garde, and art videos are the fare in the auditorium of the **Musée d'Art Moderne et d'Art Contemporain**, ✆ 04 93 62 61 62. Big-league musicians and dancers, and jazz musicians twice a month, perform at **CEDAC de Cimiez**, 49 Ave de la Marne, ✆ 04 93 53 85 95, while **Forum Nice Nord**, 10 Blvd Comte-de-Falicon, just off the A8 at Nice-Nord, ✆ 04 93 84 24 37, is a major venue for modern dance and world music.

From April onwards rock, jazz, and other concerts take place in the outdoor **Théâtre de Verdure** in Jardin Albert Ier. There are several small theatres in Vieux Nice with imaginative productions, such as **Théâtre du Cours**, 5 Rue de la Poissonnerie, © 04 93 80 12 67, and **Théâtre de La Semeuse**, 21 Rue St-Joseph, © 04 93 92 85 08. Molière and other classics are showcased at **Théâtre de l'Alphabet**, 10 Blvd Carabacel, © 04 93 13 08 88, and in the new **Théâtre de Nice**, by the contemporary art museum, © 04 93 80 52 60.

Nice's nightlife is divided between expensive clubs and bland hotel piano bars, and the livelier bars and clubs of Vieux Nice, which come and go like ships in the night. Some of the most jumping joints are the ex-pat havens in Vieux Nice, noisiest of which is the British-owned **Chez Wayne**, 15 Rue de la Préfecture, © 04 93 13 46 99 (*open 10 am–midnight, reservations obligatory at weekends*), a pub and restaurant with live music every night. Fiddlers fiddle at the **Scarlett O'Hara**, 22 Rue Droite, © 04 93 80 43 22. The Dutch go boozing at the funky **De Klomp**, 6 Rue Mascoïnat, near Place Rossetti, © 04 93 92 42 85, with live jazz and a hedonistic atmosphere (not for tee-totallers or anti-smokers). Other night music in Vieux Nice is Brazilian, at the **Ship**, 5 Rue Barillerie, © 04 93 80 46 76, accompanied by cuisine from the Americas (135F menu) and Californian wines, of all things. **Hole in the Wall**, at 3 Rue de l'Abbaye, © 04 93 80 40 16, is just that: a small hole serving large beers, big fresh burgers, and live music on an unfeasibly small stage. In the north of Vieux Nice, **Jonathan's** beer cellar, 1 Rue de la Loge, © 04 93 62 57 62, serves food, lit by candles, and the 1970s-inspired 'live' music is hosted by Jonathan himself: wait long enough and he might treat you to his Rolf Harris impersonation. For clubbing and dancing, **Alizé**, 75 Quai des Etats-Unis, © 04 93 80 06 40, is fast, and full of sailors, of course; and **Le News Rock**, 9 Passage E. Négrin, © 04 93 87 76 30, is much younger, both in its music and clientele. Near the Gare Routière on the north side of Ave Felix Faure is the modern and stylish **Bar Sud**, with iron chairs and sliced wood tables, cool stone walls, tapas and delicious panini for 25F and live music some nights for a 20s/30s crowd.

Other tempting places for a drink or snack include the 19th-century **Grand-Café de Turin** (or **Chez Jo L'Ecailler**), 5 Place Garibaldi, © 04 93 62 66 29, serving some of the best, cheapest oysters in town (and other shellfish in non-R months, *open until 11 in summer, closed June*).

Cagnes to Cannes

The deep Greek of the Mediterranean licked its chops over the edges of our febrile civilization.

Zelda Fitzgerald

The stretch of the Riviera between Nice and Cannes is just about as dense and febrile and excessive as old Europe ever gets—'one vast honky-tonk' declared Noel Coward back in 1960: too many cars, villas, theme parks, and marinas full of yachts the size of tankers, too many gift shops in the lovely *villages perchés*, too many Parisians and movie stars in Cannes and too many technocrats in Sophia-Antipolis, the 'Silicon Valley of the Riviera'. The scenery, especially up around the Gorges du Loup, is decidedly excessive, and you can be bedazzled by the perfumes at Grasse and surplus of art that crowds the coast: Renoir in Cagnes, Léger in Biot, more Matisse in Vence, Picasso in Antibes and Vallauris, and all the contemporary greats up at the dazzling Fondation Maeght. There are so many good restaurants at Mougins, you hardly dare go out for a walk. Nothing succeeds like excess.

Beaches

Between Nice and Antibes the shore is as rocky as the eastern side of the Côte. But purists should make for Antibes, where the sand starts in earnest. There are two public beaches in Antibes: the best lie south of the town centre, just before the Cap, with views back across the Baie des Anges to the Alps.

Juan-les-Pins, blessed with fine sand, is also cursed with countless private beach clubs. Public beaches exist here—try further west towards Golfe-Juan. Cannes has even more snooty beach clubs, but here too there is a public beach right in front of the Palais des Festivals. Further west towards Mandelieu the beach is beautifully sandy, and free.

best beaches

Antibes: Port and south of centre on D2559.

Cannes: Palais des Festivals and west to Mandelieu.

Cagnes

West of Nice runs the river Var, the wet but politically prickly border between France and Savoy, whose dukes were usually allied to France's rivals—England, Spain, or Austria. As bridges over the Var were periodically blown up, for centuries people crossed the water sitting on the shoulders of two strong men. Nowadays in the maelstrom of traffic and overbuilding it's hard even to notice the Var at all. Across the river lies the bloated amoeba of Cagnes, divided into three cells—overbuilt Cros-de-Cagnes by the sea with a Hippodrome; Cagnes-sur-Mer, further up, site of Renoir's house, the happiest of all artists' shrines in the south; and medieval Haut-de-Cagnes on the hill, notorious in the 17th and 18th centuries for the indecorous pastimes and the brilliant parties held in its castle before the Revolution—beginning a long tradition of artsy decadence and futility chronicled in Cyril Connolly's *The Rock Pool* (1936), in which Zelda Fitzgerald's carnivorous Greek Mediterranean becomes merely 'the tideless cloaca of the ancient world'.

Getting Around

There are **train stations** in both Cagnes-sur-Mer and Cros-de-Cagnes (for information, call ✆ 04 93 22 46 47) and a continuous service of **minibuses** from Cagnes-sur-Mer station up the steep hill to Haut-de-Cagnes. There's a massive **underground car park** just outside the village entrance, and restricted parking in the serpentine streets of the old village (beware of parking by the police station at the back of the château). **Buses** from Nice to Vence stop in Cagnes-sur-Mer, where you can also **hire a bike** at Cyclette Marcel, 5 Rue Pasqualeni, ✆ 04 93 20 64 07.

Cagnes-sur-Mer ✉ 06804: 6 Blvd Maréchal-Juin, ✆ 04 93 20 61 64 (closed Sun). Also 20 Ave des Oliviers, ✆ 04 93 07 67 08, 🖩 04 93 07 61 59.

market days

Cagnes-sur-Mer: Wednesday and Friday mornings. **Cros-de-Cagnes**: Tuesday and Thursday mornings.

Cagnes-sur-Mer: Musée Renoir

Ave des Colettes, open 10–12 and 2–5, summer 10.30–12.30 and 1.30–6, closed Tues and 20 Oct–9 Nov; adm; ✆ 04 93 20 61 07.

There is only one thing to do in sprawling Cagnes-sur-Mer: from central Place Général-de-Gaulle follow Ave Auguste-Renoir up to Chemin des Colettes, to Les Colettes, where Renoir spent the last 12 years of his life. Stricken with rheumatoid arthritis, Renoir followed his doctor's advice to move to warmer climes and chose Cagnes, where 'one's nose is not stuck in the mountains'; in 1903 he purchased an ancient olive grove to build a villa in. Rejuvenated by the climate, Renoir produced paintings even more sensuous and voluptuous than before, and there's no contrast more poignant than that of colour-saturated *Grandes Baigneuses* (in the Louvre) and the photograph in the museum of the painter's hands, so bent and crippled that they're painful even to look at. 'I pay dearly for the pleasure I get from this canvas,' he said of one portrait that he especially liked, painted with brushes strapped to his hands. It was also in Cagnes that Renoir first experimented with sculpture, by proxy, dictating detailed instructions to a young sculptor.

In 1989, the museum's collection of portraits of Renoir by his friends was supplemented with 10 canvases the master himself painted in Cagnes. The north studio, with his wheelchair and easel, looks as if Renoir might return any minute—even the chicken wire he put over the window to keep out the children's tennis balls is in place. You can wander freely through the venerable olive grove; the only drastic change from Renoir's day is the view down to the sea.

Haut-de-Cagnes

Spared the worst of the tourist shops, intricate, medieval Haut-de-Cagnes has become instead the fiefdom of contemporary artists, thanks to the UNESCO-sponsored *Festival International de la Peinture*. The crenellated **Château-Musée Grimaldi**, ✆ 04 93 20 85 57 (*open*

Wed–Sun, 10–12 and 2–5 in winter, 10.30–12.30 and 1.30–6 in summer, closed Tues; adm) was built by the first Rainier Grimaldi in the 1300s, at a time when there were a hundred excess male Grimaldis prowling the coast, looking for a castle to call home. This particular branch of the family held on to Cagnes until the Revolution; its most famous twig was Henri, a good friend of Louis XIII, who convinced his cousin in Monaco to put himself under the protection of France rather than Spain.

A handsome inner courtyard tiered with galleries provided all the castle's light and air. In the vaulted halls on the ground floor there's a **Musée de l'Olivier**, where among the presses you may find a small machine for pressing coins, not olives, used by the Marquis to counterfeit the king's coin (he was arrested in 1710, by the Comte d'Artagnan of the Musketeers). Upstairs are Henri Grimaldi's ornate reception rooms, topped by *The Fall of Phaeton* (1624) by the Genoese Giovanni Andrea Carlone, one of those hysterical *trompe-l'œil* ceiling paintings of floating horse stomachs and testicles that the Italians were so fond of. In another room, the **Donation Suzy Solidor** contains 40 paintings donated by the free-living chanteuse and cabaret star, each a portrait of herself, each by a different artist—Van Dongen, Dufy, Kisling, Friesz, Cocteau, and so on. On the next floor, the **Musée d'Art Moderne Méditerranéen** is dedicated to the above and other painters who have worked on the coast.

Villeneuve-Loubet and Escoffier

To the southwest of Cagnes, on another hill dominated by another medieval castle, Villeneuve-Loubet is a small village known for its fishing, a visit by François Ier (where he signed a ten-year peace treaty with Charles V in 1538) and Marshal Pétain, hero of the First World War, who was working as a farmer and wine grower before accepting the summons to govern France from Vichy. The event that really put it on the map, however, happened in 1846, when Auguste Escoffier came into the world here to become 'the chef of kings and the king of chefs'—the king in question being Edward VII, who encouraged Escoffier and the hotelier César Ritz to move to London, thus making the Savoy and the Carlton citadels of class and cuisine. Escoffier's birthplace is now the **Musée de l'Art Culinaire**, 3 Rue A. Escoffier, © 04 93 20 80 51 (*open 2–6, closed Mon, holidays, and Nov*), but don't come looking for nibbles or scratch-and-sniff exhibits of his creations. Instead there's a 19th-century Provençal kitchen; an autographed photo of soprano Nellie Melba, thanking Escoffier for calling his new peach dessert after her; a collection of the chef's radical light menus which seem incredibly elaborate nowadays; and the sugar sculptures Escoffier loved, still prepared by local *pâtissiers* for saccharine competitions that put the kitsch back in kitchen. There's also a **Musée Militaire**, Place de Verdun, © 04 93 22 01 56 (*open 10–12 and 2–5, closed Mon and holidays*).

Villeneuve-Loubet-Plage is another kettle of fish, home of those concrete ziggurats you may have already noticed, looming over the Bay of Angels with all the charm of totalitarian Mesopotamia. They are part of the **Marina Baie des Anges** built in the 1970s, before the French regulated building on the coast—too late indeed for the once beautiful stretch between here and Cannes.

Cagnes ✉ *06800*   ***Where to Stay and Eating Out***

Haut-de-Cagnes

The luxury choice for this niche of the coast is Haut-de-Cagnes's ★★★**Le Cagnard**, Rue Pontis-Long, © 04 93 20 73 21, ✆ 04 93 22 06 39 (*menus*

begin at 300F), with sumptuous comforts discreetly arranged to fit in with the 12th-century architecture. Nearly every room has a private terrace, but the largest and most magical belongs to the hotel's excellent restaurant, serving delicacies such as pigeon stuffed with morels and foie gras. *Open all year.* You can dine for less at **Les Peintres**, 71 Montée de la Bourgade, ✆ 04 93 20 83 08 (*menus 190 and 310F*), where the walls are covered with paintings and the tables with warm homemade bread and Provençal dishes. *Closed mid-Nov–mid-Dec, Wed.*

Cagnes-sur-Mer

None of the restaurants here stands out, but the 40 different kinds of fresh chocolates do at **L'Oiseau d'Or**, 2 Place Général-de-Gaulle, ✆ 04 93 20 80 54, including *grimaldines*, flavoured with fresh orange juice.

St-Paul-de-Vence and Vence

Inland from Cagnes are two towns as bound up with contemporary art as any in the whole of France. St-Paul-de-Vence is the home of the wonderful Fondation Maeght, while Vence has a unique chapel painted by Matisse. D.H. Lawrence and Marc Chagall died in Vence, a pleasant enough old town where real people still live amongst the writers, artists, and perfectly tanned Martians with their faces lifted, stretched, and moulded into tautly permanent frowns.

Getting There

There are frequent **buses** from Cagnes-sur-Mer to La Colle-sur-Loup, St-Paul-de-Vence and Vence, and connections nearly every hour from Nice. La Gaude can be reached by bus from St-Jeannet and Cagnes-sur-Mer (but not from Vence); Tourrettes-sur-Loup and Le Bar-sur-Loup are on the Vence–Grasse bus route.

Tourist Information

St-Paul-de-Vence ✉ 06570: 2 Rue Grande, ✆ 04 93 32 86 95, ✇ 04 93 32 60 27.
Vence ✉ 06140: Place du Grand Jardin, ✆ 04 93 58 06 38, ✇ 04 93 58 91 81.

market days

Vence: every morning: fruit, vegetables and flowers, Place Surian, Place du Grand Jardin and Place Clemenceau, Tuesday and Friday: clothes, Place Clemenceau; Wednesday: fleamarket, Place Clemenceau; Saturday (*all day*): arts and crafts, Place Clemenceau.

St-Paul-de-Vence

Between Cagnes and St-Paul the D6 winds above the river Loup, passing through **La Colle-sur-Loup**, a village once famous for its roses, that now earns its keep from the overspill of tourists from St-Paul-de-Vence, its mother town. For La Colle was founded in 1540, when François Ier showed his gratitude to St-Paul-de-Vence for standing up to the assaults of his arch-rival, Emperor Charles V, by financing a rampart around the town. Some 700 houses had to be demolished to make room for the king's gift, obliging the displaced populace to move elsewhere.

Reduced in size, **St-Paul-de-Vence** became a '*ville fortifiée*' and still preserves a *donjon* watchtower dating from the 12th century, as well as François's costly ramparts. A cannon captured from Charles V is embedded near the town gate, a gate much more accessible these days than the simple wooden door of the restaurant **La Colombe d'Or**, down in the square. Its first owner, an unschooled farmer named Paul Roux, fell in love with modern art and for 40 years accepted paintings in exchange for hospitality from the impoverished artists who flocked here after the First World War—including Picasso, Derain, Matisse, Braque, Vlaminck, Léger, Dufy, and Bonnard. By the time he died he had accumulated one of France's greatest private collections but strictly for viewing by those who can at least afford a meal.

If you're prone to claustrophobia, visit St-Paul early, before its little lanes are clogged with visitors and baskets of artsy trinkets. From its ramparts, to the north, you can see the odd, sphinx-shaped rock called the **Baou de St-Jeannet**, that was painted into the uncanny landscape of Nicolas Poussin's *Polyphème*. There's a handsome fountain along Rue Grande, and the church of the **Conversion de St-Paul**, sumptuously furnished with Baroque stuccoes, woodwork and paintings.

Fondation Maeght

> *Here is an attempt at something never before undertaken: creating a world with which modern art can both find its place and that other-worldliness which used to be called supernatural.*

> Speech by André Malraux at the inauguration of the Fondation, 1964

Set back in the woods up on Route Passe-Prest, the **Fondation Maeght**, ✆ 04 93 32 81 63, @ 04 93 32 53 22 (*open daily July–Sept 10–7; Oct–June 10–12.30 and 2.30–6; adm*) is the best reason of all for visiting St-Paul. Its fairy godparents, Aimé and Marguerite Maeght, were art dealers and friends of Matisse and Bonnard who decided, in the early 1960s, to create an ideal environment for contemporary art, and for its creators. They hired Catalan architect José-Luis Sert, a pupil of Le Corbusier and good buddy of Joan Miró, to design the setting—'building' seems too confining a term for these walls that are 'a play between the rhythms of the interior and exterior spaces', as Sert himself described them. The various levels of the building follow the changes in ground level; the white 'sails' on top collect rainwater for the fountains; 'light traps' in the roof are designed to distribute natural light evenly, although the quality of light varies from room to room.

The permanent collection, which includes nearly every major artist of the past 50 years, is removed during the Foundation's frequent exhibitions of young artists and retrospectives of established ones. But you'll always see the works incorporated into the walls, windows and gardens—Miró's *Labyrinth*, a garden path lined with delightful sculptures and a ceramic half-submerged Egg; a wet and wobbling tubular fountain by Pol Bury, a mobile by Calder, mosaics by Chagall, Tal-Coat, Braque and Ubac, Léger's *Flowers, Birds and Bench*, and Giacometti's stick-figured cat and elongated people, reminiscent of Etruscan bronzes at their quirkiest. The Foundation also has a cinema and a studio for making films, art workshops, and one of the world's most extensive art libraries.

St-Paul-de-Vence ✉ *06570*　　　　　**Where to Stay and Eating Out**

To stay in St-Paul-de-Vence, have buckets of money and book months in advance in the summer, especially to sleep among the 20th-century art in ★★★**La Colombe d'Or**, Place des Ormeaux, ✆ 04 93 32 80 02, @ 04 93 32 77 78 (*à la carte only, around 400F*). The rooms are full of character, the pool is heated, the terrace lovely. The restaurant, where Yves Montand and Simone Signoret celebrated their wedding, and Arnold Schwarzenegger hosted his 1993 Cannes Film Festival bash, is more a feast for the eyes than for the stomach, but you won't go wrong with its traditional groaning platters of hors-d'œuvres and grilled meats. *Closed Nov–mid Dec.* In the centre, in the 16th-century ★★★★**Le St Paul**, 86 Rue Grande, ✆ 04 93 32 65 25, ✆ 04 93 32 52 94, the interior designers let their hair down to create unusual but delightful juxtapositions of medieval, surreal, Egyptian and Art Deco elements. Its equally attractive restaurant has a summer terrace. The more moderately priced ★★★**Le Hameau**, 528 Rte de La Colle, ✆ 04 93 32 80 24, ✆ 04 93 32 55 75, has lovely views over the orange groves and a swimming pool (no restaurant). *Closed mid-Nov–21 Dec and 7 Jan–mid-Feb.* Cheapest of all is ★★**Les Remparts**, 72 Rue Grande, ✆/✆ 04 93 32 09 88 (*menus from 280–480F*): pleasant rooms with baths, and a good affordable restaurant with a superb terrace. With its own *boules* court, large covered terrace and grand Parisian-style mirrored interior, **Café de la Place**, ✆ 04 93 32 80 19, is a good lunch or coffee stop. A couple of minutes by car from St-Paul, **Le Ste Claire**, Espace Ste Claire, ✆ 04 93 32 02 02, ✆ 04 93 32 01 32, is traditional but not dull.

Vence

I live among rocks, which happy fate
Has sprinkled liberally with roses and with jasmine,
Trees carpet them from foothill to summit,
Rich orange groves blossom in the plains;
The emerald in their leaves reveals its hue,
On the fruit shines gold, and silver on the flower.

Antoine Godeau, on Vence

Sister city of Ouahigouya in Burkina Faso, Vence lies 3km from St-Paul and 10km from the coast, sufficiently far to seem more like a town in Provence than a Riviera fleshpot. Roman *Vintium*, it kept up its regional prestige in the Middle Ages as the seat of a bishopric (albeit the smallest in France) with a series of remarkable bishops. Two are now Vence's patron saints: Véran (449–481), an alumnus of the seminary of St-Honorat near Cannes, and Lambert (1114–54). Lambert had to confront the claims of the new baron of Vence, Romée de Villeneuve, knighted by Raymond Bérenger V of Provence after Romée arranged for Bérenger's daughters the four most strategic marriages of all time—to the kings of England, France (St Louis) and Naples, and the German emperor. Although Romée earned a mention in Dante's *Paradiso* (an apocryphal story telling how he began and ended his career as an impoverished pilgrim), as baron he set a precedent of quarrelling with the bishop of Vence that lasted until the Revolution abolished both titles. Alessandro Farnese was head of Vence's see from 1508 to 1511—one of the 16 absentee bishoprics he accumulated thanks to his beautiful sister Giulia, the mistress of Pope Alexander IV, who slept with enough cardinals to get her brother elected Paul III. But best-loved of Vence's bishops was Antoine Godeau (1639–72), a dwarf famed for his ugliness, a gallant poet and 'the wittiest man in France'. Appointed the first member of the Académie Française by Cardinal Richelieu, Godeau tired of it all by the time he was 30, took holy orders and devoted himself to reforming his see—rebuilding the cathedral, and founding tanneries and scent industries.

Although a fair amount of villa sprawl extends on all sides, the **Vieille Ville** has kept most of its medieval integrity. Enter the walls by way of the west gate, the fortified **Porte du Peyra**: the **Place du Peyra**, just inside, was the Roman forum and is still the site of the daily market. Roman tombstones are incorporated in the walls of the **Ancienne Cathédrale**, a rococo church full of little treasures—the pre-Christian sarcophagus of St Véran; the tomb of Bishop Godeau; Merovingian and Romanesque fragments of stones and birds, especially in the chapel under the belfry; a spluttery mosaic by Chagall; reliquaries donated by Alessandro Farnese; and, best of all, the stalls with lace-fine carvings satirizing Renaissance customs and mores, sculpted by Jacques Bellot in the 1450s. Also in and around the Vieille Ville is the **Centre d'Art VAAS**, 14 Traverse des Moulins, ☎ 04 93 58 29 42, ⊕ 04 93 58 30 83 (*closed Tues and Sat*), which boasts an art school, sculpture garden, and *boutique* or shop.

West, outside the walls, **Place du Frêne** is named in honour of a majestic ash tree planted here in 1538 to commemorate visits by François Ier and Pope Paul III; the 17th-century château built here by Vence's plucky barons is now used for exhibitions. Vence's **Saturday market** spills beyond the confines of the city, and all that's home grown, crafted or made is exhibited with worthy pride. Trawl the stalls and you may well find something way above the ordinary (Olivier de Celle hunts out his woods with the passion of a truffle-hunter, and carves them into fruits so beautiful they're hard not to touch). You'll be hurried by the crowds and the sweet stench of bakeries browning new wares, and pancakes hissing and crisping from trollies on the corners.

Matisse's Chapelle du Rosaire

From Vence, follow Ave des Poilus to the route for St-Jeannet/La Gaude, or take the mini-train in summer from the main square, 30F. Open Tues and Thurs 10–11.30am and 2.30–5.30, and Wed, Fri, Sat 2.30–5.30 during school holidays. Adm.

Matisse arrived in Vence in 1941 to escape the bombing along the coast, and fell seriously ill. The 'White' Dominican sisters nursed him back to health, and as a gift he built and decorated the simple **Chapelle du Rosaire** for them. Matisse worked on the project well into his 80s, from 1946 to 1951, using long bamboo poles to hold his brushes when he was forced to keep to his bed, designing every aspect of the chapel, down to the priest's robes. He considered the result his masterpiece, an expression of the 'nearly religious feeling I have for life', the fruit 'of a life consecrated to the search for truth'.

Probably the most extraordinary thing about these decorations by the most sensual of Fauves is their lack of colour, except in the geometrically patterned stained glass windows that occupy two walls and which give the interior an uncanny glow. The other walls are of white faïence, on which Matisse drew black line drawings of St Dominic holding a Bible, and the Virgin and Child, the Crucifixion and the fourteen Stations of the Cross. None of the figures has a face, but they're powerfully drawn and compelling in their simplicity.

Vence ✉ *06140*   ***Where to Stay and Eating Out***

Vence has more choice and lower prices than St-Paul—unless you check into the opulentissimo ★★★★**Château St-Martin**, 3km from Vence on Rte de Coursegoules (Ave des Templiers), ☎ 04 93 58 02 02, ⊕ 04 93 24 08 91 (*lunch menu 400F*), a set of villa-*bastides* built around a ruined Templar fortress. The 12-hectare park has facilities for riding, fishing, tennis and a heart-shaped pool installed at the request of Harry Truman, who never had such luxuries back in Independence, Missouri. The restaurant is equally august, with prices to match. *Closed mid-Oct–mid-April.* ****Relais Cantemerle**, 258 Chemin Cantemerle, ✆ 04 93 58 08 18, ✆ 04 93 58 32 79 (*menu 210F*), is decorated with Art Deco bits and pieces from the gutted Palais de la Méditerranée in Nice. Set in its piney garden, with terraces and a pool, the Cantemerle's restaurant serves some of the finest food in Vence (try the *St Pierre à la fondue de poivrons et tomates*). *Closed Oct–Easter.*

** **Diana**, Ave des Poilus, ✆ 04 93 58 28 56, ✆ 04 93 24 64 06, is right in the historic centre of Vence and has single and double rooms, some with kitchenettes. **La Roseraie**, 14 Ave H.-Giraud, ✆ 04 93 58 02 20, ✆ 04 93 58 99 31, offers a garden of magnolias and cedars, with an enormous home-made breakfast, by an impeccable pool. Sadly there's no longer a restaurant, but the owner's passion has been channelled into antiques, Salernes tiles a-plenty, and lovely ironwork. Beware the two top-most rooms which are noisy and cramped.

Hidden away in the centre of Vence, the charming yet unpretentious *Closerie des Genêts**, 4 Impasse Marcellin-Maurel, ✆ 04 93 58 33 25 (*rooms 180–280F*), has quiet rooms, a garden and a decent restaurant. For gastronomy, you won't go wrong or hungry at **Auberge des Templiers**, 39 Ave Joffre, ✆ 04 93 58 06 05 (*menus 120–250F*), which although not innovative, is just elegant and traditional French— lamb, foie gras and fish. *Closed Mon.* More Provençal regional cuisine and good fresh fish can be found at **La Farigoule**, 15 Ave Henri-Isnard, ✆ 04 93 58 01 27 (*menus 130–160F*). *Closed Tues, Wed lunch, 9–30 Nov.* In the Vieille Ville, the quaint **Le Pigeonnier**, Place du Peyra, ✆ 04 93 58 03 00, makes its own pasta and ravioli, as well as fish. *Closed Sat lunch and Mon, and Dec–Mar.* **Le Pêcheur du Soleil**, on Place Godeau (behind the church), is fine, as long as you won't be dazzled by the choice of 500 different pizza toppings. But at the unprepossessing-looking **Crêperie Royale**, 14 Rue Isnard, over the warm breath of strong spirit you will be served—a rarity in France—real tea, made and brewed with sweet leaves from a tin. Don't be tempted by the plaque on the door of **La Vieille Douve**, 10 Ave Henri-Isnard, ✆ 04 93 58 10 02, as 'douve' means ditch.

Excursions around Vence, and the Gorges du Loup

Vence makes an excellent base for exploring the countryside, especially if you have your own car—otherwise the only connections are the once- or twice-daily buses from Nice to St-Jeannet and Gattières.

Ten km beyond the Chapelle du Rosaire, the wine-making village of **St-Jeannet** balances on a terrace beneath the distinctive *Baou*, a sheer 400m rock that dominates the surrounding countryside. A two-hour path from the Auberge de St-Jeannet leads to the summit, with views stretching to the Alps. A narrow road continues south to the *village perché* of **La Gaude**, unspoiled despite the giant Y-shaped IBM research centre along the way. Alternatively, continuing northeast on D2210, are three other *villages perchés* that have yet to sell their souls to Mammon: **Gattières**, **Carros** on a 300m rock over the Var crowned by a 13th-century château, and **Le Broc**, 4km up the Var on D2209, with a Canavesio in its church. Another excursion from Vence takes you through the austerely beautiful **Clues de Haute Provence** by way of the **Col de Vence**, 975m up and affording an incomparable, breathtaking view of the coast from Cap Ferrat to the Esterel (take D2 north).

The most popular excursion of all is to loop-the-Loup, so to speak, around the upper valley of the Loup river, starting on D2210. On the way you can call at the **Château Notre-Dame des Fleurs**, 2.5km from Vence on Route de Grasse, ✆ 04 93 24 52 00 (*open daily 11–7 except Sun/Mon; adm*), a 19th-century castle built over the ruins of an 11th-century Benedictine abbey, which used to be home to the deliciously named Musée du Parfum et de la Liqueur, but it is now sadly yet another contemporary art gallery.

Some essential oils, especially of violets, originate in **Tourrettes-sur-Loup**, 2.5km further on. Its medieval core of rosy golden stone has often been compared to an Algerian town, the houses knitted together so that their backs form a wall defended by the three small towers that give the village its name. Tourrettes grows more violets than any town in France, and in March all the façades are covered with bouquets for the *Fête des Violettes*. But in the summer Tourrettes turns into a veritable *souk*, where you can purchase handmade fabrics, jewellery, marionnettes, ceramics, household items and more. The village **church** has a triptych by the school of Ludovico Brea and a Gallo-Roman altar dedicated to Mercury, while the **Chapelle St-Jean**, at the village entrance, has naïve frescoes mixing biblical tales with local life, painted by Ralph Souplaut in 1959.

Before heading into the Gorges du Loup, take a short detour south at **Pont-du-Loup** to **Le Bar-sur-Loup**, scented by its plantations of oranges, jasmine, roses and violets. The village surrounds the château of the lords of Bar, a branch office of the counts of Grasse (one of whom grew up here to become the Admiral de Grasse, who chased the British out of Chesapeake Bay, so Washington could blockade Yorktown and win the American War of Independence). Legend has it that one of his 15th-century ancestors held a wild party here in the middle of Lent, during which the guests all dropped dead. Mortified, the lord commissioned an itinerant artist from Nice to commemorate the event by painting a curious little *Danse Macabre*, now in the tribune of the church of **St-Jacques**: the elegant nobility dance to a drum, unaware that tiny demons of doom echo the dance on their heads. Death, grinning, mows them down, while busy devils extract their souls in the form of newborn babies and pop them into the mouth of Hell. The church also has a retable by Ludovico Brea and, on the door, beautiful Gothic/Renaissance panels representing St Jacques, carved by Jacques Bellot of Vence. Not to be missed in **Pont du Loup** is the **Confiserie Florian**, ✆ 04 93 59 32 91 (*open every day 9–12pm and 2–6pm*), where jams, jellied fruits, crystallized flowers, chocolates and sweets are made before your eyes, by men in white hats and blue aprons. The factory's quaint and full of antique kitchen furniture, but best is the free tasting at the end of each tour.

North of Pont-du-Loup, D6 leads into the steep, fantastical cliffs of the **Gorges du Loup**, cooled by waterfalls—one next to the road falls a sheer 45m—and is pocked by giant *marmites*, or glacial potholes. The largest of these is up at **Saut-du-Loup**, and in spring the river broils through it like a witch's cauldron. At Pont de Bramafan you can cross the gorge and head back south. Looming ahead is **Gourdon**, 'the Saracen', a brooding eagle's nest converted into yet another rural shopping-mall of crafts and goodies. Its massive rectangular **château** was built in the 1200s over the Saracen citadel, and heavily restored in 1610. Inside are a pair of museums (✆ 04 93 09 68 02; *open 11–1 and 2–7 summer, 2–6 only in winter, closed Tues in winter, adm*): the **Musée Historique** with antique arms and armour, the odd torture instrument in the dungeon, a Rembrandt self-portrait, and Marie-Antoinette's writing-desk, while upstairs, a **Musée de Peinture Naïve** features a small portrait by the Douanier Rousseau and works by his French and Yugoslav followers. The panoramic three-tiered castle gardens were laid out by Le Nôtre, although now most of the plants are alpine. You can take a spectacular two-hour walk on the **Sentier du Paradis** from Gourdon to Pont-du-Loup, or sneak a preview of lunar travel by driving up the D12 (or walk along the GR4 from Grasse) on to the desolate **Plateau de Caussols**, boasting the driest, clearest air in France—hence an important observatory. French film directors often use it for Western or desert scenes, the very kind used these days for selling French cars and blue jeans.

Where to Stay and Eating Out

Tourrettes-sur-Loup ✉ 06140

★★Auberge des Belles Terrasses, Rte de Vence, ✆ 04 93 59 30 03, 📠 04 93 24 19 86 (*menus 92F and 140F*), has basic but pleasant rooms with views from its terraces and a good little restaurant. For comfortable, clean rooms and a view of orange trees and distant sea, head for **★★La Grive Dorée**, 11 Route de Grasse, ✆ 04 93 59 30 05 (*menus 98F, 130 and 175F*). Its simple restaurant offers *coq au vin* and *médaillon de lotte aux légumes*.

Le Bar-sur-Loup ✉ 06140

Stop for lunch with local shopkeepers and *gendarmes* at **L'Amiral**, 8 Place Francis-Paulet, ✆ 04 93 09 44 00 (*menus at 98 and 150F*), in an impressive 18th-century house that belonged to Admiral de Grasse. The dishes on the menu change daily, and are always spot on for freshness and value. Be sure to reserve for dinner in the summer. *Closed Wed.*

Back towards the Coast: Biot

Between Cagnes and Cannes, the *résidences secondaires* battle for space with huge commercial greenhouses and fields of flowers destined for the scent distilleries of Grasse, a paroxysm of fragrance and colour powerful enough to make a sensitive soul swoon. Set in a couple of miles from the sea, Biot (rhymes with yacht) is a handsome village endowed with first-rate clay—in Roman times it specialized in wine and oil jars large enough to contain Ali Baba's forty thieves. In 1955, Fernand Léger purchased some land here in order to construct a sculpture garden of monumental ceramics—then died 15 days later. In 1960 his widow used the land to build a superb museum and garden to display the works he left her in his will. Come late in the day if you want to see more of Biot and less of the human race.

Getting There

Biot's train station is down by the sea at La Brague, and you will have a steep 5km walk from here up to the village. Buses approximately every hour from Antibes stop at the station en route to Biot.

Tourist Information

6 Place de la Chapelle, ✆ 04 93 65 05 85, 📠 04 93 65 70 96.

To the right of the entrance to Biot, the **Musée National Fernand Léger** (at Chemin du Val de Pome, ☎ 04 92 91 50 30; *open July–Oct 11–6; Nov–Mar 10–12.30 and 2–5.30; April–June 10–12.30 and 2–6, closed Tues; adm;* ☎ *04 92 91 50 30; guided tours by appointment*) is hard to mistake behind its giant, sporty ceramic-mosaic designed for the Olympic stadium of Hannover. Opened in 1960, the museum was enlarged in 1989 to provide more space for the 348 paintings, tapestries, mosaics and ceramics that trace Léger's career from his first flirtations with Cubism back in 1909—although even back then Léger was nicknamed the 'tubist' for his preference for fat noodly forms. After being gassed in the First World War, he recovered to flirt with the Purist movement founded by his buddies Le Corbusier and Amédée Ozenfant around 1918, a reaction to the 'decorative' tendencies of Cubism. Purism was to be the cool, dispassionate art of the machine age, emotionally limited to a 'mathematical lyricism', and Léger's scenes of soldiers and machines fitted the bill. After teaching at Yale during the Second World War, he returned to France with a keen interest in creating art for the working classes, using his trademark style of brightly coloured geometric forms to depict workers, factories, and their pastimes. The new wing of the museum contains Léger's ceramics, mosaics and other works—most notably the tapestres called *La Création* (1922) and *Liberté*, the latter illustrating the eponymous poem by his friend Paul Eluard.

The presence of the museum has boosted the local ceramic and glass industry; across from the museum at **La Verrerie de Biot**, Chemin des Combes, ☎ 04 93 65 03 00, you can watch workers make glass suffused with tiny bubbles (*verre à bulles*). Tiny workshops dotted around the big Verrerie, below the town walls, all sell bubbly glassware more cheaply than the museum shop. More ceramics and glass can be seen in the charming tiny **Musée d'Histoire et de Céramique Biotoises** in the walled town, ☎ 04 93 65 54 54 (*open Wed–Sun, 10–6; adm*); most of the pieces, and 400 photographs, were donated by villagers. The town itself, and the roads leading down to the station, are crammed with art and pottery galleries, and workshops of individual artists, of widely varying quality.

Guarded by 16th-century gates, Biot itself has retained much of its character, especially around central **Place des Arcades**. A hundred years ago, the accents in this charming square would be Genoese—Biot's original population was decimated by the Black Death, and the village was only resettled in 1460, when the Bishop of Grasse invited in 50 families from Genoa. The church they built among the arcades has two excellent 15th-century altarpieces: the red and gold *Retable du Rosaire* by Ludovico Brea and the recently restored *Christ aux Plaies* by Giovanni Canavesio, who was married to a Biotoise.

With his bright colours and often playful forms, Léger is one artist children usually like. Afterwards you can take them to **La Brague** by the sea, to watch the performing dolphins and whales at **Marineland**, the oldest of its kind in Europe (*open daily from 10am, performances from 10.30am, with nocturnal performances at 9.30pm in July and Aug; adm*). Next door to it at **Aquasplash**, you can play otter yourself on the slides (*open daily in summer, 10–7,* ☎ *04 93 33 49 49 for both attractions*), or watch the silent pretty creatures at **La Jungle des Papillons**, a live butterfly zoo, ☎ 04 93 33 55 77 (*open all year, 10–5*).

Biot ✉ *06410*   **Where to Stay and Eating Out**

There aren't many choices in Biot, but in the medieval centre, ★**Arcades**, 16 Place des Arcades, ☎ 04 93 65 01 04, ✆ 04 93 65 01 05 (*280F plus*), is a delightful old hotel in a 15th-century building, furnished with antiques. The amiable restaurant below does a genuine *soupe au pistou* and other Provençal favourites. *Closed Sun eve, Mon.* For a special feast, reserve a table at least a week in advance at ★★**Auberge du Jarrier**, Passage de la Bourgade, ✆ 04 93 65 11 68, in an old jar-works, with a magical terrace, friendly service and a superb four-course seasonal 300F Provençal menu that puts the Côte's *haute cuisine* budget-busters to shame. *Closed Mon eve, Tues.* For a quick lunch, **3615 Code Café**, 44bis Impasse St-Sébastien, ✆ 04 93 65 61 61, has a large sunny garden at the back, with a 55F cold buffet.

Antibes, Juan-les-Pins and Vallauris

Set on the largest of the Côte's peninsulas, Antibes started out as the Greek trading colony of *Antipolis*, 'the city opposite' Nice. But these days it's also the antithesis of the Nice of retired folks soaking up the rays: Antibes belongs to the young, who scoot, bike and skate like their counterparts in California to *collège* and *lycée*, and the aspiring young who frequent the mega-white boats that measure over a hundred yards long, moored shoulder-to-shoulder, vying to see which has the most high-tech communications systems or the most advanced surface-to-air missile launcher. Here the *de rigueur* Riviera poodle has been supplanted by the terrier, labrador and spaniel, or the even more exotic breeds kept by the chi-chi employees at Sophia-Antipolis. On the other side of luxurious Cap d'Antibes are the sandy beaches of Juan-les-Pins, where you can swing all night, especially to the tunes of the Riviera's top jazz festival. Inland from here is Vallauris, another ceramics village, this one synonymous with Picasso.

Getting Around

Antibes' **train station**, is near the edge of town, along the Ave Robert-Soleau towards Nice at Place P. Semard, ✆ 04 93 99 50 50, and has frequent trains to Nice and Cannes. **Buses** (✆ 04 93 34 37 60) for Cannes, Nice, Nice airport, Cagnes-sur-Mer, and Juan-les-Pins depart from Place de Gaulle; others leave from Rue de la République. From Golfe-Juan buses leave every 20 mins for Antibes.

Tourist Information

Antibes ✉ 06600: 11 Place de Gaulle, ✆ 04 92 90 53 00, ✆ 04 92 90 53 01.

Juan-les-Pins ✉ 06160: 51 Blvd Guillaumont, ✆ 04 92 90 53 05, ✆ 04 92 90 53 01 (*write to them to book tickets for the jazz festival*).

Golfe-Juan ✉ 06220: 84 Ave de la Liberté, ✆ 04 93 63 73 12.

Vallauris ✉ 06220: Square du 8 Mai 1945, ✆ 04 93 63 82 58, ✆ 04 93 63 95 01 (*open all year*).

market days

Antibes: Cours Masséna: fruit and veg, flowers, rolls of fabric, wicker-work a-plenty (*6am–1pm sharp, every day July–Aug, otherwise daily except Mon*); Place Nationale: fleamarket, other people's bits and pieces (*Thursdays, and Saturdays, 7am–6pm*); Place du Tribunal: clothes market (*Tuesdays/Saturdays*), and Parking de la Poste : clothes market (*Saturday am*).

Antibes and the Musée Picasso

Now all the gay decorative people have left, taking with them the sense
of carnival and impending disaster that colored this summer...

Zelda Fitzgerald, 1925

Antibes has been a quieter place since the Fitzgeralds and their self-destructive high jinks set a precedent no alcoholic writer or artist has been able to match. The frolicking now takes place over at Juan-les-Pins, which took off as a resort shortly after F. Scott and Zelda's holiday, leaving Antibes to tend its rose nurseries. After the war, when developers cast an eye over to Antibes, there were enough building restrictions intact to keep out most of the concrete. Even so, inlanders regard the town with a jaundiced eye: instead of 'go to hell' they say *'Vai-t'en-à-n-Antibo!'*

A relic of Antibes' earlier incarnation as France's bulwark against Savoyard Nice are its seawalls, especially the massive 16th-century **Le Fort Carré**. Though it's recently been bought by the town of Antibes, it is not possible to visit. It provides a decorative backdrop for Antibes' pleasure port, big enough to moor even the 285ft behemoths of the ridiculously rich. The handsome 17th- and 18th-century houses of Vieil Antibes look over their neighbours' shoulders towards the sea, obscuring it from **Cours Masséna**, the main street of Greek Antipolis. Here the morning **market** sells a cornucopia of local produce, from *fromage de chèvre aux olives* to a profusion of cut flowers that leave the paintings in Antibes' galleries pale by comparison. From the Cours, Rue Sade leads back to café-filled Place Nationale and the **Musée Peynet**, ℗ 04 92 90 54 32 (*open daily 10–12 and 2–6, closed Mon and hols*), offering a queasy journey back to the 1960s paved with the love postcards drawn by Raymond Peynet, the father of the genre.

Back towards the sea, Tour Gilli houses the **Musée de la Tour**, ℗ 04 93 34 50 91, devoted to the costumes, furniture, household items and tools of Antibes' fisher-folk of yore (*open only Wed, Thurs and Sat afternoons*). The best sea views are monopolized by the **Château Grimaldi**—a seaside castle built by the same family who ran most of this coast at one time or another, and who had possession of Antibes from 1385 to 1608. It became a history museum in the 1920s, and for six months in 1946, the owner, Romuald Dor, let Picasso use the second floor as a studio. Picasso, glad to have space to work in, even if it was cold and damp, quickly filled it up in a few months, only later discovering to his annoyance that all along Dor had intended to make his efforts into the **Musée Picasso**, ℗ 04 92 90 54 20 (*open summer 10–6, winter 10–12 and 2–6, closed Mon and hols; adm*). As it is, and despite a post-war lack of canvases and oil paint (he used mostly fibro-cement and boat paint), you can't help but get the feeling that Picasso was exuberantly happy, inspired by the end of the war, his love of the time, Françoise Gillot, and the mythological roots of the Mediterranean, expressed in *La Joie de Vivre, Ulysse et ses Sirènes* and 220 other paintings, drawings and ceramics. Among the other artists represented, note the eight striking works that Nicolas de Staël painted in Antibes shortly before he committed suicide (or merely fell out of the upstairs window) in 1955. Outside, the garden is crammed with sculptures, while below, a speedboat crosses the sea like a slow rip in a blue canvas.

Just across the street is the **Church of the Immaculate Conception**, where a leaflet in your chosen language entreats you to 'Listen...listen to the silent echo of prayers down the ages...' but you'll have to listen hard for silence over the Almighty Muzak. Built over a Greek temple, it's a hotchpotch of art and idols, gawpers, hawkers, and rows of burning candles, dedicated to

St Sebastian and St Roch. Further south, at the end of Promenade Amiral-de-Grasse, the Vauban-built Bastion St-André houses the **Musée d'Histoire et d'Archéologie**, ℰ 04 92 90 54 35 (*open Tues–Sun 10–12 and 2–6; closed Mon*), where Greek and Etruscan amphorae, monies and jewels dredged up from the sea and soil trace the history of Antibes.

Cap d'Antibes

Further south along the peninsula (follow the scenic coastal D2559) the beautiful, free, sandy beach of **La Salis** marks the beginning of Cap d'Antibes, scented with roses, jasmine and the smell of money—there's more concentrated here than almost anywhere else in France. Jules Verne was among the first to retreat here, where he found the inspiration for *Twenty Thousand Leagues under the Sea*; nowadays, to maintain the kind of solitude and high-tech luxury enjoyed by Captain Nemo aboard the *Nautilus*, the owners of the Cap's villas need James Bond security systems and slavering Dobermanns. At 62 Boulevard du Cap is the lovely **Jardin Thuret**, ℰ 04 93 67 88 00 (*with a villa which can't be visited, but the garden's free, Mon–Fri 8–6, closed weekends and holidays*), laid out in 1866 as an acclimatization station, where the first eucalyptus was transplanted to Europe (the park now contains over 100 varieties).

The **Plateau de la Garoupe** is the highest point of the headland, with a **lighthouse**, a grand view stretching from Bordighera to St-Tropez, and the ancient seamen's **Chapelle de la Garoupe**. Its two naves, one 13th-century and one 16th-century, hold a fascinating collection of ex votos, the oldest one commemorating a surprise attack on Antibes by Saracen pirates. At the tip of the peninsula is **Villa Eilenroc**, ℰ 04 93 67 74 33 (*gardens open Wed pm only, closed school and bank holidays; adm free*), and further west, a 12th-century tower holds the **Musée Naval et Napoléonien**, Ave Kennedy, ℰ 04 93 61 45 32 (*open 9.30–12 and 2.15–6, closed Sat afternoons, Sun*), with ships' models and items relating to Napoleon's connections with Antibes—he left Madame Mère and his sisters here during the siege of Toulon and began 'The Hundred Days' at nearby Golfe-Juan.

The cape is practically synonymous with the **Grand Hotel du Cap**, built in 1870 and one of the very first on the coast to feature an outdoor swimming pool. It played a major role in the creation of the Riviera's summer season, when popular American socialites Gerald and Sara Murphy began to come down here from Paris in 1923, discovering the hitherto unheralded joys of sunbathing on the beach when Antoine Sella, the owner of the Grand Hotel, stayed open in July and August in an attempt to recoup losses from a bad winter season. They had the place to themselves, along with Picasso's family and a Chinese couple. That same summer, top trend-setter Coco Chanel astonished everyone with her suntan. A fad was born. In 1925, Sella created Eden Roc, still rated as the most beautiful place for a swim and a tan on the whole Riviera. The Murphys, famous for holding the very best parties, bought a house on the beach, where they created and lived the carefree but elegant sunny seaside existence that became the essential myth of the Riviera, sharing it with everyone who happened by, including Zelda and Scott Fitzgerald, the latter of whom based his characters Dick and Nicole Diver in *Tender is the Night* on the Murphys.

Juan-les-Pins

When a good idea is in the air, it's not uncommon for different people to pick up on it. In 1924 Edouard Baudoin, a Nice restaurateur, saw a film about Miami Beach and was inspired to recreate it on the Côte. He found his location at Juan-les-Pins amongst the silver sands and pines of the best natural beach on the Riviera, and bought some land and opened a restaurant and a little casino. As it had suddenly become desirable to bake brown on the beach, Baudoin's investment flourished, attracting the attention of the ever-acquisitive Frank Jay Gould, who bought Baudoin out, built roads and injected the essential money and publicity to help Juan-les-Pins really take off. By 1930 it was the most popular and scandal-ridden resort on the Riviera, where women first dared to bathe in skirtless suits. The presence of Edith Piaf and Sidney Bechet boosted its popularity in the 1950s; all the young come here from Antibes and further (the rich and posh go to Nice). It's still going strong, not a beauty but a brash and sassy tart of a resort, with nightclubs and a magnificent jazz festival in the last two weeks of July.

Golfe-Juan

Next up the coast is **Golfe-Juan**, with its pines, sandy beach and pleasure port, famous as the very spot where Napoleon disembarked from Elba on 1 March 1815, proclaiming that 'the eagle with his national colours will fly from bell tower to bell tower all the way to the towers of Notre-Dame'. An obelisk and a column commemorate the landing, which in fact was slightly less than momentous: the locals quickly arrested a few of his men, a cold reception that decided the eagle to sneak along the back roads to Paris. In one of many Napoleonic coincidences, Bonaparte, as he landed, met the Prince of Monaco, who informed him that he was on his way to reclaim his tiny realm after being removed during the Revolution. 'Then, Monsieur, we are in the same business,' Napoleon told him, and each continued on his way, the Prince to his orange groves, Napoleon to Waterloo.

Vallauris

Two km inland from Golfe-Juan, **Vallauris** has two things in common with Biot: it was given an injection of Genoese in the 1400s and was famous for its pottery, in this case useful household wares. Because of competition with aluminium, the industry was on its last legs in 1946 when Picasso rented a small villa in town and met Georges and Suzanne Ramié, owners of the Poterie Madoura. Playing with the clay in their shop, Picasso discovered a new passion, and spent the next few years working with the medium. He gave the Ramiés the exclusive right to sell copies of his ceramics, and you can still buy them at **Madoura**, just off Rue du 19 Mars 1962. Thanks to Picasso, 200 potters now work in Vallauris, some talented, others trying.

In 1951 the village asked Picasso if he would decorate a deconsecrated chapel next to the castle. The result is the famous plywood paintings of *La Guerre et la Paix*, said to have taken Picasso less time to do than if a house-painter had painted the wall. The work was as spontaneous as *Guernica* was planned, and every bit as sincere (it's known as the **Musée National Picasso**, Place de la Libération, © 04 93 64 16 05 (*open 10–12 and 2–6; July and Aug 10–7, closed Tues*). The same ticket admits you to the **Musée Municipal** (*same details*) up in the castle, which used to have many of Picasso's original pieces until art thieves struck in 1989; now to be seen are the winners of the ceramic Biennale and paintings by Italian abstract master Alberto Magnelli. There's more Picasso in Place Paul-Isnard: a rather grumpy bronze man with a sheep.

Sophia-Antipolis

Meanwhile, as all this modern art appreciation and nightclubbing goes on around Antibes, 15,000 international business people are punching away on their new generation computers in 'France's Silicone Valley', the spooky new town complex of Sophia-Antipolis off D103, north of Vallauris, where cars are directed Scalextrix-style around endless bends and roundabouts. Created in 1969 and funded in part by Nice's chamber of commerce, it seems popular with executives: Air France's international reservations network is here, as well as Dow Corning, Toyota and others.

Where to Stay and Eating Out

Antibes ✉ 06600

A short walk from central Antibes is ★★★**Mas Djoliba**, 29 Ave de Provence, ✆ 04 93 34 02 48, 🖷 04 93 34 05 81, a serendipitous *mas* in a small park with a heated pool. You can combine pleasure with thalassotherapy and beauty treatments at ★★★**Thalazur**, 770 Chemin des Moyennes Breguières, ✆ 04 92 91 82 00, with four heated pools, saunas, and a doctor on duty. *Open all year.* ★**L'Auberge Provençale**, 61 Place Nationale, ✆ 04 93 34 13 24, 🖷 04 93 34 89 88, is a cosy house under the plane trees, with Provençal furniture and canopied beds. There are only 7 rooms, so reserve long in advance.

Cap d'Antibes' ★★★★**Hôtel du Cap Eden Roc**, Blvd Kennedy, ✆ 04 93 61 39 01, 🖷 04 93 67 76 04, is still very much there, set in an idyllic park overlooking the Iles de Lérins, where the rest of the world seems very far away. No hotel on the Riviera has hosted more celebrities, film stars or plutocrats; you could easily drop 1000F at the exalted restaurant, the Pavillon Eden Roc. *Closed mid-Oct–April.* A more reasonable choice in Cap d'Antibes is ★★★**La Gardiole**, 74 Chemin de La Garoupe, ✆ 04 93 61 35 03, 🖷 04 93 67 61 87, with large, luminous rooms set in a pine wood and a magnificent wisteria over the terrace. Rooms vary greatly in price; half-board is obligatory in season. *Closed Nov–Feb.* Near the bus station, ★**Le Nouvel Hôtel**, 1 Ave du 24-Août, ✆ 04 93 34 44 07, 🖷 04 93 34 44 08, has twenty rooms which fill up rapidly in summer.

In Roman times, Antibes was famous for its *garum*—a sauce made of salted tuna guts left to dry in the sun. You can eat nearly anything else that was once seaworthy at **De Bacon**, in Cap d'Antibes, on Blvd de Bacon, ✆ 04 93 61 50 02, as stylish and elegant as its perfectly prepared seafood and *bouillabaisse*, at classy prices: lunch menus at 250F. In the same price range, try some of the Côte's finest *nouvelle cuisine* at the renowned **La Bonne Auberge**, on the N7 near La Brague, ✆ 04 93 33 36 65. Chef Jo Rostang's son Philippe has inherited the kitchen, and has already made a name for his *Salade de homard aux ravioles de Romans* and *Millefeuille Bonne Auberge à l'ancienne*; the lunch menu is good value at 195F. More reasonable choices abound in Antibes: **Les Vieux Murs**, ✆ 04 93 34 06 73, on the Promenade Amiral-de-Grasse (near the Picasso museum, looking out over the road to the sea) is cool and spacious, with wooden décor, and serves well-presented traditional food made modern. *Closed Sun eve, Mon.*

For good Provençal favourites there's **Chez Olive**, 2 Blvd Maréchal-Leclerc, ✆ 04 93 34 42 32. *Closed Mon and last 3 weeks in Dec*. Don't be tempted by the aroma of *bruschetta* next to the market on Cours Masséna; it's glorified cheese on toast. Instead, head for the **Comic Strips Café**, 4 Rue James-Close, ✆ 04 93 34 91 40, for crammed-full just-baked baguettes, every sort of salad, and sticky but unpretentious cakes. It's informal and as jolly and bright as the comic library downstairs. *Open 12–10pm summer, 12–8pm winter*. The **Café Sans Rival**, 5 Traverse du 24-Août, ✆ 04 93 34 12 67, not far from the *gare routière* yet off the beaten tourist track, is a tiny wooden-floored shop fitted to the ceiling with coffee beans, teas, herb teas, rice cakes, rye breads, fat sultanas and all things wholesome and *complet*. You can perch outside, drink *real* cappuccino and eat cake. *Open 8.30–7, closed Mon*. **L'Oursin**, 16 Rue de la République, ✆ 04 93 34 13 46 (*menus begin at 99F*), is famous for fresh fish. *Closed Sun eve, Mon*.

Juan-les-Pins ✉ 06160

Juan isn't exactly made for sleeping, but it makes sense to stay if you want to join in the late-night revelry. Unlike Antibes, everything closes tight from November to Easter. There are two grand survivors from the 1920s: the beautiful Art Deco hotel ★★★★**Juana**, not on the sea but in a lovely garden facing the pines on Ave Georges Gallice La Pinède, ✆ 04 93 61 08 70, 🖷 04 93 61 76 60, with a private beach and heated pool. The resort's top restaurant, the luxurious **La Terrasse**, ✆ 04 93 61 20 37 (*lunch menus from 280–640F, or à la carte*), boasts delicate dishes imbued with all the freshness and colour of Provence, and excellent wines to match from the region's best vineyards. The second palace, ★★★★**Belles Rives**, Ave Baudouin, ✆ 04 93 61 02 79, 🖷 04 93 67 43 51 (*menus start at 220F and rise steeply*), offers de luxe rooms, vintage 1930, facing the sea. There's a private beach and jetty, and a good restaurant with a fine view over the gulf, or you can eat on the beach.

More reasonably priced beds may be found at ★★★**Hôtel des Mimosas**, in quiet Rue Pauline, 500m from the sea, ✆ 04 93 61 04 16, 🖷 04 92 93 06 46, where the rooms have balconies overlooking the pool and garden. Or at ★★ **Le Pré Catelan**, set among the palms at 22 Ave des Palmiers, ✆ 04 93 61 05 11, 🖷 04 93 67 83 11, with a private beach only a short walk away.

An excellent array of sea and land dishes fill the menu of **Le Bijou**, directly on the sea on Blvd du Littoral, ✆ 04 93 61 39 07; during the Cannes festival it's a good place to find the stars tucking into a *bouillabaisse* (*300F*). Slightly cheaper is **Le Capitole**, 26 Ave Amiral-Courbet, ✆ 04 93 61 22 44 (*at 60F and 98F; reduced menu price mid-week and all week in summer*), with a charming welcome and generous menus. *Closed Tues*.

Entertainment and Nightlife

There's plenty to entertain, all along the Route de Biot. Be one of the 600,000 who visit **Marineland** each year; it's Europe's largest marine park, with sea-lions, sea-elephants, dolphins, whales, seals and penguins (or *manchots*, which means 'armless' in French) and a great hit with the kids. Get closer to the animals at **La Petite Ferme**, and a chance to wet yourself at **Aquasplash**, complete with a pool with waves. For the timid and the adventurous there's **Mini-Golf** and **Adventure-Golf**. **La Jungle des Papillons** is for butterfly fanciers and **Antibe Land, Luna Park** for whosoever chooses (same number for all: ✆ 04 93 33 49 49). *Open June–Sept*. If you've lost all your money at the gaming or dining tables, then **Parc Exflora** on the N7 at Antibes-les-Pins is a free park full of flora.

Four to five boats a day sail to the **Iles de Lérins** between 9am and 4pm, from Ponton Courbet, Juan-les-Pins (✆ 04 92 93 02 36), or Quai Saint-Pierre, Porte de Golfe-Juan (✆ 04 93 63 45 94) for 60F.

But the best fun to be had is in the **Vieille Ville** (of Antibes), full of *confiseries* and *pâtisseries*; a mêlée of locals, lubbers, sailors and who knows who—a mix reflected in the gamut of polyglot newspapers, even the British grubbies. At **Antibes Books** (formerly Heidi's English Bookshop), 24 Rue Aubernon, ✆ 04 93 34 74 11 (*open daily*), Heidi's one word answer to why-did-you-come-to-the-South-of-France is 'hedonism'; yet she runs the local community centre, and a tiny **theatre** below the bookshop. If you're homesick, baked beans, Marmite, tea and crumpets can be got at the English supermarket in the **Galerie du Pont**.

For cinema there's **Cinéma Casino**, 6–8 Ave du 24-Août, ✆ 04 93 34 04 37 (*adm 45F*), but mostly the nightlife keeps you moving: in Antibes, the famous **La Siesta**, on the road to Nice, ✆ 04 93 33 31 31, which operates as a beach concession by day, with activities for kids, and at night turns into an over-the-top nightclub and casino where thousands of people flock every summer evening to seven dance-floors, fountains, and fiery torches.

The whole of Juan's swinging during the jazz festival. In Juan, '*ça bouge,*' the young say; they move it at **Whisky à Gogo**, La Pinède, ✆ 04 93 61 26 40; older shakers and movers bop at **Voom Voom**, 1 Blvd de la Pinède, ✆ 04 92 93 90 00. If you can't get in, amongst others there's **Le Bureau**, Ave G.-Gallice, ✆ 04 93 67 22 74 (*Thurs–Sun*).

Grasse

It was Catherine de' Medici who introduced artichokes to the French and the scent trade to Grasse. Although it may seem obvious that a town set in the midst of France's natural floral hothouse should be a Mecca for perfume-making, Grasse's most important industry throughout the Middle Ages was tanning imported sheep-skins from the mountains of Provence and buffalo-hides from the town's Italian allies, Genoa and Tuscany. Part of the tanning process made use of the aromatic herbs that grew nearby, especially powdered myrtle which gave the leather a greenish lustre.

In Renaissance Italy, one of the most important status symbols an aristocrat could flaunt was fine, perfumed gloves. When Catherine asked Grasse, Tuscany's old trading partner, to start supplying them, the Grassois left the buffalo hides behind to become *gantiers parfumeurs*. When gloves fell out of fashion after the Revolution they became simply *parfumeurs*, and when Paris co-opted the business in the 1800s, the townspeople concentrated on what has been their speciality ever since—distilling the essences that go into that final costly tiny bottle. And in that, this picturesque but unglamorous hilltown, with approximately 30 *parfumeries*, leads the world, even though most of the flower fields that surrounded Grasse only 40 years ago have now been planted with poxy, boxy villas.

Getting There

There are no trains, but there are frequent buses from Cannes to Grasse; they leave from directly to the left of the railway station. Grasse's *gare routière* (✆ 04 93 36 37 37), is on the north side of town, at the Parking Notre-Dame-des-Fleurs. Leave your car here or in one of the other places just outside the centre: Grasse's steep streets are narrow for motorists.

Tourist Information

Palais des Congrès, ✆ 04 93 36 66 66, ✉ 04 93 36 86 36.

market days

Place aux Aires: daily except Monday; and Place aux Herbes: Wednesday morning fleamarket.

Vieille Ville

Grasse's name may be the same as the French for 'fat', but it comes from *Grâce*—the state in which its original Jewish inhabitants found themselves once they converted to Christianity. In the Middle Ages it was an independent city-state on the Italian model, with close ties to the republics of Genoa and Pisa—a relationship witnessed these days by the austere Italian style of its architecture. During the 13th-century turmoil between the Guelphs and the Ghibellines, the town put itself under the protection of the Count of Provence. Today, a large percentage of the population hails from North Africa: the perfume magnates themselves live in Mougins and surrounding villages.

The one place where they often meet is at the morning food and flower market in arcaded **Place aux Aires** near the top of the town, where the handsome Hôtel Isnard (1781) with its wrought-iron balcony looks as if it escaped from New Orleans. From here Rue des Moulinets and Rue Mougins-Roquefort lead to the Romanesque **Cathédrale Notre-Dame-du-Puy**, its spartan façade similar to churches around Genoa, matched by its spartan nave. The art is to the right: the *Crown of Thorns* and *Crucifixion*, by Rubens at the age of 24, before he hit the big time; a rare religious subject by Fragonard, the *Washing of the Feet*; and, most sincere of all, a triptych by Ludovico Brea. Across the Place du Petit-Puy, a plaque on the **Tour de Guet** (the former *évêché*) commemorates the Grassois poet Bellaud de la Bellaudière, whose songs of wine and women, the *Obras et Rimos Provençalos* (1585), are the high point in Provençal literature between the troubadours and Mistral.

Place du Cours and Four Museums

The Cannes road leads into Grasse's promenade, **Place du Cours**, with pretty views over the countryside. Close by at 23 Blvd Fragonard is the **Musée Jean-Honoré Fragonard**, 23 Blvd Fragonard, ✆ 04 93 40 32 64 (*open daily summer 10–7, winter 10–12 and 2–5; closed Mon, Tues in Oct–May, and all of Nov*), in a 17th-century home belonging to a cousin of Grasse's most famous citizen, Jean-Honoré Fragonard (1732–1806). Son of a *gantier parfumeur*, Fragonard expressed the inherent family sweetness in chocolate-box pastel portraits and mildly erotic rococo scenes of French royals trying their best to look like well-groomed poodles. Some of these are on display, along with copies of *Le Progrès de l'amour dans la cœur d'une jeune fille*, which even his client, Mme du Barry, Louis XV's most beautiful mistress, rejected as too frivolous (the originals are in the Frick Collection in New York). Losing La Barry's favour was the beginning of the end for Fragonard; he lost her, and most of his other clients, to the guillotine and in 1790 he washed up in Grasse feeling very out of sorts, until one very hot day in 1806 he died from a cerebral haemorrhage induced by eating an ice-cream.

Just north of the Cours, at 2 Rue Mirabeau, the **Musée d'Art et d'Histoire de Provence**, ✆ 04 93 36 01 61 (*same hours as Villa Fragonard*), has its home in the 1770 Italianate mansion built by the frisky sister of Count Mirabeau of Aix, who was married to one of several degenerate Marquis who pepper the history of Provence—this one, the Marquis de Cabris, is remembered in Grasse for having covered the walls of the city with obscene graffiti about the local women. Besides Gallo-Roman funerary objects, *santons* and furniture in all the Louis styles, there's Count Mirabeau's death mask, his sister's original *bidets*, an exceptional collection of faïence from Moustiers and Apt, and paintings by Granet. At 8 Cours Honoré-Cresp, the **Musée International de la Parfumerie**, ✆ 04 93 36 01 61 (*same hours as Villa Fragonard*), displays lots of precious little bottles from Roman times to the present, plus Bergamot boxes of the 1700s and Marie-Antoinette's travel case, while around the corner in Blvd du Jeu-de-Ballon, the **Musée de la Marine**, ✆ 04 93 40 11 11 (*open winter Mon–Sat 10–12.30 and 2–6; daily summer 10–12.30 and 1.30–7*) is devoted to the career of the intrepid Admiral de Grasse, hero of the American War of Independence.

Parfumeries

It's hard to miss these in Grasse, and if you've read Patrick Süskind's novel *Perfume* the free tours may seem a bit bland. The alchemical processes of extracting essences from freshly cut mimosa, jasmine, roses, bitter orange etc. are explained—you learn that it takes 900,000 rosebuds to make a kilo of rose essence, which then goes to the *haute couture* perfume-bottlers and hype-merchants of Paris. Even more alarming are some of the other ingredients that arouse human hormones: the genital secretions of Ethiopian cats, whale vomit, and Tibetan goat musk.

Tours in English are offered by **Parfumerie Fragonard** at 20 Blvd Fragonard, ✆ 04 93 36 44 65, and at Les 4 Chemins, on the Route de Cannes; **Molinard**, 60 Blvd Victor-Hugo, ✆ 04 93 36 01 62, and **Gallimard**, 73 Rte de Cannes (N85), ✆ 04 93 09 20 00. The visits are free, and they don't seem to mind too much if you don't buy something at the end.

Around Grasse: Dolmens and Musical Caves

The Route Napoléon (N85), laid out in the 1930s to follow the little emperor's path to Paris, threads through miles of empty space on either side of medieval **St-Vallier-de-Thiey** (12km). Things were busier here around 800 BC, when the people built elliptical walls with stones as much as 2m high. An alignment of 12 small **dolmens**, most of them buried under stone tumuli, stands between St-Vallier and St-Cézaire-sur-Siagne; a balanced flat rock nearby is known as the *pierre druidique* (St-Vallier's tourist office in Place du Tour has a map). Just to the southwest, signposted on the D5, there's a subterranean lake in the **Grotte de la Baume Obscure**, ✆ 04 93 42 61 63 (*open Mon–Fri 10–5, weekends 10–7; adm*). **Cabris**, 6km west of Grasse on the D4, a *village perché* once favoured by Camus, Sartre and Antoine de Saint-Exupéry, is now a town of artisans and perfume executives. The D11 and D13 to the west lead to more caves: the red **Grottes de St-Cézaire**, ✆ 04 93 60 22 35 (*open 2.30–5, in summer 10.30–12 and 2.30–6, July/Aug 10.30–6, closed Nov–Feb except Sun 3–5; adm*), where the iron-rich stalactites, when struck by the guide, make uncanny music. **St-Cézaire-sur-Siagne** itself is an unspoiled medieval town; its white 13th-century cemetery-chapel built on pure, sober lines, is one of the best examples of Provençal Romanesque near the coast.

Grasse ✉ 06130

There is the **Grasse Country Club** at 1 Rte des 3 Ponts, ✆ 04 93 60 55 44, 📠 04 93 60 55 19, which is small, exclusive and expensive. ★★★**Best Western Hôtel des Parfums**, Blvd Eugène-Charabot, ✆ 04 92 42 35 35, 📠 04 93 36 35 48, has pretty views, a pool, sauna and jacuzzi, and offers a 1½hr 'Introduction to Perfume' that takes you into the secret heart of the smell biz, lending you a 'nose' to help create your own perfume. Modern ★★**Hôtel du Patti**, overlooking the Monoprix supermarket in the centre of medieval Grasse on Place du Patti, ✆ 04 93 36 01 00, 📠 04 93 36 36 40, has very comfortable rooms, all with air conditioning and TV.

Grasse's culinary specialities are if anything, *grasses*, especially *sous fassoun* (cabbage stuffed with pig's liver, sausage, bacon, peas and rice and cooked with turnips, beef, carrots, etc.) or *tripes à la mode de Grasse*. For lunch underneath the arches, head to **Les Arcades**, Place aux Aires, ✆ 04 93 36 00 95 (*menus from 80F*), with Provençal dishes and fishes.

St-Vallier-de-Thiey ✉ 06460

Here there's a charming choice: ★★**Le Préjoly**, Place Rougière, ✆ 04 93 42 60 86, 📠 04 93 42 67 80, with 17 rooms in a large garden, most with terraces, and an excellent restaurant frequented by film stars up from the Cannes Film Festival (*menus at 96F upwards*).

Mougins

Cooking, that most ephemeral of arts, is the main reason most people make a pilgrimage to Mougins, a luxurious, fastidiously flawless village of *résidences secondaires*, with more gastronomy per square inch than any place in France, thanks to the magnetic presence of Roger Vergé (*see* below). But there are a few sights to whet your appetite before surrendering to the table: a **Musée de la Photographie**, at 67 Rue de l'Eglise, ✆ 04 93 75 85 67 (*open 2–11pm July and Aug, 1–6 at other times, closed Tues and Nov*), with changing exhibitions, often featuring the work of Jacques Lartigue, who lived in nearby Opio. Other exhibitions take place in the old village **Lavoir** (wash-house) in the pretty Place de la Mairie. Two km southeast of Mougins, Picasso spent the last 12 years of his life in a villa next to the exquisite hilltop **Chapelle de Notre-Dame-de-Vie**, a 12th-century priory founded by monks from St-Honorat, and rebuilt in 1646.

Appropriately located just off the *autoroute* to Cannes, at the Aire des Breguières, the de luxe **Musée de l'Automobiliste**, Chemin Font de Currault, ✆ 04 93 69 27 80 (*open 10–6, 7 summer; adm*), is a modernistic cathedral to the car.

Mougins ✉ *06250*

In 1969 chef Roger Vergé bought a 16th-century olive mill near Notre-Dame-de-Vie and made it into the internationally famous luxury ★★★★ **Le Moulin de Mougins**, Notre Dame de Vie, ✆ 04 93 75 78 24, 📠 04 93 90 18 55. Of late, France's gourmet bibles have been sniffing that the mild-mannered celebrity chef, author of *The Cuisine of the Sun* (1979), has lost a bit of his touch—and little faults seem big when you shell out 1000F for a meal. But it's still a once-in-a-lifetime experience for most, in the most enchanting setting on the Côte. *Closed end of Jan–Feb.* If you can't get a table, Vergé's shop in central Place du Com.-Lamy, with tableware and a selection of the master's sauces, may offer some consolation.

The *nouvelle cuisine* and chocolate desserts at the hôtel-restaurant ★★★★**Les Muscadins**, at the village entrance, 18 Blvd Courteline, ✆ 04 92 28 28 28, ✆ 04 92 92 88 23 (*menus 175F and up*), have received excellent reviews, and the hotel has sumptuous bedrooms of charm and character. *Closed mid-Jan–mid-Mar.* Mougins even has affordable restaurants like **Feu Follet**, Place de la Mairie, ✆ 04 93 90 15 78, ✆ 04 92 92 92 62, offering excellent menus (*rognons de veau à la graine de moutarde*) for 128–158F. *Open all year, daily.*

Cannes

In 1834, the 3000 fisherfolk and farmers of Cannes were going about their business when Lord Brougham, retired Lord Chancellor, and his ailing daughter checked into its one and only hotel, stuck in the village because a cholera epidemic in France had closed the border with Savoy. As they waited, Lord Brougham was so seduced by the climate and scenery that he built a villa, where he spent every winter. English milords and the Tsar's family played follow-my-leader, and flocked down to build their own villas nearby. 'Menton's dowdy. Monte's brass. Nice is rowdy. Cannes is class!' was the byword of the 1920s. Less enthusiastic commentators mention the dust, the bad roads, the uncontrolled building, and turds bobbing in the sea. If nothing else, the French Riviera proper ends with a bang at Cannes. The spunky sister city of Beverly Hills, France's Hollywood, and a major year-round convention city (Cannes was the first place on the Côte d'Azur to note that business travellers spend over three times as much per head as tourists), Cannes offers a moveable feast of high fashion, showbiz trendiness, overripe boutiques, and glittering nightlife. Depending on your mood, and perhaps on the thickness of your wallet, you may find it appalling or amusing, or just plain dizzy. You can always catch the next boat to the offshore Iles de Lérins, some of the most serene antidotes to any city.

Getting There

By train: The frequent *Métrazur* between St-Raphaël and Menton, and every other train whipping along the coast, calls into the station at Rue Jean-Jaurès. For information call ✆ 08 36 35 35 35, but have some extra French wits about you, as it's an unforgiving computerized system that flits you from place to place.

By bus: There is a multiplicity of private bus companies, all arriving and departing from different places; though there is one central number, ✆ 04 93 39 18 71, at Place de l'Hôtel de Ville.

By boat: Every hour in the summer, the glass-bottomed boat, *Nautilus*, at Jetée Albert-Edouard, departs for tours of the port and its sea creatures; tickets 80F.

Boat trips out to the Iles de Lérins, ✆ 04 93 39 11 82, depart from the *gare maritime*, Allées de la Liberté, approximately every hour, and much less frequently between

October and June. The general tour is a whirlwind trip—you're no sooner there than it's time to go back; you're best off going to one island at a time.

By bike: You can rent bikes at the train station or at Location Mistral, 14 Rue Georges-Clemenceau, ✆ 04 93 39 33 60.

Cannes ✉ *06400*   ***Tourist Information***

Palais des Festivals, 1 La Croisette, ✆ 04 93 39 24 53, 📠 04 93 99 84 23, closed Sun; another office is in the **Gare SNCF**, ✆ 04 93 99 19 77.

Post office: 22 Bivouac Napoléon, ✆ 04 93 06 26 58.

market days

Marché Forville: daily (except Mon in summer, Mon–Tues in winter); Saturday flea market in the Allées de la Liberté.

La Croisette and the Cannes Film Festival

Besides ogling the shops, the shoppers and their dogs there isn't much to see in Cannes. Characterless luxury apartment buildings and boutiques have replaced the gaudy Belle Epoque confections along the fabled promenade **La Croisette**, its glitter now clogged by incessant traffic in the summer, its lovely sands covered by the sun-beds and parasols of the beach concessions. The shoreline is divided into 32 sections (you can get a map), all memorably named as 'Waikiki', 'Le Zénith' and 'Long Beach' (which is all of several metres long). One rare public beach is in front of the fan-shaped **Palais des Festivals**, a 1982 construction that may have been the prototype for one of Saddam Hussein's cosier bunkers. **Hand-prints** of film celebrities line the '*Allée des Etoiles*' by the '*Escalier d'Honneur*' where the limos pull up for the festival. Outside May, this orange monster engorges conventioneers attending events such as the Festival of Hairdressing or Dentistry.

The **Cannes festival** was founded to rival Mussolini's new Venice film festival: the French were not about to let the Fascists have all the starlets to themselves. The first edition, slated to start 1 August 1939, was cancelled owing to a party-pooper named Hitler. The second festival, in 1946, where 50 journalists swilled complementary rosé wine, set the tone from the start: the competition bit (every film won a prize) was only an excuse for a week of carousing; the real festival would always be outside the screenings. The essential ingredients of sex and scandal were added to the glamour in 1954, when the décolletage of newcomer Sophia Loren grabbed the headlines away from Gina Lollobrigida, and English starlet Simone Silva removed her brassiere all together. Two years later, the sensation was Brigitte Bardot, who coyly spun her skirts to reveal her *petites culottes*. In the 1990s the starlets strip down completely, hoping to attract attention, any kind of attention from the 6000 journalists and thousands of wheeler-dealers from around the world who come to market their wares in what has become the film industry's biggest trade fair. The fun and wild times manage to co-exist with business, sometimes from unexpected quarters. In 1993, a ship full of raw Russian sailors anchored within spitting distance of the Palais des Festivals with a contraband cargo of vodka and smoked salmon. The next day, most of the jurors slept through the films in competition. For all the present emphasis on glitter, tourist Cannes still remembers its English roots. Behind the Carlton Hotel, at 2–4 Rue Général-Ferrié, the **Holy Trinity Church** was rebuilt in 1971 on the site of its 19th-century predecessor, preserving some Victorian odds and bobs: a mosaic, glass medallions of the arms of the archbishop of Canterbury and the bishop of Gibraltar and other Anglican paraphernalia. Built in ferro-concrete, the church's chief glories are its stained glass and seventies style, enough to give points to your collars and make you reach for your wedges. The vicar willl be pleased to conduct a tour.

The Old Port and Le Suquet

The **Vieux Port**, with its bobbing fishing-boats and plush, luxury craft, is on the other side of the Palais des Festivals. Plane trees line the **Allées de la Liberté**, where the flower market and Saturday flea market take place. Two streets further back, narrow pedestrian **Rue Meynadier** is the best place to buy cheese (Ferme Savoyarde), and fresh pasta (Aux Bons Raviolis), near the sumptuous **Forville** covered market. Cannes' cramped old quarter, **Le Suquet**, rises up on the other side of the port, where the usual renovation and displacement of the not-so-rich is just beginning. At the city's highest point, the monks of St-Honorat built the square watchtower, the **Tour du Mont Chevalier** in 1088, and their priory is now the **Musée de la Castre**, *©* 04 93 38 55 26 (*open April–June 10–12 and 2–4; July–Sept 10–12 and 3–7; Oct–Mar 10–12 and 2–5, closed Tues*), a little museum at a little price (*10F*), with an archaeological and ethnographic collection donated by a Dutch Baron in 1873, containing everything from Etruscan vases to pre-Columbian art and a 40-armed Buddha.

A good way to get Cannes into proportion is to see it by night. Climb up through Le Suquet to **La Tour**, and join the lovers to look beyond the white boats and lights.

The Iles de Lérins: Saint-Honorat and Sainte-Marguerite

When Babylon begins to pall, you can take refuge (and a picnic, for the island restaurants are dear) on a delightful pair of green, wooded, traffic-free islets just off the coast. Known in antiquity as Lero and Lerina, they are now named after two saints who founded religious houses on them at the end of the 4th century: little **Ile Saint-Honorat** and the larger **Ile Sainte-Marguerite**. According to legend, when St Honorat landed on the islet that bears his name in 375, he found it swarming with noxious snakes and prayed to be delivered of them. They immediately dropped dead but the stench of the cadavers was so hideous that Honorat climbed a palm tree and prayed again, asking for the bodies be washed away. God obliged again, and in memory the symbol of the island became two palm trees intertwined with a snake.

Saint Honorat shares with Jean Cassien of St-Victor in Marseille the distinction of introducing monasticism to France. The island became a beacon of light and learning in the Dark Ages; by the 7th century, St-Honorat had 4000 monks, and 100 priories and lordships on the mainland (including Cannes, which belonged to the monastery until 1788). Its alumni numbered 20 saints, including St Patrick, who, before going back to Ireland, trained here and picked up some tips on dealing with pesky snakes.

The monastery was also a big boon to local sinners: a journey to St-Honorat could earn a pilgrim an indulgence equal to a journey to the Holy Land. Other visitors, especially Saracen pirates, were not as welcome. To protect themselves, the monks built a fortress, connected to the abbey by means of an underground tunnel. Although the abbey is long gone, the evocative, crenellated **donjon** remains strong, lapped by the wavelets on three sides, mellowed by sea and time; within there's a vaulted cloister and chapel, and a terrace with views that stretch to the Alps. In 1869 Cistercians from Sénanque purchased St-Honorat, rebuilt the abbey (men only are admitted on weekdays, there's not much to see) and have done all they could to preserve the islet's natural beauty and serenity, so close to and yet so far from the sound and fury of Cannes.

Sainte Marguerite, and the Man in the Iron Mask

Legend has it that Marguerite, sister of St Honorat, founded a convent on this island, but it broke her heart that her austere brother would only come to visit her when a certain almond tree blossomed. Marguerite asked God to make him come more often, her prayer was answered when the almond tree miraculously began to bloom every month.

Ste-Marguerite has nicer beaches than St-Honorat, especially on the south end of Chemin de la Chasse. On the north end stands the gloomy **Fort Royal**, built by Richelieu as a defence against the Spaniards (who got it anyway) and improved by Vauban in 1712. By then the fortress mainly served as a prison, especially for the mysterious Man in the Iron Mask, who was transferred here from Pigneroles in 1687, and then ended up in the Bastille, in 1698. Speculation about the man's identity continues at least to amuse historians (who insist that the mask was actually leather): was he Louis XIV's twin, as Voltaire suggested, or, according to a more recent theory, the gossiping son-in-law of the doctor who performed the autopsy on Louis XIII and discovered that the king was incapable of producing children? Later prisoners included six Huguenot pastors who dared to return to France after Louis XIV's revocation of the Edict of Nantes, and were kept in solitary confinement until all but one of them went mad.

Festivals

The **Festival International du Film** erupts for 12 days beginning around the second week of May with a hurricane of hype, *paparazzi*, journalists, movie stars, gawking fans and characters who come every year, like the trucker from Kansas who's a dead ringer for Liz Taylor and flounces up and down the Croisette signing autographs. There are some 350 screenings, but most of the tickets are reserved for the cinema people themselves, while 10 per cent go to the Cannois, who bestow the *prix populaire* on their favourite film. The few seats left over go on sale at the Palais' box-office a week before the festival. From 4–14 July, the **Festival Américain** brings in jazz and country music.

Cannes ✉ 06400

Where to Stay

expensive

Although there are sizeable discounts if you come to Flash City in the off-season, you can't book too early for the film festival or for July and August. Cannes' two tourist offices offer a free reservation service, but they won't be much help at that time of year if you want a room that costs less than a king's ransom; if, however, you possess one of those, you can drop a considerable lump of it at the ★★★★**Carlton**, 58 La Croisette, ✆ 04 93 06 40 06, ✉ 04 93 06 40 25, one of the great landmarks of the Riviera, with its two black cupolas, said to be shaped like the breasts of the *grande horizontale* Belle Otero, the Andalusian flamenco dancer and courtesan of kings. Given a thorough renovation by its new Japanese owners, the seventh floor has been endowed with a pool, casino, beauty centre, and more. In the same category, the traditional ★★★★**Majestic**, 14 La Croisette, ✆ 04 92 98 77 00, ✉ 04 93 38 97 90, is the movie stars' favourite with its classic French décor, heated pool, private beach, etc. A third, the ★★★★**Martinez**, 73 La Croisette, ✆ 04 92 98 73 00, ✉ 04 93 39 67 82, has kept its Roaring Twenties character, but with all imaginable modern comforts, including tennis courts, a heated pool and, from the seventh floor, grand views over the city.

moderate–inexpensive

If you aren't in Cannes on an MGM expense account, there are other alternatives, such as the elegant, stuccoed ★★★**Bleu Rivage**, 61 La Croisette, ✆ 04 93 94 24 25, ✆ 04 93 43 74 92, a renovated older hotel amidst the big daddies on the beach where rooms overlook the sea, or the garden at the back. The 19th-century ★★★**Molière**, 5–7 Rue Molière, ✆ 04 93 38 16 16, ✆ 04 93 68 29 57, sits in the midst of a garden, with bright rooms and terraces. Another quiet choice, the modern ★★**Sélect**, 16 Rue Hélène-Vagliano, ✆ 04 93 99 51 00, ✆ 04 92 98 03 12, has air-conditioned rooms, all with bath, while **Le Chanteclair**, 12 Rue Forville, ✆/✆ 04 93 39 68 88, has decent doubles with showers. *Closed Nov.* The **youth hostel** is at 35 Ave de Vallauris, ✆/✆ 04 93 99 26 79.

Eating Out

expensive

Good food follows money, and Cannes is well-endowed with opportunities for gastronomic indulgence. Two of the top restaurants on the whole Riviera are here: **La Palme d'Or** in the Martinez hotel, ✆ 04 92 98 74 14, has a fabulous Art Deco dining room; the Alsatian cook, Christian Willer, prepares dishes including *salade de pigeonneau* or a succulent *agneau de Sisteron persillé* (*menus 350F and 580F*). *Closed mid-Nov–mid-Jan, Mon, Tues and Sun, open daily during Festival*. **La Belle Otero**, ✆ 04 92 99 51 10, is on the 7th floor of the Carlton (*see* above)—and the seventh heaven of gastronomy. If *loup de Méditerranée en croustillant de parmesan poêlée de légumes niçois* doesn't make your mouth water, then be guided by numbers; it shares two Michelin stars with the Palme d'Or. *Closed Sun, Mon, and Tues lunchtime*. **Le Royal Gray**, by the luxurious Lebanese hyper-mall at 6 Rue des Etats-Unis, ✆ 04 93 99 76 60, ✆ 04 92 99 26 10, is a citadel where ingredients such as fresh shrimp from Tunisia and tiny morels from Canada go to create extraordinarily rare and delightful dishes, at rarefied prices—although there's a tempting 205F weekday lunch menu that definitely bears thinking about. *Open all year*.

moderate–inexpensive

For affordable seafood and fine views of its original habitat, try *bouillabaisse* and a pretty good *aïoli* at the nautical **Lou Souléou**, 16 Blvd Jean-Hibert, ✆ 04 93 39 85 55. **Au Bec Fin**, 12 Rue du 24-Août, near the station, ✆ 04 93 38 35 86, serves good food and plenty of it, with a wide selection of *plats du jour* for 98F. *Closed Sat eve, Sun*. Spread out along the Vieux Port, **La Pizza**, 3 Quai St-Pierre, ✆ 04 93 39 22 56, has fine pizzas, *saltimbocca à la Romana*, a very passable *tarte aux pommes* and a congenial atmosphere. *Open until 2–4am in the summer*. **Le Grand Café**, Rue Felix Faure, ✆ 04 93 99 93 10, has a promenade view for people-watching and grilled sardines and huge margaritas served by an assortment of chatty young waiters. If you want to star-spot, a **Planet Hollywood** has recently opened right on the Croisette.

If you want your stars on celluloid, choose between **Les Arcades**, 77 Rue Félix-Faure, ✆ 04 93 39 00 98; **Olympia**, 5 Rue d'Antibes, ✆ 08 36 68 00 29; and **Star**, 98 Rue d'Antibes, ✆ 04 93 39 11 79—all of which sometimes show v.o. films (*version originale*).

Otherwise, the fleshpot will keep you entertained if you have the wherewithal to afford it. Its casinos draw in some of the highest rollers on the Riviera, although the adjoining casino discos are fairly staid. There's **La Grande Aventure**, at 50 La Croisette, ✆ 04 93 68 43 43, where you can eat 'theme cuisine' while you gamble away the readies, or the **Casino Croisette**, in the Palais des Festivals, ✆ 04 93 38 12 11.

To get into the most fashionable clubs (those with no signs on the door) you need to look like you've just stepped off a 30m yacht to get past the sour-faced bouncers. **Jimmy'Z** at the Casino in the Palais des Festivals, ✆ 04 93 38 12 11, ✆ 04 93 68 00 07 after 11pm, is a glitzy showcase billing itself '*La discothèque des stars*': it's certainly for those with stars in their eyes—gamblers, their ladies and mainstream music (*11pm–dawn*). There's usually live music to go with the food at **La Chunga**, 72 La Croisette, ✆ 04 93 94 11 29 (*meals about 300F*). *Open 8.30pm–dawn.* **Le Whisky à Gogo** has a well-heeled crowd grinding away to the top of the pops, at 115 Ave de Lérins, ✆ 04 93 43 20 63. Cannes also has a gay bar of long standing: **Zanzi-Bar**, 85 Rue Félix-Faure, ✆ 04 93 39 30 75 (*6pm–6am*); newer on the scene, **Disco 7** at 7 Rue Rougière, ✆ 04 93 39 10 36 (*90F cover charge*), has dancing and a transvestite show. *Open 11.30pm–6am.*

Côte d'Azur: L'Esterel to Bandol

Where the shores of the eastern Riviera tend to be all shingle, the beaches of the western Côte d'Azur are mostly soft sand. The crowds, cars, art, yachts, boutiques and prices are less intense as well, with the outrageous exception of St-Tropez, the pretty playground of the jet set and dry-martini louts on yachts. But just behind these careless seaside pleasures-grounds bulge two of the world's most ancient chunks of land, the prodigious porphyry Esterel and the dark, forested Maures, and tucked in between you'll find museums of post-Impressionism, music boxes, ships' figureheads and booze; Roman ruins and a tortoise reserve; an island national park and the oldest baptistry in France; and to begin, the most Gothic of follies, Henry Clews' little house of horrors in La Napoule.

Beaches

This region contains some of the most enticing beaches in France. From Cannes to St Tropez the dramatic corniche road offers glimpses down to small sandy coves hiding between jagged rocks. This is

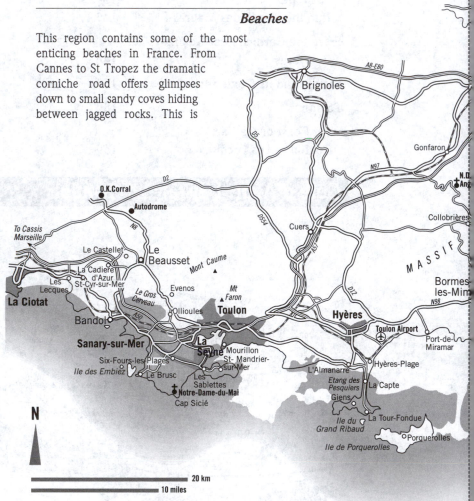

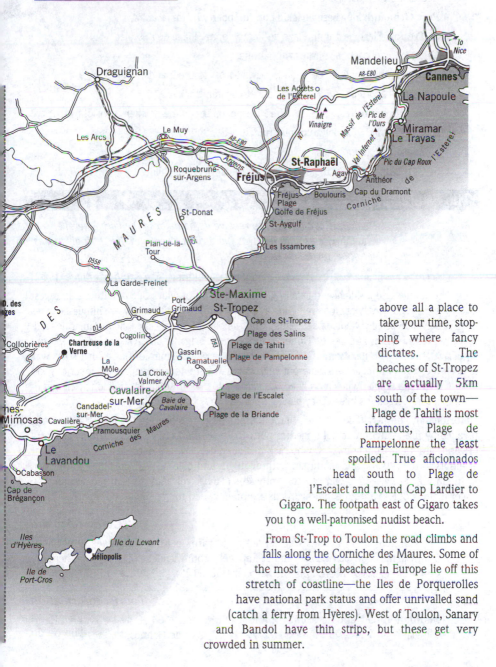

above all a place to take your time, stopping where fancy dictates. The beaches of St-Tropez are actually 5km south of the town—Plage de Tahiti is most infamous, Plage de Pampelonne the least spoiled. True aficionados head south to Plage de l'Escalet and round Cap Lardier to Gigaro. The footpath east of Gigaro takes you to a well-patronised nudist beach.

From St-Trop to Toulon the road climbs and falls along the Corniche des Maures. Some of the most revered beaches in Europe lie off this stretch of coastline—the Iles de Porquerolles have national park status and offer unrivalled sand (catch a ferry from Hyères). West of Toulon, Sanary and Bandol have thin strips, but these get very crowded in summer.

131

St-Aygulf: long sand, lots of space, but crowded in summer.

Les Issambres: as above.

Port Grimaud: long beach backing on to Spoerry's *cité lacustre*.

St-Tropez: Plage de Tahiti, Plage de Pampelonne, Plage de l'Escalet.

Gigaro: long beach, favourite with families.

St-Clair: just outside Le Lavandou; views across to the islands.

Cap de Brégançon: wilder coves, off the beaten track.

Ile de Porquerolles: Plage de Notre Dame, or any of the northern coastal beaches.

Ile du Levant: Héliopolis, premier nudist beach.

Hyères: large town beach.

St Cyr: 2km of fine sand, gentle slope, perfect for small children.

The Esterel

The Esterel is supposed to receive its name from the fairy Esterelle, who intoxicates and deceives her ardent lovers and thus fittingly makes her home on the Coast of Illusion.

Douglas Goldring, *The South of France* (1952)

Between Cannes and St-Raphaël this fairy Coast of Illusion provides one of nature's strangest interludes: a wild *massif* of blood-red cliffs and promontories, with sandy or shingle beaches amid dishevelled porphyry boulders tumbling into the blue blue sea—the kind of romantic landscape where holy hermits like St Honorat and unholy brigands like Gaspard de Besse felt equally at home. The handsome Gaspard, from a bourgeois family of Besse-sur-Issole, was himself the stuff of romance—a generous highwayman with courtly manners, a lover of good food and wine, a scholar who entertained the jury at his trial in Aix by reciting long passages of Homer and Anacreon in Greek. They hanged him anyway.

Unfortunately, the virgin cork forests that once hid Gaspard's band in the Esterel have been ravaged by fire—environmental tragedies with the side-effects of clearing sites for property brigands and their cement-mixers, who race neck-and-neck with the forestry service's gallant attempts to reforest the arid mountain with drought- and disease-resilient pines and ilexes. Come in the spring, when wild flowers ignite this Fauvist volcanic fairyland; in summer, to lower the risk of real fires, the internal roads are often closed to traffic.

Getting Around

The Corniche de l'Esterel is well served by 5 **trains** per day and **buses** (2 per hour from Cannes) between Cannes and St-Raphaël. From Mandelieu-La Napoule there are **boats** to the Iles de Lérins from the harbour (*see* p.125), ✆ 04 93 49 15 88, 50F.

Tourist Information

Mandelieu-La Napoule ✉ 06210: Rue Jean-Monnet, ✆ 04 93 49 14 39; Blvd Henri Clews, ✆ 04 93 49 95 31, 🖷 04 92 97 99 57; Ave de Cannes, ✆/🖷 04 92 97 99

27,☏ 04 92 97 67 79. **Agay** ✉ 83700: Blvd de la Plage, ☏ 04 94 82 01 85, ☏ 04 94 82 74 20.

Mandelieu-La Napoule

Golf is what makes Mandelieu famous. There are nine- and eighteen-hole courses; the first was laid out a hundred years ago by the nephew of the Tsar, the latest by an American. The brochures speak of 'panoramas to stop you from breathing'. If you recover your breath, down below on the coast its sister town, La Napoule, has the usual beaches and hotels and the nuttiest folly ever built by a foreigner on this shore, the **Fondation Henri Clews**, ☏ 04 93 49 95 05 (*open for tours Mon–Fri, at 3 and 4; closed Tues, and 1 Nov–1 Mar*), a pseudo-medieval fantasy castle beautifully set on Pointe des Pendus (hanged men's point), built by a pseudo-medieval artist, Henry Clews. Born in 1863 into a wealthy American banking family, Clews was a sculptor and designer who fancied himself the Don Quixote of the 20th century. In 1917 he bought the Château de la Napoule, a ruined fort first built by the Saracens, and converted it into his 'La Mancha', his refuge from the modern world, especially scientists, reformers, members of the middle class, and democrats. Once installed, Henry and his wife Marie rarely left their fairytale world—Henry designed the costumes, for themselves and the servants; they filled the place with exotic birds and liked nothing better than to stage dramatic dinner parties that to the bewildered guests seemed to come straight out of Hollywood. Henry's personal mythology, 'Humormystics', is still amply illustrated throughout: monsters and grotesques, human figures and animals, many in egg and phallic shapes with cryptic inscriptions, carved in stone out of his private quarry in the Esterel with the help of 12 stone-cutters.

Corniche de l'Esterel

Laid out by the French Touring Club way back in 1903, the Corniche (N98) is dotted with panoramic belvederes overlooking the extraordinary red, blue and green seascapes below. The largest beaches of sand or shingle are served by snack wagons in the summer, and in between, with a bit of climbing, are rocky coves and nooks you can have all to yourself. Heading south from La Napoule, **Théoule-sur-Mer**, which claims to be only 10 minutes from Cannes' Croisette, has small beaches and an 18th-century seaside soap factory converted into a castle, which isn't bad compared to **La Galère** (the next town east on the same road), infected in the 1970s by a private housing estate which looks as if it were modelled on cancer cells. This is a suburb of fashionable **Miramar**, where the best thing to do is walk out along **Pointe de l'Esquillon** for the view of the sheer cliffs of **Cap Roux** plunging into the sea. The nearby slopes and jagged shore, pierced with inlets and secret coves, belong to the villas and hotel of **Le Trayas**.

Beyond Le Trayas, a road at **Pointe de l'Observatoire** ascends to the **Grotte de la Ste-Baume**, where St Honorat resided as a hermit when four-star views were free of charge. Meanwhile the Corniche road itself twists and turns towards **Anthéor** and the Esterel's biggest resort, **Agay**, a laid-back village set under porphyry cliffs, around a perfect horseshoe bay rimmed with sand and pebble beaches. In 1944 the American 36th Division disembarked just to the west at the **Plage du Dramont**, where you can pick up the path to the **Sémaphore du Dramont**, for panoramas over the Gulf of Fréjus. The place seems to have made an impression in Neolithic times: there's a menhir and other, rather mysterious engraved stones on the ancient road from Dramont to Agay.

The Esterel: Inland Routes

From Cannes, the N7 follows the path of the Roman Via Aurelia, passing through the bulk of the Esterel's surviving cork forest. This is ravishing scenery, ravished by the world that wants to see it: it is possible to see it underneath all its tourists, at least at dawn. The high point of the trip, both literally and figuratively, is **Mont Vinaigre**, rising to 600m; from the road a short path leads to its summit and a fantastic viewing platform in an old watchtower. Other hairpinning roads begin in Agay and lead to within easy walking distance of the Esterel's most dramatic features: the hellish **Ravin du Mal-Infernet**, and the panoramic **Pic de l'Ours** and **Pic du Cap Roux**, where the Esterel is at her most stunning, and the Coast of Illusion a flaming vision of colour and light.

Where to Stay and Eating Out

Mandelieu-La Napoule ✉ 06210

In Mandelieu, golf enthusiasts can sleep near their favourite sport at the modern ★★★**Hostellerie du Golf**, 780 Ave de la Mer, ✆ 04 93 49 11 66, 🖷 04 92 97 04 01, equipped with a pool and spacious rooms with terraces. La Napoule's ★★★★**Ermitage du Riou**, Ave Henri Clews, ✆ 04 93 49 95 56, 🖷 04 92 97 69 05, is a luxurious refuge built like a Provençal *bastide*, with a garden and pool overlooking the sea. The much more affordable ★★**La Calanque**, Blvd Henri Clews, ✆ 04 93 49 95 11, 🖷 04 93 49 67 44, has a shady terrace and views of the sea and Clews' folly. *Closed Nov–Mar.* For dinner, try the *soupe de poissons* or *plateau de fruits de mer* at **Le Boucanier**, by the Port de Plaisance, ✆ 04 93 49 80 51; good 150F menu.

Le Trayas ✉ 83700

Right on the sea, ★★**Le Relais des Calanques**, Corniche de l'Esterel, ✆ 04 94 44 14 06, 🖷 04 94 44 10 93 (*menus from 85F*), has 14 rooms, a pool and a good fish restaurant on a terrace over the red sea rocks. There's a superb **Auberge de Jeunesse** (cards required), ✆ 04 93 75 40 23, 🖷 04 93 75 43 45, but as usual it's hard to reach—a 2km march uphill from the station (last bus from the train station 7.30pm), so ring ahead; and in summer, book. *Closed Jan–mid-Feb.*

Anthéor ✉ 83700

At ★★**Les Flots Bleus**, on the N98, ✆ 04 94 44 80 21, 🖷 04 94 44 83 71 (*menus from 98F*) all rooms have grandiose views of the sea and Esterel. The seafood served on the terrace is fresh and copious. *Closed Oct–Mar.*

Agay ✉ 83700

There are mostly campsites here, and among the handful of hotels the most comfortable is the isolated ★★★**Sol e Mar**, at Plage Le Dramont, ✆ 04 94 95 25 60, 🖷 04 94 83 83 61, right on the sea, with two salt-water pools and a restaurant with adequate food but tremendous views. ★★★**France Soleil**, ✆ 04 94 82 01 93, 🖷 04 94 82 73 95, in Agay itself, is a reliable choice on the beach. *Open Easter–Oct only.* Up along the N7, just beyond Mt Vinaigre, the **Auberge des Adrets**, ✆ 04 94 40 36 24, is a lonely inn (dating back to 1653) once a notorious haunt of bandits like Gaspard; it now has a simple but bandit-less restaurant.

Between the Esterel and the Massif des Maures, in the fertile little plain of the river Argens, St-Raphaël and Fréjus are the big noises on the coast between Cannes and Hyères. After the fireworks of the Esterel, St-Raphaël has—guess what?—more beaches, holiday flats and yachts, swollen so big as to merge with its venerable neighbour Fréjus (*Forum Julii*), a market town and naval port on the *Via Aurelia* founded by Julius Caesar himself to rival Greek Marseille. Octavian made it his chief arsenal, to build the ships that licked Cleopatra and Mark Antony at Actium. Even today, Fréjus is a garrison town, with France's largest naval air base.

Getting Around

By train: St-Raphaël is the terminus of the *Métrazur* trains that run along the coast to Menton. Other trains between Nice and Marseille call at both St-Raphaël and Fréjus stations, making it easy to hop between the two towns; St-Raphaël also has direct connections to Aix, Avignon, Nîmes, Montpellier and Carcassonne, and it's a mere 6hrs 15mins on the TGV direct from Paris.

By bus: Both towns have buses for Nice and Marseille (*gare routière* ✆ 04 94 95 24 82), more pricey ones for St-Tropez and Toulon (SODETRAV, ✆ 04 94 95 24 82) and buses inland for Bagnols, Fayence and Les Adrets (Gagnard, ✆ 04 94 95 24 78).

By boat: Les Bateaux Bleus, ✆ 04 94 95 17 46, depart regularly from the Quai Albert 1er, to St-Tropez and St-Aygulf, and make day excursions to the Iles de Lérins and Ile de Port Cros, as well as jaunts around the Golfe de Fréjus and its *calanques* (creeks); be sure to reserve ahead in July and Aug. The *Capitaine Nemo* will submerge you in the murky depths.

Bike hire: Cycles Michel, ✆ 04 94 51 45 56, and **Cycles Trevisan**, ✆ 04 94 53 74 02, both in Fréjus. For mountain bike excursions into the Esterel, contact **Grenouillet** in Agay, ✆ 04 94 82 81 89; also call ✆ 04 94 40 85 70 for **horses**.

Tourist Information

St-Raphaël ✉ 83702: Rue Waldeck Rousseau, ✆ 04 94 19 52 52, 🖷 04 94 83 85 40. **Fréjus** ✉ 83601: 325 Rue Jean-Jaurès, ✆ 04 94 51 83 83, 🖷 04 94 51 00 26. **Fréjus-Plage** ✉ 83600: Blvd de la Libération, ✆ 04 94 51 48 42, summer only.

market days

St-Raphaël: daily; Place Victor-Hugo and Place de la République for produce; and Place Ortolan for fish. **Fréjus:** Wednesday and Saturday mornings, in front of the city hall; Sun morning fleamarket.

St-Raphaël

Once the fiefdom of the ambitious François Léotard, leader of the centre-right UDF party, and now of his successor Elie Brun, St-Raphaël has money if not much heart. Its once glittering turn-of-the-century follies and medieval centre were bombed to smithereens in the war, sparing only the Victorian-Byzantine church of **Notre-Dame** in Blvd Felix-Martin, and the **Eglise des Templiers** or St-Pierre (1150), with its Templar watchtower, in Rue des Templiers (just north of the station). This is the third church to occupy the site, re-using the same old Roman stones—one in the choir vault is carved with something you won't often see in church: a flying phallus, an ancient charm for averting evil (Pompeii has lots of them). If the church is closed, pick up the key at the adjacent **Musée Archéologique**, © 04 94 51 26 30 (*open mid-Sept–mid-June 10–12 and 2–5, closed Sun; June–Sept 10–12 and 3–6; closed Tues*). For centuries there were rumours of a sunken city off St-Raphaël, apparently confirmed by the bricks that divers kept bringing to shore. Jacques Cousteau went down to see and found, not Atlantis, but a Roman shipwreck full of building materials. Some are displayed here along with a fine collection of amphorae.

Fréjus: the Roman Town

Founded in 49 BC, *Forum Julii* was the first Roman town of Gaul, but not the most successful; the site was malarial and hard to defend, and eventually the river Argens silted up, creating the vast sandy beach of **Fréjus-Plage** but leaving the Roman harbour, once famous for its size, high and dry a mile from the sea. A path tracing the ruined quay begins at Butte St-Antoine, south of central Fréjus, but even then it's hard to picture a hundred Roman galleys anchored in the weeds. Its one monument, the **Lanterne d'Auguste**, isn't even Roman, but a medieval harbourmaster's lodge built on a Roman base.

Other fragments of *Forum Julii* are a long hike across the modern town—Fréjus is one place where those ubiquitous ridiculous tourist trains come in handy. Best preserved is the ungainly, greenish **Amphithéâtre Romain**, Rue Henri-Vadon (*open 9.30–12, 2–6.30; winter 9–12, 2–4.30; closed Tues*), flat on its back like a beached whale with the rib arches of its *vomitoria* exposed to the sky. Arches from a 40km **aqueduct** still leapfrog by the road to Cannes; north, on Ave du Théâtre Romain, the vaults of the **Théâtre Romain** (*same hours*) survived, although the seating had to be replaced (the coastal road once ran right through its middle). Rock concerts and bull fights now fill the bill.

Le Cité Episcopale: the Oldest Baptistry in France

On a map marked with walls that once contained *Forum Julii*, modern Fréjus looks like the last lamb-chop on a platter. The Saracens had much of the rest in the 10th century, coming back seven times to pillage and destroy the bits they missed. When the coast was clear in the 12th century, the Fréjussiens rebuilt their **Cathédral St-Léonce** in Place Formigé, and in the 16th century gave it a superb pair of **Renaissance doors** carved with sacred scenes, a violent Saracen massacre, and portraits of aristocratic ladies and gents, including King François Ier. Inside, over the sacristy door, there's a *retable de Ste-Marguerite* (*c.* 1450) by Jacques Durandi, of the School of Nice. The cathedral was the centre of a mini **cité épiscopale** incorporating a crenellated defence tower, a chapterhouse and a bishop's palace (*guided tours daily April–Sept 9–7, other times 9–12 and 2–5; closed Tues; adm*). The tour includes the **Baptistry**, the one bit of Fréjus the Saracens missed: late 4th century, octagonal (like all early baptistries, it was modelled after the original, built in the 320s by Constantine in Rome) and defined by eight black granite columns with white capitals lifted from the Roman forum.

Fairest of all is the 12th-century **Cloister**, with slim marble columns and a 14th-century ceiling, coffered into 1200 little vignettes, of which a third still have curious paintings that comprise a whole catalogue of monkish fancies: grotesques, mermaids, animals, portraits, and debaucheries. Upstairs, the **Archaeology Museum** has a collection of finds from *Forum Julii*, among them a perfectly preserved mosaic, a fine head of Jupiter, and a copy of the superb two-faced bust of Hermes discovered in 1970.

Just off Place Formigé at 53 Rue Sieyes are two **Atlantes**, all that remains of the house of the Abbé Sieyes (1748–1836), pamphleteer of the Revolution, deputy at the Convention and mastermind of the 18th Brumaire coup that brought Napoleon to power.

Around Fréjus

Just outside Fréjus stand a pair of remarkable monuments recalling the rotten days of the First World War, when states supplemented their manpower by importing men from the colonies to fight wars that weren't theirs. The Vietnamese built a colourful **Pagode Hong Hien** as a memorial to their 5000 dead, 2km from the centre on the N7, *✆* 04 94 53 25 29 (*open daily 9–12 and 3–6.30*), while the Sudanese sharpshooters at the local marine base built a **Mosquée Missiri** (a concrete reproduction of the Missiri Mosque at Djenne, Mali) on Rte de Bagnols-en-Forêt, 5km from Fréjus by way of the N7 and D4 towards Fayence). Further along the D4, the **Musée des Troupes de Marine** covers the history of the marines from 1622 to the present (*open daily exc Tues and Sat, summer, 10–12, 3–7; afternoons only in winter*). Another mile further on at Le Capitou you can drive and walk through the **Parc Zoologique**, *✆* 04 94 40 70 65 (*open daily, 10–7.30*), where parrots and yaks don't look too out of place under the parasol pines.

Ten km up the River Argens from St-Aygulf (Fréjus' resort suburb to the west), the picturesque 16th-century village of **Roquebrune-sur-Argens** offers a break from coastal craziness with a wine and orchid centre that boasts the largest mulberry tree in France. Along the road to Le Muy, the **Rochers de Roquebrune** form a peculiar red baby *massif* that toddled away from the Esterel.

Where to Stay and Eating Out

St Raphaël ✉ 83700

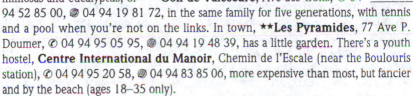

The town of the archangel is rich in pricey campsites, but a few hotels stand out. The best choices are outside the centre, like ★★★**La Potinière**, in Boulouris, 5km east, *✆* 04 94 95 21 43, *✆* 04 94 95 29 10, a modern hotel dedicated to sports (pool, tennis, sailing) and R and R, set in a park of mimosas and eucalyptus, or ★★★**Golf de Valescure**, Ave des Golfs, *✆* 04 94 52 85 00, *✆* 04 94 19 81 72, in the same family for five generations, with tennis and a pool when you're not on the links. In town, ★★**Les Pyramides**, 77 Ave P. Doumer, *✆* 04 94 95 05 95, *✆* 04 94 19 48 39, has a little garden. There's a youth hostel, **Centre International du Manoir**, Chemin de l'Escale (near the Boulouris station), *✆* 04 94 95 20 58, *✆* 04 94 83 85 06, more expensive than most, but fancier and by the beach (ages 18–35 only).

The most genial place to eat, **L'Arbousier**, 6 Ave de Valescure, *✆* 04 94 95 25 00 (*menus from 140F, closed Wed*), combines charm and excellent, aromatic gourmet food for half the price you'd pay elsewhere. *Mousseline de sole* and fresh pasta are among the fare at **Les Terrasses de L'Orangerie**, Promenade René Coty, *✆* 04 94 83 10 50, (*menus from 99F; closed Sun eve, Mon and Jan*). Otherwise go for the Friday special 155F *aïoli* menu at **Pastorel**, 54 Rue de la Liberté, *✆* 04 94 95 02 36 (*other menus 160 and 195F*), an excellent address since 1922, with a pleasant-no-nonsense proprietress and a garden terrace. *Closed Sun eve and Mon.*

Fréjus ✉ 83600

***Résidence du Colombier**, Rte de Bagnols, ✆ 04 94 51 45 92, 📠 04 94 53 82 85, is perfect for families with rooms in bungalows, each with a private garden and terrace, spread out in a pine-wood, plus a heated pool, archery, *pétanque*, volleyball, etc. *Open till the end of Oct. Rooms must be booked through ULVF at Firminy,* ✆ *04 77 56 66 09.* The ***Aréna**, 139 Rue du Gén. de Gaulle, ✆ 04 94 17 09 40, 📠 04 94 52 01 52, offers colourful, air-conditioned rooms, a pool, and good food in old Fréjus. The best of the cheapies, quiet *Bellevue**, is by the cathedral in Place Paul-Vernet, ✆ 04 94 51 39 04, 📠 04 94 57 35 20. There's a pleasant **Auberge de Jeunesse** 2km from Fréjus' historic centre in a large park east on the N7, ✆ 04 94 53 18 75, 📠 04 94 53 25 86; from the intermittently used Fréjus station take bus no.7; there is a much handier shuttle-bus from the station at St-Raphaël. It also has a camp-site. *Open all year.* For dinner, **La Romana**, 155 Blvd de la Libération at Fréjus-Plage, ✆ 04 94 51 53 36 (*menus 75–125F*), offers a seaside setting and an honest *soupe de poisson*, along with Italian and Provençal favourites. *Closed Sun eve and Mon, exc in season.* Near the cloister, **La Cave Blanche**, Place Calvini, ✆ 04 94 51 25 40 (*menus from 80F*) has a wide choice of classics in a medieval dining room. *Closed Sun eve, Mon, Jan–Mar.* For sparky *nouvelle cuisine* try **Les Potiers**, 135 Rue des Potiers, in town near Place Agricola, ✆ 04 94 51 33 74 (*impressive 120–165F menus*). Or eat for less from the popular *crêperie/saladerie* **Cadet Rousselle**, 25 Place Agricola, ✆ 04 94 53 36 92 (*around 60F*).

Entertainment and Nightlife

Beer-lovers can chug one hundred varieties at Fréjus-Plage's **Maison de la Bière**, 461 Blvd de la Libération, ✆ 04 94 51 21 86. For more strenuous entertainment, gamble and dance at the **Casino de St-Raphaël** and its **Madison Club**, Square de Gand, ✆ 04 94 95 01 56; try **Le Kilt**, 130 Rue Jules-Barbier, ✆ 04 94 95 29 20 for disco; or the **Coco-Club** music bar at Port Santa Lucia, ✆ 04 94 95 95 56.

The Massif des Maures

Between Fréjus and Hyères, the coast bulges out and up again to form the steep rolling hills and arcadian natural amphitheatres of the ancient Massif des Maures. Although it lacks the high drama of the Esterel, this mountain range (760m at its highest point) is as much of a geological oddball, its granite, gneiss and schist completely unrelated to the limestone that dominates the rest of Provence. The name Maures is derived from *maouro*, Provençal for black, describing its dark, deep forests of umbrella and Aleppo pines, chestnuts and cork. For centuries the latter two trees provided the main source of income of the few inland villages.

Until the 19th century this was the most dangerous coast in France. The Saracens made it their chief stronghold in the area in 846, building forts (*fraxinets*) on each hill to watch for ships to plunder, and to defend themselves from the Franks. They were finally forced out in the campaign of 972, led by William of Provence, who was greatly assisted by a knight from Genoa named Grimaldi, the first of that family to make waves. But although the pirates had to abandon their *fraxinets*, they hardly abandoned the coast, and maintained a reign of terror that continued until 1830, when the French captured Algiers.

Ste-Maxime and Port Grimaud

In the seaside conurbation spread between Fréjus and St-Tropez, the only place that may tempt a detour is Ste-Maxime, a modern resort town with a beach of golden sand facing St-Tropez. It willingly takes the overflow of fashionable and bankable holidaymakers from the latter, an attractive proposition as it's easy to commute by frequent boat to the capital of see-and-be-seen; St-Tropez may not look far but it's two hours' traffic jam away in high season. If you do stay there's the **Musée des Traditions Locales**, © 04 94 96 70 30, opposite the port. The remarkable **Musée du Phonographe et de la Musique Mécanique**, is in the unlikely setting of the wooded Parc de St-Donat, © 04 94 96 50 52, 10km north towards Le Muy on the D25, or take the Le Muy bus from Ste-Maxime (*open Easter–Oct, 10–12 and 2–6, closed Mon, Tues; adm*). Exhibits include one of Edison's original phonographs of 1878, an accordion-like 'Melophone' of 1780, a 1903 dictaphone, and an audio-visual '*pathégraphe*' to teach foreign languages, built in 1913.

From Ste-Maxime, the road passes through **Port Grimaud**, a pleasure port designed in 1968 by Alsatian architect François Spoerry, inspired by the lagoon complexes around St Petersburg, Florida, where wealthy home-owners, like Venetians, can park their boats by the front door. The traditionally styled, colourful houses themselves are a preview of the real McCoys in St-Tropez; the pseudo-Romanesque **church**, sitting on its own islet, has annoying stained glass windows designed by the late op artist Vasarely.

Ste-Maxime ✉ *83120*   ***Where to Stay and Eating Out***

 For all the usual 4-star comforts, including parking, pool, private beach and gastronomic restaurant, ★★★★**La Belle Aurore** will oblige, at 4 Blvd Jean-Moulin, © 04 94 96 02 45, 🖷 04 94 96 63 87. *Open Mar–Oct, otherwise intermittently.* ★★★**Le Petit Prince**, 11 Ave St-Exupéry, © 04 94 96 44 47, 🖷 04 94 49 03 38, is a small, modern hotel, 50m from the beach, with a parking garage and no-nonsense charm enough to make you believe you might even be welcome. There's no restaurant, but they are in happy cahoots with **Le Dauphin**, 10 Ave Charles de Gaulle, © 04 94 96 31 56, where you can expect pretty but not elaborate good food fresh from the kitchen: the rabbit in mustard is gourmet quality, and rather than decide on a dessert, simply order a selection that come in miniature dishes. Also good, ★★**Le Revest**, 48 Ave Jean-Jaurès, © 04 94 96 19 60, 🖷 04 94 96 32 19, is moderate in price, central, with parking and a pool, and **Domaine du Calidianus**, Blvd Hortensias, © 04 94 96 23 21.

There are over 80 restaurants in Ste-Maxime. Aside from Le Dauphin, try **Le Lotus Bleu**, 30 Ave Gén. Leclerc, © 04 94 49 28 00, for *cassolette de la mer*, and Thai/Vietnamese specialities.

St-Tropez

It made the headlines in France when St-Tropez's mayor forced the discos to close at 2am and declared the beaches off limits to dogs, inciting the fury of 'Most Famous Resident' Brigitte Bardot, that crusading Joan of Arc of animal rights who married a National Front politician and in a recent autobiography referred to her son as a 'tumour'. But then again BB has always been a bit ahead of the rest of us, ever since she came down here to star in Roger Vadim's *Et Dieu créa la femme* in 1956 and incidentally made this lovely fishing village into the national show-case of free-spirited fun, sun and sex, all boxed in the glitter litter of fashion and wealth. Everyone who wants to be associated with these desirable things tries to squeeze into St-Tropez in the summer, booking one of the few hotel rooms nearly a year in advance, or just coming down for the day for a gawk at the yachts.

The French fondly call this St-Trop'—pronouncing the 'p', to avoid saying St-Too-Much, though in the summer it really is: too many people (100,000 on an average day) clogging the roads, lanes and beaches; too much rubbish; too many artists hawking paintings around the port; too many crowded cafés and restaurants charging unholy prices. At other times of the year it's easier to understand what started all the commotion in the first place—although beware that in winter St-Tropez, the only town on the Côte d'Azur that faces north, can be extremely blustery.

History: Proto-National Front Ligurians and Celebrity Cosmetics

One of the strangest but most prophetic legends along the coast has it that St-Tropez's first incar-nation, the Greek colony Athenopolis, was founded by Praxiteles' famous model Phryne, who had a face like a toad but the body of a goddess. Put on trial in Athens for unseemly behaviour, she lifted up her skirt, astonishing the jury with her charms, and was acquitted on condition that she leave Athens. She ended out here in the Wild West of antiquity, married to a Ligurian chief-tain. Together they founded Athenopolis, but the story has a sad end: Phryne was sacrificed to the Ligurian gods with the request that they please keep foreigners away in the future.

In AD 68, Torpes, a Christian officer of Nero, was beheaded in Pisa. As anyone who has studied the *Lives of the Saints* knows, the Romans had no lack of ingenuity in dealing with martyrs; in this case, they buried Torpes' head in Pisa, and put his body in a boat with a dog and a cock, who were to slowly devour it. But the animals had no appetite, and their boat floated safely to Athenopolis (the Roman *Heraclea Cacabria*) which eventually adopted St Torpes' name. The saintly trunk was hidden and lost during the Saracen attacks, one of which destroyed St-Tropez in 739.

St-Tropez was repopulated in 1470 with settlers imported from Genoa. Good King René of Provence exempted them from taxes in return for defending the coast, and until the 1600s the Tropéziens enjoyed a special autonomous status under their *Capitaines de Ville*. Their most glorious moment came on 15 June 1637, when they courageously beat off an attack by 22 Spanish galleons, an event annually celebrated in the *Bravade des Espagnols*. Later invaders were more successful. The first famous visitor from the outside world, Guy de Maupassant, drifted into the port in 1880s and in his pre-syphilitic madness gave the villagers a preview of the 1960s. In 1892, the post-Impressionist painter Paul Signac was forced by the weather to anchor his yacht at St-Tropez; enchanted, he bought a villa called La Hune and invited his friends down to paint. St-Tropez was a revelation to many: Matisse, who had previously worked in a rather dark style, came down in 1904 and produced his key, incandescent picture of nudes on a St-Tropez beach, *Luxe, calme, et volupté*, and joined the Fauvist revolution begun by Signac's friends Derain, Vlaminck, Van Dongen and Dufy; today their hot-coloured canvases illuminate the town's museum.

Writers, most famously Colette, joined the artists' 'Montparnasse on the Mediterranean' in the 1920s, but even then thoughts of making a franc out of fashion and beauty were in the air; Colette herself had a shop in the port selling Colette-brand cosmetics in the 1930s. The third wave of even more conspicuous invaders, Parisian existentialists and glitterati, began in earnest in the 1950s, when Françoise 'Bonjour Tristesse' Sagan and Bardot made it the pinnacle of chic. Back then Sartre could sit in the Café Sénéquier and write Les Chemins de la liberté in peace, but these days he'd be hard put to it to even think, with all the showbiz comets who come to be seen and the paparazzi who dutifully come to snap them when they appear. Joan Collins has a house here, so has George Michael, and Elton John's manager paid £7m in 1995 to join the set. Guest appearances have been made by Prince Albert, Clint Eastwood, Naomi Campbell, Robert De Niro, Jack Nicholson, Rupert Everett and even a cavorting once-royal duchess (for an oral pedicure).

Getting Around

On its peninsula, St-Tropez is a dead end; the one road leading into it (D98A), and the lanes leading off to the beaches, are packed solid from June to August.

By bus: Besides the St-Raphaël–Hyères coastal bus (for info contact SODETRAV Hyères 47, Ave Alphonse-Denis, © 04 94 12 55 12, or the gare routière at St-Tropez © 04 94 12 55 12, there's a regular bus in season linking Toulon to St-Tropez (contact SODETRAV Toulon © 04 94 92 20 80). Note that there's no place at all to leave your luggage if you want to stop off en route.

By boat: You may be better off catching a boat from St-Raphaël (gare maritime © 04 94 95 17 46) or Ste-Maxime (MMG © 04 94 96 51 00).

Bike hire: The ghastly traffic makes bike and moped hire a good alternative (**M.A.S.**, 5 Rue Quaranta, near Place Carnot, © 04 94 97 00 60; open daily, closed Oct).

Should you need a **horse** to gallop away, contact © 04 94 56 16 55; or buzz off in a **helicopter, RCE Helistation Za**, © 04 94 43 39 30, ◉ 04 94 43 39 60.

Tourist Information

The **Maison du Tourisme du Golfe de St-Tropez/Pays des Maures**, © 04 94 43 42 10, ◉ 04 94 43 42 78, at the N98/D559 junction just before the traffic gridlock, is a touristic godsend. Cool, calm and collected, with fountains and sculptured pools, this is the Var tourist board's pièce de résistance. The helpful staff will call ahead to St-Tropez to book hotels, advise on restaurants, excursions both coastal and inland, wine tours, and generally provide a thoroughly pleasant introduction to the area. If you miss them, head into St-Tropez, and the office at Quai Jean-Jaurès, © 04 94 97 45 21, ◉ 04 94 97 82 66.

market days

Tuesday and Saturday.

Musée de l'Annonciade

Place Grammont, © 04 94 97 04 01; open Oct–May 10–12 and 2–6, June–Sept 10–12 and 3–7, closed Tues, holidays and Nov; adm.

If everything about St Tropez in the summer fills you with dismay, let this be your reason to visit. Housed in a 17th-century chapel next to the port, the Annonciade concentrates on works by painters in Paul Signac's St-Tropez circle, post-Impressionists and Fauves who began where Van Gogh and Gauguin left off and blazed the trail for Cubism—and blaze they do, saturated with colour that takes on a life of its own with Vlaminck (Le Pont de Chatou) and Derain

(*Westminster Palace* and *Waterloo Bridge*). Seurat's small but fascinating *Canal des Gravelines* (1890) gives an idea of his mathematical, optical treatment of Impressionism, a style his disciple, Signac, moved away from while in St-Tropez. Other highlights include Braque's *Paysage de l'Estaque*, painted in homage to Cézanne; Matisse's *La Gitane* (1906); Vuillard's *Deux Femmes sous la Lampe*, Bonnard's *Nue devant la Cheminée* and key works by Van Dongen, Friesz, Dufy, Marquet and Cross.

From the Port to the Citadelle

Just outside the museum, the **port** is edged with the colourful pastel houses that inspired the Fauves, a scene that regains much of its original charm if you can get up before the trippers and the scores of hack painters who block the quay. The view is especially good from the **Môle Jean Réveille**. In the street above, the church of **St-Torpes** contains the gilt bust of St Torpes and a sculpture of his little boat, carried in the *bravades*. Seek out Place de l'Ormeau, Rue de la Ponche and Place aux Herbes, poetic corners of old St-Tropez that have refused to shift into top gear. You can look down on the shiny roof tiles from the 16th- to 18th-century *citadelle* at the top of town (or visit its little **Musée de la Marine**, © 04 94 97 06 53 (*open 10-6, closed Tues*). Another essential ingredient of St-Tropez is the charming Place Carnot, better known by its old name of **Place des Lices**, an archetypal slice of Provence with its plane trees, its Tuesday and Saturday market, its cafés and eternal games of *pétanque*.

Beaches, and St-Tropez's Peninsula

Although the beaches begin even before you enter St-Tropez, those famous sandy strands where girls first dared to bathe topless (circumventing local indecency laws by placing Coke bottle tops over their nipples), skirt the outer rim of the peninsula. In the summer minibuses link them with Place Carnot, a good idea as beach parking is as expensive as the beaches themselves. **Plage des Graniers** is within easy walking distance, but it's the most crowded. A path from here skirts Cap de St-Tropez and, in 12km, passes **Plage des Salins** (4km direct from St-Tropez), the gay beach **Neptune**, and ends up at the notoriously decadent **Plage de Tahiti**, the movie stars' favourite. Tahiti occupies the north end of the 5km **Plage de Pampelonne**, lined with cafés, restaurants, and luxury concessions where any swimming-costumes at all are optional. On the other side of Cap Camarat, **Plage de l'Escalet** is hard to reach, but much less crowded and free (take the narrow road down from the D93); from L'Escalet you can pick up the coastal path and walk in an hour and a half to the best and most tranquil beach of all, **Plage de la Briande**.

The centre of the peninsula, swathed with Côtes de Provence vineyards, is dominated by two villages of sinuous vaulted lanes and medieval houses: **Gassin**, up a dizzy series of hairpin turns, and below it the larger **Ramatuelle**. Both were Saracen *fraxinets*, and both have caught serious cases of artsy fashion flu from St-Trop, but they still make refreshing escapes from the anarchy down below. In Ramatuelle's cemetery you can see the romantic tomb of actor Gérard Philipe (*Le Diable au Corps* and *Fanfan la Tulipe*), who was only 37 when he died in 1959.

Festivals

Not to be missed if you're anywhere in the vicinity, the *Bravade des Espagnols* (15 June) sees St-Tropez's finest lads and lasses in 18th-century uniforms and Provençal costumes for a morning procession of the relics of St Torpes. At every square the bands stops playing as the 'soldiers' fire an earsplitting fusillade from their blunderbusses straight into the stone pavement. St Torpes himself is honoured with an even more important two-day shooting-spree *bravade* in the middle of May.

Besides the *Bravades*, the most exciting annual event in St-Tropez is the **Nioulargue** (last week of September and the first week of October). The oldest and most beautiful yachts in the world take on the autumn billows, accompanied by a parade of Rolex watches, blond but balding British sailors, and Germans with an air of practised hauteur.

Shopping

Although many of the once trendsetting boutiques are now owned by designchains, a few exclusive shops remain for die-hard St-Trop fans: **Vilebrequin**, Blvd Louis-Blanc, for 99 colours of ballet slippers; **Gas**, Place Sibilli, specializing in costume jewellery made of coral and turquoise; **Rondini**, 16 Rue Clemenceau, for the famous *sandales tropéziennes*, invented in 1927 on the Roman gladiator model; **Sugar**, Rue Victor-Laugier, for cotton tops and shorts, and **Galeries Tropéziennes** for fabrics, espadrilles, garden furniture and everything else.

St-Tropez ✉ *83990*   ## Where to Stay

If you haven't already booked a hotel long ago, forget about arriving in St-Tropez on the off-chance between June and September. There are acres of campsites in the area, although in the summer they are about as relaxing as refugee camps; the tourist offices keep tabs on which have a few inches to spare. As for prices, expect them to be about 20 per cent higher per category than anywhere else on the coast. And if you come in the off season, beware that most hotels close in the winter.

If money's no object, there's the celebrated ★★★★**Byblos**, Ave Paul Signac, © 04 94 56 68 00, ✆ 04 94 56 68 01, built by a Lebanese millionaire, designed like a *village perché*, with rambling corridors, patios, and opulent rooms. In the middle there's a magnificent pool, and the nightclub is one of most desirable to be seen in. *Closed mid-Nov–mid-Mar.* The *luxe, charme et volupté* of the Relais & Châteaux ★★★★**Résidence la Pinède**, Plage de la Bouillabaisse, © 04 94 97 04 21, ✆ 04 94 97 73 64, has given it the current fashion edge; dining *à la carte* in its gourmet restaurant will set you back about 700F. Similarly swish, but perched on a hill, the ★★★★**Bastide de Saint-Tropez**, Rte des Carles, © 04 94 97 58 16, ✆ 04 94 73 64, has an even better restaurant, **L'Olivier**: served in a garden of oleander, figs, palms, eucalyptus and parasol pines, the food is flamboyant, generous, and unexceptionally delicious; *morue demi-sel en ratatouille minute* or *carré d'agneau au riz parfumé et sa brochette d'abats* (*menus 120–290F*). Picasso's old watering hole, ★★★**La Ponche**, 3 Rue des Remparts, © 04 94 97 02 53, ✆ 04 94 97 78 61, located in a group of old fishermen's cottages—a charming, romantic nook to entice your special darling—if you can spare a grand a night. *Closed Nov–Mar.* Or you can sleep in the port overlooking the yachts at ★★★**Le Sube Continental**,© 04 94 97 30 04, ✆ 04 94 54 89 08, the oldest hotel in town and an historic monument to boot. *Open all year.*

The more moderate ★★★**Lou Troupelen**, Chemin des Vendanges, © 04 94 97 44 88, ✆ 04 94 97 41 76, has quiet rooms in an old farmhouse for under 500F in season (*closed end Oct–Mar*); at **★★Les Lauriers**, in the centre at Rue du Temple, ✆ 04 94 97 04 88, 📠 04 94 97 21 87, has modern rooms in a garden in a similar range. *Closed mid-Nov–mid-Dec and Jan–mid-Feb.* Anything cheaper should be reserved a light year in advance: the sweet and intimate garden-hotel **★La Romana**, Rue des Conquêtes, ✆ 04 94 97 70 38, with a good Italian/French restaurant. *Hotel open April–Oct; restaurant open summer only.* And at the entrance of town **★Les Chimères**, Port du Pilon, ✆/📠 04 94 97 02 90. *Closed 12 Nov–15 Dec: ask for a room on the garden.*

St-Tropez ✉ 83990

Most of St Trop's gourmet bastions are in its hotels (*see* above, and below), but for pure atmosphere and the best creative food in town, book a table on the terrace at the **Bistrot des Lices**, 3 Place des Lices, ✆ 04 94 97 29 00; Laurent Tarridec's remarkable 175F lunch may be one of the high points of your holiday (*other menus 280 and 340F*). To be seen with the likes of George Michael, Claudia Schiffer or Carla Bruni, try **Chez Yvan**, Place de la Garonne, ✆ 04 94 97 89 65, with a single, but excellent 190F menu that changes daily. At **L'Echalote**, 35 Rue du Général-Allard, ✆ 04 94 54 83 26, you can beef up on your black puddings, and all things meaty (*menus from 150F*).

Ramatuelle ✉ 83350

This includes all the hotels along Tahiti and Pampelonne beaches. For self indulgence, you can't beat the **★★★★Château de la Messardière**, Rte de Tahiti, ✆ 04 94 56 76 00, 📠 04 94 56 76 01, a late 19th-century folly on a height overlooking the sea; ultra comfortable, with a superb panoramic restaurant, with exquisite, exotic dishes you'll find no where else (*menus from 240F*). *Closed Nov–Mar.* Or try **★★★La Figuière**, Rte de Tahiti, ✆ 04 94 97 18 21, 📠 04 94 97 68 48, an old farmhouse in the middle of a vineyard, with a relaxed atmosphere, tennis, and a pool, or the less expensive **★★★La Ferme d'Augustin**, Plage de Tahiti, ✆ 04 94 55 97 00, 📠 04 94 97 40 30, set in a garden a stone's throw from the sea. The views are enchanting further up among the vineyard terraces at **★★★Le Baou**, Rue Gustave-Etienne, ✆ 04 94 79 20 48, 📠 04 94 79 28 36, which also has a heated pool and restaurant serving delicious sunny Provençal treats like *daube de Saint-Pierre* and *dos de loup au caviar d'aubergine* (*menus 180–300F*). At Cap Camarat, **Chez Camille**, ✆ 04 94 79 80 38, is reputed for its *bouillabaisse* (300F) and other concoctions from the briny deep (*menus from 185F, closed Tues, Oct–Mar*).

Gassin ✉ 83580

★Bello Visto, Place des Barrys, ✆ 04 94 56 17 30, 📠 04 94 43 45 36, offers simple, relatively inexpensive rooms next to Gassin's magnificent belvedere, but again, book early for a chance of staying in one. The restaurant (*open April–Oct only, menu 120F*) has a pleasant terrace. On the outskirts of Gassin, **Auberge La Verdoyante**, 866 Ave de Coste-Bugade, ✆ 04 94 56 16 23, seems lost in the countryside, an old Provençal manor with a fine view, serving old Provençal dishes (*menus from 138F, reservations advised*). *Closed Wed exc. eves July and Aug; and Nov–Easter.*

The bars in Place des Lices provide an entertaining sideshow in which to pass the average evening, especially the resolutely old-fashioned **Café des Arts**, © 04 94 97 02 25, with its zinc bar and crowd of St-Germain-des-Prés habitués (closes after the Nioulargue). By the port, **Sénéquier**, © 04 94 97 08 98, is a St-Trop institution, but note that all the Joe Cools sit in the back. Younger bars include **La Bodega de Papagayo**, on Quai d'Epi, © 04 94 97 76 70. Dancing and much besides goes on until dawn at St-Trop's clubs. Try **Le Bal** by the new port, © 04 94 97 14 70, or **Les Caves du Roy** at Hotel le Byblos, © 04 94 56 68 20. Don't take it personally if you have trouble getting in: St-Tropez's bouncers have a reputation to uphold.

Into the Massif des Maures

Beckoning just a short drive from the coastal pandemonium are the quiet chestnut woodlands of the Massif des Maures, or at least what's left of them after a quarter of the forest burned in 1990; note that some of the few roads that penetrate the mountain may be closed in dry summers. The main walking path through the hills, the GR9, begins at Port Grimaud and passes through La Garde-Freinet on its way west to Notre-Dame-des-Anges; if you're going by road, the most rewarding route is the D14, beginning at Grimaud.

Getting Around

Grimaud and Cogolin are stops on the St-Raphaël–Hyères **bus** routes. Other villages are much harder to reach by public transport: two buses a day go from Le Lavandou to La Garde-Freinet, and there's but one linking La Garde-Freinet and Grimaud to Toulon.

Tourist Information

Cogolin ✉ 83310: Place de la République, © 04 94 54 63 17, ✆ 04 94 54 10 20.
Grimaud ✉ 83310: Blvd des Aliziers, © 04 94 43 26 98, ✆ 04 94 43 32 40.
La Garde-Freinet ✉ 83680: Place Neuve, © 04 94 43 67 41, ✆ 04 94 43 08 69.
Collobrières ✉ 83610: Blvd Caminat, © 04 94 48 08 00, ✆ 04 94 48 05 62.

market days

Cogolin: Wednesday and Saturday. **Grimaud**: Thursday. **La Garde-Freinet**: Wednesday and Sunday. **Collobrières**: Thursday and Sunday.

Inland from St-Tropez: Cogolin and Grimaud

Perhaps by now you've noticed signs advertising pipes from **Cogolin**, not an especially pretty town but a busy one. For once the craftsmen are not just loose ends from Paris selling artsy gimcracks to tourists; for over two centuries the famous pipes of Cogolin have been carved from the thick roots of the briars (*erica arbores*) that grow up to 6m high in the Maures (visits at 58 Ave G. Clemenceau, *daily 9–12 and 2–7*). A second craft was started up in the 1920s by Armenian immigrants, who introduced their ancestral art of hand-knotted wool rugs, the origin of a local industry that now sells its *tapis de Cogolin* to the best addresses in Paris and the Arab emirates (watch the carpets being woven Mon–Fri at **La Manufacture de Tapis de**

Cogolin, Blvd Louis-Blanc, ✆ 04 94 54 66 17). Another important industry harvests an ancient swamp to make top-quality reeds for saxophones. And Provence's only bamboo forest provides the raw material for Cogolin's furniture. Cogolin's church of **St-Saveur** has some pretty Renaissance art inside, especially a Florentine wood triptyque (1540), but the pilgrims who come to Cogolin are more likely to be French film buffs: the grand-daughter of Pagnol's favourite character actor has opened the **Musée Raimu** in his memory, 18 Ave G.-Clemenceau, ✆ 04 94 54 18 00 (*open daily 10–12 and 3–6*) packed full of memorabilia from his most famous films.

Unlike Cogolin, **Grimaud** is all aesthetics and boutiques. A former Saracen and Templar stronghold, it can hold its own among the most perfect *villages perchés* on the coast, crowned by the ruined castle of the Grimaldis, after whom the village is named. The Romanesque church of **St-Michel** is in surprisingly good nick; from here, Rue des Templiers (formerly Rue des Juifs), lined with arcades of 1555, passes the **House of the Templars**. This is one of the few surviving structures in Provence built by that religious and military order of knights founded in Jerusalem during the First Crusade in 1118. Before their wealth, influence and secret rites incited the deadly envy of King Philip the Fair of France and Pope Clement V, the Templars acquired extensive properties in exchange for their military services. They often built their castles and churches in Jewish or Saracen quarters, both to learn from their ancient wisdom and to protect them from the Christians—hence the damning charge of heresy raised against them by Pope and King, who conspired together to dissolve the order in 1307.

La Garde-Freinet, and a Museum Dedicated to Pigeons

When Charles Martel defeated the Moorish invaders at Poitiers in 732 and pushed them back to Spain, a few managed to give the Franks the slip and escape into Provence, where they generally made a nuisance of themselves (but are also credited with introducing the tambourine, medicine, and flat roof tiles). Their strongholds, or *fraxinets*, gave their name to La Garde-Freinet, a large village full of medieval charm and British ex-pats. A path, past chestnuts said to be 1000 years old, ascends to the site of the Saracen fortress (the standing walls are from the 15th century); from here look-outs would signal the approach of fat merchant ships down to the pirates' cove of St-Tropez.

One of the arts brought to Provence by the Saracens was working in cork, which involves stripping the tree of its outer layer of bark during certain years when the tree can survive the loss; the bark is then boiled, cut into strips, boiled again, and set to dry and season for six months before being carved into bottle stoppers; this was the chief industry in the 19th century. Below the village on the D558, Europe's first **Musée de la Colombophilie**, ✆ 04 94 43 65 32, (*open 3–6, closed Tues and Sun*) is a haven for pigeon fanciers, with hundreds of the flying doo-droppers on display, plus videos of great moments in pigeon history.

Collobrières and a Village of Tortoises

Six km off the D14 from Grimaud stands the moody, ruined **Chartreuse de la Verne**, ✆ 04 94 43 45 41 (*open 11–6, closed Tues and whole of Nov; adm*), founded in 1170 in a beautiful if one of the most desolate corners of France. Rebuilt several times before it was abandoned and burned in the Revolution, the vast Carthusian complex (great and small cloisters, guest house, church and porch) is mostly of interest for its use of local stone—a combination of reddish schist and hard greenish serpentine. Since 1983, restoration work has been carried out by the brothers of Bethlehem. Near the crossroads for the Chartreuse, a minor road leads to the *maison forestière* Ferme Lambert, where you can ask permission to see the two largest **menhirs** in Provence (11ft and 10ft high) and the largest chestnut tree, the **Châtaignier de Madame** (33ft in circumference). The air is sweet in the biggest settlement of the western Maures, **Collobrières**, an attractive old village scented with chestnuts being ground into paste and purée or undergoing their apotheosis into delectable *marrons glacés*.

Due north of Collobrières, narrow roads squiggle up through the forests to **Notre-Dame-des-Anges**, a sanctuary sitting on top of the highest point in the Var, with brave views over the Maures. Further squiggles north, just east of **Gonfaron** (on the N97) will bring you to the **Village des Tortues**, ✆ 04 94 78 26 41 (*open daily 9–7, closed Dec–Feb, when a notice on the gates explains that 'the tortoises are sleeping'*), devoted to saving France's last native land tortoise, the yellow and black Hermann's tortoise of the Maures. Some 1200 tortoises live at this non-profit-making centre until they reach the age of three, when they are released into the Maures where the lucky ones will live to be 80. The best months to visit are April and May when the tortoises mate, June when they lay their eggs, and September when they hatch.

Where to Stay and Eating Out

Grimaud ✉ 83310

Open all year, **★★★Le Côteau Fleuri**, Place des Pénitents, ✆ 04 94 43 20 17, 🖶 04 94 43 33 42, is a comfortable inn built in the 1930s on the quiet western outskirts of town, with grand views over the Maures; its restaurant serves reliably good Provençal dishes (*filet de rouget au pistou* and *carré d'agneau*); the lunch menu at 150F is good value. For more great views and silence, but with a pool and tennis and a video library to boot, try the intimate **★★★La Boulangerie**, Rte de Collobrières, ✆ 04 94 43 23 16, 🖶 04 94 43 38 27. *Open Easter–Sept*. In dining rooms full of *santons*, indulge in a gourmet spread of lobster salad, seafood, or thyme-scented *selle d'agneau* at **Les Santons**, Rte Nationale, ✆ 04 94 43 21 02 (*menus 215F and up*). *Closed Wed, Jan–mid-Mar*. Pennywise, the best bet for food is the **Café de France**, Place Neuve, ✆ 04 94 43 20 05, an old stone house with a summer terrace and an average 125F menu. *Closed Tues*.

La Garde-Freinet ✉ 83680

In the centre, there's **★La Sarrazine**, ✆/🖶 04 94 43 67 16, with simple rooms and a good restaurant with very filling menus (*65, 110 and 120F for fish*).

Collobrières ✉ 83610

Collobrières has just two hotels, **★Notre-Dame**, 15 Ave de la Libération, ✆ 04 94 48 07 13, with adequate rooms and a garden; and **Hotel Restaurant des Maures**, 19 Blvd Lazare Carnot, ✆ 04 94 48 07 10, 🖶 04 94 48 02 73; both have restaurants and are open all year. Ring ahead to ensure there's a table at **La Petite Fontaine**, Place de la République, ✆ 04 94 48 00 12, where you can dine on ribsticking polenta, rabbit in garlic sauce, mushrooms in season and the local wine, amid quirky curios and antique tools (*menus 110F and 145F; closed Sun eve, Mon, and 2 weeks Feb and Sept*).

Apart from fashionable pockets like Bandol and Cassis, the Corniche des Maures is the last glamorous hurrah of the Côte d'Azur, where celebrities and other big money types have villas among the pines and flowers by the silver sand. No railways come between the towns and the sea, but the main road in season is a slow purgatory of fed-up motorists and bus passengers.

Getting Around

Besides the slow and expensive **buses**, there are summer **boat connections** from Cavalaire-sur-Mer and year-round services from Le Lavandou to the Iles d'Or. To explore the hinterlands, you can **rent bicycles** at **Planet Glissa**, 15 Ave des Ilaires, ℰ 04 94 71 16 50, or scooters at **Moto Start**, Ave Maréchal-Juin, ℰ 04 94 71 25 38.

Tourist Information

Cavalaire-sur-Mer ✉ 83240: Maison de la Mer, ℰ 04 94 01 92 10, ℰ 04 94 71 00 61.

Le Lavandou ✉ 83980: Quai Gabriel-Péri, ℰ 04 94 71 00 61, ℰ 04 94 64 73 79.

Bormes-les-Mimosas ✉ 83230: Place Gambetta, ℰ 04 94 71 15 17, ℰ 04 94 64 79 57.

market days

Bormes-les-Mimosas: Wednesday morning. **Pin-de-Bormes**: Tuesday morning. **Le Lavandou**: Thursday morning.

Baie de Cavalaire

The bay on the underside of the St-Tropez peninsula, with its clear coves and large beaches of silken sand, has been given lock, stock and barrel to the property promoters. **La Croix-Valmer** is all new although the story of its name dates back to Emperor Constantine who, as mere co-emperor of Gaul, was on his way to Rome when he saw a cross lit against the sky here, telling of his future destiny as the victor at the Milvian bridge in Rome—where he would see another cross—and his role as the first Christian emperor. The longest beach in the bay is at **Cavalaire-sur-Mer** which, like La Croix-Valmer, is more popular with families than movie stars. Between Cavalaire-sur-Mer and Le Rayou Canadel, the **Domaine du Rayol**, Ave des Belges, ℰ 04 94 05 32 50 (*open April–Nov 9.30–12.30 and 2.30–6.30; July–Sept 9.30–12.30 and 4.30–8*) is well worth a stop for its Mediterranean gardens with global flora, including South African, New Zealand, Mexican and Californian species. For a quiet detour inland, take the narrow D27 from Canadel-sur-Mer west of Cavalaire to **La Môle**, a tiny village with a two-towered château, where Antoine de Saint-Exupéry (pilot and author of *The Little Prince*) spent much of his youth.

Le Lavandou and Bormes-les-Mimosas

Persevering west past Cap Nègre and the exclusive villages of **Pramousquier** and **Cavalière** you find the big boys on the Corniche, the fishing port and resort of **Le Lavandou** and **Bormes-les-Mimosas**, a cute hyper-restored medieval enclave that added the mimosas to tart up its name in 1968, although the honour of first planting and commercializing these little yellow Mexican ball blooms goes to Cannes, where in 1880 a gardener carelessly tossed a branch someone had given him into a pile of manure and *voilà*, the next morning he had the lovely flowers that are now the totem of the Côte d'Azur. Bormes' outskirts, **La Favière**, was once the favourite resort of the White Russian community in Paris, because the steep hills descending towards Cap Benet reminded the founder—Chekhov's granddaughter—of the Crimea. All this has since been spoiled by Bormes' hideous pleasure port, the building of which was challenged by residents and was declared completely illegal in French courts. Typical of the corruption that plagues the coast, the marina blithely continues to exist as a legal fiction.

Le Lavandou, where Bertolt Brecht and Kurt Weill wrote *The Threepenny Opera* in 1928, is a good place in which to empty your wallet on seafood, watersports, boutiques and nightclubs. For a freebie, take the walk out along the coast to Cap Bénat. If you have a car or bike, don't miss the little coastal wine road, beginning at **Port-de-Miramar**, west of Le Lavandou (take D42 off the N98); it passes Cap de Brégançon and its fortified château (the official summer retreat of the President of France) and leads southeast to the delicious beach at **Cabasson**, with a campsite and hotel. Although the beach is crowded in the summer, it stands out as the one corner of the Côte d'Azur free from the scourge of cement.

Where to Stay and Eating Out

Bormes-les-Mimosas ✉ 83230

The best hotel in the commune, ★★★**Les Palmiers**, 240 Chemin du Petit Fort, ✆ 04 94 64 81 94, 📠 04 94 64 93 61, is a steep drive south along the D41 to Cabasson, and is only a few minutes from the sea; its restaurant serves solid classic food which is a good thing because board is obligatory in the summer (*menus from 140F*). In Bormes itself the ★★★**Grand Hôtel**, 167 Rte de Baguier, ✆ 04 94 71 23 72, 📠 04 94 71 51 20, is splendidly located and very reasonably priced for its category. In the centre of the medieval town, the ★**Provençal**, at 37 Rue Plaine des Anes, ✆ 04 94 71 15 25, 📠 04 94 64 71 45, has pretty white-painted rooms, a pool and a restaurant with a 95/145F menu and good views. *Closed Dec*. ★**Le Bellevue**, 12 Place Gambetta, ✆ 04 94 71 15 15, has rooms with views over palm trees and a nest of red roofs, and a terrace restaurant serving simple but scenic food (*menus at 80F and 140F*).

Good regional fare awaits at **La Tonnelle**, Place Gambetta, ✆ 04 94 71 34 84, where tables are set under a gallery of vines, and the food is made entirely from local ingredients with the finesse of a master and perfectionist. The prices are very reasonable by Côte standards (*menus from 95 to 250F, closed Wed, exc in season*). In a 12th-century guardhouse, **Lou Portaou**, 1 Rue Cubert-des-Poètes, ✆ 04 94 64 86 37, serves excellent seasonal, regional dishes (*168F menu*). *Closed Tues*.

Le Lavandou ✉ 83980

For luxury and style, the extragavant ★★★★**Les Roches**, 1 Ave des Trois-Dauphins, ✆ 04 94 71 05 07, 📠 04 94 71 08 40, set magnificently over the *calanques* 4km east of Le Lavandou at Aiguebelle, has lovely, bright rooms furnished with antiques, marble bathrooms, a private beach and pool and tennis. The restaurant is just as palatial, and presided over by an extremely talented young chef, who waves a magic spoon over the typical ingredients of Provence (*menus from 295F*). The less extravagant but charming

***Belle Vue**, at St-Clair on Chemin du Four des Maures, ✆ 04 94 71 01 06, 🖷 04 94 71 64 72, is as good as its name, with views over the coast. The good value **L'Escapade**, 1 Chemin du Vannier, ✆ 04 94 71 11 52, 🖷 04 94 71 22 14, is a small but very cosy hotel in a quiet lane, with air conditioning and TV.

For imaginative preparations of the day's catch, try **Au Vieux Port**, Quai G.-Péri, ✆ 04 94 71 00 21 (*menus from 98F*). On Plage St=Clair, the summery **Les Tamaris St-Clair**, ✆ 04 94 71 02 70, offers fresh grilled fish, *bouillabaisse* and *langoustes* that will warm the cockles of your heart (*à la carte only 200–300F, closed 15 Nov–15 Dec, 10 Jan–10 Feb*).

Hyères and its Golden Isles

Known as *Olbia* by the Greeks from Marseille, who founded it in 350 BC, as *Pomponiana* by the Romans, and as *Castrum Arearum* ('town of threshing floors') during the Middle Ages, Hyères claims to be the original resort of the Côte d'Azur, with a pedigree that goes back to Charles IX and Catherine de' Medici, who wintered here in 1564. It knew its greatest fame in the early 19th century, when people like Empress Josephine, Pauline Borghese, Victor Hugo, Tolstoy and Robert Louis Stevenson built villas here and invited one another to teas and soirées, before it faded genteelly from fashion in the 1880s. For despite its mild climate and lush gardens, Hyères was, unforgivably, three miles from the newly popular seaside. But the town had more than one egg in its basket, and has since made the most of its salt pans on the peninsula, exploited since ancient times, and its nurseries of date palms (developed from a Californian species adaptable to sand and salinity), most of which are exported to Saudi Arabia and the Arab emirates. Now 'Hyères-les-Palmiers' if you please, it has recently won a national award for its parks and gardens.

Getting Around

By air: Hyères-Toulon Airport (✆ 04 94 89 83 83) is served mainly by Air France from Paris (for national information, call ✆ 0 802 802 802).

By train: Hyères is a dead end, linked to Toulon but nowhere else; the station is 1.5km south of town.

By bus: Buses are tricky. Telephone first: SODETRAV, 47 Ave Alphonse Denis, ✆ 04 94 12 55 12, serves west to Toulon and east to Le Lavandou. City buses link Hyères to Hyères-Plage and the Giens peninsula.

By boat: Boats for all three of Hyères islands—Porquerolles, Port-Cros and Le Levant—depart at least twice a day, year-round, from **Port d'Hyères** (✆ 04 94 12 54 40) and **Le Lavandou** (✆ 04 94 71 01 02) with additional sailings in the summer. There are more frequent connections from **La Tour-Fondue**, at the tip of the Giens peninsula, to Porquerolles (✆ 04 94 58 21 81) and in summer, boats also sail from Toulon to Porquerolles. Note that inter-island connections are more rare; check the schedules before setting out.

Tourist Information

Hyères ✉ 83400: Rotonde Jean-Salusse, Ave de Belgique, ✆ 04 94 65 18 55, 🖷 04 94 35 85 05.

Hyères: Place de la République, Tuesday; Place de la Vicomtesse de Noailles, Tuesday, Thursday and Saturday; Ave Gambetta, Saturday; Place Massillon, every morning.

local wine

Côte des Iles: Exquisite but rare. Try some at **Domaine de la Courtade**, at La Courtade, Porquerolles, © 04 94 58 31 44 (*open for visits by appointment*).

Hyères

Mit Palmen und mit Ice-cream, ganz gewöhnlich, ganz gewöhnlich... (With palms and ice-cream, quite common, quite common...) so Bertolt Brecht, and so Hyères. There isn't much to do but take a brief wander into the Vieille Ville, beyond **Place Massillon**. Here stands the **Tour St-Blaise**, a remnant from a Templar's lodge, and on top of a monumental stair, the collegiate church of **St-Paul** (1599) (*open Wed–Sat, 10.30–6 only in winter*) with 400 ex votos dating back to the 1600s. The Renaissance house next to St-Paul doubles as a city gate, through which you can walk up to **Parc St-Bernard** with Mediterranean plants and flowers.

At the upper part of the park, the so-called Château St-Bernard or **Villa de Noailles** was designed as a *château cubiste* by Robert Mallet-Stevens in 1924 for art patron Vicomte Charles de Noailles, the financier of the first film by Cocteau, *Blood of the Poet* (1930) and Salvador Dali and Luis Buñuel's *L'Age d'Or*—which nearly got Noailles excommunicated. Austere cement on the outside, furnished with pieces commissioned from Eileen Gray and designers from the Bauhaus, this vast villa was a busy hive of creativity between the wars—it even stars in Man Ray's murky 1929 film *Le Mystère du Château de Dé*. You can visit during exhibitions, or the exotic garden, the Parc St Bernard, any day for free. There are plans to link the Noailles' garden to that of Edith Wharton, author of *The Age of Innocence*, who lived on the same slope in a former convent of Ste-Claire, and even encompass the little house where Robert Louis Stevenson stayed. Further up the hill are the hollow walls and towers of the **Vieux Château** with an overview of Hyères' peninsula and jumble of hills.

In 1254, when Louis IX returned to France from the Crusades, he disembarked at Hyères and went to pray in the 13th-century Franciscan church in Place de la République, now named **St Louis** in his honour. Inside, the main thing to see is a set of *santons* too large to move (*open 2.30–5*). Below, in Place Th.-Lefebvre, the heart of 19th-century Hyères, a **Musée Municipal**, (*open 10–12 and 3–6; closed Sat, Sun and Tues*) houses the the fragmentary remains of Hyères' Greek and Roman seaside predecessors, as well as two engraved menhirs and a Celto-Iberian figure holding two heads, similar to the statues at Roquepertuse in Aix.

Further south, on Ave Gambetta, you can relax in the **Jardin Olbius-Riquier** amongst the palms and rare tropical and semi-tropical trees, cacti, a lake, and a small zoo for the kids, with birds, ponies etc. (*open 9–6*). Two neo-Moorish villas from the 1880s remain in this part of town: the **Villa Tunisienne** in Ave Beauregard and the **Villa Mauresque** in Ave Jean-Natte.

The Giens Peninsula

Over the centuries the island that was Giens has been anchored to the continent by two sandbars whose arms embrace a salt marsh, the **Etang des Pesquiers**. Although the link has historically been dodgy—Giens became an island again in the storms of 1811—it hasn't stopped people from building villas and hotels, especially on the isthmus at **La Capte**. The barren west arm, dotted by shimmering white piles of salt, is traversed by the narrow *route du sel* beginning at **Plage de l'Almanarre**. In 1843, the archaeologist king, Frederick VII of Denmark, excavated the ruins of the Greek-Roman town at **Almanarre**, but most of it has since been reclaimed by the sand; there are curious Merovingian tombs in the village's 12th-century **Chapelle St-Pierre**. The salt road ends in **Giens**, a quiet little hamlet under a ruined castle that was the last home of the 1961 Nobel-prize-winning poet St-John Perse, who is buried in the cemetery. To the south, **La Tour-Fondue** is the principal port for Porquerolles, although beware that the often violent seas around the peninsula have caused scores of ship-wrecks. In 1967, an intact cargo ship dating from the Roman republic was found in the Golfe de Giens, with sealed amphorae containing a clear liquid with reddish mud on the bottom—the ultimate fate of red wine aged too long.

The Iles d'Hyères

Known as the *Stroechades* or 'chaplet' by the ancient Greeks, and in the Renaissance as the *Iles d'Or*, owing to the shiny yellow colour of their rock, Hyères' three islands are voluptuous little greenhouses that have seen more than their share of trouble. In the Middle Ages they belonged to the monastery of St-Honorat, and attracted pirates like moths to a flame; in 1160, after the Saracens carried off the entire population, the monks gave up and just let the pirates have the islands. The expansion of the Turkish Empire throughout the Mediterranean in the 16th century made the kings of France sit up and notice the Saracens, and in 1515 an attempt was made to preach a crusade against the Hyères pirates, but the crusading spirit was long past. François Ier had a golden opportunity to install the then homeless Knights of St John on Porquerolles, but the two parties couldn't agree on terms, and the Knights settled for Malta, then belonging to Spain, paying their famous rent of one golden falcon. François had to build his own forts and send settlers to man them against Charles V and every other sea predator, but again the pirates carried everyone off.

Henri II, son of François, thought he had a good idea in populating the islands with criminals and malcontents. By this time, however, France had found the solution to her piracy problem: becoming allies with them and the Turks. On one memorable occasion in 1558, the French navy had a big party on Porquerolles to help the notorious Barbarossa and his cut-throats cele-brate the end of Ramadan. Then the inhabitants of the islands spoiled Henri's plans by following their instincts and becoming pirates themselves, capturing numerous French ships and once even pillaging the naval base in Toulon. It took another century to eradicate them. Later rulers rebuilt the island's forts. In the late 19th century, they were variously used to quarantine veterans of the colonial wars and as sanctuaries for homeless children: Levant and Porquerolles became Dickensian orphanages and juvenile penal colonies. In both cases the young inmates rebelled, and many were killed. Industrialists opened sulphur plants on the islands that no other place in France would have tolerated, and the navy bought Le Levant in 1892 and blew it to pieces as a firing range. In the 1890s fires burned most of the forests on Porquerolles and Port-Cros. Fortunately, in this century, the French government has moved decisively to protect the islands; strict laws protect them from the risks of fire and developers.

Porquerolles

Largest of the three, Porquerolles stretches 7km by 3km and has the largest permanent popu-lation, which in the summer explodes to 10,000. Its main village, also called Porquerolles, was founded in 1820 as a retirement village for Napoleon's finest soldiers and invalids. It still has a colonial air, especially around the central pine-planted **Place d'Armes**, the address of most of Porquerolles' restaurants, bars, hotels and bicycle hire shops. Even the village church was built by orders of the Ministry of War, and has military symbols on the altar. Although the cliffs to the south are steep and dangerous for swimming, there are gentle beaches on either side of the village, especially **Plage Notre-Dame** to the east and **Plage d'Argent** to the west.

Between Porquerolles and Giens the now deserted little islet of **Grand Ribaud** was used in the early 1900s for 'spiritualist experiments' and other research by one Dr Richet, who also imported kangaroos. The kangaroos liked the islet, we are told, but banged themselves to untimely deaths by jumping too exuberantly on the sharp rocks.

Port-Cros

Although barely measuring a square mile, Port-Cros rising to 195m is the most mountainous of the three islands. Since 1963 it has been a national park, preserving not only its forests of pines and ilexes, recovered from a devastating fire in 1892, but nearly a hundred species of birds; brochures will help you identify them as you walk along the mandatory trails. There are a selection of these: the *sentier botanique* is for visitors pressed for time, while at the other end of the scale there's a 10km *circuit historique* for the lucky ones who have a packed lunch and all day. Two curiosities of the island are its abundant native catnip and its *euphorbe arborescente*, which loses all its leaves in the summer and grows new ones in the autumn. Like the national park in the Florida Keys, Port-Cros also protects its surrounding waters, rich in colourful fish and plant life. There's even a 300-metre 'path' which divers can follow from Plage de la Palud to Rascas islet, clutching a plastic guide sheet that identifies the underwater flora.

Ile du Levant: The Full Monty 365 Days a Year

The French navy still hogs almost all this flowering island, but they no longer use it for target practice. Nowadays, they test aircraft engines and rockets, which are marginally quieter. The island's remaining quarter is occupied by **Héliopolis**, France's first nudist colony (1931). Anyone who's been to St-Tropez and other fashionable Côte beaches will find the ideal of a specially reserved nudist area quaint by now, but Héliopolis still has its determined Adams and Eves, especially because it's so warm: 60 members of the colony stick it out here all year.

Hyères ✉ *83400*   ***Where to Stay and Eating Out***

Hyères Town

The newly opened ★★**Acropole**, 45 Ave Victoria, ✆ 04 94 35 42 22, ☏ 04 94 35 51 98, is the most comfortable in town, with TV and air conditioning. In the centre, the immaculate ★**Hôtel de la Poste**, Ave Lyautey, ✆ 04 94 65 02 00, is the best of the cheapies. *Open all year.* Or if you'd rather be near the sea, try the delightful ★★★**Les Pins d'Argent**, Blvd de la Marine, ✆ 04 94 57 63 60, ☏ 04 94 38 33 65, surrounded by trees, with a pool and warm welcome, and delicious food at fair prices (*menus 100–180F*). Or little ★**La Reine Jane**, by the sea at Ayguade, ✆ 04 94 66 32 64, ☏ 04 94 66 34 66, with good rooms and food at bargain prices. For a more elaborate dinner, try the delicious *turbot au beurre d'herbe tendre* at the dove-decorated **La Colombe**, at Impasse Vieille, La Bayorre, ✆ 04 94 65 02 15 (*menu 135F*).

Ile de Porquerolles

There are seven hotels on the island, all priced above the odds and all booked months in advance in the summer. The ★★★**Mas du Langoustier**, ✆ 04 94 58 30 09, @ 04 94 58 36 02, is a romantic old inn between the woods and a long sandy beach, with lovely rooms and a superb restaurant, where the chef imaginatively combines the best ingredients of Provence—*filet de rouget poêlé purée d'amandes* or *St Pierre rôti fondue de poireaux* (*menu 400F*). Of the other hotels, ★★**Les Glycines**, Place d'Armes, ✆ 04 94 58 30 36, @ 04 94 58 35 22, is small and charming, and open all year. ★★**Sainte-Anne**, ✆ 04 94 58 30 04, @ 04 94 58 32 26, is a bit dilapidated but stays open longer than the rest; half pension, but good food. Also try **Il Pescatore**, ✆ 04 94 58 30 61, for all things fish: not just the predictable *bouillabaisse* but *carpaccio* and *sashimi*. Eat on the restful terrace overlooking the boats bobbing in the port.

Port-Cros

There is only one choice on paradise, and it needs to be booked long in advance: the pricey but tranquil and casual ★★★**Le Manoir**, ✆ 04 94 05 90 52, @ 04 94 05 90 89, among the eucalyptus groves, which also has a fine little restaurant (*menus from 260F*). *Closed Nov–May.*

Ile du Levant

If you can bare it, Ile du Levant with a greater selection of hotels makes a good base for visiting Port-Cros. The best is ★★★**Héliotel**, ✆ 04 94 05 90 63, @ 04 94 05 90 20, set in the mimosas and greenery, boasting a pool, a piano bar, a little beach down below and a restaurant with pretty views over the other islands. *Open Easter–Sept.* In Place du Village, ★**La Brise Marine**, ✆ 04 94 05 91 15, @ 04 94 05 93 21, is at the summit of the islet, with pretty rooms situated around a patio with a pool. *Closed Oct–May.*

Entertainment and Nightlife

With bar life in Toulon restricted to seedy sailors' bars and nefarious goings-on in the old town, most Toulonnais head to Hyères for a night out, crowding the bars and clubs. The liveliest bar in Hyères is **L'Estaminet**, ✆ 04 94 65 06 52, at 14 Rue de Limans; for a bop, try **Le Rêve**, La Capte, ✆ 04 94 58 00 07 (Fri and Sat nights only in winter, nightly in July and Aug).

Toulon

> *Lauso la mar e ten-ten terro.*
> *(Praise the sea but stick to the land.)*
>
> Provençal proverb

If Provençal traditionalists (and they are landlubbers all) look upon the cosmopolitan Côte d'Azur as an alien presence, they feel equally ill-at-ease in the south's two great ports, Toulon and Marseille: to the Provençal they are dangerous, salty cities, populated by untrustworthy strangers and prostitutes. But while Marseille is essentially a city of merchants and trade, Toulon has always been the creature of the French navy, and whatever piquant charms its old port and quarter once had were bombed into oblivion in the Second World War.

History

For some reason the deepest, most majestic natural harbour in the Mediterranean tempted neither the Greeks nor the Romans. Instead Toulon (originally *Telo Martius*) was from Phoenican times a centre for dyeing cloth, thanks to its abundant murex shells (the source of royal purple) and the dried red corpses (*kermès*) of the *coccus illicis*, an insect that lived in the surrounding forests of oaks. Toulon's destiny began to change when Provence was annexed to France in 1481. The first towers and walls went up under Louis XII in 1514; Henri IV created the arsenal, but it was Louis XIV who changed Toulon forever, making it the chief port of France's Mediterranean fleet, greatly expanding the arsenal and assigning Vauban the task of protecting it with his star-shaped forts, built by forced labour. It was during this period that Toulon became the most popular tourist destination in Provence, when well-heeled visitors came to see not the new navy installations, but the miserable galley slaves—Turkish prisoners, African slaves, criminals and later, Protestants—chained four to an oar, where they worked, ate and slept in appalling conditions.

Toulon's history is marked by three disasters. In 1720, nature's neutron bomb, the plague, killed 15,000 out of 26,000 inhabitants. The second disaster began after the execution of Louis XVI, when Toulon's royalists had confided the city to the English and their Spanish and Sardinian allies. In 1793, a ragamuffin Revolutionary army of volunteers and ruffians under the painter Carteaux, fresh from massacring 6000 people in Lyon, arrived at the gate of Toulon and began an ineffectual siege of two months. A young Napoleon Bonaparte came on the scene, and convinced the commissioners to put him in charge of the artillery. Bonaparte turned his guns to the west side of the harbour, on the English redoubt of Mulgrave, so well fortified that it was nicknamed 'Little Gibraltar' (now Fort Caire), and captured it by 19 December. In spite of the opposition of the English commander Samuel Hood, the allies decided to abandon Toulon to its fate. The thousands who couldn't escape were mercilessly slaughtered by the Jacobins. The hitherto unknown Bonaparte, promoted to brigadier-general, became the darling of the Convention. Although the Revolutionaries hailed the galley slaves as 'the only decent men of the infamous city', convicts (like Jean Valjean in *Les Misérables*) continued to be sentenced to the *bagnes* (penal camps) in Toulon until the 1850s. In 1860 the convicts were packed off out of sight to Devil's Island in French Guyana.

The city's most recent sufferings began in 1942, when the Germans took the city by surprise, and the Vichy Admiral Laborde blocked up the harbour by scuttling the entire Mediterranean fleet to keep it from falling into the hands of the enemy. On 15 August 1944, after flattening the picturesque old port with aerial bombing raids, the Allies landed and the French army, under Général De Lattre de Tassigny, recaptured Toulon, but not before the entrenched Germans blew up the citadel, the harbour and the dockyards. Toulon was rebuilt quickly, although without a great sense of design or beauty. Recently dark clouds have threatened Toulon's horizon: the shipbuilding yards in La Seyne have been under continuous threat of closure, and the ugly forces of reaction succeeded in electing France's first National Front deputy, followed in June 1995 by the election of a National Front mayor whose xenophobic, anti-cultural antics have been a national affront.

Getting Around

Toulon is the major transport hub of the region, and anyone dependent on public transport will find it hard to avoid.

By air: Toulon's airport is out near Hyères (for information, ✆ 04 94 22 81 60, for Air Inter's reservations, ✆ 04 94 89 83 83).

By train: The train station is on the northern side of Toulon in Place Albert Ier, with four daily TGVs to Nice and Marseille, four also direct to Paris (taking just over 5hrs), and frequent connections up and down the coast and to Hyères.

By bus: For St-Tropez and the coast between Hyères and St-Raphaël, catch a SODE-TRAV bus in the adjacent *gare routière*, ✆ 04 94 93 11 39. Other buses will take you frequently to Hyères, Bandol, La Seyne, Six-Fours and Sanary, and to inland towns like Brignoles, Draguignan, Aix and St-Maximin. From Quai Cronstadt, sea-buses go to La Seyne, Les Sablettes and St-Mandrier. City bus info ✆ 04 94 03 87 03.

By boat: From May to September there are daily sailings to Corsica and weekly sailings to Sardinia, (SNCM, Ave de l'Infanterie-de-Marine, ✆ 04 94 16 66 66). Companies departing from Quai Cronstadt offer tours of Toulon's anchorages, the *grande rade* and *petite rade*, and the surrounding coasts and islands: **Le Batelier de la Rade**, ✆ 04 94 46 24 65 (year-round tours of the *rades* and all three Iles d'Hyères); **Transport Maritime Toulonnais**, ✆ 04 94 23 25 36, (tours of the *rades*); **Catamaran Alain III**, ✆ 04 94 46 29 89 (tours of the *rades* and their battleships); **SNRTM**, ✆ 04 94 62 41 14 (tours of the *rades* and mini-cruises, and from 15 June–15 Sept a regular service to the Iles d'Hyères).

Tourist Information

Toulon ✉ 83000: Place Raimu, ✆ 04 94 18 53 00, 🖷 04 94 18 53 09.

The main **post office** is at Rue Jean-Bartolini, ✆ 04 94 16 66 20.

market days

Every morning except Monday on Cours Lafayette—don't miss it; fleamarket, every morning, Place Ste Musse.

Central Toulon

From the train station, Ave Vauban descends to Ave Général-Leclerc; on the left at No. 113 are the **Muséum d'Histoire Naturelle**, with stuffed birds and beasts (*open daily, 9.30–12 and 2–6*) and **Musée d'Art** (*open daily, 1–7*), containing an above-average collection of paintings and sculptures, although there's only room to display a fraction of the works by Breughel, Annibale Carracci, Fragonard, Vernet and Pierre Puget; there's also an especially strong contemporary collection (Bacon, Arman, Yves Klein, Christo, etc.). Avenue Vauban continues down to the large formal gardens of **Place d'Armes**, decorated with ordnance from the adjacent arsenal, one of the biggest single employers in southeast France with some 10,000 workers. Alongside the arsenal in Place Monsenergue are miniature versions of the ships that it once made, displayed in the **Musée de la Marine** (*open 10–12 and 1.30–6, 2.30–7 in summer, closed Tues and holidays; adm*). France's great Baroque sculptor and architect Puget started out in Toulon carving and painting figureheads for the ships, and the museum has works by his followers. The grand Baroque entrance to the building itself is the original Louis XIV arsenal gate of 1738.

The best surviving works of Puget in Toulon are the two **Atlantes** (1657) on Quai Cronstadt, *Force* and *Fatigue*, whose woe and exhaustion may well have been modelled on the galley slaves. They once supported the balcony of the old Hôtel de Ville, and were packed off to safety just before the bombings in the last war. Off the Quai, **Rue d'Alger**, now a popular evening promenade, used to be the most notorious street in Toulon's **Vieille Ville**, or 'Le petit Chicago', the pungent pocket of the pre-war town. Blocked off from the sea by rows of new ugly buildings, the Vieille Ville's narrow streets have become almost respectable.

Come in the morning to take in the colourful fruit and vegetable market in Cours Lafayette, and the fish market in Place de la Poissonerie. At 69 Cours Lafayette there's the dingy **Musée Historique du Vieux-Toulon** (*open 2–6 daily, closed Sun*) with sketches by Puget and historical odds and ends. Around the corner is the **cathedral,** 17th-century on the outside and Romanesque-Gothic within, although its features are barely discernible in the gloomiest interior in the south of France. At the top of the adjacent pedestrian quarter is Toulon's prettiest fountain, the 18th-century **Fontaine des Trois Dauphins**. North of the three dolphins is Toulon's main street, Boulevard de Strasbourg, site of the **Opéra**, ☏ 04 94 92 70 78, the biggest opera-house in Provence, noted for its acoustics, with an interior inspired by Charles Garnier.

Mont Faron

Toulon looks better when seen from a distance. Bus 40 will take you to Boulevard Amiral-Vence in Super-Toulon, site of the terminus of the little red funicular that runs 9–5.30 (later in summer), to the top of 535m Mont Faron (there's a narrow hairpin road circuit as well, beginning in Ave E.-Fabre). Besides a tremendous view over the city and its harbours, there's the **Musée du Mémorial du Débarquement** (*open daily, 9.30–12.30 and 2.30–6, except Mon; adm*), devoted to the August 1944 Allied landing in Provence, with models, uniforms and 1944 newsreels. It shares the summit with a large wooded park, two restaurants, and a **zoo** (*open daily 10–7, May–Sept, closed mornings in winter; adm*).

Around the Harbour

Bus 3 from in front of the station or on Ave Général-Leclerc will take you to the **Plage du Mourillon**, Toulon's largest beach and site of the city's oldest fort, Louis XII's 1514 **Grosse Tour** or Tour Royale that once guarded the eastern approaches to Toulon with its rounded walls, 16–24ft thick. In later years the lower part, excavated in the rock, was used as a prison and now contains an annexe of the Musée Naval, with more figureheads in a baleful setting. The west shore of the *Petite Rade* is Toulon's business end, especially the yards and industry at **La Seyne**. To the south, at L'Aiguillette, stood 'Little Gibraltar' near **Fort Balaguier**, another English stronghold that fell to Bonaparte; this now contains the **Musée Naval du Fort Balaguier** of Napoleana (*open Wed–Sun 10–12 and 2–6; adm*). Further south is the residential suburb of **Tamaris**, once the home of officers and their families, and where George Sand wrote her novel *Tamaris* in 1861. In the 1880s, the mayor of nearby Sanary purchased much of Tamaris in the hopes of turning it into a resort. This mayor had a more exciting career than most: born Michel Marius in Sanary in 1819, he was employed by the Ottoman Empire as a builder of lighthouses, a job he performed so well that the Sultan made him a pasha before sending him home in 1860 with a fat pension. Inspired by what he had seen in Turkey, Michel Pasha commissioned a number of fantasy neo-Moorish buildings in the area, especially Tamaris' **Institute of Marine Biology**. The resort was a flop, but a fad for neo-Moorish confections swept across the Riviera at the turn of the century.

Prices are about a third less than on the fashionable Côte, and fall even lower in the off-season. The most elegant place to sleep and eat in Toulon is ★★★**La Corniche**, 17 Littoral F.-Mistral, at Mourillon, ℗ 04 94 41 35 12, ✆ 04 94 41 24 58, a cleverly designed modern Provençal hotel, air-conditioned and near the beach. The restaurant, **Le Bistrot**, built around the massive trunks of three maritime pines, not only serves refined seafood and dishes such as *selle d'agneau en rognonnade* but also has one of the best wine cellars for miles around (*menus from 130–240F*). In the pedestrian zone, not far from the opera, ★★**Du Dauphiné**, 10 Rue Berthelot, ℗ 04 94 92 20 28, ✆ 04 94 62 16 69, is a comfortable friendly older hotel, air-conditioned, with guarded parking. Nearby, the friendly ★**Le Jaurès**, 11 Rue Jean-Jaurès, ℗ 04 94 92 83 04, ✆ 04 94 62 16 74, is the top bargain choice; the rooms all have baths. If that's full, try ★**Molière**, near the opera at 12 Rue Molière, ℗ 04 94 92 78 35, ✆ 04 94 62 85 82. *Closed Jan*.

Eating Out

If they don't go to the aforementioned Bistrot at La Corniche, the Toulonnais in search of a special meal drive 20km northeast to Cuers to eat at **Le Lingousto**, Rte de Pierrefeu, ℗ 04 94 28 69 10, located in an old *bastide*, where the freshest of fresh local ingredients are transformed into imaginative works of art—langoustines with fresh pasta, omelettes with *oursins* (sea urchins), cheeses that have 'worked' to perfection and divine chocolate desserts (*menus 180–380F*). *Closed Jan–Feb*. **Le Lido**, Ave Frédéric Mistral, ℗ 04 94 03 38 18, has nice, nautical décor, and a window on to the kitchen where you can watch your fresh fish being prepared (*menus 90, 135 and 195F*). **Le Jardin du Sommelier**, 20 Allée Amiral-Courbet, ℗ 04 94 62 03 27, provides gastronomic Provençal cuisine with wines to match in its small, intimate dining-room, perfect for '*un tête à tête en amoureux*' (*200F upwards*). *Closed Sat lunch and Sun*. For *moules* and good home-made *frites* try **La Frégate**, 237 Ave de la République, ℗ 04 94 92 97 60, for a thrifty 40F. Pizzas come at about the same price, and it's one of the few places in Toulon where you can eat late. The jovial and friendly **Le Cellier**, 52 Rue Jean-Jaurès, ℗ 04 94 92 29 78, has a good little 95F menu, including wine. *Closed Sat and Sun*.

Entertainment and Nightlife

Pick up a paper or copy of *Le Petit Bavard* to tell you what's really going on. Toulon has some good theatre, dance and jazz. Northwest of Toulon (Ollioules), a 17th-century tower was converted in 1966 into a handsome **Théâtre National de la Danse et de l'Image**, ℗ 04 94 22 74 00, to host cultural events, especially the July Festival de la Danse et de l'Image—although at the time of writing Toulon's mayor is fighting to restrict its artistic freedom. In July, there's the **Jazz is Toulon** festival, ℗ 04 94 36 33 61. There's opera and inane comedies in the winter at the **Opéra**, Blvd de Strasbourg, ℗ 04 94 92 70 78. The likes of Elton John and Lenny Kravitz play at Toulon's **Zenith-Oméga** concert hall, on Blvd Commandant-Nicolas, ℗ 04 94 22 66 77, which is rapidly becoming the number one rock venue in the south of France.

Slap bang in the centre is the **Pathé Liberté**, 4 Place de la Liberté, ✆ 04 36 68 20 22, with six screens and comfortable seats. The same cinema has a big brother—**Pathé Grand Ciel**, opposite the university at La Garde (same ✆ as Pathé Liberté); 12 screens and v.o. (*version originale*) films. There's no lack of bars, both straight and gay, especially around Rue Pierre-Sémard, but they're not places where you'll feel comfortable alone. Toulon society prefers the bars along Littoral Frédéric-Mistral on Mourillon beach, or drives to Hyères or Le Lavandou.

West Coast of the Var: Toulon to Les Lecques

West of Toulon, the coast tosses out the curious peninsula of Cap Sicié with the old town of Six-Fours before ending in a string of small towns with sandy beaches: Sanary, fashionable Bandol, one of the coast's great wine towns, and Les Lecques. Offshore you can be entertained on Paul Ricard's two little islets, or amuse yourself exploring the hills, woods, vineyards and gorges around Ollioules, La Cadière-d'Azur and Le Castellet.

Getting Around

Six-Fours and Sanary are easiest reached by **bus** from Toulon. The **train station** in Ollioules is halfway between the town and Sanary, with bus connections to both. Bandol is on the Toulon–Marseille TGV; for **bus** information call ✆ 04 94 74 01 35.

In Bandol, you can **hire a bike** to explore the beautiful hinterlands at **Holiday Bikes** 127 Route de Marseille, ✆ 04 94 29 03 32 (closed Oct–Mar), or catch some waves by hiring **windsurfers and surf boards** from the **Société Nautique de Bandol**, ✆ 04 94 29 42 26.

Tourist Information

Ollioules ✉ 83190: 16 Rue Nationale, ✆/✉ 04 94 63 11 74 (mornings only). **Bandol** ✉ 83150: Allée Vivien, ✆ 04 94 29 41 35, ✉ 04 94 32 50 39, website www.bandol.org.

market days

Sanary: Wednesday morning. **Bandol**: daily, with a big market on Tuesday morning.

local wine

Bandol: next to Bandol's tourist office, the Maison des Vins du Bandol sells most of the labels and has a complete list of all the estates open for visits (✆ 04 94 29 45 03). A few to mention: Domaine des Salettes, at La Cadière-d'Azur (✆ 04 94 90 06 06); the organic Domaine de la Tour du Bon, at Le Brulat du Castellet (✆ 04 94 32 61 62); Domaine Ray-Jane, at Le-Plan-du-Castellet (✆ 04 94 98 64 08); the Comte de Saint-Victor's estate of Château de Pibarnon, at La Cadière-d'Azur, (✆ 04 94 90 12 73); Domaine de la Laidière, at Sainte-Anne d'Evenos (✆ 04 94 90 37 07).

Around Cap Sicié: Six-Fours

Cap Sicié, like a clenched fist punching the sea, takes the brunt of the wind and rough swells from the west. If you can, avoid the depressing main roads and urban sprawl that cut across the peninsula from Les Sablettes to Sanary, and take the **Corniche Varoise**, a minor road that circles the cliffs of the Cap. The cliffs tower up to 335m over the sea at **Notre-Dame-du-Mai**, named after a sanctuary much esteemed by sailors, who always approached it barefoot. On the west side of the peninsula, the little port of **Le Brusc**, set amid cliffs and pines, has two or three departures every hour for **Ile des Embiez**, owned by Paul Ricard, the *pastis* baron. Ricard has left the seaward side of the island alone, but facing the mainland he is busy developing what he calls 'the leisure centre of the future', a vast pleasure port and the **Fondation Océanographique Ricard** (*open daily 10–12.30 and 1.30–6.45, and from 2pm Sat*), with 100 different species from the Mediterranean.

The rough winds and waves off Cap Sicié's west coast offer an exciting challenge to surfers and windsurfers who get their kicks at **Brutal Beach** and **Plage de Bonnegrâce**, part of the commune of **Six-Fours-les-Plages** (from the Latin *sex furni*). The village once stood on the isolated mountain nearby, but was destroyed in the 19th century to build the **fort** (no entry, but you can drive up to the barbed wire outside for the view). Two churches were spared: a 10th-century **oratory** on the road to Le Brusc, commemorating a victory over Saracen pirates, and the 12th-century Collegiate church of **St-Pierre-aux-Liens** (*open daily, 2.30–6*), built in pure Provençal Romanesque over a 5th-century baptistry; Palaeo-Christian coins and gems found here are displayed in a case. The church has a number of medieval works of art, including a polyptych of Provence's favourite saints by Jean de Troyes (1520). The niche behind the altar, built to hold the Eucharist, was until 1914 (when the practice was banned) used by the faithful to deposit scraps of cloth taken from the clothes of dead relatives when they came to pray for their souls.

North of here, off the D63, is the stone-built **Chapelle Notre-Dame-de-Pépiole** (*usually open after 3*), with its three little barrel-vaulted naves modelled after the earliest Syrian churches. It goes back to at least the 8th century, the date of fragments of Islamic ceramics found inside, and may even be Carolingian.

Sanary-Sur-Mer, Ollioules and the Big Brain

Provençal for St Nazaire, Sanary is a little resort of pink and white houses and a sandy beach, one picked out by the Kislings and Aldous Huxley as good places to live, far from the Babylon further east. After 1933, Huxley was joined by the cream of anti-Nazi German intelligentsia, led by Thomas and Heinrich Mann and Bertolt Brecht. But Sanary was not far enough away, and under the Vichy régime many Germans were rounded up and imprisoned in an internment camp near Aix. On Sanary's promontory, the chapel **Notre-Dame-de-Pitié** has a delightful collection of naïve ex votos.

Ollioules' funny name comes from olives, although these days it's better known for its wholesale Mediterranean flower market. The town itself has all the typical Provençal charms—arcaded lanes, a medieval castle and a Romanesque church—and numerous artisans who make barrels, bird-cages, nougat, olive woodwork, goats' cheese and the like.

A kilometre north of town, just past the romantic ruins of an 18th-century oratory, the Celto-Ligurian Iron Age *oppidum* of **La Courtine** is built on a basalt rock and covered with wild roses planted by two frustrated amateur archaeologists when they got tired of digging. You can still make out the dry-stone walls and wells. Over 300 Greek coins engraved with the features of Hercules and Hecate were discovered here, donated to a sanctuary destroyed by Romans in 123 BC.

Around **Evenos**, a restored *village perché* just to the north off the N8, the dramatic scenery makes for good walks, especially in the fantastical yellow-tinted **Gorges d'Ollioules**, a natural Gothic landscape much admired by Victor Hugo. The D220 from Ollioules leads on to the wooded mountain ridge of **Le Gros Cerveau** or 'Big Brain', a curious name of uncertain derivation and site of another *oppidum*. It, too, has strange rock formations and is pitted with caves, where 'witches' hid in the time of Louis XIII.

Bandol

Sheltered from the ravages of the mistral, travellers will find Bandol either a preview or a *déjà vu* of the typical Côte d'Azur town: pretty houses and lanes festooned with flowers, palm trees, boutiques, a casino, the morning market in Place de la Liberté, and an over-saturation of villas on the outskirts. But Bandol has something most of the Riviera hotspots lack—its own excellent wine and a little island, **Ile de Bendor**. A barren six-hectare rock when Paul Ricard bought it with his *pastis* fortune in 1950, it is now a little adult playground, a masterpiece of architectural dissonance from the 1950s and '60s—Ricard himself hopes that it will some day fall in ruins and become 'a 20th-century Delos'! There's a diving and windsurfing school, a nautical club that organizes yacht races, an art school and gallery, a business centre, hotels, and the **Exposition Universelle des Vins et Spiritueux**, ✆ 04 94 29 44 34 (*open Easter–Sept 10.15–12 and 2.15–6, closed Wed; adm free*). The building is decorated with frescoes by art students and the displays of 8000 bottles and glasses from around the world will whet your thirst for some Bandol AOC.

Apart from wine, Bandol offers its visitors pink flamingos, toucans, cockatoos, and disgusting Vietnamese pigs in a lovely exotic garden of tropical flora at the **Jardin Exotique et Zoo de Sanary-Bandol**, Route du Beausset, 3km east on the D559 (*open 8–12 and 2–7, closed Sun am, adm*). This is near the *Moulin de St-Côme*, where you can tour the most important olive press in the Var (or in December and January, watch it at work) and buy a bottle of *huile d'olive vierge extra* to take home.

North of Bandol are a pair of medieval wine-producing *villages perchés*, both restored, both lovely nonetheless, and neither as virgin as their olive oil. **La Cadière-d'Azur** sits on a hill with cliffs sliced sheer on the north side, with views out to the Massif de Ste-Baume. **Le Castellet** is perched even more precariously over its sea of vines. Much refurbished, it looks like a film set, and indeed has often been used as such (Marcel Pagnol got here first, for his *Femme du Boulanger*); its 12th-century church is attractively austere, although the same cannot be said of the streets full of arty shops. East of here (follow D26 towards the N8), the 16th-century agricultural villlage of **Le Beausset** sits on a plain 2.5km from the 12th-century **Chapelle Notre-Dame-du-Beausset-Vieux** (*open daily July–Sept, Sat and Sun only other times*), with a basalt altar that once served as a millstone in an olive press, *santons* from the 16th century, and ex votos.

Les Lecques and St-Cyr-sur-Mer

West of Bandol, **Les Lecques** is an unpresuming family resort with a long fine sand beach, set in front of the old Bandol AOC town of **St-Cyr-sur-Mer**, which has something in common with New York—a **Statue of Liberty**, a scale model of Bartholdi's grande dame in Place Portalis. It also offers the cool, wet delights of **Aqualand**, ✆ 04 94 32 08 52, where you can dump the kids—or yourself—down the slides (*open June–Sept*). Les Lecques itself is one of several places that claim to be ancient *Tauroentum*, a colony of Greek Marseille where Caesar defeated Pompey in a famous naval battle and gained control of Marseille. But most of the finds in Les Lecques so far have been Roman, as displayed in the **Musée de Tauroentum** on the road to La Madrague (*open June–Sept 4–7, closed Tues; other times weekends only 2–5*). The museum protects the remains of two Roman villas built around the year AD 1, with mosaics and bits of fresco, vases and jewellery, and outside, an unusual two-storey tomb of a child. A lonely coastal path (marked with yellow signs) begins near the museum and continues to Bandol; along the way are little *calanques* for quiet swims.

Where to Stay and Eating Out

Le Brusc ✉ 83140

At **Le Saint-Pierre**, 47 Rue de la Citadelle, ✆ 04 94 34 02 52, 'Marcel, the king of *bouillabaisse*' will fill you to the brim with the offerings on his delicious menus, mostly fish (*from 90–198F, with a well-priced bouill-abaisse at under 200F*).

Bandol ✉ 83150

The delightful pink ★★★**Master Ker Mocotte**, 103 Rue Raimu, ✆ 04 94 29 46 53, ✆ 04 94 32 53 54, once belonged to the Toulon-born Raimu—the best actor in the world, according to Orson Welles. It has a seaside garden and private beach and pool, and offers facilities for water sports. The restaurant offers a summer grill in gardens above the Mediterranean, and as much as you can eat for 130F. *Open all year*. Its cheaper annexe, the villa **Coin d'Azur** looks directly over the beach. On Ile de Bendor there's Ricard's ★★★**Delos**, ✆ 04 94 32 22 23, ✆ 04 94 32 41 44, with big, comfortable rooms decorated in extravagant bad taste—but the views of the sea below and the many watersports make up for it. West of the port, the exceptionally pleasant ★★**L'Oasis**, 15 Rue des Ecoles, ✆ 04 94 29 41 69, has a cool, shady garden, a short walk from the beach. *Open all year.*

L'Auberge du Port, 9 Allée J.-Moulin, ✆ 04 94 29 42 63, is Bandol's gourmet rendezvous, specializing in seafood, where you can go the whole hog on a 250F *menu dégustation* ; other menus begin at 120F.

Le Castellet ✉ 83330

Next to the medieval gate, ★**Le Castel Lumière**, ✆ 04 94 32 62 20, ✆ 04 94 32 70 33, has six rooms and an excellent restaurant, partially furnished with antiques, with panoramic views (*menus from 175–250F*). *Closed Sun eve and Mon; July and Aug open daily exc. Mon, Tues and Wed lunchtime.* Outside of the village, ★★**Castel Sainte-Anne**, 2km northwest on the D 26, ✆ 04 94 32 60 08, ✆ 04 94 32 68 16, is a cosy niche that won't break the bank, with a terrace, garden, pool and inexpensive restaurant.

La Cadière-d'Azur ✉ 83740

The one hotel in the village, ★★★**Hostellerie Bérard**, Rue Gabriel-Péri, ✆ 04 94 90 11 43, ✆ 04 94 90 01 94, is a charming and luxurious place to stay: a 16th-century convent building with a shady terrace, a heated pool, gardens, and a good restaurant with splendid views, serving delicately perfumed dishes (*try the carré d'agneau with basil, menus from 160F*).

AIX. — THE CLOISTER OF ST. SAUVEUR CATHEDRAL

Metropolitan Provence

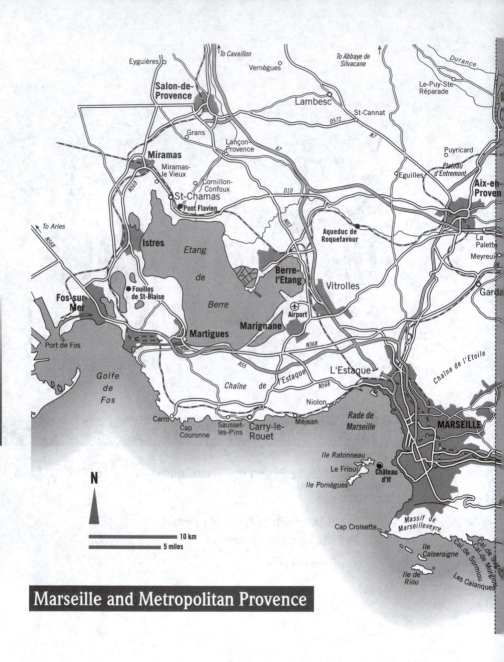

Marseille and Metropolitan Provence

Although this is the business end of Provence, the most densely populated, hurly-burly, industrial and everything-else-you've-come-to-get-away-from part of Provence, the region holds several trump cards: elegant and lively Aix-en-

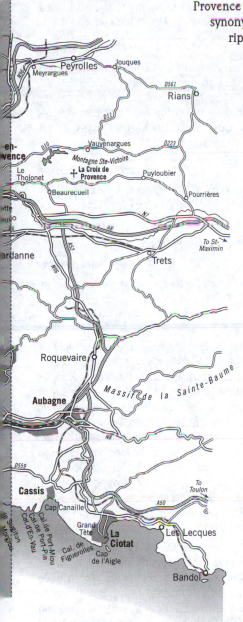

Provence with its incredible markets and countryside synonymous with Cézanne; a tumultuous coastline ripped into the bones of the earth between La Ciotat and Marseille; and Marseille itself, every bit as good as its magnificent setting, as bad as any big port city, and as ugly as the fish in its heavenly *bouillabaisse*. Another plus: state-funded museums in the department of the Bouche de Rhône (and there are some good ones—only Paris has more than Marseille) charge only 10F admission.

Beaches

The beach at Cassis is pretty, with a dramatic backdrop of cliffs, but it gets crowded in summer. Marseille possesses an artificial town beach, lively at all times of the year, but for more adventurous sand head into the *calanques*. Boats run from Cassis and Marseille. West of Marseille, La Côte Bleue is the playground of the Marseillais and gets crowded at weekends in summer. The beaches are mediocre; the best is at Carro. For real sand continue west to the Camargue.

best beaches

Cassis: sand and cliffs.

Calanques: walk the cliff-top path and descend at will (*see* p.167).

Marseille (Plage du David): soccer, kites, skateboards and windsurfers; an action beach, artificial pebbles.

Sausset-les-Pins: sand and caravans.

Carro: the furthest from Marseille, hence the quietest.

La Ciotat, Cassis and the *Calanques*

Before settling down and creating the broad, smooth bay that permits the existence of Marseille, the Provençal coast bucks and rears with the fury of wild horses. La Ciotat, halfway between Toulon and Marseille, is a shipbuilding, hard-nosed and gritty town, while well-heeled Cassis is endowed with a dramatic setting, a bijou harbour and delicate wine.

Getting Around

La Ciotat is a main stop for **trains** between Marseille and Toulon; regular **buses** (℡ 04 42 08 90 90) cover the 3km from the station to the Vieux Port. Cassis' train station is just as far from the centre but has less frequent services; if you're coming from Marseille, take one of the frequent coaches that drop you off at Blvd Anatole France, near the tourist office. For **bike hire** the best is **Lleba Cycles,** 1 Ave Frédéric-Mistral, ℡ 04 42 83 60 30, in La Ciotat.

Tourist Information

La Ciotat ✉ 13600: Blvd Anatole France, ℡ 04 42 08 61 32, 🖷 04 42 08 17 88. **Cassis** ✉ 13260: Place Baragnon, ℡ 04 42 01 71 17, 🖷 04 42 01 28 31.

market days

La Ciotat: Tuesday and Sunday. **Cassis**: Wednesday and Friday.

local wine

Cassis: visit the vast, ancient *caves* of Clos Sainte-Magdeleine (℡ 04 42 01 70 28), or Château de Fontcreuse, Route de La Ciotat (℡ 04 42 01 71 09).

La Ciotat: the World's First Film Set

A safe anchorage with fresh water and beaches, protected from the winds by a queerly eroded rock formation known as the Bec de l'Aigle (the 'eagle's beak'), La Ciotat has seen ancient Greeks, pirates, fishermen and, since the time of François I, shipbuilders—though instead of galleys to battle the Empire, the yards now produce vessels to transport liquefied gas. La Ciotat has also given the world two momentous pastimes: first, motion pictures, pioneered here in 1895, when Auguste and Louis Lumière filmed a train pulling into La Ciotat station (*L'Entrée d'un train en gare de La Ciotat*), a clip that made history's first film spectators jump out of their seats as the locomotive seemed to bear down upon them; the **Eden Théâtre** where they were shown, on 28 December 1895, is the oldest surviving cinema. And second, *pétanque*, that most Provençal of sports, which came into being here in 1907 when one old-timer's legs became paralysed and he could no longer take the regulation steps before a throw, as laid down in the laws of *boules*. The rules were changed for him and, as everyone enjoyed working up less of a sweat, they stuck.

Most visitors to La Ciotat keep to the beaches and pleasure port around **La Ciotat-Plage,** but it's the business side of things, around the **Vieux Port,** that affords the best loafing; in the evening the shipyard cranes resemble luminous mutant insects from Mars. The **Musée Ciotaden,** 51 Rue des Poilus (*open 4–7, Sun 10–12, closed Tues and Thurs*), is dedicated to the history of La Ciotat and its shipyards. Beyond the latter, amid the wind-sculpted rocks and dishevelled Mediterranean flora of the Bec de l'Aigle is the cliff-top **Parc du Mugel** (Bus 3 from the Vieux Port). Avenue de Figuerolles continues from here to the red pudding-stone walls and pebble beach of the **Calanque de Figuerolles,** with its hunchback monkish rock formation, once painted by Braque. Floating off shore, the wee **Ile Verte** can be reached by boat from Quai Ganteaume.

The nicest hotels are at La Ciotat-Plage, beginning with the ★★★**Miramar**, 3 Blvd Beaurivage, ✆ 04 42 83 09 54, ✉ 04 42 83 33 79, a classy, updated old hotel amid pine groves, by the beach; half-board is mandatory in the summer, but its restaurant, **L'Orchidée**, ✆ 04 42 83 09 54 is the best in town (*menus from 125F*). ★**Beaurivage**, 1 Ave Beaurivage, ✆ 04 42 83 09 68, is a good budget choice, while in town ★★**La Rotonde**, 44 Blvd de la République, ✆ 04 42 08 67 50, ✉ 04 42 08 45 21, is your best bet near the Vieux Port. Quai Stalingrad near the shipyards has the widest choice of restaurants with cheap menus, most—surprise, surprise—featuring seafood. For something different, leave France behind for the **République Indépendente de Figuerolles**, a grand name for a *chambres d'hôte* (*260F for a double*) on the beach at the Calanque de Figuerolles, ✆ 04 42 08 41 71, ✉ 04 42 71 93 39, with a good restaurant that becomes Russian between November and May, with a great 120F menu.

Route des Crêtes

If you can sneer at vertigo and laugh in the face of tenuous hairpin turns, ignore the main road between La Ciotat and Cassis and twist and turn along the 17km **Corniche des Crêtes**. Alternatively, a footpath cuts through the road loops and takes about 4 hours. Your pains will be amply rewarded with plunging views from the highest cliffs in France: the **Falaises de Soubeyran**, or 'Big Head' (399m), and craggy **Cap Canaille**. From Pas de la Colle the road and path descend to the ancient Gallo-Roman *Portus Carcisis*, now known as Cassis.

Cassis and the *Calanques*

The old coral-fishing village of Cassis, with its fish-hook port, white cliffs, beaches and quaint houses spilling down steep alleyways, was a natural favourite of the Fauve painters. Since their day, the village has made the inevitable progression from fishing to artsy to chic, and beyond the purse of most fishermen and artists. The swanky modern Casino Municipal does a roaring trade thanks to its proximity to the gambling-mad Marseillais, and in the summer so many tourists descend on the little port it's often elbow room only, here and on the pebbly **Plage de Bestouan**. And when they're not counting wads of banknotes, the Cassidans bestir themselves to make one of the most delicious, fragrant white wines of Provence.

Until 1990 Cassis had yet another profitable trade: exporting crystal white stone, hewn from the sheer limestone cliffs that stand like a great jagged sea wall between Cassis and Marseille. Here and there the cliffs are pierced by startling tongues of lapis lazuli-mini fjords known as *calanques*. The nearest *calanque*, **Port-Miou** is accessible by car or foot (a 30-minute walk): here the hard,

Cassis Harbour.

white stone was cut for the Suez Canal. Another mile's hike will take you to **Port-Pin**, with a pretty beach, and another hour to **En-Vau**, the most beautiful of them all, with a small skinny dippers' beach tucked under the sheer cliffs, where daring human flies dangle from threads (you can also reach En-Vau with less toil from a car park on the Col de la Gardiole). Serious walkers can continue along GR 98 all the way to Marseille. **Note,** however: after being ravaged by forest fires in 1990 the paths to the *calanques* are strictly off limits from the beginning of July to the second Saturday in September, when the only way to visit is by motor boat from Cassis port; excursions depart frequently throughout the day.

Cassis ✉ *13260* **Where to Stay and Eating Out**

Don't expect any bargains in trendy Cassis. Most spectacular, perched on the promontory overlooking Cassis bay, is ★★★★**Les Roches Blanches**, Ave des Calanques, ✆ 04 42 01 09 30, 🖷 04 42 01 94 23. Rooms are a tad small, but very comfortable; there's a private beach and sun terraces, and as usual half-board is mandatory in season. Set amid lemon groves and bougainvillea, ★★★**Les Jardins du Campanile**, Rue Favier, ✆ 04 42 01 84 85, 🖷 04 42 01 32 38, is a lovely Provençal-style oasis, with a pool. *Closed Nov–Mar*. Just above the port, in a quiet park, ★★★**Le Royal Cottage**, 6 Ave du 11 Novembre, ✆ 04 42 01 33 34, 🖷 04 42 01 06 10, also has a pool, air conditioning and well equipped rooms—but no restaurant. Book months in advance for the more reasonable ★★**Grand Jardin**, 2 Rue Pierre Eydin, ✆ 04 42 01 70 10, 🖷 04 42 01 33 75. Otherwise try ★★**Laurence**, 8 Rue de l'Arène, ✆ 04 42 01 88 78, 🖷 04 42 01 81 04, with a view up to the château. *Closed mid-Nov–1 Mar*. West of Cassis, in a magnificent setting overlooking the *calanques*, France's most remote youth hostel, **La Fontasse**, Col de la Gardiole, ✆ 04 42 01 02 72, is a dusty drive or an hour's walk from town or the Marseille–Cassis bus stop *Les Calanques*. It's not for sissies—beds, lights, and cold water are the only creature comforts (45F a head, bring your own food).

The local, rosy-pink sea-urchins, *oursins*, often crop up on the menu in the company of other sea creatures at the excellent **La Presqu'île**, in Quartier de Port-Miou, ✆ 04 42 01 03 77; menus from 165F or ask what's best and eat *à la carte*. *Closed Nov–Mar and Sun eve*. Among the many places on the waterfront, **Chez César**, 21 Quai des Baux, ✆ 04 42 01 75 47, has reasonably priced food in a Marcel Pagnol decor. *Closed Mon eve, Tues, Jan*. Also on the waterfront, overlooking the château, **Nino**, 1 Quai Barthélemy, ✆ 04 42 01 74 32, has tasty fish soup and grilled prawns on a summery seaside terrace (*menus from 96F*). *Closed Sun eve, Mon*.

Marseille

Marseille isn't a city; it's a shock.

Marseille tourist office

Amid Provence's carefully nurtured image of lavender fields, rosé wine and *pétanque*, Marseille is the great anomaly, the second city of France (although Lyon is close) and the world's eighth-largest port. Like New York, it has been the gateway to a new world for hundreds of thousands of new arrivals—especially Corsicans, Armenians, Jews, Greeks, Turks, Italians, Spaniards and Algerians. Many immigrants have gone no further, creating in Marseille perhaps the most varied mix of cultures and religions in Europe, 'the meeting place of the entire world' as Alexandre Dumas called it. It is traditionally the great anti-Paris, ever defiant of central authority and big-wigs in any form, be they Julius Caesar, Louis XIV, Napoleon, Hitler or De Gaulle.

Unfortunately, Marseille also shares some of New York's less savoury traits: racial hostility towards whoever was the last off the boat, the petty crooks and hardened gangsters of the French mafia, or *milieu*, heroin and prostitution rings, political and financial scandals, and an international reputation put about by films like *The French Connection*. Unemployment is disproportionately high and xenophobia thrives: the National Front holds the reins in the industrial suburb of Marignan, and in the spring of 1995 a young immigrant was shot dead after a struggle over National Front bill posters.

'These Marseillais make Marseilles hymns, and Marseilles vests, and Marseilles soap for all the world; but they never sing their hymns, or wear their vests, or wash with their soap themselves,' wrote Mark Twain. So what *do* they do? Marseille (pop. 800,000) is a great unknown, a metropolis of 111 villages that in its 2600 years has contributed precious little to Western civilization; it is the eternal capital of great expectations, 'a city that's been waiting for Godot', according to an editor in one of Marseille's young publishing houses. There are hints (in theatre, the plastic arts, and research) that its long bottled-up juices are ripe and ready to flow. It has recently been declared a Ville d'Art, which translates, on a practical level, into state funds for restoration of its historic monuments, and the new RPR city government seems determined to make Marseille not only respectable, but also welcoming to visitors; if nothing else it comes as an unclogging shot of *pastis* to the blood after the Côte d'Azur.

History

The story goes that in 600 BC Greek colonists from the Ionian city of Phocaea, having obtained the approval of the gods, loaded their ship with olive saplings and sailed towards Gaul. They found a perfect bay, and their handsome leader Protis went to the local king to obtain permission to found a city. It just so happened that that very day the king was hosting a banquet for the young men of his land, after which, according to tradition, his daughter Gyptis would select her husband. Protis was invited to join, and, thanks to his great beauty, was chosen by the princess. For his new wife's dowry, Protis asked for the land the Greeks coveted near the mouth of the Rhône, including the Lacydon (the *Vieux Port*). He named the new city Massalia.

Massalia boomed from the start; by 530 BC it had its own treasury at Delphi, and its own colonies, from Málaga to Nice; it traded for tin with Cornwall and its great astronomer Pytheas explored the Baltic and in 350 BC became the first scientist to accurately calculate latitudes. As a commercial rival of Carthage, the city allied itself with Rome in the Punic Wars, and profited from the latter's conquests in Spain and Gaul. By the 2nd century BC, Massalia had a population of 50,000, and they were ruled by a merchant oligarchy whose political astuteness was admired by Aristotle and Cicero. This astuteness failed them when they sided with Pompey, calling down the vengeance of Caesar, who conquered their city after a long siege and seized all of Massalia's colonies, with the exception of Nice and Hyères. Yet even after the 2nd century AD, when Massalia adopted Roman law, it remained a city apart, the westernmost enclave of Hellenism, with famous schools of Greek rhetoric and medicine.

As the Pax Romana crumbled, Marseille nearly went out of business, taking hard knocks from Goths, Franks, Saracens and then more Franks again in the 700s under Charles Martel. Plagued by pirates, business stayed bad until the 11th century, when the Crusaders showed up looking for transport to the Holy Land. This was the best get-rich-quick opportunity of the Middle Ages, and although Genoa and Venice grabbed the biggest trading concessions in the Levant, Marseille too grew fat on the proceeds. Briefly a republic, the city's real power soon passed to a merchant oligarchy; between 1178 and 1192 the big boss was the cultivated En Barral, patron of two of Provence's greatest troubadours, the mad Peire Vidal and Folquet of Marseille (*see* p.58).

Trumped by Kings: Charles d'Anjou to Louis XIV

When Charles d'Anjou acquired Provence in 1252, he confiscated Marseille's entire fleet to make good his claim on Sicily. Thanks to the monumental arrogance of the Angevins, the ships were annihilated in the revolt of the Sicilian Vespers (1282). With its legitimate commerce undermined by its own rulers, Marseille became a den for pirates and went into such a decline that it became an easy target for the Angevins' rival, Alfonso V of Aragon, who destroyed as much of it as he could in 1423.

Coming under French rule in 1481 meant, for Marseille, tumbling headlong into the power-grasping scrum known as the Wars of Italy (1494–1559). The city's galleys went to war again, this time for François I, earning the fury of Emperor Charles V, who sent his henchman, the rebel Constable of Bourbon, to besiege the city. Marseille resisted heroically, and François I showed his gratitude by giving the city the freedom to trade at will in the eastern Mediterranean. Once again the money rolled in, to be pumped into new industries, especially soap and sugar.

Marseille's longing to be left alone to mind her own affairs put her squarely at odds with Louis XIV; for 40 years the city thumbed its nose at his Solar Majesty while scrambling to retain its autonomy. By 1660, the King had had enough, and opened up a great breach in Marseille's walls, and humiliated the city by turning its own cannons back on itself. The central authority that Louis forced on Marseille was dangerously lax when it came to issues crucial to the running of a good port—like quarantine. The result, in 1720, was a devastating plague that spread throughout Provence.

Tunes, Booms and Busts

Marseille buried its dead and went right back to business. New markets in the Middle East, North Africa, and America made it Europe's greatest port in the 18th century. Its industries (soap, woollens, porcelain, tarot cards) blossomed—then withered away in the Revolution, which for ten years bitterly divided workers and the oligarchy. The former did their share in upholding of the Revolution; as 500 volunteers set off for Paris in July 1792, someone suggested singing the new battle song of the Army of the Rhine, recently composed by Rouget de l'Isle. It caught on, and as the Marseillais marched along, they improved the rhythm and harmonies. By the time they reached Paris, the 'song of the Marseillais' was perfected and became the hit tune of the Revolution, and subsequently, the most rousing and bloodcurdling of national anthems.

But as the Revolution devolved into the Terror, Marseille was found so wanting in proper politics that it was known in Paris as the *ville sans nom*. Any building that had sheltered an anti-Revolutionary was demolished, including the famous monastery of St-Victor. The misery continued under Napoleon, who was added to the list of Marseille's bogeymen when he provoked the continental blockade by the British and ruined trade. Recovery came with the

Second Empire, the conquest of Algeria in 1830, and the construction of the Suez Canal. Soon Marseille was more prosperous than ever, and more populous, with some 60,000 new immigrants every decade between 1850 and 1930—Greeks and Armenians fleeing the Turks, Italians fleeing Fascism, and later, Spaniards fleeing Franco.

After becoming one of the first French cities to vote socialist (1890), Marseille's reputation took a nosedive. Corruption, rigged elections and an open link between the Hôtel de Ville and the bosses of the *milieu* were so rampant that in 1938 Paris dissolved the municipal government and ran the city at a distance. Yet the '30s also saw the release of Marcel Pagnol's classic Marseillais film trilogy *Marius*, *Fanny* and *César*, which helped create throughout France an insatiable appetite for *operette marseillaise*; even Josephine Baker sang the tunes of Marseille's great songwriter, Vincent Scotto.

In 1953, Marseille elected a socialist mayor—Gaston Deferre, the antagonist of De Gaulle, who reigned until his death in 1986. Deferre oversaw rapid, and difficult changes: a sharp decline in trade when France lost its colonies, and a population that exploded from 660,000 in 1955 to 960,000 in 1975. To accommodate the new arrivals (mostly North Africans and French refugees from Algeria) the city infested itself with the shoddy high-rise housing that scars it to this day. Unemployment rose as the traditional soap and fat industries plummeted, and new projects such as the steel-mills and port at Fos failed to provide as many jobs as expected—fuelling the racial tensions and organized crime that still give the city a rough reputation.

Even when the city, or at least its revered soccer team, L'Olympique de Marseille, won the European championship in 1993, the team got itself banned from 1994 European competition on charges of match fixing and bribery. The team's flamboyant ex-owner, maverick politician, businessman and Euro-deputy Bernard Tapie futilely denied everything and had to serve time.

Less well known than all the scandals is Marseille's reorientation, for the first time in its history, away from the Mediterranean and towards Europe. New high-speed rail links are being built, and a canal will link the Rhône with the Rhine by 2010. Marseille is now the most important research centre in France after Paris, home of a major science university, inventor of a new fifth-generation computer language, and site of COMEX, the world's leading developer of underwater technologies.

Getting There

By air: Marseille's airport is to the west at Marignane; call ☏ 04 42 78 21 00 for flight information. (Air France, ☏ 0 802 802 802). A bus every 20 minutes (☏ 04 91 50 59 34) links the airport with the train station, Gare St-Charles, and takes 25 minutes.

By train: Gare St-Charles is the main train station, and the only one in France that could star in a Busby Berkeley musical, with its big stagey staircase, draped with buxom statues representing Asia and Africa. There are connections to nearly every town in the south, and the TGV will get you to Paris in 4 hours and 40 minutes.

By boat: Ferries sail to Algeria (politics permitting) Corsica, Sardinia and Tunisia; contact SNCM, 61 Blvd des Dames, ☏ 04 91 56 30 10; reservations ☏ 04 91 56 35 86, ✉ 04 91 56 35 86.

By metro and bus: Marseille runs an efficient bus network and two metro lines: the metro is safe, quick and highly efficient, but the buses can be an experience. Pick up the useful *plan du réseau* at the tourist office or at the RTM (Réseau de Transport

Marseillais) information desk by the Bourse, 6–8 Rue des Fabres, ✆ 04 91 91 92 10. Tickets are 8F, valid for an hour, and are transferable between the bus and metro. At night a number of buses (Fluobus) run from the Canebière across town. The coach station, ✆ 04 91 08 16 40, is behind the train station at 3 Place Victor Hugo, with connections to Aix, Cassis, Nice, Arles, Avignon, Toulon and Cannes. RTM also has guided tour buses: the *Bus Pagnol*, for sites associated with Pagnol's childhood, and a *Histobus*, a tour of historic Marseille.

By taxi: if you need a taxi, call ✆ 04 91 03 60 03 or ✆ 04 91 05 80 00, and make sure the meter is switched on at the start of your journey.

Car hire: some car hire firms are in the Gare St-Charles, including **Avis**, ✆ 04 91 08 41 80. Others include **Hertz**, at 16 Blvd Charles Nédelec (1er), ✆ 04 91 14 04 24, and **Thrifty**, 8 Blvd Voltaire, ✆ 04 91 05 92 18.

Tourist Information

By the Vieux Port, at 4 La Canebière, ✆ 04 91 13 89 00, ✉ 04 91 13 89 20 (open Mon–Sat 9–7 in winter, 8.30–8 in summer, Sun 10–5). Also in the train station, ✆ 04 91 50 59 18. Check at 4 La Canebière for tours of the Opéra and the Vieux Port forts and 'Taxi Tourisme'—four different set-price taxi tours of the city (145–515F), with an English cassette guide to expain what's what.

The central **post office** is at 1 Place de l'Hôtel des Postes (1er), ✆ 04 91 15 47 31.

Emergencies: Hospital, 264 Rue St-Pierre, ✆ 04 91 38 60 00.

Special Information Centres exist for **young people**, at the very helpful CIJ, 4 Rue de la Visitation, ✆ 04 91 24 33 50; **disabled visitors**, at the Office Municipal pour Handicapés et Inadaptés, 128 Ave du Prado (8e), ✆ 04 91 81 58 80; and **crime victims**, at AVAD, 56 Rue Montgrand (6e), ✆ 04 91 33 11 91, which will help out if you're robbed.

Orientation

Marseille, with 111 neighbourhoods and 16 *arrondissements*, is one of Europe's largest cities, sprawling over twice as many acres as Paris. The northern neighbourhoods are the poorest, the first addresses of many new immigrants; the Panier (*see* below) and neighbourhoods around the station constitute the North African quarters, lively during the day but uncomfortable to wander in after dark. The southern neighbourhoods, with their parks and access to the beaches, are distinctly more monied and sanitized. A circle of hills divides the city from the mainland, physically and psychologically.

The Vieux Port, the heart of the city since its founding, is now used only for pleasure craft and boats out to the islets of Frioul and the Château d'If, while commercial port activities are concentrated to the north in the *Rade de Marseille*. To the south of the Vieux Port, where the golden Virgin of Notre-Dame de la Garde towers high over her beloved city, the Parc du Pharo marks the start of a *corniche* road along the coast to Cap Croisette, lined with coves, beaches and restaurants, with a mountain, Marseilleveyre, that you can climb at the end for a view of all of the above.

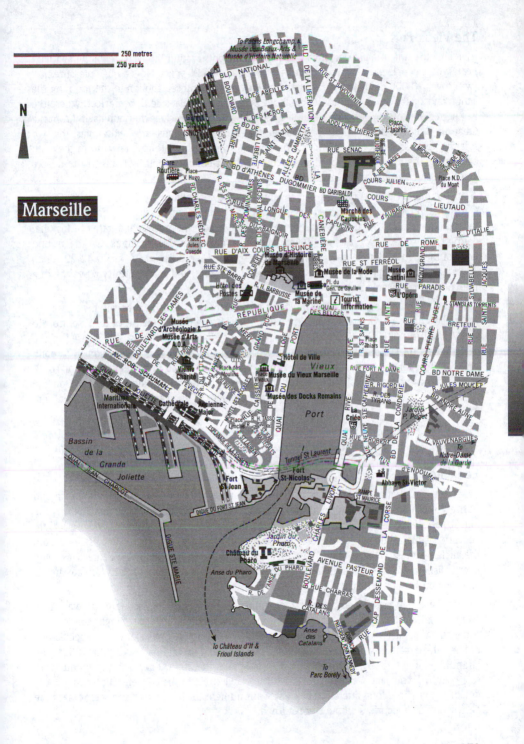

Marseille

To Palais Longchamp,
Musée des Beaux-Arts &
Musée d'Histoire Naturelle

Scale: 250 metres / 250 yards

N

Gare
St-Charles
(SNCF)

BLD NATIONAL

R. DES ABEILLES

R. DES HÉROS

BD DE LA LIBERATION

R. ST SAVOURNIN

Place
J. Jaurès

R. ADOLPHE THIERS

ST MICHEL FONTAINE

BD DE LA LIBERTÉ

ST BAZILE

Gare
Routière

Place
V. Hugo

BD d'ATHÈNES

ALLÉES GAMBETTA

RUE SÉNAC

Place N.D.
du Mont

BOULEVARD VOLTAIRE

BD CHARLES NÉDÉLEC

R. DES PTES. MARIES

RUE DES DOMINICAINES

RUE DES DOMINICAINES

BD DUGOMMIER

BD GARIBALDI

COURS JULIEN

R. D'AUBAGNE

LIEUTAUD

Place
Jules
Guesde

RUE D'AIX

COURS BELSUNCE

Marché des
Capucins

CAPUCINS

CANEBIÈRE

RUE DE

ROME

R. D'ITALIE

RUE STE-BARBE

RUE D'AIX

Musée d'Histoire
de Marseille

Musée de la Mode

RUE ST FERRÉOL

R. STANISLAS TORRENTS

Hôtel des
Postes

R. H. BARBUSSE

COLBERT

Musée de
la Marine

Pl. du
Gén. de Gaulle

Musée
Cantini

L'Opéra

RUE PARADIS

BRETEUIL

RUE SYLVABELLE

RUE ST JACQUES

Musée
d'Archéologie &
Musée d'Arts
A.O.A.

RÉPUBLIQUE

GRAND RUE

Tourist
Information

QUAI
DES BELGES

Place
Thiars

R. ST SAËNS

RUE SAINTE

RUE PIERRE PUGET

COURS

BOULEVARD DES DAMES

RUE DE LA

BOULEVARD DES DAMES

Vieille
Charité

Place des
Moulins

Hôtel de Ville

Vieux

Musée du Vieux Marseille

RUE FORT N. DAME

BD NOTRE DAME

BD JULES MOULET

QUAI DE LA JOLIETTE

Gare
Maritime
Internationale

Cathédrale

Ancienne-
Major

Place
Lenche

Musée des Docks Romains

Port

La
Criée

RUE NEUVE STE CATHERINE

R. RIGORD

R. DES
TYRANS

BD ANDRÉ AUNE

Jardin
P. Puget

R. VAUVENARGUES

To
Notre-Dame
de la Garde

Bassin
de la
Grande
Joliette

QUAI JEAN CHARCOT

R. H. TASSO

QUAI

RIVE NEUVE

R. ROBERT

BD DE LA CORDERIE

Tunnel St Laurent

d'ENDOUME

Abbaye St-Victor

Fort
St-Jean

Fort
St-Nicolas

CHARLES LIVON

RAMPE
ST MAURICE

DESSEMOND DE LA CORSE

DIGUE DU FORT ST JEAN

Jardin du
Pharo

Château du
Pharo

BOULEVARD DU PHARO

AVENUE PASTEUR

DIGUE STE MARIE

Anse du Pharo

R. DE L'ANSE

RUE CHARRAS

R. DES
CATALANS

C.F.P.

To Château d'If &
Frioul Islands

Anse
des
Catalans

CORNICHE PRÉSIDENT JOHN KENNEDY

To
Parc Borély

The Vieux Port

Marseille the urban mangrove entwines its aquatic roots around the neat, rectangular Vieux Port, where people have lived continuously for the past 2600 years. Now a huge pleasure port (with over 10,000 berths) its cafés have fine views of the sunset, though in the morning the action and smells centre around the Quai des Belges and its boat-side **fish market**, where the key ingredients of *bouillabaisse* are touted in a racy *patois* as thick as the soup itself. From the Quai des Belges *vedettes* sail to the Château d'If and Frioul islands (*see* below), past the two bristling fortresses that still defend the harbour: to the north, **St-Jean**, first built in the 12th century by the Knights of St John, and to the south **St-Nicolas**, built by Louis XIV to keep a close eye on Marseille rather than the sea.

A bronze marker in the Quai des Belges pinpoints the spot where the Greeks first set foot in Gaul. And yet Marseille concealed its age until this century, when excavations for the glitzy new shopping mall, the Centre Bourse, revealed the eastern ramparts and gate of Massalia, dating back to the 3rd century BC, now enclosed in the **Jardin des Vestiges**. On the ground floor of the Centre Bourse, the **Musée d'Histoire de Marseille** (© 04 91 90 42 22, *open Mon–Sat 12–7*), displays models, everyday items, mosaics, and a 3rd-century BC wreck of a Roman ship, discovered in 1974.

Elaborate antique models of later ships that sailed into the Vieux Port and items related to Marseille's trading history are the main focus of the **Musée de la Marine et de l'Economie de Marseille**, © 04 91 39 33 33 (*open 10–12 and 2–6, closed Tues*). It's housed in the 1860 **Palais de la Bourse**, France's oldest stock exchange, built under Napoleon III to obliterate an unrepentant democratic quarter that spilled much blood in the Revolution of 1848. But this corner, stock exchange or not, remained a vortex for violence: a plaque on the Canebière side of the Bourse recalls that King Alexander of Yugoslavia was assassinated here in 1934.

Just up La Canibère from here, at No. 11, the **Musée de la Mode**, © 04 91 56 59 57 (*open Tues–Sun 12–7; adm*) has Chanel clothes and other pieces from the 1930s to the present.

Le Panier

On sunny afternoons the Marseillais laze like contented cats in the cafés lining the north end of the Vieux Port, a custom probably as old as the city itself. Rising up behind them is the oldest part of the city, known rather oddly as the Panier or 'Basket' after a popular 17th-century cabaret, although its irregular weave of winding narrow streets and stairs date from the ancient Greeks. When the well-to-do moved out in the 18th century, the Panier was given over to fishermen and a romanticized underworld; guides were published to its 'private' hotels and the hourly rates of their residents.

Before the war it was a lively Corsican and Italian neighbourhood, and later its warren of secret ways absorbed hundreds of Jews and other refugees from the Nazis, hoping to escape to America. In January 1943, Hitler cottoned on and, in collusion with local property speculators, ordered the dynamiting of everything between the Vieux Port and halfway up the hill, to the Grand'Rue/Rue Caisserie. Given one day to evacuate, the 20,000 departing residents were screened by French and German police, who selected 3500 for the concentration camps, sent out of the city in a long line of tram cars. A monument in the quarter commemorates the destruction and deportees who never returned.

Two buildings were protected from the dynamite: the 17th-century **Hôtel de Ville** on the quay, and behind it, in Rue de la Prison, the **Maison Diamantée**, Marseille's 16th-century Mannerist masterpiece, named after the pyramidical points of its façade. It holds the **Musée du Vieux Marseille** (*due to be reopened after a major restoration*), a delightful attic where the city stashes its odds and ends—Provençal furniture; an extraordinary relief diorama made in 1850 by an iron merchant, depicting the uprising of 1848; 18th-century Neapolitan Christmas crib figures and *santons* made in Marseille; playing and tarot cards, long an important local industry; and poignant photos of the Panier before it was blown to smithereens. Some of the cheap housing thrown up after the war in Place du Mazeau has been demolished in turn to make way for a museum dedicated to the flamboyant sculptor and native Marseillais César.

The dynamite that blew up the lower Panier was responsible for revealing the contents of the **Musée des Docks Romains**, 2 Place Vivaux, ✆ 04 91 91 24 62 (*open daily 10–5 winter, 11–6 summer; adm*), built over a stretch of the vast 1st-century AD Roman quay, where wine and grains were stored in *dolia* or massive jars. Exhibits describe seafaring in the ancient Mediterranean. One last survivor of the pre-war Panier is the oldest house in Marseille, the **Hôtel de Cabre** (1535), a Gothic-Renaissance confection on Grand'Rue. The city's oldest café, the 1903 **Café de Parisien**, with colourful mosaics and stuccoes intact, is just up on Place Sadi-Carnot.

The Panier retains its original crusty character atop the well worn steps of **Montée des Accoules** and around **Place de Lenche**, once the market, or *agora* of the Greeks: lanky cats prowl, laundry flaps, cement mixers grind away, people sit on the sidewalk in kitchen chairs— it still feels more Greek than French, although that may soon change: a five-year programme to rehabilitate 1700 of the Panier's 3000 homes and flats has just begun, with the ground floors set aside for shops of 'touristic interest'. Signs point the way through the maze to the top of Rue du Petit-Puits and the elegant **Vieille-Charité**, designed by Pierre Puget, a student of Bernini and court architect to Louis XIV—and a native of the Panier. Built by the city fathers between 1671 and 1745 to take in homeless migrants from the countryside, this is one of the world's most palatial workhouses: three storeys of arcaded ambulatories in pale pink stone, overlooking a court with a sumptuous elliptical chapel crowned by an oval dome—a curvaceous Baroque work forced into a straitlaced neo-Corinthian façade in 1863. Although the complex became a barracks after the Revolution, it returned to its original purpose in 1860, housing families displaced first by the construction of the Bourse and later by the Nazis' destruction of the Panier. By 1962, the Charité was in so precarious a state that everyone was evacuated, and Le Corbusier, happening through, warned the city it was in danger of losing a masterpiece. A long restoration ensued, and in 1985 it reopened as a cultural centre.

The Charité's middle gallery houses the excellent **Musée d'Archéologie Méditerranéenne**, ✆ 04 91 14 58 80 (*open daily except Mon, 10–5 winter, 11–6 summer; adm*), featuring a collection of ancient Mediterranean artefacts. The remarkable Egyptian art (second in France, after the Louvre) has a range of fine art and sculpture to everyday bric a brac and cat, ibis and crocodile mummies; there are beautiful works from ancient Cyprus, Susa, Mesopotamia, Greece (including a good section of vases) and pre-Roman and Roman Italy. Another section is devoted to the reconstructed **Sanctuary of Roquepertuse** from Velaux, near Aix. Built by a headhunting Celto-Ligurian tribe called the Salians, the sanctuary has pillars pierced with holes to hold skulls, a lintel incised with the outline of four horse heads (who symbolically transported the dead soul), and Buddha-like figures sitting in the lotus position. Similar temples found in Entremont (*see* p.199) and Mouriès suggest a common religion, perhaps a chthonic cult in which warriors went to commune with the spirits of their dead heroes. The Charité also houses the **Musée d'Arts Africains, Océaniens et Amérindiens** (*same hours*) with a fascinating collection of ritual artefacts, especially those dealing with more recent cultures obsessed with human heads and skulls, particularly in the Amazon and Vanuatu.

Just to the north, looming over the tankers and cargo ships drowsing in Marseille's outer harbour basin, are the two 'majors'. The striped neo-Byzantine, empty and unloved **Cathédrale de la Major** (*closed Mon and 12–2*) was built in 1853 with the new money coming in from the conquest of Algeria—enough to make it the largest church built in France since the Middle Ages. The pile is held up by 444 marble columns; predictably, somehow, the monster is not only ugly but dangerous, and has to be encased in nets to keep passers-by from being brained with bits of falling stone. Its Romanesque predecessor, the **Ancienne-Major**, is in better nick, in spite of having its transept brutally amputated for the new cathedral (note the poor angel, gesturing sadly without a hand). If the interior has reopened after restoration, don't miss the Ancienne-Major's crossing, a fantasy in brick that sets an octagonal dome on four stepped conical squinches, a typically Provençal conceit. One chapel has a *Descent from the Cross* (early 1500s), by Nicolas della Robbia, and the altar of *SS. Lazarus, Martha, and Mary Magdalene* in Carrara marble is by Francesco Laurana (1475–81), considered by Anthony Blunt to be 'the earliest purely Italian work on French soil'. What you never get to see is the Ancienne-Major's old curiosity shop of relics: part of Jesus' cradle and one of His tears, St Peter's tooth, and best of all, the fishbones left over from the feast at the Sermon on the Mount.

South of the Vieux Port: Quai de Rive Neuve and St-Victor

In the last decade, this part of the Old Port has made a comeback: at lunchtime and on summer evenings half of Marseille descends on its bars, restaurants, theatres and clubs on the quay, Rue Saint-Saens and Place Thiars. The oldest cultural institution here is **Opéra**, two blocks south of the port in Place Reyer, built in 1924 and graced with Art Deco Greek gods, and a pure Art Deco interior (*see* the tourist office for tours). Two streets back, at 19 Rue Grignan, a *hôtel particulier* houses the **Musée Cantini**, © 04 91 54 77 75 (*open 10–5, closed Mon; adm*) and its modern art and frequent special exhibitions. Permanent displays include Paul Signac's shimmering *Port de Marseille*, and the first Cubist views of L'Estaque that Dufy painted with Braque in 1908; the greater part of the Cantini's post 1960 works have been moved into the new Musée d'Art Contemporain (*see* p.180).

On **Quai de Rive Neuve** you'll find ship chandlers' shops, restaurants, and the national theatre, **La Criée**, installed in a former fish auction house (*see* below). For better or worse, its presence has tamed the once salty Rive Neuve bars, including the **Bar de la Marine**, no longer recognizable as the set for the famous card-playing scene in Marcel Pagnol's *Marius*. Further along the *quai*, steps lead up to battlemented walls and towers good enough for a Hollywood castle, defending one of the oldest Christian shrines in Provence, the **Abbaye St-Victor**. St-Victor was founded in AD 416 by St Jean Cassien, formerly an anchorite in the Egyptian Thebaid. One account has it that he brought with him from Egypt the mummy of St Victor, though the more popular version says Victor was a Roman legionary who converted to Christianity, and slew at least one sea serpent (see the relief over the door) before being ground to a pulp between a pair of millstones.

St-Victor may be Marseille's oldest church, but it's no fuddy duddy: like Broadway it has an electronic sign at the entrance reeling off news, and the side aisles are equipped with TV screens so all the parishoners can view mass at the high altar—doings Jean Cassien never imagined 1600 years ago when he excavated the first chapels into the flank of an ancient stone quarry near a Hellenistic necropolis, which he expanded for Christian use as a *martyrium* (rock-cut burials surrounding the tomb of a martyr). In the 11th century, when the monks of St-Victor adopted the Rule of St Benedict, they added the church on top, turning the old chapels into a labyrinthine **crypt** (*open 9–7; adm*). Although now well lit, this curious termitary, with ceilings ranging from 6 to 60ft high, is suffused with ancient mystery—some of the beautifully sculpted sarcophagi date from the 3rd century AD and were found to contain seven or eight dead monks crowded like sardines, proof of the popularity of an abbey that founded 300 monastic houses in Provence and even Sardinia. Then there's the 5th-century sarcophagus of St Jean Cassien, showing the saint preaching among the columns, and the cave-like 5th-century chapel, carved with a pair of weird old faces and stained green with moss, traditionally enshrining one of Marseille's three Black Virgins (supposedly Christian adaptations of Artemis, the patroness of Massalia). A primordial Candlemas rite begins here every 2 February: the archbishop comes to bless green candles before the Virgin, who gets to go out in a procession that ends at the abbey's bakery, where small loaves (*navettes*) are baked in the shape of boats—a similar custom, in the temples of Isis, once heralded the start of the navigation season. The faithful then take the green candles home to light at wakes as a symbol of rebirth.

Notre Dame de la Garde

Below St-Victor is Louis XIV's **Fort St-Nicolas**, and beyond that, the **Château du Pharo** (bus 83 from the Vieux Port), built by Napoleon III as a gift for his wife, the Empress Eugénie, who never got around to seeing it. The gardens, with striking views over the port, are used for concerts and summer theatre under the stars; beyond are the *calanques* (*see* p.180). The prize 360° view, however, is from Marseille's watchtower hill—an isolated limestone outcrop towering 162m above the city, crowned by **Notre-Dame de la Garde**, a neo-Byzantine/Romanesque pile with an unfortunate resemblance to a locomotive (a killer walk, and even fairly hair-raising to drive; let bus 60 do the work, from Place aux Huiles on Quai de Rive Neuve). This landmark supports France's largest golden mega-Madonna, 33ft high and shining like a beacon out to sea. In 1214 a monk of St-Victor built the first chapel here, and over the decades it gained a reputation for the miracles performed by a statue of the Virgin, Marseille's 'Bonne Mère'. The chapel's florid Second Empire architecture attracted some real bombs when the Nazis made it their headquarters and last stand, and you can still see some of the dents. But besides the view, the main attraction is the basilica's great **collection of ex votos**, painted by fishermen and sailors.

La Canebière

Before La Canebière itself was laid out in Louis XIV's expansion scheme of 1666, this area was the ropemakers' quarter. The hemp they used has given its name to Marseille's most famous boulevard—*chanvre* in French, but in Provençal more like the Latin *cannabis*—a not entirely inappropriate allusion, for this was the high street of French *dolce far niente*, an essential ingredient of music-hall Marseille, which could swagger and boast that 'the Champs-Elysées is the Canebière of Paris'. In its day La Canebière sported grand cafés, fancy shops and hotels where travellers of yore had their first thrills before sailing off to exotic lands, but these days La

Canebière—or 'Can o' beer' as English sailors know it—has suffered the same fate as the Champs-Elysées: banks, airline offices and heavy traffic. Trees would do it a world of good.

Some of the Canebière's old pizzazz lingers in the lively streets to the south around 'Marseille's stomach', the **Marché des Capucins**, a grazer's heaven, where the air is filled with tempting, exotic smells. Here, too, is Noailles station, the last resting-place for the city's retired omnibuses and tramways (**Galérie des Transports**, ✆ 04 91 54 15 15, *open 11–6 summer, 10–5 winter, closed Sun and Mon*); Marseille's last working tram still has its terminus here. Behind this hurly-burly stretches the **Cours Julien**, a favourite promenade and *pétanque* court, lined with many antique shops, galleries and several trendy restaurants.

North, and perpendicular to La Canebière, extends another tarnished grand boulevard, **Cours Belsunce**. Until 1964 No. 54 was the site of the famous neo-Moorish/Art Nouveau music-hall where Maurice Chevalier and Fernandel once starred, and where Tino Rossi and Yves Montand had their stage débuts. Now the Cours leads only to the **Porte d'Aix**, a fuzzy-minded Roman triumphal arch, vintage 1823, erected to Louis XVI or Liberty or both, adorned with statues of virtues such as Resignation and Prudence, whose heads (much like Louis XVI's) suddenly fell off in 1937 and rolled down the street. This quarter, like the Panier, is now mostly North African: Marseille's mosque is just on the other side of the arch.

Palais Longchamp and Environs

In 1834 Marseille suffered a drought so severe that it dug a canal to bring in water from the Durance. This 80km feat of aquatic engineering ends with a heroic splash at the **Palais Longchamp**, a delightfully overblown nymphaeum and cascade, populated with stone felines, bulls, and a buxom allegory of the Durance (Ⓜ Longchamp-Cinq-Avenues; bus 80 from La Canebière). Behind the palace stretch the public gardens, an observatory (one of four in this city, which has been the home of many famous astronomers) and a little zoo; in the right wing of the palace itself, some of the same creatures are embalmed in the **Musée d'Histoire Naturelle**, sharing space with their fossilized ancestors (*open 10–12 and 2–6, closed Tues and Wed am*).

The left wing of the Palais Longchamp houses the **Musée des Beaux Arts**, ✆ 04 91 14 59 30 (*open daily 10–5 winter, 11–6 summer; adm*). Formed around art 'conquered' by Napoleon's army, it has some second-rate canvases by Italian masters such as Perugino, and stagey burlesques like Rubens' violent *Boar Hunt* (in which ladies daintily watch the spurting blood) or Louis Finson's *Samson and Delilah* (1600), with a nasty Delilah tugging the ear of a very dirty-footed Samson. The mood changes with Michel Serre's scrupulously dire *Scenes of the Marseille Plague of 1720*, where a large percentage of the plague's 40,000 victims are shown dropping like flies while healthy rich men in suits prance by on horseback, looking politely sympathetic.

These same gentlemen never dismounted to assist Marseille's native artists, either—even an establishment figure like Baroque sculptor, architect, and painter Pierre Puget (1671–1745); the rooms devoted to him feature models for buildings and a lovely square that Marseille regretfully never built. Then there's Françoise Duparc, a follower of Chardin (1726–76), who worked most of her life in England; and the satirist Honoré Daumier (1808–97), who went to prison for his biting caricatures of Louis-Philippe's toadies, here represented by Spitting Image-style satirical busts modelled after his drawings. Here, too, is Van Gogh's roving, bohemian precursor, Adolphe Monticelli (1824–86), who sold his paint-encrusted canvases of frag-mented colour for a day's food and drink in the cafés along La Canebière. Also of note are paintings by Provençal pre-Impressionists, especially 18th-century scenes of Marseille's port by Joseph Vernet and sun-drenched landscapes by Paul Guigou.

Just across Boulevard Longchamp at 140, the **Musée Grobet-Labadié** (*open daily 10–5 winter, 11-6 summer, closed Mon; adm*), contains a private collection as interesting for its eclecticism as for any individual painting, table, plate, instrument, tapestry, or iron lock.

Heading South: Le Corbusier and Mazargues

The building that achieves speed will achieve success.

Le Corbusier

To pay your respects to Modular Man, take bus 21 from the Bourse down dreary Boulevard Michelet to the *Corbusier* stop. In 1945, at the height of Marseille's housing crisis, the French government commissioned Le Corbusier to build an experimental **Unité d'Habitation**, derived from his 1935 theory of 'La Cité Radieuse'. Le Corbusier thought the solution to urban *anomie*, transport, and housing problems was to put living-space, schools, shops, and recreational facilities all under one roof, in a building designed according to the human proportions of Leonardo da Vinci's Renaissance man-in-a-circle, reborn as Le Corbusier's wiggly Modular Man symbol. You can see the Man in relief on the concrete *pilotis*, or stilts, the most revolutionary aspect of the building. Le Corbusier, who knew the future role of cars, intended that the ground level should be for parking.

For a city like Marseille, where people enjoy getting out and about at ground level, the building was a ghastly aberration, and they nicknamed it the *casa de fada* or 'house of the mentally deranged'. Plans for other *unités* were stifled and in 1952 the state sold the flats off as co-ops. But architects were entranced; for the next 30 years thousands of buildings in every city in the world went up on *pilotis*, before everyone realized that the Marseillais were right all along: it was madness to deprive a building of its most important asset, a ground floor. The Unité's genuinely good points, unfortunately, had few imitators—each of its 337 flats is built on two levels and designed for maximum privacy, each with fine views over the mountains or sea. Of the original extras, only the school, the top-floor gym, and the communal hotel for residents' guests (*see* 'Where to Stay', below) have survived.

Bus 21 continues towards **Mazargues**, a once-fashionable *banlieue* under the Massif de Marseilleveyre, famous in the 19th century for its climate. And when its residents died, at a ripe old age, they often chose to be remembered in the local **cemetery** by a mini-monument to their life's work—there are stone hedge-clippers, fishing boats, hoes and, on the tomb of an omnibus driver, a tramway.

Marseille's Corniche and Parc Borély

Why go to the Riviera when Marseille has one of its very own? From the Vieux Port, you can catch bus 83, and pass the Parc du Pharo, to Corniche Kennedy, a dramatic road overlooking a dramatic coast that must have reminded the ancient Greek colonists of home—now improved with artificial beaches, bars, restaurants, villas and nightclubs.

Amazingly, until the road was built in the 1850s, the first cove, the picture postcard **Anse des Catalans**, was so isolated that the Catalan fisherfolk who lived there as squatters in the ruins of the old Lazaretto (or quarantine station) could hardly speak French. This now has the most popular (and the only real) sandy beach. From the bus stop *Vallon des Auffes* you can walk down to the fishing village of **Anse des Auffes** ('of the ropemakers'), isolated from the corniche until after the Second World War and still determinedly intact. Other typical quarters with still more piquant names lie further on: **Anse de Maldormé** and **Anse de la Fausse Monnaie**. As soon as the corniche was built, the wealthy families of Marseille planted grand villas along it: the Château Talabot is one of the most spectacular of these.

The *corniche* then descends to the artificial **Plages Gaston Deferre**, where a copy of Michelangelo's *David* holds court at the corner of Ave du Prado, looking even more smugly ridiculous than he does in Florence. Beyond the big fellow opens the cool green expanses of **Parc Borély**, with a botanical garden, duck ponds, and the **Château Borély**, an 18th-century palace built according to the strictest classical proportions for a wealthy merchant, unique for its surviving interior decoration. Behind it, Avenue de Hambourge leads into Sainte-Anne, another former village, where César's Giant Thumb emerges at the Avenue d'Haïfa, signalling the vast new **Musée d'Art Contemporain** at No.69, ✆ 04 91 72 17 27 (*open daily exc Mon 11–6, winter till 5; adm*), with a large collection of post-war art.

The *Calanques* and Grotte Cosquer

To continue along the coast from Parc Borély, you'll need to change to bus 19, which passes by another beach and the **Musée de la Faïence**, open since 1995 in the 19th-century Château Pastré at 157 Ave de Montredon, ✆ 04 91 72 43 47 (*open daily exc Mon, 11–6, winter 10–5; adm*), with an exceptional collection of faïence from Neolithic times to the present, concentrating on the famous ware made in Marseille and Moustiers, beginning in the 17th century. Bus 19 poops out just after **Calanque du Mont Rose**, Marseille's nudist beach. Bus 20 from here continues to **Cap Croisette**, a miniature end-of-the-world at the base of the Massif de Marseilleveyre—forming a backdrop to the fishing hamlet in the **Calanque des Goudes**—and the pebble beach at **Calanque de Samena**, facing the islets of Maître and Tiboulen. The road gives out at the narrow **Calanque de Callelongue**, where the GR 98 coastal path to Cassis begins. Another path from here leads in two hours to the summit of Marseilleveyre (432m), with grand views over Marseille, its industrial *rade*, and islands.

In 1991, the next *calanque*, the beautiful chalky jagged **Calanque de Sormiou**, made national headlines when local diver Henri Cosquer discovered a hollow 40m under the sea that hid the entrance to a tunnel. Cosquer swam up the tunnel, and after 200m found himself in a subterranean cave above sea level, to his astonishment covered with paintings of running bison, horses, deer and the ancestors of the modern penguin. Along with the art, Cosquer found 'negative' handprints, made by blowing colour around a hand to create its outline on the wall. Similar 'artists' signatures' mark the famous painted caves in the Dordogne. Although first dismissed as a forgery, mainly because no similar works have ever been found in Provence, the **Grotte Cosquer** is now recognized by prehistorians as a contemporary of Lascaux (*c.* 27,000 BC). At the time, when much of the northern hemisphere's water was concentrated in Ice Age glaciers, the level of the Mediterranean was much lower, so that the entrance of the cave was on dry land. The climate of Provence was also considerably colder—hence the bison and penguins. To protect the art, the cave has been walled up.

Sormiou and the more distant *calanques* can be most painlessly reached from Marseille by boat, operating mid-June to mid-September from the Quai des Belges (Groupement des Armateurs Côtiers Marseille, ✆ 04 91 55 50 09). Alternatively, take bus 21 from La Canebière to the end of the line (Luminy) and walk 40 minutes to **Calanque de Morgiou**, dotted with seaside *cabanons*, or to the wilder **Calanque de Sugiton**.

The Château d'If and Frioul Islands

If in French means yew, a tree associated with death, and an appropriately sinister name for this gloomy precursor of Alcatraz built by François I in 1524, originally to defend Marseille from Emperor Charles V (*©* 04 91 59 02 30; *boats from the Quai des Belges, as above, departures hourly 9–7 in summer, in winter 9, 11, 2, 3.30 and 5*). Even when Alexandre Dumas was still alive, visitors came to see the cell of the Count of Monte-Cristo, and a cell, complete with escape hole, was obligingly made to show to visitors. Real-life inmates included Mirabeau, imprisoned by his father-in-law for running up debts in Aix (*see* p.191); a Monsieur de Niozelles, condemned to six years in solitary confinement for not taking his hat off in front of Louis XIV; and after the revocation of the Edict of Nantes, thousands of Protestants who either died here or went on to die as galley slaves somewhere else.

The two other islands in the Archipel du Frioul, **Pomègues** and **Ratonneau**, white as bones and nearly as dry, tortured into crags and lumps by the mistral, were originally hunting and fishing reserves that witnessed, in 1516, one of the first rhinoceroses in Europe, who rambled here en route to Pope Leo X's menagerie in Rome. Later used as quarantine islands, they are now linked by a causeway at Port du Frioul, a pleasure port designed by Le Corbusier's pupil, José-Luis Sert; scores of swimming coves can be easily reached by foot, along paths lined with aromatic herbs and plants especially adapted to the extremely dry climate. A 20-minute path leads to the **Hôpital Caroline**, built in the 1820s on Ratonneau, where the winds blow the strongest, on the theory that they would help 'purify' infectious diseases. Now used for a summer festival, the hospital has excellent views of Marseille—as Marseille was meant to be seen, from the sea—that must have been heartbreaking to the imprisoned patients.

Shopping

Rue Saint Ferreol, home of the Galleries Lafayette and Marks and Spencer, is the centre of city's shopping district. Marseille holds a remarkable market of clay Christmas crib figures, the *Foire aux Santons*, from the end of November to January; at other times, you can find *santons* at **Marcel Carbonel**, near St-Victor at 47 Rue Neuve Ste-Catherine (7e), *©* 04 91 54 26 58, and see them being made (*open 9–1 and 2–7, closed Sun and Aug*). Year-round markets include the daily old book, postcard, and record market in Place A. et F. Carli, near the Noailles métro, or the Sunday morning flea-market in Rue Frédéric-Sauvage (14e) (Ⓜ Bougainville, then bus 30). For the best in Provençal food and wine, try **Georges Bataille**, 18 Rue Fontange, *©* 04 91 47 06 23.

Sports and Activities

L'Olympique de Marseille (OM), is France's most enthusiastically supported football squad and tickets often sell out (Stade Vélodrome Municipal, Blvd Michelet (8e), *©* 04 91 71 47 00). **Windsurf boards** can be hired at **Pacific Palissades**, Port de la Pointe Rouge, *©* 04 91 73 54 37, or neighbouring **Sideral's Time Club**, *©* 04 91 25 00 90. On rainy days you can roll the rock or shoot some pool until 2am at **Le Bowling Notre-Dame**, 107 Blvd Notre-Dame (6e), *©* 04 91 37 15 05.

Marseille's top-notch hotels are the bastion of expense-account businessmen and women, while its downmarket numbers attract working girls of a different kind. Chains have bought up many of the old classics: one worth mentioning is ★★★**Mercure Vieux Port**, 4 Rue Beauvau (1er), ✆ 04 91 54 91 00, ✇ 04 91 54 15 76, overlooking the Vieux Port, where Chopin and George Sand canoodled—wood-panelled and comfortable with air-conditioned, soundproofed rooms (no restaurant). A special treat for students of architecture is the hotel restaurant incorporated into the Unité d'Habitation, ★★**Le Corbusier**, 280 Blvd Michelet (8e), ✆ 04 91 16 78 00, ✇ 04 91 16 78 28; reserve one of its 23 rooms as early as possible (*190–285F*). Near the Prefecture, ★★**Moderne**, 30 Rue Breteuil (6e), ✆ 04 91 53 29 93 has nice inexpensive rooms, with showers and TV; other palatable budget choices include ★**Montgrand**, 50 Rue Montgrand (6e) (off Rue Paradis, behind the Opéra), ✆ 04 91 00 35 20, ✇ 04 91 33 75 89, and ★★**Azur**, 24 Cours Roosevelt (1er), ✆ 04 91 42 74 38, ✇ 04 91 47 27 91, with frills such as colour TV and garden views (Ⓜ Réformés). Near the Gare St-Charles the most benign choice is the ★**Little Palace**, 39 Blvd d'Athènes (1er), ✆ 04 91 90 12 93, at the foot of the grand stair. The best of Marseille's two youth hostels is in a 19th-century château overlooking the city at 76 Ave de Bois-Luzy (12e): **Auberge de Jeunesse de Bois-Luzy**, ✆/✇ 04 91 49 06 18 (bus 6 or 8 from La Canebière, or bus K after dark; Ⓜ direction La Rose).

There's a fair smattering of choices overlooking the sea: Marseille's most refined, exclusive hotel, the Relais & Châteaux ★★★★**Le Petit Nice Passédat**, off Corniche Kennedy, at Anse de Maldormé (7e), ✆ 04 91 59 25 92, ✇ 04 91 59 28 08, is a former villa overlooking the Anse de Maldormé, with a fine restaurant, Le Passédat (*see* below). Above the Corniche J. F. Kennedy, the modern ★★★**New Hôtel Bompard**, 2 Rue des Flots Bleus (7e), ✆ 04 91 52 10 93, ✇ 04 91 31 02 14 (bus 61 from ✆ Joliette or St-Victor), seems remote from the city, set in its own peaceful grounds, with rooms overlooking a garden; those in bungalows have their own kitchenette. ★★**Péron**, 119 Corniche Kennedy (7e), ✆ 04 91 31 01 41, ✇ 04 91 59 42 01, near the Plage des Catalans, has an unusual cast-iron façade and good rooms. Or try the inexpensive ★★**Le Richelieu**, 52 Corniche Kennedy (7e), ✆ 04 91 31 01 92, ✇ 04 91 59 38 09; best rooms here are Nos.28, 29 and 30.

Eating Out

The Marseillais claim an ancient Greek—even divine—origin for their ballyhooed *bouillabaisse*: Aphrodite invented it to beguile her husband Hephaestos to sleep so that she could dally with her lover Ares— seafood and saffron being a legendary soporific. Good chefs prepare it just as seriously, and display like a doctor's diploma their *Charte de la Bouillabaisse* guaranteeing that their formula more or less subscribes to tradition: a saffron and garlic-flavoured soup cooked on a low boil (hence its name), based on *rascasse* (scorpion fish, the ugliest fish in the Med, and always cooked with its leering head attached), which lives under the cliffs and has a bland taste that enhances the flavour of the other fish, especially *fielas* (conger eel), *grondin* (gurnard), and *saint-pierre* (John Dory). On menus you'll usually find three degrees of *bouillabaisse*: simple or *du pêcheur*, made from the day's catch with a few shellfish thrown in; *royale*, with half a lobster included; or most expensive of all, *royale marseillaise*, the real McCoy, with all the right fish. When served, the fish is traditionally cut up before you and presented on a side dish of *aïoli* or *rouille*, a paste of Spanish peppers. The best, and certainly swankiest *bouillabaisse* is served at **Michel-Brasserie des Catalans**, 6 Rue des Catalans (7e), ✆ 04 91 52 30 63: you'll be mixing with politicians and showbiz people (*250F and up*). *Open every day, all year.* Or there's the reliable, traditional stuff at **Miramar**, by the Vieux Port at 12 Quai du Port (2e), ✆ 04 91 91 10 40 (*250F*). *Closed Sun and Aug.* **Le Chaudron Provençal**, 48 Rue Caisserie (2e), ✆ 04 91 91 02 37, presents an acceptable version (*200F for bouillabaisse, or a seafood menu starting at 160F*). *Closed Sun and Aug.*

But there's more than *bouillabaisse* in Marseille. For a genuine Provençal spread try **Les Mets de Provence Chez Maurice Brun**, up on the second floor at 18 Quai Rive-Neuve (7e), ✆ 04 91 33 35 38, a 50-year-old restaurant with an overwhelming four-course menu at 220F that starts with eight different hors-d'oeuvres and includes a *pichet* of Coteaux d'Aix. *Closed Sun and Mon lunch.* Cours d'Estienne d'Orves is a favourite place to go: try the new **Les Arcenaulx**, in the old arsenal at No.25, ✆ 04 91 59 80 30, serving fresh market fare next to a book shop full of art books (*menus from 135F*). Dessert mavens flock to **L'Atelier Chocolat**, 18 Place aux Huiles (1er), ✆ 04 91 33 55 00, where the meals are light to leave room for the exquisite grand finales (*lunch 80F for a plat du jour and dessert, at night around 160F*). *Closed Sat eve and Sun.* Near the Préfecture, the **Au Jambon de Parme**, 67 Rue de la Paluad, ✆ 04 91 54 37 98, serves delicious Provençal dishes in an historic building (*menu 185F*). *Closed Sun eve, Mon, and half of July and Aug.* **Le Marseillois**, Quai de Rive Neuve, a sailing boat moored stern-on, ✆ 04 91 91 61 44, has plenty of atmosphere to go with its 61 and 82F menus.

international and late-night eating

Marseille's unique ethnic mix produces an unrivalled selection of inexpensive cuisines from around the world: try **Au Feu de Bois**, 10 Rue d'Aubagne (1er), ✆ 04 91 54 33 96, ⓜ Noailles, for some of the tastiest pies in a city that takes pizza seriously (*around 60F for a big one*); **Le Roi du Couscous**, 63 Rue de la République, ✆ 04 91 91 45 46, for the best couscous in town; **Erevan**, 10 Rue Fort Notre Dame, at the Old Port (7e), ✆ 04 91 33 70 29, for Armenian. *Closed Sun.* Try **Shabu Shabu**, 30 Rue de la Paix (1e), ✆ 04 91 54 15 00, for Japanese. *Closed Aug.* Night owls can assuage their hunger pangs at **Le Mas**, by the Opéra at 4 Rue Lulli (1er), ✆ 04 91 33 25 90, open daily until 6am, offering good pasta dishes and grills for around 120F. *Closed Aug.* Then there's the even cheaper 24-hour **O'Stop**, a popular institution at 1 Place de l'Opéra, ✆ 04 91 33 85 34, with similar fill-ups whenever you need them. If you're sick of meat there's **Country Life**, at 14 Rue Venture (1e), ✆ 04 91 54 16 44 (*lunchtimes, weekdays only*), or try **La Gentiane**, 9 Rue des Trois Rois (6e), ✆ 04 91 42 88 80. *Closed Sun and Mon.*

along the beaches and the calanques

The haughty gourmet **Petit Nice Passédat** (*see above*), ✆ 04 91 59 25 92, offers ravishing food in its exotic garden (*weekday lunch menu 310F; otherwise menus*

590F plus). On the little fishing port at Vallon des Auffes, overlooking the Château d'If and Frioul islands, you can feast on *bouillabaisse* from a charter member, **Chez Fonfon**, © 04 91 52 14 38, which prides itself on the freshness of its fish; 250F and up. *Closed Sun, Mon midday, and Feb.* Next door, **L'Epuisette**, © 04 91 52 17 82, is a Marseille institution for its seafood—try the *tian de Saint-Jacques à la fondue de tomates* (*menus from 195F*). *Closed Sun eve.* Or have a fancy pizza at nearby **Pizzeria Jeannot**, © 04 91 52 11 28 (*around 110F for a full meal*). *Closed Mon.* Further out, **La Grotte**, Calanque de Cannelongue, © 04 91 73 17 79, is a favourite for pizza by the sea.

Entertainment and Nightlife

Marseille may be going on 3000 years, but the old girl's still kicking—sometimes in the wrong places, especially after 10 in the back-streets between the station and the Vieux Port, where British lorry drivers say you can get stabbed in the back and no-one would notice. But you don't have to be a brawny sailor to have a good time: Marseille has lively after-dark pockets, especially around Place Thiers, Cours d'Estienne d'Orves and Cours Julien. You can find out what's happening in *Taktik*, or *Atout Marseille* distributed free by the tourist office, or in the pages of *La Marseillaise*, *Le Provençal* or the Wednesday edition of *Le Méridional*. Or try the book and record chain **FNAC**, in the Centre Bourse, © 04 91 39 94 00 which not only has information on events, but sells tickets as well.

In the last decade, most of the cultural excitement in Marseille has been generated in its theatres—and as it likes to mention, it has more seats per capita than Paris. Since 1981, **Théâtre National de la Criée**, 30 Quai de Rive Neuve (7e), © 04 91 54 70 54, directed by Marcel Maréchal, has put on performances to wide critical acclaim. **Théâtre des Bernadines**, 17 Blvd Garibaldi (1er), © 04 91 24 30 40, puts on experimental dance and theatre. There's more of the same at **Théâtre du Merlan**, a second national theatre, at Ave Raimu (14e), © 04 91 11 19 30.

There are old movies and art films in v.o. (*version originale*) at the **Alhambra Cinemarsille**, 2 Rue du Cinéma, © 04 91 03 84 66. The three **Breteuil** cinemas also run v.o. films at 120 Blvd de Notre-Dame (6e), © 04 91 37 88 18.

The city has always had a special affinity with music: in fact Berlioz claimed that Marseille understood Beethoven five years before Paris. At the **Opéra Municipal** in Place Reyer (1er), © 04 91 55 14 99, the bill includes Italian opera and occasional ballets from the **Ballet National de Marseille** (Roland Petit), 20 Blvd Gabès (8e), © 04 91 71 03 03, @ 04 91 71 51 12. Music from all around the world is performed at **La Maison de l'Etranger**, 12 Rue Antoine Zattara (3e), © 04 91 28 24 01. The **Abbaye de St-Victor**, 3 Rue de l'Abbaye (7e), © 04 91 33 25 86, hosts a chamber music festival in Oct–Dec; the Frioul islands also host a music festival every July.

Nightlife in Marseille is concentrated in several distinct zones. Place Jean-Jaurès/Cours Julien and around is perhaps the trendiest place. Jazz, rock and reggae are all on offer at **Espace Julien**, 39 Cours Julien (6e), © 04 91 24 34 10, where there's also a café with live music many nights of the week; more music, along with chocolates, pastries, and *plats du jour* are the fare at **Chocolat Théatre**, 59 Cours Julien (6e), © 04 91 42 19 29 (*192F*). *Closed Sun.*

The nearby **Maison Hantée**, Marseille's temple of rock at 10 Rue Vian, off Rue des Trois Mages, ☎ 04 91 92 09 40, is a favourite spot, although live music has been banned because of too many complaints from the neighbours. Then there is the **Metal Café** at 20 Rue Fortia, ☎ 04 91 54 03 03. At 24 Quai de Rive Neuve, **Le Trolleybus**, ☎ 04 91 54 30 45, is a favourite place for a drink or a dance. **Le Perroquet Bleu**, 72 Bd des Dames (2e), ☎ 04 91 91 11 18, has acid jazz and funk.

Bars and Latin clubs have also sprouted up along the sea at the Plage de Borély (8e); there are a number of new places at Escale Borély, including the trendy **Café de la Plage**, with karaoke nights at 148 Ave Mendes France, ☎ 04 91 71 21 76.

West of Marseille: Chaîne de l'Estaque and the Etang de Berre

Whatever personality of its own this region once had has been thoroughly chewed and swallowed by the metropolis next door. Once sheltering attractive, out-of-the-way retreats, the Estaque coast and the broad lagoon of Berre behind it have in the last three decades totally succumbed to creeping suburbia; isolated corners that once knew only hamlets of poor fishermen now suffer some of the biggest industrial complexes in France. Still, the 'Côte Bleue', as the tourist offices call the Estaque coast, is a very attractive piece of coastline. Especially in the east, the mountains plunge straight into the sea, with sheltered *calanques* between them; there is no road along the coast until Carry-le-Rouet.

Tourist Information

Carry-le-Rouet ✉ 13620: Ave Aristide Briand, ☎ 04 42 13 20 36, ✆ 04 42 44 52 03.

Salon: ✉ 13300: 56 Cours Gimon, ☎ 04 90 56 27 60, ✆ 04 90 56 77 09.

Martigues ✉ 13500: 2 Quai Paul Doumer, ☎ 04 42 42 31 10, ✆ 04 42 80 00 97.

market days

Martigues: Thursday and Sunday. **Salon:** Wednesday.

L'Estaque to Sausset-les-Pins

Leaving Marseille on the N568, you'll pass the industrial suburb, docks and marinas of **L'Estaque** (bus 35 from the Vieux Port)—a favourite subject of Cézanne, who came to paint here off and on for 15 years, and whose vision of a new, classical Provence transformed the town's smokestacks into Doric columns. He was followed by Braque, Dufy, Marquet and others; the Marseille tourist office has a brochure pinpointing the spots where they set up their easels, but don't expect to recognize too many of the scenes. The road then crosses over the **Souterrain du Rove**, the world's longest ship tunnel. A partial collapse closed it in the 1960s, and no one has found it worth repairing since.

The reputation of **Carry-le-Rouet**, the biggest town on the coast, is based on the two very odd-looking gifts it has bestowed on the world: the horse-faced actor Fernandel and prickly-stickly sea-urchins; it celebrates the latter with a festival each February. There is a beach, often oversubscribed; Carry is fast being surrounded by the weekend villas of the Marseillais. **Sausset-les-Pins**, the next town, is much the same; however, if you press on further there are popular if often crowded beaches around **Carro** and especially **Cap Couronne**, a favourite of the Marseillais.

Martigues

On the lagoon side of the Chaîne de l'Estaque, facing inland across the Etang de Berre, the distinguished old city of **Marignane** has been completely engulfed by Marseille's sprawl and airport. In the centre of the old town, you can visit its 14th-century **château** (now the *mairie*), an eccentric work with mythological frescoes. From here, making a clockwise tour around the Etang de Berre, the next stop is **Martigues**, a sweet little city full of salt air and sailboats, not a compelling place to visit but probably a wonderful place to live. If Carry-le-Rouet serves up sea-urchins to visitors in February, Martigues can answer with its own speciality—fresh sardines—during its Sardine Festival in July and August.

Martigues sits astride the Canal de Caronte, linking the lagoon and the sea, lending it a slight but much-trumpeted resemblance to Venice. According to legend the city was founded by and named after the Roman General Marius; the oldest part of town is the Ile Brescon, at the head of the channel. One of its prettiest corners is a quay called the **Miroir des Oiseaux**, the 'mirror of birds'. On the mainland, the **Musée Ziem**, Blvd du 14 Juillet, ✆ 04 42 80 66 06 (*open 10–12 and 2.30–6.30, afternoons only in winter, closed Mon and Tues*), has paintings left to Martigues by landscape artist Félix Ziem, and works by Provençal painters Guigou, Monticelli, and Loubon, as well as archaeology exhibits.

Fos

The French, fascinated with technology, actually come to visit this gigantic industrial complex. Fos has an information centre on Ave Jean Jaurès, ✆ 04 42 47 71 96, and there are guided tours. You too might consider a drive through; in its way Fos is the most astounding, unsettling sight in Provence. Before 1965, when France's Mephistophelean economic planners commandeered it to replace the overcrowded port of Marseille, this corner of the Camargue was pristine marshland. Today it is the biggest oil port, and the biggest industrial complex, on the entire Mediterranean. In area, it is considerably larger than Marseille.

To a degree, it makes sense to concentrate unpleasant industry all in one place. But when driving past its 19km of chemical plants, steel-mills and power-lines, rising out of the void like a mirage, the senses rebel. Economically, the 'ZIP' (*zone industriel-portuaire*) is a failure; as planning, it is stupidly primitive, ecologically disastrous, and demeaning to the people who live and work in it, the perfect marriage of corporate gigantism and bureaucratic simple-mindedness.

West and North of the Etang de Berre

Along the west shore there is more of the same, engulfing ancient villages like **St-Blaise**, with a Romanesque church and a wealth of ruins currently being excavated, including a rare stretch of Greek wall. Of the two large towns, **Istres** has a Provençal Romanesque fortified church, Notre Dame de Beauvoir, and a **Musée Archéologique** filled with mostly Roman era finds discovered by divers in the Golfe of Fos, ✆ 04 42 55 50 08 (*open daily exc Tues, 2–7*). **Miramas** is more attractive, with ruins of its medieval predecessor nearby at **Miramas-le-Vieux**.

There's also a railway museum, ✆ 04 90 58 07 41. **St-Chamas**, to the southeast, has an impressive Baroque church. The Via Domitia passed this way, and over a small stream south of the village stands one of the finest and best-preserved Roman bridges anywhere, the **Pont Flavien**. Built in the 1st century AD, the single-arched span features a pair of elegant triumphal arches at the approaches, decorated with Corinthian capitals, floral reliefs and stone lions. But life went on here even earlier than that, and there are troglodyte dwellings to prove it.

North of the Etang, towards Salon, lie three attractive villages: **Cornillon-Confoux**, on a steep hill with a wide view, **Grans** and **Lançon-Provence**, the latter being home of some of the most exquisite AOC Coteaux-d'Aix-en-Provence wines.

Salon-de-Provence

The home of Nostradamus should be a more interesting place. Aix-en-Provence's disagreeable little sister, Salon is quite well-off from processing olive oil, making soap and from being home to the French air-force training school. The town seems aptly named: a little bourgeois parlour, smug and stuffy and neat as a pin. Its spirit is captured perfectly in the antiseptic, gentrified *vieille ville*, ruined by a hideous and insensitive restoration programme in the last few years. Even the antiseptic has its surprises, however: surely the snazziest tiled loos in France (underneath Place Général de Gaulle), and L'Ecole de Bergers, France's national school for shepherds.

The old quarter, surrounded by a ring of boulevards, is entered by the 18th-century **Porte de l'Horloge**, with an iron-work clock tower. In the centre, at the highest point of Salon, is the **Château de l'Empéri,** parts of which go back to the 10th century. Long a possession of the Archbishops of Arles, it now houses the **Musée Nationale de l'Empéri** (✆ 04 90 56 22 36, *open daily exc Tues, 10–12 and 2.30–6.30; adm*) and contains a substantial hoard of weapons, bric-a-brac and epauletted mannequins on horseback, covering France's army from Louis XIV to 1918, with an emphasis on Napoleon.

Nostradamus

Salon's most famous citizen was born in St-Rémy in 1503, to a family of converted Jews. Trained as a doctor in Montpellier, young Michel de Nostredame made a name for himself by successfully treating plague victims in Lyon and Aix. In 1547, he married a girl from Salon and settled down here, practising medicine and pursuing a score of other interests besides—studying astrology, publishing almanacs and inventing new recipes for cosmetics and hair dyes. The first of his *Centuries*, ambiguous quatrains written in the future tense, were published in 1555, achieving celebrity for their author almost immediately.

Nostradamus himself said that his works came from 'natural instinct and poetic passion'; in form they are similar to some other poetry of the day, such as the *Visions* of du Bellay. It may be that he had never really intended to become an occult superstar—but when the peasants start bringing you two-headed sheep, asking for an explanation, and when the Queen Regent of France sends an invitation to court, what's a man to do? Nostradamus went to Paris, and later Charles IX and Catherine de' Medici came to visit him in Salon. The Salonnais didn't appreciate such notoriety; if it had not been for Nostradamus's royal favour, they might well have put him to the torch. Now they've made up, and you can visit the **Maison de Nostradamus**, 11 Rue de Nostradamus, ✆ 04 90 56 64 31, just inside the Porte de l'Horloge (*open 9.30–12 and 2–6.30; closed Sat and Sun am*). On his death in 1566, Nostradamus was oddly buried inside the wall of the Cordeliers' church; tales spread that he was still alive in there, writing his final book of prophecies. After his tomb was desecrated in the Revolution, he was moved to the 14th-century Dominican church of **St-Laurent**, on Rue du Maréchal-Joffre, where he rests today.

The **Musée Grévin de Provence**, ✆ 04 90 56 36 30 (*open daily 9.30–12 and 2–6.30, closed Sat and Sun am*), is run by the Parisian waxwork family Grévin, which displays the history of Provence in 54 waxwork figures, from Marius' battle with the Barbarians, through a lifeless

Napoleon, to Pagnol's *Manon des Sources*. If you can face yet another museum there's **Le Musée de Salon et Le Crau**, Ave Donnadieu, © 04 90 56 28 37 (*open 10–12 and 2–6.30, closed Sat and Sun am*), with a dry, old-fashioned exhibition of costumes, furniture and paintings. East of Salon along the D572, the **Château de la Barben** once belonged to Napoleon's favourite sister Pauline Borghese and now has a little zoo on the grounds for the kids.

North of Salon on the D17 in **Eyguières** is an archetypal Provençal village, with Celtic-Greek tombs above the ruins of a medieval castle (their contents may be seen in the Dépôt Archéologique, © 04 90 57 90 64); also note the 10th-century **Chapelle-St-Vérédème**. **Vernègues**, in a forgotten corner of Provence (take the D16 northeast of Salon), has a ruined castle, and just east, the ruins of a 1st-century BC **Roman temple**.

Where to Stay and Eating Out

Carry-le-Rouet ⊠ 13620

There's plenty of seafood along the Promenade du Port; try the roast lobster or sea bass grilled with spices on the attractive seaside terraces of **L'Escale**, © 04 42 45 00 47; *menus from 320F, closed Sun eve and Mon*. If it's full there are the moderately priced and no more than ordinary **Le Calypso** on Quai Vayssiere, © 04 42 45 10 64, and **Le Madrigal** on Ave G. Montus, © 04 42 44 58 63. Since most people here have villas or are on a day-trip from the city, accommodation is scarce and functional, as at ★★**La Tuilière** on 53 Ave Draïo-de-la-Mer, © 04 42 44 79 79, 🖨 04 42 44 74 40.

Martigues ⊠ 13500

In the centre, there's ★★**Le Provençal**, 35 Blvd 14 Juillet, © 04 42 80 49 16, 🖨 04 42 49 26 71, or on the outskirts, the fancier ★★★**Eden**, Blvd Emile Zola, © 04 42 07 36 37.

Salon ⊠ 13300

If *force majeur* constrains you to spend a night in Salon, you can luxuriate at the Relais & Châteaux ★★★★**Abbaye de Ste-Croix**, 5km out of town on Route du Val de Cuech (the D 16), © 04 90 56 24 55, 🖨 04 90 56 31 12, with expensive and lovely rooms overlooking a medieval cloister. There's a swimming pool and horse-riding, an ultra-posh restaurant with shrimps flambéed in *pastis* and lamb in truffle sauce, and a big wine list. (*Rooms start at 625F*). *Closed Nov to Mar*. ★★★**Le Mas du Soleil**, 38 Chemin Saint Côme, © 04 90 56 06 53, 🖨 04 90 56 21 52, has elegant air-conditioned rooms, pool and terrace and a traditional but not predictable restaurant, with beautifully presented dishes; try the pigeon, if you can resist the tender *agneau* (*menus 170–450F*). Set in 19th-century *mas*, ★★**Domaine de Roquerousse**, north on the road to Avignon, © 04 90 59 50 11, 🖨 04 90 59 53 75, has pretty rooms in individual buildings in a park, with a pool and tennis; for something cheaper, try the bright and pretty and old fashioned ★★**Vendôme**, 34 Rue du Maréchal-Joffre, © 04 90 56 01 96, 🖨 04 90 56 48 78. Nearby an exuberantly floral 19th-century mansion, **La Salle à Manger**, 6 Rue du Maréchal-Joffre, © 04 90 56 28 01, offers a delicious if rather extravagant choice of dishes (ostrich carpaccio, for instance) to match the decor (*menus at 89F and 125F*). *Closed Sun eve and Mon*. Alternatively, dine in the 13th-century chapel that once hosted Nostradamus' mortal remains: **La Brocherie des Cordeliers**, 20 Rue d'Hozier, ✆ 04 90 56 53 42 (*excellent menus for 100F*). *Closed Sun eve and Mon.*

Aix-en-Provence

Elegant and honey-hued, the old capital of Provence is splashed by a score of fountains, a charming reminder that its very name comes from its waters, *Aquae Sextiae*—sweet water, mind you, with none of the saltiness and excesses of Marseille. For if tumultuous Marseille is the great anti-Paris, Aix-en-Provence is the stalwart anti-Marseille—bourgeois, cultured, aristocratic, urbane, slow paced, convivial. Since 1948 Aix has hosted France's most elite festival of music and opera, while its 580-year-old university not only teaches the arts and humanities to the French but instructs foreign students in the fine arts of French civilization (the more 'practical' science departments are in Marseille); if a fifth of Aix's 150,000 souls are students, another large percentage are doctors, lawyers and professors, not to mention financial and underworld nabobs who commute to Marseille. But as cultured as it is, it can never quite live down having mocked and laughed at Cézanne, the one real genius it ever produced.

History

The first version of Aix, the *oppidum* of Entremont, was the capital of the Salyens, a Celto-Ligurian tribe, who liked to decapitate their enemies and tie their heads to the tails of their horses. By 123 BC they had pulled this trick once too often on the Greeks of Massalia, who called in their Roman allies to teach them a lesson. Under Sextius Calvinus, the Romans did just that, and founded a camp by a nearby thermal spring which they named *Aquae Sextiae Salluviorum*. Only 20 years later, in 102 BC, these Latin frontiersmen woke up one day to find 200,000 ferocious Teutones with covered wagons full of wives and children at their door, en route to Italy—looking not for a place to camp but for *Lebensraum*. The strategies of the great Roman general Marius caught them unawares, and in the battle that raged around Aix, so many Teutones were killed or committed suicide that for decades Aix enjoyed bumper crops thanks to soil enriched with corpses; the mountain where Marius's final triumph took place was renamed Montagne Sainte-Victoire.

Although by the next century Aquae Sextiae was a bustling town on the Aurelian Way, invaders in the Dark Ages destroyed it so thoroughly that little survived. Only in the 11th century did Aix begin to revive: the Bourg St-Sauveur grew up around the cathedral with such vigour that in the early 13th century the counts of Provence chose it as their capital. In 1409 Louis II d'Anjou endowed the university; and in the 1450s Aix was the setting for the refined court of Good King René, fondly remembered, not for the way he squeezed every possible *sou* from his subjects, but for the artists he patronized such as Francesco Laurana, Nicolas Froment and the Maître de l'Annonciation d'Aix, and the popular festivities he founded, especially the masquerades of the Fête-Dieu (*see* below).

When René died at Aix, in 1486, France absorbed his realm but maintained Aix's status as the capital of Provence, seat of the provincial Estates, the governor, and the king-appointed Parlement—the latter institution so unpopular that it was counted as one of the three 'plagues' of Provence, along with the mistral and the Durance. In the 17th and 18th centuries, this unloved elite built themselves over 160 refined *hôtels particuliers* in golden stone, inspired by northern Italian Baroque architecture, bequeathing Aix a rich, harmonious urban fabric. Even the real plague of cholera in 1720 contributed to the city's embellishment, when it contaminated the water; once new sources had been piped in, the city built its charming fountains to receive them.

In 1789, the tumultuous Count Mirabeau became a popular hero in Aix when he eloquently championed the people and condemned Provence's Parlement as unrepresentative; in 1800, the whole regional government was unceremoniously packed off to Marseille. Aix, the 'Athens of the Midi', has found enough to keep it busy without it, tending its university, making its sweets, hosting music festivals, and as of April 1997, inaugurating a brand new thermal spa for the spring that gave the city its name.

Getting Around

By train: The station is on Rue G. Desplaces, at the end of Ave Victor-Hugo; there are hourly connections to Marseille, and others less frequently to Toulon. Central train reservations, ✆ 08 36 35 35 35.

By bus: The tumultuous coach station is in Rue Lapierre, ✆ 04 42 27 17 91, with buses every 20/30mins to Marseille and direct to the airport, and others to Avignon, Cannes, Nice, Arles and more.

By taxi: Cours Mirabeau, ✆ 04 42 21 61 61; or at night, call ✆ 04 42 26 29 30.

Bike hire is available at **Cycles Naddéo**, Ave de Lattre-de-Tassigny, ✆ 04 42 21 06 93, and **Cycles Zamette**, 27 Rue Miguet, ✆ 04 42 23 19 53.

Car hire: You can rent a car at **Rent A Car**, 35 Rue de la Molle, ✆ 04 42 38 58 29, and **ADA Discount**, 114 Cours Sextius, ✆ 04 42 52 36 36, as well as the big multinational companies. Parking isn't easy, especially on market days: try the car parks in Place des Cardeurs, Place Carnot, or by the bus station (behind the casino).

Tourist Information

Place du Général de Gaulle, ✆ 04 42 16 11 61, 🖅 04 42 16 11 62: without doubt one of the most pleasant tourist offices in the south of France. There are a host of circuits to navigate and explore, either by yourself with a map or in guided groups by foot, bus or car—in town or around the countryside, and whether your interest is painting, architecture, history or just a good walk.

market days

There's local produce every morning in Place Richelme, but Tuesdays, Thursdays and Saturdays are the days to come, when the centre of Aix overflows with good things: food in Place des Prêcheurs and Place de la Madeleine, flowers in Place de l'Hôtel de Ville, antiques and fleamarket bits in Place de Verdun, and clothes, fabrics and accessories along Cours Mirabeau; on Saturday night in the summer the stands along the Cours stay open late, all bustling and brightly lit, while the birds squawk indignantly in the trees above.

local wines

Coteaux d'Aix-en-Provence: Try Château du Seuil, in Puyricard (✆ 04 42 92 15 99); Château de Fonscolombe, Le Puy Ste-Réparade (✆ 04 42 61 89 62); Château de Calissanne, on the D10, near Lançon-Provence (✆ 04 90 42 63 03); Château St-Jean, at Port de Buc near Fos (✆ 04 42 44 70 14).

La Palette: Visit the celebrated 150-year-old Château Simone, at Meyreuil (off the D58H, ☎ 04 42 66 92 58); Château Crémade, in Le Tholonet (☎ 04 42 66 92 66).

Cours Mirabeau

Canopied by its soaring plane trees, decked with fountains and flanked by cafés, banks, pâtisseries, and *hôtels particuliers* of the 17th and 18th centuries, **Cours Mirabeau**, 'the most satisfying street in France', is the centre stage for Aixois society. Laid out in 1649 to replace the south walls, it begins in Place du Général de Gaulle, which takes the old roads from Marseille and Avignon and spins them around the pompous Second Empire fountain **La Rotonde**. Other fountains punctuate the Cours itself: the lumpy, mossy **Fontaine d'Eau Chaude**, oozing up its much esteemed 34°C water, and at the far end, the **Fontaine du Roi René**, with a fairy-tale statue of the good monarch holding up a bunch of the muscat grapes he introduced to Provence (along with the turkey and silkworm, discreetly omitted by the sculptor).

Of the fine *hôtels particuliers* on the Cours, No.12 is where Mirabeau wed the aristocratic Emilie de Covet-Marignane in 1772, after playing a dastardly trick on her. When the young lady refused his marriage proposal, Mirabeau sneaked into her house and appeared in the morning on her balcony, clad only in his nightshirt and socks, publicly compromising her virtue. In revenge, his new father-in-law refused the couple any money, and when Mirabeau ran up huge debts, he signed the order to have him imprisoned in the Château d'If. Mirabeau returned to Aix to plead in the subsequent divorce case, and despite his unparalleled eloquence he lost the appeal. Thus rebuked by his noble peers, he returned to Aix in 1789 as a member of the Third Estate and proceeded to attack their privileges—a trial run for his major role in igniting the Revolution in Paris.

Cézanne grew up at 55 Cours Mirabeau, the son of a hatter who later turned banker (on the façade you can still make out the sign of the *chapelier*). Nearby, at No.53, the elegant mirrored café **Les Deux Garçons** ('Les Deux G') has been Aix's smartest place to see and be seen since the Second World War, with a reputation and prices similar to Paris's café-citadels of artsy existentialist mumbo-jumbo; until recently North Africans were not admitted to enjoy its rarefied air. It looks across towards the weighty façade of the 1647 **Hôtel Maurel de Pontevès** (No.38), the building that inspired Aix's secular Baroque—still supported after all these years by two musclebound stone giants, 'the only ones who do any work at all on the Cours' as the saying went in the days of Aix's parliament.

South of Cours Mirabeau the straight lanes of the **Quartier Mazarin**, lined with *hôtel particuliers* and antique shops, were laid out according to the rules of Renaissance urban design by the archbishop brother of the famous cardinal. At 2a Rue du 4 Septembre, the **Musée Paul Arbaud** (*open daily 2–5, closed Sun; adm*) is the city's overflow tank for odds and ends, especially Provençal ceramics and a few hundred portraits of Mirabeau's overlarge pockmarked head.

Musée Granet

13 Rue Cardinale, ☎ 04 42 38 14 70; open 10-12 and 2-6, closed Tues Sept–May only; adm.

Walk two streets south of the Musée Arbaud, and turn left at the Fountain of the Four Dolphins (unusually equipped with teeth and scales) for the meatier archaeology and art collections of the **Musée Granet**, housed in the Priory of the Knights of Malta (1675), next to the church of **St-Jean-de-Malte**, where the Counts of Provence lie buried. The museum's

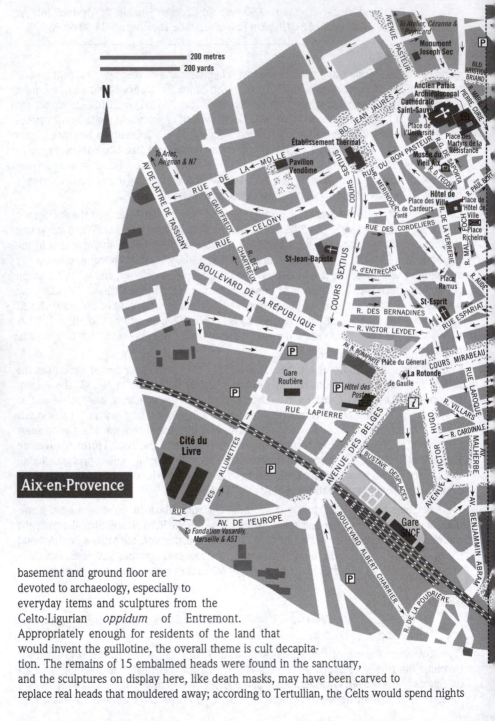

200 metres
200 yards

N

To Atelier, Cézanne &
Puyricard

Monument
Joseph Sec

AVENUE PASTEUR

BLD
ARISTIDE
BRIAND

P

Ancien Palais
Archiépiscopal
Cathédrale
Saint-Sauveur

Place de
l'Université

Place des
Martyrs de la
Résistance

Établissement Thermal

BD JEAN JAURÈS

RUE DU BON PASTEUR

Musée du
Vieil Aix

R. D. L'ÉCOLE

R.G. DE SAPORTA

PIERRE CURIE

R. PAUL BERT

To Arles,
Avignon & N7

Pavillon
Vendôme

RUE DE LA MOLLE

RUE R. GAUFFREDY

COURS SEXTIUS

RUE MÉRINDOL

Hôtel de
Ville

Place des
Fonté

Pl. de Cardeurs

Place de
l'Hôtel de
Ville

Place
Richelme

RUE DES CORDELIERS

RUE DE LA VERRERIE

R. MAL. FOCH

R. AUDE

AV DE LATTRE DE TASSIGNY

RUE CELONY

RUE

R. DES CHARTREUX

St-Jean-Bapiste

COURS SEXTIUS

R. d'ENTRECAST

Place
Ramus

BOULEVARD DE LA RÉPUBLIQUE

St-Esprit

R. DES BERNADINES

RUE ESPARIAT

R. VICTOR LEYDET

AV. N. BONAPARTE

Place du Général

COURS MIRABEAU

P

Gare
Routière

P

Hôtel des
Postes

La Rotonde

de Gaulle

RUE LAROQUE

RUE VILLARS

AV. MALHERBE

P

RUE LAPIERRE

AVENUE DES BELGES

i

HUGO

R. CARDINALE

AV. VICTOR

AV. BENJAMMIN ABRAM

Cité du
Livre

RUE DES ALLUMETTES

P

GUSTAVE DESPLACES

RUE

AV. DE l'EUROPE

To Fondation Vasarély,
Marseille & A51

BOULEVARD ALBERT CHARRIER

Gare
SNCF

P

R. DE LA POUDRIÈRE

Aix-en-Provence

basement and ground floor are
devoted to archaeology, especially to
everyday items and sculptures from the
Celto-Ligurian *oppidum* of Entremont.
Appropriately enough for residents of the land that
would invent the guillotine, the overall theme is cult decapita-
tion. The remains of 15 embalmed heads were found in the sanctuary,
and the sculptures on display here, like death masks, may have been carved to
replace real heads that mouldered away; according to Tertullian, the Celts would spend nights

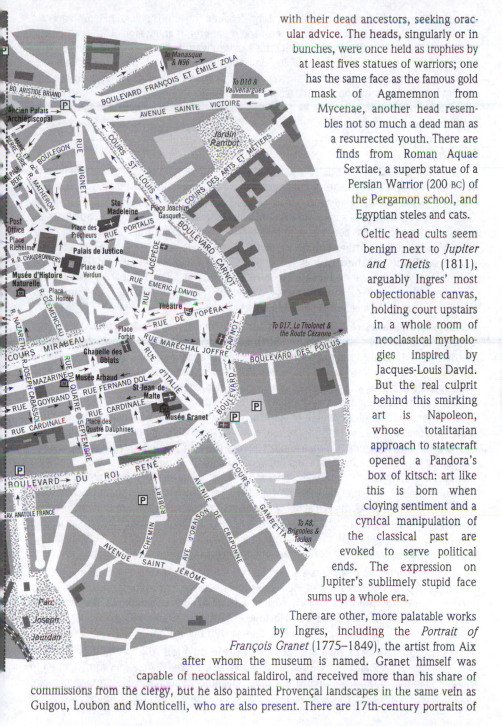

Map labels:
BD. ARISTIDE BRIAND
To Manasque & N96
BOULEVARD FRANÇOIS ET ÉMILE ZOLA
To D10 & Vauvenargues
AVENUE SAINTE VICTOIRE
Ancien Palais Archiépiscopal
Jardin Rambot
R. PIERRE CURIE
R. PAUL ET BERT
R. BOULEGON
RUE MIGNET
COURS ST-LOUIS
COURS DES ARTS ET MÉTIERS
R. MATHERON
Ste-Madeleine
Place Joachim Gasquet
RUE PORTALIS
BOULEVARD CARNOT
Post Office
Place Richelme
Place des Prêcheurs
RUE LACÉPÈDE
R.D. CHAUDRONNIERS
Palais de Justice
Place de Verdun
Musée d'Histoire Naturelle
R. C.S. Honoré
R. CLÉMENCEAU
RUE EMERIC DAVID
Théâtre
RUE DE L'OPÉRA
To D17, Le Tholonet & the Route Cézanne
R. NAZARETH
COURS MIRABEAU
Place Forbin
RUE MARÉCHAL JOFFRE
BOULEVARD DES POILUS
R. JOSEPH CABASSOL
Chapelle des Oblats
RUE DU QUATRE SEPTEMBRE
RUE MAZARINE
Musée Arbaud
RUE FERNAND DOL
RUE D'ITALIE
BOULEVARD CARNOT
RUE GOYRAND
St-Jean-de-Malte
RUE CARDINALE
RUE CARDINALE
Musée Granet
Place des Quatre Dauphines
BOULEVARD DU ROI RENÉ
AVENUE DE CRAPONNE
AVE. D'ORAISON
RUE ROBERT
COURS GAMBETTA
AV. ANATOLE FRANCE
To A8, Brignoles & Toulon
CHEMIN
AVENUE SAINT JÉRÔME
Parc Joseph Jourdan

with their dead ancestors, seeking oracular advice. The heads, singularly or in bunches, were once held as trophies by at least fives statues of warriors; one has the same face as the famous gold mask of Agamemnon from Mycenae, another head resembles not so much a dead man as a resurrected youth. There are finds from Roman Aquae Sextiae, a superb statue of a Persian Warrior (200 BC) of the Pergamon school, and Egyptian steles and cats.

Celtic head cults seem benign next to *Jupiter and Thetis* (1811), arguably Ingres' most objectionable canvas, holding court upstairs in a whole room of neoclassical mythologies inspired by Jacques-Louis David. But the real culprit behind this smirking art is Napoleon, whose totalitarian approach to statecraft opened a Pandora's box of kitsch: art like this is born when cloying sentiment and a cynical manipulation of the classical past are evoked to serve political ends. The expression on Jupiter's sublimely stupid face sums up a whole era.

There are other, more palatable works by Ingres, including the *Portrait of François Granet* (1775–1849), the artist from Aix after whom the museum is named. Granet himself was capable of neoclassical faldirol, and received more than his share of commissions from the clergy, but he also painted Provençal landscapes in the same vein as Guigou, Loubon and Monticelli, who are also present. There are 17th-century portraits of

Aixois nobility, made fluffy and likeable by Largillière and Rigaud; Dutch and Flemish masters (Teniers, Brit, Neefs, Robert Campin, Rubens, and a sumptuous anonymous 15th-century triptych of the *Adoration of the Magi*); the Italians (Alvise Vivarini, Previtali, Guercino, Preti, and the mysterious, grave 15th-century Maître de l'Annonciation d'Aix). But what of Cézanne, who took his first drawing-classes in this very building? For years he was represented by three measly watercolours (no one in Aix would buy his works), until 1984 when the French government rectified the omission by depositing eight small canvases here that touch on the major themes of his work.

Vieil Aix

North of Cours Mirabeau, the narrow lanes and squares of Vieil Aix concentrate not only some of Provence's finest architecture, but the region's most delightful shopping, especially on market days (*see* above). Enter the casbah by way of Rue Espariat from Place du Général de Gaulle, and you'll come to a cast-iron Baroque campanile and the church of **St-Esprit**, where a 16th-century retable has portraits of 12 members of the first Provençal Parlement cast in the roles of the apostles. Further up, just beyond Aix's most elegant little square, the cobbled, fountained **Place d'Albertas**, you can pop into the lavish, Puget-inspired Hôtel Boyer d'Eguilles of 1675, now the **Musée d'Histoire Naturelle** at 6 Rue Espariat, © 04 42 26 23 67 (*open 10–12 and 2–6, closed Sun am*)—well worth it for an impressive 17th-century interior, a grand stair, and a clutch of petrified dinosaur eggs.

Rue Espariat ends at Place St-Honoré, just south of the neoclassical **Palais de Justice**, a dull building of the 1760s that hardly merited the demolition of a well-preserved Roman mausoleum and the medieval palace of the counts of Provence. Aix's flea-market takes place in the adjacent Place de Verdun and **Place des Prêcheurs**, laid out in 1450 by King René for popular entertainments and executions of all sorts, including, in 1772, the burning in effigy of the Marquis de Sade and his valet after they were caught sodomizing prostitutes in Marseille. Here the former Dominican church of **Ste-Marie-Madeleine** has a pleasant Second Empire façade and paintings by Rubens and Van Loo, although the show-stopper is the central panel of the *Triptych of the Annunciation*, a luminous work of 1445 painted for a local draper—the two lateral panels are in Rotterdam and Brussels. Commonly attributed to Barthélémy d'Eyck, illuminator of King René's courtly allegories in the *Livre du Cœur d'Amour Epris* in Vienna's National Library, the central panel has provoked endless controversy over its singular, possibly heretical iconography: the angel Gabriel winged with owl feathers (a bird of evil omen) kneels in the porch of a Gothic church, decorated with a bat and a dragon. From on high, an unconventionally gesturing God the Father sends in a golden stream of breath a foetus bearing a cross, just missing a monkey's head; a vase of flowers holds poisonous belladonna.

The more orthodox blooms of Aix's flower market lend an intoxicating perfume to Place de l'Hôtel de Ville in the very heart of Vieil Aix, a lovely square framed by the stately, perfectly proportioned **Hôtel de Ville** (1671), decorated with stone flowers and fruits and intricate iron grilles, and the flamboyant **Tour de l'Horloge** (1510) with clocks telling the hour and the phase of the moon and wooden statues that change with the season.

From here, Rue Gaston de Saporta leads to the **Musée du Vieil Aix**, © 04 42 21 43 55, at No. 17 (*open 10–12 and 2–5 winter, 2.30–6 summer, closed Mon, Nov; adm*), housed in another grand 17th-century *hôtel* with another magnificent staircase. It stores some quaint paintings on velvet, a bevy of *santons* in a 'talking Christmas Crib' and marionettes made in the 19th century to represent the biblical, pagan, and local personages who figured in King René's Fête-Dieu processions.

Cathédrale Saint-Sauveur, the Tapestry Museum and Joseph Sec

Rue Gaston de Saporta continues north to Place de l'Université, once part of the forum of Roman Aix, and the **Cathédrale St-Sauveur**, a dignified patchwork of periods and styles crowned by an octagonal bell tower. The flamboyant Gothic west portal of 1340, decorated with scenes of the *Transfiguration* and the Apostles by King René, was mutilated in the Revolution and partially restored in the 1830s; only the lovely Virgin on the central pillar (under restoration at the time of writing) was spared when someone popped a red cap of Liberty on her head and made Mary a Marianne. Fortunately the Revolutionaries forgot to axe the doors; under their protective covers they have beautiful high reliefs of prophets and sibyls by Jean Guiramand of Toulon, sculpted in 1508–10 (*ask the guardian, daily exc Sun until 11.30 or from 2.30–4.30*) The interior has naves for every taste: from right to left, Romanesque, Gothic and Baroque. Tucked by the door inside the Romanesque nave, the octagonal **baptistry** dates from *c.* 375, when Aix was made a bishopric. The font is encircled by columns recycled from the temple of Apollo that once stood on this site in the forum.

The cathedral's most famous treasure, Nicolas Froment's **Triptyque du Buisson Ardent** (1476), is under restoration and can only be viewed between 3 and 4pm on Tuesdays. On the lateral panels are portraits of a well-fed King René, who commissioned the work, and his second wife, while the central scene depicts the vision of a monk of St-Victor of Marseille, who saw the Virgin and Child appear amidst the miraculous burning bush vouchsafed to Moses. The flaming green bush symbolizes her virginity (it burns without being consumed); the mirror held by the Child symbolizes his incarnation. The meticulously detailed castles in the background seem to have been inspired by Tarascon and Beaucaire.

On the same wall, from the same period, another triptych has scenes from the Passion with SS. Maximin and Mitre. Mitre, a 4th-century Greek slave serving a cruel master in Aix, was accused of sorcery and had his head chopped off by Roman soldiers. His trunk then picked up the head (already adorned with a halo) and carried it into the cathedral. The sight scared the children but made the Romans, who had a modern sense of humour, laugh until they cried, at at least according the 15th-century *Martyrdom of St Mitre*, perhaps on display in the chapel tucked behind the high altar, where the saint's 5th-century sarcophagus once emitted an ooze collected by the faithful to heal eye diseases. The high altar itself is decorated with tapestries on the lives of Christ and the Virgin made in Brussels in 1510. These originally hung in Canterbury Cathedral, but were sold by the Commonwealth, and purchased by a cathedral canon in Paris for next to nothing in 1656.

In the Baroque aisle is the striking **Altar des Aygosi** (1470), formerly attributed to Francesco Laurana, and now to Audinet Stephani, an itinerant sculptor from Cambria. On top, the *Crucifixion* is surrounded by symbols: the sun and moon on either side represent universality; the skull of Adam set at the base of the Cross is purified by the blood from Christ's wounds, while above the pelican feeds her nestlings with her own blood, according to a popular medieval misconception. Below stand SS. Anne, Marcel and Marguerite, the latter emerging from the shoulders of an embarrassed-looking dragon who swallowed her whole. The guardian on request will also unlock the airy, twin-columned, 12th-century **cloister**, with capitals daintily carved, though in an awful state of repair.

To the right and back of the cathedral, the grand 17th–18th-century residence of Aix's arch-bishops, **L'Ancien Palais Archiépiscopal**, is the setting for the festival's operas. It also houses the **Musée des Tapisseries** ✆ 04 42 23 09 91 (*open 10–12 and 2–5.45, closed Tues; adm*), containing three sets of lighthearted Beauvais tapestries, which were hidden under the roof during the Revolution and rediscovered only in the 1840s. The set known as the *Grotesques* (1689) features arabesques, animals, dancers, and musicians; there are nine rococo scenes from the story of *Don Quixote* (1740s), and four on the subject of *Jeux Russiens* (1769–93), inspired by the rustic frolics that the court of Louis XVI got up to in the backwoods of Versailles.

Just north of the cathedral on Ave Pasteur stands the 1792 **Monument Joseph Sec**, an eccentric discourse on the Revolution that spoiled those pampered bucolic daydreams. Sec, the builder, was a Jacobin who made his fortune floating timber down the Durance, and no one has ever satisfactorily explained the meaning behind the reliefs and statues of biblical char-acters, allegories, and masonic symbols he chose for his monument 'dedicated to the municipality of a law-abiding town.'

Around Aix: Cézanne, the Pavillon de Vendôme and Cité du Livre

Paul Cézanne spent an idyllic childhood roaming Aix's countryside with his best friend, Emile Zola, and as an adult painted those same landscapes in a way landscapes had never been painted before. The **Musée Cézanne**, 9 Ave Paul Cézanne, ✆ 04 42 21 06 53 (*open 10–12 and 2–5, summer 2–6, closed Tues; adm*), the studio he built in 1897, a half-kilometre north of the cathedral, has been rather grudgingly maintained as it was when the master died in 1906, with a few drawings, unfinished canvases, his smock, palette, pipe and some of the bottles and skulls used in his still-lifes. But for a better understanding of Cézanne's art, pick up the free *Circuit Cézanne* from the tourist office, a guide that points out the places he liked best to plant his easel around Aix.

Cézanne's family home at Jas de Bouffan is now dominated by the irritating black and white cubic forms of the **Fondation Vasarély**, ✆ 04 42 20 01 09, inaugurated in 1976 by the late op/geometric/kinetic artist at the height of his fame. Unpersuasively dedicated to promoting 'more human' urban develop-ment, the foundation is open 10–1 and 2–7 weekdays.

Along the boulevards west of Aix, in what was open country in 1665, a local cardinal built himself a lavish summer folly and park, the **Pavillon de Vendôme**, 32 Rue Célony, ✆ 04 42 21 05 78 (*open 10–12 and 1–5 winter, 2–6 summer; adm*). The delightful exterior includes a pair of Atlantes, who by their pained expressions have just been staring into one of Vasarély's more fiendish optical illusions. Part of the interior decor is intact, complete with 17th- and 18th-century patrician furnishings and paintings.

Just to the south of the bus station at 8 Rue des Allumettes, the modern **Cité du Livre** collects several cultural entities under its roof, including the **Bibliothèque Méjanes**, ✆ 04 42 25 98 88 (*open Tues, Thurs, Fri, 12–6, Wed and Sat 10–6*), with a rich collection of incunabula and illuminated manuscripts, some of which are usually on display; the **Fondation St-John Perse**, ✆ 04 42 25 98 85 (*open Tues–Fri 2–6*), a museum and study centre bequeathed to Aix by the French poet who won the Nobel Prize in 1960, and the **Vidéothèque Internationale d'Art Lyrique** ✆ 04 42 26 62 15 (*open*

Tues–Sat 12–6) where you can sit in a booth and take in a wide selection of celebrated operas and concerts filmed from 1950 to the present day.

Festivals

Aix publishes a free monthly guide to events, *Le Mois à Aix*, which comes in especially handy during Aix's summer festivals. Headquarters and general booking office for these is the **Comité Officiel des Fêtes**, Complexe Forbin, Cours Gambetta, © 04 42 63 06 75. The most famous is the **International Music Festival**, featuring celebrity opera and classical music during the last three weeks of July. This highbrow (and *very* expensive) affair is supplemented with lively alternative performances in the streets and smaller theatres. It is preceded by a less formal **Rock Festival**, an umbrella title that includes jazz, big band music, and chamber music during the second and third weeks of June. This is followed, in the first part of July, by the **International Dance Festival**, ranging from classical ballet to jazz and contemporary dance.

Shopping

The traditional souvenirs of Aix are its almond and glazed melon confits, *calissons*, which have been made here since 1473; buy them at **Béchard**, 12 Cours Mirabeau, © 04 42 26 06 78, or **Confiserie Brémond**, 16 Rue d'Italie, © 04 42 27 36 25, or best of all **Chez Mestre Micoulin,** in Les Tours-Venelles, © 04 42 54 13 11, a veritable citadel of sweet wizardry. **Terre du Soleil**, at 6 Rue Aude, © 04 42 93 04 54, has local, world-renowned pottery. The better grocers sell the prize winning *huile d'olive du pays d'Aix*: Aix calls itself 'the capital of the olive tree since the 18th century'. Antique lovers should pick up a list of *antiquaires* at the tourist office.

Aix-en-Provence ✉ *13100*   **Where to Stay**

 If you come in the summer during the festivals, you can't book early enough; Aix's less pricey hotels fill up especially fast (if you have a car, check where to stay around Aix as well, p.200). For luxury, there's the romantic ★★★★**Le Pigonnet**, on the outskirts at 5 Ave du Pigonnet, © 04 42 59 02 90, ✉ 04 42 59 47 77, an old *bastide* with rose arbours, pool, lovely rooms furnished with antiques, an excellent restaurant and views out over the Aix countryside (*from 600F*). Just north of the centre, the ★★★★**Villa Gallici**, Ave de la Violette, © 04 42 23 29 23, ✉ 04 42 96 30 45, is a member of the Relais & Châteaux group, with all the warm atmosphere of an old Provençal *bastide,* with charming rooms, garden, parking and pool (*from 900F*). The renovated, elegant 18th-century ★★★**Grand Hôtel Nègre-Coste**, 33 Cours Mirabeau, © 04 42 27 74 22, ✉ 04 42 26 80 93, still hoists guests in its original elevator (no restaurant), or try the ★★★**Mercure Paul Cézanne**, 40 Ave Victor-Hugo (two blocks from the train station), © 04 42 26 34 73, ✉ 04 42 27 20 95, an exceptional little hotel, furnished with antiques and serving delicious breakfasts. Two of Aix's medieval religious houses have been converted into hotels: the 12th-century convent of ★★★**Des Augustins**, just off Cours Mirabeau at 3 Rue de la Masse, © 04 42 27 28 59, ✉ 04 42 26 74 87, which has soundproofed rooms and a breakfast garden (*prices start at 600F*), and ★★★**Le Manoir**, 8 Rue d'Entrecasteaux, © 04 42 26 27 20, ✉ 04 42 27 17 97, built around a 14th-century cloister. The home of composer Darius Milhaud (who grew up in Aix)

is now a comfortable hotel, **Artea**, 4 Blvd de la République, near the bus station, *C* 04 42 27 36 00, *D* 04 42 27 28 76; don't expect any mementoes of the composer but arrive after 8pm and get a discount. Two km from the centre, the 17th-century **Le Prieuré**, Rte des Alpes, *C* 04 42 21 05 23, *D* 04 42 21 60 56, is charming, overlooking a garden designed by Le Nôtre. Cheaper choices in town include **Du Casino**, off Rue Espariat at 38 Rue Victor-Leydet, *C* 04 42 26 06 88, *D* 04 42 27 76 58; the old fashioned **France**, 63 Rue Espariat, *C* 04 42 27 90 15, *D* 04 42 26 11 47, and *Paul, near the cathedral at 10 Ave Pasteur, *C* 04 42 23 23 89, *D* 04 42 63 17 80. The modern **Auberge de Jeunesse** is out at Jas de Bouffan at 3 Ave Marcel Pagnol (bus 12), *C* 04 42 20 15 99.

Eating Out

Under the masterful touch of Jean-Marc Banzo, the lovely **Le Clos de la Violette**, 10 Ave de la Violette (just north of the cathedral), *C* 04 42 23 30 71, has long been considered the best in Aix, and does wonderful things with seafood and Provençal herbs (*lunch menu 230F, dinner menus from 300F*). Closed Sun and Mon lunch. **Le Bistro Latin**, 18 Rue de la Couronne (just north of Place du Général de Gaulle), *C* 04 42 38 22 88, features imaginative variations on local themes such as leg of lamb with herbs, at refreshingly reasonable prices (*lunch menu 87F; dinner 110F and up*). Closed Sun and Mon lunch. The shady terrace or cosy fireside at **Chez Maxime**, 12 Place Ramus, *C* 04 42 26 28 51, is the place to go for delicious meat or fish dishes, accompanied by a list of 500 wines (*lunch menus from 95F, dinner from 125F*). Closed Sun and Mon lunch. For fresh pasta and other Italian dishes, the intimate, laid back **Trattoria Chez Antoine,** 3 Rue Clemenceau (just off Cours Mirabeau), *C* 04 42 38 27 10, is a good bet (*around 120F*); the cosy, popular **La Vieille Auberge**, 63 Rue Espariat, *C* 04 42 27 17 41, serves tasty Provençal dishes at tasty prices (*menus from 78F*). Least expensive of all is the eternally popular **L'Hacienda**, 7 Rue Mérindol (near Place des Cardeurs), *C* 04 42 27 00 35, which has a 65F menu including wine. More serious drinkers should head to **Le Petit Verdot**, 7 Rue d'Entrecasteaux, *C* 04 42 27 30 12, an authentic bistro where red wines by the glass are accompanied by ancient jazz records and simple dishes or charcuterie (*lunch 80F*). Reasonable vegetarian fare is served up at **L'Arbre a Pain**, 12 Rue Constantin, *C* 04 42 96 99 95.

Entertainment and Nightlife

Outside the festival season, the large student population of 'Sex-en-Provence', as they call it, keeps a number of jazz clubs in business, such as **Hot Brass**, west of the centre on Chemin de la Plaine-des-Verguetiers, *C* 04 42 21 05 57, or **Le Scat**, 11 Rue de la Verrerie, *C* 04 42 23 00 23. For a good stomp and a beery crowd, head to **L'IPN**, downstairs at 23 Cours Sextius, *C* 04 42 26 25 17, or **Le Richèlm**, at 24 Rue Verrerie, *C* 04 42 23 49 29. Clubs outside town include **Club 88**, at La Petite Calade north on the RN 7, *C* 04 42 23 26 88.

Films in their original language are shown at **Le Mazarin**, 6 Rue Laroque, *C* 04 42 26 99 85. Or join the punters at the slots and black jack tables in the **Casino Municipal d'Aix Thermal**, *C* 04 42 26 30 33, open 10am until dawn just off La Rotonde.

Aix-urbia: East around Montagne Ste-Victoire

The rolling countryside around Aix is the quintessence of Provence for those who love Cézanne: the ochre soil, the dusty green cypresses—as still and classical as Van Gogh's are possessed and writhing—the simple geometry of the old *bastides* and villages and the pyramidal prow of the bluish-limestone Montagne Ste-Victoire.

Along the south flank of the Montagne Ste-Victoire runs the **Route Cézanne** (D17), beginning in the wooded park and Italianate château of **Le Tholonet** (3km from Aix) where Cézanne often painted the view towards the mountain, which haunts at least 60 of his canvases ('I am trying to get it right,' he explained). The entire 60km route around Montagne Ste-Victoire is striking and unspoiled, the mountain's wild shoulders covered with maquis and holm oaks, growing back after a devastating fire in 1989, or tamed with vineyards. **St-Antonin-sur-Bayon** is home to the **Maison du Ste-Victoire**, an information centre on the mountain; the GR 9 begins nearby.

The **ascent of the Montagne Ste-Victoire** takes about two hours, and there's a 17th-century stone *refuge* with water and a fireplace if you want to spend a night. Crowning the precipitous west face, the 55ft **Croix de Provence** has been here, in one form or another, since the 1500s. Legend has it that Marius stood on the spot, watching his troops annihilate the Teutones; then, at the urging of his sibyl Martha, had 300 defeated chieftains brought up and tossed into the **Garagaï**, Ste-Victoire's mighty chasm. One legend claims the floor of the Garagaï is occupied by an enchanted lake and meadows, abode of the legendary Golden Goat of Provence; shepherds, they say, would lower their sick sheep and cows down on ropes to graze the therapeutic grass. Other stories claimed that the chasm was the entrance to hell, or linked to the Fountain of Vaucluse (in fact, fluoride released here surfaced there three months later). In the 17th century, curiosity reached such a pitch that the Parlement in Aix offered a condemned man his freedom if he would agree to be lowered into the Garagaï and tell what he found. Carefully trussed, the man went down, but was strangled in the ropes before he reached the bottom.

Further east the D17 passes through **Puyloubier**, a pleasant wine village, as is **Pourrières**, in spite of being named after *Campi putridi*, the fields of putrefaction, where the unburied corpses of the Teutones rotted after Marius's victory. A trophy was erected to Marius here, showing the victorious general carried shoulder-high on his shield by his soldiers. From Pourrières the mountain circuit winds through the pines (D25), and at Le Puits-de-Rians, veers back west towards Aix through the steep, forested Vallée de l'Infernet (D10). Northern approaches to the summit of Ste-Victoire begin at Les Cabassols or **Vauvenargues**. The 14th-century **Château de Vauvenargues**, strikingly set apart from the village, was the home of Luc de Clapiers (1715–47), author of the *Introduction à la connaissance de l'esprit humain*, in which he wrote that 'the highest perfection of the human soul is to make it capable of pleasure'. In 1958, the château was purchased by Picasso, who probably would have agreed with him; Picasso's grave is on the grounds, but off limits along with the rest of the château ('No admittance! Don't insist! The museum is in Paris!').

Puyricard and the Arc Valley

Four km to the north of Aix, overlooking the modern city, is the plateau where the city's story began, the Celto-Ligurian **Oppidum of Entremont**. For a place that lasted less than a century—it was founded in the 2nd century BC and destroyed by the Romans in 122 BC—it was an impressive achievement, its clusters of stone houses once sheltering some 5000 souls.

You can trace the foundations of the large public building that produced the Granet museum's sculptures (*open 9–12 and 2–6 exc Tues; bus 20 from the BNP on Cours Sextius every half hour*). The same bus continues north to Puyricard, and the **Chocolaterie Puyricard**, 420 Route du Puy Ste Réparade, ✆ 04 42 96 11 21, ✆ 04 42 21 47 10, where some of the most delectable (and expensive) fresh chocolates you'll ever taste are made in the traditional way.

To the west of Aix, the D64 continues to the three-tiered **Aqueduc de Roquefavour** (1847), twice as high as the Pont du Gard and built across the steep valley of the River Arc to bring the waters of the Durance to Marseille. The wooded setting is delightful—the Arc is the river where Cézanne painted his famous proto-Cubist scenes of bathers. The edge of the Arc valley is dotted with old farms and *villages perchés*: **Eguilles**, north on the D543; and south, off the busy Aix-Marseille routes, lofty **Cabriès** and **Mimet**. An old village often painted by Cézanne, **Gardanne**, has remained unchanged, defended by an ugly ring of industry and highways.

Where to Stay and Eating Out

Le Tholonet ✉ 13100

With views over Ste-Victoire, the family-run **La Petite Auberge du Tholonet**, south of the centre on D64E, ✆ 04 42 66 84 24, features local produce, good country fare and a number of vegetarian dishes (*menus 85–250F*). *Closed Sun eve and Mon.*

Beaurecueil ✉ 13100

Just ten km from Aix, just off the N 7, the ★★★**Relais Sainte-Victoire**, ✆ 04 42 66 94 98, ✆ 04 42 66 85 96, is a ravishing place to stay or eat, complete with a swimming pool, a gourmet restaurant with a lovely terrace and, above all, tranquillity. Air-conditioned rooms with terraces start at 400F; book early. *Closed Jan and Feb.*

Puyloubier ✉ 13114

Isolated on the flanks of Ste-Victoire, between Puyloubier and St-Antonin, the **Domaine de Saint-Ser**, ✆ 04 42 66 37 26, makes wine and has a small hotel for guests who want to get away from it all. Stop for a well prepared *cuisine du terroir* in the village at **Les Sarments**, an old country inn at 4 Rue qui Monte, ✆ 04 42 66 31 58 (*around 170F*), which is run by the same family as the Relais Sainte-Victoire.

Vauvenargues ✉ 13126

There's one hotel, **Moulin de Provence**, ✆ 04 42 66 02 22, with 12 simple rooms and a breakfast terrace overlooking Picasso's castle.

Roquefavour ✉ 13122

In the Arc valley, next to the aqueduct, ★★**Arquier**, ✆ 04 42 24 20 45, ✆ 04 42 24 29 52, offers peaceful rooms immersed in trees, with a pleasant restaurant and terrace along the river.

Gardanne ✉ 13320

Twelve km from Aix, ★★**L'Etape Lani**, Rte CD6, in Bouc Bel Air, ✆ 04 42 22 61 90, ✆ 04 42 22 68 67 (*menus from 140F*), has comfortable, well equipped and quiet rooms and a pool set in a pine wood; the restaurant features light, delicate and delicious seasonal dishes. *Closed Sun eve, Mon, and late Aug.*

MOUSTIERS - SAINTE - MARIE.

The Provençal Alps

The Côte d'Azur has an admirably spacious back garden, rolling over mountains and plateaux from the Italian border to the valley of the Durance, and covering the better part of three *départements*. Yet it has only two towns of any size in it, Digne and Draguignan. Between them are plenty of wide open spaces, landscapes on an Arizonan scale including even a Grand Canyon worthy of the name.

But is there really anything up here to tempt you away from the fleshpots of the Côte d'Azur? The stars of this huge and diverse area are beyond doubt the spectacular mountains, Italianate villages and frescoed churches of the Alpes-Maritimes, inland from Monaco

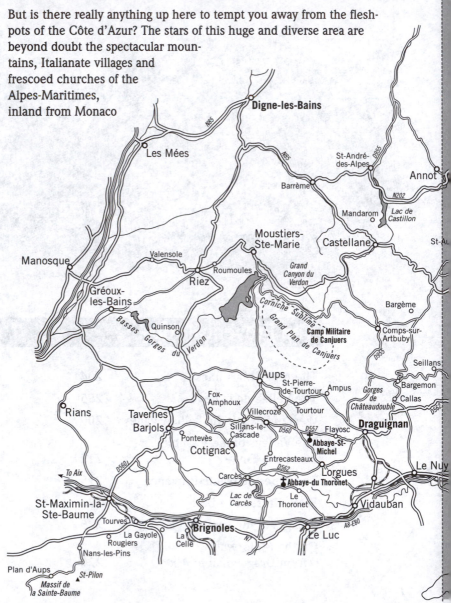

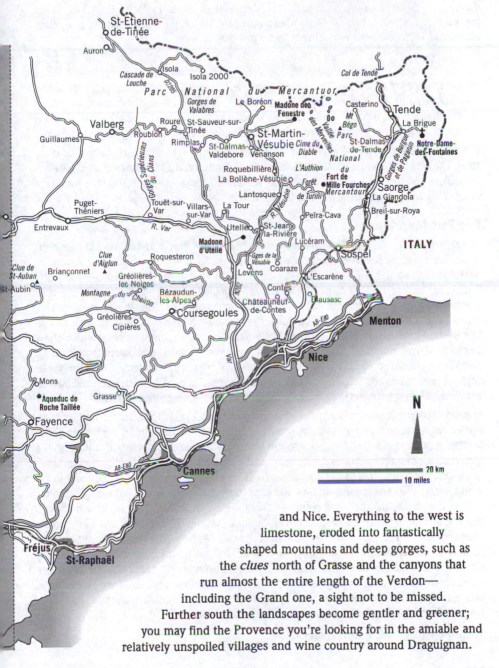

and Nice. Everything to the west is limestone, eroded into fantastically shaped mountains and deep gorges, such as the *clues* north of Grasse and the canyons that run almost the entire length of the Verdon—including the Grand one, a sight not to be missed. Further south the landscapes become gentler and greener; you may find the Provence you're looking for in the amiable and relatively unspoiled villages and wine country around Draguignan.

The Alpes-Maritimes

Lacet means a shoelace, or a hairpin turn. It's a word you'll need to know if you try to drive up here, on the worst mountain roads in Europe, designed for mules and never improved. When you see a sign announcing '20 *lacets* ahead', prepare for ten minutes in second gear, close encounters with demented lorry drivers, and a bad case of nerves.

So, what do you get for your trouble, in this corrugated department where the Alps stretch down to the sea? For starters these are real Alps—arrogant crystalline giants, which make their contempt felt as we crawl through the valleys beneath. Up in Switzerland, they would have enough altitude to make the geography books. Close to the sea, their numbers aren't overwhelming—but if you think 2803m Mt Bégo is a foothill, try climbing it. Bégo is a holy mountain, an Ararat or a Mount Meru, a prehistoric pilgrimage site for the ancient Ligurians.

The scenery defies any travel writer's verbiage, a jigsaw-puzzle panorama at the turn of every *lacet*. The best parts have been set aside as the **Parc National du Mercantour**. In the valleys of the Roya and the Tinée, there's another attraction—all those *lacets* will also take you to the some of the finest Renaissance painting in the Midi.

The Parc Mercantour

The highest regions of this *département* are contained in the **Parc National du Mercantour**, stretching along the Italian border for over 128km, and joining with the adjacent Argentera National Park in Italy to make a unique preserve of alpine and Mediterranean wildlife. Established only in 1979, it consists of a central 'protected zone', a narrow strip of the most inaccessible areas, including the Vallée des Merveilles with its prehistoric rock carvings (*see* below), and a much larger 'peripheral zone' that includes all the villages from Sospel to St-Etienne-de-Tinée and beyond. There are many excellent hiking trails, some of which allow you to cross over into Italy. The park rangers, all local people, have an excellent reputation for helpfulness and knowledge. They enforce some strict rules in the protected zone: no tents, dogs, or fires, no motor vehicles (though all-terrain vehicles have recently been allowed on trails only, as an experiment), and no collecting flowers, insects or anything else.

The most spectacular alpine fauna, and the sort you're most likely to see, are the birds of prey: golden eagles, falcons and vultures. A recent addition, reintroduced from the Balkans after becoming extinct here, is the mighty *gypaète barbu* (lammergeyer), a 'bearded' vulture with a bizarre face, orange-red feathers, black wings and a reputation for carrying off lambs and children. On the ground, there's the ubiquitous stoat, or ermine, popping out of the snow in his white winter coat and looking entirely too cute to be made into royal coat linings, also his bulkier cousin the marmot, and plenty of boars, foxes, *mouflons* (wild mountain sheep), chamois and, in the more inaccessible places, *bouquetins* (ibex). All of these have been rapidly increasing in number since the establishment of the park. As for wildflowers, the symbol of the park is the spiky *saxifrage multiflora*, one of 25 species found here and nowhere else. Edelweiss exists, but is as elusive as anywhere else. Beyond these exotic blooms, there is a tremendous wealth of everything that grows. Blue gentians and anemones are everywhere, plus hundreds of other species, in micro-climates that range from Mediterranean to alpine. Half the flowers of the whole of France are represented here.

There are several **Park Information Centres**:

Tende ✉ 06430: Gare de St Dalmas, ✆ 04 93 04 67 00.

Casterino (Vallée des Merveilles): Maison de la Minière, ✆ 04 93 04 68 66. Summer only.

St-Martin-Vésubie ✉ 06450: Rue Kellermann Sérurier, Place de la Mairie, ✆ 04 93 03 23 15 or 04 93 87 86 10.

St-Etienne-de-Tinée ✉ 06660: Quartier de l'Ardon, ✆ 04 93 02 42 27.

St-Sauveur-sur-Tinée ✉ 06420: on the D2205, ✆ 04 93 02 01 63.

In Nice, there is a helpful information centre for the Parc National du Mercantour at 23 Rue d'Italie, ✆ 04 93 87 86 10.

The Vallée de la Roya

As you climb up into the mountains from the coast, you'll see evidence of the prosperous peasant culture these mountains once supported. Terraced vineyards and fields line the lower slopes, most no longer in use.

Getting Around

In all the hinterlands of Provence, this is the region most difficult to navigate by car, and the most convenient for **public transport**. One of the best ways to see the Vallée de la Roya is from that alpine rarity—a **train**. The railway line from Nice that runs to Cuneo in Italy offers spectacular scenery and serves all of the local villages: L'Escarène, Sospel, Breil, St-Dalmas and Tende (five each, daily). One train a day goes on to Turin. At the Sospel station, don't miss the historic train cars permanently parked here, including an old Orient Express.

Sospel also has four daily **buses** (no.910) to and from Menton, which take twenty minutes. There is a regular bus service from Nice to L'Escarène and Contes—some five a day, and also five a day from Nice to Lucéram, and a range of buses from Sospel into the smaller valleys (✆ 04 93 04 01 24).

Tourist Information

Sospel ✉ 06380: on the Pont Vieux, ✆ 04 93 04 18 44, 🖷 04 93 04 19 96.

Breuil-sur-Roya ✉ 06540: at the Mairie, ✆ 04 93 04 99 76, 🖷 04 93 04 99 70.

Tende ✉ 06430 : ✆ 04 93 04 73 71.

market days

Sospel: Thursday. **Breuil**: Tuesday. **Saorge**: Saturday. **Tende**: Wednesday.

Sospel

Travelling along the road from Nice, Sospel greets you with rusty cannons and machine guns, pointing out over the road from **Fort St-Roch** (*open daily June–late Aug, 2–6 exc Mon, April, May, Sept and Oct weekends only*). The fortress, almost entirely underground, shows only a few blockhouses, in a sort of military Art Deco; it dates from a 1930s counterpart of the Maginot Line. Inside, exhibits show details of its short career. The fort was designed to keep the Italians out, which it did with ease until the French surrender in 1940. Four years later, in

September 1944, Sospel found itself on the front line again—the vexing *sitzkrieg* of the Provençal mountains, where the Allies had no effort to spare for a serious advance. The Germans held out in Sospel until almost the end of the war.

Through all that, the town suffered considerable damage, now entirely, and lovingly, restored, including Sospel's landmark, the **Pont Vieux**, the base of which dates back to the 10th century. The tiny tower in the middle of the bridge was the toll on the **salt road**; in the Middle Ages, salt from the flats of Toulon and Hyères was taken by boat to Nice, and from there by convoys of mules to Piedmont and Lombardy. Now the toll bridge houses the tourist information office.

The Cathedral of **St-Michel**, in a handsome arcaded square, retains its original 12th-century bell tower, but the rest has been Baroqued with charming tastelessness inside and out, including a wonderful circus-tent baldachin over the altar, dripping with gilt and tassels; a chapel to the left discreetly hides a fine *Annunciation* by Ludovico Brea, as well as another retable of the Virgin in a Gothic frame, possibly also by Brea or one of his followers. Don't miss a wander around the narrow winding streets of the rest of the old town, and another arcaded square, **Place St-Nicolas** with a 15th-century fountain, on the other side of the bridge.

Breil and Saorge

To the north, the D2204 is the best route into the Vallée de la Roya, with only a few dozen *lacets* and one mountain pass; the other route, following D93 and the N204, is slightly shorter, but it passes two border crossings in and out of Italy. **Breil-sur-Roya**, the first town in the French part of the valley, has two peculiar attractions: the unidentifiable black pseudo-turkeys who live in the River Roya under the bridge, and the 18th-century church of **Sancta-Maria-in-Albis**, with large cracks in its ill-formed walls that seem ready to bring the place down around the ears of the faithful. Inside is another retable attributed to Brea, though not a very good one. Further north, the village of **La Giandola** sits among the olive groves that once were the valley's only resource, and beyond that come the **Gorges de Saorge**.

After the gorges, the village of **Saorge** is a magnificent sight—neat rows of Italian slate-roofed, green-shuttered houses, perched on a height like some remote Byzantine monastery, punctuated by church steeples with cupolas of coloured tiles. Saorge guards the Roya valley, and the Piedmontese made it a key border stronghold. You won't see more than ruins of their fort today—it was destroyed after a young commander named Bonaparte took it during the wars of the Revolution.

Saorge is just as attractive from close up, an ancient border village with customs and a dialect all its own, a little bit Occitan and a little bit Ligurian Italian; instead of rue or via on the street signs, you'll see *caréra* or *chu* or *ciassa*. The streets, stairways more often than not, climb and dive and duck under arches. The sights require a kilometre's hike to the outskirts: the 18th-century **Franciscan Monastery**, in elegant Piedmontese Baroque, and beyond that the 11th-century chapel of the **Madonna del Poggio**, with Renaissance frescoes including a *Marriage of the Virgin*. West of Saorge, you can penetrate into the southernmost corner of the Mercantour National Park, up the narrow D40 into the **Forêt de Caïros**.

Vallée des Merveilles

Before going further, understand that the Roya is a cul-de-sac; there's no way out besides retracing your steps or continuing through the Tende tunnel to Cuneo, Italy. After Saorge, the mountains close in immediately, with the **Gorges de Bergue et de Paganin**; these end at the village of **St-Dalmas-de-Tende**, once the border post between France and Italy and now the gateway to the Vallée des Merveilles.

From about 1800 BC, the Ligurian natives of these mountains began scratching pictures and symbols on the rocks here. They kept at it for the next 800 years, until over 100,000 inscriptions decorated the valley: human figures, religious symbols (plenty of bulls, horns and serpents), weapons and tools. Most defy any conclusive interpretation—circles, spirals and ladders or chequerboard patterns of the kind found all over the Mediterranean; the Val Camonica in northern Italy has even more carvings, from the same era. Why they were made is an open question; one very appealing hypothesis is that this valley, beneath Mont Bégo, was a holy place and a pilgrimage site, and that the carvings can be taken as ex votos made by the pilgrims.

The presence of these symbols has brought the valley some notoriety—superstition gave the surroundings place names like Cime du Diable ('Devil's Peak') and Valmasque (*masco*, or mask, was an old local word for sorcerer). The first person to study the site systematically was an Englishman, Clarence Bicknell, in the early part of this century. As the prime attraction of the Parc Mercantour, the valley gets its share of visitors these days. Besides the carvings, the landscape itself is worth the hike, including a score of mountain lakes, mostly above the tree line, all in the shadow of the rugged, uncanny **Mont Bégo**, highest of the peaks around the Roya; the mountain's name, as far as anyone can tell, comes from an Etruscan god of storms.

Don't just wander up here like some fool tourist, looking for Neolithic etchings. Plan the trip out beforehand, with advice from the Park Information Offices. They will probably recommend a guided tour; the symbols are plentiful, but nonetheless inconspicuous and hard to find. Apart from the summer months, many will be covered in snow. To tour the valley is *at least* a 20km round-trip trek from the *refuge* at Les Mesches, at the end of the road west from St-Dalmas; there are hotels in nearby **Casterino** (*see* below) and *refuges* within the park if you want to stay over; make arrangements at the park office. Jeep-taxis can also take you around (expensively) from St-Dalmas.

La Brigue and Notre-Dame-des-Fontaines

Vittorio Emanuele II, the last king of Piedmont-Sardinia and the first of unified Italy, may have been utterly useless at his job, but as a hunter few crowned heads could match him. When he arranged to give away the County of Nice in 1860, he stipulated only that the Upper Roya, above St-Dalmas-de-Tende, be left for him as a hunting reserve (to add to a few others he had, strung out across Italy, including the famous Isle of Montecristo). The few inhabitants had already voted (under French supervision) for union with France; suspiciously, 73 per cent of the electorate abstained. But this had to wait until 1947, when another plebiscite was held and the valley became France's latest territorial acquisition.

Tende, a dour slate-roofed *bourg,* is the only town. No longer a dead end since the road tunnel through to Italy was built, it has become a busy place by local standards. It has the ruined castle of the Lascaris, long-time feudal lords of the Roya, and a late Gothic church, **Ste-Marie-des-Bois**, with a pretty sculpted Renaissance portal, painted façade and ceiling. Don't miss its cemetery, built on steps for lack of space. On Ave du 16 Septembre 1847, the **Musée des Merveilles**, *©* 04 93 04 32 50, has copies and photos of the rock engravings, as well as ethnographic exhibits on prehistoric life up to the 18th century.

East of St-Dalmas-de-Tende, the D143 takes you into La Brigue, a minute region (partly in Italy) that grows apples and pears and raises trout. **La Brigue**, the tiny capital, has some fine painting in its church of **St-Martin**, another late Gothic work of the 1400s: three altarpieces by Ludovico Brea and his followers, along with Italian paintings from the 17th and 18th centuries. The people who live in La Brigue seem to have an elevated opinion of tourists, since the only ones who pass through have come a long way to see their paintings and, more importantly, those by Giovanni Canavesio at **Notre-Dame-des-Fontaines**, 4km from the village of La Brigue. The name comes from seven intermittent local springs, miniature versions of the Fontaine de Vaucluse, gushing out of the rock or stopping according to pressure and the water-table; these can still be seen, though now they are on the Italian side of the border.

The Upper Roya may not have been much of an economic or strategic gain for France, but artistically it was a real prize—the country's total number of good Renaissance frescoes went up considerably. Giovanni Canavesio, from Piedmont, is not well known outside his own region, but he was a painter in the best north Italian Renaissance tradition: bright colours, exquisite, stylized draughtsmanship and an ability to put genuine religious feeling in his frescoes that recalls Fra Angelico. His works in this rural chapel, done in the 1490s, include 26 large scenes of the *Passion of Christ* in the nave, and on one of the side walls a tremendous **Last Judgement**. Around the choir, on the triumphal arch, he painted scenes from the Life of Mary, from the *Birth of Mary* at the upper left to the *Presentation at the Temple* at the bottom right.

The frescoes in the choir itself are by another hand, Giovanni Baleison. Done in the 1470s, in a more old-fashioned style that still shows the influence of Byzantium, these include the *Four Evangelists* on the vaulted ceiling, the four *Doctors of the Church* under the arch, and more scenes from the Life of Mary.

Where to Stay and Eating Out

Sospel ✉ 06380

There's little choice between the five hotels in Sospel: **★★Des Etrangers**, 7 Ave de Verdun, *©* 04 93 04 00 09, *@* 04 93 04 12 31, is marginally the more expensive, and has a pool. *Closed Dec–Feb.* A mile from the centre, **★★L'Auberge Provençal**, Route de Menton, ✆ 04 93 04 00 31, has a *terrasse* with a magnificent view over Sospel. *Closed Nov–11 Dec.* Outside Sospel off the D2566 towards Moulinet at La Vasta (you will need a car) the *chambre d'hôte*, **Domaine du Paraïs**, ✆ 04 93 04 15 78, was a villa taken over by officers during the war, and has now been proudly restored by its owners. You must stay a minimum of two nights; book ahead (*280F for two*).

L'Escargot d'Or, at 3 Rue de Verdon, ✆ 04 93 04 00 43, is the best place to eat in Sospel, specializing in meat fondues and menus start at only 115F. Ring to reserve, and to check they're open out of season—they'll close if they anticipate a quiet night. *Closed Fri.* In Place St Michel, you can lunch slapbang opposite the cathedral at the vegetarian **T+** (Thé Plus), ✆ 04 93 04 06 28, where you will be welcomed and served bubbling pots by a lady who travelled the world before stopping to settle here.

Breil-sur-Roya ✉ 06540

Breil-sur-Roya is not the most enchanting place to stay in the Roya, but it has several hotels, including the comfortable modern **★★Castel du Roy**, spread out among several buildings near the river on the Route de Tende, ✆ 04 93 04 43 66, 🖷 04 93 04 91 83, with a pool and a highly rated restaurant, *closed Nov–Feb*; and the functional **★★Le Roya** in the village square, ✆ 04 93 04 48 10, 🖷 04 93 04 92 70. *Closed Feb.* L'Etoile, ✆ 04 93 04 41 61, offers ravioli, rabbit, and trout at reasonable prices.

Saorge ✉ 06540

There is only one hotel in Saorge, **Le Bellevue**, ✆ 04 93 04 51 37, reasonably priced (*160–200F*) and open all year. On the N204, 2km to the north at Fontan, there is a simple but adequate inn: **Restaurant de la Roya**, ✆ 04 93 04 50 19, with cheap rooms and a popular restaurant serving a 95F menu. For lunch, **Lou Pountin** on Rue Revelli, ✆ 04 93 04 54 90, makes excellent pizzas (*75F menu*).

La Brigue ✉ 06430

The best choice of the three hotels here is **★★Le Mirval** on Rue St-Vincent Ferrier at the west end of the village, ✆ 04 93 04 63 71, 🖷 04 93 04 79 81; some rooms have good views, and the management can arrange a trip (expensive) into the Vallée des Merveilles. *Closed Nov–Mar* .

Casterino ✉ 06430

If you're doing the Merveilles on your own, it's convenient to start from Casterino, a hamlet at the end of the D91; the nicest of the three hotels here is **★Les Melèzes**, ✆ 04 93 04 64 95, 🖷 04 93 04 95 96, with small but comfortable rooms and a good restaurant (*rooms 200–290F*). *Closed mid-Nov–27 Dec.* Also with a restaurant is **★Marie-Madeleine**, ✆ 04 93 04 65 93, 🖷 04 93 04 77 65; try the smoked trout. *Closed 11 Nov–Christmas.*

West of Sospel: the Paillon Valley

There is some painting here too, in the rugged mountains between Sospel and the valley of the Var. The Italian influence shows itself in another way–the road map looks like a plate of spaghetti, with more twists and bends than anywhere in the *département*. Lacking a mule, you'll need to return to Sospel to get out of the Roya.

Getting Around

All the villages in the Paillon are served by at least two buses a day from Nice.

Tourist Information

Coaraze ✉ 06390: at the village entrance, ✆ 04 93 79 37 47.

Contes ✉ 06390: Place Albert-Ollivier, ✆ 04 93 79 13 99 (afternoons only).

L'Escarène

The D2204 west will take you to L'Escarène, a lovely Italianate village that served as a posting station between Turin and Nice. From the bridge you can see the houses overhanging the river, and you can visit the **Chapelle des Pénitents-Blancs**, with spectacular rococo stucco decoration. There are some peculiar landscapes to the south: stone quarries on the road to Nice that have carved out a huge, nearly perfect ziggurat (perhaps the Médecins of Nice could tunnel inside and make it their family tomb); the road is sometimes closed in the mornings for blasting. In the hills above, around Blausasc, 19th-century deforestation has left a lunar wasteland of bare rock; the government is currently building water channels to keep the erosion from spreading.

Lucéram

North of L'Escarène, **Lucéram** is an old shoe of a village, well-worn and a bit out at the toes. Full of arches and tunnels like Saorge, it has some remains of walls and towers on the mountain-side, a steep but pleasant excursion if you want to circumnavigate them. The church of **Ste-Marguerite** is second only to Notre-Dame-des-Fontaines as an artistic attraction. Amidst the gaudy Baroque stucco of the interior, the altarpieces of the Nice school seem uncomfortably out of place. The best, with an innocence and spirituality matched by few other saintly portraits, is the *Retable de Ste-Marguerite* over the main altar, attributed to Ludovico Brea. Marguerite, a martyr of Antioch, is another popular Provençal dragon-slayer, often confused with Ste-Martha (*see* Tarascon, p.299). Brea made her exceedingly lovely; the Tarasque-like demon at her feet obviously never stood a chance. The other retables around the church include *SS Peter and Paul* (with the keys and sword); *St Claude, St Lawrence* (with his gridiron, upon which he was barbecued) and *St Bernard*, all by unknown 15th-century artists; Giovanni Baleison contributed a good one of *St Anthony of Padua* (1480) in the Chapelle du Trésor, keeping company with a **Trésor** of awful clutter: reliquaries, monstrances and statuettes. Outside the church, the **Chapelle St-Jean** was built by the Knights of St John—the Knights of Malta, who had a commandery here. Its beautiful exterior is painted to imitate precious marble (though the inside is still full of electricity generators).

If you have the time, there are some worthwhile digressions into the mountains around Lucéram, beginning just outside the village with two more chapels with frescoes by Giovanni Baleison, similar to his work at Notre-Dame-des-Fontaines: **St-Grat** (on the road towards L'Escarène) and **Notre-Dame-de-Bon-Coeur** (on the road for Coaraze; the sacristan in Lucéram has the keys for both). East of Lucéram, a half-hour climb up into the hills, there is a wild spot with a huge circular prehistoric wall, the site of a fortified village from the time of the inscriptions in the Vallée des Merveilles, with a fine view of holy Mont Bégo.

North of Lucéram, the D21 and D2566 take you past Peïra-Cava, a resort for the French military and their families, to the **Forêt de Turini**, centred around a 1520m mountain pass, the Col de Turini, at the tip of three river valleys. Up above the pass are several old forts, near the summit of Mont L'Authion, an eyrie that commands almost all the Alpes-Maritimes. These were one of the Germans' last redoubts in the war; signs of the battle are still evident, especially around the **Fort des Mille Fourches**, reduced, incredibly, by bombardment from the sea in 1945.

The Devil's Tail, and Other Tales

A long tour on the D2566/D15 west from Lucéram (7km for the crow, 19 for you) will take you with some difficulty to **Coaraze**, a village that is a magnet for attracting stories. One is its name, *Caude Rase* in medieval times, or the 'cut tail' of the Devil. The villagers back then somehow trapped Old Nick, who had to give up his tail like a lizard to get away. Coaraze has also attracted its share of artists lately; one has given the village centre a lizard mosaic to commemorate the event. Other artists, including Cocteau, have contributed a number of colourful ceramic **sundials** around the village. Another legend deals with the abandoned village of **Roccasparvière**, an hour's walk from Coaraze in the mountains. Queen Jeanne of Provence, the story goes, once took refuge from her enemies here. The plot differs in every version, but in most of them someone in the village kills Jeanne's twin sons, and serves them up for dinner. '*Roc, méchant roc,*' Jeanne cursed. '*Un jour viendra où plus ne chantera ni poule ni coq.*' No chickens indeed are singing in Roccasparvière today, but spoilsport historians say it was because the village well dried up.

Another tortuous 10km south of here on the D15, **Contes** has its stories too. One fine day in 1508, the village was attacked by a horde of caterpillars. Apparently it was not the first time; the area has a colourful species the French call *chenilles processionnaires*, who enjoy a promenade in town every now and then. This time, the Contois had had enough; they called in the Bishop of Nice, who brought inquisitors and exorcists, and made anathemas and proclamations until the caterpillars finally grew uncomfortable and went home. Such affairs were not uncommon, especially in old France. Animals, too, were considered subject to God's law; horses and dogs occasionally went on trial for their indiscretions when times were dull. Contes has another altarpiece in the Brea manner in its church, and down by the river a well-preserved **forge** with a water-powered hammer, near the communal olive oil press. Here, and in many villages in the mountains, the oil presses are still in use. Across the river, and 9km up in the Ferion mountains, there is another abandoned village to explore, 2km outside **Châteauneuf-de-Contes** (*but note: the road is open weekends and holidays only*).

Where to Stay and Eating Out

Chic sophistication goes only as far as the foothills. In these mountains, so close to Nice and Monte Carlo, you'll find both food and accommodation surprisingly basic and humble.

Lucéram ✉ 06440

In the centre of Lucéram, **La Bocca Fina**, © 04 93 79 51 54, serves a 75F menu during the week, 85F at the weekend. At the top of Col de Turini, you can stop for the view and lunch at the **★★Trois Vallées**, a handsome chalet in the woods at Moulinet,

© 04 93 91 57 21, @ 04 93 79 53 62, on roast boar and such (*160–250F; rooms 320–600F*).

Coaraze ✉ 06390

Coaraze, with its sundials and restored houses, seems to get more visitors than the other villages, perhaps because of the most attractive mountain hideaway in the area. Despite having no star, the **Auberge du Soleil**, © 04 93 79 08 11, @ 04 93 79 37 79, is a dreamy location at the top of the village, a pool, and a fine restaurant with a memorable view from the terrace. This end of the village is closed to traffic—call ahead if you need help with your baggage. The restaurant has an excellent menu. (*Hotel prices begin at 360F for a double.*) *Closed mid-Nov–mid-Mar.*

Contes ✉ 06390

There is a less expensive alternative in Contes, the ***Auberge le Cellier**, 3 Blvd Charles-Alunni, © 04 93 79 00 64, with only five rooms and a simple but nourishing restaurant (*menu 80F*).

The Valleys of the Vésubie and the Tinée

The extensive valley of the River Vésubie is almost completely isolated from the regions to the east; from Lucéram the only ways across are the D21/D2566/D70 through the Col de Turini, or the miserable D2566/D73 directly over the mountains. There's an equally tortuous route from Contes—the D815/D19.

Getting Around

There are no trains in either the Vésubie or the Tinée valleys, and the coach service is sketchy. St-Martin-Vésubie can be reached by **coach** from the *gare routière* in Nice (Cars TRAM, © 04 93 89 47 14); **buses** for St-Sauveur and St-Etienne in the Tinée also leave from here. Roads in this area are as difficult as those to the east; service stations are few so keep your tank full.

Tourist Information

Levens ✉ 06670: © 04 93 79 71 00.

St-Martin-Vésubie ✉ 06450: Pl Félix Faure, © 04 93 03 21 28, @ 04 93 03 20 21.

Levens to Lantosque

The Vésubie flows into the Var near **Levens**, a big walled village on a small plain. Beneath it, the main road up the valley, D2565, follows the scenic **Gorges de la Vésubie**. From St-Jean-la-Rivière, at the end of the gorge, a winding 15km detour leads to the sanctuary of the **Madone d'Utelle**, one of the most popular pilgrimage sites in Provence, with a chapel full of naïve ex votos to Notre-Dame-des-Miracles, many from sailors, and a spectacular view as far as the sea. **Lantosque**, the next village up the valley from St-Jean, is a humble place, regularly shaken by landslides and earthquakes. Lantosque was occupied by the Austrians in the Revolution. One of them must have been *un bon coq*, as the French say; it's a joke in the other villages that you can always find someone in Lantosque named Otto.

St-Martin-Vésubie

At the top of the valley, St-Martin is the only town for a great distance in any direction, and a base for tackling the upper part of the Mercantour. It's as unaffectedly cute as a town can be, and once it was a spa of some repute. In the delightful and shady town square is an old fountain where the mineral waters used to flow, with inscriptions testifying to their 'organoleptic properties'. The medieval centre is traversed by a lovely street (Rue Dr Cagnoli) with a mountain spring flowing down a narrow channel in the middle, as in a garden of the Alhambra. On this street you'll see an impressive Gothic mansion, the **Maison des Contes de Gubernatis**, and the parish church, housing an altarpiece attributed to Brea and a polychrome wooden statue of the Virgin from the 1300s.

In the vicinity, **Venanson** is a beautiful village up in the mountains above St-Martin, with a small church full of frescoes by Giovanni Baleison. To the east, up into the Parc Mercantour on the D94, the **Sanctuaire de la Madone de Fenestre** was an ancient holy site near the present Italian border; the name comes from a natural window in a nearby mountain peak. The chapel has burned four times. In the Middle Ages the Templars held the site; they were massacred in the 14th century, and their ghosts were often seen in the neighbourhood. Hiking trails from here can take you on a very scenic route to the Vallée des Merveilles. Another road from St-Martin, the D89, leads northwest up a valley between the peaks of Mont Archas and Cime du Piagu to the resort village of **Le Boréon**; this is a lovely area, with many hiking trails, a waterfall (near the village) and some mountain lakes near the Italian border.

The Valley of the Tinée

There's nothing splashy or spectacular about the Tinée. People who love the Mercantour follow the slow D2205 along its length, from the N202 out of Nice, up to the protected zone of the Parc; skiers flock in winter to the modern resorts of Isola 2000 and Valberg. But outside their punctual visitations, there is a sort of pious hush in this valley, serenely beautiful even by alpine standards. In the lower part of the valley, the scenery is as much indoors as out; prosperity in the 15th and 16th centuries allowed the villages of the Lower Tinée to decorate their modest churches with fine Renaissance frescoes by artists of the Nice school.

The river flows into the Var with a climax, at the **gorges**, across the mountains from Utelle; to the northeast, **La Tour** has frescoes of 1491 in its **Chapelle des Pénitents-Blancs**. The traditional subjects are represented: the *Passion* and a colourful *Last Judgement*, with Christ sitting on a rainbow and allegorical figures of the Seven Deadly Sins riding on fantastical animals, accompanying the damned to hell.

The next paintings are at **Clans**, in two chapels just outside the village: **St-Antoine** offers more Sins, from an unknown, late 15th-century hand; they accompany some 20 rather peculiar scenes from the *Life of St Anthony*—cooking eggs and exorcizing female demons. **St-Michel** has frescoes by an Italian named Andrea de Cella, *c.* 1515, including St Michael 'fishing for souls', an odd conceit that goes back to Byzantine art. The parish church in the centre of the village has pictures too: surprisingly, a rare late medieval hunting scene. Next up the valley, there is a pleasant detour on the D2565 through Valdeblore, the only reasonable road through to the Vésubie. It begins at **Rimplas**, and the nearby **Chapelle de la Madeleine**, a conspicuous landmark occupying a gorgeous site overlooking the valley; and continues through **St-Dalmas-Valdeblore**, where there is a large and sophisticated Romanesque church: the **Eglise de l'Invention de la Sainte-Croix**, with fragments of its original frescoes.

Continuing up the Tinée, the next stop is **St-Sauveur-sur-Tinée**, throbbing metropolis of the valley, with its 496 souls. From here the D130 follows the Vionène valley west, through the rugged and lovely villages of **Roure** and **Roubion**. The former, set amidst the biggest larch forest in Europe, has more painting: a Brea (attributed) altarpiece in the church of **St-Laurent**, and unusual frescoes of the lives of St Sebastian and St Bernard in the chapel outside the village—all these chapels outside villages, incidentally, are a regional peculiarity, set outside the gates as if to avert evil influences, and often dedicated to plague saints like Sebastian. Roubion has a Sebastian chapel too, with another frescoed set of Deadly Sins. Continuing in this direction, the next town is the modern ski resort of **Valberg**. There is alpine scenery in these parts but little else; the best of it is in the long, lonely canyons stretching south off the D30/D28: the **Gorges Supérieures du Cians** and the **Gorges de Daluis**.

The uppermost part of the Tinée, following the D2205, runs through the northern half of the Parc Mercantour, never more than a few kilometres from the Italian border. After St-Sauveur come the **Gorges de Valabres**, decorated with an EDF electric plant that somehow managed to sneak inside the park borders. **Isola**, on the other side of the river, has some more appealing sights, both just off the D2205: a magnificently tall waterfall, the **Cascade de Louch**, and an impressive Romanesque bell tower, the only survival of an abbey washed away by a flood 300 years ago.

A good road takes you up to the Italian border and **Isola 2000**, a British-built, modern, concrete ski resort that does good business due to its proximity to the coast. Everywhere else to the north is at ski level, and almost all the villages have learned to bend their lives and habits to the seasonal invasions of the ski-bunnies.

If you haven't yet had enough Renaissance frescoes, you may also want to follow the Tinée to its source. In **Auron**, the 12th-century church of **St-Erige** has a sequence of paintings of that obscure Provençal saint, along with the Parisian St Denis, a stranger in these parts. **St-Etienne-de-Tinée** has two painted rural chapels: **St-Sébastien** with a cycle of works by Canavesio and Baleison, in very bad shape, and the chapel of the **Couvent des Trinitaires** where the subject is, of all things, the great naval victory of the Venetians and Spaniards over the Turks at Lepanto in 1571.

Where to Stay and Eating Out

Lantosque ✉ 06450

On the way up to the Parc Mercantour, there's a gracious country hotel in Lantosque: the **★★★Hostellerie del'Ancienne Gendarmerie**, ✆ 04 93 03 00 65, 🖷 04 93 03 06 31. The 'former police station' occupies a pretty hillside site, with garden-side rooms and a pool. The restaurant specializes in trout and *escargots* (*menus 165F and 285F*). *Closed Nov–Jan*.

St-Martin-Vésubie ✉ 06450

★★La Bonne Auberge, ✆ 04 93 03 20 49 🖷 04 93 03 20 69, is as good as its name, a welcoming and pretty place on the main Place Félix Faure, with nice rooms starting at 200F and a cosy cellar restaurant with a boar's head over the chimneypiece—grilled chops, *escargots*, *civet du lapin* and profiteroles (*menus at 90F and 140F*). Small wonder that this is where Nice's soccer team prepares for matches. *Closed Dec, Jan*. If the Auberge is full, settle for the modern **★Des Alpes** across the square, ✆ 04 93 03

21 06. *Closed Jan.* Outside of St-Martin, **de Boréon**, ✆ 04 93 03 20 35, in the village of the same name, is a chalet-style place with a few simple rooms and a good restaurant, serving 80–170F menus including *truite aux amandes*, and homemade desserts *Closed Nov–Mar.* Also in Le Boréon, **★Le Cavalet**, ✆ 04 93 03 21 46, 🖷 04 93 03 34 34, is a simple abode in a dreamy lakeside setting, at the forest edge. The excellent restaurant is open only at lunchtime (*menus from 85F*), whilst *demi-pension* is required for hotel guests. Open all year, as is the simple **Bella Vista**, up at Venanson, ✆ 04 93 03 25 11. In St-Martin, you can step out for some of the best pizza this side of the border—baked in a proper pizza oven—at **La Treille**, Rue Dr Cagnol, ✆ 04 93 03 30 85; also pasta and more ambitious dishes (*90–150F, weekends only in winter*). On the Place du Marché, **La Trappa**, ✆ 04 93 03 21 50, serves up mountain fare and heady house wine (*90F and 120F menus*). *Closed Mon.*

The Tinée Valley

Don't expect anything out of the ordinary in the sparsely populated, little-visited Tinée valley: simple country inns with restaurants are the rule, like the **Auberge St-Jean** in **Clans** (✉ 06420), ✆ 04 93 02 90 21; or in **St-Etienne** (✉ 06660), **★★La Pinatelle**, Blvd d'Auron, ✆ 04 93 02 40 36, 🖷 04 93 02 47 90 (*menus from 85F*). These two, and most of the others, require half-board in the summer. At **Valdeblore** (✉ 06420) there is a *ferme-auberge* called **Chalet du Val de Blore** on the D2565 west of St-Dalmas, ✆ 04 93 02 83 29, 🖷 04 93 02 83 06: four simple rooms in a modern chalet with Italian-Niçoise home cooking. When in the mountains, look out for locally made liqueurs, an alpine speciality: *myrtille* (bilberry), pear, or something called *genépi meunier*—made from an Alpine herb that is closely related to absinthe.

The Alpes de Haute-Provence

> *Clearly we find ourselves in a place that is out of the ordinary. You need a strong character, and a little bit of soul.*
>
> Jean Giono

There is something of the Wild West in this *département*, complete with lofty plateaux and canyons, including a Grand one. Provence's wide open spaces are full of lavender fields and fresh air, a place to white water raft, hang glide, ride, climb or hike: the Maison des Alpes-de-Haute-Provence, 19 Rue du Docteur Honnorat, ✉ 04005 Digne-les-Bains, ✆ 04 92 31 57 29, 🖷 04 92 32 24 94, publishes a free and an extremely useful, practical guide (*Sports and Leisure Activities in the Open Air*) on how and where to indulge in your favourite sport.

Getting Around

Buses are so rare they aren't worth the trouble, but it can be fun seeing this region by the scenic, recently modernized narrow gauge rail-line familiarly called the ***Train des Pignes***, from Nice to Digne; it follows the Var, and a few trains stop at villages along the way: Villars, Puget-Théniers, Entrevaux and Annot—five a day at the most. This is not the SNCF, but a separate line called *Chemin de Fer de Provence* (in Digne, call ✆ 04 92 31 01 58 for details).

Puget-Théniers ✉ 06260: ✆ 04 93 05 05 05, open July and August only.

Entrevaux ✉ 04320: at the Porte Royale, ✆ 04 93 05 46 73, ✆ 04 93 05 43 91.

Castellane ✉ 04120: Rue Nationale, ✆ 04 92 83 61 14, ✆ 04 92 83 76 89. Ask about the guided tours organized by the *mairie*.

Riez ✉ 04500: 4 Allée Louis Gardiol, ✆ 04 92 77 82 80, ✆ 04 92 77 79 67.

Digne ✉ 04000: Le Rondpoint, ✆ 04 92 36 62 62, ✆ 04 92 32 27 24.

market days

Moustiers: Friday. **Riez**: Wednesday and Saturday. **Digne**: Wednesday and Saturday.

Villars to Entrevaux along the N202

The N202 is the east–west traffic chute, following the upper Var, and the only convenient way to get through the mountains north of Grasse. It isn't scenic, though the gravelly, impossibly blue Var makes a refreshing sight alongside; it may however be an antidote to claustrophobia after traversing too many gorges. The trip begins with a local novelty—wine—at **Villars-sur-Var**. The centre of the only, tiny AOC wine region in the mountains, Villars was almost abandoned before the awarding of the *dénomination* in the 1970s. Production has vastly increased since then, and you'll occasionally see this variety of Côtes-de-Provence in trendy restaurants on the coast—perhaps more for its curiosity value than for anything else. The village church has a few Renaissance pieces: a retable of *St John the Baptist*, and an Italian fresco of the *Annunciation*, both anonymous works of the early 1500s.

Next comes a postcard shot: **Touët-sur-Var**, seemingly pasted up on the side of a cliff, with much of its medieval defences still intact in case anyone tries to storm the place. **Puget-Théniers**, the biggest village on this stretch of the Var, is more open and welcoming, a shady oasis after the stark mountain landscapes, where you may stop for lunch and look at more pictures—two genuine jewels among a number of altarpieces in the parish church: Antoine Ronzen's *Notre-Dame de Secours* and Mathieu d'Anvers' *Passion*, both done about 1525. A monument by Aristide Maillol in the town square commemorates Puget's pride: a local boy named Auguste Blanqui, who became a journalist and one of the leaders of the Paris Commune in 1870, which he paid for by spending 36 years in prison.

Under the sweeping twist of its cliffs, **Entrevaux** is the strategic key to the valley. There has been a fort of some kind here since Roman times, and its present incarnation is particularly impressive—the work of Louis XIV's celebrated engineer Vauban, high above the village,

Entrevaux.

complete with Second World War additions. At the time it was built the French-Piedmontese border was only a few miles away (it is now the departmental boundary between Var and Alpes-Maritimes). The entrance is a **fortified bridge**, rebuilt by Vauban on medieval foundations. Around the village, vestiges of its old garrison days can be seen: barracks and powderhouses, and an ancient **drawbridge**, still in working order, behind the 17th-century **cathedral**. There's a honeycomb of buildings and narrow alleys where people are living; if you wander through the smelly damp alleys there are flowers high up in the windows, duvets thrown over the sills in the mornings. The serious part of the **fort** is a hard 15-minute climb if you're fit; take water, a sunhat, some historical imagination and a 10-franc piece for the turnstile and you're on your own to explore the derelict tunnels and dungeons—once deliciously dangerous, now undergoing restoration to make them safe. The landscape below, with the little *Train des Pignes*, is as unlikely as an alpine train set. Try to get up there before 9am, when the first of the coaches are beginning to fit themselves in below. Harley fans will enjoy Entrevaux's **Musée de la Moto**, © 04 93 79 12 70 (*open April–Sept 10–12 and 2–7; free*), a collection of motorcycles from 1901 to 1967.

The *Clues* and the Esteron Valley

South of the Var is a grim and lonely region; you can see Nice and Cannes from the summit of the **Montagne du Cheiron** in its centre, but from here the Riviera beaches seem a world away. A *clue*, or more properly *cluse*, is a transverse valley, formed between the limestone folds of the mountains; here the name is given to the many narrow gorges that make life and communications in the area difficult. Local villages are humble and crumbling and few, and the roads across are winding and exasperating. From Puget, the D2211A/D17 takes you to **Roquesteron**, a fortified village divided into two parts (before 1860 one was Piedmontese, one French); west of the village, a bad road, the D10, leads off into the isolated **Clue d'Aiglun**, perhaps the most dramatic of the *clues*, with a big waterfall.

The more southerly route—with a choice of roads running east–west, some conveniently reached from Vence or Nice—passes some lovely *villages perchés*: **Bézaudun-les-Alpes**, **Coursegoules**, **Gréolières** and **Cipières** (follow D1/D8/D2, from Carros on the Var, north of Nice), all starting to be colonized by people from the Riviera. Gréolières, under the Montagne du Cheiron, has an enormous ruined castle; from here you can follow the D603 into the **Gorges du Loup** towards Grasse, or take the D2/D802 on to the Cheiron and the new ski station of **Gréolières-les-Neiges**.

Where to Stay and Eating Out

Being the only good road across this region, the N202 has the best selection of places to stay and eat, with a few rather better than the average *routier*.

Touët-sur-Var ✉ 06710

The **Restaurant des Chasseurs**, © 04 93 05 71 11, has a few rooms, but does most of its business serving fish and game to appreciative locals; ravioli and rabbit stew figure (*menus at 110–180F*).

Puget-Théniers ✉ 06260

There are two hotels: **★★Alize** on Rue Alexandre Barety, © 04 93 05 06 20, 📠 04 93 05 14 14, and **★★Langier** on Place A. Conil, © 04 93 05 01 00, 📠 04 93 05 06 20, which is picturesque, but has a noisy bar and uncomfortable beds. For dining you won't do better than **Les Acacias**, Le Planet, ✆ 04 93 05 05 25, featuring duck, pigeon, and rabbit prepared in imaginative ways (*menus from 75–160F*). *Closed Mon and Jan.*

Entrevaux ✉ 04320

Entrevaux, with so many tourists, surprisingly has only one hotel, the unstarred **Vauban**, ✆ 04 93 05 42 40, and a *chambre d'hôtes*, ✆ 04 93 05 06 91. A good stop for lunch, **L'Echauguette** has outside tables on the central Place de la Mairie, ✆ 04 93 05 49 60, with menus (*75F and 110F*), including some seafood and, for starters, a salad served with the local speciality, a beef sausage called *secca*. Or try the **Pont Levis**, Place Louis Moreau, ✆ 04 93 05 40 12, for good home cooking and a great view of fort, village and valley.

The Lac du Castillon, Mumbo Jumbo and Castellane

After Entrevaux, the Var turns northwards, while the main road continues west, past the modest mountain resort of **Annot** and the **Gorges du Galange**. Further west the country becomes even stranger and lonelier; long monotonous stretches lull you to sleep until suddenly the road sinks into a wild gorge, or confronts a patch of striated mountains that look like gigantic *millefeuille* pastries tumbled over the landscape. Grey is the predominant colour, making a startling contrast with the opaque blue sheet of the **Lac de Castillon**, backed up behind the Barrage de Castillon, a mighty 293ft concrete dam begun in 1942 under the Vichy government, with a distinctly grim, wartime look about it. **St-André-des-Alpes**, on the north end of the lake, is France's hang-gliding capital. And what is that warped theme park on the west shore? Why, that's **Mandarom Shambhasalem**, the centre of Aumism, a fruit cake of a cult that half bakes bits of every religion into its batter. You can visit most afternoons (road up from Castellane).

Castellane, south of the lake, has become the capital of the Grand Canyon, the base for visiting one of the greatest natural wonders in Europe. It's centred round a pretty square of plane trees where boules is played, and people amiably hang about. But its edges are deep in up-to-the-minute sports shops supplying slick whizz-gimicry for any sport you could or couldn't conceive. There is a pretty *mairie* and a church, where the 597ft ascent up the Castellane's landmark square rock begins: pick up the key for the chapel on top from outside the *curé*'s house, or collect it on your way up from the last person coming down. Castellane's motto 'Napoleon stopped here. Why don't you?' comes from its spot on the **Route Napoléon**, the road taken by the emperor on his return from the island of Elba, now a tourist trail starting from his landing point at Golfe Juan and ending at his destination, Grenoble.

The Grand Canyon of the Verdon

The most surprising thing about the Grand Canyon du Verdon is that it was not 'discovered' until 1905. That the most spectacular canyon on the continent could be so overlooked speaks volumes about the French—their long-held aversion to nature, which they are now working so enthusiastically to correct, and the traditional disdain of Parisian authorities for the Midi. The locals always knew about it, of course; agriculturally useless and almost inaccessible, the 21km canyon had an evil reputation for centuries, as a haunt of devils and 'wild men'. Even after a famous speleologist named Martel brought it to the world's attention at the beginning of the century, many Frenchmen weren't impressed. In the '50s the government decided to flood the whole thing for another dam (the tunnels they dug are still visible in many places at the bottom); when the plan was finally abandoned, it was for reasons of cost, not natural preservation.

The name 'Grand Canyon' was a modern idea; when the French became aware of its existence, comparisons with that grand-daddy of all canyons in Arizona were inevitable. It does put on a grand show: sheer limestone cliffs as much as a half-km apart, snaking back and forth to follow the meandering course of the Verdon; in many places there are vast panoramas down the length of it. There are roads along both sides, though not for the entire distance. Most of the best views are from the so-called **Corniche Sublime** (D71) on the southern side; if you want to explore the bottom, ask about trails and the best way to approach them (it's a long trek) at the tourist information office in Castellane.

The lands south of the Canyon are some of the most desolate in France; you will find them either romantic or tiresome depending on your mood. But either mood will be definitively broken when columns of tanks and missile-carriers come rattling up the road. The army has appropriated almost all of this area, the **Grand Plan de Canjuers**, for manoeuvres and target practice; you'll see their base camp on the D955 towards Draguignan.

Directly west of the Canyon, a less spectacular section of the Verdon has indeed been dammed up, forming the enormous **Lac de Ste-Croix**; there is yet another dam further downstream, and the next 40km of the river valley are under water too: the **Gorges du Verdon**, in parts as good as the Canyon, but sacrificed forever to the beaverish Paris planners. It's wild country on both sides, and access is limited since the roads are few. Beyond the dam on the way to Manosque and the Lubéron, **Gréoux-les-Bains**, with its above-average number of launderettes and poodles, is a favourite with the rheumatic set who treat their aching bones to a jolt of sulphurous, radioactive water at the baths. The Bains bit is a clinical, eerie, hairdresser-smelling place, with New Age oddities on sale as if by money-changers at the temple. Gréoux was a fashionable resort in the early 1800s, when Napoleon's tearaway sister Pauline Borghese dropped by, but that's about it. The village turns its back on the shabby **castle**, built in the 12th century by the Templars, which occasionally is used as a theatre too (*open Wed for guided tours only, 2.30 in winter, 4 in summer*).

Riez and Moustiers

The **Plateau de Valensole**, north of the Verdon and the Lac de Ste-Croix, is a hot, dry plain of olive and almond trees, and one of the big lavender-growing areas of Provence—come in July to see it in full bloom. **Riez**, in the middle, is an old centre for lavender-distilling, now become adapted to tourism. Ruined medieval houses have been restored, and artists and potters have moved in. It's pretty but bustling, a good place to dawdle in. Riez was an important Celtic religious site, though it isn't clear exactly which deity it honoured. Testimonies to later piety can be seen at the western edge of town, thought to have been the centre of Roman-era Riez: four standing columns of a Roman **Temple of Apollo**, and a 6th-century **Baptistry** that is one of the few surviving monuments in France from the Merovingian era; octagonal, like most early Christian baptistries, it has eight recycled Roman columns and capitals; all the rest was heavily restored in the 1800s. Inside is a small **museum** of archaeological finds, including an altar with bull horns, ✆ 04 92 77 82 80 (*open April–Oct 9–12 and 2–6, otherwise by appointment only; adm*). Inside the medieval gates are two pretty fountains recycled from Roman remains, and a number of modest palaces and chapels that recall Riez's prosperity in the 16th to 18th centuries.

To the east, some 15km on the D952, **Moustiers-Ste-Marie** gets all the attention, spectacularly hanging on the west cliffs of the Grand Canyon du Verdon. Like Castellane on the other side, it is a popular base for visiting the Canyon, and busy in summer. The town will be familiar to anyone who haunts the museums of the Midi, as Moustiers in the old days was Provence's famous centre for painted ceramics. The blue and yellow faïences, usually painted with country scenes or floral designs, were often works of art in their own right; first popular in the time of Louis XIV, they were made here as late as the 1870s. Today a large number of potters, some talented and some pretty awful, clutter the village streets, capitalizing on the perfect clay of the region (and on the tourists). You can compare their efforts with the originals at the **Musée de la Faïence**, a small collection on Place du Presbytère, © 04 92 74 61 64 (*open daily exc Tues, April–Oct 9–12 and 2–6, July and Aug till 7, otherwise school holidays only, same hours; adm*).

In the middle of the village is the deep-set 12th-century **parish church** with a kink in it. Moustiers' other distinction, as everyone in Provence knows, is the **Cadeno de Moustié**, a 783ft chain suspended between the tops of two peaks overlooking the village. A knight of the local Blacas family, while a prisoner of the Saracens during the Crusades, made a vow to put it up if he ever saw home again; the star in the middle comes from his coat of arms. The original (thought to be solid silver, but really plated) was stolen in the Wars of Religion, and a replacement didn't appear until 1957. A climb up under the chain will take you to the **chapelle Notre-Dame-de-Beauvoir** where a notice piously requests that pilgrims do not write on the walls but inscribe their names on the heart of the Virgin instead.

Also Worthy of Your Attention...

Riez in French is a plural imperative: laugh! **Digne** means 'worthy', and one suspects a degree of deliberate etymological mutation in the gradual name change from the local Gaulish tribe, the *Bodiontici*, whose capital this was, to Roman *Dinia*, and finally to *Digne*. The capital of *département* number 04 (Alpes de Haute-Provence), and the only city in a long stretch of mountains between Orange and Turin, over in Italy, Digne has one thriving boulevard of cafés and touristic knick-knackery mixed with smart shoe-shops, posh chocolates and more than one bookshop. The town has recently rediscovered its role as a spa, and you will be given a glossy pamphlet in the tourist office consisting entirely of pictures of people smiling in the thermal baths. In the minuscule medieval centre is the crumbling, down-at-heel, 15th-century **Cathédrale de St-Jérome**, and its surrouding brightly painted houses stand shoulder to shoulder with some daring grey municipal buildings. Out of town (27 Avenue du Maréchal Juin) is something entirely unexpected: the **Fondation Alexandra David-Neel**, © 04 92 31 32 38, the former home of a truly remarkable Frenchwoman who settled here in her 'Himalayas in miniature' after a lifetime exploring in Tibet (*guided tours with her former secretary, daily in summer at 10.30, 2, 3.30 and 5, otherwise at 10.30, 2 and 4*). Ms David-Neel called this house *Samten Dzong*, the 'castle of meditation', and Tibetan Buddhist monks attended her when she died here in 1969, at the age of 101. The Dalai Lama has since come twice to visit; there are exhibits of Tibetan art and culture, photographs, and also Tibetan crafts on sale. In summer there are up to 40 people crammed into this tiny museum, so be prepared to wait in the garden. If you don't speak French, they will be happy to play the commentary in English.

At Place Paradis in an old bunker in the hillside is the **Museum of the Second World War**, © 04 92 31 54 80 (*open May–Oct Wed 2–6, out of season first Wed of each month*). At St Benoit, the **Geology Centre**, © 04 92 31 51 31 (*open April–Nov, 9–12 and 2–5.30, til 4.30 Fri; closed Sat and Sun*) houses the largest geology collection in Europe, including an impressive wall of ammonites. And at 64 Blvd Gassendi, the **Musée Municipal**, © 04 92 31 45 29 (*open July and Aug daily exc Mon 10.30–12 and 1.30–6, Sun until 5, other times Tues–Sun 1.30–5.30; adm*), has a collection of mostly 19th-century Provençal painters, archaeological finds and local curiosities. Follow Blvd Gassendi to the eastern edge of town, passing the peculiar neoclassical **Grande Fontaine** (1829), and you will find Digne's former cathedral, **Notre-Dame-du-Bourg**, a large Lombard-style Romanesque building of the 1100s, complete with a bell tower of that date, a deep-set Romanesque arch below a beautiful rose window, and inside some fragments of frescoes.

Where to Stay and Eating Out

St-André-des-Alpes ✉ 04170

Hang gliders in the know stay at the welcoming **★★L'Auberge du Parc**, Place Charles Bron, © 04 92 89 00 03, ℡ 04 92 89 17 38; the huge portions in the restaurant feature game dishes, mushrooms and other traditional country fills, and unusual items liked smoked mutton and *genépi* sorbet (*menus at 80F, 130F and 165F*). *Closed Jan.*

Castellane ✉ 04120

★★Ma Petite Auberge, 8 Blvd de la République, © 04 92 83 62 06, ℡ 04 92 83 68 49, is inexpensive and acceptable for a short stay. *Closed Nov–April.* **★★★Nouvelle Hôtel du Commerce**, Place de l'Eglise, © 04 92 83 61 00, ℡ 04 92 83 72 82, is friendly and comfortable. *Closed Nov–Easter*. At the foot of the rock next to the church, **Hôtel La Forge**, © 04 92 83 62 61, ℡ 04 93 83 65 81, has a terrace from which to view the village and the walkers going up and down the *roc*. The best way to see the Canyon is from the glassed-in restaurant terrace of the **★★Grand Canyon**, 14km east of the village of Aiguines, at the Falaise des Cavaliers, looking 300m down onto the Verdon, © 04 94 76 91 31, ℡ 04 92 76 92 29. *Closed Oct–April.*

Moustiers-Ste-Marie ✉ 04360

This region isn't quite as wild as the badlands to the east; after a day's tramping through the Grand Canyon du Verdon you can sleep in comfort and splurge for a memorable dinner at celeb-chef Alain Ducasse's 17th-century **La Bastide de Moustiers**, just outside the village at La Grisolière, © 04 92 70 47 47, ℡ 04 92 70 47 48, at the foot of the village, with seven individually fashioned rooms, jacuzzi, pool, riding stable etc. (*rates begin at 800F*). The food is predominantly local, picked fresh from the kitchen garden, and innovative (herb and vegetable tart, spit-roasted baron of lamb followed by cherries baked in batter) (*menus from 195F*). *Closed Dec–mid-Mar.* Up in the village and rather more affordable, is the **★★Belvédère**, © 04 92 74 66 04, ℡ 04 92 74 62 31. *Closed mid-Nov to Jan*. For dinner, **Les Santons**, Place de l'Eglise, © 04 92 74 66 48, enjoys a gorgeous setting on top of the village overlooking the torrent; the refined Provençal cooking matches the views (*menus 160–300F*). *Closed Mon eve; book.*

On the road to Riez at Roumoules (✉ 04500) **Le Vieux Castel**, ✆ 04 92 77 75 42, has been restored by its owners, the Allègres. It's tranquil, elegantly simple and far less expensive than anywhere else. Try the *table d'hôte*, if you can stand the other guests, and sit at the huge table, medieval-style. The formula of courteous no-nonsense hospitality works; the Allègres are currently restoring a large monastery down the road just outside Moustiers, partially open soon.

Quinson ✉ 04500

Further south, in the middle of the Gorges du Verdon, ****Relais Notre Dame**, ✆ 04 92 74 40 01, ✆ 04 92 74 02 10, has a garden and swimming pool, but most importantly a real, warm welcome and very good food. *Closed mid-Dec–mid-Mar* .

Digne ✉ 04000

Digne can be a civilized, urban oasis after too many empty spaces. There's a distinguished hotel in a restored 17th-century monastery: ******Du Grand Paris**, 19 Blvd Thiers, ✆ 04 92 31 11 15, ✆ 04 92 32 32 82, with an excellent restaurant featuring classic cuisine, truffles and seafood; *rooms 400–490F. Closed Christmas–Mar* . Next door is the family-run *****Mistre**, 65 Blvd Gassendi, ✆ 04 92 31 00 16, less of a grand hotel, and a bit less pricey, but just as comfortable. ****Le Provence**, 17 Blvd Thiers, ✆ 04 92 31 32 19, ✆ 04 92 31 48 39, is central and comfortable (*rooms starting at 200F*), and a good restaurant. **Hôtel du Petit St-Jean** 14 Cours des Arès, ✆ 04 92 31 30 04, ✆ 04 9236 05 80, might look quaint but your view—if you have one—will be tainted with the whiff of chip oil from the neighbouring restaurant. If you have to stay here, eat elsewhere.

From Grasse to Aix

Getting Around

Driving in this southern half of the Provençal mountains will prove much less trouble than the areas to the north and east; **roads** are better and service facilities more common. You can take the A8/E80 motorway straight across and miss everything—but the villages to the east and west of Draguignan offer some of the most delightful opportunities for casual touring in Provence—good bicycling country too. Two possible itineraries for you: from Fayence (west of Grasse on D562) to Le Muy, through the lovely villages along the D19 and D25 (the latter is the wine route); or from Draguignan, travel west on the D557, dipping into the mountains on the D77 for Aups, then the D22 for Sillans-la-Cascade and Cotignac, and west again (D32) to Fox-Amphoux or Barjols.

The main Provençal **railway** follows the motorway from Aix and Marseille to Cannes; for Draguignan you'll usually have to change at Les Arcs. Draguignan and Brignoles are well served, unlike almost everywhere else. Draguignan is also the hub for village **buses**, though as always these are few and generally inconvenient: several daily to Grasse, stopping at Bargemon, Seillans and Fayence along the way, and several daily in the other direction, to Tourtour and Aups, with at best one or two to the other villages.

Fayence ⊠ 83440: Place Léon Roux, ℃ 04 94 76 20 08, ⊛ 04 94 84 71 86.

Draguignan ⊠ 83300: 9 Blvd Clemenceau, ℃ 04 94 68 63 30, ⊛ 04 94 47 10 76.

Seillans ⊠ 83440: Le Valat, ℃ 04 94 76 85 91, ⊛ 04 94 76 84 45.

market days

Fayence: Tuesday, Thursday and Saturday. **Draguignan**: Wednesday and Saturday.

Fayence, Mons and Seillans

The first leg of this journey, as far as Draguignan, is close enough to the coast to have become thoroughly colonized by the holiday-home set. **Fayence**, a large village of moderate cuteness, has plenty of Englishmen and estate agents. Built on a steep hillside like Grasse, its road winds back and forth up to the centre, which is pleasant enough: there is a *mairie* perched on an arch over the main street, a forgotten 18th-century church and a view not to be missed from the Tour de l'Horloge at the very top of the village. North of Fayence, there is some lovely, wild countryside; off the D37, **Roche Taillée** has a Roman aqueduct still in use—but don't expect the Pont du Gard. This one is entirely carved out of the rock, along a steady descent of some 5km. Also from the D37, you'll see the towers of an impressive 17th-century castle, the **Château de Beauregard**, a private home. Further north, **Mons** is a beautiful and strange village of narrow streets overhung with arches. The language of its inhabitants still conserves some Ligurian Italian words; the people of Mons were totally wiped out in the Black Death of 1348, and colonists from the area around Genoa and Ventimiglia were brought in to replace them. There are a large numbers of **dolmens** in the area; some are inaccessible on the base of the Canjuers army camp, the borders of which are only 2km away.

West of Fayence, the farmhouses may now all be bijoux holiday-homes, but the scenery is delicious; the main road, the D562 to Draguignan, is fine, but even better is the winding D19/D25, passing through three pretty villages. **Seillans** has been occupied since the time of the Ligurians, giving it some two and a half millennia to perfect its charm, with cobbled streets leading up to the restored castle. It's one of the most beautiful villages in France, and like the others, it's got a plaque to prove it. The village lives on flowers, and was the last home of Max Ernst. **Bargemon**, further west, is just as old; behind its medieval gates are several fountains and a 15th-century church with a Flamboyant portal and heads sculpted by Pierre Puget. From here you can take a detour north, through the thoroughly depressing Canjuers military zone to **Bargème**, the highest village in the Var (3589ft), still encircled by its walls and ruined castle, although only two people live there year round to enjoy it.

Last before Draguignan is **Callas**, under a ruined castle. The D25 south of Callas, as far as Le Muy, is a beautiful drive through forests, with the **Gorges de Pennafort** and a waterfall along the way; it is also one of the best wine roads in the region, with a few places to stop and sample Côtes-de-Provence along the way (*see* p.229).

Draguignan

Draguignan gets a bad press, especially from the timid English: ugly, depraved, full of soldiers; *avoid it if you can...* Under the garish Provençal sunlight, we watched a young fellow on the Boulevard de Maréchal Joffre being run in by a pair of municipal policemen—clean-shaven, brutishly intelligent, all dressed up, military-style, in black and silver like American cops. Beautiful women waltzed by, swinging their handbags and smiling at the unfortunate; flaccid shop-keepers squinted furtively through immaculately clean windows.

After the Casino at Monte Carlo, there's no better free theatre in Provence. Tough, sharp-edged Draguignan is not French so much as French Colonial. The Army owns it—it's the biggest base in France—and its dusty palm-shaded boulevards (laid out in 1849 by Baron Haussmann, *préfect* of the Var, who treated the town to a trial run of his urban planning efforts in Paris) pass the national schools of artillery and military science. Draguignan's symbol is the *drac*—yet another Provençal dragon, chased out by an early bishop, though its fire-spitting image can still be seen everywhere. Draguignan could be Saigon or Algiers or Dakar, a cinematic fantasy in a wreath of *Gauloise* smoke, waiting for the Warner Bros cameras to capture Bogart, Lorre and Greenstreet conspiring in some tawdry nightclub.

Anyhow, have your papers in order, and try not to exceed the speed limits. Touring in Provence you'll be bound to pass through here once or twice, and it's a pleasant stop, really. The Saturday market is especially good, and there are a few things to see: the 17th-century **Tour de l'Horloge**, Draguignan's architectural pride; a small **Musée Municipale** on Rue de la République, ✆ 04 94 47 28 80 (*open 9–12 and 2–6, closed Sun, Mon am, and hols*), with a picture gallery (including the *Child blowing a Soap Bubble*, by Rembrandt, and a portrait by Camille Claudel, and faïences from Moustiers). The **Musée des Arts et Traditions Populaires**, at 15 Rue de la Motte, ✆ 04 94 47 05 72 (*open daily exc Sun morning and Mon, 10–12 and 2–6; adm*), is a complete, didactic overview of everything you'll never see in the real Provence any more—from mules to silk culture, along with reconstructions of country life. There's a large **American war cemetery** and Memorial on Boulevard John Kennedy, with a bronze map tracing the route of the 150,000 men of the 7th army who disembarked in the south of France in the two weeks following D-Day. And just outside town, on the D955 towards the Verdon Canyon, is one of the biggest and most spectacular dolmens in Provence, the **Pierre de la Fée**; the table stone weighs over 20 tonnes.

Where to Stay and Eating Out

Fayence ✉ 83440

There are inexpensive hotels, including the ★**Hotel Restaurant de la Fontaine**, Route de Fréjus, ✆/✆ 04 94 76 07 59; but the only places you're likely to remember are the ★★★**Moulin de la Camandoule**, Chemin Notre-Dame-des-Cyprès, ✆ 04 94 76 00 84, ✆ 04 94 76 10 40, a lovely old olive-oil mill, prettily restored (by a British couple) with all the amenities—pool, garden, etc. and a restaurant; *menus 185F and 285F*, half pension obligatory from Mar–Oct (*460–685F per person*) and the small starless **Sousto**, 4 Rue du Paty in the centre, ✆ 04 94 76 02 16, with its charming rooms equipped with kitchenettes overlooking the valley. For refined, sunny cuisine, head out of town for **Le Castellaras**, Route du Banegon, ✆ 04 04 94 76 13 80; try the courgette flowers stuffed with ratatouille; great wine list, too (*menus from 185F*). *Closed Tues*. In the centre, **Le Poelon**, Rue Font de Vin, ℗ 04 94 76 21 64 (*menus at 75 and 120F*), is small, cheerful and well-recommended. *Closed Oct–Easter*.

Seillans ✉ 83440

The much-lauded ★★★**Deux Rocs**, Place Font d'Amont, ℗ 04 94 76 87 32, 🖂 04 94 76 88 68, offers a matriarchal welcome as well as the odd bombs from the army firing range. Near perfect food, crowned with sublime desserts: a favourite with Americans (*menus from 145F*). The alternative is ★★★**De France Clariond**, Place du Thouron, ℗ 04 94 76 96 10, 🖂 04 94 76 89 20, which is not as quaint, but busy with its swimming pool overlooking the valley. *Closed Nov–Jan*. Don't miss **La Chirane**, ℗ 04 94 76 96 20, for a meal—a converted stable underneath the houses halfway up the hill, painted jolly blue, and with tables outside looking down over the lower village. Run by an Alsatian, there's live jazz monthly; reserve on Saturday nights. Specialities include chicken in garlic, ham from the bone, and home-baked bread. *Closed Tues and Sat afternoons*.

Bargemon ✉ 83620

Bargemon is a good place to rest without breaking the bank. There are simple, inexpensive hotels, like the ★★**Auberge des Arcades** on Ave Pasteur, ℗ 04 94 76 60 36, 🖂 04 94 76 68 33, and one fine restaurant with an outside terrace: the **Restaurant Pierrot**, Place Chauvier, ℗ 04 94 76 62 19; *menus 86–260F*.

Draguignan ✉ 83300

Don't expect red-carpet treatment in military Draguignan; the only really decent place is outside town, clean, modern and colourless—but with a view: ★★★**Les Etoiles de l'Ange** on the D557 towards Lorgues, ℗ 04 94 68 23 01, 🖂 04 94 68 13 30. The best restaurant, **Le Galoubet**, 23 Blvd Jean-Jaurès, ℗ 04 94 68 08 50, serves good seafood; try the *fillet de saint-Pierre* with leeks (*menus from 98F*). *Closed Mon eve and Sun eve and the last fortnight in Aug*.

Villages of the Central Var

Heading west from Draguignan, there are two choices; if aesthetics are a bigger consideration than time, don't bother with the A8 motorway or the parallel road through Brignoles and St-Maximin (for which, *see* below); instead, take the D557 or 562 directly west for a leisurely tour through some of Provence's loveliest and most typical landscapes. Though this area gets its share of foreign and Parisian summer folk, it isn't quite chic—compared to similar but totally colonized places like the Lubéron. But there's enough lavender and blowing cypresses, plenty of wine, and a dozen relentlessly charming villages that won't trouble you with any strenuous sightseeing.

Tourist Information

Aups ✉ 83630: Place de la Mairie, ℗ 04 94 70 00 80.
Barjols ✉ 83670: Blvd Grisolle, ℗ 04 94 77 20 01.

market days

Aups: Wednesday and Saturday. Truffle market on Thursdays.

From Lorgues to Aups

Lorgues is the first village, with a complete ensemble of 18th-century municipal decorations, proof that the *ancien régime* wasn't quite so useless after all: a fountain, the huge, dignified church of **St-Martin**, and the inevitable avenue of venerable plane trees, one of the longest and fairest in Provence. To the north, along the D10, you'll pass the **Monastery of St-Michel**, a recently refounded Russian Orthodox community; its handmade wooden chapel, a replica of a Russian church, may be visited. Further north, there are a number of pretty villages around the valley of the Nartuby: **Ampus**, **Tourtour**, over-restored but up on a height with views down to the sea, and **Villecroze**, with its vaulted lanes. At the edge of the Plan de Canjuers, Villecroze is built up against a tufa cliff; there is an unusual park at the base of it, with a small waterfall and a cave-house dug into the rock in the 16th century.

Aups was a Ligurian settlement, and a Roman town; its name comes from the same ancient root as *Alps*. It has a reputation for being different; a monument in the town square records Aups' finest hour, when the citizens put up a doomed republican resistance to Louis Napoleon's coup of 1851. The village is known in the region for its Thursday truffle market, held through the winter months. The village church is oddly below surface level; the ground level around it was raised to avoid the frequent flooding of the old days. Aups, like the other villages, has not completely escaped Riviera modernism. The **Musée Simon Segal**, ✆ 04 94 70 12 98 (*adm*), founded by an eponymous Russian artist, has his and other 20th-century works and is on Ave Albert I. **Salernes**, south of Aups, has been known for over 200 years as a manufacturer of tiles: the small, hexagonal terracotta floor-tiles called *tomettes* that are as much a trademark of Provence as lavender. They still make them, and in a day when French factory-made tiles all come in insipid beige, they are at a premium. Lately Salernes' factories and individual artisans have been expanding into coloured ceramics and pottery; there are a few shops in the village and factory showrooms on the outskirts. With such a workmanlike background, the village itself is rather drab, with a medieval fountain and a simple 13th-century church in the centre.

Further west, **Sillans** has lately been calling itself Sillans-la-Cascade, to draw attention to the 36m waterfall just south of the village (it dries up in summer); beyond that **Fox-Amphoux** is worth a visit just to hear the locals pronounce the name; this minuscule and well-restored village of stepped medieval alleys sits on a defensible height. There is a ruined castle, and on the trail to the hamlet of Amphoux, an odd cave-chapel, **Notre-Dame-de-Secours**, hung with ex votos, many from sailors.

Thoronet Abbey

South of Salernes, **Entrecasteaux** is dominated by a 17th-century castle, completely restored in the 1970s by a Scotsman named McGarvie-Munn; visitors are admitted, but there's nothing to see and the fee is exorbitant. Further south, the artificial **Lac de Carcès** has been a favourite with fishermen since the dam was built in the 1930s. To the east are the biggest bauxite mines in France, which are playing hell with one of the most impressive medieval abbeys in Provence.

The **Abbaye de Thoronet**, ✆ 04 94 60 43 90 (*open Mon–Sat 9–7 summer, 9–12 and 2–7 Sun; 9.30–12.30 and 2–5 winter; adm*), was the first Cistercian foundation in Provence, on land donated by Count Raymond Berenger of Toulouse in 1136; the present buildings were begun about 1160. Like most Cistercian houses, it was in utter decay by the 1400s; and like so many other medieval monuments in the Midi, it owes its restoration to Prosper Mérimée, Romantic novelist (*Carmen*, among others) and State Inspector of Historic Monuments under Napoleon III; he chanced upon it in 1873, when most of the roof was gone, the galleries were overgrown with bushes and the only beings dining in the refectory were cows.

It often seems as if the restoration is still under way; you may find it full of props, scaffolding and concrete piers, as its keepers experiment desperately to keep Thoronet from being shaken to pieces by the bauxite lorries rumbling past on the D79. The mines themselves (nearby, but screened by trees) have caused some subsidence, and cracks are opening in the walls. Nevertheless, this purest and plainest of the Cistercian 'Three Sisters' of Provence (with Silvacane and Sénanque) is worth a detour. Following the stern austerity of Bernard of Clairvaux, it displays sophisticated Romanesque architecture stripped to its bare essentials, with no worldly splendour to distract a monkish mind, only grace of form and proportion. The elegant stone bell tower would have been forbidden in any other Cistercian house (to keep local barons from commandeering them for defence towers), but those in Provence got a special dispensation—thanks to the mistral, which would have blown a wooden one down with ease. There are no such compromises in the blank façade, but behind it is a marvellously elegant interior; note the slight point of the arches, a hint of the dawning Gothic—Thoronet was begun in the same year as France's first Gothic churches, in the north at St-Denis and Sens. The **cloister** with its heavy arcades is equally good, enclosing a delightful stone fountain-house. There's a cellar to visit, too, to see how the monks fared, and a modern chapel.

Cotignac and Barjols

Its inhabitants might be unaware of it, but **Cotignac** is one of the cutest of the cute, a Sunday supplement-quality Provençal village where everything is just right. There are no sights, but one looming peculiarity: the tufa cliffs that hang dramatically over it. In former times these were hollowed out for wine cellars, stables or even habitations; today there are trails up to them for anyone who wants to explore; at the base of the cliffs there is a meadow where Cotignac holds its summer music festival.

Westwards on the D13/D560, the landscapes are delicious and drowsy; **Pontevès** will startle you awake again, a castle with a remarkable setting atop a steep conical hill. Long the stronghold of the Pontevès family, feudal rulers of most of this region, the apparition loses some of its romantic charm after the climb up; there's nothing inside but a few houses, *La Poste* and a food shop. Three km further on, **Barjols** has little cuteness but much more character. This metropolis of 2000 souls owes its existence to leather tanning, an important industry here for the last 300 years. There is still one shoe factory left, but Barjols is now little more than a market town, although it retains an urban and somewhat sombre air: elegant rectangular squares of the 18th century, and moss-covered fountains and *lavoirs* similar to the ones in Aix—hence its nickname 'the Tivoli of Provence'. If you stop in at the tourist office you can get a '*circuit des fontaines*' to guide you round all forty-two of them.

To see Barjols at its best, you'll have to come on 16–17 January, the feast of St Marcel (Marcellus, the 4th-century pope) whose gaudy relics, stolen in the Middle Ages from a Provençal monastery, can be seen in the 16th-century parish church. There'll be a bit of dancing (*la danse des tripettes*) and, equally unusual for Provence, the essentially pagan slaughter and roasting of an ox, accomplished to the sound of flutes and *tambourins*.

Lorgues ✉ 83510

Lorgues, 13km from Draguignan, is a more pleasant place to stop over if you're passing through the area; the venerable, classy hotel in the centre, a bit down on its luck but still comfortable, is the **Hôtel du Parc**, 25 Blvd Clemenceau, ✆ 04 94 73 70 01, with a restaurant (*65F and 235F menus; rooms start at 120F*). The **Brasserie du Parc** next door does a great *café au lait*. There are several decent restaurants in the centre, but for a better than average meal locals go to **Chez Pierrot**, 18 Cours de la Republique, ✆ 04 94 67 67 15. For something extra special, book a table at **Bruno**, an old *mas* at Campagne Mariette, ✆ 04 94 73 92 19, ✆ 04 94 73 78 11, where the chef does wonderful things with truffles (*menu at 270F*). *Closed Sun eve and Mon.* There are also three luxurious rooms, at prices in the ozone layer (*750F*).

Tourtour ✉ 83690

Tourtour, easily the poshest of the villages in this region, also has the most luxurious accommodation: the Relais & Châteaux ★★★★**Bastide de Tourtour**, Montée St Denis, ✆ 04 94 70 57 30, ✆ 04 94 70 54 90, a modern complex with pool, tennis and all the amenities, including a highly reputed restaurant with a blend of Provençal cooking and *nouvelle cuisine* (*menus 160F for lunch, 220–300F eve*). Charming and more affordable, ★★★**Le Mas des Collines**, Route de Villecroze, ✆ 04 94 70 59 30, ✆ 04 94 70 57 62, is a pleasant little hotel, offering tranquillity, air-conditioned rooms and a pretty pool overlooking the valley below Tourtour. There are only three pricey rooms at **Les Chênes Verts**, 2km on the route de Villecroze, ✆ 04 94 70 55 06, ✆ 04 94 70 59 35, but the wonderful food is the strongest magnet, classical and featuring lobster, seafood, truffles, and game in season, prepared to classical perfection. *Closed Tues eve, Wed, and Jan.* Three km east at St-Pierre-de-Tourtour, the ★★★**Auberge St-Pierre**, ✆ 04 94 70 57 17, is a find—an up-to-date working farm built around a hotel; exceptional rooms in an 18th-century house and a fine restaurant, with authentic Provençal food (largely the farm's own produce) (*menus 160F and 200F*). It also offers a swimming-pool, horse-riding and other activities.

Salernes ✉ 83690

In Salernes, the ★**Hôtel Allègre**, 20 Rue Rousseau, ✆ 04 94 70 60 30, ✆ 04 94 70 78 34, is another old establishment, like the one in Lorgues, with a bit of faded grandeur and some of its 1920s decor intact. The cooking's a bit faded too; you'll do better with a simple *magret* or stewed rabbit at **La Fontaine** on Place 8 Mai 1945, ✆ 04 94 70 64 51 (*outside tables, menus from 78F*). *Closed Sun eve, Wed, and Jan.* If you're going to **Sillans** (✉ 83690), the first thing you'll see, right on the D32, is the **Restaurant des Pins**, ✆ 04 94 04 63 26, ✆ 04 94 04 72 71, a very popular restaurant in an old stone house, serving grilled meats with shrimps for openers on 80–170F menus, also a few rooms at 240F, but book early for the summer. *Closed Jan and Feb.*

Fox-Amphoux ✉ 83670

One of the most pleasant village inns in Provence is in Fox-Amphoux: the ★★★**Auberge du Vieux Fox**, ✆ 04 94 80 71 69, ✆ 04 94 80 78 38, with rooms overlooking the Place de l'Eglise, and a delightful restaurant; try the *carré d'agneau*, *menus 135–270F*. In **Cotignac** (✉ 83570) ★★★**Lou Calen**, 1 Cours Gambetta, ✆ 04 94 04 60 40, 🖷 04 94 04 76 64, is an unexpectedly stylish hotel-restaurant in the centre of the village, with a lovely hidden garden and pool; only eight rooms, and as many (more expensive) suites; also a somewhat unexciting restaurant, menus 99F and upwards (half *pension* obligatory in season).

Off the Motorway: from Draguignan to Aix

With the Var's rocky coast, and the mountains behind it, the only easy route across the *département* is a narrow corridor through Brignoles and St-Maximin-la-Ste-Baume. The French have obligingly plonked down a motorway across it, successor to the Via Aurelia and the old St-Maximin pilgrims' route as the great high road of Provence.

Tourist Information

St-Maximin-la-Ste-Baume ✉ 83470: Place de Ville, ✆ 04 94 59 84 59, 🖷 04 94 59 82 92.

Brignoles ✉ 83170: Parking des Augustins, ✆ 04 94 69 01 78.

market days

Brignoles: Saturday. **St-Maximin**: Wednesday.

local wines

Côtes de Provence: With 57 cooperatives and 350 private cellars, Côtes-de-Provence wine is easily sampled, especially along the signposted 400km Route des Vins, which you can pick up at Le Luc or Le Muy from the A 8 or N 7 or at Fréjus, Les Arcs, and Puget-sur-Argens. Two of the best-known producers are at Trets, on D56 east of Aix: Château Ferry-Lacombe (✆ 04 42 29 33 69), and the 1610 Château Grand'Boise (✆ 04 42 29 22 95). You can also try: Domaine de St-Baillon, on the N 7 at Flassans-sur-Issole (✆ 04 94 69 74 60); Domaine Richeaume at Puyloubier (✆ 04 42 66 31 27); and at La Londe-les-Maures (west of Bormes-les-Mimosas) Domaines Ott, Clos Mireille, Route de Brégançon (✆ 04 94 66 80 26).

Coteaux Varois: this old *vin de pays* has recently been elevated to the ranks of VDQS. Visit the organic Domaine de Bos Deffens, on the Cotignac road just east of Barjols; or compare both Côtes-de-Provence and Coteaux Varois at Château Thuerry, set in a magnificent wooded landscape at Villecroze (✆ 04 94 70 63 02).

Les Arcs and Le Luc-en-Provence

Picking up the D555 south of Draguignan, you'll pass through **Les Arcs**, a well-exploited village of stepped streets, pink stone and ivy. Next comes **Le Luc-en-Provence**, practically strangled by the motorway and the parallel national routes but a game town nevertheless, with another steep medieval centre, a castle on top, and a restored Romanesque church flanked by an unusual hexagonal tower from the 1500s. To entertain the hordes of coast-bound tourists there's a **Musée Régional du Timbre Poste**, in a 17th-century château on Place de la Convention, ✆ 04 94 47 96 16 (*open all summer and by appointment*), and another small museum in a 16th-century church, the **Musée Historique du Centre Var**, 24 Rue Victor Hugo, ✆ 04 94 60 90 70 (*open mid-May to Mid-Oct, Mon–Sat 3–6*) with a collection ranging from fossils and Neolithic finds to medieval art.

Brignoles

The biggest date in Brignoles' history, perhaps, is 25 September 1973, when several thousand dead toads rained down from the sky, an event that does not seem to be commemorated in any way. Little else has ever happened here. This gritty but somehow likeable place earns its living mining bauxite. It has an attractive medieval centre, and a museum to remember.

Le Musée du Pays Brignolais (Regional Museum)

Closed Mon and Tues, otherwise 9–12 and 2.30–6; adm; © 04 94 69 45 18.

Situated at the top of the old town, on Place du Palais des Comtes de Provence in a palace that was those counts' summer residence, Brignoles' incredible curiosity shop has grown to fill the whole building since a local doctor began the collection in 1947. Amidst two big floors packed full of oil presses, fossils, cannon-balls, reliquaries and roof tiles, you'll see some things you never dreamed existed. In the place of honour, near the entrance, is the original model of a great invention by Brignoles' own Joseph Lambot (1814–87): the **steel-reinforced concrete canoe**. Contemporary accounts on display suggest the thing floated, though the idea somehow never caught on. Lambot probably never collected a *sou* for his revolutionary new construction technique, since found to be better adapted to skyscrapers.

Admittedly, a hard act to follow, but just across the room is a provocative **sarcophagus**, dated *c.* AD 175–225, nothing less than the earliest Christian monument in France. Well sculpted and well preserved, the imagery is a remarkable testament to religious transition. The centre shows a familiar classical scene, a seated god receiving a soul into the underworld—but whether the god is Hades, Jesus, or another remains a mystery. Also present are Jesus as the 'Good Shepherd' (the most common early Christian symbol), a figure that may be St Peter (fishing, figuratively, for souls), another that seems to be a deified Sun, and another early Christian symbol, an anchor. The sarcophagus is believed to be Greek, possibly made in Antioch or Smyrna; how it got here no one knows.

Nearby is a rare but badly worn Merovingian tombstone, and a part of the counts' palace, the **Chapel of St-Louis-d'Anjou**, a Provençal bishop who may be better known in California—the town of San Luis Obispo is named after him. The chapel houses a hoard of gaudy church clutter, with Louis' chasuble and rows of wax saints under glass. After that, you may inspect a **reconstructed Provençal farm kitchen**, and a **reconstructed mine tunnel**. Other prizes await on the second floor: a **plywood model of Milan Cathedral** by a local madman, a stuffed weasel, and large collections of owls and moths. Local painters are exhaustively represented: some of the finest works are 19th-century ex votos in the French tradition, with the Virgin Mary blessing people falling off wagons and out of windows. Even after all this, Gaston Huffman's *Allegory of Voluptuous Folly* takes the cake, a medieval conceit in a modern style, with a delicious lady in a little boat enjoying the caresses of a cigar-smoking pig. Rue des Lanciers, the spine of old Brignoles, begins opposite the museum's front door, passing the 13th-century **Maison des Lanciers**, where the counts' guards stayed when they were visiting.

West of Brignoles are two sights of interest off the main road, both of which you'll need to talk your way in to visit: first the half-ruined **Abbaye de la Celle**, an ancient foundation (started in the 6th century) that made a reputation for itself due to the open licentiousness of its nuns, and which was dissolved in 1770; the buildings are now part of a farm. Second, also on a farm, off the D205 6km east of Tourves, is the **Chapelle de la Gayole**, an early Romanesque cemetery chapel in the shape of a Greek cross (built in 1029, though parts of it go back to the 700s).

St-Maximin-la-Ste-Baume

For proof that Provençal sunlight softens the Anglo-Saxon brain, consider St-Maximin. 'Considerable charm', gushes one guidebook; 'another pretty Provençal village', yawns another. Prosper Mérimée, back in 1834, got it right: 'Saint-Maximin is a miserable hole between Aix and Draguignan.' It hasn't changed. The general atmosphere of bricks and litter is reminiscent of some burnt-out inner-city in the Midlands or Midwest. It is hard to imagine a place in such a state of total, lackadaisical decrepitude in the midst of a prosperous region.

But once upon a time, the Miserable Hole was a goal for the pious from all over France. According to legend, the site was the burial place of the Magdalene (*see* Stes-Maries-de-la-Mer, p.331) and her companions St Maximin, the martyred first bishop of Aix, and St Sidonius. Their bodies, supposedly hidden from Saracen raiders in a crypt, had disappeared, and were conveniently 'rediscovered' in 1279 by the efforts of Charles II of Anjou, Count of Provence. Inconveniently, the body of the Magdalene was already on display at the famous church of Vézelay, in Burgundy. Nevertheless, an ambitious basilica and abbey complex was begun, and eventually the Pope was convinced or bribed into declaring St Maximin's relics the real McCoy. The pilgrim trade made St-Maximin into a town; among the visitors were several kings of France, the last being Louis XIV. There were wild times during the Revolution; St-Maximin renamed itself 'Marathon', and was briefly under the command of Lucien Bonaparte, who was calling himself 'Brutus'. This most devoutly revolutionary of Bonapartes saved the basilica from a sacking. As the local legend tells it, an official from Paris came down to oversee its liquidation, but Brutus had him greeted with the *Marseillaise*, played all stops out on the church's great organ.

Basilica Ste-Marie-Madeleine

After its ramshackle, unfinished façade, on a desolate square decorated only by a faded Dubonnet sign, the interior seems an apparition: the only significant Gothic building in Provence. Despite the prevailing gloom, and the hosts of awful, neglected 18th- and 19th-century chapels and altars, the tall arches of the nave and the lovely apse, with its stained glass, leave an impression of dignity and grace. The original decoration is spare: coats of arms and effigies of Charles of Anjou and Queen Jeanne on some of its capitals. Among the later additions, the most impressive is the enormous, aforementioned **organ**, almost 3000 pipes and all the work of one man, a Dominican monk named Isnard (1773). Another Dominican, Vincent Funel, was responsible for the lovely choir screen (1691). To the left of the high altar, the retable of the *Passion of Christ* (1520), by an obscure Renaissance Fleming named Ronzen, has some surprising backgrounds: the Papal Palace in Avignon, the Colosseum and Venice's Piazzetta San Marco. Stairs lead down to the **crypt**, a funeral vault from the 4th or 5th century AD, where the holy sarcophagi remain with a host of eerie reliquaries.

The Couvent Royal

The monastery attached to Ste-Marie-Madeleine was a 'royal' convent because the kings of France were its titular priors. After losing it in the Revolution, the Dominican Order bought back the monastery and church in 1859. Apparently St-Maximin proved too depressing even for Dominicans; they bolted for Toulouse in 1957, leaving the vast complex in a terrible state. Restorations have been going on fitfully since the '60s. The buildings include the imposing **hospice** from the 1750s (now the town hall), to the left of the basilica's façade; the rest, behind it, now houses an institute for cultural exchanges. The best part is the **cloister**, with Lebanon cedars and a charming subtropical garden in the centre. One of the arcades is a Gothic original of 1295 (*guided tours of the cloister and basilica available, open all year; adm*).

The Massif de la Ste-Baume

If you're heading towards Marseille or the coast from here, you might consider a detour into this small but remarkable patch of mountains. Rising as high as 975m, and offering views over the sea and as far north as Mont Ventoux, the massif shelters a small forested plateau called the **Plan d'Aups**. This is a northern-style forest, including maple, beech and sycamore, as well as scores of species of wild flowers and other plants not often seen around the Mediterranean. They have remained in their primeval state because the massif is holy ground, the site of the cave (*Sainte-Baume*, or holy grotto) where according to legend the Magdalen spent the last years of her life as a hermit. The cave, furnished as a chapel, was part of the pilgrimage to St-Maximin since the Middle Ages, and can be seen today along the D80. Monastic communities grew up around the site, and you may visit the 13th-century Cistercian **Abbaye de St-Pons**, near the loveliest part of the forests (the Parc de St-Pons).

Where to Stay and Eating Out

Les Arcs ✉ 83460

Les Arcs, strategically located on the road to the Côte d'Azur, has spawned one exceptional hotel-restaurant. ★★★**Le Logis du Guetteur**, Place du Château, ✆ 04 94 73 30 82, ✆ 04 94 99 51 10, is located at the top of the old town, a lavishly restored castle dating in parts from the 11th century, with a garden and pool; some rooms have wonderful views. The restaurant serves ambitious *haute cuisine* : smoked salmon, stuffed sole, and elaborate desserts (*menus from 135F*). *Closed 15 Jan–15 Feb.*

Brignoles ✉ 83170

Brignoles has plenty of inexpensive hotels, most of them dives; try the centrally located ★**Le Carami**, over a simple restaurant at 11 Place Caramy, ✆ 04 94 69 11 08. Something more elegant can be found outside town: the ★★**Château de Brignoles**, Ave Dréo, ✆ 04 94 69 06 88,✆ 04 94 69 59 76, just on the eastern edge of Brignoles, offers peace and quiet in an old farm, with pool and tennis. A little further east, at the village of **Flassans-sur-Issole** ✉ 83340, is a gracious and friendly farm hotel, ★★**La Grillade au Feu de Bois**, with sixteen rooms and a restaurant with admirable home cooking (on the N7, ✆ 04 94 69 71 20).

Dining in Brignoles' medieval centre, the best bet is **L'Assiette Gourmande**, on Rue Gradalet, ✆ 04 94 59 04 48; the cooking is both Italian and French—you can have *carpaccio* or pizza for starters, and there is a shady outdoor terrace (*menus 67F and 120F*). For a change, there is a good Vietnamese restaurant, the **Saigon** on Square St-Louis, ✆ 04 94 59 14 51 (*menus 55–150F*). Six km north of Brignoles, in sleepy **Montfort-sur-Argens**, **Le Relais des Templiers** Place G. Péri, ✆ 04 94 59 55 06, ✆ 04 94 59 78 76, is a peaceful place for an intimate meal: only a handful of tables, so ring ahead and ask owner chef Suzanne Hézard what's on the hob. *Closed Tues.*

If you're compelled to stay in **St-Maximin** (✉ 83470), head for the orange shutters of the ★★**Hôtel Plaisance**, 20 Place Malherbe, ✆ 04 94 78 18 39. Dining in this town is an adventure; the local speciality is limp pizza, and finding anything else can be difficult.

NWR CHATEAU - GIGONDAS.

Northern Provence: the Vaucluse

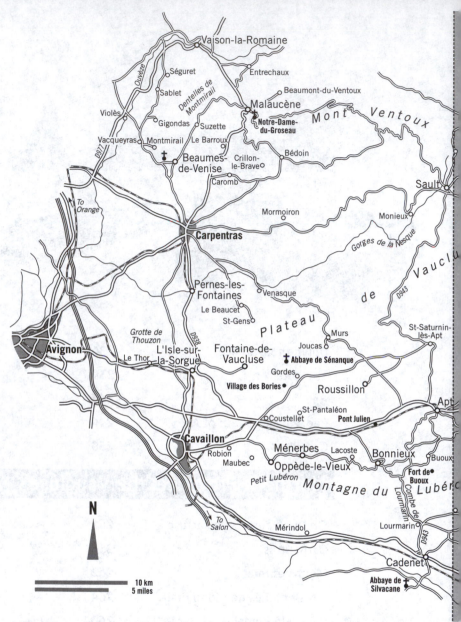

The 'Three Plagues of Provence', according to tradition, were the mistral, the Durance and the *Parlement* at Aix. The *Parlement* is ancient history, but the other two still serve to define the troublesome boundaries of this region: the long curve of the wicked, boat-sinking, valley-flooding River Durance to the south, and a line of long, ridge-like mountains, Mont Ventoux and the Montagne de Lure, to the north—folk wisdom has always credited these northern boundary-stones of Provence as the source of the

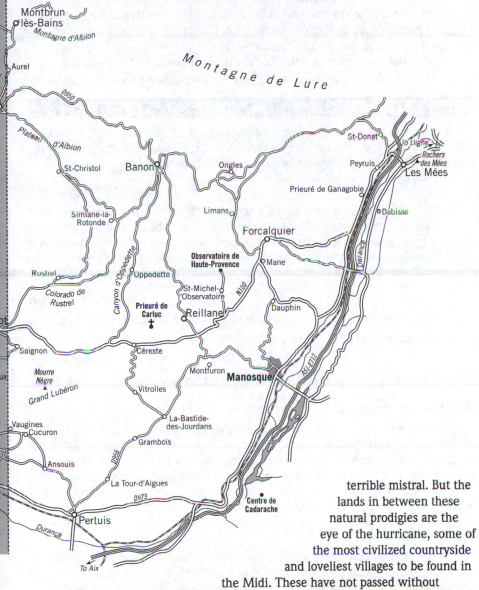

Northern Provence

terrible mistral. But the lands in between these natural prodigies are the eye of the hurricane, some of the most civilized countryside and loveliest villages to be found in the Midi. These have not passed without notice, of course, and the rural Vaucluse is now what the Côte d'Azur was forty years ago: the in-place for both the French and foreigners to find a bit of sun-splashed holiday paradise amongst the vineyards.

235

Not everything included in this section is actually in the *département* of Vaucluse (Manosque and Forcalquier are in Alpes-de-Haute-Provence); and the Vaucluse's two cities, Orange and Avignon, will be found in **Down the Rhône: Orange to Beacaire**, pp.271–304. The remainder divides neatly into three areas: the mountainous Lubéron, cradled in the Durance's arc, a *pays* of especially pretty villages; the old papal Comtat, nearer the Rhône, rich agricultural lands rightfully called the 'Garden of France'; and Provence's definitive northern wall, including the dramatic Mont Ventoux and the Dentelles de Montmirail, along with the Roman city of Vaison.

Down the Durance

The Durance was a major trade route in the Middle Ages, following the Roman Via Domitia, and religious centres grew up along it from the earliest times. These old priories, set in gentle rolling scenery, are the main attraction in this still fairly untouristed region.

Getting Around

The valley of the Durance is the main corridor for public transport. A **rail-line** passes Manosque and continues along the bottom edge of the Lubéron, serving Pertuis on its way to Aix and Marseille (five or six daily). Manosque is also the hub for **buses**, with several daily to Aix and Marseille, also one or two a day to Forcalquier and to Digne, stopping in Les Mées.

Tourist Information

Forcalquier ✉ 04300: 8 Place du Bourget, ✆ 04 92 75 10 02, 📠 04 92 75 26 76.

Manosque ✉ 04100: Place Dr Joubert, ✆ 04 92 72 16 00, 📠 04 92 72 58 98 .

market days

Manosque: Saturday. **Forcalquier**: Monday. **Banon**: Tuesday.

St-Donat and Ganagobie

Coming down from Digne and the Provençal Alps, a startling landmark punctuates your entry into the Durance valley: **Les Mées** (a Provençal word for milestones), 2km of needle-like rock formations, eroded into weird shapes overlooking the D4. There is a bridge at the village of Les Mées, crossing over to **Peyruis** and its ruined castle. Up in the hills, 5km above Peyruis, the church of **St-Donat** enjoys a wonderful setting on a little wooded plateau. This graceful building, one of the earliest Romanesque monuments in Provence (11th-century), was built for pilgrims visiting the relics of St Donat, a 5th-century holy man from Orléans who ended his life as a hermit here.

Of all the holy sites down the Durance, the one most worth visiting is the **Priory of Ganagobie**, just down the N96, south of Peyruis, ✆ 04 92 68 00 04, in a setting as lovely as that of St-Donat (*open daily 3–5, closed Mon*). Founded in the 9th century as a dependency of Cluny, the remarkable church was built some 200 years later. Its portal, though rebuilt in the 1600s, still has its original tympanum relief: a **Christ in Majesty** with the four Evangelists, one of the finest such works in Provence. Inside is another rare decoration,

mosaics with geometric designs and peculiarly styled animals done in red, black and white; discovered and restored in the 1960s, they were part of the church's original pavement.

Ganagobie used to have the relics of a certain St Transit; he is not found in any hagiography, and it seems that in the Middle Ages the habit of carrying holy relics in procession on a holiday (a *transit*) led to the invention of a new saint. Such things happened all the time in the Midi. (And there must have been some Provençaux colonists involved in a similar occurrence very much later, in New Orleans. The faithful in one parish there still beseech favours at the altar of Ste Expédite. A statue of a female saint had arrived during the building of the church; no one knew who she was—but they found her name on the packing crate.) Ganagobie is still a monastery, but you can visit; don't be confused by the roads—coming from the north, the village of Ganagobie is up a separate side road; you'll want the D30, about 3km further south. The lovely area around the Priory is a great place for a picnic, or for some unambitious hiking along the old trails, with a few *bories* (*see* p.252), medieval quarries and views over the valley.

Forcalquier, Mane and Around

Nowadays on the drowsy side, a bit too large and funky to attract the holiday home restoring crowd, Forcalquier only bestirs itself on Mondays for its market. Yet in the old days, in the 11th and 12th centuries, it was a miniature capital of a small fry mountain state, whose counts often made life difficult for the counts of Provence. Alphonse II managed to swallow it up in 1209, by marriage, but later Provençal rulers like Raymond Berenger V made Forcalquier a favoured residence throughout the 1300s. They left few traces: an obelisk in front of the stern Gothic cathedral commemorates Marguerite de Provence-Forcalquier, wife of St Louis; there's a Gothic fountain with the warrior angel and monkey faces in Place St-Michel, and Europe's only **listed cemetery**, its ancient yew hedges trimmed to form the arcades of a cloister (*open daily 9–5*). A tower and other scanty remains of Forcalquier's **citadel** overlook the town, next to an octagonal chapel crowned by a statue of the Virgin, honouring Pope Urban II who came here to raise men and money for the First Crusade. There's the well-restored 13th-century **Couvent des Cordeliers**, © 04 92 75 02 38, parts of which were originally the counts' palace, given to the Franciscans by Raymond Berenger V; it has medieval art, a Franscian cloister garden, and frequent exhibitions in summer (*guided tours July–Sept, at 11, 2.30, 3.30, 4.30 and 5.30; May, June, and Oct at 2.30 and 4.30; adm*). The **Musée Municipal**, in the Hôtel de Ville has a small collection of antiquities, old furniture, ceramics from Moustiers and Apt, and items from daily life (*open July–Sept 10–12 and 3–7, closed weekends and Mon am, others times Mon–Fri 2–6; adm*).

The lands around Forcalquier are some of the most beautiful in this part of Provence, full of oak forests and sheep meadows, rustic and peaceful and not yet as touristy as the Lubéron to the south. Six km south, in **Mane**, the 12th-century Benedictine **Prieuré (Musée) de Salagon**, © 04 92 75 19 93 (*open April–June 2–6, July and Sept 10–12 and 2–7, Oct–11 Nov Sat, Sun only 2–6*) was built on the site of a Gallo-Roman farm and 5th-century Christian cemetery. Beautifully restored by the Conseil Général, the priory has a medieval and medicinal gardens and houses the frequent exhibitions of the Alpes de Lumières, an organization dedicated to preserving and documenting local culture and customs. Mane's 18th-century **Château de Sauvan**, © 04 92 75 23 13, owned by a friend of Marie Antoinette, is a fine example of French classicism, with period furnishings (*guided tours July and Aug daily exc Sat at 3.30, other times Sun and hols only at 3.30, or by reservation; adm*).

Twelve km southwest of Forcalquier, **Saint-Michel-l'Observatoire**, © 04 92 76 60 04, was attracted to the area by a study in the 1930s that found that the *pays de Forcalquier* had the cleanest, clearest air, and the least fog of anywhere in France; there are guided tours, sadly only during the day, with films, a look at photos and the telescope (© 04 92 70 64 00, *Oct–Mar Wed, 3pm, April–Sept Wed between 2 and 4, and the first Sunday of each month between 9.30 and 11; adm*). This is also a region of *villages perchés*: **Dauphin**, just to the south of Forcalquier, and **Oppedette**, to the west, overlooking the scenic canyon of the River Calavon. To the north, **Limans,** under brooding bald Montagne de Lure, is famous for its rather luxurious 16th-century *pigeonniers*, while **Banon** to the northwest, is synonymous with Provence's most famous sheep's cheese. Most impressive of all, perhaps, is **Simiane-la-Rotonde**, set high on a small plateau. The *'rotonde'* is a peculiarly shaped 12th-century **donjon** dominating the village, © 04 92 75 62 15, with Romanesque carvings around what may have been a chapel— all that's left of a feudal castle (*open daily Apr–June 3–5.30, July–mid-Sept 10–12.30 and 3–7, otherwise by reservation only*). Simiane is by far the most chic of the villages in this area, with plenty of restored second homes; it's a charming place nevertheless, with a late Gothic church and an old **covered market** supported on stone pillars.

Manosque

By far the biggest town in this part of the Durance valley (pop. 20,000), Manosque is unavoidable. Nicknamed 'Manosque la Pudique' by François 1er after a beautiful girl from the village who disfigured herself rather than surrender to his unwanted advances, it was for centuries a drowsy place, with no other distinction than being the home town and lifetime abode of Jean Giono (1895–1970). Today it presents the spectacle of a Provençal village out of control. Acres of concrete suburban sprawl press against the hilltop medieval centre, and the traffic can be as ferocious as Marseille's. The culprit is Cadarache, France's national nuclear research centre, a huge complex to the south across the Durance, begun in 1959; most of its workers live around Manosque.

Manosque's tidy, teardrop-shaped centre, an oasis amidst the sprawling disorder, is entered by two elegant 14th-century gates, the **Porte Saunerie** and the **Porte Soubeyran**, designed more for decoration than defence. Inside are two unremarkable churches on quietly lovely squares: **St-Sauveur**, made in bits and pieces from the 1200s to the 1700s, but attractive nevertheless, and **Notre-Dame-de-Romigier**, with a Renaissance façade; the altar here is an early Christian sarcophagus with reliefs of the Apostles. Manosque has a pair of newer attractions just outside the historic centre. A handsome 19th-century mansion *hôtel particulier* holds the **Centre Jean Giono**, just outside the Porte Saunerie at 1 Blvd Elémir Bourges (*open 9–12 and 2–6, closed Sun and Mon; adm*) is dedicated to Manosque's literary lion, with a permanent exhibit on his life and works, a library, and a *videothèque* with interviews and the films made from Giono's writings. A few doors down, the **Fondation Carzou**, in the neoclassical church at the Couvent de la Présentation, has frescoes by contemporary Armenian painter Jean Carzou based on the Apocalypse and New Jerusalem (*open 10–12.30 and 3–7, closed Tues*).

Where to Stay and Eating Out

Dabisse-Les Mées ✉ 04190

If at all possible, stop for lunch or dinner at **Le Vieux Colombier**, on the D4, © 04 92 34 32 32, 📠 04 92 34 34 26, a pleasant old farmhouse with a dovecot, appropriately specializing in succulent pigeon; superb cheese and desserts (*menus from 135 to 295F*). *Closed Wed, Sun eve and a week in Feb.*

Forcalquier ✉ 04300

One of the nicest places to stay is in the centre, in a 17th-century posthouse: the ★★★**Hostellerie des Deux Lions**, 11 Place du Bourguet, ✆ 04 92 75 25 30, ✉ 04 92 75 06 41, with lovely rooms (*300–450F*) and a justifiedly popular restaurant, with menus that change daily and the best local cheeses and wines. *Closed Jan and Feb.* Less expensively, there is the not-so-grand but perfectly acceptable ★★**Grand Hôtel**, 10 Blvd Latourette, ✆ 04 92 75 00 35, ✉ 04 92 75 06 32, with a garden out back. Out in the pretty countryside around Forcalquier, ★★**Le Colombier**, 3km south at Mas Les Dragons, ✆ 04 92 75 03 71, ✉ 04 92 75 14 30 is a prettily restored mas, with a shady garden and pool. Similar, in a Revolutionary era farm, the ★★**Auberge Charembeau**, 2.5km east on the Route de Niozelles, ✆ 04 92 70 91 70, ✉ 04 92 70 91 83, also with a pool; no restaurant, but the rooms have kitchenettes. There's also a bed-and-breakfast *ferme-auberge*, the **Ferme de Bas-Chalus**, 2km from Forcalquier, ✆ 04 92 75 05 67, ✉ 04 92 75 39 20.

Manosque ✉ 04100

Manosque has a good selection of hotels, though nothing really special, from the modern but pleasant ★★**Le Provence** on the outskirts, Quart Durance, ✆ 04 92 87 75 72, ✉ 04 92 87 55 13, or the central, quiet ★★**François I**, 18 Rue Guilhempierre, ✆ 04 92 72 07 99, ✉ 04 92 87 54 85 to the unstarred but passable **Mont d'Or**, in the centre at 8 Place de l'Hôtel de Ville, ✆ 04 92 72 13 94, ✉ 04 92 87 41 65. The only luxury hotel-restaurant in this area, the ★★★★**Hostellerie de la Fuste** (Valensole ✉ 04210), ✆ 04 92 72 05 95, ✉ 04 92 72 92 93, is across the Durance on the D4, near Oraison. The rooms are fine, in a restored *bastide* with a covered pool, but the real attraction is an elegant, highly rated restaurant, although everyone is waiting to see what a recent change of chef and staff (spring 1997) will bring (*menus from 250F*). *Closed Sun eve and Mon.*

Manosque really comes into its own at lunch-time; at number 7 Promenade Aubert-Millot, near the Porte Saunerie by the statue of a dog, look for a crowded hole-in-the-wall with no sign: **Le Petit Pascal**, ✆ 04 92 87 62 01, a one-woman oper-ation with delicious, filling home-cooking (*menus 50F, 75F, lunch only*); second choice is **Chez André**, 21 Place du Terreau, ✆ 04 92 72 03 09, with a large patio (*menus at 75–125F*). Or if you've had enough French, try Indonesian at **Restaurant Dadang**, 62 Ave J. Giono, ✆ 04 92 72 57 18. *Closed Wed.*

The Lubéron

As is the case with many a fair maiden, the Lubéron's charms are proving to be her undoing. This is Peter Mayle country, the stage set for his surprise bestseller, *A Year in Provence*. Yes, this is that magical place where the natives are endlessly warm and human, the vineyards ever-so-lovely in autumn, and the lunch in the little bistro worth writing about for pages and pages. All true, in fact—but everybody knows it, and the trickle of outsiders who began settling here in the 1950s, permanently or in holiday homes, has now become a flood.

How you experience the Lubéron will also depend on what time of year you come. Most of the year it's as quiet as a graveyard; in summer it can seem like St-Tropez-under-the-Poplars, with vast crowds of Brits, Yanks and Parisians milling about, waiting for lunch-time. It's hard to imagine why anyone would want to come here in August, but if you insist, make sure you have your hotel reservations months in advance.

The Regional Park

EAGLE OWL 'DUCAS'   BONELLI'S EAGLE

Like many parts of rural Provence, the Lubéron presents a puzzling contrast—how these villages became such eminently civilized places, set amidst a landscape (and a population) that is more than a little rough around the edges. The real Lubéron is a land of hunters stalking wild boar over Appalachian-like ridges, and weatherbeaten farmers in ancient Renaults full of rabbit cages and power tools. There are other regions of Provence, equally scenic and rustic, that merit being frozen into a nature preserve, but the Lubéron was the one most in danger of being destroyed by a rash of outsiders and unplanned holiday villas. The **Parc Régional du Lubéron** was founded in 1977, a cooperative arrangement between the towns and villages that covers most of the territory between Manosque and Cavaillon; quite a few (often where the mayor is an estate agent or a notary) have decided not to participate at all. The Lubéron is not an exceptional nature area like the Mercantour. Still, the Park is doing God's work, protecting rare species like the long-legged Bonelli's eagle, a symbol of the Midi that needs plenty of room to roam and is nearing extinction; most of all, it is a reasonably effective legal barrier to keep the Lubéron from being totally overwhelmed by the kind of building madness that wrecked the Côte d'Azur.

EGYPTIAN VULTURE   WILD BOAR

Park Information: the **Maison du Pays du Lubéron**, 1 Place Jean Jaurès in Apt, with exhibits, slide shows and a gift shop; ✆ 04 90 04 42 00, ✆ 04 90 04 81 15.

Getting Around

Public transport is woefully inconvenient in the Lubéron; it's possible to get around the villages, but just barely. Apt is on an SNCF branch line, with a few **trains** daily to Cavaillon and Avignon. **Buses** from Apt leave from the Place de la Bouquerie by the river; there are one or two daily to Roussillon, to Avignon, to Aix, stopping at Bonnieux, Lourmarin, Cadenet and Pertuis; also one to Digne, stoping at Céreste. Cavaillon is on the main Avignon–Marseille rail line, and there are also buses to L'Isle-sur-la-Sorgue, Pernes-les-Fontaines and Carpentras (several daily), to Apt and Avignon, and very occasionally to Bonnieux and other western Lubéron villages.

Finding a **horse** is no problem in most areas; in Cucuron, try the Gîte Equestre La Rasparine, ✆ 04 90 77 21 46; and in St-Martin (north of Pertuis), phone ✆ 04 90 68 38 59.

La Tour d'Aigues ✉ 84240: in the château, ✆ 04 90 07 50 29, 📠 04 90 07 35 91.

Cadenet ✉ 84160: Place du Tambour ✆ 04 90 68 38 21; includes a shop for Cadenet's basket-weavers, the village's old craft speciality.

Lourmarin ✉ 84160: Ave Philippe de Girard, ✆/📠 04 90 68 10 77; summer only.

market days

Pertuis: Friday; farmers' market Wednesday and Saturday. **La Tour d'Aigues:** Tuesday. **Cucuron:** Tuesday. **Lourmarin:** Friday. **Cadenet:** Monday; also Saturday in summer.

The Pays d'Aigues

The southern end of the Park, the Pays d'Aigues, is the sleepier corner of the Lubéron, a rolling stretch of good farmland sheltered by the Grand Lubéron mountain to the north. **Pertuis**, a busy crossroads town along the D973, is the modest capital of *pays*, with a bit of an aristocratic air; it earned the *fleur de lis* on its arms for its loyalty to the French crown during the Wars of Religion. Prosperity in the 1600s has left it a number of fine buildings in the historic centre. Of the smaller villages, a few stand out: **Grambois** to the northeast, is a neatly rounded hilltop hamlet, a Saracen stronghold in the 8th–10th century and later one of the twelve citadels of Provence. Some walls remain, but the crenellated tower belongs to the church of **Notre-Dame-et-St-Christophe**. Both its patrons are represented in art inside: a good Renaissance altarpiece of the Virgin, and an original 14th-century fresco of St Christopher, and best of all, an anonymous 16th-century polyptych of John the Baptist, considered one of the masterpieces of the Provençal school. **Ansouis**, north of Pertuis on the D56, is a *village perché* built around the sumptuously furnished **Château de Sabran**, ✆ 04 90 09 82 70 (*open daily, exc Tues in winter, 2.30–6*), first mentioned in print in 961 and still in the hands of the original family: a Henry IV monumental stair leads to Flemish tapestries, Italian Renaissance furniture, portraits and later Bourbon bric-a-brac. The atmosphere is wonderfully snooty, but they let us in to visit just the same. The **Musée Extraordinaire G. Mazoyer**, ✆ 04 90 09 82 64 (*open 2–6, closed Tues*), has some of this and some of that—sculptures, stained glass, and other work by the namesake; also fossils, and displays on underwater life.

For an airier, more pleasant castle without the bric-a-brac, try **La Tour-d'Aigues**, just to the east. The **Château** here, in fact, doesn't even have a roof. The Baron of Cental was still making repairs to damage caused by a fire in 1782 when the Revolution came, and the local peasantry torched the place for good. What's left is a thoroughly elegant Renaissance shell, begun in 1555 by an Italian architect, Ercole Nigra, imitating the styles then fashionable in Paris. The entrance, a massive triumphal arch, carved with trophies, was inspired by the Roman arch at Orange. One of the château's side towers has been rebuilt, and the Conseil de Vaucluse, which now owns it, plans to restore the rest a little at a time as funds are available. There is a small **museum** in the cellar, ✆ 04 90 07 50 29, exhibiting both pottery and the history of Aigues (*open daily exc Tues, Sat, and Sun morning; summer 10–12 and 1.30–7, winter 9.30–11.30 and 2–3; adm*). La Tour also has an unusual Romanesque church, **Notre-**

Dame-de-Romegas, with an apse at either end—originally built facing the east, it was turned around in the 1600s when some clerical stickler for the rules had a second apse built.

Heading west, and still on the the the south flank of Montagne du Lubéron, **Cucuron** was found perfect enough to be used as the set for *Le Hussard sur le toit* (The Horseman on the Roof), the recent film adaptation of a novel by Jean Giono; the view of the same roofs is especially pretty from the Donjon St-Michel. Cucuron's market takes place on the banks of its little lake, surrounded by ancient plane trees. The D56 leads on to **Vaugines**, a lovely little place (itself the setting for many scenes in *Manon des Sources* and *Jean de Florette*) and Lourmarin.

Lourmarin and Cadenet

Further west, into the heart of the Lubéron, **Lourmarin** was the last home of Albert Camus. This is an unusual village, densely packed almost to the point of claustrophobia; many of its houses have tiny courtyards facing the street—too cute for its own good, as few villages even in the Lubéron are so beset by tourists. Its landmark is a grand bell tower, so everyone always knows what time it is, and its main attraction is another 16th-century **château**, © 04 90 68 15 23 (*open for guided tours at 11, 2.30, 3.30, 4.30, except Tues in Nov–Mar; more times in July and Aug; adm*), the residence of the Counts d'Agoult for three centuries; its last Countess was the mother of Franz Liszt's three children, one of whom, Cosima, married Richard Wagner. Well restored, 'the Villa Medicis of Provence' as it's called, is now the property of the Académie of Aix, who use it for cultural programmes, concerts and exhibitions. The rooms have rare furnishings (don't miss the Aztec fireplace) and art, including a lovely *Lute Player* by the school of Leonardo da Vinci and a collection of engravings by Piranesi. If you are looking for the co-founder of existentialism, Albert Camus is buried on the left-hand side of the pretty cemetery, next to his wife.

Cadenet, a big village overlooking the rocky bed of the Durance, is only 5km away, but the difference is like day and night. An ancient place, Cadenet began as a pre-Celtic *oppidum*; even older are some of the cave dwellings that can be seen in the cliffs behind the village (others were refuges for persecuted Waldensian Protestants in the 1500s). It's also a very attractive village. On the Place du Tambour, one of the focal points of the Monday market, is the bronze statue of Cadenet's favourite son, André Estienne, a 15-year-old drummer boy who once managed a difficult river crossing for Napoleon's troops—wading right in and beating the charge under direct Austrian fire. The embarrassed soldiers could only follow. Have a peek inside the parish church, **St-Etienne**, on the northern edge of town. The baptismal font has well-preserved reliefs of a Bacchic orgy; scholars call it 3rd-century, but disagree over whether it was originally a sarcophagus or a bathtub. A new **Musée de la Vaunerie**, © 04 90 68 24 44 (*open Apr–Oct 10–12 and 2.30–6.30, closed Tues and Sun am*), is dedicated to Cadenet's age old occupation: wicker work and basketry.

West of Cadenet, **Mérindol** isn't much to look at, but worth a mention as a symbol of a very dark page of the Lubéron's history. When plagues and war depopulated the region in the 1300s, immigrants from the Alps and from Italy came to work the land. Many were peaceful, hard-working Waldensian dissenters; when the Reformation began, the authorities could no longer tolerate them. In 1540, the Parlement of Aix oversaw the burning of 19 Waldensian villages in the Lubéron, including Mérindol, and Lourmarin as well. Over 3000 innocents were butchered, and hundreds more were sent off to the King's galleys. The ruins of

Mérindol's castle house a Waldensian memorial; also note the curious onion domed tower, called a 'Saracen bulb' in French.

Abbaye de Silvacane

Open daily exc Tues, 9–12 and 2–5; adm; ℗ 04 42 50 41 69.

Life as a medieval Cistercian was no picnic. Besides the strict discipline and a curious prejudice against heating, there was always the chance the Order might send you to somewhere in the middle of a swamp. They built this, the first of the 'Three Sisters of Provence', in just such a location because they meant to reclaim it—the 'forest of rushes' (*silva cana*), south of the Durance, 7km from Cadenet. It took a century or two, but they did the job, as you can see today from the fertile farmlands around Silvacane. A Benedictine community had already been established here when the Cistercians arrived in 1147. Work began on the present buildings soon after, partially financed by the barons of Les Baux, and Silvacane became quite prosperous. Bad frosts in the 1300s killed all the olives and vines, starting Silvacane on its long decline. When the government bought the complex to restore it in 1949, it was being used as a barn.

The church is as chastely fair as its younger sisters at Sénanque and Thoronet, perhaps more austere and uncompromising still; even the apse is a plain rectangle. Of sculptural decoration there is hardly any (though scores of masons' marks on the columns and vaulting). The adjacent **cloister** now contains a herb garden, around a lovely broken fountain. Note the capitals on the arcades, carved, oddly, with maple leaves.

Where to Stay and Eating Out

Pertuis ✉ 84120

If you're passing through at lunch time, stop at **Le Boulevard**, 50 Blvd Pecout, ℗ 04 90 09 69 31 for tasty and kindly priced Provençal classics (*menus from 98F*). *Closed Sun eve, Wed and 23 Aug–10 Sept.*

La-Bastide-des-Jourdans ✉ 84240

Coming down from Manosque, there is a pleasant hotel on the D27/D956 to La Tour-d'Aigues: the picture postcard ★**Auberge du Cheval Blanc**, ℗ 04 90 77 81 08, ✆ 04 90 77 86 51, with a restaurant that specializes in game dishes and trout on an outdoor terrace (*rooms are 220–360F*).

La Tour-d'Aigues ✉ 84240

The best bet for lunch is ★★**Les Fenouillets**, just outside the village on the D956, ℗ 04 90 07 48 22, ✆ 04 90 07 34 26. Rooms are simple, but there's a swimming-pool, and an inexpensive restaurant with outdoor tables.

Lourmarin ✉ 84160

Lourmarin, small as it is, has become the chic rendezvous in the southern Lubéron. One of the classiest establishments to open here in recent years is ★★★★**Le Moulin de Lourmarin**, ℗ 04 90 68 06 69, ✆ 04 90 68 31 76, on the western perimeter of the village on Rue du Temple. A one-time olive mill with views over the château and nearby hills, now Provençal meets Art Nouveau in its tasteful decoration, whilst the restaurant serves attractive and delicious Provençal dishes (*rooms 500–1200F*). Just east of the village on the Route de Vaugines is a similarly immaculately restored farmhouse, the ★★★**Hôtel de Guilles**, ✆ 04 90 68 30 55, ✉ 04 90 68 37 41, beautifully decorated, with lots of antiques and all the amenities: tennis court, pool and gardens. For something less expensive, there's **Le Paradou,** Route d'Apt, ✆ 04 90 68 04 05, ✉ 04 90 08 54 94, in a dreamy setting north of Lourmarin on the D943, at the entrance to the Combe de Lourmarin (*rooms 190–230F*). Or, for even less, **La Villa St Louis**, 35 Rue Henri de Savournin, ✆ 04 90 68 39 18, ✉ 04 90 68 10 07, on the edge of the village, a charming *chambres d'hôte* in a 19th-century house run by the warm and affable Mme Lassallette. Lourmarin can also offer some of the best restaurants in the Lubéron. **La Fenière**, on Rue du Grand Pré in the centre, ✆ 04 90 68 11 79, combines expert, innovative cooking with old Provençal favourites: batter-fried courgette flowers and a hearty *daube* (*menus 190–490F*). C*losed Sun eve and Mon.* Overlooking the Château, **Le Bistrot**, Ave Raoul Dautry, ✆ 04 90 68 29 74, offers a choice of Provençal or Lyonnais cuisine (*menus at 85F and 115F*). *Closed Thurs and last two weeks in Aug and 20 Dec–mid-Jan.* Another good bet, **La Récréation**, 15 Rue Philippe de Girand, ✆ 04 90 68 23 73, with a terrace facing the castle—fresh Provençal fare and good lamb dishes with garlic for 95 or 125F. *Closed Wed.*

Cadenet ✉ 84160

Cadenet, less expensive and touristy than Lourmarin, is a good alternative for a stay in this region. The newish ★★**Mas du Colombier,** Route de Pertuis, ✆ 04 90 68 29 00, ✉ 04 90 68 36 77 is a pleasant place with a pool and good restaurant, in the middle of an old vineyard (*menus start at 86F*). *Closed Jan.* The ★★**Hôtel Aux Ombrelles**, Avenue de la Gare south of the village on the D943, ✆ 04 90 68 02 40, ✉ 04 90 68 06 82, combines nice inexpensive rooms with a fine restaurant. The truffle omelettes are very popular, but there's a wide choice of menus (*100F –150F*). *Closed Dec–Jan.* Even cheaper, but acceptable, is the old hotel-restaurant ★**De Commerce**, 2 Ave Gambetta, ✆ 04 90 68 02 35. Delicious simple fish and meat dishes are served on the panoramic terrace at **Stefáni**, 35 Ave Gambetta, ✆ 04 90 68 07 14 (*menus from 110, weekday lunch 68F*). *Closed Wed.*

Northern Lubéron: Along the N100 to Apt

Coming from Forcalquier, this route follows the northern slopes of the mountains, generally much more scenic country than the other side, with pretty villages like **Reillane**, almost deserted a century ago, but now making a comeback, even attracting a few artists; and **Céreste**, with its Roman bridge, a village that grew up as a stopping point on the Via Domitia. Between the two, you can make a excursion to the **Prieuré de Carluc**, with a 12th-century Romanesque chapel and unique ruins of the original early Christian priory, partly carved out of a rocky outcrop; like Notre-Dame du Groseau on Mont Ventoux (*see p.263*), this was an ancient religious site, built around a sacred spring; the ruins around the rock include a Gallo-Roman cemetery (*guided tours July and Aug 3.30–7; adm*).

The narrow roads south of the N100 are some of the most beautiful in the Lubéron, passing through **Vitrolles** or through **Montfuron**, with its lofty ruined castle, on their way to the Pays d'Aigues. There are also several hiking trails, from Vitrolles or from **Saignon** 5km southeast of

Apt, leading up to the summit of the Grand Lubéron, the **Mourre Nègre**, with views that take in all of the Vaucluse and beyond. Saignon itself is a beautiful *village perché* between two crags, with a well-preserved 12th-century church of **Ste-Marie**, with a curious lobed façade and a reliquary of the True Cross inside.

Apt

The capital of the Lubéron (pop. 15,000 and growing) also claims to be the 'World Capital of Candied Fruits', with one big factory and plenty of smaller concerns that make these and every other sort of sweets. There is a certain stickiness about Apt; everyone in the Lubéron comes here for the huge, animated Saturday market, but no one has ever admitted to liking the place, at least not in print. Roman *Colonia Apta Julia*, a colony refounded over a Celtic village, was the capital of the area even then. Despite languishing for a few dark centuries, before being rebuilt in the 1100s, the streets still bear traces of a rectangular Roman plan, bent into kinks and curves through the ages.

Tourist Information

28 Ave Philippe de Girard, ✆ 04 90 74 03 18, ✉ 04 90 04 64 30.

market day

Saturday; Tuesday, farmers' market in Cours Lauze de Perret, from June to October.

The Cathedral, and More Dubious Provençal Saints

We can guess that the **Rue des Marchands**, the main shopping street, roughly follows the course of its Roman predecessor. It leads to the **Tour de l'Horloge** (1567), the bell tower of Apt's old cathedral of **Ste-Anne**. Begun in the late 12th century and tinkered with incessantly until the 18th, the ungainly exterior conceals a wealth of curiosities within. There is fine 14th-century stained glass in the apse, and an early Christian sarcophagus and an odd golden painting of John the Baptist in two chapels on the north side; also an interesting **trésor** with books of hours, reliquaries and some Islamic ivories. Another trophy from the east is a linen banner, brought back from the Crusades by a lord of Simiane; as its origin was forgotten, it came to be revered in Apt as the **Veil of St Anne**.

Few regions of Europe had such a longing for relics as Provence in the Dark Ages. Other peoples, the Germans and Venetians, had a kleptomanic urge to steal holy bones when no one was looking; the Provençaux, showing less initiative but greater imagination, simply invented them. We met St Transit at Ganagobie (*see* above), and the **crypt** here has two more. According to legend the bones of St Anne, the mother of Mary, were miraculously discovered in this crypt in the 700s, occasioning the building of the first cathedral. In those days, any early Christian burial dug up was likely to be elevated to saint status; beyond that, scholars guess the Anne invented for the occasion was less the biblical figure than a dim memory of the primeval pan-European mother goddess, who was known as Ana, or Dana, to the Celts, the Romans (*Anna Perenna*), and nearly everyone else. Next to her are the bones of 'St Auspice', claimed to be Apt's first bishop—really the sacred auspices of pagan times (divination from bird flight or from the organs of sacrificed animals), another verbal confusion like St Transit.

Fruits and Fossils

Apt also has a good, well-laid-out **museum** at 27 Rue de l'Amphithéâtre, © 04 90 74 00 34 (*open June–Sept 10–12 and 2–5; daily exc Tues and Sun; in winter Mon, Wed, Thurs and Fri 2–5, Sat 10–12 and 2–5; adm*), with archaeological finds going back to the Palaeolithic period, late Roman sarcophagi, recent Roman and medieval finds from the centre of Apt, painted ex votos and a display of Apt's once flourishing craft of faïence, which had its heyday in the 18th century. The town's other attraction is the **Maison du Parc**, 60 Place Jean Jaurès, © 04 90 04 42 00 (*open daily exc Sun 9–12 and 1.30–6, till 7 in summer*), the headquarters and information centre of the Regional Park; it has exhibits on the region's natural life, including a push-button Palaeontology Museum for the children, an interesting gift shop, and all the information you'll ever need on the wild areas of the Lubéron. Finally, you can take a tour of the **Apt-Union Factory**, west of town on the N100, © 04 90 76 31 31, where they make most of those crystallized fruits. It's an interesting process; they suck the water out of the fruit and replace it with a sugar solution—a bit like embalming.

Apt ✉ 84400   ***Where to Stay and Eating Out***

As rooms in the smaller villages are hard to come by, you'll probably find yourself staying in Apt. One of the most pleasant is outside town, the ★★**Relais de Roquefure**, on the N100, 4km west, © 04 90 04 88 88, ✇ 04 90 74 14 86, an old stone-built inn with a pool and an inexpensive restaurant (*rooms 210–350F*). Closed Jan–mid-Feb. The ★★★**Auberge du Lubéron** on the river at 17 Quai Léon Sagy, © 04 90 74 12 50, ✇ 04 90 04 79 49 (*menus 130–345F*); the speciality is rabbit with figs, and other dishes with *confit d'Apt*. Also in the centre is ★★**Le Palais** in Rue Dr Albert Gros, © 04 90 04 89 32, which includes a pizzeria with an 85F lunch menu and other dishes apart from pizza, particularly a good *ratatouille*. Closed Nov–1 Apr. For a delightful meal with all the trimmings (the vegetables are especially ravishing), head out 5km northwest to Gargas and **Bernard Mathys**, © 04 90 04 84 64, a lovely restaurant in an 18th-century house (*menus 160, 250 and 350F*). Closed Tues and Wed. For a simple lunch in central Apt, tuck into a choice of inexpensive pies and salads at **Dame Tartine**, by the hollow plane tree in Rue de la République. In Saignon, the **Auberge du Presbytère**, © 04 90 74 11 50, ✇ 04 90 04 68 51, is worth the detour: two 10th- and 11th-century buildings at the centre on Place de la Fontaine, with a magnificent view over the Lubéron, charming homey rooms (*220–420F*) and a fine intimate restaurant with a 160F menu; remember to book. Closed Dec–Jan.

Red Villages North of Apt

Technically this isn't part of the Lubéron, though it is within the boundaries of the Regional Park. Above Apt, on the southern slopes of the Plateau de Vaucluse, the geology changes abruptly. The plateau is mostly limestone, which erodes away to make caves and water tricks like the Fontaine-de-Vaucluse (*see* below). This particular part has sandy deposits full of iron oxides—ochre, the material used in prehistoric times as skin-paint, and later to colour everything from soap to rugs. Centuries of mining have left some bizarre landscapes—cliffs and pits and peaks in what the locals claim are '17 shades of red', also yellow and cream and occasionally other hues besides.

Roussillon ✉ 84220: Place de la Poste, ✆/🖶 04 90 05 60 25.

Bonnieux ✉ 84480: 7 Place Carnot, ✆ 04 90 75 91 90, 🖶 04 90 75 92 94.

market days

Roussillon: Thursday. **Lacoste**: Tuesday. **Bonnieux**: Friday. **Oppède**: Saturday.

local wine

Côtes-du-Lubéron: This wine is produced in an extraordinary, high-tech works at the Château Val-Joanis in Pertuis (✆ 04 90 79 20 77, 🖶 04 90 09 69 52). On the other hand, Château de l'Isolette, on the main road between Bonnieux and Apt (✆ 04 90 74 16 70), is run by the Pinatels, a family that has been making wine since the 1500s. It has won scores of medals, as has Château La Canorgue (Rte du Pont-Julien, ✆ 04 90 75 81 01).

Rustrel to Roussillon

Rustrel, northeast of Apt on the D22, was one of the mining towns until 1890. The huge ruddy mess they left is called the **Colorado**; there are marked routes around it for tourists. From here, the D179 west takes you to **St-Saturnin-lès-Apt** (St Saturnin is probably the Roman god Saturn). Inside a modern ring of bungalows, this old village had little to do with mining, but it has always grown nice red cherries; there are plenty of ruins, including a castle and bits of three different sets of walls (13th- to 16th-century), a windmill for a landmark also a simple Romanesque chapel from the 1050s. **Roussillon**, to the southwest, occupies a spectacular hilltop site, and well it should, for centuries of mining have removed nearly everything for miles around. The *Association Terre d'Ochres*, an organization that wants to get the business going again, has an information centre in the village, and can direct you on a walk through the old quarries, known locally as the *Sables de Roussillon*. Samuel Beckett spent the war years exiled in Roussillon; rural peace and quiet gave him a nervous breakdown. Roussillon was the 'Peyrane' in the late Laurence Wylie's *Village in the Vaucluse* (*see* p.490); the one place that readers will recognize from the 1950s is the Bar Castrum, with its old poster of the film *Marius* on the wall.

Roussillon

South of Roussillon, near the meeting of the N100 and D149 (south of the N100), is a well-preserved Roman bridge, the **Pont Julien**. The little stone village of **Joucas** just northwest is quiet and uncommercial; north of here at Murs, you can pick up the scenic D4 across the Plateau de Vaucluse and its gorges to **Venasque** (*see* p.257).

Villages of the Petit Lubéron

West of Apt, and south of the N100, is a string of truly beautiful villages that have become the high-rent district of the Lubéron, one of the poshest rural areas in France. Don't come here looking for that little place in the country to fix up; it's all been done, as long as 40 years ago. The first to arrive were the Parisians, including many artists, intellectuals and eccentrics, giving the place a reputation as 'St-Germain-in-the-Lubéron'. Since the '60s, a wave of outsiders looking for Provençal paradise, including many Americans, have transformed the place. None of this is readily apparent, apart from the infestations of swank villas on many hillsides outside the Regional Park boundaries. The villagers, a bit richer now, take it in their stride and carry on as they always have—separate worlds, existing side by side.

Biggest and busiest of the villages, **Bonnieux** is also one of the loveliest, a belvedere overlooking all the Petit Lubéron. The ungainly modern church at the bottom of the village contains four colourful 16th-century wood paintings of the *Passion of Christ*; the other attraction, so to speak, is the **Musée de la Boulangerie**, on Rue de la République, © 04 90 75 88 34 (*open 10–12 and 3–6.30, closed Tues in Jan and Feb*), which as the name suggests will tell you everything you wanted to know about Provençal bread. There are some wonderfully scenic excursions from here: take the D36/D943 south to Lourmarin; this is the only good road across the spine of the Lubéron, and passes through a long and beautiful gorge called the **Combe de Lourmarin**. East of Bonnieux off the D943 a side road, the D113, takes you up into the mountains, passing the slender, elegant Romanesque bell tower of the **Prieuré de St Symphorien**, and up to the hamlet of **Buoux**; above it, the ruined medieval **Fort de Buoux** offers tremendous views over the heart of the Lubéron. Nearby is the beginning of a **nature trail** marked out by the Regional Park, with informative placards on the Lubéron's flora and fauna all along the way.

Lacoste, west of Bonnieux on D109, is a trendy *village perché*, home to an American school run by the Cleveland Institute of Art. Overlooking the village is a gloomy ruined **castle**, the home of no less a personage than the Marquis de Sade (d. 1814). The French are a bit embarrassed by the author of *120 Journées de Sodome*, but he certainly wasn't insane, and he is a literary figure of some note, taking to extremes the urge for self-expression that came with the dawn of the Romantic movement. He did have his little weaknesses, which kept him in and out of the calaboose for decades, on charges such as pushing 'aphrodisiac bonbons' on servant girls, and worse. Scion of an old respectable Provençal family, he spent a lot of time here when Paris grew too hot for him. Oddly enough, the Marquis seems to have been a descendant of Petrarch's Laura—Laura de Sade (*see* 'Avignon', p.282). The thought of it obsessed him for life, and he saw her in visions in the castle here. The castle, burned in the Revolution, is currently undergoing a slow restoration (*open to group visits if you reserve two weeks ahead; © 04 90 75 80 39*).

Continuing along the D109, you come to **Ménerbes**, honey-coloured, artsy and cuter than cute (with an attitude to match). As the former home of Peter Mayle—he's escaped to California—it now attracts fans of *A Year in Provence* who come to pay homage and buy a postcard—there's not much else to do. Ménerbes is so narrow, from some angles it looks like a ship, cruising out of the Lubéron toward Avignon; at the top is a small square, about 18ft across, with balconies on either side. The D188 from here takes you amongst waves of vines, to, fittingly, the world's first and only corkscrew museum, **Le Musée du Tire-Bouchon** at Domaine de la Citadelle, ✆ 04 90 72 44 77 (*open 10–12 and 2–6 daily, closed Sat, Sun and hols in winter*), just to the west of Ménerbes. Created by a French film producer, the museum houses a collection of weird and wonderful bottle poppers, from 17th-century attempts, to a bejewelled Cartier deluxe model, to an extensive display of pornographic corkscrews. From here the D188 continues through grand scenery almost to the top of the Petit Lubéron, and **Oppède-le-Vieux**, with its even gloomier ruined castle, one that can be explored. Perhaps it has a curse on it; this was the home of the bloodthirsty Baron d'Oppède, leader of the genocide against the Waldensians in the 1540s. The road west of Oppède, by way of Maubec and Robion towards Cavaillon is equally pretty; **Maubec** with its Baroque church, may be the Luberon village of your dreams.

Where to Stay and Eating Out

St-Saturnin ✉ 84490

St-Saturnin is a friendly village and though a bit out of the way it is a good, reasonably priced choice for a base; stay at the delightfully old-fashioned ★★**Hotel des Voyageurs**, a Logis de France on Place Gambetta, ✆ 04 90 75 42 08, @ 04 90 75 50 58, *closed Jan*, or at the **Saint Hubert**, with eight rooms on Place de la Fraternité, ✆ 04 90 75 42 02, @ 04 90 75 49 90, which has a slightly better restaurant, with a pretty terrace; menu, as daily posted on the chalk board (*130F*). *Open all year*. Note the 'wallpaper' in the bar.

Roussillon ✉ 84220

One of the few real luxury places is in Roussillon, the ★★★**Mas de Garrigon**, ✆ 04 90 05 63 22, @ 04 90 05 70 01, is a well-restored farmhouse with all the amenities, lovely rooms and a gourmet restaurant; but both, unfortunately, are woefully over-priced; (*590–800F for a room, menus 140–350F*). *Restaurant closed Dec.* Just outside the centre, ★★**Des Ocres**, Route de Gordes, ✆ 04 90 05 60 50, @ 04 90 05 79 74, is pleasant and lots cheaper, with convenient parking; there's also a *chambre d'hôte* at the very top of the town, ✆ 04 90 05 62 99. For a simple meal, try **Le Val des Fées**, ✆ 04 90 05 64 99, in Rue R. Casteau, with lovely views over the ochre from its terrace (*menus 100–255F*).

Joucas ✉ 84220

The panoramic road from Joucas to Murs is dotted with fine hotels, including two of the most prestigious (and pricey) in the Luberon: ★★★★**Le Phébus**, ✆ 04 90 05 78 83, @ 04 90 05 73 61, all done in exquisite taste, with views over the bizarre red hills of Roussillon, and a garden, pool, tennis and excellent restaurant where the chef perks up his Provençal dishes with the freshest herbs (*menus from 160F*). *Closed mid-Oct to mid-Mar*. Here, too, is ★★★★**Le Mas des Herbes Blanches**, ✆ 04 90 05 79 79, @ 04 90 05 71 96, a sumptuous Relais & Château spread in an old mas, in a beautiful setting and with all the fixings. *Closed Jan and Feb*. The same road also has a pair of more modest country hotel/restaurants with pools: **★★La Bergerie**, ✆ 04 90 05 78 73, @ 04 90 05 73 41, with 20 rooms (*from 280 to 350F*), and the more intitmate and refined **Le Mas du Loriot**, ✆ 04 90 72 62 62, @ 04 90 72 62 54, with only six rooms in a new Provençal *mas* (*270–500F*).

Bonnieux ✉ 84480

Bonnieux's lovely **★★★Hostellerie du Prieuré**, ✆ 04 90 75 80 78, @ 04 90 75 96 00 occupies a 17th-century priory in the village centre; rooms with a view and a garden. *Closed Nov–Mar*. Inexpensively, there is the **★Hotel César** on Place de la Liberté, ✆ 04 90 75 99 35. Neighbouring **Le Pistou** serves local produce on its imaginative menu (*100–200F*). **Le Fournil**, on lovely Place Carnot, ✆ 04 90 75 83 62 has a dining room excavated in the cliff and light fresh fare (*menus from 90 to 160F*). *Closed Mon*. At the **Rendez-vous des Artistes**, 2 Victor Hugo, ✆ 04 90 75 99 58, Japanese tour groups stop by for lunch for the excellent fish; it's quieter in the evening, and in the off season live music is featured twice a week (*around 130F*).

To really get away from it all, there's an isolated hotel above **Buoux** (✉ 84480), near the Fort, the **★Auberge des Seguins**, ✆/@ 04 90 74 16 37, Les Seguins (off the D113); simple rooms and home-cooking in a memorable setting, half-board obligatory.

Menerbes ✉ 84560

★★★Le Roy Soleil, in an olive grove at Le Fort, along the Route des Beaumettes, ✆ 04 90 72 25 61, @ 04 90 72 36 55, occupies a 17th-century building overlooking Menerbes, with a pool and tennis and excellent restaurant. *Closed mid-Oct to mid-Mar*.

Oppède-le-Vieux ✉ 84580

Once a stable, now a plesant country hotel, **★★Le Mas des Capelans**, on the N100, ✆ 04 90 76 99 04, @ 04 90 76 90 29, has a pool and terrace and playground. *Open mid-Feb to mid-Nov*. Eat beneath ruined medieval walls at **L'Oppidum**, Place de la Croix, ✆ 04 90 76 84 15, which serves good-value local produce alongside local works of art (*menus 68F to 158F*).

Cavaillon

Lacking anything more compelling, Cavaillon is famous for its melons. As one of the biggest agricultural market towns in France, it ships a million tons or so of these and all the other rich produce of the surrounding plains to Paris every year. Back in the last century, Alexandre Dumas loved the melons so much that he agreed to supply the local libraries with his books in exchange for a dozen melons a year.

Tourist Information

Cavaillon ✉ 84300: Place F. Tourel, ✆ 04 90 71 32 01, @ 04 90 71 42 99.

Monday; it competes with Apt's as the most important in the Vaucluse.

Roman Cavaillon

Cavaillon is built under a steep hill overlooking the Durance, the **Colline St-Jacques**, where a Neolithic settlement has been uncovered by a medieval chapel; it is a short climb up from central Place du Clos, with views on top stretching from Ventoux to the Alpilles. Roman-era Cavaillon has left behind only a 1st-century AD **arch**, at the foot of the hill. Unlike the arches of Carpentras and Orange, this one probably doesn't mark any particular triumph; it is four-sided, a *quadroporticus*, and like the only similar construction, the Arch of Janus in Rome, it probably was a simple decoration for—appropriately enough—a market-place; its decorative reliefs, mostly fruits and flowers, are now too eroded to be seen very clearly.

Cavaillon's other attractions include a small **Archaeological Museum**, ☎ 04 90 76 00 34, in the chapel of the Musée de l'Hôtel-Dieu on Cours Gambetta (*closed Tues*); the odd shaped, rather forbidding Romanesque cathedral of **Notre-Dame-et-St-Véran**, with a tatterdemalion 17th-century interior and a pretty cloister; and an ornate 18th-century **synagogue**, similar to the one in Carpentras, with a small museum, on Rue Hébraïque (*open 10–12 and 2–5*). Before the Revolution, Cavaillon had the biggest Jewish population in the papal enclave; among them were the ancestors of the composer Darius Milhaud. Segregated in a tiny ghetto around the synagogue, the community prospered despite occasional gusts of papal persecution; after the Revolution, most of Cavaillon's Jews moved to the larger cities of Provence, and there are none living in the town today.

Cavaillon ✉ *84300*   ***Where to Stay and Eating Out***

Even though the *parc* has become a car park, the old **★★Hôtel du Parc**, Place F. Tourel, ☎ 04 90 71 57 78, ☎ 04 90 76 10 35, is still a pleasant place to stay. Slightly more expensive, there's the equally venerable and well-kept **★★Toppin**, 70 Cours Gambetta, ☎ 04 90 71 30 42, ☎ 04 90 71 91 94.

The **Fin de Siècle**, 46 Place du Clos, ☎ 04 90 71 12 27, by the Roman Arch, is a good bet, named for its old-fashioned decor, with treats like stuffed chicken breast and salmon cakes on even the cheaper menus (*menus 89–200F*). *Closed Sun.* The café next door is a listed monument. At 5 Place Philippe de Cabassole, opposite the market, the eccentric **Le Pantagruel**, ☎ 04 90 76 11 30, doubles as an atmospheric wine bar and bistrot, unders its big stone arches (*125F menu Provençal, 155F menu dégustation*). *Closed Sun and Mon lunch.* Opposite the station, **L'Oustau**, ☎ 04 90 76 04 58, offers generous 105F menus. *Closed Sun.* If you need a change from French, there are Indian, Tex-Mex, Vietnamese and others along Boulevard Gambetta.

On the Plateau de Vaucluse

The Plateau de Vaucluse is the high ground that runs between the Luberon and Mont Ventoux to the north. Beware that both Gordes and the Fontaine-de-Vaucluse can get crowded by the heaving coachload in the summer.

Gordes ✉ 84220: Le Château, ✆ 04 90 72 02 75, 🖅 04 90 72 04 39.

Fontaine-de-Vaucluse ✉ 84800: Chemin de la Fontaine, ✆ 04 90 20 32 22, 🖅 04 90 20 21 37.

market days

Gordes: Tuesday.

Gordes

The first thing you'll notice about this striking *village perché* is that it has a rock problem. They have it under control; the vast surplus has been put to use in houses and sheds, and also for the hundreds of thick stone walls that make Gordes seem more like a south Italian village than one in Provence. The stones made agriculture a bad bet here, so the Gordiens planted olives instead, and became famous for them—at least until the terrible frost of 1976 killed off most of the trees. But without ever asking for it, Gordes has found something easier and more profitable: art tourism, with exhibitions and concerts in the summer.

Gordes was a fierce resistance stronghold in the war and suffered for it, with wholesale massacres of citizens and the destruction of much of the village; after the war the village was awarded the Croix de Guerre. All the damage the Nazis did has been redeemed; the village centre, all steep, cobbled streets and arches, is extremely attractive. At the centre, you may see flocks of well-scrubbed art students lounging on the steps of the imposing château built by the lords of Simiane in the 1520s. They are making their pilgrimage to an avant-garde that no longer exists. Even the rear guard–a 'didactic museum' of the works of the late Hungarian op art/poster artist Vasarély–has ducked out of Gordes, apparently for good, victim of an unseemly quarrel over money between Vasarély's heirs and the management. If you're disappointed, the Galerie Pascal Lainé in Place du Château has a permanent exhibit of his works.

To see what real art's all about, walk over to Gordes' parish church of **St-Fermin**, with a memorable 18th-century interior of purple, pink and gilded jiggumabobs, a lodge brother's fantasy seraglio. A statue of the Magdalen on the right looks down on it with a jaundiced eye. The **Château** itself (*open 10–12 and 2–6; adm*) has a superb Renaissance fireplace, the second largest in France, and a hodge podge of art in the Musée Pol Mara up on the second and third floors.

Around Gordes: Les Bories, and Another Bore

Across the Midi they are called *bories*, or *garriotes*, or *capitelles*, or a dozen other local names. In Provence there are some 3000 of them, but the largest collection in one place is the **Village des Bories** southwest of Gordes, off the D2 (*open daily 9–8 summer, 9–5.30 winter; adm*). A *borie* is a small dry-stone hut, usually with a well-made corbelled dome or vault for a ceiling. From their resemblance to Neolithic works (like the *nuraghi* of Sardinia) they have always intrigued scholars. Recently it has been established, however, that though the method of building goes way back, none of the *bories* you see today is older than the 1600s. Elsewhere they are usually shepherds' huts, but these are believed to have been a refuge for the villagers in times of plague. This group of 12 *bories* has been restored as a rural museum. You'll see other *bories* all around Gordes; some have been restored as holiday homes, and one has even become an expensive restaurant. Determined *borie*-hunters should also tour the large concentrations in the countryside around Bonnieux, Apt, Buoux, St-Saturnin, and Saumane, north of Fontaine-de-Vaucluse.

South of Gordes, there is a beautiful, simple Romanesque church at the hamlet of **St-Pantaléon**. West of that, watch out for the well-publicized **Musée du Vitrail** or Musée du Moulin des Bouillons ✆ 04 90 72 22 11 (*closed Tues*), where another little Vasarély has set up shop near the oldest intact olive-oil press in France. There are indeed exhibits on the history of stained glass, and others on Marseille soap, but their only purpose is to suck you into the adjacent gallery to look at the high-priced and gruesome work of Duran and others. Further south still, at **Coustellet**, the **Musée de la Lavande**, ✆ 04 90 76 91 23 (*open 10–12 and 2–6, closed Mon*) reveals all you have ever wanted to know about lavender, and more.

Abbaye de Sénanque

The loveliest of the Cistercian Three Sisters lies 4km north of Gordes on the D177. The church may be almost a double of the one at Thoronet (*see* pp.226–7), but built in the warm golden stone of the Vaucluse and set among lavender fields and oak groves, it makes quite an impression. Now it is in the hands of the same cultural association that controls the abbey at St-Maximin-la-Ste-Baume; oddly enough they use the place for studies of Saharan nomads, and there is a room of exhibits on the subject. The Benedictine monks of Ile St-Honorat, who hold the title, seem interested in occupying it again, so Sénanque's status is uncertain. Meanwhile, it is a favourite venue for summer concerts, often of medieval music.

The **church** (*open daily 10–12 and 2–6, closed Sun am; adm*), begun about 1160, shows the same early Cistercian seriousness as Thoronet and Silvacane, and has been changed little over the centuries; even the original altar is present. Most of the monastic buildings have also survived, including a lovely **cloister**, the *chauffoir*, the only heated room, where the monks transcribed books, and a refectory with displays giving a fascinating introduction to Sénanque and the Cistercians.

Fontaine-de-Vaucluse

Over a century ago, explorers found the source of the Nile. They're still looking for the source of the little Vaucluse river called the Sorgue. It's underground; the best spelunkers in France have been combing the region's caves for decades without success, and in 1983 a tiny, specially made submarine probe (the *Sorguonaute*) sent back data from some 250m below the surface of the **Fontaine-de-Vaucluse**, where the Sorgue makes its daylight debut, through a dramatic gaping hole in a cliff in the beautiful narrow valley the Romans called *Vallis Clausa*— the origin of *Vaucluse*. A second probe, *Sorguonaute II*, was sent down in 1984, and imploded soon after immersion; finally, in 1985, a sophisticated device usually used in oil exploration— the *Modexa 350*—plunged to a sandy bed 312m below the surface, though the passages that carry the stream into this remain unexplored.

Medieval legends record St Véran, patron of Cavaillon, dispatching a dragon near the source—a sure sign this was an ancient holy place, given the close connection between underground water and mythological serpents everywhere in Europe. The more prosaic Romans channelled the water into an aqueduct, remains of which can still be seen along the D24 towards Cavaillon. In later times, among those attracted by Provence's greatest natural wonder was Petrarch, who beginning in 1327 spent many seasons in a villa by the river bank writing his *De Vita Solitaria* , until 1353 when a band of brigands sacked the village and frightened him back to Italy.

The Fontaine is still an exquisite place, but the 540 or so residents of the town of Fontaine-de-Vaucluse have not been able to keep the place from being transformed into one of Provence's more garish tourist traps. To reach it, from the car park next to the church, you'll have to walk a noisy 2km gauntlet of commerciality, everything from *frites* stands to a museum of authentic Provençal *santons*, and a museum of medieval torture instruments. Incredibly, many of the attractions are worthwhile. There is **Norbert Castaret's Subterranean World**, a museum of underground rarities and informational exhibits overseen by France's best-known cave explorer (*open 10–12 and 2–6; closed Tues, Jan and Feb*) and **Vallis Clausa**, a paper-mill powered by old wooden wheels in the river that keeps up an old craft tradition on the Sorgue, making paper the 15th-century way for art books and stationery (*open 10–8, closed Tues: guided tours and sales*). Most surprising of all, in a sharp modern building, is the **Musée de l'Appel de la Liberté**, *✆* 04 90 20 24 00 (*open 10–7 July and Aug, 10–12 and 2–6 winter, weekends only mid-Oct–Dec and Mar–mid-April, closed Tues*), a government-sponsored institution that opened in 1990 and recaptures the wartime years vividly with two floors of explanatory displays, vignettes of daily life under the Nazis, newsreels and magazines, weapons and other relics. As at Gordes, Resistance life around Fontaine-de-Vaucluse was no joke; among the exhibits is a tribute to Fontaine's own mayor, Robert Garcin, whose aid to the *maquis* earned him a one-way ticket to Buchenwald in 1944.

Finally, there is the source itself, well worth the trouble even in its off-season. In the spring, and occasionally in winter, it pours out at a rate of as much as 200 cubic metres per second, forming a small, intensely green lake under the cliff. From the late spring until autumn it is greatly diminished, and often stops overflowing altogether (the water appears slightly further down the cliff); its unpredictability is as much a mystery as its source. It is a beautiful spot; if you're ambitious, it is also the beginning of two excellent hiking trails (GR 6 and 97), leading up into some of the most scenic parts of the Plateau de Vaucluse. More easily, you can climb up to the romantically ruined 13th-century **château** overlooking the spring, once owned by Petrarch's friend Philippe de Cabassole.

Before you leave, have a look at the village church, **Ste-Marie-et-St-Véran**. Begun in 1134, this lovely Romanesque building incorporates Roman and Carolingian fragments, including some bits of floral arabesques and the columns and capitals around the altar. The cornice outside is decorated with winsome rows of human and animal faces. Inside, there is the 6th-century Merovingian tomb of St Véran, and a good painted altarpiece of the *Crucifixion*, donated in 1654 by the village's *confrérie* of papermakers. Also on the way out, peek in at the **Musée Pétrarque**, *✆* 04 90 20 37 20 (*open mid-April–mid-Oct 10–12 and 2–6.30 summer, closed Tues*), a subdued look at the life and times of the poet during his stay in the town. Also note the column, erected in 1804 by the Athenaeum Valclusianum to celebrate the 500th anniversary of his birth.

Where to Stay and Eating Out

Gordes ✉ 84220

Gordes is big business; several fancy villa-hotels have sprung up on the outskirts, but the whole Gordes scene is expensive, over the top, and a bit exploitative of the credulous, who want it and deserve it. If you must, there's ★★★**La Mayanelle**, Rue de la Combe, ✆ 04 90 72 00 28, 📠 04 90 72 06 99, just below the centre on the Cavaillon road; unpretentious, comfortable, and a good bargain, with an authentic Provençal kitchen and an outdoor terrace. Some rooms have a grand view. Another honest establishment, outside the village, the ★★**Auberge de Carcarille**, southwest of town on the D2, ✆ 04 90 72 02 63, 📠 04 90 72 05 74, is a carefully restored *mas*, with pretty rooms, some with balconies, and a reasonable restaurant specializing in fish and game (*menus 98, 140 and 180F*). The tourist office has a list of the many *chambres d'hôtes* in the area. **Restaurant Tante Yvonne**, Place du Château, ✆ 04 90 72 02 54, is a solid choice for lunch, with a few unusual specialities (*menus 135 and 190F*). *Closed Sun eve and Wed.*

Fontaine-de-Vaucluse ✉ 84800

Fontaine-de-Vaucluse, in spite of its touristic vocation, is a quite pleasant place in which to stay or dine. The ★**Hostellerie Le Château**, ✆ 04 90 20 31 54, 📠 04 90 20 28 02, in Fontaine's old *mairie*, overlooking the Sorgue, has an outdoor terrace (behind glass, so you won't get splashed by the water-wheel in front). Excellent cooking on menus from 85 to 145F includes delicate sautéed frogs' legs and *truite en papillotte*; also three nice inexpensive rooms. ★★**Le Parc**, near the river and centre at Les Bourgades, ✆ 04 90 20 31 57, 📠 04 90 20 27 03, is a simple but pretty hotel wrapped in roses; its restaurant serves some of the best Italian food in Provence (*150F*). *Closed Nov–mid-Feb.* Trout is featured on nearly all the menus in town. The closest restaurant to the spring isn't a bad one: **Philip**, Chemin de la Fontaine, ✆ 04 90 20 31 81; mostly fish, on 105F and 155F menus, with an outside terrace by the river. *Closed Nov–Easter.*

From Cavaillon to Carpentras

Until the Revolution, the western Vaucluse plains from Cavaillon north to Vaison-la-Romaine were known as the *Comtat Venaissin*, a county that was a part of the papal dominions in France, though legally separate from Avignon. St Louis had stolen the territory from the Counts of Toulouse in 1229, part of the French kings' share of the booty after the Albigensian crusade, and Philip III passed it along to the popes in 1274 to settle an old dispute. It was a worthy prize—medieval irrigation schemes had already made the rich lands of the Comtat the 'Garden of France', an honorific it holds today as the most productive agricultural region in the country. Besides Cavaillon's famous melons, this small area has 5 per cent of all France's vineyards, including its best table grapes, and still finds room to grow tons of cherries, asparagus, apples and everything else a Frenchman could desire. All this intensive agriculture doesn't do the scenery any harm, and passing through it you'll find some fat, contented villages that make the trip worthwhile.

Tourist Information

L'Isle-sur-la-Sorgue ✉ 84800: Pl de l'Eglise, ✆ 04 90 38 04 78, 📠 04 90 38 35 43.

Le Thor ✉ 84250: Place 11 Novembre, ✆ 04 90 33 92 31.

Pernes-les-Fontaines ✉ 84210: Place du Comtat Venaissin, ✆ 04 90 61 31 04, 📠 04 90 61 33 23.

L'Isle-sur-la-Sorgue: Thursday and Sunday. Antique market Sunday, year round. **Le Thor**: Saturday. **Pernes-les-Fontaines**: Saturday.

L'Isle-sur-la-Sorgue

The Sorgue, that singular river that jumps out of the ground at Fontaine-de-Vaucluse and makes fly fishermen happy all the way to the suburbs of Avignon (it's one of France's best trout streams), has one more trick to play before it reaches the Rhône. At L'Isle-sur-la-Sorgue, it briefly splits into two channels to make this Provençal Venice, a charming town of 17,000 souls, an island indeed. In the Middle Ages, as a scrappy semi-independent commune, L'Isle-sur-la-Sorgue dug two more channels, and put the water to work running mills and textile factories; when trouble came, as during the Wars of Religion, the town knew how to keep out invaders by flooding the surrounding plains and making itself even more of an island.

Today, L'Isle-sur-la-Sorgue still makes fabrics and carpets, but it is best known as the antiques' centre of Provence, with a number of permanent shops on the southern edge of town, around Avenue des Quatre Otages, and a big 'Antiques Village' by the train station, open on Sundays (some booths open Sat and Mon also). Circumnavigating the town is a pleasant diversion, passing a number of old canals and wooden **mills**, some still in use, and houses with little front terraces built over the rushing water. There are two mills along Rue Jean Théophile, a street that will also take you to the 18th-century **Hôtel-Dieu**, with a sumptuous chapel and a perfectly preserved pharmacy of that era that can be visited, an ensemble of Moustiers faïence and ornate carved wood. There are frequent art exhibitions in an 18th-century palace, the **Hôtel Donadel Campredon** at 2 Rue Dr Tallet, © 04 90 38 17 41 (*open 10–1 and 2.30–6.30 summer; 9.30–12.30 and 2.30–5.30 winter, closed Tues*). And finally, right in the centre, is the town's beached whale of a church, 17th-century **Notre-Dame-des-Anges** (*open Tues–Sat 10–12 and 3–5, also Sun and Mon in July and Aug from 3–6*) sprawling across Place de l'Eglise. Even in a region full of marvellously awful churches, this one is a jewel, a mouldering imitation of Roman Baroque outside and gilt everything within. Opposite the façade, note the old firm of Fauques-Beyret, the prettiest drapery shop in Provence, with a fine Art Nouveau front; inside and out, nothing seems to have changed since the turn of the century.

West of L'Isle-sur-la-Sorgue, the N100 leads to **Le Thor**, with one of the best Romanesque churches in Provence, carrying the intriguing name of **Notre-Dame-du-Lac**. Begun about 1200, it is a work of transition, the Provençal Romanesque giving way to Gothic influences, as seen in the pointed vaulting of the nave. The sculptural decoration is spare but elegant, emphasizing the perfect symmetry of one of the last great medieval buildings in this region. Some 3km north of Le Thor on the D16 is the **Grotte de Thouzon** (*open daily in July and Aug, 9.30–7; rest of year 10–12 and 2–6; adm*). Of all the caves in Provence, this may be the one most worth seeing—weird and colourful, with rare needle-slender stalactites hanging down as much as 10 feet.

Pernes-les-Fontaines

L'Isle-sur-la-Sorgue's tiny neighbour to the north, Pernes-les-Fontaines has only a single drowsy stream passing through it, the Nesque. In the 18th century, perhaps out of jealousy, the Pernois took it into their heads to build decorative fountains instead. They got a bit carried away, and now there are 37 of them, or one for every 190 inhabitants, so that no one is ever far from a soulful plash. The fountains contribute a lot to making Pernes one of the most thoroughly delightful towns in the Vaucluse. It is an introspective place, still turning its back on the world, sheltering inside a circuit of walls that was demolished a hundred years ago, to be replaced by a ring of boulevards. Pernes is for walking; the Pernois have used the centuries to make their town an integrated work of art, looking exactly the way they want it to look; there's a surprise around every corner—or at least, a fountain.

Starting from the centre, the old **bridge** over the Nesque is embellished at both ends, with the 16th-century **Porte de Notre-Dame**, the **Cormorant Fountain** and the small chapel of **Notre-Dame-des-Graces**, from the same era. Behind it, the 12th-century church of **Notre-Dame-de-Nazareth** includes some Gothic chapels and reliefs of Old Testament scenes. The relative simplicity of its interior, in contrast to so many other Provençal churches, is a reminder of Pernes' earnest Catholicism through the centuries (one of its current economic mainstays, incidentally, is making the communion hosts for all the churches of France). Note the **Tour d'Horloge**, once the keep of the castle of the Counts of Toulouse, now crowned with a pussy cat weather vane (*you can climb up daily, 10–5*). Ask at the Tourist Office for a guide to take you around to the **Tour Ferrande**, on Rue Gambetta. This unassuming medieval tower, next to a fountain with carved grotesques, contains some of the oldest frescoes in France (*c. 1275*): vigorous, primitive scriptural scenes, Charles of Anjou in Sicily, St Sebastian and St Christopher, and a certain Count William of Orange battling against a giant.

East of Pernes-les-Fontaines is a very odd place, **Le Beaucet** (on the D39 south of St-Didier), where the people used to live in cave houses, some of which can still be seen, along with a ruined castle; above it, in the mountains, a source similar to Fontaine-de-Vaucluse has given rise to one of the biggest pilgrimage sites in Provence, a well-decorated chapel dedicated to the 12th-century **St-Gens**, a rain-maker and tamer of wolves. **Venasque**, further east, was the old capital of the Comtat Venaissin, and gave the county its name. Though a pretty village, and lately fashionable, nothing is left of its former distinction but the usual ruined fortifications and a venerable **baptistry**, really a 6th-century Merovingian funeral chapel reworked in the 1100s. The twisting D4, connecting Carpentras and Apt, was the main road of the Vaucluse in medieval times; it is still an exceptionally lovely route, passing eastwards from Venasque through the **Forêt de Venasque** and some rocky gorges on the edge of the Plateau de Vaucluse.

Where to Stay and Eating Out

L'Isle-sur-la-Sorgue ✉ 84800

L'Isle-sur-la-Sorgue can be a delightful place for a stay, when not being ravaged by summer tour buses, and its accommodation is fine. Outside the town there is a restored inn from the 1700s, the ★★★**Mas de Curebourse** (at Velorgues, 2km south of town on the D938, Route de Caumont, ✆ 04 90 38 16 58, 🖷 04 90 38 52 31), with a pool and extensive gardens, thirteen rooms, and a restaurant where the Lubéron lamb in garlic sauce is a treat (*menus from 175F*). In town, ★**La Gueulardière** on Route d'Apt, right in the centre, ✆ 04 90 38 10 52, 🖷 04 90 20 83 70, has cosy rooms and a garden terrace for dining; specialities of the house include salmon terrine and duck with olives. The best budget hotel is **Le Bassin** on Ave du Général de Gaulle, ✆ 04 90 38 03 16, 🖷 04 90 89 40 83, by the river, with a simple restaurant. Fish in a number of tasty forms is served on the lovely terrace over the river at **Le Vivier de la Sorgue**, Cours

Fernande-Peyre, ✆ 04 90 38 52 80 (*menus from 95F*). *Closed Sat lunch and Sun eve.* Also good, **Le Carré d'Herbes**, 13 Ave des Quatre-Otages, ✆ 04 90 38 62 95 serves Provençal specialities with an exotic touch in a dining room full of antiques (*menus from 98F*). *Closed Tues eve and Wed.*

Pernes-les-Fontaines ✉ 84210

Pernes-les-Fontaines offers two two-star hotels: the ★★**L'Hermitage**, on Route de Carpentras, ✆ 04 90 66 51 41, ✆ 04 90 61 36 41; and the ★★**Prato Plage**, ✆ 04 90 61 31 72, ✆ 04 90 61 33 34, with 20 rooms from 280 to 400F, slightly less expensive than its competitor. Both are open all year round. The ★★**Mas de la Bonoty**, off the D28 to Saint Didier, on the Chemin de Bonoty outside the village, ✆ 04 90 61 61 09, ✆ 04 90 61 35 14, also has a restaurant with creditable 145–195F menus and stunning views up to Mt Ventoux. *Closed Jan–mid-Mar.* For some of the best Italian food in Provence—*spaghetti alle vongole, carpaccio, tiramisù*—get a table at **Le Palépoli**, Route de Carpentras, ✆ 04 90 61 34 00 (*menus from 98–180F*). *Closed Sat lunch.*

Venasque ✉ 84210

Auberge de la Fontaine, Place de la Fontaine ✆ 04 90 66 02 96, ✆ 04 90 66 13 14 has five pricey rooms (*750F*) and the best food in the village: eat upstairs in the charming dining room (*menus from 80F*). *Closed Dec–Mar.*

Carpentras

The average French town of 30,000 or so, unless it has some great historical importance or major monument, is likely to be a rather anonymous place. Carpentras isn't. Perhaps because of its long isolation from the rest of France, under papal rule but really run by its own bishops, Carpentras has character and a subtle but distinct sense of place. A bit unkempt, and unconcerned about it, immune to progress and to any sudden urges for urban renewal, it is nevertheless an interesting place to visit. There are some cockeyed monuments, and some surprises. The rest of Provence pays Carpentras little mind; ask anyone, and they'll probably remember only that the town is famous for caramels, mint-flavoured ones called *berlingots*.

Getting Around

Carpentras is the node for what little there is of **coach transport** in the northern Vaucluse, with good connections to Avignon (some going by way of Pernes-les-Fontaines and L'Isle-sur-la-Sorgue) and Orange, one to Marseille; also one or two a day to Vaison-la-Romaine and some villages of the Dentelles de Montmirail, including Beaumes-de-Venise and Gigondas. Almost all of these stop at Place Aristide-Briand, on the ring boulevard. There are also several daily SNCF **trains** to Orange and Avignon.

Tourist Information

170 Allée Jean-Jaurès, ✆ 04 90 63 00 78, ✆ 04 90 60 41 02.

market day

Friday morning (truffles from Dec until Feb).

Into the Centre

As in so many other French towns, you'll have to cross a sort of motorway to get into the centre: a ring road of boulevards that was created when the town walls were knocked down in the last century (it's one-way and very fast; miss a turn and you'll have to go all the way around again; the French find these very entertaining). One part of the fortifications remains, the towering 14th-century **Porte d'Orange**, built in the 1360s under Pope Innocent IV.

If you can get in, you'll find an amiable and lively town, especially when the gorgeous produce of the Comtat farmers rolls in for Friday market. The stands fill half the town, but the centre is Rue des Halles, with the **Passage Boyer**, an imposing glass-roofed arcade, built by Carpentras' unemployed in the national public works programme started after the 1848 revolution.

Cathédrale St-Siffrein

Undoubtedly this is one of the most absurd cathedrals in Christendom. So many architects, in so many periods, and no one has ever been able to get it finished and get it right. Worst of all is the mongrel façade—Baroque on the bottom, a bit of Gothic and who knows what else above—like a mutt with a spot around its eye, likeable somehow, the kind that follows you home and you end up keeping him. Begun in the 1400s, remodellings and restorations proceeded in fits and starts until 1902. Some of the original intentions can be seen in the fine flamboyant Gothic portal on the southern side, called the **Porte Juive** because Jewish converts were taken through it, in suitably humiliating ceremonies, to be baptized. Just above the centre of the arch is Carpentras' famous curio, the small sculpted *Boule aux Rats*—a globe covered with rats. The usual explanation is that this has something to do with the Jews, or heretics. But bigotry was never really fashionable among 15th-century artists, and more likely this is a joke on an old fanciful etymology of the town's name: *carpet ras*, or 'the rat nibbles'.

The interior, richly decorated in dubious taste, includes some stained glass of the 1500s (much restored) and an early 15th-century golden triptych (left of the high altar) by the school of Enguerrand Quarton, an island of calm among so much busy-ness. The sacred treasures are in a chapel on the left: the relics of St Siffrein, one of the most obscure of all saints, not even mentioned in any early hagiographies; and the *Saint-Mors*, the 'holy bridle bit', said to have been made by St Helen out of two nails of the Cross as a present for her son, Emperor Constantine (*closed Sat and Sun*). Next to the cathedral, the **Palais de Justice** (1640) is the former Archbishop's Palace, occupying the site of an earlier palace that, for the brief periods that popes like Innocent IV chose to stay in Carpentras, was the centre of the Christian world. The present building, modelled after the Farnese Palace in Rome, contains some interesting frescoes from the 17th and 18th centuries including mythological scenes, and also views of Comtat villages and towns (ask the concierge to show you around).

The Triumphal Arch and the Secret Cathedral

Everyone knows that if you walk around a church widdershins (against the sun: counter-clockwise), you'll end up in fairyland, like Childe Harolde. Try it in Carpentras, and you'll find some strange business. The 28ft Roman **Triumphal Arch**, tucked in a corner between the Cathedral and the Palais de Justice, was built about the same time as that of Orange, in the early 1st century AD. Anyone who hasn't yet seen Orange's would hardly guess this one was Roman at all. Of all the ancient Provençal monuments, this shows the bizarre Celtic quality of Gallo-

Roman art at its most stylized extreme, with its reliefs of enchained captives and trophies. In the 1300s, the arch was incorporated into the now-lost Episcopal Palace. By 1640, when it was cleared, it was serving an inglorious role separating the archbishop's kitchens from his prisons. Originally, it must have connected the palace with the Romanesque cathedral.

Now, look at the clumsily built exterior wall of the present cathedral, opposite the arch. There are two large gaps, through which you can have a peek at something that few books mention, and that even the Carpentrassiens themselves seem to have forgotten: the **crossing and cupola** of the 12th-century cathedral, used in the rebuilt church to support a bell tower (later demolished) and neglected for centuries. In its time this must have been one of the greatest buildings of Provence, done in an ambitious, classicizing style—perhaps too ambitious, since its partial collapse in 1399 necessitated the rebuilding. The sculpted decoration, vine and acanthus-leaf patterns, along with winged creatures and scriptural scenes, is excellent work; some of it has been moved to the town museum.

The Synagogue and Museums

Behind the cathedral and palace, two streets north up Rue Barret, is the broad Place de l'Hôtel de Ville, marking the site of Carpentras' Jewish Ghetto. Before the Revolution, over 2000 Jews were forced to live here in unspeakable conditions, walled in and forced to pay a fee any time they wanted to leave. A small population remains one that is only just recovering from the trauma of a brutish desecration incident in the local Jewish cemetery, a crime that went unsolved for years and stirred up passions, rumours and bitterness on a national scale until March 1997, when a few local skinheads finally confessed, and apologized in court. All that remains of the old ghetto is the **Synagogue** at the end of the square. Built in 1741, it has a glorious decorated interior in the best 18th-century secular taste (*open Mon–Thurs, 10–12 and 3–5, Fri 10–12 and 3–4*). Other attractions in town include the **Hôtel-Dieu** on Place Aristide Briand, an 18th-century hospital with another well-preserved pharmacy and an attractive chapel, containing the tomb of Carpentras' famous bishop (1735–73) and civic benefactor, the Monseigneur d'Inguimbert (*open Mon, Wed, and Thurs 9–11.30*). This hospital is his monument, along with the important library he left to the town and the beginning of the collections in the **Musée Comtadin-Duplessis** on Blvd Albin-Durand (the ring road), © 04 90 63 04 92. Here are displayed artefacts and clutter from Carpentras' history, old views of the town, as well as 16th- and 17th-century paintings, many by local artists (*open daily exc Tues 10–12 and 2–4;, adm*).

Carpentras ✉ *84200*   ***Where to Stay and Eating Out***

Carpentras somehow manages to be left out of the annual tourist visitations, and accommodation here is limited. For something cosy in the centre, there is the elegant old ★★**Le Fiacre**, 153 Rue Vigne, © 04 90 63 03 15, ✆ 04 90 60 49 73, in an 18th-century building, near the Syndicat d'Initiative. The budget choice is the ★**Hôtel du Théâtre**, 7 Ave Albin Durand, © 04 90 63 02 90, on the ring boulevard, where the friendly proprietor may try to corner you into a game of chess.

It's hard to miss **Les Rives d'Auzon**, 47 Boulevard du Nord (the ring boulevard that encircles Carpentras, opposite the Porte d'Orange), © 04 90 60 62 62; it comes in Fauvist colours throughout, and serves delicious bright Provençal dishes with verve;

excellent vegetarians dishes (*lunch menus at 85 and 110F; others 130F and 158F*). *Closed Sat lunch, Sun, and Mon lunch.* For original cooking, try **Le Vert Galant** on Rue des Clapiès, ✆ 04 90 67 15 50 (*150–270F for strictly fresh seafood*). If the day's catch is unspectacular, you won't go wrong with their *suprême de pigeon* or grilled lamb either. *Closed Sat lunch, Sun, and 3 weeks in Aug.* **L'Orangerie**, 2 Place M. Charretier, ✆ 04 90 60 11 61, is a similar place both in price and in its innovative tinkering with old local favourites: the lamb flavoured with mint (unheard of!), also a memorable seafood platter, *délices aux fruits de mer*; (*menu 88F (lunch only), otherwise up to 200F*). *Closed Mon.* For less than a 100F note, you won't do better than the popular and friendly **Le Marijo**, 73 Rue Raspail, ✆ 04 90 60 42 65, sometimes serving genuine fresh seafood, or at least a well-cooked trout, 55–120F. *Closed Sun eve.*

Between Carpentras and Mont Ventoux, and the Gorges de la Nesque

Heading north for Mont Ventoux and Vaison-la-Romaine, you might consider a slight detour to the east, along the D974; towards the village of **Bédoin**, a small resort below Mont Ventoux famous for its enormous forest, you will pass Carpentras' **aqueduct**—not Roman but a 17th-century work, and impressive nevertheless. **Crillon-le-Brave**, just west, was the birthplace of Henri IV's companion-at-arms and has a belvedere with splendid views onto Mont Ventoux; **Caromb**, west of the D974 on the D55, is an attractive village that has kept parts of its medieval fortifications, as well as a surprisingly grand church, **Notre-Dame-et-St-Maurice**, with a wealth of Renaissance decoration inside. From here the skyline is dominated by **Le Barroux**, a dramatically perched village built around a 13th-century château (*open for tours in the summer*) that belonged to the Seigneurs of Baux. Follow the signs in the village up to the lofty Benedictine **monastery of Ste-Madeleine**, set in a geometrical lavendar garden, a fine example of Provençal Romanesque—built in the late 1970s. Come at 9.30am (Sundays at 10) to hear the fifty monks sing Gregorian chant for an uncanny journey straight back to the days when Romanesque was spanking new.

Or take a tour through the centre of the Plateau de Vaucluse, on the D942 almost as far as Sault, then return on the D1. Few ever take it, though they miss the most spectacular scenery the Vaucluse has to offer: the dry, rugged **Gorges de la Nesque**, leading to Sault and the Plateau d'Albion (*see* below). **Monieux**, at the eastern end of the Gorges, is a strange and isolated village that seems to have grown out of the rocky cliffs. There are caves and underground streams in the neighbourhood; experiments with dyeing the water have suggested that one of the sources of the Fontaine-de-Vaucluse may be here.

Where to Stay and Eating Out

Le Barroux ✉ 84330

Just below the monastery, surrounded by flower beds and acres of woods, the ★★★**Hostellerie François Joseph**, Chemin des Rabassières, ✆ 04 90 62 52 78, ✆ 04 90 62 33 54 is so quiet that guests awaken to birdsong; there's a pool and bright rooms are all well equipped with TV and mini bar, and many with kitchenettes as well (*from 300F*). *Closed Dec–mid-Mar.* Down by the crossroads for Caromb, you can dine well on refined, traditional dishes at **Le Four à Chaux**, ✆ 04 90 62 40 10.

Crillon le Brave ✉ 84410

The ★★★★**Hostellerie de Crillon le Brave**, ℰ 04 90 65 61 61, ✆ 04 90 65 62 86, is a sunny, sumptuous hotel in an old manor house, run by Peter Chittick, a Canadian infatuated with Provence. Glorious views of Mont Ventoux are supplemented with the hotel's helpful guide to walks in the area.

Mont Ventoux

You can pick it out from almost anywhere on the plains around Carpentras, a commanding presence on the northern horizon. **Mont Ventoux**, a bald, massive humpbacked massif over 20km across, is the northern boundary stone of Provence, and it has always loomed large in the Provençal consciousness. For the Celts, as for the peoples who came before them, it was a holy place, the Home of the Winds; excavations early this century at its summit brought to light hundreds of small terracotta trumpets, a sort of ex voto that has never been completely explained. Winds, in Provence, inevitably suggest the mistral, and as the source of that chilling blast Mont Ventoux has always had a somewhat evil reputation among the people; medieval Christians sought to exorcize it, perhaps, with the string of simple chapels that mark its slopes.

Mountain climbers will find a special interest in Mont Ventoux, if only because the sport was invented here. Petrarch, that admirably modern soul, went up with his brother in 1336—this, according to historian Jacob Burckhardt, was the first recorded instance of anyone doing such an odd thing simply for pleasure. The experience had an unexpected effect on the poet. Reading a passage from his *Confessions of St Augustine* at the summit, he was seized with a vision of the folly of his past life, and resolved to return to Italy: '...and men go forth, and admire lofty mountains and broad seas, and roaring torrents, and the course of the stars, and forget their own selves in doing so.' For us the trip will be easier, if perhaps less profound; Edouard Daladier, the Carpentrassien who became French Prime Minister in the 1930s, had a road built to the top (the D974).

Tourist Information

Malaucène ✉ 84340: Place de la Mairie, ℰ 04 90 65 22 59.

Sault ✉ 84390: Ave de la Promenade, ℰ 04 90 64 01 21, ✆ 04 90 64 15 03.

market days

Malaucène: Wednesday.

local wine

Côtes-du-Ventoux: Englishman Malcolm Swan has an estate at Domaine des Anges. A 15th-century glassworks, Domaine La Verrière at Goult (ℰ 04 90 72 20 88, ✆ 04 90 72 40 33), has been transformed into another of the area's best sources of wine. Or visit the purpose-built winery on the outskirts of Orange, La Vieille Ferme (ℰ 04 90 34 64 25).

Malaucène and the Fountain of Groseau

The base for visiting the mountain is **Malaucène**, an open, friendly village on the road from Carpentras to Vaison. Piled under a little conical nib of a hill, its landmark is the enormous church-cum-fortress of **St-Michel-et-St-Pierre**, built in 1309 by Pope Clement V. From here, the D153 was the ancient route around Mont Ventoux, passing a pair of medieval chapels and a ruined defence tower around the village of **Beaumont-du-Ventoux** (it now peters out into a hiking trail, the GR 4). The D974, into the heart of the massif, passes a pre-Celtic site dedicated not to wind, but water. **Notre-Dame-du-Groseau** marks the spot today, an unusual 11th-century octagonal chapel. Originally this was part of a large monastery, now completely disappeared. Pope Clement V used it as his summer home, and his escutcheon can be seen painted inside (the *curé* at Malaucène has the key). But this was also a holy spot in remotest antiquity; the iron cross outside the chapel is planted on a stone believed to have been a Celtic altar. *Groseau* comes from *Groselos*, a Celtic god of springs; the object of veneration is a short distance up the road, the **Source du Groseau**, pouring out of a cliff face. The Romans, as they did at Fontaine-de-Vaucluse, channelled the spring into an aqueduct for the city of Vaison; fragments of this can still be seen.

Further up the mountain, the almost permanent winds make themselves known and vegetation becomes more scarce (despite major reforestation programmes in this century). The D974's big day comes, almost every summer, when the Tour de France puffs over it, probably the most tortuous part of the race; it was here that the English World Champion Tommy Simpson collapsed and died in 1967. The top of Ventoux (1890m) is a gravelly wasteland, embellished with communications towers and a meteorological observatory. Coming down the eastern side of the mountain takes you into one of the least-visited backwaters of Provence, a land of shepherds, boar and *cèpes*. There are a few attractive villages: **Sault**, on its outcrop, surrounded by bucolic landscapes, forests, and lavendar fields, with a quirky **Musée Municipal** of fossils, village curios and archaeology, even a mummy (℡ 04 90 64 02 30, *open Mon, Wed and Sat in July and Aug, rest of year by appointment*); and further north, two medieval *villages perchés*, **Aurel** and **Montbrun-les-Bains**. South of Sault, the lonely **Plateau d'Albion** takes its name (like the English Albion, the Alps and the Provençal village of Aups) from an ancient Indo-European root meaning white—from the odd limestone mountains around it, that seem to be covered in snow. The landscape can be a bit eerie, even more so when you consider that much of this territory, around the village of St-Christol, has been taken over for a complex of bases where France keeps most of its nuclear missiles.

Where to Stay and Eating Out

Malaucène ✉ 84340

Malaucène makes a good base for Ventoux and the Dentelles de Montmirail. By St-Michele, the peaceful ★★★**Hostellerie Le Chevalerie**, Rue des Remparts, ℡ 04 90 65 11 19, @ 04 90 12 69 22 has the most comfortable rooms in town; the restaurant, with a charming terrace, specializes in fancy fare—truffles, foie gras, tournedos (*menus at 143 and 200F*). *Closed in July and part of Aug.* The clean and shipshape ★★**L'Origan**, is in the centre on Cours des Isards, ℡ 04 90 65 27 08, @ 04 90 65 12 92; the restaurant offers some hearty cooking—dishes such as guinea-fowl with *morilles*, on menus of 80F, 100F and 120F. *Closed Nov–Mar*. Opposite, ★★**Le Venaissin**, ℡ 04 90 65 20 31, @ 04 90 65 18 03 is similar. For the best cooking in the area, follow the signs to **La Maison** in Hameau de Piolon, outside Beaumont-du-Ventoux, ℡ 04 90 65 15 50, where there's only one 140F menu with a wide selection of dishes, many with a touch of the southwest; *try the pintadeau en croûte. Closed Mon, Tues and Wed lunches, and Oct–Easter.*

Around Mont Ventoux: Sault and Aurel ✉ 84390

In Sault, facing Mont Ventoux, the ★★★**Hostellerie du Val de Sault**, Ancient Chemin d'Aurel, ✆ 04 90 64 01 41, 🖷 04 90 64 12 74, is a handsome new hotel 760m up, with only 11 rooms surrounded by trees and gardens, and equipped with a pool, gym, tennis and sauna and good restaurant. *Closed mid-Nov–Mar.* The ★**Relais du Ventoux**, in Aurel, ✆ 04 90 64 00 62, has plain but comfortable rooms and a restaurant with no surprises on the 85F menu. *Closed mid-Nov–mid-Mar.* East of the summit of Ventoux, at the corner of the D164 and D974, the **Chalet-Reynard**, ✆ 04 90 61 84 55, is the only restaurant for miles, a cosy, wood-lined bar where the local lumberjacks tuck into boar and a *pichet de rouge* at lunchtime (*menus from 98F*).

Les Dentelles de Montmirail

Montmirail's 'lace' is a small crown of dolomitic limestone mountains, opposite Mont Ventoux on the other side of Malaucène. Eroded by the wind into a lace-like fantasy of thick columns and spikes, the peaks form an ever-changing pattern as you circle around them. This is superb walking country, and superb wine country: stroll up a thirst.

Tourist Information

Gigondas ✉ 84190: Place du Portail, ✆ 04 90 65 85 46, 🖷 04 90 65 88 42.

Beaumes-de-Venise ✉ 84190: Cours Jean-Jaurès, ✆/🖷 04 90 62 94 39.

market days

Beaumes-de-Venise: Tuesday.

local wines

Côtes-du-Rhône Sud: Gigondas, Vacqueyras, and Beaumes-de-Venise.

Gigondas: The Cave des Vignerons de Gigondas (✆ 04 90 65 86 27, 🖷 04 90 65 80 13) is responsible for 20 per cent of the total Gigondas production. Individual estates worth visiting are: the Domaine Piaugier, Sablet (✆ 04 90 46 96 49, 🖷 04 90 46 99 48); the Domaine les Pallières in Gigondas (✆ 04 90 65 85 07); and the Domaine Les Goubert (✆ 04 90 65 86 38, 🖷 04 90 65 81 52), also in Gigondas.

Vacqueyras: A minute region just to the south of Gigondas; some of the finest wines are made by a Provençal-speaking Pole named Jocelyn Chudzikiewicz at the Domaine des Amouriers, Les Garrigues, Sarrians (✆ 04 90 65 83 22, 🖷 04 90 65 84 13). Or try the Château de Montmirail, in Vacqueyras (✆ 04 90 65 86 72, 🖷 04 90 65 81 31).

Beaumes-de-Venise: The locals find the English habit of treating Beaumes as a dessert wine eccentric; they drink it as an aperitif or best of all, with a foie gras starter. The local cooperative, near Notre Dame d'Aubune makes a very good example. The two leading estates are Domaine Durban, ✉ 84190 Beaumes de Venise (✆ 04 90 62 94 26, 🖷 04 90 65 01 85), and La Vieille Ferme (✆ 04 90 34 64 25), on the outskirts of Orange.

Wine and Antiques

The ideal overview of the Dentelles is along the D90 from Malaucène to Beaumes-de-Venise, passing by way of **Suzette**, a cluster of sunbleached stone houses and a bar/pizzeria enjoying a dream-like vision of the mountains at their most fantastical. If you're in no hurry, steep semipaved roads from Suzette plunge into the heart of the mountains for more of the same, towards Séguret to the west (*see* below) or north to **Crestet** a half-abandoned, half-restored *village perché* with a castle, more fabulous views, and an art centre with changing, and usually quirky exhibits.

The D90 takes you into Côtes-du-Rhône country (*see* above), beginning with **Beaumes-de-Venise**, the metropolis of the Dentelles, where the worthies sit out on the wall sunning themselves like fat cats. There's a ruined castle to explore, and a small archaeological museum. Don't expect any canals: the name Beaumes comes from the Provençal word for cave, and the Venise from a corruption of Comtat Venaissin—the papal county. North along the D81, the Romanesque chapel of **Notre-Dame-d'Aubune** overlooks the Comtat plain, with a lofty bell tower decorated with classical pilasters. A track leads up the Côte Balméenne, where terraces were settled by the Celto-Ligurians, Greeks, Romans and Saracens. After the archaeologists had their way with it in the 1980s, the terraces have been replanted with olive, almond and fruit trees.

Vacqueyras, a dusty little crossroads devoted entirely to wine, has a by-road up to **Montmirail**, a spa once famous for its purgative waters. Sold off after the Second World War, a Greek shipping tycoon now owns the grand Victorian villa, while the rest of the spa is now a hotel (*see* below). A few km north of Vacqueyras, **Gigondas**, like so many wine villages in the south, is much smaller than its fame: sweet and small, overlooking the immaculate vineyards, full of shops to *dégust* the eponymous red nectar. The château on top of the village has been turned into a modest outdoor sculpture garden. The extremely helpful tourist office sells maps of the paths through the Dentelles: the GR 4 passes nearby, and steep white roads back to Beaumes or to the Col du Cayron and Lafare (south of Suzette) for more lovely Dentelles scenery.

Sablet, north of Gigondas, is another pretty, hard-working wine village packed on a hill, with old covered lanes to explore. Most of the passing tourists hone in on **Séguret**, built on a terrace over the vine-striped Ouvèze plain. It bears the burden of being 'One of the Most Beautiful Villages in France' with a fair amount of grace: there's no room for cars, and none for more than a handful of artists and *santonniers*. Note the funny weathered faces on the 14th-century Fontaine des Mascarons. Séguret is a good base for hiking; there are two trails (GR 4 and 7) and one village track that passes through a gap in the Dentelles to the eastern side. The back road to Vaison-la-Romaine is steep but beautiful.

Where to Stay and Eating Out

Beaumes-de-Venise/Vacqueyras ✉ 84190

The **Auberge St-Roch** on Ave Jules Ferry, ✆ 04 90 65 08 21, ✉ 04 90 65 05 07, has a modest restaurant that does seafood and local dishes (*closed mid-Nov–Mar*). In the village centre, there's a little bed and breakfast, ✆ 04 90 62 93 98 with lace curtains and balconies. In Vacqueyras, the modern ★**Hôtel Restaurant des Dentelles**, ✆ 04 90 65 86 21, offers 2-star comfort (at 2-star prices), and only so-so food in the restaurant: other possibilities are ★★**Le Pradet**, Route de Vaison, ✆ 04 90 65 81 00, ✉ 04 90 65 80 27, a quiet new complex on the edge of the village, or the ★★★**Hôtel de Montmirail**, once part of the spa, ✆ 04 90 65 84 01, ✉ 04 90 65 81 50, with pool, garden, and restaurant (*rooms 255–410F*).

Gigondas ✉ 84190

In the middle of a Gigondas vineyard, ****Les Florets**, Route des Dentelles, ✆ 04 90 65 85 01 has simple rustic rooms and plenty of peace and quiet. In the centre of the village there are a couple of places to dine: **L'Oustelet**, in a neoclassical building in Place du Portail, ✆ 04 90 65 85 30, does good beef in wine (*menus 100–140F*); *closed Sun eve and Mon*; or the **Cafe de la Poste**, ✆ 04 90 65 89 62, a bar/restaurant (*with simple 55 and 75F menus*); *closed Mon eve and Tues*. In **Violès** (✉ 84150) just west of Gigondas, **Le Mas de Bouvau**, Route de Cairanne, ✆ 04 90 70 94 08, ✆ 04 90 70 95 99, a charming family-run hotel-cum-restaurant in the vines, serving specialities from southwest France: duck confit, magret, foie gras pigeon and rabbit (*menus at 130–265F*). *Closed Sun eve and Mon except in July and Aug.* Also in Violès, there's a pleasant bed and breakfast, **La Farigoule,** in an old farm house at Le Plan de Dieu, ✆ 04 90 70 91 78; they also rent bikes. *Open Easter–Oct.*

Séguret ✉ 84110

The *****Domaine de Cabasse**, ✆ 04 90 46 91 12, ✆ 90 46 94 01, part of a Côtes-du-Rhône estate on the D23 towards Sablet; a few comfortable rooms with terraces (*200–650F*), a pool, and an excellent restaurant that has truffles in season and other rather extravagant dishes year-round (*menus 140–170F, more at weekends*). *Closed Jan, Feb and Mar.* *****La Table du Comtat**, in the village, ✆ 04 90 46 91 49, ✆ 04 90 46 94 27 is well known for refined dishes such as *bohémienne d'agneau en tourtière et sa côte en beignet* (*menus 160–250F*). *Closed Tues eve and Wed out of season*. For simpler fare, head for **Le Mesclun** also in the village, ✆ 04 90 46 93 43, and its à la carte selection of local delights (*around 150F*). *Closed Mon.*

Vaison-la-Romaine

Vaison, in all its 2400 years, has never been able to make up its mind which side of the River Ouvèze it wanted to be on. Locals have always been wary of the river's mighty potential for destruction, and the town's peregrinations from bank to bank have left behind a host of monuments, including extensive Roman ruins. Such circumspection was proved justified in 1992 when, on the night of 22 September, the Ouvèze burst its banks and swept away houses, caravans, bridges and roads, drowning 30 people in one of the worst French floods this century. The town's riverside is still being rebuilt, and the scars of the tragedy are yet to heal. Yet, as the tourist office proclaims, the best way to support Vaison is to continue to visit. The Roman ruins were untouched, and life goes on: Vaison is a pleasant and beautiful place (with a good market if you are staying locally), and despite the summer crowds, if you're interested in the Romans or the Middle Ages it will be a mandatory stop on your Provençal agenda. The recently created Vaison Festival draws large crowds from July to September, when theatre groups, choirs and musicians from France and the world gather for performances in venues ranging from the Roman amphitheatre to the town's car parks. For information contact the tourist office, or call the festival organizers, ✆ 04 90 36 00 78.

Tourist Information

Place du Chanoine Sautel, ✆ 04 90 36 02 11, ✆ 04 90 28 76 04. There is a vast car park across the street for visitors.

Vaison-la-Romaine (the lower town): Tuesday.

History

Vaison began on the heights south of the Ouvèze as a Celtic *oppidum*. In the late 2nd century BC, the Romans took control and refounded it as *Vasio Vocontiorum*, a typical colony on the gentler slopes to the north of the river. For an out-of-the-way site, Vasio prospered spectacularly for the next five centuries, an *urbs opulentissima* with a large number of wealthy villas and as many inhabitants as it has today (about 6000). Vaison survived the age of invasions better than many of its neighbours; church councils were held here in the 6th century, a time when the city could afford to begin its imposing cathedral.

For the following centuries, bishops ruled in Vaison as the city gradually declined. Perhaps in the 700s, the Counts of Toulouse acquired the site of the old Celtic *oppidum* and built a castle on it. They carried on a chronic quarrel with the bishops; meanwhile most of the people were abandoning the Roman town (and the bishops) for the freedom and safety of the heights, the beginnings of what is now the Haute-Ville. In the 1300s Vaison fell into the hands of the pope, along with the rest of the Comtat Venaissin, and did not become part of France until the Revolution. In the 1900s, on the move once more, the Vaisonnais were abandoning the Haute-Ville for the river bank. In 1840, the first excavations were undertaken in the Roman city. Vaison nevertheless had to wait for a local cleric, the Abbé Sautel, to do the job seriously. He dug from 1907 until 1955, financed mostly by a local businessman.

The Ruins

> *Open daily 10–12 and 2–4.30, closed Tues in winter; 9–12 and 2–6.45 in summer; same adm for both, also includes cathedral cloister.*

The Abbé uncovered almost 11 hectares of Roman Vaison's foundations, while the modern town grew up around the digs. There are two separate areas, the **Quartier de la Villasse** and the **Quartier de Puymin**; their entrances are on either side of the central Place Abbé-Sautel, by the Tourist Information pavilion. Vaison's ruins are an argument for leaving the archaeologists alone; with everything sanitized and tidy, interspersed with gardens and playgrounds, there is the unmistakable air of an archaeological theme park. The Villasse is the smaller of the two areas; from the entrance, a Roman street takes you past the city's **baths** (the best parts are still hidden under Vaison's post office) and the **Maison au Buste d'Argent**, a truly posh villa with two *atria* and some mosaic floors. It has its own baths, as does the adjacent **Maison au Dauphin**; beyond this is a short stretch of a **colonnaded street**, a status embellishment in the most prosperous Roman towns.

The Puymin quarter has more of the same: another villa, the **Maison des Messii**, is near the entrance. Beyond that, however, is an *insula*, or block of flats for the common folk, as well as a large, partially excavated quadrangle called the **Portique de Pompée**, an enclosed public garden with statuary that was probably attached to a temple. On the opposite side of the *insula* is a much-ruined *nymphaeum*, or monumental fountain. From here you can walk uphill to the **theatre**, restored and used for concerts in the summer, and the **museum**, displaying the best of the finds from the excavations. You'll learn more about Roman Vaison here than from the bare foundations around it; there is a model of one of the villas as it may have looked. All the items a Roman museum must have are present: restored mosaics and fragments of wall painting, some lead pipes, inscriptions, hairpins and bracelets, and of course statuary: municipal notables of Vaison, a wonderful monster *acroterion* (roof ornament) from a mausoleum, and a few marble gods and emperors—including a startling family portrait with the Emperor Hadrian completely naked and evidently proud of it, next to his demurely clothed Empress Sabina, smiling wanly.

The Cathedral of Notre-Dame-de-Nazareth

The French, with their incurable adoration of anything Roman, go on forever about the ruins and neglect Vaison's real attraction, one of the most fascinating medieval monuments of the Midi. A treasure-house of oddities, it is a reminder that there is more to the art and religion of the Middle Ages than meets the eye, and much of significance that is lost to us forever. It stands a half-km west of the ruins, on Avenue Jules Ferry.

The church was begun in the 6th century. Its **apse** is the oldest part; looking at it from the outside, you'll see where excavations have uncovered the dressed Roman stones and drums of columns that were recycled to serve as a foundation. The rest of the structure dates from a rebuilding that began in the 1100s, including some handsome sculptural decoration around the portals, cornices and bell tower. The first clues to the mystery of this church can be seen near the top of the façade: a rectangular **maze**, and a triangular figure that may be a mystic representation of the Sun. Even with this, the exterior is subdued, and the muscular perfection of the columns and vaults inside comes as a surprise. The 12th-century nave is Romanesque at its best, but still the eye is drawn down it to the magnificent, arcaded interior of the apse. There is nothing like this apse in France; it is a place to muse on time and fate—the last surviving work of Roman Provence, the wistful farewell of a civilization that can be heard across the centuries. Almost incredibly, the 6th-century marble **altar** is still present, carved in a beautiful wave-like pattern. Also here are the original bishop's throne, and benches set around the semicircle of the apse where the monks would sit: the earliest form of a choir, as in the churches of Ravenna. In the medieval nave, some of the decoration is as provocative as that on the façade. At the rear, near a column that survives from the original basilica, you'll notice the figure of an unidentifiable 'hairy person', extending a hand in a gesture of benediction. Elaborate masons' marks are everywhere. Odd figures of the Evangelists embellish the squinches of the fine octagonal cupola; behind one of them, high up, on the second column on the right side of the nave, is what appears to be a little *devil*. You'll meet his big brother in the cloister.

The Cloister

Look around as you enter. Grinning over the ticket-booth to the cloister is Vaison's most famous citizen—Old Nick himself, with horns and goatee, carved into the stone as big as life. This is not a personage one usually sees portrayed in cathedral cloisters, and no one has ever come up with an explanation for his presence here—one unlikely guess is that it's really Jesus, superimposed over a crescent moon. This is a small but graceful cloister from the 1100s, with a number of finely carved capitals (one with a pair of entwined serpents) and architectural fragments displayed around the walls.

And if you think the Devil and all the other curiosities were simply fanciful decoration, look up from the cloister at the Latin verse inscription, running the entire length of the church's southern cornice:

I exhort you, brothers, to triumph over the party of Aquilon [the north], faithfully maintaining the rule of the cloister, for thus will you arrive at the south, in order that the divine triple fire shall not neglect to illuminate the quadrangular abode in such a way as to bring to life the arched stones, to the number of two times six. Peace to this house.

The medieval Latin is in parts obscure enough for other interpretations to be possible, but these tend to be even stranger. The twelve stones seem to be pillars of the cloister, the 'quadrangular abode'. The rest is lost in arcane, erudite medieval mysticism, wrapped up with the architecture and unique embellishments, and undoubtedly with a monastic community that was up to something not entirely orthodox. Like most medieval secrets, this one will never be completely understood.

Chapelle St-Quenin

A bit of a climb to the north, on Avenue de St-Quenin, you can continue in this same vein of medieval peculiarity. **St-Quenin**, a chapel dedicated to a 6th-century bishop who became Vaison's patron saint, fooled people for centuries into thinking it a Roman building. Its apse, unique in France, is triangular instead of the usual semicircle, and crowned with a cornice that includes fragments from Roman buildings as well as primitive reliefs that may date from Merovingian times. It is difficult to ascribe any special significance to this odd form. Probably built in the 11th or 12th century, it may be simply an architectural experiment, typical of the creative freedom of the early Romanesque. On the front of the chapel is a Merovingian-era relief of two vine shoots emerging from a vase, a piece of early Christian symbolism that has become the symbol of Vaison.

The Haute-Ville

From Roman and modern Vaison, the medieval version of the town is a splendid sight atop its cliff, a honey-coloured skyline of stone houses under the castle of the Counts of Toulouse. Almost abandoned at the turn of the century, the Haute-Ville is becoming quite chic now, with restorations everywhere and more than a few artists' studios. You reach it by crossing the Ouvèze on a **Roman bridge**, still in good nick after 18 centuries of service (although it had to be repaired after the last floods; note the plaque, in Latin) then climb up to the gate of the 14th-century fortifications, next to the **Tour Beffroi**, the clock-tower which is the most prominent sight of the Haute-Ville's silhouette. The cobbled streets and the shady **Place du Vieux-Marché** with its fountain are lovely; trails lead higher up to the 12th- to 14th-century **castle**, half-ruined but offering a view.

Vaison-la-Romaine ✉ *84110*   **Where to Stay and Eating Out**

Vaison has plenty of room, and in the crowded summer months you might end up here even if you had preferred to be in one of the villages of the Dentelles—for a compromise, try the **★★Hôtel Les Auric**, ☏ 04 90 36 03 15, a modernized old farmhouse with a pool, west of Vaison on the D977 and convenient to both. *Closed Dec–April*. In town, staying up in the Haute-Ville is not entirely convenient—but it can be very gratifying: **★★★Le Beffroi**, Rue de l'Evêché, ☏ 04 90 36 04 71, 🖷 04 90 36 24 78, is a picturesque 16th-century house, furnished to match, a bargain for its category. *Closed Dec–mid-Mar*. **★★Le Burrhus**, 1 Place Montfort, ☏ 04 90 36 00 11, 🖷 04 90 36 39 05, offers comforable rooms with an Art Deco touch, with a shady terrace to relax on. *Closed mid-Nov to mid-Dec.* The budget choice is the old ★**Théâtre Romain**, Rue Abbé Sautel, ✆ 04 90 28 71 98, ✉ 04 90 36 20 71, in the centre, very accommodating, though some rooms can be noisy. The restaurant serves standard 100–160F menus.

Vaison was something of a gastronomic desert until 1995, when young Olivia and Didier Rogne opened **Le Brin d'Olivier**, 4 Rue du Ventoux, ✆ 04 90 28 74 79, an intimate, romantic place with an inner courtyard, the ideal place to feast on Olivia's fresh, imaginative Provençal cuisine, where fresh herbs hold pride of place (*lunch menu at 70F, other from 120–180F*). *Closed Wed and Sat lunch, and first fortnight Dec.* In the Haute-Ville, **La Fête en Provence** on Place du Vieux Marché, ✆ 04 90 36 36 43, serving its own *foie gras de canard*, followed by a *magret* or lamb with olives, on a bargain 90–240F menu. *Closed mid-Nov–mid-April, Wed.* For a change, there are West Indian specialities at **Le Colibri** on Cours Taulignan, ✆ 04 90 36 09 18 (*menus 80–135F*). *Closed Mon.*

Avignon.

Down the Rhône: Orange to Beaucaire

Despite Frédéric Mistral's best efforts in the epic 1896 *Poème du Rhône*, this is not a lyrical river, neither fair of face nor full of grace. Its nickname *malabar*, the strongman, describes it well: deep and swift-flowing with muscular currents, its banks like bulging biceps, its secret depths hosting legendary man-eating monsters such as the Tarasque and Drac. For the Rhône is a Saturday's child and has to work for a living: after serving the industries and nuclear plants to the north, it does it all again in Provence, at France's biggest centre for the processing of nuclear waste, at Marcoule, at the hydro-electric plant and Satanic mills of Avignon's industrial quarter, and at the paper mills near Tarascon.

Historically most of the Rhône's traffic has come south with the current, ferrying the blond barbarians, the eaters of *frites* and drinkers of beer, down to the sultry Mediterranean. The river also divided the spoils: Provence, on the east bank, owed allegiance to the emperor and pope; Languedoc, on the west, belonged to the kingdom of France after the Albigensian crusade. Rhône boatmen called the banks not port and starboard, but Empire and Kingdom. On the empire's side are Orange, with its famous Roman theatre, Châteauneuf-du-Pape and Avignon, where 14th-century popes spent what Petrarch called their 'Babylonian exile', and Tarascon, favoured home of Provence's Good King René.

Orange

There seems to have been a settlement of some kind around the hill of St-Eutrope in prehistoric times, and the city dates its chronicles from 35 BC—enough time for all imaginable Oranges to have come and gone. The present incarnation must be one of the sadder ones, a miasmic provincial town with a few cosy corners among the prevailing drabness. Fate, or the lack of a bypass road, has made its streets a kind of Le Mans for heavy lorries, fouling the air, menacing pedestrians and coating the old houses with a sooty film. Nevertheless there are two ancient monuments unmatched in France, and some surprises besides. You'll probably like it best on a Sunday, when the law bans trucks from the road.

History

Rome took good care of its soldiers; keeping its word by them was one secret of the empire's success. Nine years after Julius Caesar's death, many veterans of the Second Gallic Legion were ready for their promised retirement. The pattern was already set. Rome would establish a colony for them in the lands they conquered, often replacing a native village they had destroyed; the veterans farmed their allocated lands, and could look forward to real wealth in their declining years as the colony grew into a town. The colony that became Orange was called *Colonia Julia Secundanorum Arausio*. Exceedingly prosperous throughout Roman times, Orange survived the Visigothic conquest in 412; it was the site of two Church councils in the following decades. The chronicles are largely blank from then until the mid-12th century, when the city's feudal lord was Raimbaut d'Orange, troubadour and patron of troubadours. Even then, history was on the back-burner; the city and its hinterlands were often in

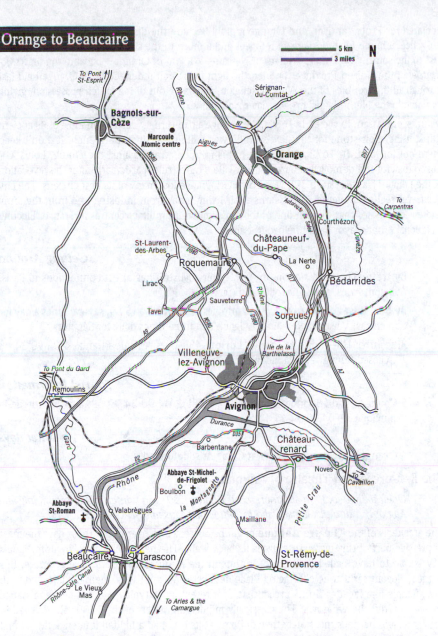

hock to pay Raimbaut's debts, while he presided over the most brilliant of Provençal courts. He died in 1173, at the age of only 29, and Orange passed to the Counts of Baux. In the 1300s it was a thriving place, with a municipal charter and even a university. In 1530, the city became the property of the German House of Nassau, just in time for the Reformation and the most unusual page of the city's history, an odd chance that would let Orange lend its colour to the Dutch, the Northern Irish, the Orange Free State and Orange, New Jersey. The Nassaus declared for Protestantism, and Orange rapidly became the dissenters' chief stronghold in Provence, a home for thousands of refugees and a thorn in the side of arch-Catholic Avignon, just to the south. Soon after, William of Nassau—William of Orange—became the first *stadhouder* of the United Provinces and led the fight for Dutch independence. Orange held fast through all the troubles of the Wars of Religion, and came out of it a Dutch possession, giving its name to the Netherlands' present-day royal family.

Maurice of Nassau, in the early 1600s, did Orange a bad turn by destroying most of its ancient ruins, using their stone for the new wall he was building against the French. It didn't keep them out for long. In 1672, during one of his frequent wars against the Dutch, Louis XIV seized the city and demolished its wall and castle. French rule, particularly after the revocation of the Edict of Nantes (*see* p.39), was a disaster; Orange lost many of its best citizens. The city has never really recovered, but it earns a fair living today from industry, and from the army and air-force bases that make it one of the most important military centres in France. Electing a National Front mayor hasn't helped it, either.

Getting Around

By train: The train station on Ave Frédéric Mistral has direct connections to Paris, Avignon, Arles, Marseille, Nice and Cannes.

By bus: Buses depart from Cours Portoules, ✆ 04 90 34 15 59, several times a day for Carpentras, Vaison-la-Romaine, Avignon and three times daily for Séguret.

Bike hire: Hire a bike at **Cycles Lurion**, 48 Cours Aristide Briand, ✆ 04 90 34 08 77. Closed Sunday and Monday.

Tourist Information

5 Cours Aristide Briand, ✆ 04 90 34 70 88, ✉ 04 90 34 99 62; also 15 Rue de la République, ✆ 04 90 34 44 44.

market days

Orange: Thursday mornings at Cours Aristide Briand.

The Best-preserved Theatre of Antiquity

Open daily 9–6.30 in summer, 9.30–12 and 1.30–5 in winter, guided tours July and Aug only; adm; ticket also valid for Municipal Museum; ✆ 04 90 51 17 60.

The architects of the **Théâtre Antique** might be distressed to hear it, but these days the most impressive part of this huge structure is its back wall. 'The best wall in my kingdom,' Louis XIV is said to have called it. If the old prints in the municipal museum are accurate, this rugged, elegant sandstone cliff facing Place des Frères-Mounet was originally adorned with low, temple-like façades. In its present state, it resembles a typical Florentine Renaissance palace, without the windows. The classically minded architects of the 1400s all travelled in Provence, and perhaps this stately relic of Rome at its best had a hidden influence that would have made its architects proud.

Built in the early 1st century AD, the theatre is a testimony to the culture and wealth of Arausio. Like the Colosseum in Rome, it even had a massive awning (*velum*), a contraption of canvas and beams that could be raised to cover most of the 9000 spectators. All over the Mediterranean, theatres fell into disuse in the cultural degradation of the late empire. This one was probably already abandoned when it burned in the 4th or 5th century. In the Middle Ages other buildings grew up over the ruins; old prints show the semicircular tiers of seats (*cavea*) half-filled in and covered with ramshackle houses. The site is typical for a Roman theatre, backed into the hill of St-Eutrope where the banks of seats could be built on the slope. These have been almost completely restored. Since 1869, Orange has used the theatre for a summer festival called *Les Chorégies*. Mistral and the Félibres (*see* pp.55–6) were active in its early years, when Greek and Roman plays were often on the bill; today contemporary drama and opera are more common.

Unlike Greek theatres, which always opened to a grand view behind the stage, those of the Romans featured large stage buildings, serious architectural compositions of columns, arches and sculptured friezes. This is what the great exterior wall is supporting; Orange's stage building (35m high) is one of two complete specimens that remain to us (the other is at Aspendos, in Turkey), though the fragments of its decoration are mostly in the municipal museum across the street. A statue of Augustus remains, in the centre, over an inscription honouring the people of Arausio and welcoming them to the show. Outside the theatre, foundations of a temple have been excavated, along with a semicircular ruin that may have been a nymphaeum, or a gymnasium.

The Musée Municipal

Open daily 9–7 in summer, 9–12 and 1.30–5.30 in winter; adm; ticket also valid for the Roman theatre.

Save some time for this bulging curiosity shop, directly opposite the theatre on Place des Frères-Mounet; it is one of the most fascinating town museums in Provence. As expected, the main rooms are given over to Roman art, including an exceptional frieze of satyrs and amazons from the theatre. The *plan cadastral* (land survey) is unique: a stone tablet engraved with property records for the broad Roman grid of farmland between Orange and Montélimar. The first pieces of it were discovered in 1856, though no one guessed what they were until the rest turned up, between 1927 and 1954; since then they have been a great aid to scholars in filling in some of the everyday details of Roman life and law.

Climbing the stairs into the upper levels of the museum, you'll pass rooms of Dutch portraits and relics of Nassau rule, and a collection of works by the Welsh impressionist Frank Brangwyn (who was, in fact, born in Bruges). The most unexpected exhibit is the **Salle des Wetters**, a remarkable relic of the Industrial Revolution in France. The Wetters were a family of mid 18th-century industrialists who produced *indiennes*, printed cotton cloth much in demand at the time. They commissioned an artist named G. M. Rossetti to paint a record of their business; this he did (1764) in incredible detail, on five huge, colourful, naïve canvases showing every aspect of the making of *indiennes*.

Old Orange and the Triumphal Arch

Touring old Orange does not handsomely reward the visitor; walk up the **Hill of St-Eutrope** for a view over the town and a look at the foundations of the castle destroyed by the French. In the city centre, there is only an utterly pathetic cathedral, begun in 529 over a Temple of Diana and rebuilt to death between 1561 and 1809. One thing Orange does have is original street names—sometimes unintentionally hilarious ones, like the *Impasse de Parlement*.

Rue Victor-Hugo, roughly following the route of the ancient Roman main street, or *cardo major*, is the axis that leads to Orange's other Roman attraction. The **Triumphal Arch**, built

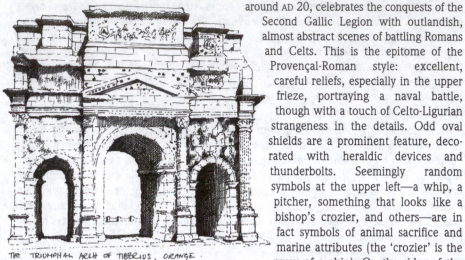

THE TRIUMPHAL ARCH OF TIBERIUS, ORANGE.

around AD 20, celebrates the conquests of the Second Gallic Legion with outlandish, almost abstract scenes of battling Romans and Celts. This is the epitome of the Provençal-Roman style: excellent, careful reliefs, especially in the upper frieze, portraying a naval battle, though with a touch of Celto-Ligurian strangeness in the details. Odd oval shields are a prominent feature, decorated with heraldic devices and thunderbolts. Seemingly random symbols at the upper left—a whip, a pitcher, something that looks like a bishop's crozier, and others—are in fact symbols of animal sacrifice and marine attributes (the 'crozier' is the prow of a ship). On the sides of the arch are heaps of arms—'triumphs'—that were to influence the militaristic art fostered by rulers such as Emperor Charles V in the Renaissance. A little over a half-century before this arch was built, Orange was still Rome's wild frontier, and art such as this evokes it vividly. Note the standards the legionaries are carrying: not the expected Roman eagle, but a boar.

When frontier days returned to Orange, in the Middle Ages, the arch was expanded into a castle by Raymond of Baux. It is said that Raymond arranged it so that the battle reliefs would be a wall of his dining hall; we have his arrogance to thank for their relatively good state of preservation.

Orange ✉ 84100   *Where to Stay and Eating Out*

The best bet in the centre of Orange is the ★★★**Arène**, Place de Langes, ℂ 04 90 11 40 40, ✆ 04 90 11 40 45: pleasant, with a good restaurant, on a quiet square where you can't hear the lorries. *Closed Nov–mid-Dec.* There are a number of decent budget choices: the ★★**St-Florent**, 4 Rue du Mazeau, ℂ 04 90 34 18 53, ✆ 04 90 51 17 25; ★★**Acigaloun**, near the theatre at 4 Rue Caristie, ℂ 04 90 34 10 07, ✆ 04 90 34 89 76, all rooms with bath and TV.

For lunch after looking over Orange's theatre, try one of the restaurants on Rue du Pont Neuf, or Place Sylvian where the pretty **Le Yaca**, ℂ 04 90 34 70 03, has appetizing menus (*from 75F to 125F). Closed Tues eve and Wed.* **Le Pigraillet**, ℂ 04 90 34 44 25, on Colline St-Eutrope, a wooded park overlooking the Rhône, is an unforgettable place to spend a warm summer's night: clients may use the swimming pool before eating for a luxurious 155F. *Closed Sun eve and Mon.*

Around Orange: Sérignan-du-Comtat and the 'Virgil of Insects'

Eight km northeast of Orange on the D976 will allow you to pay your respects to the great entomologist, botanist, scientist, and poet Jean-Henri Fabre (1823–1915). Although born into poverty, the largely self-taught Fabre qualified as a *lycée* teacher of sciences in Avignon, only to be fired in 1870 for explicitly describing the sex life of flowers to a night class of spinsters. Left without means, he borrowed money from his friend John Stuart Mill and settled in Orange for nine years, cranking out books on popular science on the average of one every four months—he would produce over a hundred in his life. He made enough in royalties to pay back his debts and in 1879 to buy an abandoned property in Sérignan that he called **L'Harmas**, the 'fallow land', ✆ 04 90 70 00 44 (*generally open daily except Tues 9–11.30 and 2–6, 2–4 winter, but ring ahead to make sure*). Fabre walled in the garden and planted a thousand species of flower and herb, letting them run wild to create the perfect environment for his true passion: observing insects. Over the years he wrote ten volumes of *Souvenirs entomologiques*, works of such beauty that he was twice nominated for the Nobel Prize (in literature).

L'Harmas was purchased by the state in 1922, and has been left as it was during Fabre's life: you can see his curious apparatus for observing insects, his collections of fossils, shells, rocks, insects, plants, eggs, coins, bones and letters from Darwin. Most extraordinarily of all is the display of a selection of his 700 watercolours of the fungi of the Vaucluse, so real that you can hardly believe they are only two-dimensional. The village has erected a statue to Fabre, magnifying glass in hand, in front of the convex Baroque façade of the parish church, and you can visit his grave in the village cemetery.

Serignac-du-Comtat ✉ *84830*   ***Where to Stay and Eating Out***

On the edge of the village, the grand old ★★★**Hostellerie Le Vieux Château**, Route de Ste-Cécile, ✆ 04 90 70 05 58, 📠 04 90 70 05 62, has only six rooms, but they're all you could ask for in the way of comfort and quiet; there's a pool and restaurant with a 100F lunch menu, 145F in the evening. For a cheaper lunch, try the nearby **Vieille Auberge La Venus**, ✆ 04 90 70 08 48, where 98F will get you a plate of salmon ravioli and duck marinated in Gigondas. *Closed Sat lunch and Sun eve.*

South of Orange: Châteauneuf-du-Pape

> *Je veux vous chanter, mes amis,*
> *Ce vieux Châteauneuf que j'ai mis*
> *Pour vous seuls en bouteille:*
> *Il va faire merveille!*
>
> *Quand de ce vin nous serons gris,*
> *Vénus applaudira nos ris:*
> *Je prends à témoin Lise,*
> *La chose est bien permise!*

(My friends, I want to sing you / Of this old Châteauneuf that I've bottled just for you / It will work miracles! / For when this wine makes us tipsy / Venus will crown our mirth / I take Lise as my witness / No one will mind if I do!)

Pope John XXII's drinking song

Place du Portail, ✆ 04 90 83 71 08, ✉ 04 90 83 50 34.

local wines

Châteauneuf-du-Pape: *see* below.

Tavel: you can visit the two best-known producers in the village by ringing ahead: the de Bez family at the Château d'Aquéria (✆ 04 66 50 04 56), and the prize-winning Domaine de la Mordorée (✆ 04 66 50 00 75).

Lirac: Domaine Duseigneur at St-Laurent-des-Arbres (weekdays, ✆ 04 66 50 02 57); Château St-Roch in Roquemaure (✆ 04 66 82 82 59).

You'll begin to understand why Châteauneuf's wines are so expensive when you pass through the vineyards, between Orange and Avignon. Blink, and you'll miss them. This pocket-sized wine region, tucked between the outskirts of Avignon and Orange, has become one of the most prosperous corners of France; every available square inch is covered with vineyards of a rare beauty, so immaculately precise and luxuriant they resemble bonsai trees.

Châteauneuf-du-Pape, the very attractive village that gives the wine its name, has not resisted the temptation to become the Midi's foremost oenological tourist trap; along the main street, there are few grocers or boutiques, but plenty of wine shops. In places it is hard to see the buildings for the signs, advertising other shops or the winemakers' estates.

Legend has it that one of the first things Clement V did on leaving Rome was to inspect his vineyards north of Avignon. In 1316, his successor John XXII, a celebrated imbiber, did him one better by building a castle here, which the Avignon popes used as a summer residence—a 14th-century Castel Gandolfo. Sacked by the Protestants in the Wars of Religion, it was finally blown up by the retreating Germans in 1944; two crenellated walls still stand. Even if you don't like ruins or crowds, brave the hordes anyway to see the huge plain below you, and the Rhône muscling away to the west on its way south to Avignon. Down on the plain, on the road to Avignon, you can taste chocolate, if you're bored of wine (Chocolaterie Artisanale, ✆ 04 90 83 54 71).

Châteauneuf-du-Pape

An inspiration to both popes and lovers, Châteauneuf-du-Pape's reputation has remained strong through the ages; to safeguard it in 1923 its growers agreed to the guarantees and controls that formed the basis for France's modern *Appellation d'Origine* laws. Several factors combine to give the wine its unique character: the alluvial red clay and pebbly soil, brought down by a Rhône glacier in the Ice Age; the mistral which chases away the clouds and haze, letting the sun hit the grapes like an X-ray gun; and the wide palette of 13 varieties of grapes that each winemaker can choose from: grenache, syrah, cinsault, mourvèdre, terret noir, vaccarèse, counoise, and muscardin for the reds; and clairette, bourboulenc, roussane, picpoul and picardan for the whites, 30 years ago dismissed as mere novelties and today celebrated as some of Provence's top wines—pale blond with greenish highlights and a fresh, floral bouquet.

Because of the complex blends that give Châteauneuf its voluptuous qualities, the grapes are sorted by hand—unique among southern wines. The end result must have the highest alcoholic minimum of any great French wine (12.5%), a level achieved by spacing the vines a good 2m apart to soak up the maximum amount of sun, and from the heat-absorbing pebbles underneath the vines that keep the grapes toasty after dark. Light, soft, and fast to mature, Châteauneuf-du-Pape red can be enjoyed much earlier (often in three years) than its Rhône rivals, and only gets better the longer you can wait.

In its home town, the wine is not exactly hard to find, and even in the cellars it's not cheap. The tourist office distributes a map of the vineyards: perhaps the best known of the many excellent wineries that welcome visitors are **Château Le Nerthe**, with its fascinating ancient cellars, ✆ 04 90 83 70 11, or the vaulted cellars of **Château de la Gardine**, ✆ 04 90 83 73 20. In Bédarrides, the vineyards of **Domaine du Vieux Télégraphe**, 3 Route de Châteauneuf, ✆ 04 90 33 00 31, occupy a rugged promontory topped by a tower once used for optic telegraphic experiments.

The three finest estates are in a class of their own and have such highly individual styles as to be unmistakable even tasted blind. **Clos des Papes**, ✆ 04 90 83 70 13, is run by the highly intelligent and innovative Paul Avril. Avril is alone in employing humidifiers in his cellar to alleviate the drying effects of the mistral wind in particular and the heat in general. As a consequence his wines have the best-defined fruit of the region and are the most elegant. With age Avril's Châteauneuf-du-Pape can taste like expensive claret. The wines of **Château de Beaucastel**, in Courthézon, ✆ 04 90 70 41 00, have been consistently among the top wines of the *appellation*. The most extraordinary source of Châteauneuf-du-Pape and possibly one of the country's most interesting wines is made by Jacques Raynaud at **Château Rayas**. Raynaud's cellar has been described as the most filthy and disorganized in France, and it is only fair to warn you he has a well-deserved reputation for being very inhospitable. One well-known wine merchant, and one not used to anything other than gracious hospitality when visiting growers, turned up on time for a pre-arranged rendezvous to find the place deserted. After nearly an hour's wait, the hapless fellow got back into his car and pulled out of the driveway. Looking back in his rearview mirror he caught a glimpse of Raynaud clambering out of the ditch in which he had been hiding! Raynaud may be difficult to visit but his wines are a must for all keen wine lovers. They are the product of a bygone era—wines of incredible concentration and depth with the capacity to age 20 years or more. Wines such as these are increasingly rare in an age when technology, which has helped to ensure that most wine is well made, also means that too many are sound but mediocre.

Châteauneuf-du-Pape ✉ *84230*   ***Where to Stay and Eating Out***

 It's difficult to imagine how such a sweet old hotel-restaurant could survive in a tourist trap like Châteauneuf-du-Pape, but if you're passing through do stop at **La Mère Germaine**, Place de la Fontaine, ✆ 04 90 83 54 37, ✉ 04 90 83 50 27. There are fine rooms, decorated with antiques (290F) while the restaurant serves tantalizing dishes such as *pistou de morue fraîche* and the succulent *flan de chèvre au caramel de miel épicé*. Menus at 135, 185 and 245F; the adjacent brasserie offers a 69F *plat du jour* and dessert. *Closed Sun eves and Mon, and 10–31 Jan.* For an even more luxurious stay, there's the ★★★★**Château des Fines Roches**, 2km south on the D17, ✆ 04 90 83 70 23, ✉ 04 90 83 78 42, an imposing but entirely fake crenellated castle (19th-century)

with gardens, set among the vineyards south of Châteauneuf; elegant and quite expensive, the kitchen shines in seafood dishes and elaborate desserts (*menus 195F, 270F*). *Closed mid-Dec–Feb.* In a restored 18th-century sheepfold, ★★★**La Sommellerie**, D17 towards Roquemaure, © 04 90 83 50 00, ✆ 04 90 83 51 85, is a peaceful place to sleep, with rooms overlooking the pool or vines; the restaurant, presided over by Pierre Paumel, *Maître cuisinier de France,* serves delicately perfumed Provençal dishes and fish trucked up daily from the coast. Don't miss his reproductions of Van Gogh's paintings—in spun sugar (*menus from 170–360F*). *Closed Sun eve, Mon and Feb.*

The Right Bank of the Rhône, through Rosé-tinted Glasses

Once you cross the Rhône into the Gard, the land takes on a more arid and austere profile, its knobby limestone hills and cliffs softened by crowns of silver olives and the green pin-stripes of vines, especially in the river bend north of Villeneuve along the D976. The landmark here is **Roquemaure**, where Pope Clement V died his peculiar death (*see* p.56) in its ruined castle, although it's not his ghost who haunts it, but that of a lovely but leprous queen who was quarantined in the tower. Roquemaure's church of **St-Jean Baptiste**, opened by Clement V in 1329, has sheltered since 1868 the relics of a certain St Valentine, which it celebrates with a Festival of Lovers in 19th-century costume (Terni, in Umbria, which enshrines the relics of its 3rd bishop Valentine in a basilica and celebrates his feast day on 14 February would be surprised to learn this). The church also houses a superb organ of 1680, built for the Cordeliers in Avignon and transferred here in 1800.

The D976 continues west to the charming little village of **Tavel**, a place just as haunted—by wine fiends slaking their thirst on the pale ruby blood of the earth; **Lirac**, 2km north, is even smaller; a pretty kilometre's walk to the west of the village leads to the **Sainte-Baume**, a cave holy since time immemorable, where a statue of the Virgin was discovered in 1647; a hermitage was built on the outside of the cave chapel. North, little **St-Laurent des Arbres** was owned by the medieval bishops of Avignon, and has a fortified Romanesque church built in 1150, a tower, and a castle keep.

Where to Stay and Eat

Roquemaure ✉ 30150

Large gardens, swimming pool, and old-fashioned rooms combine to make a restful stay in the 18th-century ★★★**Château de Cubières**, Route d'Avignon, © 04 66 82 64 28, ✆ 04 66 90 21 20; the annexe has modern, but equally stylish rooms. The restaraunt, independent of the hotel, is excellent, serving classics from the South and the rest of France, including tasty roast pigeon with figs and prunes (*menus from 165F*). *Closed Sun eve, Mon and Mar*). In nearby **Sauveterre**, the 18th-century ★★★**Hostellerie de Varenne**, © 04 66 82 59 45, ✆ 04 66 82 84 83, is set in a beautiful park with enormous trees (*rooms vary from 360–700F*); the chef serves seasonal specialities, with plenty of fish on the menu, with helpful wine suggestions from the chef (*from 160F*). *Closed Wed.* Roquemaure's ★★**Clement V**, Route de Nîmes, © 04 66 82 67 58, ✆ 04 66 82 84 66, is an excellent, moderately priced alternative, with a pool and small gym.

Tavel ✉ 30126

The ★★★**Auberge du Tavel**, Voie Romaine, ✆ 04 66 50 03 41, 📠 04 66 50 24 44, offers charming, quiet, well equipped rooms, and has a good restaurant (*menus from 125F*). *Closed Sun eve, Mon and Feb.* In the centre, the **Hostellerie du Seigneur**, in Place Seigneur, ✆ 04 66 50 04 26, has seven pleasant rooms in an old house, covered with creeper (*from 180F*); half *pension* in season, but the restaurant isn't bad at all (*menus at 98 and 140F*). In **St-Laurent-des-Arbres**, dine at **La Louisia**, on the N580, ✆ 04 66 50 20 60, where the young chef prepares fresh and imaginative meals (*menus from 115F*). *Closed Sun eve, Mon and first half of Sept.*

Avignon

Avignon has known more passions and art and power than any town in Provence, a mixture of excitement whipped to a frenzy by the mistral. But even the master of winds has never caused as much trouble as the papal court, a vortex of mischief that ruled Avignon for centuries, trailing violence, corruption and debauchery in its wake. 'In Paris one quarrels, in Avignon one kills,' wrote Hugo. In Avignon Petrarch's platonic, courtly love for Laura was an aberration. 'Blood is hot there,' wrote an anonymous writer in the 1600s, 'And the most serious occupation in the land is the search for pleasure…even most of the husbands are accommodating in love, and allow their wives the same freedoms they enjoy themselves.'

Avignon still has a twinkle in its eye; it is alive, ebullient, and has been one of France's most innovative cities ever since the Italian Renaissance filtered through here to the rest of Europe. As the cultural and publishing centre of the south, it rocked the cradle of the Félibrige, the Provençal literary movement (*see* p.55) and since the war has been the stage for Europe's most exciting theatre festival. Charming it's not, but as an old Provençal proverb puts it: *Quau se lèvo d'Avignoun, se lèvo de la resoun* or 'He who takes leave of Avignon takes leave of his senses.'

History

Rome, *anno domini* 1303. Anarchy reigns: popular riots, regular visits from foreign armies, and clans waging medieval gang war in the streets, turning the tombs of the Caesars into urban fortresses. The papacy, though in the thick of it all, usually kept the papal person himself in places like Viterbo and Anagni for safety's sake—as it had the arrogant intriguer Boniface VIII, now fresh in his grave. Boniface's arch-enemy, Philip the Fair of France, has just bribed the conclave to elect a Frenchman, Clement V. Philip also suggested that the new pope flee the inferno of Rome for the safer havens of the Comtat Venaissin in Provence—and Clement didn't have to be asked twice.

The Church had picked up this piece of Provence real estate as its spoils after the Albigensian Crusade. Isolated within it was the little city-republic of Avignon, belonging to the Angevin Counts of Provence—old papal allies, who welcomed their illustrious visitor. Clement V always intended to return to Rome, but when he died the French cardinals elected a former archbishop of Avignon, John XXII (1316–34), who moved the Curia into his old episcopal palace and greatly enriched the papacy (through alchemy, it was rumoured: *see* p.56). Although he enlarged the palace with the proceeds, it still wasn't roomy enough for his successor, Benedict XII (1334–42), who replaced it with another palace, or for Clement VI (1342–52), who added another. It seemed that the popes meant to stay forever, especially after 1348 when Clement purchased Avignon outright from the young Angevin Countess of

Provence, Jeanne I of Naples, for the sale price of 80,000 florins and an absolution for her possible involvement in the suspicious strangulation of her husband.

Meanwhile all the profits that the 14th-century papal machine generated—from tithes and the sale of indulgences, pardons, offices, and the visits of pilgrims—went to Avignon instead of Rome. Overcrowding, debauchery, dirt, luxury, plague, blackmail, and crime came with the deal—troubles exasperated by papal tolerance that admitted outcasts from everywhere else into Avignon, as long as they could pay. Such refugees included not only common criminals but also Jews and, during the Schism, heretics. The Italians, mortified at losing their cash cow during this 'Babylonian captivity', expressed their self-righteous indignation through the long-time Avignon resident Petrarch: 'Avignon is the hell of living people, the thoroughfare of vice, the sewers of the earth... Prostitutes swarm on the papal beds.' Yet these same popes summoned the best *trecento* artists from Italy, especially from Siena, who perfected in Avignon the elegant, courtly, fairy-tale style of painting known as International Gothic. And when he wasn't being outraged, Petrarch wrote incomparable love sonnets to his beloved Laura, a mysterious figure believed to have been an ancestress of the Marquis de Sade.

In 1377, Avignon's population rose to 30,000 souls, a third of them under religious orders. In that year St Catherine of Siena convinced the seventh Avignon pope, Gregory XI, to return to Rome. The pope came, he saw, he sickened, but before he could pack his bags to return to Avignon, he died. The Roman mob seized their chance, and physically forced the cardinals to elect an Italian pope who would re-establish the papacy in Rome. When the French cardinals escaped the Romans' clutches, they sparked off the Great Schism by electing a French anti-pope, Clement VII, and went back to Avignon. A Church council, held in Pisa 30 years later to resolve the conflict, only ended in the election of yet a third pope. In 1403 the French went over to the Rome faction and sent in an army to persuade Avignon's second anti-pope, Benedict XIII, to leave for his native Catalunya—where he spent the rest of his life bitterly raining anathemas and excommunications on all and sundry.

When the Church finally settled on one pope, Avignon and the Comtat Venaissin settled in for three and a half centuries of relaxed rule by cardinal legates, under whom the debauchery and violence continued, although on a more modest level. The party really ended when the Comtat Venaissin was incorporated into France during the Revolution in a blood rite of atrocities and the destruction of centuries of art and architecture.

But even as part of France, Avignon has maintained its lively international character. Publishers who first set up shop with the popes stayed on under the cardinal legates, beyond the bounds of French censorship (there were 20 in town before the Revolution); in the 1850s they took on a new life publishing the works of the Félibrige. In 1946, actor Jean Vilar founded the Avignon Festival of Theatre and Film, the liveliest and most popular event on the entire Provençal calendar.

Getting Around

By air: Avignon's airport is at Caumont, ✆ 04 90 81 51 15.

By train: The train station is outside the Porte de la République, central bookings on ✆ 08 36 35 35 35; Avignon is on the Paris–Marseille TGV line, and has frequent links to Arles, Montpellier, Nîmes, Orange, Toulon and Carcassonne.

By bus: The bus station is also outside the Porte de la République, next to the train station (Blvd St-Roch, ✆ 04 90 82 07 35): plenty of daily buses to Carpentras,

Cavaillon St-Rémy and Orange, four to Arles, five to Nîmes, one early morning run to Nice, Aix and Cannes, along with six others to Aix, three for Marseille and Salon, six for Fontaine-de-Vaucluse, and some services to the Pont du Gard, Uzès, Châteaurenard, Châteauneuf-du-Pape and Tarascon. For Villeneuve-lez-Avignon, take city bus no.11 from in front of the post office (buy tickets on board).

By boat: Travellers of yore always approached Avignon by boat, a thrill still possible on the **tourist excursion boat** *Le Cygne* from Beaucaire, ℓ 04 66 59 35 62, or with a **lunch or dinner cruise** on *Le Miréio*, based at Allées de l'Oulle, ℓ 04 90 85 62 25, ⦿ 04 90 85 61 14; the food is delicious and an afternoon's exploration of Arles is included in the price. Or spend a week on the Rhône and Saône on the *Princesse de Provence* (April–Nov), ℓ 04 78 39 13 06. In July and August, the **Bateau-Bus** makes regular trips between Avignon and Villeneuve, starting from the Allées de l'Oulle. There are several other cruise boats; the tourist office has complete information.

Car and bike hire: Inexpensive car hire firms are **VEO**, 51 Ave Pierre Sémard, ℓ 04 90 87 53 43, and **Eurorent**, 3 Ave Saint Ruf, ℓ 04 90 86 06 61. Bike hire shops in Avignon are: **Aymard**, 80 Rue Guillaume Puy, ℓ 04 90 86 32 49; **Richard Masson**, Place Pie, ℓ 04 90 82 32 19; and **Transhumance** (for all-terrain and mountain bikes), located in the main tourist office (summer only), ℓ 04 90 95 57 81.

Tourist Information

The helpful office is at 41 Cours Jean Jaurès, ℓ 04 90 82 65 11, ⦿ 04 90 82 95 03 (open Mon–Sat, daily during the Festival). There is also an office at the Pont St-Bénézet (the famous medieval bridge), open Tues–Sun in winter, daily the rest of the year (same hours as above).

The **post office** is on Cours Président-Kennedy, just inside the Porte de la République near the rail station.

market days

 Covered market Tues–Sun at Les Halles in Place Pie; bric-a-brac on Sat in Place Crillon; flower market Sat morning and flea-market Sun morning in Place des Carmes; travelling market Sat and Sun morning at Rempart St-Michel.

The Famous Half-Bridge

From the Rhône Avignon is a brave two-tiered sight: in front rise the sheer cliffs of the **Rocher des Doms**, inhabited since Neolithic times, and behind it, the sheer man-made cliffs of the Palais des Papes, the same colour as the rock, and almost as haphazard a pile. The ensemble includes the **walls** that the popes wrapped around Avignon: bijou, toothsome garden walls ever since Viollet-le-Duc re-crenellated them and filled in the moat in 1860.

From the walls, four arches of a bridge leapfrog into the Rhône, sidle up to a waterbound two-storey Romanesque chapel (the lower half is dedicated to St Nicholas, patron of the Rhône boatmen), and then stop abruptly mid-river, long before reaching Villeneuve-lez-Avignon on the distant bank. This is the famous **Pont St-Bénézet**, or simply the Pont d'Avignon, begun in 1185 (*open daily April–Sept 9–6.30, Mar and Oct, 9–1 and 2–5; Nov–Feb daily exc Mon, 9–1, 2–5; adm; ℓ 04 90 85 60 16*). It was built at a time when all bridges were the work of either devils or saints; in this case a shepherd boy named Bénézet, obeying the mandates of heaven, single-handedly laid the huge foundation stones. Originally 22 arches and half a mile

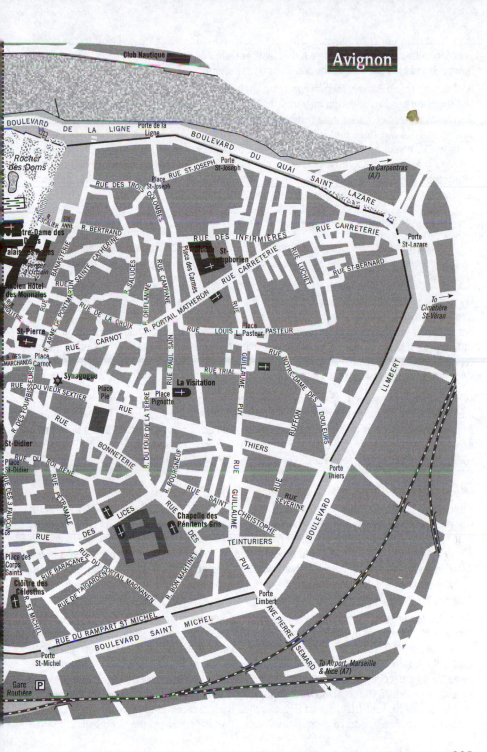

Avignon

Club Nautique

BOULEVARD DE LA LIGNE
Porte de la Ligne

BOULEVARD DU QUAI SAINT LAZARE

Rocher des Doms

Porte St-Joseph

To Carpentras (A7)

Place St-Joseph
RUE ST-JOSEPH

RUE DES TROIS COLOMBES

RUE CARRETERIE

Porte St-Lazare

ESCALIER ANNE
STE

otre-Dame des
Doms
alais des Papes

R. BERTRAND

RUE DES INFIRMIERES

St-
phorien

RUE CARRETERIE

RUE LUCHET

RUE ST-BERNARD

Verger
a Urbain

RUE BANASTERIE

Place des Carmes

ncien Hôtel
des Montiales

RUE DE PONTMARTIN

RUE SAINTE CATHERINE

R. SALUCES

RUE CAMPANE

R. ORIFLAMME

RUE

To Cimetière St-Véran

RUGIERE

R. ARME

RUE DE LA CROIX

St-Pierre

RUE CARNOT

R. PORTAIL MATHERON

RUE LOUIS
Place
Pasteur

PASTEUR

R. DES
MARCHANDS

Place
Carnot

RUE PAUL SAIN

RUE TRIAL

RUE GUILLAUME

RUE NOTRE-DAME DES 7 DOULEURS

Synagogue

DU VIEUX SEXTIER

R. DES FOURBISSEURS

Place
Pie

RUE

RUE DUFOUR DE LA TERRE

La Visitation
Place
Pignotte

RUE PUY

BUFFON

LIMBERT

St-Didier

RUE DU ROI RENE

Place
St-Didier

RUE

BONNETERIE

THIERS

Porte
Thiers

RUE DES 3 FAUCONS

RUE PETRAMALE

RUE BOURGNEUF

RUE SAINT

RUE GUILLAUME

RUE SEVERINE

RUE

BOULEVARD

DES

LICES

Chapelle des
Pénitents Gris

RUE CHRISTOPHE

Place des
Corps
Saints

RUE BARACANE

RUE DU PORTAIL MAGNANEN

RUE DES

TEINTURIERS

RUE PUY

Cloître des
Célestins

RUE DE L'AGARDEN

R. BON MARTINET

Porte
Limbert

AVE PIERRE

R. ST MICHEL

RUE DU RAMPART ST MICHEL

BOULEVARD SAINT MICHEL

SEMARD

To Airport, Marseille
& Nice (A7)

Porte
St-Michel

Gare
Routière

long, the bridge enriched Avignon with its tolls: its presence was a major factor in the popes' decision to live here. In 1660 the Avignonais got tired of the constant repairs it demanded, however, and abandoned it to the monsters of the Rhône.

And did they ever '*danse, tout en rond*' on their bridge, as the nursery song would have it? No, the historians say, although they may well have danced *under* it on the mid-river **Ile de la Barthelasse**, formerly a hunting reserve and headquarters for many of Avignon's prostitutes and thieves. It was here that in later years the Avignonais came for Sunday picnics. The Félibres liked to bring pretty 'Félibresses' here to recite poetry. In the summer, people still come to cool off in its Olympic-size pool. Next to the bridge, a new exhibition hall boasts a multivision show in seven languages called the **Musée en Images**, relating the history of Avignon (*daily 9–7; Oct through Feb, daily exc Mon 9–5; adm*).

The Palais des Papes

> *Open daily April–Oct 9–7, Sept till 8; Nov–Mar 9–12.45 and 2–6; adm. Last ticket 45mins before closing time. Optional guided tours in English at 3pm; © 04 90 27 50 71.*

For a curious sensation, park directly under the popes' palace and take the lift up to the traffic-free **Place du Palais**. Once crowded with houses, the square was cleared by anti-pope Benedict XIII to emphasize the message of the Palace's vertical, impregnable walls: 'you would think it was an Asiatic tyrant's citadel rather than the abode of the vicar of the God of peace,' wrote Mérimée. But the life of a 14th-century pope justified paranoia. The entrance is up the steps, in the centre of Clement VI's façade.

What is harder to realize is that the life of a 14th-century pope and his cardinals, courtiers, mistresses and toadies, was also extremely luxurious. The palace was spared destruction in the Revolution only to end up serving as a prison and a barracks, and until 1920 its bored residents amused themselves by chipping off frescoes to sell to tourists, so that on most of the walls the only remaining decoration is an extraordinary variety of masons' marks.

Old Palace: Ground Floor

After crossing the **Cour d'Honneur**, the great courtyard dividing Benedict XII's stern Cistercian Palais Vieux (1334–42) and Clement VI's flamboyant Palais Neuf (1342–52), the tour begins in the **Jesus Hall**, so called for its decorative monograms of Christ. Once used to house the pope's treasure and account books, it now contains a hoard of maps, views of old Avignon and curios like a pair of 17th-century bell-ringing figures, or *Jacquemarts*. The most valuable loot would be stored behind walls 10ft thick in the windowless bowels of the **Angels' Tower**, its ceiling supported by a single stone pillar like an enormous palm tree.

Next, the **Consistory**, where the cardinals met and received ambassadors; as its lavish frescoes and ceiling burned in 1413, it now displays 19th-century portraits of Avignon's popes and Simone Martini's fresco of the *Virgin of Humility*, detached from the cathedral porch in 1960. Under the fresco, the restorers found Martini's *sinopia*, or initial line sketch, etched in the stone. As an artist could only paint a small patch of fresh, wet plaster a day, such *sinopie* were essential to maintain the composition, and these, as is often the case in Italy, give a clearer idea of the painter's intent than the damaged fresco itself. Traces of *sinopie* in situ are in the **Chapelle St-Jean**, dedicated to both Johns, the Baptist and the Evangelist. Matteo

Giovannetti of Viterbo, a *trecento* charmer who left the bulk of his work in Avignon, did the frescoes for Clement VI; saints float overhead in starry blue landscapes (recall that at the time ultramarine blue paint was even more expensive than gold). On one wall, John's head is blissfully served to Herod at table, as if in a restaurant.

Old Palace: First Floor

The tour continues to the first floor and the banqueting hall, or **Grand Tinel**, hung with 18th-century Gobelin tapestries. Although big enough for a football pitch, the Grand Tinel was too small to hold all the cardinal-electors who would gather in a conclave ten days after a pope's death. Masons were brought in to accommodate them: the arches on the far end were knocked down to give the cardinals more room to manoeuvre (in both senses of the word), while the doors and windows were bricked up to keep them from bringing in more food and endlessly prolonging the conclave. The trick always worked, for the appetites of the 14th-century Curia were Pantagruelian—the adjacent **Upper Kitchen** boasts a pyramidal chimney that could easily handle a roast elephant, or the menu of Clement VI's coronation feast: 1023 sheep, 118 cattle, 101 calves, 914 kids, 60 pigs, 10,471 hens, 1446 geese, 300 pike, topped off by 46,856 cheeses and 50,000 tarts, all consumed by just 3000 guests—some 16 tarts per person, with a few thousand left over for the pope's midnight snack. Off the Grand Tinel, more delightful frescoes by Matteo Giovannetti decorate the **Chapelle St-Martial**, celebrating the French saint who came from the same Limousin village as Benedict XII.

The New Palace

The tour continues from the Grand Tinel to the pope's **Anti-chamber**, where he would hold private audiences, and continues to the **Pope's Bedroom** in the Tower of Angels, a room covered with murals of spiralling foliage, birds, and birdcages. It leads directly into the New Palace and the most delightful room in the entire palace, the **Chambre du Cerf**, Clement VI's study, where he would come 'to seek the freedom of forgetting he was pope'. In 1343 he had Matteo Giovannetti (probably) lead a group of French painters in depicting outdoor scenes of hunting, fishing, and peach-picking that not only quickened the papal gastric juices, but expressed what was then a revolutionary new interest in the natural world, where flowers and foliage were drawn from observation rather than copying a 'source'.

The arrows direct you next to the **Sacristy**, crowded with statues of kings, queens, and bishops escaped from Gargantua's chessboard, followed by Clement VI's **Great Chapel**, longer even than the Grand Tinel and just as empty, though the altar has recently been reconstructed. The **Robing Room** off the chapel contains casts of the Avignon popes' tombs. Revolutionaries bashed most of the figures that once adorned the elaborate **chapel gate**; through the bay window in front of this, the pope would bless and give indulgences to pilgrims. A grand stair leads down to the flamboyant **Great Audience Hall**, where a band of Matteo Giovannetti's *Prophets* remain intact, along with outline sketches of a *Crucifixion* that would have been splendid if it had ever been completed.

Around the Palace: Notre-Dame-des-Doms

Before spray paint and tagging, the posterity-minded had to record their passing with family emblems. None did it better than the family of the Borghese pope, Paul V; his nephew, legate in Avignon, produced the striking 1619 **Hôtel des Monnaies**, or mint, just across from the Palais des Papes, where reliefs of the Borghese dragon and eagle prance in garlands of fruit salad. To the left of the palace is Avignon's cathedral, **Notre-Dame-des-Doms**, built in 1150, its landmark square bell tower ridiculously dwarfed by a massive gilt statue of the Virgin added in 1859, an unsuccessful attempt to make the church stand out next to the overwhelming papal pile. The interior has been fuzzily Baroqued, but it's worth focusing on the good bits: the dome at the crossing, with an octagonal drum pierced with light, the masterpiece of this typically Provençal conceit; the 11th- or 12th-century marble bishop's chair in the choir; and in a chapel next to the sacristy, now the **Trésor** (*adm*), the flamboyant *Tomb of John XXII* (d. 1334) by English sculptor Hugh Wilfred, mutilated in the Revolution, and restored in the 19th century with a spare effigy of a bishop on top to replace the smashed pope. Next to the cathedral, ramps lead up to the oasis of the **Rocher-des-Doms**, now a garden enjoying panoramic views from the Rhône below to Mount Ventoux rising on the right.

Musée du Petit Palais

Open 9.30–12 and 2–6, closed Tues; July and Aug, 10–6; adm; © 04 90 86 44 58.

Overlooking the Rhône at the end of the Place du Palais stands the **Petit Palais**, built in 1318 and modified in 1474 to suit the tastes of Cardinal Legate Giuliano della Rovere—one day to become Michelangelo's patron and nemesis, as Pope Julius II. In 1958, the Petit Palais became a museum to hold all the medieval works remaining in Avignon.

Although the scale of the Petit Palais can be daunting, it contains rare treats from the dawn of the Renaissance by artists hailing for the most part from Siena or Florence. But Avignon gets its say as well: the sculptures and pretty courtly frescoes from the 12th to the 14th century in the first two rooms demonstrate the city's role in creating and diffusing the late International Gothic style. The third room contains some fascinating fragments of the 35ft, 8-storey **Tomb of Cardinal Jean de Lagrange** (1389), which stood in Avignon's church of St-Martial before the Revolution. One bit that survived was the *transi*, or relief of the decomposing corpse that occupied the lowest level of the tomb and was carved with morbid anatomical exactitude. Such *mementi mori* would soon become popular in northern France, always used to contrast the handsome effigy of the deceased while alive. The mouldering Cardinal Lagrange is one of the earliest, perhaps the prototype of the genre.

The next six rooms glow with the gold backgrounds (the better to show up in dim churches) of 14th- and early 15th-century Italian painting. Nearly all depict the Virgin and Child, a reflection of the cult of Mariolatry and chivalric ideals of womanhood that began where the troubadours left off. Although the subject matter is repetitive, it makes it easy to trace the medieval revolution in art and seeing, back in the good old days when art was content merely to imitate nature and not try to outdo her. The iconic, Byzantine flatness of the earliest paintings (see especially Paolo Veneziano's *Virgin* (1340), remarkably never restored in its 650 years) begins to give way to a more natural depiction of space, composition and human character after the innovations of Giotto in Italy (see especially Taddeo Gaddi, Pseudo Jacopino di Francesco, Lorenzo Monaco, and Gherardo Starnina). Meanwhile, Sienese artists, following the lead of the great Duccio di Buoninsegna, took up a more elegant, stylized line and richer colours (see Simone Martini and the many works by Taddeo di Bartolo).

The taste of Avignon's popes for Sienese art made the latter the strongest influence in the International Gothic style forged at the papal court (room 8), a style which the Sienese kept at long after the Florentines had moved on to new things—see Giovanni di Paolo's *Nativity* (1470), or Pietro di Domenico da Montepulciano's kinky *Vierge de Miséricorde* (1420), a delicate portrayal of a congregation sheltered under the Virgin's mantle, while a band of flagellants whip themselves in robes with custom-cut backs. Bridal chests (*cassoni*) were often used to illustrate cautionary tales for women: in room 9, see Domenico de Michelino's *cassone* panels of 1450 on the story of Suzanna and the Elders.

Renaissance Gems, Sacred and Profane

Beyond the *salon de repos* hangs the museum's best-known work, Botticelli's *Virgin and Child*, a tender, lyrical painting of his youth inspired by his (and Leonardo da Vinci's) master, Verrocchio. The next few rooms offer nothing as striking until room 15 and its four delightful narrative panels from bridal chests (*c.* 1510) by the Maestro dei Cassoni Campana. This unknown master's meticulous, miniaturist style is as rare as the subject of his cautionary tale: *The Minotaur*, beginning with Queen Pasiphae of Crete's love for a white bull, resulting in the birth of the Minotaur. The third panel shows Ariadne, her ball of twine, and Theseus slaying the Minotaur in an exquisite circular labyrinth.

The sacred equivalent of the *cassoni* is in room 16b: the *Sacra Conversazione* by Venetian Vittore Carpaccio, lyrical master of charm, colour and incidental detail. Carpaccio has added a landscape dominated by a natural rock bridge, where episodes from the lives of SS. Jerome, Augustine and Paul the Hermit take place.

Lastly, rooms 17–19 are devoted to works by French artists in Avignon, who after 1440 formed one of the most important schools of French Renaissance art. Influenced by the realism of Flemish oil painting (introduced to Avignon by Benedict XIII) and the almost abstract, decorative lines of the Italians, it concentrates on strong, simple images, as in the altarpiece *Virgin and Child between two Saints* (1450), by the school's greatest master, Enguerrand Quarton, with a pair of luminous shutters with SS. Michael and Catherine on the reverse by Jossé Lieferinxe.

Place de l'Horloge and Quartier des Fusteries

Just below the Place du Palais, an antique carousel spins gaily in the lively centre of old Avignon: **Place de l'Horloge**, site of the old Roman forum, now full of buskers and holiday layabouts. The timepiece of its name is in the 1363 tower of the Hôtel de Ville; this originally belonged to a Benedictine monastery on the site, but was secularized with a clock and two **jacquemarts** who sound the hours. They aren't the only archaic figures here: many first-time visitors do a double-take when they notice the windows on the east side of the square filled with *trompe-l'œil* paintings of historic personages, who all are linked in some way to the city.

Behind the Hôtel de Ville lies the **Quartier des Fusteries**, thus named for the wood merchants and carpenters, who had their workshops here in the Middle Ages, which were replaced in the 18th century with *hôtels*: in one, the **Maison aux Ballons** (with little iron balloons on the window sills) at 18 Rue St-Etienne, Joseph de Montgolfier discovered the principle of balloon flight in 1782 when he noticed how his shirt, drying by the fire, puffed up and floated in the hot air. From the Quartier des Fusteries, the steep picturesque lanes of the **Quartier de la Balance** wind back up to the Place des Papes.

Off Place de l'Horloge and Rue St-Agricol, Rue du Collège-du-Roure leads to the fine mid 15th-century **Palais du Roure**, ✆ 04 90 80 80 88, marked by a flamboyant gate topped by intertwining mulberry branches in memory of the Taverne de Mûrier that it replaced. Equally flamboyant was the 19th-century descendant of the Florentine family who built it, the Félibre poet Marquis Baroncelli-Javon, who preferred to spend his time as a cowboy in the Camargue and lent this town-house to Mistral as a headquarters for his Provençal-language journal *Aïoli*. It now houses a study centre and exhibits on the language (*free guided tours Tues at 3pm, and by appointment*). Rue St-Agricol is named after the recently restored Gothic church of **St-Agricol** (1326); its treasure is the *Doni Retable*, a rare Provençal work from the Renaissance. At No.19 is the **Librairie Roumanille**, founded in 1855 by the Avignon poet Joseph Roumanille, father of the Félibrige (*see* p.55). The bookshop published the movement's first masterpiece, Mistral's epic *Miréio* (1859) and continues to put out books in Provençal.

Museums: Vouland, Calvet, Requien, Lapidaire and Mont de Piété

At the end of Rue St-Agricol curves Rue Joseph-Vernet, lined with 18th-century *hôtels*, antique shops, pricey restaurants and cafés. The kind of overly ornate, spindly furniture, porce-lains, and knick-knacks that originally embellished these mansions is on display nearby in Rue Victor Hugo's **Musée Louis Vouland**, © *04 90 86 03 79* (*open June–Sept 10–12 and 2–6, otherwise 2–6, closed Sun and Mon*).

More exciting are the contents of the handsome Hôtel de Villeneuve-Martignan, at 65 Rue Joseph-Vernet, first opened to the public as a 'cabinet of curiosities' in the late 1700s by collector Esprit Calvet. Now the **Musée Calvet**, © 04 90 86 33 84 (*open 10–12 and 2–6, closed Tues; adm*), and recently reopened after a long restoration, it offers something for every taste: 6000 pieces of wrought iron, Greek sculpture, 18th-century seascapes by Avignon native Joseph Vernet and paintings of ruins by Hubert Robert and Panini, mummies, a portrait of Diane de Baroncelli (grandmother of the Marquis de Sade), a bust of a boy by Renaissance sculptor Desiderio da Settignano, tapestries, prehistoric statue-steles, dizzy kitsch paintings of nude men, as well as an excellent collection of 19th- and 20th-century paintings by Corot, Guigou, Soutine, Daumier, Dufy, Morisot, Utrillo, Seurat, Toulouse-Lautrec, Vlaminck and Rouault.

Adjacent to the Calvet museum, the **Musée Requien**, © 04 90 14 68 56, is Avignon's fuddy-duddy natural history collection (*open Tues–Sat 9–12 and 2–6*), where a 81lb beaver found in the Sorgue steals the show. At 27 Rue de la République, in the chilly 17th-century chapel of a Jesuit College, are the sculptures of the **Musée Lapidaire**, © 04 90 85 75 38 (*open daily exc Tues, 10–12, 2–6*). It's worth popping in for the 2nd-century BC (or Merovingian) man-eating *Tarasque de Noves*, each hand gripping the head of a Gaul, while an arm dangles from its greedy jaws; or for its statues of Gallic warriors, looking much nattier in their mail than Asterix. There is good Renaissance sculpture as well, but the best is in the nearby church of **St-Didier** (1359), just to the north in Place St-Didier: Francesco Laurana's polychrome **reredos** of Christ bearing the Cross, called *Notre-Dame du Spasme* for the spasm of pain on Mary's face; it was one of the first Renaissance sculptures to reach France, executed for Good King René in 1478. Opposite, in the first chapel on the left, are Florentine frescoes *c.* 1360, uncovered in 1952.

More 14th-century frescoes have recently been restored opposite the church in the **Livrée de Ceccano**, now the town library. Nearby, at 5 Rue Laboureur, the treasures of a serious art collector named Jean Angladon-Dubrujeaud have been opened to the public as Avignon's newest museum, the **Fondation Angladon-Dubrujeaud** (*open Wed–Sun, 1–6pm; adm*). These include Renaissance and Art Deco furniture, bronzes and African art, but mainly a fine assortment of modern painting never before seen: works by Modigliani, Picasso, Manet, Degas and Cézanne, as well as the only Van Gogh on display in Provence, called *Les Wagons de Chemin de Fer*. The **Musée du Mont de Piété**, 6 Rue Saluces, ✆ 04 90 86 53 12 (*open Mon to Fri, 8.30–11.30 and 1.30–5.30*), the oldest pawnbroker's in France, now houses not only the town archives, but the *conditions des soies*, or silk conditioning, once the town's wealth.

The Eastern Quarters

From Place St-Didier, Rue du Roi René is lined with chiselled palaces, one built on the site of the church of Ste-Claire (No. 22) where Petrarch first saw his Laura on Good Friday 1327. ('It was the day when the sun darkened, as God/Himself vanished into death, when I was taken,' he wrote). Laura died, probably of the plague, in 1348, and was buried nearby in the Franciscan **Couvent des Cordeliers**, by the corner of Rue des Lices and Rue des Teinturiers; only the Gothic bell tower survived the fury of the Revolution. In 1533, a humanist from Lyon claimed to have found her tomb in the church, and such was Petrarch's reputation that François I made a special trip to Avignon to see it.

Rue des Teinturiers, the most picturesque street in Avignon, was named after the dyers and textile-makers who powered their machines on water-wheels in the Sorgue, two of which survive. Shaded by ancient plane trees, crossed by little bridges, it is a pleasant place to dawdle over a beer or dinner.

Rue des Teinturiers turns into Rue Bonneterie on its way to Avignon's shopping district and Place Pie, home of the ugly-duckling new **market**, although the produce inside is fit for a swan. Another evocative street, Rue Vieux Sextière, once the site of the Jewish Ghetto, is the address of Avignon's 19th-century synagogue, while just beyond Place Carnot, **St-Pierre**'s flamboyant façade boasts a set of beautifully carved walnut doors (1551). Facing St-Pierre, Avignon's cosiest museum, **Musée Aubanel**, ✆ 04 90 82 95 54 (*private, free visits on request*), is dedicated to printing in Avignon, and to the romantic poet and Félibre Théodore Aubanel, whose family still owns one of Avignon's oldest publishing houses.

From Place St-Pierre, Rue Carnot continues to another charming square, the Place des Carmes, dominated by the 14th-century **St-Symphorien,** or White Friars', Avignon's biggest church, with a pretty cloister refurbished as a Festival venue. Visitors in the last century would continue from here along Rue Carreterie, out of the city gate and down the Lyon road to the **Cimetière St-Véran**, a romantic, shady park where John Stuart Mill and his wife Harriet are buried. Harriet died at the Hôtel d'Europe in 1858, a loss so devastating for the philosopher of utilitarianism that he lived in a house by the cemetery until he himself died in 1873. Another celebrated tomb belongs to Maurille de Sombreuil, who became a heroine during the Revolution when, to save the life of her father, the governor of the Invalides, she drank a goblet of human blood. Contemporaries noted that she always ordered white wine with her meals after that.

Festivals

In 1947 Jean Vilar with his Théâtre National Populaire founded the **Avignon Festival**, with the aim of bringing theatre to the masses. It is now rated among the top international theatre festivals in Europe, and Avignon overflows in July and August with performances by the Théâtre National in the Palais des Papes, and others throughout the city; the cinemas host films from all over the world, and churches are used for concerts (the **Maison Jean Vilar**, 8 Rue de Mons,

© 04 90 86 59 64, is the nerve centre and hosts exhibitions, films, and lectures the rest of the year). For festival bookings and information contact the **Bureau du Festival d'Avignon**, 8 bis Rue de Mons, Avignon 84000, © 04 90 27 66 30. During the festival Avignon's squares and streets overflow with fringe (or 'Off') performers. To receive the Off programme, send a stamped envelope, with 11.50F, to Avignon Public Off., BP5 75521 Paris cedex 11, or call © (1) 48 05 20 97. Otherwise, there seems to be some sort of festivity every month, whether horses are your passion (the *Cheval Passion*, January), Baroque art (April), a Triathlon (May) or of course fireworks on 14 July. The fortnightly broadsheet *Rendez-Vous*, from the tourist office, is an exhaustive map of what exactly's going on.

Shopping

Pâtisseries, especially around Rue Joseph Vernet, sell Avignon's gourmand speciality, *papalines*, made of fine chocolate and a liqueur, *d'Origan du Comtat*, distilled from 60 herbs picked from the slopes of Mont Ventoux, and said to be a sure cure for cholera. You will find all the regional specialities, garlic, olives, honey, pastis, goat's cheese, *fougasse,* and the omnipresent *herbes de Provence*. If you're not going to Aix, don't fail to buy some delicious diamond-shaped almond *calissons d'Aix* here. Also there are essential oils, *santons,* bold Provençal fabrics, local pottery and soaps. Behind the Hôtel de Ville in Place des Puits-de-Boeufs, the **Maison des Pays de Vaucluse**, © 04 90 85 55 24, has a large display of regional products and crafts.

Avignon ✉ *84000*   ***Where to Stay***

 Avignon gets full to the brim in July and August, when it's imperative to book ahead (and when many places raise their rates). Note that there are other choices just across the river in Villeneuve, and a huge number of chain hotels in all price ranges spread around the suburbs and major road entrances. The Avignon area can offer alternative accommodation, with a large number of *gîtes* and rooms in private homes, some on the idyllic Ile de la Barthelasse. For one of these, contact the **Réservation de meubles de tourisme** office, 21 Rue College de la Croix, © 04 90 80 47 17, ● 04 90 80 47 18.

Oldest, and still classically formal with its Louis XV furnishings, the ★★★★**Hôtel d'Europe**, 12 Place Crillon, © 04 90 14 76 76, ● 04 90 85 43 66, was built in the 1500s, and converted to an inn in the late 1700s. Napoleon stayed here, as did the eloping Browning and Barrett. Avignon's newest hotel, ★★★★**Cloître Saint-Louis**, is just within the walls near the station, at 20 Rue du Portail Boquier, © 04 90 27 55 55, ● 04 90 82 24 01. Built in 1589 as part of the Jesuit school of theology, the beautiful cloister is an island of tranquillity. Rooms are austerely modern; meals are served under the portico or by the rooftop swimming pool. ★★ **Mercure Palais des Papes**, 1 Rue Gérard Philipe, © 04 90 82 47 31, ● 04 90 27 91 17, has the best views of the Palace, modern soundproofed rooms and air conditioning; or for even more quiet, you can try a 16th-century farmhouse on the Ile de la Barthelasse: ★★**La Ferme Jamet**, Chemin de Rhodes (off Pont Daladier), © 04 90 86 88 35, ● 04 90 86 17 72, has rooms ranging from traditional Provençal in style to a gypsy caravan, around tennis courts and a swimming pool.

Cheaper bets include the bright and charming **★Mignon**, 12 Rue Joseph Vernet, ☎ 04 90 82 17 30, 🖾 04 90 85 78 46, with small but modernized rooms; the friendly **★★Hôtel d'Angleterre**, 29 Bd Raspail, ☎ 04 90 86 34 31, 🖾 04 90 86 86 74 (*closed Jan*); and the quieter **★★Saint-Roch**, with a delightful garden just outside the walls of Porte St-Roch at 9 Rue Mérindol, ☎ 04 90 82 18 63, 🖾 04 90 85 82 49. The **★Innova**, near the station at 100 Rue Joseph Vernet, ☎ 04 90 82 54 10, 🖾 04 90 82 52 39, is run by a jolly family with a dog, cat, and two canaries in tow. The hotel **★Splendid** isn't, but it is cheap: off Rue de la République at 17 Rue A. Perdiguier, ☎ 04 90 86 14 46, 🖾 04 90 85 38 55. Otherwise, Ile de la Barthelasse has four **camping sites**, one of which, **La Bagatelle**, ☎ 04 90 86 30 39, 🖾 04 90 27 16 23, has dormitory rooms in the summer.

Eating Out

Avignon's gourmet bastion for the past 60 years, **Hiély-Lucullus**, 5 Rue de la République, ☎ 04 90 86 17 07, is a resolutely old-fashioned place, with a first-floor dining room. The kitchen refuses to conform to any label, but never disappoints with its *tourte* of quail and *foie gras*, a legendary *cassoulet des moules aux épinards* and for dessert, *pudding aux fruits à la crème vanille*, accompanied by carafes of Châteauneuf-du-Pape or Tavel (*menus 140–210F and up*). Its less expensive sister restaurant, **La Fourchette** at 17 Rue Racine, ☎ 04 90 85 20 93, serves as good for less, with menus from 100F; a choice of 12 desserts and wine by the carafe. The popular **Le Bain Marie**, at 5 Rue Pétramale, ☎ 04 90 85 21 37, serves traditional French fare with a 138F menu. **Entrée des Artistes** has the added advantage of its location in quiet Place des Carmes, ☎ 04 90 82 46 90 (*menus 120F and up*).

Le Petit Bedon, 70 Rue Joseph-Vernet, ☎ 04 90 82 33 98, is quickly becoming an Avignon institution for well-prepared dishes seldom found elsewhere, like *lotte au Gigondas*, monkfish cooked in wine (*lunch menu 100F, 150F in the evening*). For something different there's **Le Tournesol**, at 64 Rue Bonneterie, ☎ 04 90 14 00 31, for Polynesian dishes starting at only 60F; **Izmir**, 72 Place des Corps Saints, ☎ 04 90 82 66 90, for döner kebab, or full Turkish dinners at 90F and up; or go global with a feast of 'world cuisine' and live music at **Woolloomoolloo**, 16 bis Rue des Teinturiers, ☎ 04 90 85 28 44 (*100F and up*). For lunch, pop into **Terre des Saveurs**, at the northern end of Rue St-Michel, a vegetarian-oriented place with plenty of omelettes and pasta dishes, many with wild mushrooms; 68F lunch menu, or a 78F non-vegetarian special, which might be a grilled fish or *aiguillettes de canard*.

Around Avignon

If your pockets are deep enough, in easy driving distance of Avignon are three exceptional hotel/restaurants: **★★★Hostelleries Meissonnier**, 30 Ave de Verdun, 30133 Les Angles (4km west on D900), ☎ 04 90 25 41 68, which has 16 luxurious rooms and a glorious restaurant specializing in Provençal cuisine of the highest order—even the tomatoes taste better here, especially in the lovely garden (*a true bargain 100F menu, and others up to 420F*); **★★★Auberge de Cassagne**, 450 Allée de Cassagne, 84130 Le Pontet, 5km north on the N7, ☎ 04 90 31 04 18, which has a pool, tennis courts, and access to a golf course; the food (fillet of red mullet with lime, followed by pear *croquant* in bitter chocolate) and wine cellar are perfect (*menus 220–380F*); and 5km east, on the N107 (follow the Ave d'Avignon), ★★★★**Le Jardin des Frênes**, 645 Ave les Vertes-Rives, 84140 Montfavet, ✆ 04 90 31 17 93 (*lunch menus 195F*), which is a Relais et Châteaux member, set around a beautiful garden and pool; antiques furnish the rooms. Half-board mandatory in season, but the food, with imaginative delights like salmon with truffles in a sweet and sour sauce, is as marvellous as the setting.

Entertainment and Nightlife

Outside July and August, Avignon's best source of information on cultural events is the **Centre d'Action Culturelle**, Hôtel de Brantes, 2 Rue Petit Fusterie, ✆ 04 90 80 80 53. Try to take in a performance by one of Provence's most talented theatre companies, **Le Chêne Noir**, 8 Rue Ste-Catherine, whose range covers the classics to the avant-garde (✆ 04 90 86 58 11). The same theatre is also the home of the jazz club **AJMI**, ✆ 04 90 86 08 61, featuring live music every Thursday at 9pm (membership cards available at the door). Avignon's oldest permanent company, the **Théâtre des Carmes**, performs in the restored Gothic cloister of the Eglise des Carmes (HQ at 6 Place des Carmes, ✆ 04 90 82 20 47). Quality old and new films in their original language are shown at the five halls of the **Cinemas Utopia** at 4 Rue Excalier Ste Anne and 5 Rue Figuière, ✆ 04 90 82 65 36.

There are three more cinemas: **Pathé Palace**, 38 Cours Jean Jaurés, ✆ 08 36 68 20 22; **Capitole**, 3 Rue Pourquery de Boisserin, ✆ 04 90 82 24 27; and **Cinema Vox** at 22 Place de l'Horloge, ✆ 08 36 68 03 70. Outside of all that culture, nightlife is rather limited. For rock and zebras head to **Pub Z** at 58 Rue Bonneterie, ✆ 04 90 85 42 84, and its bar decked out in black and white stripes, or try **Le Yucatan** disco near the station at 46 Blvd St-Roch, ✆ 04 90 27 00 84, or check your *Rendez-Vous*.

Villeneuve-lez-Avignon

In 586, on Puy Andaon, the rock that dominates Villeneuve-lez-Avignon, a Visigoth princess-hermit named Casarie died in the odour of sanctity (holiness smells like crushed violets, apparently). In the 10th century, Benedictines built the abbey of St-André to shelter her bones and lodge pilgrims on the route to Compostela. St-André grew to become one of the mightiest monasteries in the south of France, and in 1226, when Louis VIII besieged pro-Albigensian Avignon, the abbot offered the king co-sovereignty of the abbey in exchange for royal privileges. And so what was once an abbey town became a frontier fortress of the king of France, a new town (*ville neuve*) and a heavily fortified one, in case the pope over the river should start feeling frisky. But Villeneuve was soon invaded in another way; wanton, squalid Avignon didn't suit all tastes, and the pope gave permission to his cardinals who liked it not-so-hot to retreat across the Rhône into princely *livrées cardinalices* (palaces euphemistically 'freed' from their original owners by the Curia). Though a dormitory suburb these days, Villeneuve still maintains a separate peace, well-fed cats snoozing in the sun, leisurely afternoons at the *pétanque* court and some amazing works of art.

Getting Around and Tourist Information

From Avignon, bus no.11 runs every half-hour from the train station or Porte de l'Oulle to Villeneuve. Place Charles-David is the best place to park and has the tourist information office as well, ℰ 04 90 25 61 33, ℰ 04 90 25 91 55; in summer there is an office on Rue de la République near the Chartreuse. Note that everything except the Chartreuse is closed on Tuesdays and in February.

market days

Thursday morning on Place Charles-David.

Around Town

In 1307, when Philip the Fair ratified the deal that made Villeneuve royal property, he ordered a citadel to be built on the approach to Pont St-Bénézet and be named after guess who. As times grew more perilous, this bright white **Tour Philippe-le-Bel** (*open Oct–Mar 10–12 and 2–5.30; Easter through Sept 10–12.30 and 3–6, closed Tues and in Feb*) was made higher to keep out the riff-raff, and from its terrace, reached by a superb winding stair, it offers splendid views of Avignon, Mont Ventoux and on a clear day, the Alpilles.

From here, Montée de la Tour leads up to the 14th-century **Collégiale Notre-Dame**, once the chapel of a *livrée* and now Villeneuve's parish church. From Villeneuve's Chartreuse (Charterhouse) it has inherited an elaborate marble altar of 1745, and it contains a copy of the Enguerrand Quarton's famous *Pietà de Villeneuve-lez-Avignon* (the original is in the Louvre) but the church's most famous work, a beaming, swivel-hipped, polychrome ivory statue of the Virgin carved in Paris out of an elephant's tusk *c.* 1320, has been removed to safer quarters in the nearby **Musée Pierre-de-Luxembourg**, ℰ 04 90 27 49 66 (*same hours as Tour Philippe-le-Bel; adm*), housed in yet another *livrée*.

The museum's other prize is the masterpiece of the Avignon school: Enguerrand Quarton's 1454 *Couronnement de la Vierge*, one of the greatest works of 15th-century French painting, commissioned for the Charterhouse (*see* below). Unusually, it portrays God the Father and God the Son as twins, clothed in sumptuous crimson and gold, like the Virgin herself, whose fine sculptural features were perhaps inspired by the ivory Virgin. Around these central figures the painting evokes the spiritual route travelled by the Carthusians through vigilant prayer, to purify the world and reconcile it to God. St Bruno, founder of the Order, saints, kings, and commoners are present, hierarchically arranged, while the landscape encompasses heaven, hell, Rome and Jerusalem, and local touches like Mont Ste-Victoire and the cliffs of the Estaque.

La Chartreuse and Fort St-André

From the museum, take Rue de la République up to No. 53, the **Livrée de la Thurroye**, the best-preserved in Villeneuve; a cardinal would maintain a household of a 100 or so people here. Further up the street and up the scale rises what was the largest and wealthiest charterhouse in France, the **Chartreuse du Val-de-Bénédiction** (*open daily April–Sept 9–6; Oct–Mar 9.30–5.30; adm*). This began as the *livrée* of Etienne Aubert who, upon his election to the papacy in 1352 as Innocent VI, deeded his palace to the Carthusians for a monastery. For 450 years it was expanded and rebuilt, granted immense estates on either side of the Rhône by kings and popes, accumulated a precious library, two more cloisters, and works of art, and in general lived high on the hog by the usual Carthusian standards. In 1792, the Revolution forced the monks out, and the Charterhouse was sold in 17 lots; squatters took over the cells and outsiders feared to enter the cloisters after dark. Now re-purchased and beautifully restored, the buildings house the CNES (the Centre National des Écritures du Spectacles), where playwrights and others are given grants to work in peace and quiet in some of the former cells; it hosts seminars, exhibitions, and performances, especially during the Avignon festival.

Still, the sensation that lingers in the Charterhouse is one of vast silences and austerity, the hallmark of an order where conversation was limited (originally) to one hour a week; monks who disobeyed the rule of prayer, work, and silence ended up in one of the seven prison cells around the laundry in the Great Cloister—each with a cleverly arranged window on the prison chapel altar. Explanations (in English) throughout offer an in-depth view of Carthusian life: one cell has been furnished as it originally was. It was Pierre Boulez who discovered that the dining hall, or **Tinel**, has some of the finest accoustics in France (designed so that all could hear the monk who read aloud during meals). In the Tinel's chapel are ruined 14th-century frescoes by Matteo Giovannetti and his school: originally their work covered the walls of the huge **church**, now bare except for their masons' marks and minus its apse, which collapsed. The star attraction here is **Innocent VI's tomb**, with an alabaster effigy under a fine Gothic baldachin. Innocent was solemnly reburied here in 1960: a hundred years ago the tomb was used as a rabbit hutch.

Gazing down into the Charterhouse from the summit of Puy Andaon are the formidable bleached walls of **Fort St-André**, built by the French kings around the old abbey in the 1360s, not only to stare down the pope over the river but to defend French turf during the heyday of the *Grandes Compagnies* (bands of unemployed mercenaries, who pillaged the countryside and held towns to ransom). The two round towers afford a famous vantage point over Avignon. Jumbly ruins are all that remain of the once splendid abbey of St-André, amid beautiful Italian gardens—sumptuous in the springtime—restored and presided over by Roseline Bacou, a former curator at the Louvre.

Villeneuve-lez-Avignon ✉ *30400*   ***Where to Stay and Eating Out***

Villeneuve makes an attractive alternative to Avignon, and has some notable lodgings in its own right. The exquisite ★★★★**Le Prieuré**, centrally located in Place du Chapître, ✆ 04 90 15 90 15, 🖂 04 90 25 18 20, gives you the option of sleeping in the 14th-century *livrée*, where the rooms are furnished with antiques, or in the more comfortable annex by the swimming pool; gardens, tennis, and a remarkable restaurant that does delightful things with seafood and truffles (*gourmet lunch menus at 195F*). *Closed Nov–10 Mar.* At ★★★**La Magnaneraie**, 37 Rue Camp-de-Bataille, ✆ 04 90 25 11 11, 🖂 04 90 25 46 37, you can choose between the old-fashioned rooms in a former silkworm nursery, or another modern annex; it too has been endowed with a pool, gardens, and Le Prieuré's rival for the best restaurant in town (*menus 170F and up*). For a less expensive sojourn into history, there's the charming 16th-century ★★**L'Atelier**, 5 Rue de la Foire, ✆ 04 90 25 01 84, 🖂 04 90 25 80 06, with a walled garden in the centre of town, or the 17th-century ★★**Les Cèdres**, 39 Blvd Pasteur, ✆ 04 90 25 43 92, 🖂 04 90 25 14 66, named after its ancient cedars, with a pool and a bungalow annexe. *Closed Nov–Mar.* Several old buildings in Villeneuve have been beautifully restored as *chambres d'hôtes*, among them **Les Jardins de la Livrée**, 4 bis Rue Camp de Bataille, ✆ 04 90 26 05 05, with a walled garden, pool, and parking (*about 300F*); the restaurant is good too (try the cannelloni stuffed with salmon in dill cream); *menus from 120–150F.* Cheapest of all is the **Hostel YMCA**, in a former clinic above the river at 7 bis Chemin de la Justice, ✆ 04 90 25 46 20, 🖂 04 90 25 30 64, with superb views of the Rhône and a pool to boot. *Closed Nov–Mar.*

Besides the aforementioned hotel restaurants, you'll have to book ahead to get a table at **Aubertin**, an intimate place under the porticoes in Place Meisonnier, ✆ 04 90 25

94 84, to savour delicacies such as red mullet tartines, with *pistou* and fried aubergines. *Closed Mon.* **Chez Fabrice**, 3 Blvd Pasteur, ✆ 04 90 25 52 79, is a local boy, who specializes in seafood, served in a charming dining room or in the garden; save room for the mousse au chocolate in a strawberry *coulis (menus from 105F).* *Closed Sun eve, Mon and most of Sept.* **La Maison**, 1 Rue Montée du Fort St-André, ✆ 04 90 25 20 81, is an old favourite, with a traditional 110F menu and friendly service. *Closed Wed, Sat lunch and Tues eve.*

Between Avignon and Tarascon: La Montagnette

Just south of Avignon and the confluence of the Durance, the Rhône curves to accommodate La Montagnette, a micro-region that is still something of a best kept secret, close to the tourist fleshpots of Provence and yet distant in spirit, self contained and serene. The Montagnette itself is a striking, 10km-long white outcrop of white stone, isolated from its sisters in the Alpilles and surrounded by orchards, a bijou landscape that **Barbentane** fits into like an old shoe—a friendly old town that so loved its *farandole* that a man who could not dance it would not be considered a fit husband. It is still defended by the 14th-century **Tour Angelica**, its medieval gates, and near the church, the arcaded Renaissance **Maison des Chevaliers**. Outside the walls, the **Château**, ✆ 04 90 95 51 07 (*open Easter–Oct, 10–12 and 2–6, other times Sun only; adm*), was built in 1674, not for defence, but pleasure, by the Marquis de Barbentane, the king's ambassador to Tuscany. It would not look out of place in the Ile de France: the furnishings are Louis XV and Louis XVI but the builder's Italian tastes permeates the other decoration.

On the D35 south of Barbentane, **Boulbon** was known as Bourbon until 1792, when the guillotine cut into the name's popularity. Still defended by its fairy tale 10th-century walls built dramatically into and onto the rocky escarpment overlooking the Rhône, Boulbon is known for its unique 1 June *cérémonie du St-Vinage*, in honour of its patron saint Marcellin: the men of the village each bring a full bottle of wine to the saint's Romanesque chapel and hear the gospel in Provençal, after which the wine is blessed and God is toasted with a mighty swig. The bottle is then corked and for the rest of the year the blessed wine is used as a sovereign remedy for grave illnesses.

Leaving Barbentane on the D35E will bring you to the **Abbaye St-Michel-de-Frigolet**, ✆ 04 90 95 70 07, founded around the year 1000 (*guided tours by a monk 2.30 Mon to Sat, 4 Sun*). The word Frigolet comes from the Provençal *férigoulo*, or thyme, a healthy, invigorating herb that scents the air of La Montagnette. The monks of Montmajour (*see* p.315), enervated by the swamps, would come up here for a

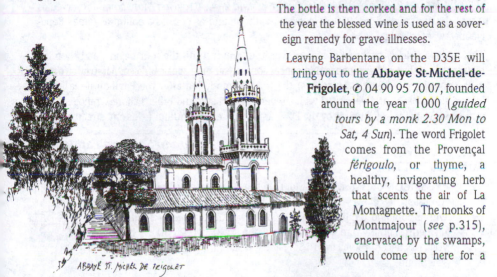

ABBAYE ST. MICHEL DE FRIGOLET

cure—some of it in the form of a liqueur called *Le Frigolet*, still distilled and on sale at the monastery. It may also have an effect on sterility: in 1632, Anne of Austria, barren after 20 years of marriage, prayed in the Romanesque chapel of the Conception Immaculée for a son, and soon after gave the world Louis XIV. In gratitude the queen sent the sumptuous gilt *boiseries* that frame 14 turgid Mignards. Another celebrity to pass through was the young Frédéric Mistral, who attended an improvised school here, where lessons were bartered for food.

The Petite Crau

East of Barbentane and the Montagnette, **Châteaurenard** is one of Provence's main wholesale fruit and vegetable markets, a big bustling place under its plane trees, lording over the rich verdant plain of the **Petite Crau**, a large marshland drained by the Romans, planted with market gardens and orchards of cherries and apricots, protected from the huffing and puffing of the mistral by hedgerows and poplars—nothing at all like the rocky waste of the 'big' Crau (*see* p.328). Two proud towers on Châteaurenard's hill are all that remain of the castle that first belonged to Reinardus, a friend and ally of Charles Martel, who was killed below its walls fighting the Saracens; his wife Emma took over the command and fought bravely, keeping the enemy at bay, then died of a broken heart. Her ghost haunts the **Tour de Griffon**, with a little museum and views over the Lubéron and Alpilles (*open 10–12 and 2–6, closed Jan and Feb*). Five km east of Châteaurenard, **Noves** claims to have been the home, or summer residence, of Petrarch's Laura.

In 1830, Mistral was born in **Maillane**, southwest of Châteaurenard, and spent as much time as possible there until he died in 1914. It's been bypassed by the main routes, leaving a quaint, dusty nowhere with two old-fashioned bars in the *place,* dogs sleeping in the middle of the streets, and a *tabac* selling keychains sporting Mistral's mug—the only noticeable effort by the locals to cash in on their Nobel prize-slinging hero (he *does* look like Buffalo Bill). The house the master Félibre had built after 1876 is now the **Musée Mistral**, ✆ 04 90 95 74 06 —don't mistake it for the rotting concrete *Centre F. Mistral*, which is something else (*open 9.30–11.30 and 2.30–6.30, Oct–Mar 10–11.30 and 2–4.30, closed Mon; adm*). Preserved as it was the day he died in 1914, it is 'as sympathetic and as cosy as a coffin' as James Pope-Hennessy described it.

The guide, a sinewy cockerel of a man, won't let you in until the tour begins, and then his high-speed spiel won't be stopped. No concessions if you only speak English. **Mistral's tomb**, in the ghastly, gravelly graveyard over the road, is modelled after the Pavillon de la Reine Jeanne at Les Baux, and decorated with a seven-pointed star and other Félibre symbols. If you can, leave Maillane southwards by the D27, and travel over beautiful fields and streams.

Where to Stay and Eating Out

Barbentane ✉ 13570

Castel Mouisson, at the foot of the Montagnette in Quartier Castel Mouisson, ✆ 04 90 95 51 17, ✆ 04 90 95 67 63, is a typical Provençal hotel, with a pool and tennis and bikes to borrow. *Closed mid-Oct–mid-Mar.* In the centre, little white ***St-Jean, 1 le Cours, ✆ 04 90 95 50 44, is open all year, has decent rooms from 180F, and a restaurant with a good, substantial 95F menu.

The **Hostellerie de Frigolet**, at St-Michel-de-Frigolet, ✆ 04 90 90 52 70, 🖷 04 90 95 75 22, is run by the Prémontrés monks: 36 rooms for guaranteed quiet retreats for a day or two or even a month; book through the Service Hostellerie, Abbaye St-Michel-de-Frigolet, 13150 Tarascon. *Closed Feb.*

Châteaurenard ✉ 13160

★★Les Glycines, 14 Ave Victor Hugo, ✆ 04 90 94 10 66, 🖷 04 90 94 78 10, makes a simple and reasonably priced base, with an average restaurant (*from 90F*).

Noves ✉ 13550

Away from it all, in a 15-hectare forest, the Relais & Châteaux **★★★★★Auberge de Noves**, 2km northwest on the D28, ✆ 04 90 24 28 28, 🖷 04 90 24 28 00, is a superb *bastide* converted three generations ago by the Lalleman family into one of the most prestigious Provençal hotels. Lovely air-conditioned rooms, endowed with every comfort (from 1150F); tennis and pool are in the grounds, riding and golf are nearby. The restaurant is a serious gastronomic temple, serving a seductive mix of regional and traditional dishes matched with a superb wine cellar (*menus begin at 180F*).

Tarascon

Few towns in Provence are as determinedly unglamorous as Tarascon. Most of the houses are not only unrestored but cry out for a lick of paint; garages outnumber craft shops; even the poodles look like real dogs instead of topiary hedges. Meanwhile the rival fairy-tale castles of Tarascon and Beaucaire muse at each other across the Rhône like the embodiments of a bi-communal Walter Mitty daydream, reminders of heroism, romance, international markets, man-eating monsters, and Alphonse Daudet's buffoonish anti-hero Tartarin, who never told a lie but, under the hot sun, was prone to imagine things. Provençal nationalists accuse Daudet (a native of Nîmes) of creating a stereotype that only heightened Paris's already smug attitude towards the Midi, to which Daudet replied that 'All Frenchmen have in them a touch of Tarascon.'

Getting Around

Nearly every east–west **train** from Provence to Languedoc stops in Tarascon. **Buses** run regularly between Beaucaire, Tarascon, Nîmes, and Avignon (✆ 04 66 29 27 29; other lines, from Tarascon's station, go to Arles, Boulbon, St-Rémy and Cavaillon (✆ 04 90 93 74 90).

Bike hire in Tarascon: **Cycles Christophe**, 70 Blvd Itam, ✆ 04 90 91 25 85, and **Motobécane**, 1 Rue E. Pelletan, ✆ 04 90 91 42 32.

Tourist Information

59 Rue des Halles, ✆ 04 90 91 03 52, 🖷 04 90 91 22 96.

market day

Tuesday.

Tarascon and St Martha

All centuries have quirks that seem quaint to later generations: tulip-bulb speculation in the 18th, ladies' bustles in the 19th, muzak in the 20th. In the 11th and 12th centuries, it was a mania for the bodily parts of saints, a fad so passionate that a sure candidate for the inner circle, such as St Francis, had bodyguards from Assisi in his dying days to prevent rival towns from kidnapping him. If it had no fresh relics, every town with a saintly legend attached to it began digging for bones; and in Tarascon, *voilà*, in 1187 they just happened to stumble across the relics of St Martha. The pious 9th-century legend told how she found Tarascon bedevilled by a Tarasque, a man-eating amphibian whose ancestors are portrayed in Celtic sculpture chomping on human heads. Martha neatly tidied away the monster by showing it a Cross, lassoing it with her girdle, then ordering it to the bottom of the Rhône, never to return. The new-found relics attracted so many pilgrims that the 12th-century **Collégiale Ste-Marthe** was enlarged in the 13th and 16th centuries into a curious Romanesque/Gothic hybrid. The church was badly bombed in the Second World War, but even worse mischief had been done earlier in the Revolution, when the great south portal of 1197 was shorn of its sculptures. Nowadays the chapels of the attractive five-aisled Gothic nave are filled with the efforts of Mignard and Parrocel, masters of the Baroque fruitcake style, while in the crypt (part of the original 1197 church) there's a king-sized statue of Martha from 1400 and the slightly later and much more refined *effigy of Jean de Cossa*, Seneschal of Provence, attributed to Francesco Laurana.

The Château du Tarascon

Open 9–7 summer, 9–12 and 2–5 winter; adm; © 04 90 91 01 93.

Rooted in a limestone rock over the Rhône, Tarascon's château gleams like white satin between the sun and water, a storybook feudal castle with crenellations and moat, named after the one character in Tarascon's history actually rounded out in flesh and blood. Good King René earned the 'Good' in his name for his good appetite and fondness for the good things of life, as well as the good sense not to let troubles or sorrows, of which he had many, get under his skin. He spent the last decade of his life (1471–80) surrounded by poets and artists in Tarascon, in this castle begun in 1401 by his father, Louis II of Anjou. After René's death and Provence's annexation to France, it underwent the usual conversion into a prison.

While the exterior is all business, the interior was designed with the good taste of René in mind—flamboyant and elegant, and now eloquently empty except for ten 17th-century tapestries on the Life of Scipio and a collection of 18th-century pharmaceutical pots. In the courtyard there are busts of the king and his second wife, Jeanne de Laval; here and there sculptural titbits and faded ceiling panels offer clues of the original decoration; graffiti by British sailors imprisoned here between 1754 and 1778 recall the castle's later use. And taking in the precipitous views from the top, you can see why no one ever tried to sneak up on it; or why, during the Revolution, Tarascon never needed to invest in a guillotine.

Elsewhere around Town

Perhaps because they haven't been prettified to death as in some Provençal towns, the streets of Tarascon, lined with rose, lemon and ochre houses with pots of geraniums in the windows and laundry flapping in the breeze, make a delightful place to wander around. The main **Rue des Halles** is still covered by medieval arcades. Halfway up it from the tourist office you'll find the Franciscan **Cloître des Cordeliers** (1450s), now used for special exhibitions (*open 10–12 and 2–5.30, summer 3–7, closed Jan and Feb*). At the top of Rue des Halles stands the handsome **Hôtel de Ville** (1648)—compare it to Beaucaire's, built 30 years later; the ceilings and original consuls' stalls are still intact. Near here at 39 Rue Proudhon, the **Musée Souleiado**, © 04 90 91 08 80 (*open by appointment only*), is run by Souleiado (Provençal for 'sun-ray piercing through clouds'), France's leading manufacturer of block-printed textiles. Founded here in 1938 by Charles Deméry in the hopes of reviving a 200-year-old Tarascon industry, the museum holds 40,000 18th-century fruitwood blocks—still the basis for all the company's patterns. Brought back to fashion in the 1950s on such diverse backs as Bardot's and Picasso's, Souleiado's colour-drenched prints can be purchased in the nearby shop, or in any of their many boutiques in the south of France.

Lastly, there's the so-called **House of Tartarin**, © 04 90 91 05 08, across from a Fiat garage at 55 bis, Boulevard Itam (*open Oct–Mar 9–12 and 1.30–5; summer April–Sept 9.30–12 and 2–7*). The modern Tarasconnais say they have forgiven Daudet for making them ridiculous, for in the age of Tourist Man he has also made them famous. Daudet claimed that the character of Tartarin was derived from his cousin, a big game hunter whom Daudet accompanied on a lion hunt in Algeria, but there's another version: in the original story, published as a newspaper serial, Tartarin was named Barbarin after an old Tarasconnais family—the head of which had rejected the author's suit for the hand of his daughter. The family threatened to sue if Daudet used their name in his novel, so he changed it to the fictional Tartarin, then got his own back by making the whole town the butt of his jokes. Inside are mementoes from the three Tartarin novels, and photos from the plays and films. The garden has been planted to fit the books' exotic flora and baobab tree, where Tartarin held court with his tall tales.

Also on display is the famous **Tarasque**, a moustachioed armadillo covered with red spikes. Scholars argue whether the monster is named after the town or vice versa; when King René founded the *Jeux et Courses de la Tarasque* in 1474, it was given a thick carapace to hide the men that made it walk, while fireworks blasted out of its nostrils and the people sang '*Lagadigadèu, la Tarasco, Lagadigadèu!* ,' or 'Let her pass, the Tarasque, let her dance.'

Festivals

Nowadays the *Fêtes de la Tarasque* take place for five days around St John's Day (24 June), and include bonfires, costumes, bullfights, cavalcades, dances, opera (the *Miréio* of course), and—yes—someone dressed up like Tartarin.

Tarascon ✉ *13150*　　　　　　　　　**Where to Stay and Eating Out**

In a large park of tall pines, heading towards the Alpilles, ★★★**Hôtel Mazets des Roches**, Route de Fontvieille, © 04 90 91 34 89, 📠 04 90 43 53 29, offers comfort and quiet in modern, air-conditioned rooms, a restaurant, pool, tennis courts, and bike rentals. *Closed Nov–Mar.* In the centre, ★★★**De Provence**, 7 Blvd Victor Hugo, © 04 90 91 06 43, 📠 04 90 43 58 13, occupies a *hôtel particulier* and offers big rooms, big baths, colour TV and breakfast on your own balcony. *Closed mid-Dec–mid-Jan.* More modest, though hardly less spacious, are the rooms at ★★**Le Saint-Jean**, 24 Blvd Victor Hugo, © 04 90 91 13 87, 📠 04 90 91 32 42; it is connected to one of Tarascon's best restaurants, with the best value menu at 145F. Of the cheapies, try the **Hôtel du Rhône**, by the station in Place de la Gare, © 04 90 91 03 35. There are 65 beds in the well-kept **Auberge de Jeunesse**, 31 Blvd Gambetta, © 04 90 91 04 08, 📠 04 90 91 54 17; lodgers can take advantage of the hostel's inexpensive bike hire. Victuals are cheap, if not *cordon bleu. Open Mar–Dec.* ★★**Le Terminus** opposite the station in Place Colonel Berrurier, © 04 90 91 18 95, 📠 04 90 91 08 00, proposes 16 different entrées and 10 main dishes, as well as inexpensive rooms.

Beaucaire

Beaucaire can match Tarascon's stories tit for tat. It, too, was plagued by a river monster, called the Drac—a dragon in some versions, or a handsome young man—who liked to stroll invisibly through Beaucaire, before luring his victims into the Rhône by holding a bright jewel just below the surface. When the Drac became a father, he kidnapped a washerwoman to nurse his baby for seven years, during which time the woman learned how to see him when he was invisible. Years later, during one of his prowls through Beaucaire she saw him and greeted him loudly. He was so mortified that he was never seen again, although like the Tarasque he makes an annual reappearance in proxy, the first weekend in June. Beaucaire was also the setting of one of the most charming medieval romances: of Aucassin, son of the Count of Beaucaire, and his 'sweet sister friend' Nicolette, daughter of the King of Carthage, whom Aucassin loved so dizzily that he fell off his horse and dislocated his shoulder, among other adventures.

But in those days Beaucaire was on everyone's lips. It was here, in 1208, that a local squire assassinated Pope Innocent III's Legate, who had come to demand stricter measures against the Cathars. It gave Innocent the excuse he needed to launch the Albigensian Crusade against Beaucaire's overlords in Toulouse, and all their lands in Languedoc. In 1216, when the war was in full swing, Raymond VII, the son of the Count of Toulouse, recaptured the town from its French occupiers, who took refuge in the castle. As soon as word reached Simon de Montfort, he set off in person to succour his stranded men and to teach Beaucaire a lesson, besieging the town walls, while his troops took up the fight from inside the castle, so that Beaucaire was sandwiched in a double attack. The siege lasted 13 weeks before the troops in the castle ran out of food and surrendered and Simon de Montfort had to admit to one of his very few defeats. In gratitude Raymond VI granted Beaucaire the right to hold a duty-free fair. But five years later the town was gobbled up by France along with the rest of Languedoc, and lost all its rights and freedoms.

In 1464 Louis XI, eager to win Beaucaire to his side, restored its freedoms and fair franchise; soon its *Foire de la Ste-Madeleine* became one of the biggest in western Europe. For ten days in July, merchants from all over the Mediterranean, Germany and England would wheel and deal in the wooden booths of the *pré*, a vast meadow on the banks of the Rhône; by the 18th century, when the fair was at its height, Beaucaire (with a population of 8000) attracted some 300,000 traders. So much money changed hands that Beaucaire earned as much in a week as Marseille did in a year. The loss of Beaucaire's duty-free privileges just after Napoleon lost at Waterloo put an end to the fair, and since then Beaucaire has had to make do with traffic on the Rhône and Rhône–Sète Canal (now the town's pleasure port), its quarries and its wine, ranging from good table plonk to the more illustrious AOC Costière du Gard. But if you come in the spring, you can try one last legacy of the great fair in Beaucaire's *pastissoun*, patties filled with preserved fruits introduced by merchants from the Levant.

Tourist Information

24 Cours Gambetta, ✆ 04 66 59 26 57, 🖃 04 66 59 68 51.

market days

Thursday and Sunday, Place de la Mairie and Cours Gambetta.

The Château and Historic Centre

Louis XI's restoration of Beaucaire's rights paid off for a later Louis (XIII); in 1632, when the château was invested by the troops of the king's rebellious brother, Gaston d'Orléans, the loyal citizens forced them out. To prevent further mishaps Richelieu ordered Beaucaire's castle razed to the ground. But after demolishing the south wall, the shell was left to fall into ruins romantic enough for an illustration to *Aucassin and Nicolette,* a fitting background to the **Les Aigles de Beaucaire,** © 04 66 59 29 72, displays of the falconer's art, in medieval costume (*hourly 2–5 from Easter to 1 Nov, closed Wed, July and Aug daily 3–6; adm*). There are sweeping views of the Rhône and the old fair grounds, the Champ de Foire, from the 80ft **Tour Polygonale**, while in the castle gardens below, the **Musée Auguste Jacquet**, (*open April–Sep 10–12 and 2.15–6.45, Oct–Mar 10–12 and 2–5.15, closed Tues and hols; adm*) has finds from Roman Beaucaire (then clumsily called *Ugernum*), including a fine statue of Jupiter on his throne, and another of the lusty Priapus found in a villa; there's a geological collection, popular arts, and advertizing posters and mementoes from the fair.

From the Château, arrows point the way to the venerable **Place de la République**, shaded by giant plane trees, and the grand, elegant Baroque church of **Notre-Dame-des-Pommiers** (1744), which perhaps more than anything proves how many annual visitors this town of 8000 once expected. It replaced a much smaller Romanesque church, but conserves, on its exterior transept wall (facing Rue Charlier), a superb 12th-century **frieze**, depicting Passion scenes in the same strong, lively relief as at St-Gilles-du-Gard. The stately French classical **Hôtel de Ville** (1683) in Place G. Clemenceau was designed by Jacques Cubiol and bestowed on Beaucaire by Louis XIV who wanted to provide Beaucaire with a monument worthy of its importance: note Louis' sun symbols on the façade, the town's coat-of-arms set in the Collar of St Michael (the French equivalent of the Order of the Garter—Beaucaire was the only town in France awarded the honour) and Beaucaire's motto: 'Renowned for its Fair, Illustrious for its Fidelity.' The other *hôtels* you can't stay in aren't anywhere near as magnificent, though if it's a holiday, there are likely to be some dramatic bull follies in the **Arènes**: a hundred bulls are brought in for the *Estivales*, a week-long recreation of the medieval market and other celebrations in late July.

Around Beaucaire: Roman Wine and Roads, and Troglodyte Monks

The outskirts of Beaucaire are home to two new yet old attractions: **Le Vieux Mas**, 8km south on the Route de Fourques, is a living evocation of a Provençal farmhouse at the turn of the century, with a working blacksmith and other craftsmen, farm animals, and regional products (*open daily exc Jan, 10–7; adm*). The second, the **Mas des Tourelles**, 4km southwest at 4294 Route de Bellegarde (© 04 66 59 19 72, *open April–5 Nov, daily, 2–7*), is more original: since 1909 archaeologists have been working on the 210-acre vineyard of Château des Tourelles (owned by the Durands for 250 years), excavating a huge 1st-century AD agricultural estate that produced olives, wheat and wine, complete with a pottery factory capable of producing 4000 amphorae a day. The current Durand in charge, Hervé, became so fascinated with the digs that together with the National Centre for Scientific Research, he has recreated a Gallo-Roman winery—come during the harvest to watch the grapes gathered and pressed in the old Roman way and later bottled, or rather amphora-ed, in jars from 5 to 1000 litres for transport, wrapped in straw to keep them from breaking. You can taste and buy the result, although there's no way of knowing how close it comes to the stuff quaffed by Nero and Co:

the Romans added lime, egg whites, plaster, clay, mushroom ashes, and pork blood to 'improve' their wines, and Durand does not. Beaucaire's Roman incarnation *Ugernum* made its living transferring goods (including its wine) along the Roman 'super highway' the **Via Domitia** that linked Rome to Spain. An 8km stretch of this has come through in remarkably good nick, especially in a place known as **Les Bornes Milliaires** (take D999 1km northwest past the train tracks, turn left 800m, following the Enclos d'Argent lane). Nowhere else along the route have the milestones survived so well: these three, on the 13th mile between Nîmes and *Ugernum*, were erected by Augustus, Tiberius, and Antoninus Pius.

In the same area, the unique and vaguely spooky **Abbaye St-Roman**, 4km up D999, ✆ 04 66 59 26 57 (*open April, May, June, Sept 10–6; July and Aug 10–7, closed Mon; other times Sat and Sun only, 2–5; adm*), was founded in a cave in the perilous 5th century and labouriously carved out of the living rock. It was mentioned in the chronicles in 1363, when Pope Urban V made it a *studium*, a school open even to the poorest children, but by 1537 it had lost its importance and was engulfed in the construction of a fortress; when the fortress in turn lost its importance in the 19th century and was destroyed, the abbey was rediscovered: the chapel, with its remarkable abbot's chair, the subterranean cells, the water cisterns and wine press, and 150 rock-cut tombs in the necropolis. East of Beaucaire, **Valabrègues** 'the most Provençal town of Languedoc', was cut off from the rest of the Gard when the Rhône changed its bed. Surrounded by clumps of osier, it makes its living from wicker and basketry: learn all about it in the **Musée de la Vannerie**, ✆ 04 55 59 23 41 (*open Easter–Oct, Wed–Sun 3–6*).

Beaucaire ✉ *30300* | ***Where to Stay and Eating Out***

***Les Doctrinaires**, Quai Général de Gaulle, ✆ 04 66 59 23 70, ✉ 04 66 59 22 26, was before the Revolution the home of the Doctrinaire fathers of Avignon, now metamorphosed into a fetching, old-fashioned hostelry. Half-board is obligatory in season, but eating 'in', in the pretty courtyard, is pleasant (*menus from 95F*). ****Robinson**, 2km north on the Route de Remoulins, ✆ 04 66 59 21 32, ✉ 04 66 59 00 03, has 30 rooms set in acres and acres of countryside, with pool, tennis, playground etc. and restaurant (*menus at 80F and 160F*). In the centre near the dike, **Napoléon**, 4 Place Frédéric-Mistral, ✆ 04 65 66 59 05 17, offers comfortable rooms with bath (*from 170F*); in 1793, Napoleon, while still unknown, visited the fair, wrote a little booklet called the *Supper at Beaucaire*, a dialogue of merchants on the subject of Federalism. You can have your own memorable supper at Beaucaire at **Le Sénéchal**, near the castle at 49 Blvd du Maréchal-Joffre, ✆ 04 66 59 23 10: well prepared French classics, followed by a score of cheeses and desserts (*menus from 105–205F, closed Sun eve, Mon*).

For a real escape, hire a **houseboat** and make the leisurely loop down the Rhône–Sète canal to the Camargue, west to Aigues-Mortes and up the Languedoc canal past St-Gilles to Beaucaire. Try **Connoisseur Cruisers**, 14 Quai de la Paix, ✆ 04 66 59 46 08, ✉ 04 66 59 27 19.

ARLES AMPHITHEATRE

Down the Rhône: Alpilles, Crau, Camargue

The Rhône that flows so majestically from the Swiss Alps down half of France comes to a rather messy end in the Camargue, dithering indecisively through a delta of swamps, salt-pans and sand-dunes. And yet if all the chapters of this book had to compete in a talent show, this would be the one to beat. It has wild bulls, horses and pink flamingos; it has the cowboys, gypsies and the fancy dress of the Arlésiennes; it has Roman ruins, the best Romanesque art, and the most romantic stories, worthy of Sir Walter Scott; it has the sharpest mountains, a plain so uncanny that it took a myth to explain it, and the mistral-whipped landscapes painted by Van Gogh; it has the biggest bull-ring, France's only AOC hay (from Arles), and all the aluminium ore you could ask for.

St-Rémy-de-Provence and the Alpilles

Getting Around

Though there are no trains, St-Rémy is a crossroads, surrounded by several big towns; consequently the **coach service** is slightly better than in most places. All leave from Place de la République, across from the church: at least one a day to Arles, Tarascon, Cavaillon and Aix; more frequently to Avignon. You can easily walk to Les Antiques (*see* p.308) and Glanum, but buses from St-Rémy to Les Baux are rare and inconvenient. The latter is better connected to Arles, with four or five buses a day, stopping at Fontvieille.

The Alpilles are not too steep for **cycling** in most places; the Syndicat d'Initiative in St-Rémy has a list of bike-hire firms. You might enjoy a tour around the southern slopes of the Alpilles, near St-Rémy, looking for the spots where Van Gogh painted many of his famous landscapes.

Tourist Information

St-Rémy ✉ 13210: Place Jean-Jaurès, on the way to Les Antiques, ✆ 04 90 92 05 22, 🖷 04 90 92 38 52.

market day

St-Rémy: Wednesday morning.

St-Rémy-de-Provence

Enclosed by a garland of boulevards lined with plane trees, St-Rémy's tranquillity has attracted its share of the famous: Nostradamus was born here, Gertrude Stein spent years here, Charles Gounod stayed here while writing his opera based on Mistral's *Mireille*, and Princess Caroline drops in for discreet visits (St-Rémy used to belong to the family). Vincent Van Gogh spent his tragic last year in the asylum, which during the First World War was commandeered to hold interned Germans—the one who got Van Gogh's room was Albert Schweitzer.

Nowadays St-Rémy is home to a good many artists, and there are always exhibitions going on. The newest attraction is the bizarre-looking organ in the church of **St-Martin** on Blvd Marceau. Built only in 1983, it is said to be one of the finest in the world; the Organ Festival in August pulls out all the stops, as do the Saturday afternoon concerts in summer and autumn. Older attractions are two fine Renaissance palaces, both around Place Flavier, behind

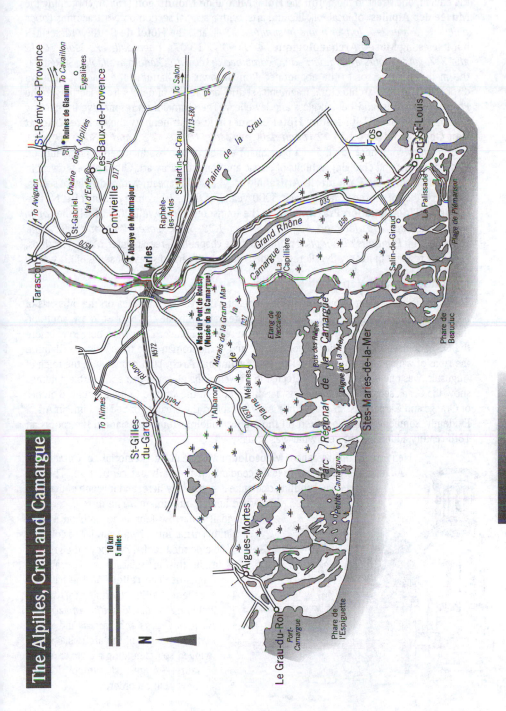

The Alpilles, Crau and Camargue

N

10 km
5 miles

St-Rémy-de-Provence
To Cavaillon
Ruines de Glanum
Eygalières
To Salon
Les-Baux-de-Provence
Chaîne des Alpilles
St-Gabriel
Val d'Enfer
To Avignon
Fontvieille
D17
St-Martin-de-Crau
Plaine de la Crau
D5
N113-E80
N570
Tarascon
Raphèle-les-Arles
Abbaye de Montmajour
Arles
Grand Rhône
Fos
Port-St-Louis
D5
D35
D36
La Palissade
Plage de Piémanson
La Camargue
La Capillière
Salin-de-Giraud
N572
Rhône
Petit
Mas du Pont de Rousty
(Musée de la Camargue)
Marais de la Grand Mar
D37
de
la
Etang de Vaccarès
Bois des Rièges
Phare de Beauduc
l'Albaron
D570
Méjanes
Plaine
Digue de la Mer
Parc Régional de la Camargue
Stes-Maries-de-la-Mer
To Nîmes
St-Gilles-du-Gard
D58
Petite Camargue
Aigues-Mortes
Le Grau-du-Roi
Port-Camargue
Phare de l'Espiguette

the church, one street to the north: the **Hôtel Mistral de Mondragon** (1550), containing the **Musée des Alpilles**, of local folk life and arts, with a special section on Nostradamus (*open daily 10–12 and 2–5, longer hours in summer, adm*); and the **Hôtel de Sade**, with a small but interesting **Musée Archaeologique**, © 04 90 92 13 07 (*open daily exc Mon, 10–12 and 2–7, guided tours every hour; adm; combined ticket with Glanum available*). St-Rémy is the medieval successor to the abandoned Roman town of Glanum (*see* below); finds on display here include architectural fragments, statues and reliefs of deities from Hermes to the Phrygian god Attis, and Roman glass and jewellery. The Grimaldi representative in St-Rémy lived in the beautiful 18th-century **Hôtel Estrine**, in Rue Estrine, now the **Centre Vincent Van Gogh**, © 04 90 92 34 72 (*open daily exc Mon, 10.30–12.30 and 2.30–6.30; adm; closed Jan–Mar*), where you'll find a permanent exhibit of photos, documents, and a film on Van Gogh's life, and changing exhibits of classic and contemporary art. Other places to visit in the centre include the **Parfumerie Artisanale** at 34 Blvd Mirabeau, with a display of scents, classic bottles, and others dating back 3000 years, or the 12th-century **Chapelle Notre-Dame de Pitié Donation Prassinos**, near the tourist office on Ave Durand Maillane (*open daily April–Sept 2–6, July and Aug 3–7; winter 1.30–5.30, closed Wed and Sat; adm*), containing 11 *Peintures du Supplice* painted for the chapel by Greek painter Mario Prassinos, long-time resident of nearby Eygalières, a video on the artist and displays of some of his works.

Les Antiques, and Van Gogh's Asylum

The Romans had a habit of building monuments and impressive mausolea on the outskirts of their towns, along the main roads. Just a 15-minute walk from the centre of St-Rémy, south on the D5, stand two of the most remarkable Roman relics in France. They were here long before the D5 of course; originally they decorated the end of the Roman road from Arles to Glanum, the ruins of which lie just across the D5. The **Triumphal Arch**, built probably in the reign of Augustus, was one of the first to be erected in Provence. Its elegant form and marble columns show the Greek sensibility of the artists, far different from the strange Celtic-influenced arches of Orange and Carpentras. In the Middle Ages it inspired the creators of St-Trophime in Arles. Evidently, someone long ago carted off the top for building stone; the slanted tile roof is an 18th-century addition to protect what was actually left.

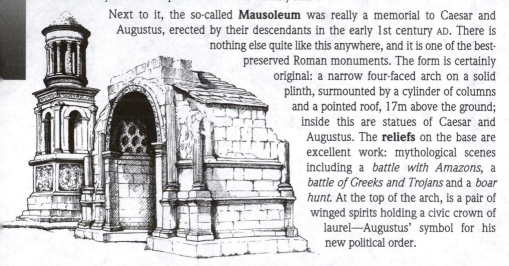

Next to it, the so-called **Mausoleum** was really a memorial to Caesar and Augustus, erected by their descendants in the early 1st century AD. There is nothing else quite like this anywhere, and it is one of the best-preserved Roman monuments. The form is certainly original: a narrow four-faced arch on a solid plinth, surmounted by a cylinder of columns and a pointed roof, 17m above the ground; inside this are statues of Caesar and Augustus. The **reliefs** on the base are excellent work: mythological scenes including a *battle with Amazons*, a *battle of Greeks and Trojans* and a *boar hunt*. At the top of the arch, is a pair of winged spirits holding a civic crown of laurel—Augustus' symbol for his new political order.

Just across the road from Les Antiques, a shady path leads to the monastery of **St-Paul-de-Mausole**, in a beautiful setting with gardens all around. Founded in the 900s, the complex includes a simple Romanesque church and a cloister. In 1810, the monastery buildings were purchased for use as a private hospital. This is the place Vincent Van Gogh chose as a refuge from the troubles of life in the outside world, in May 1890, not long after he chopped off his ear. He spent a year here, the most intense and original period of his career, painting as if possessed—150 canvases and over 100 drawings, including many of his most famous works, such as the *Nuit Etoilée* ('Starry Night') and *Les Blés Jaunes* ('Cornfield and Cypress Trees'). The blueish mountains in the background of this work and many others are the Alpilles. Appropriately enough, the patients and staff of the hospital have taken a keen interest in art therapy: you can see the results on the walls of the lovely cloister, as well as some interesting carved capitals (*open daily 9–6, until 5 in the winter*). Van Gogh painted the impressive Greco-Roman quarries (*La Carrière de St-Rémy*) just down the road, writing that it resembled a Japanese drawing. In the midst of the quarries, excavated in the rock, the **Mas de la Pyramide** (*open daily 9–12 and 2–5, till 7 in summer; adm*) is one of the oldest farmhouses in the region—it dates at least from the 8th century—and contains typical Provençal furnishings.

Glanum

Glanum began as a Celtic settlement—a proper town, really, under a heavy cultural influence from the Greeks at nearby Marseille. The Romans snatched it around 100 BC, under Marius, but not until the great prosperity of the Augustan empire did the city begin to bloom. Almost all of the ruins visible today (as well as Les Antiques) date from this period. In a prelude to the fall of the Empire, the Franks and Alemanni ranged throughout Gaul in the 250s and '60s. In one of their last hurrahs before the recovering Roman legions drove them out, they sacked Glanum in 270. After that, the townspeople relocated to a healthier and safer site, today's St-Rémy; silt washed down from the Alpilles gradually covered the city, and it passed out of memory until the 19th century, when some accidental finds alerted archaeologists to its presence. Excavations began in 1921, and have since uncovered a fascinating cross-section of Glanum, including its Forum.

More than Vaison-la-Romaine or anywhere else in France, this is the place to really feel at home in the Roman world. But you'll have to work for it; only the foundations remain, and recreating Glanum will require a bit of imagination (see the museum in the Hôtel de Sade first). From the entrance, to the left are the **Maison des Antes** and the **Maison d'Atys**, two typical wealthy homes built around peristyle courtyards. The latter had apparently been transformed into a sanctuary of Cybele and Attis; this cult was one of the most popular of the mystery religions imported from the east in imperial times.

Across the street are remains of a fountain and the **thermae** (baths), with mosaics, a *palestra* (exercise yard) and a *piscina* (pool). Next door is a building with an *exedra* that was probably a temple; altars to Silenus were found inside. In this part of the street the **sewers** have been uncovered. The **Forum** wasn't very impressive, by the standards of most Roman towns, and it is hard to make anything out today from the confusion of buildings from various ages that have been excavated. Beyond it, to the right, are foundations of temples; to the left are bases of another fountain and a monument. The street closes at a **gate** from Hellenistic times that was retained as the city expanded outside the original walls. Also retained was the **nymphaeum** beyond it, to the left; these decorated fountains were a common feature of Greek cities, built to allow travellers to refresh and clean up before entering the town.

St-Rémy gets heaps of tourists, and consequently has a wide choice of places to stay; it makes a convenient base for visiting the Alpilles and the Camargue. Most are on the outskirts, such as ★★★★**Le Vallon de Valrugues**, Chemin de Canto Cigalo, ✆ 04 90 92 04 40, 🖷 04 90 92 44 01, which waits to spoil you with lovely Provençal-style rooms, pool, sauna, jacuzzi, putting green and delicious meals (including lots of seafood and truffles, in season) in the palatial restaurant serving the best gourmet feasts in town (*menus from 190F*). The 19th-century ★★★★**Château des Alpilles**, D31, ✆ 04 90 92 03 33, 🖷 04 90 92 45 17, is outside the busy one-way rush of traffic round the centre, yet just a few steps out of town, in a park of trees, some rare, and a tennis court and pool. It's all mirrors, period furniture and creature comforts; restaurant for hotel guests only. An old country mansion has been converted into the ★★★**Castelet des Alpilles**, 6 Place Mireille, ✆ 04 90 92 07 21, 🖷 04 90 92 52 03, with pretty rooms and a lovely terrace under a century-old cedar. *Closed Nov–Easter.*

Near the ruins, the ★★**Villa Glanum**, 46 Ave Van Gogh, ✆ 04 90 92 03 59, 🖷 04 90 92 00 08; is family-run and has some surprising amenities for an inexpensive hotel: a pool and garden, also a restaurant. *Closed Nov–Feb.* ★★**Des Arts**, 30 Blvd Victor Hugo,✆ 04 90 92 08 50, 🖷 04 90 92 55 09, has comfortable rooms, as well as the oldest and most popular restaurant in St-Rémy (*menus 95F, 125–160F*). Be warned, the centre is noisy, but if you want to look out onto the *place* as you wake, try ★★**Le Cheval Blanc**, 6 Ave Fauconnet, ✆ 04 90 92 09 28, 🖷 04 90 92 69 05; the owners are cheerful, and it's adequate (and has a garage). For dining in central St-Rémy, you won't do better than the panoramic terrace of **La Maison Jaune**, 15 Rue Carnot, ✆ 04 90 92 56 14, especially if you plump for the 225F menu of Provençal specialities (*lunch menu 100F, others at 165 and 275F*). *Closed Sun eve and Mon.* Vegetarians (and others) will find joy among the bric-à-brac at **L'Assiette de Marie**, 1 Rue Jaume Roux, ✆ 04 90 92 32 14; try the lasagne. Good wine list, and one menu at 169F. For something cheaper, try **Le Bistrot des Alpilles** 15 Blvd Mirabeau, ✆ 04 90 92 09 17; you'll get generous fresh pasta, great desserts and a pleasant terrace. *Closed Sun.*

The Chaîne des Alpilles

The ruins were nice, but there is an even greater treat ahead. The five twisting kilometres of the D5 that take you from Les Antiques into the heart of the Alpilles are, in fact, one of the greatest sensual experiences Provence can offer. Van Gogh and cypresses, lushness and flowers are left behind; in a matter of minutes the road has brought you to another world. This world, incredibly, is at most 16km across, and a stone's throw from the swamps of the Camargue and the sea. It is made of thin, cool breezes and brilliant light; its colours are white and deep green—almost exclusively—in an astringent landscape of limestone crags and patches of scrubby *maquis*.

Tourist Information

Les Baux ✉ 13520: Impasse du Château, ✆ 04 90 54 34 39, 🖷 04 90 54 51 15.

Fontvieille ✉ 13990: 5 Rue M. Honorat, ✆ 04 90 54 67 49, 🖷 04 90 54 69 82.

Coteaux des Baux-de-Provence: A good source is the organic Domaine de La Vallongue in Eygalières (✆ 04 90 95 91 70). Try also the organic Mas Cellier in St-Rémy (✆ 04 90 92 03 90); and in Les Baux the Mas Ste-Berthe (✆ 04 90 54 39 01).

Les Baux-de-Provence

A l'asard, Bauthezar! ('Kill'em at random, Balthazar!')

Battle cry of the Seigneurs des Baux

From as early as 3000 BC, this exotic massif attracted residents. The Alpilles are full of caves, many of which were once inhabited. The Ligurians took advantage of its natural defences to found an important *oppidum* at Les Baux, a steep barren plateau in the centre of the massif, 11km from St-Rémy. In the Middle Ages, this made the perfect setting for the most feared and celebrated of Provence's noble clans. The Seigneurs des Baux are first heard of in the 900s. 'A race of eaglets, vassals never', as their slogan went, they never acknowledged the authority of the French king, the emperors, or anyone else, and their impregnable crag in the Alpilles allowed them to get away with it. They claimed to be descended from Balthazar, one of the magi at Bethlehem, and put the Christmas star on their feudal escutcheon.

The symbol was never a harbinger of glad tidings to their neighbours, however; for the next two centuries the lords of Baux waged incessant warfare on all comers, and occasionally on each other, gradually becoming a real power in Provence. They did it with flair, and the chronicles are full of good stories about them: one seigneur once besieged the castle of his pregnant niece, and sent sappers to undermine her bedchamber. And they met memorable ends; one was stabbed to death by his wife, another flayed alive when he fell into the hands of his enemies. All the while, the family headquarters at Les Baux maintained a polished court where troubadours were always welcome. It ended with a bang in 1372, when an even nastier fellow took over the clan: Raymond de Turenne, a distant relation who was also a nephew of Pope Gregory IX. Taking advantage of confused times, in the reign of Queen Jeanne, this ambitious and bloodthirsty intriguer found enough support, and enough foreign mercenaries, to bring full-scale civil war to Provence, bringing it the same kind of misery to which the rest of France had become accustomed in the Hundred Years War.

When the last heir of Les Baux died in 1426, the possessions of the house were incorporated into the County of Provence. That isn't quite the end of the story; in the 1500s Les Baux began to thrive once more, first under Anne of Montmorency, who rebuilt the seigneurs' castle in the best Renaissance taste, and later under the Manvilles, who inherited it from him and made it a Protestant stronghold in the Wars of Religion. Cardinal Richelieu finally put this eternal trouble-spot to rest in 1632, demolishing the castle and sending the owners the bill for the job. Until the Revolution, the remains of Les Baux were, like St-Rémy, in the hands of the Grimaldis of Monaco.

After the demolition, the village that surrounded the castle of Les Baux almost disappeared; Prosper Mérimée, in the 1830s, reported only a few beggars living among its ruins. But Provençal writers kept the place from being forgotten, men such as Mistral (born at Maillane, near St-Rémy) and Alphonse Daudet, whose famous windmill is just over the Alpilles (*see* below). In the last 50 years, Les Baux has become the second-biggest tourist attraction in France after the Mont St-Michel. The village below the castle has been rebuilt and repopulated in the worst way, and whatever spark of glamour survives in this tremendous ruin, you have to run the gauntlet of shops peddling trinkets, scowling dolls, herbs and *santons* to reach it.

The first sight to greet you as you trudge up from the car park is an elegant carved Renaissance fireplace, open to the sky and standing next to a souvenir shop. Trudge a bit further, bearing right, and you will come to the **Musée des Santons** on Place Louis Jou, which you could give a miss. Up the street, past the ramparts, is the **Porte d'Eyguères**, which until the 18th century was the only entrance to the city.

Up the Rue de la Calade you will come to the Place de l'Eglise, where the 16th-century **Hôtel des Porcelets** has now become the **Musée Yves Brayer**, © 04 90 54 36 99 (*open April–Sept 10–12 and 2–6.30, closed Jan–mid-Feb; adm*). Brayer (1907–90), a respected figurative painter, left his major works here, pictures of Spain and Italy as well as Provence; you can get a preview of his work in the 17th-century **Chapelle des Pénitents Blancs** opposite, where he frescoed scenes of a shepherds' Christmas (*same hours, free*). St-Vincent, in same square, dates from the 12th and 16th centuries. This is probably the coolest and least crowded place in Les Baux, and there's a Cistercian nave and stained glass by Max Ingrand (1955) donated by Rainier of Monaco. The domed turret with gargoyles on the south side is a Lanterne des Morts, a rare medieval survival: whenever anyone died in Les Baux, it would be announced by a flame.

Otherwise in the village are the **Hôtel Jean de Brion** and the **Hôtel de Manville**, on the Grand' Rue. The first houses the **Fondation Louis Jou**, © 04 90 54 34 17, containing Jou's engravings, as well as pre-20th-century ones, engravings by Dürer, Rembrandt and Goya and early books. In the second is the **Musée d'Art Contemporain**, © 04 90 54 34 03, and the **Hôtel de Ville**. Both these and the Hôtel des Porcelets date from the architectural development of the 16th century, before the castle was destroyed.

Next, to the **Citadel** (*8.30–7.30, till 9 in summer, til 5 in the winter; adm*), and a new museum to keep the tramping tourists from the thing itself. The **Musée d'Histoire des Baux** is perfectly nice, with illustrations and archeological finds as well as models in glass cases, to give you an overview, or to save you the walk over the site outside if the mistral's blowing.

When you see Les Baux itself the ambience changes abruptly—a rocky chaos surrealistically decorated with fragments of once-imposing buildings. The path leads through this '**Ville Morte**' (on the left are remains of the hospital and the chapelle Saint-Blaise, where you can watch a slide show on the olive tree) to the tip of the plateau, where there is a monument to Provençal poet Charlon Rieu, and a grand view over the Alpilles.

Turning back, the path climbs up to the château itself, with bits of towers and walls everywhere, including the apse of a Gothic chapel cut out of the rock, and the long eastern wall that survived Richelieu's explosives, dotted with finely carved windows. What looks like a monolithic honeycomb is really a 13th-century pigeonry. Medieval siege engines have been reconstructed to add something of the spirit of the gangsters who built the place. The only intact part is the **donjon**, a rather treacherous climb to the top for a bird's-eye view over the site.

An Infernal Valley and a Blonde Sorceress

Beneath Les Baux, on the western side, the **Pavillon de la Reine Jeanne** has nothing to do with the famous queen, but is a pretty Renaissance garden folly of 1581. The road that passes it will take you in another 3km to the **Val d'Enfer**, the wildest corner of the Alpilles, a weird landscape of eroded limestone, caves and quarries. One thing the Alpilles has a lot of is aluminium ore—*bauxite*, a useless mineral until the process for smelting it was discovered in the last century. Now there are bauxite mines all over southern Provence; those to be seen here are exhausted, but Jean Cocteau took advantage of the landscape to shoot part of his last film, *Testament d'Orphée*. Today the quarries host one of Les Baux's big attractions: the **Cathédrale des Images**, © 04 90 54 38 65 (*open daily 10–7; adm*), a slick show where thirty projectors bounce giant pictures over the walls, the theme of the show changing annually.

Off the D27A, near the crossroads for Les Baux, the **Col de la Vayède** holds scanty remains of the pre-Roman *oppidum*; the lines of the walls can be traced in some places, and there are bits of wall and no fewer than three necropolises, with small niches carved into the rock to hold the ashes of the deceased. On the side of the hill facing the D27A, you can climb up a dirt path to see the mysterious relief called the **Trémaïé**. Neatly carved on a smoothed rock face are three figures and an effaced Latin inscription. It seems to be a Roman funeral monument, but local legend has it that the figures represent Marius, his wife, and a blonde Celtic sorceress named Marthe who helped Marius in his campaigns against the Teutones. Another relief, less well preserved, can be seen a few hundred metres to the south. Finally, for hikers, there is the GR6 trail, which traverses the best parts of the Alpilles from east to west, including Les Baux.

Les Baux ✉ *13520*   ***Where to Stay and Eating Out***

Les Baux, with its tourist hordes, isn't the most desirable place to stop over—and you'll have to pay a lot for the privilege. For a memorable splurge, if you can bear the disdainful hauteur, there's ★★★★l'**Oustau de Baumanière**, Route d'Arles, © 04 90 54 33 07, ✆ 04 90 54 45 29. In magical surroundings in the Val d'Enfer, it's a restored farmhouse with all the amenities, and has a highly rated restaurant (two Michelin stars) and a spectacular terrace view. Seafood is the star: salmon, *langoustines* and such, and there are sumptuous desserts and a formidable wine list (over 100,000 bottles) of Provençal treasures (*menus 470 and 730F, but here you're just as well off choosing à la carte.*) *Closed Jan and Feb* . Nearby, the charming ★★★★**Cabro d'Or**, D27, © 04 90 54 33 21, ✆ 04 90 54 45 98, has recently undergone a complete rehab and offers similar facilities for kinder prices (fom 630F), as well as the expertise of a chef trained with Ducasse and Robuchon (*menus from 250F*). *Closed Mon and Tues lunch in winter.*

You can do as well for half the price at the ★★★**Mas d'Aigret**, literally cut into the rocks just below Les Baux (east on the D27), © 04 90 54 33 54, ✆ 04 90 54 41 37. Some rooms have great views, others open onto the gardens; there is a pool, and attention to every detail. Half *pension* is great value for money—unlike most hotels, you can chose whatever you like from the menu, but even if you're not staying this is *the* place to dine in Les Baux: the restaurant is just as good as the Baumanière's (home-produced *foie gras,* breads, own-smoked salmon, and fresh local produce) (*lunch is a tremendous bargain for 130F; other menus range from 90 to 350F*). *Closed Jan–Mar.* The village itself has only a few tourist-oriented places: try the ★★**Hostellerie de la Reine Jeanne**, © 04 90 54 32 06, ✆ 04 90 54 32 33, relatively cheap, with a bird's eye view. *Closed Nov–Mar.*

St-Gabriel and Fontvieille

The eastern half of the Alpilles is the more scenic, and if you're heading in that direction, lonely roads like the D78 and D24 make worthwhile detours that won't take you more than a few kilometres out of the way; **Eygalières**, on the D24B, is a lovely village with a ruined castle.

Along the western fringes of the Alpilles, on the D33, you will pass the canal port of *Ernaginum*, later called St-Gabriel, which flourished from Roman times until the Middle Ages. You won't see anything; the drying-up of the old canal doomed the city to a slow death, and Ernaginum has disappeared more completely than any ancient city of Provence, leaving only the impressive 12th-century church of **St-Gabriel** standing alone in open fields. There is little to see inside—and it's never open anyhow; the real interest is one of the finest Romanesque façades in the Midi. Very consciously imitating Roman architecture, it shows a stately portal with a triangular pediment, flanked by Corinthian columns. There are excellent sculpted reliefs on and above the tympanum: an *Annunciation, Daniel in the Lions' Den* and *Adam and Eve*, apparently just realizing they have no clothes on.

DAUDET'S MILL MUSEUM.

From here, the only village on the way to Arles is **Fontvieille**, best known for the **Moulin de Daudet**, south on the D33, a rare survivor among the hundreds of windmills that once embellished every hilltop of southern Provence. Alphonse Daudet never really lived here, but his *Lettres de Mon Moulin*, a collection of sentimental tales of the dying life of rural Provence in the late 1800s, is still popular across France today. The windmill has become a museum of Daudet, with photographs and documents. Two kilometres further south, there are sections of two Roman **aqueducts** that served Arles, along with vestiges of a **Roman mill**, unique in Europe. This huge installation was a serious precursor to the Industrial Revolution, using the flow of the water to power 16 separate mills, along a stretch of canal over a kilometre long; nothing like it has been found anywhere else. There's no tourist tic tac, not even a railing. Give Daudet a miss for this.

The Hypogeum of Castellet

On the D17, at the crossroads with the D82, you will find a very ruined castle that once belonged to the Counts of Provence. The surrounding area, a low, flat-topped hill called Castellet, contains one of the most unusual and least-known Neolithic monuments in France. The **Hypogeum** consists of four covered avenues, carefully carved out of the rock or earth, under tumuli that have long since disappeared. They were made as collective tombs about 3500 BC or later, by the Ligurians or their predecessors, and probably also served as a kind of temple. Many have carvings, cup-marks and sun-symbols, inside or near their openings. The sites are not marked, and you may have to scramble and scout to find their narrow, trapezoidal entrances in the undergrowth. All are within 200m of the D17, three south of the road and one north.

From Castellet, you'll see another hill, the **Montagne de Cordes**, about a half-kilometre to the south. Like Castellet, this was an island in Neolithic times. Nearby Montmajour (*see* below) was a third. The Cordes is private property, and you'll need permission from the owner (in the farmhouse on the slopes) to see another remarkable tomb-temple. The **Grotte des Fées** is also known as the 'Epée de Roland'; the tapering, 230ft tunnel has two small side chambers that give it the shape of a sword.

Fontvieille, only 11km away from Les Baux, has a surprising number of hotels. There's the luxurious Relais & Châteaux ★★★★**La Régalido**, 118 Rue Mistral, ✆ 04 90 54 60 22, ✆ 04 90 54 64 29, in a restored mill with lovely gardens, including a restaurant that is a little temple of *haute cuisine* with prices to match (*menus from 280F*) serving excellent fresh seafood or roast pigeon with *morilles. Closed Jan.* Less expensively, the ★★★**Le Val Majour**, 22 Route d'Arles, ✆ 04 90 54 62 33, ✆ 04 90 54 61 67, with a pool and tennis, has well-furnished quiet rooms, and a restaurant with menus at 110 and 190F. Fontvieille has the only budget rooms in the Alpilles, at the admirable ★★**Hostellerie de la Tour**, 3 Rue des Plumelets, ✆ 04 90 54 72 21, with a pool (*closed mid-Oct–Feb*) and the more down-to-earth ★**Bernard**, 6 Cours M. Bellon, ✆ 04 90 54 70 35, ✆ 04 90 54 68 59.

You can dine well in Fontvieille. **La Cuisine du Planet**, 144 Grand Rue, ✆ 04 90 54 63 97, has an excellent three-course summer menu and great desserts at 130F; another at 165F. For appetizing home cooking, **Le Homard**, 29 Route du Nord, ✆ 04 90 52 63 97, has no lobster, but *terrine de poisson, filet de rascasse* and *cassoulet* feature on the 115F and 165F menus, washed down with local Coteaux de Baux wines. Be sure to reserve. *Closed mid-Nov–mid-Feb.*

Abbaye de Montmajour

Just before Arles, the D17 passes one of the most important monasteries of medieval Provence. Founded in the 10th century, on what was then almost an island amidst the swamps, this Benedictine abbey was devoted to reclaiming the land, a monumental labour that would take centuries to complete. By the 1300s, the monastery had grown exceedingly wealthy, a real prize for the Avignon popes, who gained control of it and farmed it out, along with its revenues, to friends and relations. Under such absentee abbots, it languished thereafter, and its great church was never completed. To give some idea of its later decadence, an attempt to reform it in 1639 included importing new monks; the old crew refused to go, and sacked the abbey before they were chased out by royal troops. Montmajour became a national property not in the Revolution, but five years earlier. The 1786 'Affair of the Diamond Necklace' was a famous swindle that involved both Marie Antoinette and the great charlatan Cagliostro. One of the principal players was Montmajour's abbot, the Cardinal de Rohan; he got caught, and all his property, including the abbey, was confiscated. The abbey did service as a farmhouse, and its church as a barn, before restorations began in 1907.

Consequently, there isn't much to see. At the church entrance you'll notice the piers, built into the adjacent wall of the cloister, that would have supported the nave had it been completed. The interior is austere and empty, but gives a good idea of the state of Provençal architecture *c.* 1200, in transition from Romanesque to Gothic. The most interesting part is the **lower church**, a crypt with an unusual plan, including a long, narrow nave and a circular enclosure under the high altar, with radiating chapels behind it; its purpose has not been explained. The **cloister** has some fanciful sculptural decoration; see if you can find the camel. Around the back of the church, you'll see a number of tombs cut out of the rock; these are a mystery too, and may predate the abbey. The mighty 218ft **donjon** was built in the 1360s for defence, in that terrible age when the lords of Les Baux and a dozen other hoodlums were tearing up the neighbourhood; next to it, the tiny chapel of **St-Pierre** (usually closed) was the original abbey church, built on the spot where St-Trophime of Arles (*see* below) had his hermitage.

Ste-Croix

A few hundred yards behind the apse of the church, in the middle of a farm, stands what was the abbey's funeral chapel, **Ste-Croix**. Don't miss it, even though you'll have to walk through the farmyard muck (it's visible from the road, near a barn). Few buildings show so convincingly the architectural sophistication of the Romanesque as this small work of the late 11th century, a central-plan chapel with apses along three sides and an elegant lantern on top. Some complex geometry and a mastery of proportions are built into this simple but perfect form, based on the Golden Section. Too much decoration would be superfluous, and there is only a discreet carved floral frieze along the cornice, along with Moorish-style interlocking arches.

Arles

Like Nîmes, Arles has enough intact antiquities to call itself the 'Rome of France'; unlike Nîmes it lingered in the post-Roman limelight for another 1000 years, producing enough saints for every month on the calendar—Trophimus, Hilarius, Césaire and Genès are some of the more famous. Pilgrims flocked here for a whiff of their odour of sanctity, and asked on their deathbeds to be buried in the holy ground of the Alyscamps. Nowadays Arles holds the distinction of being the largest *commune* in France, ten times larger than Paris, embracing 750 square km of the Camargue and Crau plains; it has given the world the rhythms of the Gypsy Kings, and the pungent joys of *saucisse d'Arles*, France's finest donkey-meat sausage.

Henry James wrote, 'As a city Arles quite misses its effect in every way: and if it is a charming place, as I think it is, I can hardly tell the reason why.' Modern Arles, sitting amidst its ruins, is still somehow charming, in spite of a general scruffiness that seems more intentional than natural. For all the tourists it gets, no town could seem less touristy; a noxious paper mill across the Rhône wafts its stink over the comfortably down-at-heel old quarters, while grass grows up between the pavement cracks around the Roman ruins and medieval palaces. Unhappily, Jeanne Calment, born here in 1876, who met Van Gogh as a young girl and for a long while the oldest person in the world, died in 1997. The city's pride in her longevity continues though, and the way to her grave is clearly marked in the cemetery at Trinquetaille.

History

In 1975, the remains of a Celto-Ligurian settlement were uncovered near the Boulevard des Lices. It's hard to imagine what its builders thought in the 6th century BC, when Greek traders from Marseille arrived and began to dicker over prices. We know at least that the Greeks were pleased, and over the years they established the site as their principal 'counter' for dealings with the Ligurians, calling it *Arelate* ('near sleeping waters' or less poetically, 'bog town'). Business picked up considerably after Marius' legionnaires made Arelate a seaport by digging a canal to Fos (104 BC). In 49 BC, the populace, tired of getting bum deals from the wily Greeks, readily gave Caesar the boats he needed to punish and conquer Marseille for siding with Pompey. In return Arles was rewarded the spoils and received a population boost with a colony of veterans from the Sixth Legion. Most important of all, it got all the business that had previously gone through Greek Marseille. A bridge of boats was built over the Rhône, and the

Colonia Julia Paterna Arelate Sextanorum was known far and wide for its powerful maritime corporations, called *utriculares* from their rafts that floated on inflated bladders.

At the crossroads of Rome's trading route between Italy and Spain and the Rhône, Arles grew rapidly, each century adding more splendid monuments—a theatre, temples, a circus, an amphitheatre, at least two triumphal arches, and a basilica. Constantine built himself a grand palace and baths as big as Caracalla's in Rome. In 395 Emperor Honorius made it the capital of the 'Three Gauls'—France, Britain, and Spain—and as late as 418 it was recorded that 'Arles is so fortunately placed, its commerce is so active and merchants come in such numbers that all the products of the universe are channelled there: the riches of the Orient, perfumes of Arabia, delicacies of Assyria…'

Arles was one of the last cities to fall to the Visigoths, only to become their capital in 476. The Franks inherited it in 536, and Saracen raids were frequent. But on the whole, the Dark Ages were not so dark in Arles; from 879 to 1036 it served as the capital of Provence-Burgundy (the so-called 'Kingdom of Arles'), a vast territory that stretched all the way to Lorraine. Most importantly, Arles was a centre of power for Christianity. Several major Church councils convened here, including one back in 314 that condemned the heresy of Donatism (the quite reasonable belief that sacraments administered by bad priests had no value). Arles' cathedral of St-Trophime became the most important church in Provence; in 597 its bishop, St Virgil, consecrated St Augustine as first Bishop of Canterbury, and as late as 1178, Emperor Frederick Barbarossa was crowned King of Arles at its altar. After a busy career in the 11th and 12th centuries as a Crusader port and pilgrimage destination, the city's special history ended in 1239 when Raymond Berenger, Count of Provence, evicted Arles' imperial viceroy. As the city declined even the sea abandoned it, leaving the former port stranded between marshes and the rocky plain of the Crau, compressed in a time capsule of Roman monuments and ancient customs.

With the improved communications of the 19th century, Arles slowly resurfaced. The Roman amphitheatre was restored. The city's women, celebrated for their beautiful Attic features, inspired Daudet's story *L'Arlésienne* (1866) and Bizet's opera (1872). Its furniture makers invented what has become the traditional south Provençal style, more elegantly rococo than the heavy pieces of northern Provence. The Félibres made much of the city for the striking costumes the women continued to wear, for its bullfights and its *farandole*, a dance in 6/4 time dating back at least to the Middle Ages.

The Arles of Van Gogh

Vincent Van Gogh was a fervent admirer of Daudet, and it may well have been his stories that first brought him to Arles in February 1888. To his surprise, the city was blanketed with snow—a very rare occurrence and, in a way, an omen. When the snow melted it revealed an Arles made mean and ugly by new embankments along the Rhône, cutting the city off from its life-blood (previously the flooding of the river had fertilized the countryside, like the Nile in Egypt). At the same time a new railway line was being installed by workers brought in from Belgium, housed in cheap ticky-tacky buildings. Arles had never looked shabbier. But Van Gogh stayed, found a room to rent in a poor neighbourhood by the station, and painted the shabby Arles around him: the *Café de Nuit* with its hallucinogenic lightbulb, *La Maison Jaune*, and *Le Pont de Langlois* (part of a ghastly irrigation project) with colours so intense in their chromatic contrasts they seem to come from somewhere over the rainbow.

Van Gogh's dream was to found an art colony at Arles, similar to the one at Pont Aven in Brittany. He begged his overbearing friend Gauguin to join him, but when Gauguin finally arrived in October he found little to like in Arles, dashing Van Gogh's hopes. The tension between the two men reached such a pitch in December that the overwrought Van Gogh went over the edge and confronted Gauguin in the street with a razor. Gauguin stared him down and Van Gogh, despising himself, went back to his room, cut off his own ear, and gave it to a prostitute. Arles was scandalized, and breathed a sigh of relief when Van Gogh voluntarily committed himself to the local hospital, or Hôtel Dieu. In May 1889 he left for the hospital in St-Rémy. Van Gogh's output in Arles was prodigious (from February 1888 to May 1889 he painted 300 canvases) but not a single one remains in the city today. His admirers, looking for the places he painted, have just as little to see: the famous bridge, yellow house, and café were destroyed in the Second World War or afterwards; only the clock in the Bar Alcazar in Place Lamartine remains as Van Gogh painted it (in *Café de Nuit)*, along with some of the ancient plane trees around the Alyscamps. To make up for its belated appreciation of the mad, lonely genius who sojourned here, Arles has converted the Hôtel Dieu (which Van Gogh also painted) into a multi-media gallery, the Espace Van Gogh, displaying the works of others.

Getting Around

By train: Arles' train station is on the northern edge of town, on Avenue Paulin Talabot. Arles has frequent connections to Paris, Marseille, Montpellier, Nîmes, Aix-en-Provence, and to all the towns along the main line to Spain; there are frequent services to Avignon and Tarascon and a less frequent service to Orange.

Arles

By bus: The bus station is just across the street, ✆ 04 90 49 38 01. There are about five daily buses to Alberon and Stes-Maries-de-la-Mer, two to Tarascon, seven to Salon, Aix and Marseile, five to Avignon, six to Nîmes and two to St-Gilles, among other destinations; in July and August, there are services to Aigues-Mortes. (Before you hurry into Arles from here, step over the road for a minute to the bank of the Rhône and admire the city on the bend of the river; an unlikely spot for an unparalleled view.)

By taxi: For a taxi day or night, call ✆ 04 90 96 90 03, Jardin d'Eté, Blvd des Lices.

Car and bike hire: **Europcar**, ✆ 04 90 93 23 24, 🖷 04 90 96 18 99, or **Hertz**, ✆ 04 90 96 75 23, 🖷 04 90 93 17 17, both in Blvd Victor Hugo. Hire a bike at the train station, or at **Dall'Oppio**, Rue Portagnel, ✆ 04 90 96 46 83 (Mar–Oct), or **Peugeot**, 15 Rue du Pont, ✆ 04 90 96 03 77.

Tourist Information

Esplanade Charles de Gaulle, next to Hôtel Jules César, ✆ 04 90 18 41 20, 🖷 04 90 18 41 29, and in the rail station, ✆ 04 90 49 36 90. If you intend to see more than two of Arles' monuments and museums, stop here to purchase the 60F **global ticket** to save money (or you can also pick one up at any of the museums). The tourist office also sells tickets for the two-hour **Van Gogh tours** of sites associated with the artist, departing every Tues and Fri at 5pm, 15 June–15 September.

The **post office**, ✆ 04 90 18 41 00, is at 5 Blvd des Lices.

market days

Saturday, Blvd des Lices and Blvd Clémenceau. Wednesday, Blvd Émile Combes. On the first Wednesday of every month there is a *foire à la brocante* on Blvd des Lices.

The Arènes and Théâtre Antique

Despite the pictures in children's history books, Rome was ruined not so much by tribes of horrid Vandals, but by the latter-day Romans themselves, who regarded the baths, theatres and temples they inherited as their private stone quarries. The same holds true of Arles' great monuments, except for the amphitheatre, called **Les Arènes**, ✆ 04 90 96 03 70 (*open April–Sept 9–7, Oct–Mar 10–4.30*), all of 10ft wider than its rival at Nîmes. As enormous as it is, the amphitheatre originally stood another arcade higher, and was clad in marble; as in most public buildings in the Roman empire no expense was spared on its comforts. An enormous awning operated by sailors protected the audience from the sun and rain, and fountains scented with lavender and burning saffron helped cover up the stink of blood spilled by the gladiators and wild animals below. This temple of death survived in good repair because it came in handy. Its walls were tricked out with towers by Saracen occupiers and used as a fortress (like the theatres of Rome), and from the Middle Ages on it sheltered a poor, crime-ridden neighbourhood with two churches and 200 houses, built from stones prised off the amphitheatre's third storey. These were cleared away in 1825, leaving the amphitheatre free for bullfights, and able to pack in 12,000 spectators. The first was held in 1830, to celebrate the capture of Algiers.

But a different fate was in store for the **Théâtre Antique** (*same hours as Arènes*), just south of the Arènes: in the 5th century, in a fury usually reserved for pagan temples, Christian fanatics pulled it apart stone by stone. A shame, because the fragments of fine sculpture they left in the rubble suggest that the theatre, once capable of seating 12,000, was much more lavish than the one in Orange. Of the stage, only two tall Corinthian columns survived; they were nicknamed 'the two widows', after being pressed into service as gibbets in the 17th and 18th centuries. The most famous statue of Roman Provence, the *Venus of Arles*, lay buried at their feet until she was dug up in 1651 and presented to Louis XIV to adorn the gardens of Versailles. Tiers of seats have been rebuilt for modern performances and costume pageants.

South of the theatre runs the **Boulevard des Lices** ('of the lists'), where large cafés under the plane trees provide ringside seats for the rollicking Saturday and monthly Wednesday morning markets. Since the 17th century the Boulevard has been the favourite promenade of the Arlésiens, where visitors like Van Gogh would go on Sunday to see the women dressed in their best costumes. On either side of the street are the **Jardin d'Eté** (with a bust of Van Gogh) and **Jardin d'Hiver** (where the 5th-century BC *oppidum* was uncovered). Just north of the Boulevard, off Rue du Président Wilson, the old Hôtel-Dieu has been converted into the **Espace Van Gogh**, including the town's library; it's worth a look inside for the lovely, colourful courtyard, restored to look just as it did when Van Gogh painted it. Here, as elsewhere around Arles, the town has put up reproductions of his works all over the place.

Place de la République: St-Trophime

From Boulevard des Lices, Rue Jean Jaurès (the Roman *cardo*) leads to the harmonious **Place de la République**, an attractive square on the Roman model, with a fountain built around a granite **obelisk** that once stood in the *spina* (or barrier) of the circus. Overlooking this pagan sun needle is one of the chief glories of Provençal Romanesque, the cathedral of **St-Trophime**.

The original church, built by St Hilaire in the 5th century and dedicated to St Stephen, was rebuilt at the end of the 11th century, and the great **Portal** added in the next, one of the best-preserved ensembles of Romanesque sculpture in the Midi. Inspired by the triumphal arches of Glanum and Orange, its reliefs describe the *Last Judgement*, mixing the versions of the Apocalypse and Gospel of Matthew. As angels blast away on their trumpets, the triumphant Christ sits in majesty in the tympanum, accompanied by the symbols of the four Evangelists, the 12 Apostles, and a gospel choir of 18 pairs of angels. On the left side, St Michael weighs each soul, separating the good from evil for their just desserts in the after-life—the fortunate in their long robes are delivered into the bosoms of Abraham, Isaac and Jacob, while the damned, naked and bound like a chain gang, are led off in a conga-line to hell: as in all great Romanesque art, the figures on this portal seem to dance to an inner, cosmic rhythm. The large saints set back in the columned recesses below are, from left to right: Bartholomew, James the Minor, Trophime as bishop, John the Evangelist, Peter (over the man-eating lions), Paul, Andrew, Stephen (being stoned), James the Major and Philip. Van Gogh found it admirable but 'so cruel, so monstrous, like a Chinese nightmare, that even this beautiful example of so good a style seems to me to belong to another world and I am glad not to belong to it...'

After the sumptuous portal, the spartan nudity of the long, narrow nave is as striking as its unusual height. Aubusson tapestries from the 17th century hang across the top, and there are several Palaeochristian sarcophagi along the sides. The best decoration, however, is by a Dutchman named Finsonius, who came down to Arles in 1610. Like Van Gogh, he stayed, mesmerized by the light and colour, and met a bad end, drowning in the icy Rhône in 1642. St-Trophime has three of his paintings: in the crossing, a beautiful *Annunciation* (1610), the *Stoning of St Stephen* over the triumphal arch in the nave, and on the right, a singular *Adoration of the Magi*, with nightmare architecture and animals in attendance.

The Cloister

Same opening hours as the Arènes—but come around mid-day if you want to see the sculptures at their best.

Around the corner in Rue du Cloître is the entrance to St-Trophime's cloister. No other in Provence is as richly and harmoniously sculpted as this, carved in the 12th and 14th centuries by the masters of St-Gilles. Because Arles was as anti-Revolutionary as a town could be, this masterpiece was spared the wanton vandalism that destroyed so much elsewhere.

The north gallery is the oldest, supported by two monumental pillars adorned with statues; those of *St Peter* and *St Trophime* on the northwest are masterpieces of the classically influenced Arles school. The capitals in the Romanesque north and east galleries are carved with scenes from the New Testament, their figures moving to the same rhythms as those on the portal. The capitals of the more severe Gothic gallery to the south are carved with the *Life of St Trophime*, while on the west the capitals closely resemble the south gallery of Montmajour's cloister: note the *Magdalene* kissing Christ's feet, and *St Martha* with her Tarasque.

Hôtel de Ville and les Cryptoportiques

Sharing Place de la République with the church of St-Trophime is Arles' palatial **Hôtel de Ville**, built in 1675 after plans by Hardouin-Mansart, architect of the Hall of Mirrors at Versailles; here, his virtuoso signature is in the remarkable flat vaulting of the vestibule. Facing the inner courtyard are remnants of older civic buildings: sections of the 12th–15th-century palace of the *podestats* (or prefects of the Holy Roman Emperor), and the town hall of 1500, with a Roman tympanum and bell tower modelled after the mausoleum of Glanum.

Just around the corner on Rue Balze is the cryptoporticus of the forum, or **les crypto-portiques** (*open April–Sept 9–7, Oct–Mar 10–4.30; adm*). These are entered through a long-unused Jesuit church, with an unusual wooden vaulted ceiling and a huge wooden Baroque retable that covers the entire apse. With the ramparts, this cryptoporticus was the first large construction of the Roman colony. Forming three sides of a rectangle measuring 289 by 192ft, these subterranean barrel-vaulted double galleries of the 1st century BC were built as foundations for the monumental Forum above. You can see a model of this Forum's original appearance in the Archaeological Museum; like the Imperial Fora in Rome, this one was built all at once, as a unified architectural grouping, consisting of a rectangle of colonnades for public business, and a temple in the centre. No one knows for sure what other purpose a cryptoporticus may have served—for storage, or perhaps, as on Rome's Palatine Hill, for cool promenades.

The Muséon Arlaten

Open Nov–Mar 9–12 and 2–5, April, May and Sept 9–12 and 2–6, June and July 9–12 and 2–7, Oct 9–12 and 2–5.30; adm.

The indefatigable Frédéric Mistral began his collection of ethnographic items from Provence in 1896; in 1904, when he won the Nobel Prize, he used the money to purchase the 16th-century Hôtel de Castellane-Laval to house his **Muséon Arlaten**, 29 Rue de la République, ✆ 04 90 96 08 23. Mistral's aim was to record the details of everyday life in Provence for future generations. The evolution of the traditional Arlésienne costume, one of Mistral's obsessions, is thoroughly documented, with adjustments made to match fashion changes in Paris. The wearing of it declined along with the use of the Provençal language, in spite of the poet's folklore parades (the 'Festivals of Virgins') in Arles' theatre. Nowadays the female museum attendants here are the last Arlésiennes to wear the traditional costume, as they sit crocheting by the windows and gossiping (not in Provençal, but French!).

Most memorable and strange are the life-size dioramas: a Christmas dinner at a *mas*, with a table groaning with wax food, a reed-thatched *cabane des gardiens*, and a visit to a new mother and her infant. The curious gifts of salt, a match, an egg and bread brought by the visitors symbolize the hope that the baby may grow to be (in the same order) wise, straight, full and good. The gallery of rituals has a prickly Tarasque retired from the procession at Tarascon, and a lock of golden hair discovered in a medieval tomb at Les Baux. One room is dedicated to the Félibrige, and another to Mistral himself, with the great man's cradle under glass.

In the courtyard, a section of the Forum was uncovered, complete with an **exedra** cut with ten niches for statues. To the north of the Muséon Arlaten, the café-filled **Place du Forum** is the centre of modern life in Arles, watched over helplessly by a **statue of Frédéric Mistral**, moustachioed and goateed like his near-double, Buffalo Bill. Mistral himself attended its unveiling in 1909, thanking his admirers, but regretting that they made him look as if he were waiting for a train.

Constantine's Baths and the Réattu Museum

From the Place de la République, Rue Hôtel de Ville leads north to the ruins of Constantine's palace, of which only part of the baths, or **Les Thermes de Constantin**, remain (*open April–Sept 9–12 and 2–7, Oct–Mar 10–12 and 2–4.30; adm*).

Across the street on the banks of the Rhône stood the Priory of the Knights of Malta, built in the 14th century. The knights, who came from all over Europe, were divided into eight *langues* or tongues, and this was the local headquarters of the *Langue de Provence*; the façade with gargoyles facing the river gives the best idea of its original appearance. After the Revolution an academic painter named Jacques Réattu purchased the priory, and his daughter made it into the **Musée Réattu**, Rue du Grand Prieuré, ✆ 04 90 49 38 34 (*open daily 9–12 and 2–7, Oct–Mar 10–12 and 2–4.30; adm*). Besides Reattu's own contributions, there are works by Théodore Rousseau, followers of Lorrain and Salvator Rosa, and one painting so marvellously, indescribably awful that it deserves a museum to itself, Antoine Rospal's portrait of himself and his family. In 1972, the museum was jolted awake with a donation of 57 drawings from Picasso, in gratitude for the many bullfights he enjoyed in Arles. Nearly all date from January 1971 and constitute a running dialogue the artist held with himself on some of his favourite subjects—harlequins, men, women, the artist and his model—and, more unusually, a Tarasque. Other Picassos in the museum include a beautiful portrait of his mother Maria from the 1920s, donated by his widow Jacqueline, and a sculpture of a woman with a violin. There are more recent works by César and Pol Bury and, upstairs, an exhibition gallery devoted to photography.

The Alyscamps

Follow Rue E. Fassin, the first street south of the Boulevard des Lices, eastwards; a 10min walk from the centre. Same opening hours as the Arènes; adm.

One of the most prestigious necropolises of the Middle Ages, the Alyscamps owed its fame to the legend of St Trophime, a cousin of the proto-martyr St Stephen who became a disciple of St Paul. Paul sent Trophime to convert Gaul, where medieval hagiographers later confused him with a 2nd- or 3rd-century Bishop of Arles of the same name. The story has it that Trophime arrived in Arles in the year 46, and held secret meetings with his new converts in the lonesome Roman cemetery of Alyscamps (believed to be a corruption of *Elisii Campi*, or Elysian Fields), which according to Roman custom was built outside the city walls, along the Via Aurelia. Trophime eventually attracted quite a following, and before he died he gave a special blessing to the Alyscamps; Christ himself attended the ceremony, and left behind a stone imprint of his knee.

Burial in such holy ground was so desirable that bodies sealed in barrels with their burial fee attached were floated down the Rhône to Arles. Some rascals in Beaucaire took to robbing the dead of their coins as they floated downstream, but they were found out when the barrels miraculously returned upstream to the scene of the crime. At its greatest extent the necropolis stretched 2.5km and contained 19 chapels and several thousand tombs, many of them packed five bodies deep. Dante mentions it in the *Inferno* (IX, 112) and it makes an appearance in numerous *Chansons de Geste*. Ariosto wrote how Charlemagne's peers, cut down at Roncevalles, were flown here and buried by angels.

The Alyscamps' mystique began to decline in 1152, when the relics of St Trophime were transferred to the cathedral. Grave-robbers pillaged the tombs, and the most beautiful sarcophagi were given away as presents to Renaissance potentates. Under Louis Napoleon the Alyscamps itself was dismembered by a railroad, a canal, factories, and a housing estate, leaving only one romantic, melancholy lane lined with empty, mostly plain sarcophagi. Of the 19 chapels, all that remains is a 15th-century chapel that now serves as the ticket booth, along with recently restored Romanesque **St-Honorat** at the far end. Its two-storey octagonal tower still stands, rebuilt in the 12th century by the monks of St-Victor in Marseille; in the apse are three Carolingian sarcophagi.

Musée de l'Arles Antique

> *Open daily April–Sept 9–7, Oct–Mar 9.30-5, closed Mon; adm; © 04 90 18 88 88, ✆ 04 90 93 69 59.*

Arles' newest museum, the **Musée de l'Arles Antique**, Presqu'île du Cirque Romain, Avenue de la 1ère D. F. L., has been erected in an eerie wasteland slightly out of town, opposite the Palais des Congrès (follow the Boulevard des Lices to its western end, and pass under the motorway); in front of the museum you'll see foundations of the curve of Arles' Roman circus. This shiny modern building houses the collected contents of several of Arles' old museums. Though the ancient works themselves are not especially noteworthy, the detailed explanations (in French) and especially the brilliant architectural models bring the Roman city back to life in a way that few museums anywhere can match. Here you'll see how the Roman sailors wired up the sailcloth awning to shade the amphitheatre, how the city centre—the Forum and temples—looked to the man in the street, how the army engineers made the floating bridge over the Rhône, and much more.

Amongst the exhibits are the pagan statues and sarcophagi of the former Musée d'Art Païen. Nearly everything here was made in the Arles region, with the exception of the beautiful white marble *Hippolytus and Phaedra sarcophagus* (2nd or 3rd century AD), with its hunting scenes. Two exceptional mosaics brought in from nearby Roman villas show the *Rape of Europa* and *Orpheus* enchanting the wild beasts; there's a graceful but damaged dancing girl, a headless statue of Mithras, the god of the legionnaires, his torso decorated with signs of the Zodiac entwined by a serpent. The large statue of Augustus was found in the theatre, as was the *Venus of Arles*, represented here by a copy made before Louis XIV had it 'restored'. Although a fairly chaste specimen as marble love goddesses go, she earned from Théodore Aubanel the most ham-handedly erotic of all Félibre poems:

> *Laisso ti pèd toumba la raubo qu'à tis ancò*
> *S'envertouio, mudant tout ço qu'as de plus bèu:*
> *Abandouno toun ventre i pountoun dóu soulèu!*
> *Coume l'èurre s'aganto à la rusco d'un aubre,*
> *Laisso din mi brassado estregne en plen toun maubre:*
> *Laisso ma bouco ardènto e mi det tremoulant*
> *Courre amouros pertout sus toun cadabre blanc!*

> *(Throw to your feet the robe that around your hips/hangs, hiding all that is most beautiful about you:/Abandon your stomach to the kisses of the sun!/As ivy entwines the bark of a tree,/Let me in my embraces clasp all of your marble;/Let my ardent mouth and burning fingers/run lovingly over your body so white!)*

Also in the museum are the contents of the former Musée d'Art Chrétien, the best collection of 4th-century Christian sarcophagi of any museum. Carved by Arlésien sculptors between the years 330 and 395, these remarkably preserved tombs make a fascinating documentary of the newly victorious faith; as their pagan ancestors carved scenes from mythology, so these early Christians spared no expense to decorate their last resting places on earth with scenes from the Old and New Testaments. Nearly every figure of importance wears a Roman toga; in the *sarcophage de Trinquetaille*, discovered in 1974, the Three Magi sport Phrygian bonnets.

Festivals and Annual Events

Arles does its best to keep its visitors entertained. The free broadsheet *Farandole* gives details of everything from theatre, concerts, fairs and exhibitions to local basketball results. Easter is celebrated by a **Feria Pascale** with four days of bull-fights, most of them Spanish *corridas* (for ticket reservations for Arènes events, call ✆ 04 90 96 03 70, ✉ 04 90 96 64 31). On 24 June, St John's Day, there are typical Arlésien dances in costume around bonfires, and the distribution of blessed bread. July is the busiest month, with a festival of music, dance and drama, the **Cocarde d'Or** bullfights, and most importantly, photography in the **Rencontres Internationales de la Photographie**, with over a dozen shows and workshops, in the Théâtre Antique. At the end of August there's the **Festival du Film Peplum**. The last bullfights of the year, on the second Sunday in September, coincide with the **Prémices du Riz** (rice harvest).

Shopping

Besides the Wednesday and Saturday **markets** (*see* p.320), you can find authentic *gardian* costumes at **Camille**, Esplanade des Lices, ✆ 04 90 96 04 94, and traditional clothes for ladies at **L'Arlésienne**, 12 Rue Pdt Wilson, ✆ 04 90 93 28 05. For colourful Provençal fabrics, try **Les Olivades**, 2 Rue Jean Jaurès, ✆ 04 90 96 22 17, or **Arlys**, 35 Rue Voltaire, ✆ 04 90 96 45 89, which also specializes in *santons*. **Cabane Soleil**, 15 Rue du 4 Septembre, ✆ 04 90 96 07 34, has enchanting locally made puppets, as well as other modern curiosities in metal and wood. Buy your *calis-*

sons d'Aix from **Puyricard**, 5 Rue Dulau, ☎ 04 90 93 46 91. Any good butcher will sell you spicy donkey-filled **saucisson d'Arles**.

Arles ✉ 13200   *Where to Stay*

Arles offers relief for the budget-bruised traveller, and charges less for more than you'll get in cities like Avignon or Aix. If you arrive without a reservation, the tourist office has a room-finding service for a small fee.

expensive

The luxurious grand-daddy of hotels in Arles is ★★★★**Jules César** (locally known as *Chez Jules*), Blvd des Lices, ☎ 04 90 93 43 20, ✆ 04 90 93 33 47, occupying a former Dominican monastery with a Caesar-ish temple porch tacked on. The rooms are vast, air-conditioned and furnished with Provençal pieces; the pool is heated and the gardens beautiful (*closed Nov–23 Dec*). Its chief competitor, ★★★★**Nord Pinus**, Place du Forum, ☎ 04 90 93 44 44, ✆ 04 90 93 34 00, has some columns from a Roman temple embedded in its façade. Once the favourite of the Félibres, poets, and literati like Stendhal, Mérimée and Henry James, it now draws the top matadors and wealthy aficionados; the premises are comfortable and full of heavy dark furniture, bullfighting posters, trophies, and the mounted heads of famous bulls; weekend hunts in the Camargue and private boat excursions to the beach are some of its offerings. *Closed Jan–Mar.*

Near the lively Place du Forum, the 12th- to 18th-century home of the Comtes d'Arlatan has been converted into the magnificent ★★★**D'Arlatan**, 26 Rue du Sauvage, ☎ 04 90 93 56 66, ✆ 04 90 49 68 45. After a warm welcome, wait for the lift standing on glass over Roman excavations; the house was built over part of the Constantine basilica, and in 1988 a Roman drain and a statue plinth from the 1st century BC were uncovered. If you're alone, ask for room 38; a single bed for half the price, if you can do without a TV and your own bathroom, located in a converted chapel overlooking the courtyard where a fountain splatters; a cherub flies at the head of your bed. ★★★**Forum**, at 10 Place du Forum, ☎ 04 90 93 48 95, ✆ 04 90 93 90 00, in another old house, doesn't have as much charm but it does have a swimming-pool (*closed for Christmas*). Just north of Arles, a traditional farmhouse and 16th-century chapel are at the core of the ★★★**Mas de la Chapelle**, Petite Rte de Tarascon, ☎ 04 90 93 23 15, ✆ 04 90 96 53 74; excellent service, a pool and tennis courts are some of the extras. On the edge of the Crau, 5km east of Arles, the ★★★**Hôtel La Fenière** in **Raphèle-les-Arles** (✉ 13280; on the N453; ☎ 04 90 98 47 44, ✆ 04 90 98 48 39), is an attractive, ivy-covered inn; nice rooms from 325F, some with air conditioning, and a restaurant with an outdoor terrace which offers Camarguaise beef, duck with olives or salmon roulades on menus from 120F.

moderate

Among the less expensive choices are ★★**St-Trophime**, 16 Rue de la Calade, ☎ 04 90 96 88 38, ✆ 04 90 96 92 19, in an old house with a central court. *Closed mid-Nov–mid-Dec, Jan*. At the ★★**Calendal**, 22 Place Pomme, ☎ 04 90 96 11 89, ✆ 04 90 96 05 84, rooms overlook a garden with palm trees. *Closed Oct–April*. To be first at the Musée Réattu in the morning, spend the night at ★★**Hôtel du Musée**, 11 Rue du Grand-Prieuré, ☎ 04 90 93 88 88, ✆ 04 90 49 98 15: an attractive converted

17th-century residence opposite the museum. Quiet, subtly chic, and above all friendly, the hotel epitomizes all Arles has to offer. *Closed Jan–mid-Feb* .

inexpensive

There are plenty of these on the streets toward the train station, including two on Place Lamartine: the bright and welcoming **★Terminus et Van Gogh**, 5 Place Lamartine, *✆* 04 90 96 12 32, and the **★France**, next door at No.3, *✆* 04 90 96 01 24, also good and slightly less expensive. The **★★Gauguin**, at 5 Place Voltaire, *✆* 04 90 96 14 35, just south of Place Lamartine, has simple but tidy rooms, some with balconies. *Closed Nov.* Arles also has an **Auberge de Jeunesse** at 20 Ave Maréchal Foch, *✆* 04 90 96 18 25. Bus from Place Lamartine (*open year-round*).

Eating Out

Lou Marquès (in the Jules César hotel, *✆*04 90 93 43 20) is Arles' elegant citadel of traditional *haute cuisine*, featuring dishes such as *croustillant de Saint-Pierre* and *carré d'agneau* with artichokes, and an excellent wine cellar (*menus 195–380F*). In Place du Forum, **Le Vaccarès**, *✆* 04 90 96 06 17, serves delicious renderings of Provence's finest dishes, using the freshest market ingredients (steamed *loup* with a citrus *compote*, *noisettes d'agneau*), washed down with the best wines from the Rhône valley (*lunch menu 98F, others up to 280F*). Set in a beautiful vaulted room from the 17th century, **Le Tourne Broche**, 6 Rue Balze, *✆* 04 90 96 16 03, serves a selection of affordable menus (*from 80F*), including items like salmon terrine and *suprême de volaille*. *Closed Mon.* **Le Côte d'Adam**, Rue de la Liberté , *✆* 04 90 49 62 29, serves up a filling *daube provençal* and other hearty favourites in two cosy rooms with a fireplace off Place du Forum (*menus 70–120F*).

For lunch after a walk through the Alyscamps, there's **Le Jardin de Manon**, 14 Ave des Alyscamps, *✆* 04 90 93 38 68: seafood, *maigrets* and such on a pretty terrace out back (*68F lunch menu, others 90 and 128F*). For a light lunch in the centre, the vegetarian **Vitamine**, 16 Rue du Docteur Fanton, *✆* 04 90 93 77 36, offers a welcome injection of greenery: 50 different salads for under 70F. *Closed Sun, but not in July.* Or for something different you could arrange a day course in Provençal cuisine run by Erick Vedel, its high priest, and his polyglot American wife Madeleine (*✆* 04 90 49 69 20).

Entertainment and Nightlife

The most sociable bars in Arles are in Place du Forum; for lazy watching-the-world-go-by, plump for a chair in Place Voltaire or Boulevard des Lices. After dark, the liveliest place in Arles is **Le Méjan/Actes Sud**, at Quai M-Dormoy, *✆* 04 90 45 56 78, a complex that includes a book and record shop, art gallery, concerts, three cinemas and films in their original language, also a bar and restaurant where you can eat for as little as 55F a head. Then there is the **Cargo de Nuit**, 7 Ave Sadi Carmet, *✆* 04 90 45 55 99, which offers live music, a philosophy night and is open till 5am Thursdays to Saturdays; and **Le Femina**, same number, at Rue Emile Zola. If you want to strut your stuff, the two discos are **Le Krystal**, at Moules, *✆* 04 90 98 32 40, and **La Camargue**, just outside Arles on the road to Stes-Maries-de-la-Mer, *✆* 04 90 97 10 95.

Plaine de la Crau

Hercules, after completing his Tenth Labour, the theft of the cattle of Geryon, passed through Provence with the booty on his way home to Greece. He had some trouble with the native Ligurians, who apparently tried to pinch the cows. One thing led to another, and before long the big fellow found himself in single-handed battle with the entire nation. As they advanced across the marshy plain, Hercules, armed only with his club, got down on his knees in despair at having nothing to throw at them. Zeus took pity on him, and sent down a shower of stones, with which the hero soon put the Ligurians to flight. This was an unaccountably important story in the mythology of the Greeks. They and the Romans put the Hercules of this battle in the sky; the northern constellation we know as Hercules they called *Engonasis*, the 'kneeler'.

The carpet of stones Zeus sent are still there for all to see, on the weird wasteland called the **Crau**, stretching from Arles to the Etang de Berre, between the Camargue and the Alpilles. The ancients found it fascinating, and many Greek and Roman writers attempted to explain it; Aristotle, a hopeless bird-brain at anything involving natural science, said the stones were formed by volcanoes, and 'rolled down naturally' to the low plain. In fact the rounded stones are alluvial deposits from the Durance, from long ago when the river followed this path into the Rhône delta.

The empty, wind-blown Crau is a major element of the Provençal mystique; Mistral, for example, dragged his poor Mireille across it before she met her sad end. Today it does its best to keep up a romantic appearance. Over 100,000 sheep make their winter home here, nibbling the tufts of grass between the stones before migrating in the old-fashioned way up to the Provençal Alps in May or June; the stone shepherd huts are still one of the few features of the Crau. The French, unfortunately, have been trying to make it disappear. Most of the northern part has been reclaimed for farmland. The rest is criss-crossed with railways, canals and roads, decorated with army firing ranges and the gigantic Istres military airport.

There are no good roads over the unspoiled parts of the Crau, and the only village, **St-Martin-de-Crau**, is a dismal spot, but you can still see something of the original effect along the N568 (for Fos and Marseille) and the N113 (for Salon), both east of Arles.

Into the Camargue

To its handful of inhabitants, the Camargue was the *isclo*, the 'island' between the two branches of the Rhône. The river's course has taken many different forms over the millennia, and the present one, with its two arms, has created a vast marshland, France's salt cellar, its greatest treasure-house of water-fowl and home of some of its most exotic landscapes. The two branches, the *Grand* and *Petit* Rhônes, really build separate deltas, leaving the space in between a soupy battleground where land and sea slowly struggle for mastery.

With its unique coastline and wild expanses, the Camargue provides a soothing antithesis to the more crowded areas of the region. It is also ideal for outdoor activities: hiking, climbing, diving, surfing or horse-riding (*see* 'Getting Around' sections below for details).

Getting Around

Due to its proximity, Arles is the traditional jumping-off point for the Camargue.

By train and bus: The only public transport to the centre of the Camargue begins at the Gare Routière in Arles: one or two buses a day each to Stes-Maries-de-la-Mer (via

Albaron) and Salin-de-Giraud. There are also one or two SNCF trains to St-Gilles from Arles. St-Gilles has regular bus connections to Nîmes (five a day), a few to Arles and one to Lunel.

On foot, horseback and by bike and jeep: Remember that the Camargue is really quite small—it's never more than 40km from Arles to the coast. It's perfect country for bicycling, and there are a few bike hire shops in Stes-Maries-de-la-Mer. Horses are even more popular; there are many places to hire one in Stes-Maries-de-la-Mer, or in Aigues-Mortes, the **Ranch del Sol** (© 04 66 53 99 83), and at l'Etang de l'Estagel, **L'Etrier** (© 04 66 01 36 76). **Destination Camargue**, © 04 90 96 94 44 (Sat & Sun © 04 90 93 42 48), organizes day and half-day trips into the Camargue by jeep.

By boat: This is another possibility: **Blue-Line** (© 04 66 87 22 66) and other firms in St-Gilles rent boats fit for a few days' trip through the Petite Camargue. At Stes-Maries-de-la-Mer and St-Gilles there are excursion boats that make short cruises around the Camargue.

History

Ancient writers recorded the people of the Camargue hunting boar in the swamp forests and actually raking fish out of the mud; besides remarking on its curiosities, the Greeks and Romans left it entirely alone. In the early Middle Ages, however, at least four monastic colonies were founded on the edges of the Camargue, not only to reclaim land but to collect that most precious of medieval commodities, salt. In this inhospitable country, all of them disappeared long ago; the most important was the Abbey of Psalmody, which became quite a power in Provence. Today only scant ruins can be seen, on a farm still called Psalmody north of Aigues-Mortes, in the region called the 'Petite Camargue' west of the Petit Rhône.

By the 1600s, the monks gave way to cowboys (*gardians*), who created large ranches to exploit the two totem animals of the Camargue: the native black, longhorn cattle that thrive on salt grass, and who have always been the preferred stock for Provençal bullfights; and the beautiful white horse, believed to have been introduced by the Arabs back in the Dark Ages. A true cowboy culture grew up, a romantic image dear to the Provençaux, and especially to Provençal writers like Mistral.

There are still a few score *gardians* in the Camargue today, keeping up the old traditions. Big changes have come to the swampland in the last century. For a while, the French threatened to dispose rationally of this land altogether, with dikes and drainage schemes turning large areas into salt-pans and rice fields. Fortunately, nature societies secured the creation of a wildlife preserve around the heart of the Camargue in 1928, and the government made a Regional Park of the area in 1970.

Flora and Fauna

First and most spectacularly, there are the flamingos (*flamants roses*), a symbol of the Camargue; several thousand of them nest around the southern lagoons. Probably no place in the Mediterranean has a wider variety of aquatic birds: lots of ducks, grebes, cormorants, curlews and ibis. The little egret is a common sight, though they spend the winter in Africa, as does the avocet, which looks like an aquatic magpie. There are also many purple herons, conspicuously striped on the head and breast. Not all are water birds; you may see an eagle or a majestic red kite (*milan royal*).

Deforestation in favour of ranches destroyed most of the natural habitat for land animals, but there are still boars, beavers, and blue frogs. Trees are rare, although there are umbrella pines and scrubby, pink-flowered tamarisks. Common plants include the purple-flowered *saladelle*, and the *salicorne*, which grows in tough clumps. Among the fauna, we nearly forgot the most important—the hard-drilling, inescapable Camargue mosquito.

The Musée de la Camargue

Open daily exc Tues, 10–4.15; April–Sept daily 9.15–6.45; adm.

It was an inspiration on the part of the Regional Park management, creating this museum in what not long ago was a working Camargue cattle and sheep ranch, the **Mas du Pont de Rousty**, 9km southwest of Arles on the D570, ✆ 04 90 97 10 82. The buildings are well-restored and documented, giving a feeling of what life was like on the *mas* a century ago. There are special exhibits on the *gardians*, on the fickle Rhône (you'll learn that 400,000 years ago it flowed past Nîmes), on Mistral's *Miréio*, and other subjects. Outside, there are marked nature trails leading deep into the surrounding swampy plain, the **Marais de la Grande Mar**. About 4km beyond the museum on the D570, little **Albaron** was one of the first inhabited centres of the Camargue; a stout medieval tower survives, built to guard Arles from any attack or pirate raid up the Petit Rhône.

CAMARGUE
'gardian' branding iron.

The Etang de Vaccarès

For all of us lazy motor tourists, the way to see the best of the Camargue is to take the D37, a left turn 4km south of the museum. After another 4km, a side road leads to the **Domaine de Méjanes**, with horse riding and canoes; on summer weekends the *gardians* put on shows of cowboy know-how, and occasionally bullfights. Call ahead, ✆ 04 90 97 10 62, for information. Further on, the D37 skirts the edges of the **Etang de Vaccarès**, the biggest of the lagoons and centre of the Camargue wildlife preserve. In some places you can see flocks of nesting flamingos year-round. A side road, the D36B, leads down to Salin-de-Giraud, passing the **Centre d'Information la Capillière**, ✆ 04 90 97 00 97 (*open daily 9–12 and 2–7*), with exhibits on flora and fauna and fascinating guided nature walks around the lagoon.

The scenery changes abruptly at **Salin-de-Giraud**, a 19th-century industrial village that works the largest saltworks in Europe: a staggering 110 square kilometre network of pans, anually producing 800,000 tonnes of salt. There's another park nature centre on the D36, **La Palissade**, ✆ 04 42 86 81 28 (*open weekdays 9–5; June–Sept, daily*), with white horses, bulls, audiovisuals, a small aquarium, walks etc., and information on the flamingo-filled Etang de Grande-Palun. The *salins* are barred from the Mediterranean by one of the longest and emptiest beaches in France, the **Plage de Piémanson** at the mouth of the Grand Rhône; the current is a bit treacherous for swimming. To get away from it all, head west of Salin for the **Plage de Beauduc** (signposted), where you'll find a couple of places that grill the day's catch. With good local maps, determined swamp fans can hike the 40km or so to Stes-Maries-de-la-Mer in summer, through the most unspoiled parts of the Camargue; a sea-wall, the **Digue de la Mer**, provides a crossing around the lagoons, and the only hazards are secluded beaches that have been taken over by bands of *naturistes*. You might even make it over to the Camargue's forest, **Bois des Rièges**, on a large island at the southern end of the Etang de Vaccarès. Though officially off limits, as part of the nature preserve, it can sometimes be reached on foot in summer.

Almost all of the accommodation in the area is in Stes-Maries-de-la-Mer (*see* below). But if you want to stay in the eastern or central parts of the Camargue, away from the tourists, there are some possibilities. One of these isolated spots, and also a good bet for lunch after visiting the Camargue museum, is **★★Le Flamant Rose** in **Albaron** (✉ 13123), ✆ 04 90 97 10 18, 🖷 04 90 97 12 47, a simple Logis de France open all year with 95–190F menus including a *salade fruits de mer* and stewed beef cowboy style—*boeuf à la gardienne.* **Salin-de-Giraud** (✉ 13129), amidst its vast salt pans, doesn't even dream of attracting tourists. The family favourite restaurant is **Le Saladelle** at 4 Ave des Arènes in the centre, ✆ 04 42 86 83 87: a wide choice on 60/120F menus, including more spicy *boeuf à la gardienne*, chops and fish, and seafood lasagne. And of course shakers of the local speciality on every table—all you can eat. There's only one place to stay in the town, the simple and basic **★La Camargue** on Blvd de la Camargue, ✆ 04 42 86 88 52.

Les Saintes-Maries-de-la-Mer

Set among the low sand-dunes, lively Saintes-Maries-de-la-Mer has an open-armed approach to visitors that long predates any interest in the Camargue and its ecological balance. For this is one of Provence's holy of holies, and if you come out of season you may still sense the dream-like, insular remoteness that made it the stuff of legend.

The pious story behind it all was promoted to the hilt by the medieval Church: after Christ was crucified, his Jewish detractors took a boat without sails or oars and loaded it with three Marys—Mary Salome (mother of the apostles James and John), Mary Jacobe, the Virgin's sister, and Mary Magdalene, along with the Martha and her resurrected brother Lazarus, St Maximin and St Sidonius. As this so-called Boat of Bethany drifted off shore, Sarah, the black Egyptian servant of Mary Salome and Mary Jacobe, wept so grievously that Mary Salome tossed her cloak on the water, so that Sarah was able to walk across on it and join the saints. The boat took them to the Camargue, to this spot where the elderly Mary Salome, Mary Jacobe, and Sarah built an oratory, while their younger companions went to spread the Gospel, live in caves and tame Tarasques. In 1448, during the reign of Good King René (who was always pinched for money) the supposed relics of the two Marys were discovered, greatly boosting the local pilgrim trade. Les Saintes-Maries became, as Mistral called it, the 'Mecca of Provence'.

A few facts blazed the trail for the legend's ready acceptance. In the 4th century, a Roman writer described a settlement on this site called *Oppidum priscum Ra*. This lent its name to the first Christian church, Notre-Dame-de-Ratis, built over the site of a spring of fresh water—where a Gallo-Roman temple had been dedicated to three sea goddesses. *Ratis* was taken to mean raft (*radeau*), hence the connection not only with the Boat of Bethany but to ancient Egypt, where in the Book of the Dead the deceased sails in a boat without oar or sail, but with the image of Ra. Even the name Mary had a familiar ring to Provence's early Christians; not only for its resemblance to the word for mother (*Matre*) but to Marius, a local cult figure after his defeat of the Teutones, and who was advised by the blonde sibyl Marthe (as pictured at Les Baux; *see* above).Today Saintes-Maries-de-la-Mer is best known for the pilgrimage of Mary Jacobe on 24 and 25 May. This attracts gypsies from all over the world, who have canonized her servant Sarah as their patron saint. The reason seems to owe something to yet another coincidence—the discovery of the relics coincided with a great convergence of gypsies in Provence in the 1440s, some of whom wandered up from North Africa and Spain, and others who crossed into Europe by way of Greece and the Balkans. The gypsies, however, claim that Sarah was not Egyptian at all, but one of their own, Sarah-la-Kâli ('the black' but also recalling the Hindu goddess Kali), who met the Boat of Bethany here and was the first of their tribe to be converted to Christianity. The Church obliged by 'discovering' the bones of Sarah in 1496.

Getting Around

By bus: There are at least two buses daily from Arles (55 mins, ✆ 04 90 96 36 25). In July and August there are direct services to Aigues-Mortes and Montpellier (✆ 04 67 06 03 73) and others to St-Gilles and Nîmes (✆ 04 66 29 52 57).

By boat: There's an hour-long cruise in the Petit Rhône from the end of March to September on the paddle steamer *Tiki III*, ✆ 04 90 97 81 68; the sporty *Soleil*, among others, offers intimate tours of the flora and fauna (✆ 04 90 97 85 89).

On horseback: Go for a ride—the best way of exploring the trails (the tourist office has a list of stables, some offering tours for beginners).

By jeep and bike: Camargue Safaris is one of many firms offering jeep tours of the Camargue, ✆ 04 90 97 86 93. Hire a bike from **Le Vélociste**, Place des Remparts, ✆ 04 90 97 83 26 (open Sept–June); **Delta Vélos**, Rue Paul Peyron, ✆ 04 90 97 84 99 (open all year); or **Camargue Vélo**, 27 Rue F.-Mistral, ✆ 04 90 97 94 55 (open Feb–Nov).

Tourist Information

5 Avenue Van Gogh (✉ 13732), ✆ 04 90 97 82 55, 📠 04 90 97 71 15.

market days

Monday and Friday mornings.

The Church

In 869, during the construction of a new church to replace the 6th-century oratory 'built' by the two Marys, the Saracens swooped down in a surprise raid and carried off the Archbishop of Arles, who just happened to be down to inspect the work. The pirates demanded a high ransom in silver, swords, and slaves for their hostage, and were dismayed when the bishop died on them—dismayed, but not so put out as to risk losing the ransom. The pirates tied his corpse in all its vestments to a throne and made off with the loot before the Christians realized the hostage was dead.

Faced with the threat of similar shenanigans, stones were shipped down from Arles at great expense to rebuild the church in 1130. The result is, along with St-Victor in Marseille, the most impressive fortified church in Provence: a crenellated ship with loopholes for windows in a small pond of white villas with orange roofs. Inside, along the gloomy nave, are wells that supplied the church-fortress in times of siege; pilgrims still bottle the water to ensure their protection by St Sarah. In the second chapel on the left, near the model of the Boat of Bethany that is carried in the procession to the sea, is the polished rock 'pillow' of the saints, discovered with their bones in 1448.

The capitals supporting the blind arches of the raised choir are finely sculpted in the style of St-Trophime. Under the choir is the **crypt**, where the relics and statue of St Sarah in her seven robes are kept; the statue has been kissed so often that the black paint has come off in patches. Here, too, is a *taurobolium*, or relief of a bull-slaying from an ancient Mithraeum, the bits scratched away long ago by women who used the dust to concoct fertility potions, along with photos and ex votos left by the gypsies. From April to mid-November, you can take a stroll below the **bell tower**, with views across the Camargue (*open 10–12.30 and 2.30–7*).

This roof walk circles the lavish **upper chapel** (*usually closed*), dedicated to St Michael, which in times of need served as a *donjon*. The coffer holding the relics of the Marys is kept here, except during the arcane *deus ex machina* rites unique to this church: during feast days the coffer is slowly lowered through a door over the altar after the singing of a special hymn, *Les Saintes de Provence*; the pilgrimage ends to the tune of *Adieu aux Saintes*, as the relics are slowly raised back into the chapel. In the 18th century this hocus-pocus had a reputation for curing madness, combined with the shock therapy of stripping the afflicted naked and throwing them in the sea. When Mistral attended the pilgrimage as a young man, a beautiful girl from Beaucaire abandoned by her fiancé dramatically flung herself across the altar just as the relics were being lowered, praying for the return of her lover. The girl made a considerable impression on Mistral and became the basis for his heroine Mireille, who arrives in Saintes-Maries-de-la-Mer to make a similar prayer and dies of too much sun and love in the upper chapel of this church.

Around Les Saintes-Maries-de-la-Mer, and Pont de Gau

Mireille, in statue form at least, lives on in the main square north of the church, while to the south in Rue Victor-Hugo the **Musée Baroncelli** is devoted to zoology, archaeology and folklore. It is named after the Camargue's secular saint, the Félibre Marquis Folco de Baroncelli-Javon (1869–1943), a descendant of a Florentine merchant family in Avignon, who abandoned all at age 21 to live the life of a *gardian*. Baroncelli spent the next 60 years herding bulls, writing poetry, and doing all he could to maintain the Camargue and its customs intact. Although by trade a cowboy, his heart was with the American Indians and other oppressed minorities; Chief Sitting Bull, in France with Buffalo Bill and his Wild West Show, smoked the peace pipe with the Marquis and named him 'Faithful Bird'.

Festivals

The *Pélerinage des Gitanes* is held on 24–25 May. The gypsies began making the pilgrimage in numbers in the mid-19th century. In 1935, thanks to the intervention of the Marquis de Baroncelli, 24 May was especially set aside as St Sarah's day. Although the famous all-night candle vigil by her statue has been abolished by killjoys, her statue is still symbolically carried to the sea by a procession of gypsies, *gardians* and costumed Arlésiennes, where in imitation of ancient rainmaking ceremonies the statue is sprinkled with sea water while all are blessed by the bishop. Afterwards, the beaches and streets are alive with music and flamenco, *farandoles*, horse races and bullfights, attended by as many tourists as gypsies. The whole ceremony happens again, with considerably fewer gypsies and tourists, on the Sunday nearest 22 October for the other Mary, Mary Salome.

There are a lot of choices in Les Saintes, but if you don't book during the summer or pilgrimages, you'll have to join the crowd on the beach. The really luxurious choices are all outside the centre, like the ★★★★**Mas de la Fouque**, 4km on the Rte d'Aigues Mortes, ✆ 04 90 97 81 02, 🖷 04 90 97 96 84, set in the midst of the Camargue, its perfect serenity complemented by a garden, heated pool, golf, and tennis. *Closed Jan and Feb*. The little pink ★★★**Mas du Clarousset**, 7km north on D85A, the Route de Cacharel, ✆ 04 90 97 81 66, offers fresh and simple decor. Each room has a private terrace, and there are horses to ride, a pool, jeep excursions and gypsy music in the excellent restaurants (*menus from 250F*). You can sleep comfortably in a *cabane de gardian* at ★★★**Le Pont des Bannes**, 3km north on the D570, ✆ 04 90 97 81 09, 🖷 04 90 97 89 28; a pool, garden and stables for the total Camargue experience. Similar facilities may be had at the annexe, ★★★**Le Mas Sainte-Hélène**, Chemin Bas-des-Launes, ✆ 04 90 97 83 29, 🖷 04 90 97 89 28, spread out along an islet in the Etang des Launes, with pink flamingos on its waterside terraces (*from 390F with breakfast*). ★**Le Delta** offers good value for price, and is situated in the centre at Pl Mireille, ✆ 04 90 97 81 12, 🖷 04 90 97 72 85.

Eating Out

This is the place to try *bœuf gardian*, or bull stewed in red wine with lots of garlic; *bouriroun*, an omelette with elvers from the Vaccarès; *salade de télines*, made of tiny shellfish with garlic mayonnaise; or *poutargue*, Camargue caviar made from red mullet eggs. Elegant **Le Brûleur de Loups**, Ave Gilbert-Leroy, ✆ 04 90 97 83 31, has a terrace overlooking the beach and more delights from the sea, like a seafood mix in white Châteauneuf-du-Pape (*menus from 168F, cheaper for lunch*). *Closed mid-Nov–Mar*. Four km north, the **Hostellerie du Pont de Gau**, on the Rte d'Arles, ✆ 04 90 97 81 53, offers jolly Provençal decor and a delicious *pot-au-feu de la mer*; *menus from 97F* (*closed Jan–mid-Feb*). Seafood lovers should get a table on the skeeter-free patio at **Le Mangio Fango**, Route d'Arles, ✆ 04 90 97 80 56; excellent Camargue bull stew, too (*menus at 150F and 195F*).

Entertainment

There are other entertainments in Les Saintes: in the summer, nightly *courses camargues* in the bullring, guitars and buskers in the streets and miles of white sand beaches. At Pont de Gau, 4km north, there's a **Centre d'Information de Ginè s** (*open summer 9–6, winter 9.30–5, closed Fri Oct–Mar*; ✆ *04 90 97 86 32*, 🖷 *04 90 97 70 82*), and a **Parc Ornitholo-gique** (*open 9–sunset, Feb–Nov 10–sunset, adm*; ✆ *04 90 97 82 62*) with walks through the marshlands and aviaries frequented by some 200 species of birds, including some rare ones.

St-Gilles-du-Gard

West of Arles, the N572 takes you through the drier parts of the Camargue. After crossing the Petit Rhône, you're in the **Petite Camargue**, in the *département* of the Gard, approaching **St-Gilles**, the only town for miles in any direction.

Place Frédéric Mistral (✉ 30800) ☎ 04 66 87 33 75, ✆ 04 66 87 16 28.

market days

Thursday and Sunday.

History

In medieval times and earlier, St-Gilles was a flourishing port, much nearer the sea than it is now. Remains have been found of a Phoenician merchant colony, and the Greek-Celtic *oppidum* that replaced it, but the place did not really blossom until the 11th century. The popes and the monks of Cluny, who owned it, conspired to make the resting place of Gilles, an obscure 8th-century Greek hermit who lived on the milk of a friendly doe, a major stop along the great pilgrim road to Compostela. The powerful counts of Toulouse helped too—the family originally came from St-Gilles. Soon pilgrims were pouring in from as far away as Germany and Poland, the port boomed with the onset of the Crusades, and both the Templars and Knights Hospitallers (who owned large tracts in the Camargue) built important commanderies. In 1116 the **Abbey Church of St-Gilles** was begun, one of the most ambitious projects ever undertaken in medieval Provence.

Destiny, however, soon began making it clear that this was not the place. As the delta gradually expanded, the canals silted up and St-Gilles could no longer function as a port (a major reason for the building of Aigues-Mortes; *see* below). The real disaster came with the Wars of Religion, when the town became a Protestant stronghold; the leaders of the Protestant army thought the church, that obsolete relic from the Age of Faith that took 200 years to build, would look much better as a fortress, and they demolished nearly all of it to that end. It was rebuilt, in a much smaller version, after 1650. What was left suffered more indignities during the Revolution, but it is a miracle that otherwise one of the greatest ensembles of medieval sculpture has survived more or less intact.

The Church Façade

This is the masterpiece of the Provençal school of 12th-century sculptors, the famous work that was copied, life-size, in the Cloisters Museum in New York. Created roughly at the same time as the façade of St-Trophime in Arles, it is likewise inspired by the ancient Roman triumphal arches. Instead of Roman worthies and battle scenes, the twelve Apostles hold place of honour between the Corinthian columns. This is a bold, confident sculpture, taking delight in naturalistic detail and elaborately folded draperies, with little of the conscious stylization that characterizes contemporary work in other parts of France. In this too, the Romans were their masters. The scheme is complex, and worth describing in detail (*see* overleaf).

Left portal: tympanum of the Adoration of the Magi (1); beneath it, Jesus' entry into Jerusalem (2). Flanking the door, a beautiful St Michael slaying the dragon (3); on the right the first four Apostles, SS Matthew and Bartholomew, Thomas and James the Lesser (4–7).

Central portal: tympanum of Christ in Majesty (8), with symbols of the Evangelists; underneath, a long frieze that runs from one side portal across to the other: from left to right, Judas with his silver (9); Jesus expelling the money-changers from the temple (10); the resurrection of Lazarus (11); Jesus prophesying the denial of Peter and the washing of the Apostles' feet

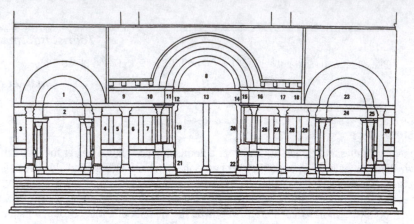

Façade of St-Gilles-du-Gard

(12); Last Supper (13); Kiss of Judas, a superb, intact work (14); Arrest of Christ (15); Christ before Pilate (16); Flagellation (17); Carrying the Cross (18). Left of the door, SS John and Peter (19); right of the door, SS James the Greater and Paul, with a soul-devouring Tarasque under his feet (20). Beneath these, at ground level, are small panels, representing the sacrifices of Cain and Abel and the murder of Abel (21); a deer hunt and Balaam and his ass, and Samson and the Lion (22).

Right portal: tympanum of the Crucifixion (23); beneath it, two unusual scenes: the three Marys purchasing spices to anoint the body of Jesus, and the three Marys at the tomb. To the left of this, the Magdalene and Jesus (24); to the right, Jesus appearing to his disciples (25). Left of the door, four more unidentifiable Apostles (26–29; note how the 12 represented here are not the canonical list; better-known figures like John the Evangelist and Paul were commonly substituted for the more obscure of the original Apostles). To the right of the door, Archangels combat Satan (30).

The Vis de St-Gilles

The 17th-century interior of the rebuilt church holds little interest, but underneath it the original, wide vaulted **crypt** (*adm*) or lower church survives (so many pilgrims came to St-Gilles that upper and lower churches were built to hold them). Behind the church, you can see the ruins of the **choir and apse** of the original, which was much longer than the present structure. Here is the 'screw' of St-Gilles, a spiral staircase of 50 steps that once led up one of the bell towers. Built about 1142, it is a tremendous *tour de force*. The stones are cut with amazing precision to make a self-supporting spiral vault; medieval masons always tried to make the St-Gilles pilgrimage just to see it. Its author, Master Mateo of Cluny, also worked on the church of Santiago de Compostela, where he is buried.

The Maison Romane

The rest of the town shows few traces of its former greatness. The medieval centre is unusually large, if a bit forlorn. Near the façade of the church, on Place de la République, is a fine 13th-century mansion, claimed to be the birthplace of Guy Folques, who became Pope Clement IV. Today this 'Maison Romane' houses St-Gilles' **Musée Lapidaire**, © 04 66 87 40 42, with a number of sculptures and architectural fragments from the church, and collections of folk life and nature of the Camargue (*open daily 9–12 and 3–7 in summer, 9–12 and 2–5 in winter, closed Jan and Sun; adm*).

St-Gilles-du-Gard ✉ 30800

Where to Stay and Eating Out

In the Middle Ages scores of pilgrims, sometimes thousands, would stay over at St-Gilles every night; try it now and the innkeepers themselves will wonder why. Best choices are ★★**Heraclée** at 30 Quai du Canal, ✆ 04 66 87 44 10, 🖷 04 66 87 13 65, not exciting but well-run; ★★**Le Cours**, 10 Ave F. Griffeuille, ✆ 04 66 87 31 93, 🖷 04 66 87 31 83, a traditional Logis de France, with a shady restaurant terrace (try the Camargue *pilaf* and frog's legs).

Aigues-Mortes

Every French history or geography schoolbook has a photo of Aigues-Mortes in it, and every Frenchman, most likely, carries in his mind the haunting picture—the great walls of the port where St Louis sailed off to the Crusades, now marooned in the muck of the advancing Rhône delta. It is as compelling a symbol of time and fate as any Roman ruin, and as magically evocative of medieval France as any Gothic cathedral.

Tourist Information

Porte de la Gardette, ✆ 04 66 53 73 00, 🖷 04 66 53 65 94; they offer historical tours of the town, year round.

Parking: there are signs around all the entrances to the town forbidding cars; these you may ignore, just as everyone else does. There will be no problem driving around Aigues or finding parking, except perhaps in July and August.

market days

Wednesday and Sunday, in Avenue F. Mistral.

History, Salt and Walls

In 1241, the Camargue was the only stretch of Mediterranean coast held by France. To solidify this precarious strip, Louis IX (St Louis) began construction of a new port and a town, laid out in an irregular grid, the better to stop the wind from racing up the streets. In 1248, the port was complete enough to hold the 1500 ships that carried Louis and his knights to the Holy Land, on the Seventh Crusade which was to bring Louis disasters both home and abroad (the town was the last he saw of France—he died in Tunis of the plague in 1270). His successor, Philip III, finished Aigues-Mortes and built its great walls. Being the only French port, by the late 13th century it was booming, with perhaps four times as many inhabitants as its present 4800, its harbour filled with ships from as far away as Constantinople and Antioch.

Aigues-Mortes means 'dead waters', and it proved to be a prophetic name. The sea deserted Aigues, and despite efforts to keep the harbour dredged, the port went into decline after 1350. Attempts to revive it in the 1830s failed, ensuring Aigues' demise, but allowing the works of Louis and Philip to survive undisturbed. Forgotten and nearly empty a century ago, Aigues now makes its living from tourists, and from salt; half of France's supply is collected here, at the enormous **Salins-du-Midi** pans south of town in the Petite Camargue (*organized visits in July and Aug, from Grau du Roi on Tues and Thurs, from Aigues-Mortes on Wed and Fri; book at the tourist office*).

Aigues-Mortes' **walls** are over a mile in length, streamlined and almost perfectly rectangular. The impressive **Tour de Constance** is a huge cylindrical defence tower that guarded the northeastern land approach to the town (*entry inside the walls on Rue Zola; ☎ 04 66 53 61 55; open daily 9.30–12 and 2–4.30 in winter, 9–7 in summer; adm*). After the Crusades, the tower became a prison to Templars and later to Protestants. One of them, Marie Durand, spent 38 years here in unspeakable conditions. On her release in 1768, she left her credo, *register* ('resist', in Provençal), chiselled into the wall where it can still be seen. The tower to the south was used as a temporary mortuary in 1431, during the Hundred Years' War, when the Bourguignons, who held the city, were suddenly attacked and decimated by their arch enemies, the Armagnacs. There were so many gruesome bodies that the Armagnacs simply stacked them in the tower, covering each with a layer of salt: hence the name, the Tower of the Salted Bourguignons.

Eight km southwest of Aigues-Mortes, **Le Grau du Roi** doubles as France's most important fishing port (after Sète) and charmless if hyper beach resort; the **Palais de la Mer**, Ave Palais de la Mer, has a good aquarium, including tanks that pass right over your head, and a small museum on the town's history (*open daily 9.30–12 and 2–6.30 Suns and holidays 10–7, May, June, Sept 9.30–8, July, Aug 10–12am; adm*). Le Grau's **Port Camargue** is nothing less than Europe's largest pleasure port, with 4350 berths. South of this stretches the **Plage de l'Espiguette**, a remarkable stretch of natural sand dunes that go on and on and on.

Activities and Entertainment

Like Les Saintes-Maries, Aigues-Mortes offers a wide selection of guided tours of flora and fauna: **Pescalune**, ☎ 04 66 53 79 47, and **Isle de Stel**, ☎ 04 66 53 60 70, offer barge tours of the Petite Camargue; four-wheel drive safari tours are run out of Le Grau du Roi by **Le Gitan**, ☎ 04 66 53 04 99, or **Camargue Aventure**, ☎ 04 66 51 90 90. Or save time and take a half-hour, 3-D film tour of the Camargue at the **Cinema 3-D Relief**, by the station at Place de Verdun, ☎ 04 66 53 68 50 (*open daily mid-Feb–mid-Nov; adm*).

Aigues-Mortes ✉ *30220*　　　　　　　　　　　　**Where to Stay and Eating Out**

Aigues-Mortes is well-served with accommodation, and top of the list is the gracious and welcoming ★★★**St-Louis**, in a distinguished and beautifully furnished 18th-century building on 10 Rue de l'Amiral Courbet, just off Place St-Louis, ☎ 04 66 53 69 61, ✆ 04 66 53 75 92. *Closed Jan–15 Mar.* Its popular restaurant, **L'Archère**, is the best in town for steaks and seafood, with good homemade desserts (*menus 79F, for lunch only, to 195F*). **Les Arcades**, 6 Blvd Gambetta, ☎ 04 66 53 81 13, ✆ 04 66 53 75 46, offers six attractive **chambres d'hôte**, some with TV, and a good inexpensive restaurant: *taureau à la gardienne* and other local favourites (*on menus 120–250F*). A good budget choice is ★**La Tour de Constance**, 1 Blvd Diderot, outside the northern wall, ☎ 04 66 53 83 50. *Closed Nov–Feb.* The Gypsy Kings got their start at **La Camargue**, 19 Rue République, ☎ 04 66 53 86 88, but even in their absence this is the liveliest and most popular place in town, with flamenco guitars strumming in the background: try to eat in the garden in summer (*fish, seafood and grilled meat, 90–160F*). Nearby, bright blue **Maguelone**, 38 Rue République, ☎ 04 66 53 74 60, has a 130F menu based on local ingredients: *tellines* in garlic, *fillet de racasse*, and a bitter chocolate *délice. Closed Jan, Feb.*

TOUR MAGNE, NÎMES

Nîmes, the Gard and Montpellier

Like most French *départements*, the Gard is named after a river—a river made famous by a feat of Roman engineering that symbolizes the Midi as boldly as the Eiffel Tower does Paris. Its spirit, or at least something intangibly classical, lingers in the Gard's luminous, sun blonde landscapes and clear air; note how often a solitary, wind-swept pine or cypress dominates the view, as if lifted straight from a painting by Claude Lorraine. The Gard's capital, Nîmes, was especially coddled by Rome and still has a full share of grand monuments; Sommières, one of the department's most charming towns, stands by its Roman bridge. The Gard is also home to Uzès, *ville d'art* and the 'First Duchy of France', and Bagnols-sur-Cèze, with its exceptional little museum of modern art, and the natural charms and vineyards of the lower valley of the Cèze.

Note that the towns on the Rhône—Beaucaire, Villeneuve-lez-Avignon, Aigues-Mortes, etc. are covered in the two preceding chapters. This chapter also includes Montpellier, Nîmes' fierce rival; we've put them in the same chapter, just to tease.

Nîmes

Built of stone the colour of old piano keys, Nîmes disputes with Arles the honour of being the 'Rome of France'—the Rome of the Caesars, of course, not of the popes: neither the Church (nor, for that matter, bossy old Paris) have ever gone down well in this mercantile, Protestant town. But after the passions of the Wars of Religion, Nîmes fell into a doze that lasted for centuries. Travellers in the 1800s found it the quintessential dusty southern city; they came to marvel at the city's famous Maison Carrée, the best-preserved Roman temple in the world, and wrote that it was so neglected it looked as if it were dedicated to the goddess of sewage.

The city has seen some spectacular change since the dynamic Jean Bousquet's election as Mayor in 1983 (since replaced in 1995 by Alain Clary). Bousquet, former head of Cacharel, Nîmes' fashionable *prêt-à-porter* firm, not only wakened Nîmes from its daydreams, but by devoting nearly 14 per cent of its budget to culture urged it to echo the ambitious efforts of upstart Montpellier, its chief rival in Languedoc. The opening of the new Carré d'Art, designed by Sir Norman Foster, has thrown down the gauntlet to Mayor Frêche of Montpellier, who now, it appears, has plans to build a modern art complex of his own. Bousquet then signed up Sir Norman to redevelop Nîmes' old centre, with plans for a 'Grand Axe' running from the Jardins de la Fontaine to surrounding smaller villages. In addition a new university has been built, specializing in law, literature and medicine. Just like the one in Montpellier.

Most Nîmois view the battle for avant-garde supremacy in this corner of France with detached amusement. For what really makes the juices flow in Nîmes is not modern architecture, but bulls. Nîmes is passionate about its *ferias*, featuring top matadors from France, Spain and Portugal and a beautiful blonde *torera*, a native of Nîmes who learned her art at the city's Ecole Française de Tauromachie.

History

Geography dealt Nîmes a pair of trump cards: first, a mighty spring, the Fontaine, whose god Nemansus was worshipped by the first known residents, the Celtic Volcae-Arecomici, and second, a position on the main route from Italy to Spain, a trail blazed by Hercules himself during his Tenth Labour, as he herded Geryon's cattle back to Greece from the Pillars that bear his name. The Romans paved his route and called it the Via Domitia, and made Celtic Nîmes into their Colonia Nemausensis. The Volcae-Arecomici Celts, unlike Astérix and Obélix, thought the Romans were just swell, and Augustus reciprocated by endowing Nîmes with the Maison Carrée, a sanctuary for the Fontaine, an aqueduct (the Pont du Gard) to augment the spring, and 7km of walls. The Nîmois celebrated Augustus' conquest of Egypt, and the arrival of a colony of veterans from the Battle of Actium, by minting a coin with a crocodile chained to a palm, a striking image that François I adopted as the city's coat-of-arms in 1535.

Nîmes declined along with Rome; the city contracted and became a mere frontier post for the Visigothic kings of Toledo. After a brief Arab occupation in the 700s, Nîmes was ruled by Frankish viscounts, who restored some of the town's old prestige in the 11th century by dominating Narbonne and Carcassonne; the Roman amphitheatre was transformed into a fort, the *castrum arenae*, whose knights played a major role in urban affairs. Nîmes, like much of Languedoc, got into trouble with the Church in the early 13th century by taking up the Cathar heresy, although at the approach of the terrible Simon de Montfort the city surrendered without a fight.

Catholicism never went down well in Nîmes, and when the Protestant alternative presented itself in the 16th century, three-quarters of the population took to the new religion immediately, and bashed the other quarter's churches and prelates. The terror reached a peak with the 1567 massacre of 200 priests, monks, and nuns known as the *Michelade*, but continued off and on until the Edict of Nantes (1598); this brought Nîmes enough peace for its Protestants to set up a prosperous textile industry, and the city seemed happy to settle down comfortably as the Huguenot capital of the south.

Louis XIV spoiled everything by revoking the Edict in 1685; troops were quartered in the Huguenots' homes, forcing them to abjure their faith or face exile or slavery aboard the king's galleys. Nîmes and the Cévennes, the wild hilly region to the north, responded with the desperate war of the Camisards, tying up an important part of the French army by inventing, or reinventing, many of the techniques used in modern guerrilla warfare. After the troubles, Nîmes went back to its second concern after religion: textiles. Its heavy-duty blue *serge de Nîmes* was reduced to the more familiar 'denim' in 1695, in London—where many of the Protestants went in exile—and it was exported widely. Some of it found its way to California, where in 1848 a certain Levi Strauss discovered it to be perfect for outfitting goldrushers. More recently Nîmes made the headlines on 3 October 1988, when violent storms in the rocky hills of the *garrigues* brought down a torrent that engulfed the city in 8ft of mud. The victory of the French Davis Cup tennis team at Nîmes' Roman arena in 1991, and the opening in May 1993 of the Carré d'Art have done much to dispel this muddy memory.

Getting Around

By air: Air Inter flies from Paris to Nîmes-Garons airport, 8km from Nîmes along Rte de St-Gilles (A 54), ✆ 04 66 70 20 11 (Air France/Air Inter: ✆ 04 66 70 08 59).

By train: Nîmes' train station, at the south end of Ave Feuchères, is a kind of arcaded train-aduct that perfectly fits *la Rome française*, ✆ 04 66 23 50 50 (direct trains to Carcassonne, Montpellier, Arles, Orange and Marseille; TGVs in 5hrs to Paris).

By bus: The bus station is just behind in Rue Ste Felicité, ✆ 04 66 29 52 00; and has departures for the Pont du Gard, Uzès, St Gilles, Aigues-Mortes, Le Grau du Roi, La Grande Motte, Avignon, and Montpellier.

Car, bike and scooter hire: Avis, 1 bis Rue de la République, ✆ 04 66 29 05 33. The baggage area at the train station has a bike hire. Scooter Hire: at **Cruz: Voitures sans Permis**, 23 Blvd Talabot, close to the train station, ✆ 04 66 29 04 40.

Tourist Information

6 Rue Auguste, near the Maison Carrée, ✆ 04 66 67 29 11, ✉ 04 66 21 81 04. They also operate a booth in the train station, which has a hotel booking service, ✆ 04 66 84 18 13. One of their maps, *Nîmes sans obstacle*, describes access for the disabled.

market days

Nîmes' organic and farmers' market takes place on Tuesday and Friday on Ave Jean Jaurès; on Monday along the same street there's a flower and flea-market. On Thursday nights in summer, the city puts on *marchés du soir* until 10pm, spread around the squares of the *centre ville*.

local wine

Costières-de-Nîmes: Near Nîmes' airport is the Château de la Tuilerie, Rte de St-Gilles, ✆ 04 66 70 07 52; or try the medal-winning Domaine des Goubins, Chemin des Canaux, just outside Nîmes, ✆ 04 66 84 39 93.

Les Arènes

Open summer 9–6.30; winter 9–12 and 2–5.30; Oct–April free guided tours; adm.

Twentieth in size, but the best-preserved of the 70 surviving amphitheatres of the Roman world, the arena at Nîmes (late 1st century AD) is just a bit smaller than its twin at Arles. Like the Maison Carrée, it escaped being cannibalized for its stone by being put to constant use—as a castle for the Visigoths and the knightly militia of the Frankish viscounts, who bricked up the arches facing the Palais de Justice and made them their headquarters—then after union with France, as a slum, where some 2000 people lived in shanties jammed into the arches, seats, and vomitoria. When restorers came in 1809 to clear it out, they had to shovel 20ft of rubbish to reach the floor where the sands (*arènes*) were spread to soak up the blood of the men and animals who died here to amuse the crowd.

When new, the arena could accommodate 24,000 people, reaching or leaving their seats in only a few minutes thanks to an ingenious system of five concentric galleries and 126 stairways. Near the top of the arena are holes pierced in the stone for the supports of the awning that sheltered the spectators from sun and rain—an idea that mayor Bousquet revived in 1988, but with a mobile plexiglass and aluminium roof that from the air looks like a giant toilet seat, but allows the amphitheatre to host events year round. The event that has packed the crowds in since 1853 is the *corrida*, a sport always close to the hearts of the Nîmois—even in ancient times, judging by the two bulls carved over the main gate.

Wandering around the outside, note the curious Siamese-twin figure embedded in the wall of the Palais de Justice, known as the *Four-Legged Man*, made of ancient sculptural fragments pieced wrongly together long ago. You may also notice Rue Bigot, named after a 19th-century fable writer from Nîmes. The name is particularly pertinent to local attitudes in the Wars of Religion. 'Bigot', after all, comes from the Old French, and refers to the first religious intolerance to shake Nîmes—the conflict between the Catholicism of the Franks and the Arianism of the Visigoths, or *Bigothi*.

Crocodiles Galore

The *hôtels* in the historic centre—the area between Les Arènes, the Maison Carrée, and the cathedral—date mostly from the 17th and 18th centuries, when Nîmes' textile magnates and financiers enjoyed their greatest prosperity. Beginning at the Four-Legged Man, **Rue de l'Aspic** (which in French evokes vipers as well as jelly) is one of the candidates for the *cardo*, the shorter of the two main streets of a Roman town. Place du Marché opens up to the left, the city's most charming square and site of a fine new **crocodile fountain** designed by Martial Raysse. Four more examples of the city's saurian emblem (donated by well-wishers to the city between 1597 and 1703) can be seen stuffed and dangling over the stair in the high-tech designer interior of the 18th-century **Hôtel de Ville**, to the right of Rue de l'Aspic. Around the corner, at 16 Rue Dorée, Nîmes' very own *Académie* meets behind the elaborate portal of the 17th-century **Hôtel de l'Académie**. This body was granted the same privileges as the Académie Française in 1682 by Louis XIV, and even today the Académiciens of Nîmes may sit with their fellows in Paris.

To the south, the amphibian community is represented in **Place de la Salamandre** named after François I's totem animal. Many Renaissance rulers had similar emblems, and used to represent them in works of art; François chose the salamander from the belief it could survive in fire—hence the first fabrics woven of asbestos were called 'salamander skins'. The salamander sculpture that once adorned this square now stands in the courtyard of the Archaeology Museum, but note the square's 17th-century **Hôtel de Chazelles**, another fine example of civic architecture.

To the north stands Nîmes' ragamuffin **Cathédrale Notre-Dame-et-St-Castor** which was consecrated in 1096 but completely flattened by rampaging Huguenots in 1597 and 1622, who spared only the campanile to use as a watchtower. Across the façade runs a vigorous frieze of the Old Testament. Lower down, and sadly damaged, are reliefs of Samson and the lions, and Alexander the Great being pulled up to heaven by a pair of griffons, coaxed by a piece of liver dangled over their heads—a favourite medieval fancy. There's a Romanesque frieze nearby, on the corner of Place aux Herbes and Rue de la Madeleine, this time adorning a rare, well-preserved 12th-century house (the **Maison Romane**).

Of course, more remarkable still is the state of that graceful little 1st-century BC temple known as the **Maison Carrée** just off the Via Domitia (*Rue Nationale, open summer 9–7, winter 9–5.30*). The best preserved Roman temple anywhere, it was built by the great General Agrippa (Augustus' right-hand man, who also built the Pantheon in Rome) and was dedicated to the imperial cult of Augustus' grandsons, Caius and Lucius, known as the 'Princes of Youth'—their 'deification' a form of flattery to the emperor. Called 'Carrée' or square, because of its right angles and 'long' square shape (85 by 50ft), its *cella* (or cult sanctuary) is perfectly intact, as are the Corinthian columns of the porch. Nîmes always found it useful for something, most notably as the meeting hall of the Consuls and least notably as a stable. It now

200 metres
200 yards

N

Nîmes

R. STÉPH. MALLARMÉ

Tour Magne

Mt Cavalier

RUE DE LA TOUR MAGNE

RUE DE COMBRET

ROUGET DE LISLE

R. DE LA LAMPÈZE

Temple de Diane

Jardin de la Fontaine

Place de la Révolution

R. CLÉRISSEAU

RUE → PASTEUR

RUE AUGUSTE

Place Maréchal Foch

QUAI DE LA FONTAINE

Pont de Vierne

BOULEVARD GAMBETTA

QUAI DE LA FONTAINE

Square Antonin

Place Aristide Briand

Place d'Assas

RUE DE ...

R. DUMURIER D'ESPAGNE

BD A. DAUDET

P

Carré d'Art

Place de la Maison Carrée

RUE GÉNÉRAL PERRIER

Maison Carrée

P

Place Jules Guesde

P

RUE DES CHASSAINTES

Eglise de Pentecôte

Théâtre Opéra

Place aux Herbes

Ste-Eugénie

AVENUE JEAN JAURÈS

RUE STANISLAS CLÉMENT

RUE ÉMILE JAMAIS

BOULEVARD VICTOR HUGO

BOULEVARD DE LA MADELEINE

RUE DE L'ÉTOILE

RUE St PAUL

St-Paul

RUE → ST-MATHIEU

RUE BECDELIÈVRE

PORTE DE FRANCE

Hôtel de Ville

Place du Marché

RUE DE L'ASPIC

Palais de Justice

RUE ÉMILE ZOLA

RUE DE L'HÔTEL-DIEU

La Placette

RUE BIGOT

Temple de l'Oratoire

Arènes

BOULEVARD DES ARÈNES

R. VERDUN

RUE DU CIRQUE ROMAIN

Place Séverine

RUE HENRI IV

RUE DE L'AQUEDUC

St François-de-Salies

Place Montcalm

RUE DE LA RÉPUBLIQUE

RUE BOURDALOUE

RUE DE LA CITÉ FOULC

RUE BRICONNET

Musée des Beaux-Arts

RUE CHARLES MARTEL

RUE DE St GILLES

RUE BOSSUET

BD. AVENUE JEAN JAURÈS

RUE DHUODA

RUE DE LA RÉPUBLIQUE

RUE HENRI IV

RUE DHUODA

SERGENT TRIAIRE

BOULEVARD

To Arles

To Airport

344

houses a small but relevant museum which includes a 1st-century painting of *personages grotesques*. The temple was originally surrounded by a colonnaded forum, similar to the Imperial Fora of Rome.

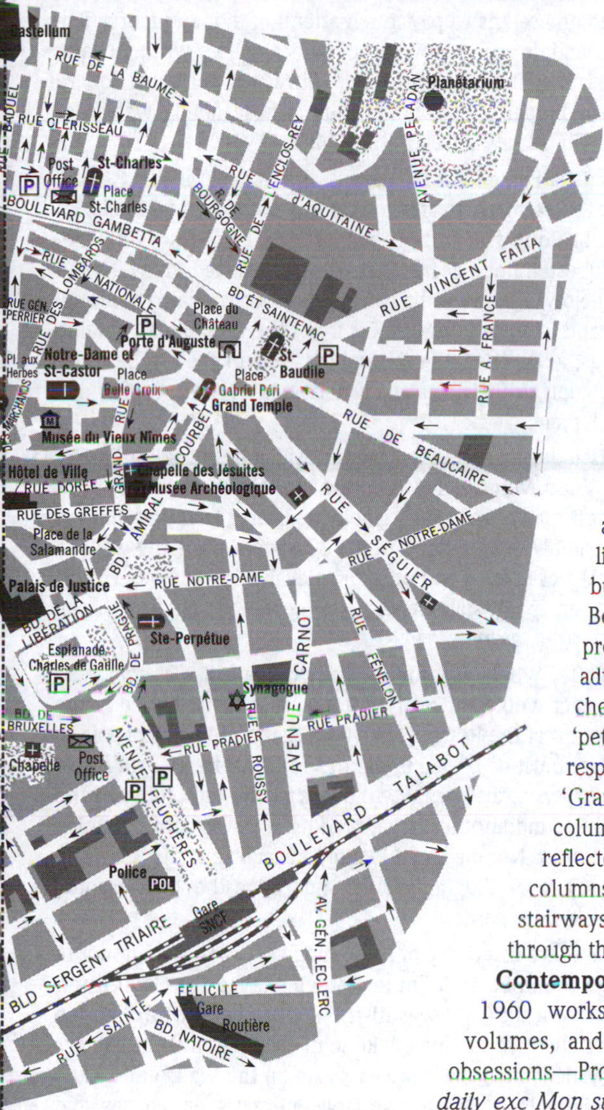
Castellum
RUE DE LA BAUME
RUE CLÉRISSEAU
RUE BADUEL
Post Office
St-Charles
Place St-Charles
BOULEVARD GAMBETTA
RUE DES LOMBARDS
RUE NATIONALE
RUE GÉN. PERRIER
Planétarium
AVENUE PELADAN
RUE DE L'ENCLOS-REY
RUE DE BOURGOGNE
RUE D'AQUITAINE
RUE VINCENT FAÏTA
RUE A. FRANCE
BD ÉT SAINTENAC
Place du Château
Porte d'Auguste
St-Baudile
Place Gabriel Péri
Grand Temple
Notre-Dame et St-Castor
Pl. aux Herbes
Place Belle Croix
RUE DES MARCHANDS
Musée du Vieux Nîmes
RUE COURBET
GRAND RUE
Hôtel de Ville
RUE DORÉE
Chapelle des Jésuites
Musée Archéologique
RUE DE BEAUCAIRE
RUE DES GREFFES
Place de la Salamandre
BD. AMIRAL
RUE SÉGUIER
RUE NOTRE-DAME
Palais de Justice
BD. DE LA LIBÉRATION
Esplanade Charles de Gaulle
BD. DE PRAGUE
Ste-Perpétue
AVENUE CARNOT
RUE FÉNELON
Synagogue
RUE PRADIER
RUE ROUSSY
BD. DE BRUXELLES
Chapelle
Post Office
AVENUE FEUCHÈRES
BOULEVARD TALABOT
Police
POL
Gare SNCF
AV. GÉN. LECLERC
BLD SERGENT TRIAIRE
RUE FÉLICITÉ
Gare Routière
RUE SAINTE
BD. NATOIRE

In his 1787 *Travels*, Englishman Arthur Young couldn't get enough of the Maison Carrée: 'What an infatuation in modern architects, that can overlook the chaste and elegant simplicity of taste, manifest in such a work and yet rear such piles of laboured foppery and heaviness as are to be met with in France.' One modern architect (and another Englishman), Sir Norman Foster, was given the chance to respond to Mr Young's gripe, on a site next to the Maison Carrée, now unimaginatively known as the **Carré d'Art.** Inaugurated in May 1993, this palace of glass and steel houses a modern art museum, audiovisual centre and extensive library, and cost 400 million francs to build. Whilst many of ex-Mayor Bousquet's critics condemned the project as further evidence of his advanced megalomania, the mayor cheerfully pointed out that his own 'petits projets' in Nîmes were merely a response to President Mitterrand's 'Grands Projets' in Paris. The ancient columns of the Maison Carrée are reflected in Sir Norman's own slender columns of steel; the walls and even the stairways are of glass to let light stream through the building. Inside, the **Musée d'Art Contemporain** on the first floor contains post-1960 works. The library has over 300,000 volumes, and is especially strong in two local obsessions—Protestantism and bullfighting (*open daily exc Mon summer 11–8, winter 11–6, similar hours for the library, adm; the museum also offers free guided tours;* ✆ *04 66 76 35 70 for details*).

Water, and Other Mysteries

A block north of the Carré d'Art is another recent project, the **Place d'Assas**, designed by Martial Raysse, as a kind of expiatory gesture, one imagines, to the two religions that went down in Nîmes without a fight: that of the Celts (the two figures in the central fountain represent the indigenous gods, 'Nemausa' and 'Nemausus') and the Cathars (the mysterious seven-pointed stars, the magic square ROTAS SATOR, and inscription LES NUAGES SONT SANS AGE). It's all a bit silly, and no one seems to pay much attention to it any more. The statue at the west end, on the other hand, is of Ernest Denis of Nîmes, whose writing championed the founding of Czechoslovakia in 1918. Just north, in the irregular polygonal Square Antonin, is a 19th-century statue of Emperor Antoninus Pius (whose family was from Nîmes), holding his hand out, as the Nîmois say, to see if it's raining.

A short stroll to the west down Quai de la Fontaine is Nemausus' first abode, the great spring that originates in the karst caverns of the *garrigue*, to gush out at the foot of Mont Cavalier. It was domesticated as the **Jardin de la Fontaine** in the 18th century by Louis XV's Chief Military Engineer of Languedoc, Jacques-Philippe Mareschal, who marshalled the waters to flow in a neo-Roman nymphaeum below a maze of balustrades and urns. Narrow, stone-walled canals surround the gardens and extend down the centre of the Quai de la Fontaine into the surrounding neighbourhoods; altogether, the ensemble is one of the loveliest city parks in France. In ancient times a complex of temples and sanctuaries stood here, of which only the so-called **Temple of Diana** remains.

Paths wind up among the flower beds and leafy arbours of Mont Cavalier to the oldest Roman monument in Gaul, the octagonal **Tour Magne**. No record of its origin or purpose has survived, though some speculate that it may have been a trophy dedicated to the opening of the Via Domitia, or a signal tower, or simply the mightiest of the 30 towers in the city wall—a sort of 'homage tower' like those of Aigues-Mortes and other medieval cities. Although 106ft high today, the tower was once half again as big; stairs spiral up to the viewing platform (*open summer 9–7, winter 10–12.30 and 1.30–6; adm*).

The Tour Magne made news in 1601, when a gardener named François Traucat read Nostradamus's prediction that a gardener would uncover an immense treasure buried in the earth. And as it was commonly believed that the Romans, like leprechauns, hid pots of gold in their ruins, Traucat decided the treasure must be buried under the Tour Magne. Henri IV gave him permission to dig (at his own expense, and with two-thirds of the loot going to the crown), but instead of finding gold, he found another large, pre-Roman tower around which the even larger Tour Magne had been built. No one could identify the rubble at the time, and the Consul of Nîmes, fearing that any more digging would undermine the Tour Magne, ordered the now bankrupt Traucat back to his garden.

Two hundred years later there was another discovery of something very rare, though not of gold, down below in Rue Lampèze: a round basin 5.5m in diameter called the **Castellum**, where the water rushing in from the Pont du Gard was distributed in the city through ten pipes of lead. The only other one to survive is at Pompeii. Like so many things in Nîmes it was built under Augustus, and to him was dedicated the city's east gate on the Via Domitia (Rue Nationale), the **Porte d'Auguste**. Built in 15 BC, it had two large entrances for vehicles, and two smaller ones for pedestrians.

Nîmes' Caesar from 1983 to 1995, Mayor Bousquet, hired Jean Nouvel (architect of Paris's Institut du Monde Arabe) to design a subsidized housing project known as **Nemausus I**. It's south of the station, off Avenue du Général Leclerc, and looks like a pair of beached ocean liners from the future. It isn't really a nice place to visit, and you wouldn't want to live there.

Museum-crawling

The former Jesuit college at 13 bis Blvd Amiral Courbet was, after the Edict of Nantes, diplomatically divided into a Protestant half and a Catholic half. Nowadays the division is between pot-shards and possums, the first half devoted to the **Musée Archéologique**, © 04 66 67 25 57, and the second to natural history (*both open 11–6, closed Mon; joint adm*). The former is filled with odds and ends for the expert, such as France's largest collection of ancient inscriptions, but there are some crowd-pleasers as well: the 4th- to 3rd-century BC figure of the *Guerrier de Grézen*, in his curved hood-helmet and belt, and nearby, a rare Celtic lintel, the *Linteau de Nages* found near the *oppidum*'s spring (*see* Nages, below). The lintel has a frieze of galloping horses and human heads—favourite Celtic motifs, but rarely carved with such pizzazz. Upstairs is a fine collection of ancient glass and everyday Roman items, Greek vases, bronze figurines and miniature altars, some bearing the mallet of the Celtic god Sucellus, whom the Romans adapted to their Silvanus.

The other half of the college is the charmingly old-fashioned **Musée d'Histoire Naturelle et de Préhistoire**, home to a collection of those mysterious menhirs-with-personality, the statue-steles. Carved with stylized faces, and sometimes with arms, a knife and a belt (*c.* 2000 BC), they are similar to those found in the Hérault, and also in Tuscany and Corsica. Large glass cases of scary masks and spears and turn-of-the-century photographs fill the ethnographic hall, and beyond, a brave little natural history collection that may be the highlight of your trip to Nîmes. It features a nine-foot stuffed moose, a beaver foetus, a wide selection of faded bats, two-headed lambs and deformed kittens, pinecone-shaped animals called pangolins, stuffed *corrida* bulls from the 1890s, two baby rabbits in formaldehyde, retrieved from the belly of a snake, and an armadillo 'captured near the Pont du Gard'. Adjacent is the Jesuit church **St-Ignace** (1678), a fine piece of Baroque architecture with an unusual pattern of vaults and openings, now used for exhibitions.

For the **Musée de Vieux Nîmes**, follow Grand' Rue behind the museums, north to Rue Lacroix. It has an exceptional collection of 19th-century textiles and 500 print designs from Nîmes' wool and silk industries—a real eye-opener for anyone who thought paisley was invented in the 1960s. There are also 17th-century carved *armoires* and painted ones from Uzès, a Charles X billiard table, thousands of socks, a 19th-century bed supported by weight lifters, plus ceramics and curios (*open daily 11–7; adm*).

The **Musée des Beaux-Arts** is on the other side of Les Arènes, 400m along on Rue Cité-Foulc, in a charming 1907 building by a local architect, who chiselled the façade with the names of Nîmes' painters and sculptors, and optimistically left plenty of room for future geniuses. In the centre of the ground floor is an enormous Roman mosaic of *The Betrothal of Admetus* surrounded by a frieze of scenes. Upstairs, look out for two Venetian paintings, an example of 15th-century retro in Michele Giambono's *Mystic Marriage of St Catherine*, and one of Jacopo Bassano's finest works, *Suzanna and the Elders* (1585), with a serene bunny rabbit in the corner. As usual, it's the Dutch paintings, with their buxom wenches and oyster-slurping sessions that one would most like to be in. Of the French offerings, the outstanding painting is Paul Delaroche's *Cromwell Looking into the Coffin of Charles I*, an 18th-century painting as memorable as its subject is odd (*open daily 11–7; adm*).

If you are tired of terrestrial culture, Nîmes small **Planetarium**, on Ave Peladan, ℰ 04 66 67 60 94, takes you to the stars with glittering displays of the universe (*open daily 11–7; adm*).

Festivals and Annual Events

To find out what's going on in Nîmes, call the 24-hour info on ℰ 04 66 36 27 27. There are usually a couple of bullfights each month in the summer, but to see the best *toreros* come for the *Ferias* at Carnival time in February or the third week of September, and especially the 10-day *Feria de Pentecôte* (Whitsun), which draws even bigger crowds than Munich's Oktoberfest. As in Seville people open up their homes as *bodegas* to take the overflow of *aficionados* from the cafés and the drinking and music go on until dawn. A recent addition to the town's calendar are the *Mosaïques Gitanes*, a festival of gypsy music and dance in mid-July, right before the Jazz Festival.

Nîmes ✉ 30000   Where to Stay

Reservations are essential during the *Ferias*, but at other times the room-finding service at the train station can usually book you a hotel.

expensive

At the top of the line, there's the ★★★★**Hôtel Impérator Concorde**, Quai de la Fontaine (near the gardens), ℰ 04 66 21 90 30, ℰ 04 66 67 70 25, a 19th-century dowager with a recent facelift; a lovely garden, TVs, air conditioning, and Nîmes' top restaurant to boot (*see* below). Another good choice in the centre is ★★★**New Hotel La Baume**, 21 Rue Nationale, ℰ 04 66 76 28 42, ℰ 04 66 76 28 45; stylish modern rooms in a 17th-century mansion with a garden terrace. If you have a car, it's a mere 8km northeast on N86 to the charming ★★★**L'Hacienda**, Chemin du Mas de Brignon, at Marguerittes (✉ 30320), ℰ 04 66 75 02 25, ℰ 04 66 75 45 58, a large farmhouse in the *garrigue*, converted into a hotel with an equally spacious swimming pool, terraces, and an excellent restaurant.

moderate

Next to the amphitheatre, the *toreros'* favourite is ★★**Le Lisita**, 2 Blvd des Arènes, ℰ 04 66 67 29 15, ℰ 04 66 67 25 32, owned by an enthusiastic bullfighting fan, Michel Caylar, who has given his rooms Spanish and rustic Languedocien furnishings. Other good choices include the delightful Art Deco ★★**Royal**, just off the esoteric Place d'Assas at 3 Blvd Alphonse-Daudet, ℰ 04 66 58 28 27, ℰ 04 66 58 28 28 (reserve early in the summer because it fills up fast), and the ★★**Plazza**, 10 Rue Roussy (off Blvd Amiral Courbet), ℰ 04 66 76 16 20, ℰ 04 66 67 65 99; an old house (with a private garage) converted into an air-conditioned hotel in 1988, with attractive retro furnishings. For a small, simple, unpretentious hotel, it is difficult to surpass the ★★**Central Hotel**, 2 Place du Château, ℰ 04 66 67 27 75, ℰ 04 66 21 77 79, with several rooms looking out over the roofs of the old city.

inexpensive

Budget choices are few, but these include the quiet ★**Des Voyageurs**, 4 Rue Roussy, ℰ 04 66 67 46 52, ℰ 04 66 76 22 30; the not-so-quiet ★**France**, 4 Blvd des Arènes, ℰ 04 66 67 23 05, ℰ 04 66 67 76 93; and the rugged and cheap ★★**De la Mairie**, 11

Rue des Greffes, ✆ 04 66 67 65 91, simple and in the historic centre. There is an **Auberge de Jeunesse**, Chemin de la Cigale, on a hill 2km from the centre (bus 20 from the train station, or bus 8 from town, stopping at Stade Villeverte), ✆ 04 66 23 25 04, 📠 04 66 23 84 27.

Eating Out

Nîmes isn't exactly famous for its restaurants, but it has some delicious specialities: *brandade de morue* (pounded cod mixed with fine olive oil), a recipe said to date back to Roman times, and *tapenade d'olives*, an appetizer made of olives, anchovies and herbs; *pélardons*, the little goat cheeses from the *garrigues*, are among the best anywhere. In the sweet category, the city is proudest of its *croquants Villaret*, almond biscuits cooked by the same family in the same oven since 1775, available at Raymond Villaret, 34 Rue Nationale.

Brandade is often on the menu at Nîmes' top restaurant, **L'Enclos de la Fontaine** (in the aforementioned Hôtel Impérator, ✆ 04 66 21 90 30), although alongside the classics the chef cooks up imaginative, subtle dishes that melt in your mouth, like veal served with fresh fig *beignets*, which seem especially fresh served outside in the garden courtyard (*menus from 180F up*). You can also eat out in a garden at **Le P'tit Bec**, 87 bis Rue de la République, ✆ 04 66 38 05 83, with a tempting selection of seasonal dishes (*menus 90–220F*). On Rue Poise, just off Blvd Amiral Courbet, **Nicolas,** ✆ 04 66 67 50 47, is one of the more affordable fine restaurants in town, and they're always busy (*69, 95 and 135F menus*). For a little more, dine on the fine cooking at **La Belle Respire**, in the unusual decor of Nîmes' former bordello, in the historic centre at 12 Rue de l'Etoile, ✆ 04 66 21 27 21. Also inexpensive for lunch are the **Bistrot du Chapon Fin**, Place du Château-Fadaise, behind Saint-Paul's church, ✆ 04 66 67 34 73, serving local dishes on its filling 68F menu (*that's lunch only— otherwise expect over 200F a la carte!*), and **Au Flan Coco**, 31 Rue du Mûrier d'Espagne, ✆ 04 66 21 84 81, a delightful tiny restaurant run by two *traiteurs* alongside their shop; the food comes fresh from the market and is whipped up before your eyes. *Closed evenings, except Sat.*

Entertainment and Nightlife

Opera, dance, and concerts take place continuously in July, August and September. Reservations and tickets for events at Les Arènes are available from the Bureau de Location des Arènes, Rue Alexandre Ducros, ✆ 04 66 67 28 02. Films in their original language are occasionally shown at **Le Sémaphore**, 25a Rue Porte de France, ✆ 04 66 67 88 04. Nîmes also has a year-round indoor/outdoor water park, the **Aquatropique**, with pools, slides, saunas, tennis, etc., located near the *autoroute* exit Nîmes-Ouest (Ville Active, 39 Chemin de l'Hostellerie, ✆ 04 66 38 31 00).

In town the hottest spots to see and be seen are **Café Napoléon** and **Café de Petite Bourse**, both on Boulevard Victor Hugo. For music, cafe-theatre and tireless animation, try **La Movida** bar, on La Placette, ✆ 04 66 67 80 90, with its flamenco feel.

By 19 BC, the fountain of Nemausus could no longer slake Nîmes' thirst and a search was on for a new source. The Romans were obsessed with the quality of their water, and when they found a crystal-clear spring called the Eure near Uzès, the fact that it was 50km away hardly posed an obstacle to antiquity's star engineers. The resulting aqueduct, built under Augustus' son-in-law Agrippa, was like a giant needle hemming the landscape, piercing tunnels through hills and looping its arches over the open spaces of the *garrigues*, and all measured precisely to allow a slope of .07 centimetres per metre. Where the water had to cross the gorge of the unpredictable river Gard (or Gardon, as it's usually called) the Roman engineers knuckled down, ordered a goodly supply of neatly dressed stone from the nearby quarries at Vers, and built the Pont du Gard, at 48m the highest of all Roman aqueducts and, along with the span in Segovia, the best preserved in the world.

Getting Around

STDG **coaches** from Nîmes, Uzès, and Avignon pass within a kilometre of the Pont du Gard 8 or 9 times a day. Note that you can no longer drive over the Pont du Gard, but will have to leave your car in one of the pay car parks on either side. **Canoe and kayak hire** is available upstream at Collias: contact Kayak Vert, ✆ 04 66 22 84 83.

Tourist Information

Pont du Gard: summer only tourist office 200m from the aqueduct on the Remoulins side of the Pont du Gard, ✆ 04 66 37 00 02.

Remoulins: 30210 Rue du Moulin d'Aure (by the eastern roundabout) ✆ 04 66 37 22 34, ✆ 04 66 37 22 01, open all year.

Pont du Gard

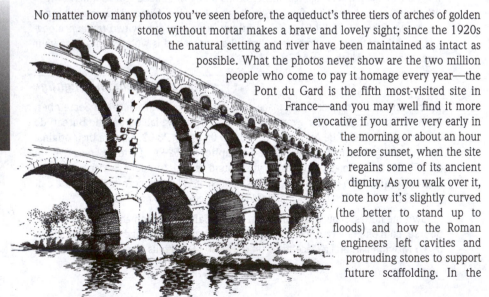

No matter how many photos you've seen before, the aqueduct's three tiers of arches of golden stone without mortar makes a brave and lovely sight; since the 1920s the natural setting and river have been maintained as intact as possible. What the photos never show are the two million people who come to pay it homage every year—the Pont du Gard is the fifth most-visited site in France—and you may well find it more evocative if you arrive very early in the morning or about an hour before sunset, when the site regains some of its ancient dignity. As you walk over it, note how it's slightly curved (the better to stand up to floods) and how the Roman engineers left cavities and protruding stones to support future scaffolding. In the

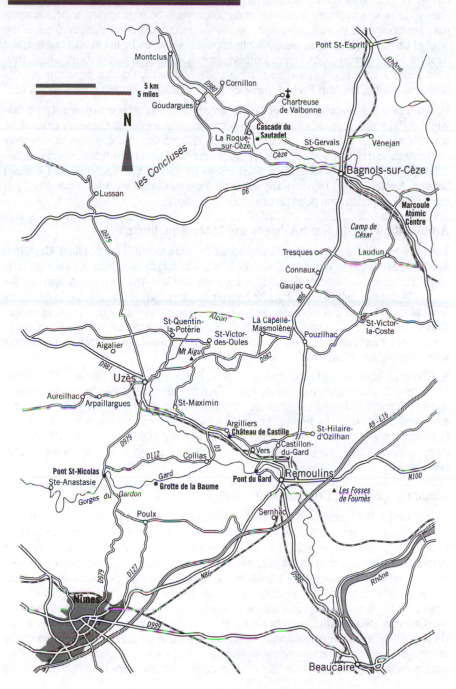

Pont St-Esprit

Rhône

Montclus

Cornillon

5 km
5 miles

Goudargues

D980

Chartreuse
de Valbonne

N

**Cascade du
Sautadet**

La Roque-
sur-Cèze

St-Gervais

Vénejan

les Concluses

Cèze

Bagnols-sur-Cèze

Lussan

D6

**Marcoule
Atomic
Centre**

D979

*Camp de
César*

Tresques

Laudun

Connaux

Gaujac

N95

Alzon

St-Quentin-
la-Potèrie

La Capelle-
Masmolène

St-Victor-
la-Coste

Aigalier

St-Victor-
des-Oules

Mt Aigu

Pouzilhac

D082

D981

Uzès

Aureilhac

Arpaillargues

St-Maximin

Argilliers

A9 - E15

D979

Château de Castille

St-Hilaire-
d'Ozilhan

Castillon-
du-Gard

D112

Collias

D3

Vers

Pont St-Nicolas

Gard

Remoulins

N100

Ste-Anastasie

Pont du Gard

Grotte de la Baume

Gorges du Gardon

▲ *Les Fosses
de Fournès*

Poulx

Sernhac

D979

D127

D86

Rhône

N86

Nîmes

D999

Beaucaire

18th century, the bottom tier was expanded to take a road. This is now limited to pedestrians, due to the damaging vibrations caused by cars. At the time of writing the scaffolding the Romans foresaw is in place—5 per cent of the stone has to be replaced. The ancient quarries have been reopened in Vers (*see* below), so the patches should blend right in. Some of the original blocks weigh six tons; many have inscriptions, a few left by the Roman builders, but most left by the *compagnons*, French journeymen masons who, as part of their training, travelled about France studying its most important monuments. On the Remoulins side, a paleolithic shelter, the **Abri Préhistorique de la Salpetrière**, is currently being excavated.

During repairs and 'remanagement' of the site, access to the top tier is closed, and it is unclear when or if it will reopen as before to allow visitors to fumble through the water channel, or brazenly walk over the top-most tiles that cover it. This top tier can be dangerous, especially on windy days: it is no more than a few feet wide, and there are no guard-rails, not to mention the big gaps where tiles have been taken out to illuminate the lime encrusted channel beneath. Paddling down the gorge and under the Pont du Gard is great fun, especially if you can avoid peak periods and potential canoe jams (*see* above).

Around the Pont du Gard: Villages and More Aqueducts

Take time to visit the pretty wine villages around the aqueduct: Just north, hilltop **Castillon-du-Gard**, exudes medieval atmosphere, even if it was mostly rebuilt in the 16th century. Other attractions include views down to the Pont du Gard and an isolated Romanesque chapel, **St-Caprais**, a favourite setting for summer concerts. East of Castillon the 11th-century **St-Hilaire-d'Ozilhan** is another charming village with an even older chapel, the 11th-century **Clastre,** standing on its own just to the south. If it's *supermarchés* or bustling sprawl you're after, there's **Remoulins**, the area's market town and gateway to the **Fosses de Fournès**, a weirdly eroded lunar landscape to the east.

Southwest of Remoulins, you can explore traces of the aqueduct in the hills around **Sernhac** (the local IGN map may come in handy here). Here the Romans dug two impressive tunnels, one for the water and one for maintenance, still bearing the grooves left by the hammers that excavated them, stroke by stroke. The extraordinarily hard calcium deposits that accumulated in the water channels were chiselled out as a prized building material in the Middle Ages: some went into the walls of the fortified Romanesque church of **St-Bonnet-du-Gard**, near Sernhac.

Columns, Columns, Columns and a Bridge

Then there are the Roman (and later) stone quarries that produced the Pont du Gard just off the Uzès road in **Vers**, another pleasant little village with another Romanesque church. Here, by the level-crossing on the D227 and down the white road a couple of hundred metres to the south, stand a few aqueduct arches in a state of romantic abandon; other vestiges may be seen between Vers and Argilliers, just off the D3bis, taking the side road that veers sharply on the left. At **Argilliers**, a Romanesque chapel and a neoclassical colonnaded funeral chapel dedicated to St Louis on the D981 mark the entrance to one of Languedoc's most curious follies, the **Château de Castille**, the private mania of Froment Fromentès, Baron de Castille (1747–1829). One of the great travellers of his day, the Baron was afflicted by a serious case of columnitis in Rome, and on his return to his estates in the Gard he erected over 200 pillars and columns, of which only some 50 survive, incorporated into garden follies, porticoes and hemicycles inspired by Bernini. Unfortunately, the estate isn't open, and you have to boldly trespass to peak into the Baron's magic garden.

South of Arguilliers, down on the banks of the river, **Collias** has a popular beach and kayak rental and paths going up and down the river from the Pont du Gard to Pont St-Nicolas. The dramatic, wild beauty of the sheer walled Gardon gorge around Collias inspired an awe of religious proportions in the past, and there are several old hermitages in caves, one near the **Grotte de la Baume**, with an 11th-century chapel (an hour's walk), and another, the **Ermitage de Collias**, in a place so beautiful that it has been classed like an historic monument. People have worshipped here since prehistoric times—there's a little chapel by the cave, a Roman bridge and fountain dedicated to Minerva. Further west, the D112 will take you to **Pont St-Nicolas**, where an impressive 13th-century bridge, made of the same lovely and reliable stone as the Pont du Gard, takes the scenic old Nîmes–Uzès road over the Gardon gorge. Just above it to the west, the 12th-century church of **Ste-Anastasie** is all that survives of the Priory of St-Nicolas de Campagnac: built with exquisite care, the church is unusually large, sober, pure and empty.

Where to Stay and Eating Out

Castillon-du-Gard ✉ 30210

Sleep in the lap of luxury at the Relais and Châteaux' ★★★★**Le Vieux Castillon**, Rue Citernasse, in the heart of this medieval village, ℗ 04 66 37 61 61, ℗ 04 66 37 28 17. The rooms are scattered on several different levels in several different houses, connected with each other by patios, tennis courts, with a stunning swimming pool perched among the gardens, and an excellent restaurant, featuring dishes with truffles (the Gard produces 15% of France's crop), *langoustines* and a wide variety of Côtes du Rhône wines (*rooms from 750F, menus at 250F and up*). *Closed Jan and Feb.* For something a tad simpler **L'Amphitryon**, Place du 8-Mai-1945, ℗ 04 66 37 05 04, serves good solid cooking, including some fish, as the name suggests (*menus from 145F*). *Closed Wed.*

Remoulins ✉ 30210

A five-minute walk from the Pont du Gard, ★★**Le Colombier**, Rte du Pont du Gard, ℗ 04 66 37 05 28, ℗ 04 66 37 35 75, has 10 comfortable rooms behind its broad awnings; or try the central ★★**Moderne Les Glycines**, Place des Grands Jours, ℗ 04 66 37 20 13, ℗ 04 66 37 01 85 (*meals from 70F to 145F*).

Vers ✉ 30210

La Béguda Saint-Pierre, on the D981 at Les Coudoulières, ℗ 04 66 63 63 63, ℗ 04 66 22 73 73, has luminous, air-conditioned rooms inside a 17th-century post station, with a quiet park and pool, restaurant and terrace (*415F*).

Collias ✉ 30210

At Collias the friendly, Art Deco ★★★**Le Castellas**, Grand' Rue, ℗ 04 66 22 88 88, ℗ 04 66 22 84 28, is spread out in two large houses, and has a good and stylish restaurant (*rooms from 410F, menus 155F and 220F*). *Closed Jan and*

Feb. **★★Le Gardon**, right on the river, ✆ 04 66 22 80 54, 📠 04 66 22 88 98, is a peaceful, pleasant and family-run Logis de France (*from 235F, menus from 75F*). *Closed mid-Oct–mid-Mar.*

Uzès, the First Duchy of France

Few towns of 8000 souls have so bold a skyline of towers, or so little truck with the modern industrial world. Uzès seems to have been vacuum-packed when its wealthy, Protestant merchants of cloth and silk stockings packed their bags and left at the Revocation of the Edict of Nantes. 'O little town of Uzès', wrote André Gide (whose father was a Uzètien) 'Were you in Umbria, the Parisians would flock to visit you!' Now they do, more or less, ever since 1962, when Uzès was selected as one of France's 50 *villes d'art*, entitling it to dig into the historical preservation funds set aside by de Gaulle's culture minister André Malraux. Houses tumbling into ruin have been repaired, creating the perfect stage for films like *Cyrano de Bergerac*.

Getting Around

Uzès is linked by frequent buses to Nîmes, Avignon and the Pont du Gard, ✆ 04 66 22 00 58. **Hire mountain and touring bikes** at Ets Payan, 16 bis Ave Général Vincent, ✆ 04 66 22 13 94.

Tourist Information

Avenue de la Libération, ✆ 04 66 22 68 88, 📠 04 66 22 95 19.

market days

Wednesday and Saturday.

The Duché and Around

Café life in Uzès engulfs most available space in and around Place Albert I, just under the residence of the dukes, or the **Duché**, ✆ 04 66 22 18 96 (*daily guided tours 15 June–15 Sept, 10–6.30, other times 10–12 and 2–6; adm exp; English translation available*). The de Crussols of Uzès, claiming a family tree that sent out its first shoots under Charlemagne, became the first dukes and peers of the realm when the Duc de Montmorency forfeited the title (along with his head) in 1632. The current title holders now spend most of their time in Paris, and have opened their grand fortified home to visitors. The oldest section, the rectangular *donjon* called the **Tour Bermonde**, was built over a Roman tower in the 10th or 11th century; its fairy-tale crenellations were designed by the inevitable Viollet-le-Duc to replace the originals destroyed in the Revolution. The Renaissance façade in the central courtyard, a three-layered classical cake of Doric, Ionic, and Corinthian orders, was constructed in 1550 and bears the motto of the dukes: *Ferro non auro* ('iron, not gold'—i.e. they were warriors, not financiers). This didn't keep the women of the family from sometimes donning the trousers: in 1565, the Duchess of Uzès became the first woman to be sent abroad as an ambassador (to Spain), and then there's the amazing Duchess Anne, heiress to the Veuve Clicquot fortune, a talented sculptress, enthusiastic huntress who rode until age 86, feminist, friend of anarchist Louise Michel (of Paris commune fame) but still an ardent monarchist (she personally financed General Boulanger's attempt to overthrow the Republic to the tune of 3 million gold écus) and the first woman in France to get a driving licence, and the first to get a speeding ticket. The tour of the Duché includes several furnished rooms and cellars.

Across Place du Duché is the attractive 18th-century **Hôtel de Ville**, while to the left of the Duché is a rock-cut **Crypt** that lost its church (the Jesuits discovered it by accident under their monastery); it is believed to date from the 4th century, has some primitive bas-reliefs of St John the Baptist and a convert. Uzès is a lot smaller than it seems, and a short wander will soon bring you to the irregular, arcaded perfectly delightful **Place aux Herbes**, with its old plane trees, for centuries the centre of public life. The nearby church of **St-Etienne**, with an attractive Baroque façade, had to be rebuilt in the 18th century after the Wars of Religion and contains a handful of good paintings.

The Cathedral and Tour Fenestrelle

Set apart from the rest of the old town on a terrace, the 1671 **Ancien Palais Episcopal** was the seat of the powerful bishops of Uzès (64 bishops reigned here between the 5th century and the Revolution). A restoration attempt in the 1970s caused the interior to cave in behind the façade, although the right wing is in good enough nick to hold the eclectic collections of the **Musée Municipal** (*open 3–6, in Nov and Dec 2–5, closed Mon*) with its fossils, ceramics, paintings, and memorabilia of the Gide family. Behind stretches the pleasant **Promenade des Marroniers**, while adjacent, the **Cathédrale St-Théodorit** was built in 1663, the third to occupy the site after its predecessors were destroyed in the Albigensian Crusade and the Wars of Religion. The quaint neo-Romanesque façade was tacked on in 1875, with the idea of making a better partner to the stunning 12th-century **Tour Fenestrelle** spared by the Protestants only because they found it useful as a watchtower. Unique in France, the 137ft tower is encircled by six storeys of double-lit windows, inspired by the Romanesque campaniles of Ravenna and Lombardy. The cathedral's interior was severely damaged during the Revolution, when it was converted into a Temple of Reason, leaving only the peculiar upper gallery with its wrought iron railing (erected right after the Revocation of the Edict of Nantes, to make room for the former Protestants) and the Cathedral's pride and joy: a splendid **organ** of 1670, the only one in France to have retained its original painted shutters. Recently restored, it is the centrepiece of the end-of-July festival, *Nuits Musicales d'Uzès*.

The peculiar building just below the terrace is the **Hôtel du Baron de Castille** (its façade adorned with—guess what—columns, tall slender ones that don't conform to any classical order but which have a charm all their own.

The funny little domed building abutting the belvedere-cum-*pétanque* courts on the far side of the cathedral is the so-called **Pavillon Racine**, named after the playwright and poet who, in spite of popular belief, never sat there because it was built a quarter of a century too late. In 1661, at the age of 22, Racine spent a year with his uncle, the Vicar-General of Uzès, during which time his family hoped he would forget his foolish love of poetry and turn to the priest-hood. Just the opposite happened. The climate, the friendly welcome, the charming girls, the food and the inscrutable patois made a great impression on the young man.

Around Uzès: the Uzège

Close enough to walk from Uzès (from Parc du Duché, follow the Chemin André Gide; the Uzès tourist office sells a map), the **Vallée de l'Alzon** is the arcadian setting of the **Fontaine d'Eure**, the spring where the Roman aqueduct to Nîmes began; you can see the large basin that regulated the flow down the canal, excavated in 1993. If you have kids, the Haribo candy company runs a **Musée du Bonbon** south of town at Pont des Charrettes, where you can watch them make little jelly crocodiles and more (*open July–Sept 10–7, other times 10–1 and 2–6, closed Mon*). Horse lovers, in July and August, can meet the 65 stallions at the national stud farm, **Les Haras Nationaux d'Uzès**, Rte d'Alès (*Tues and Fri at 3; otherwise call ahead, © 04 66 22 33 11*).

The countryside around Uzès—where fields of asparagus, cherry orchards, forests of truffle oaks and vineyards alternate with *garrigues*—is dotted with attractive old villages. One, **Arpaillargues,** 4km west on the D982, has the added attraction of the **Musée 1900** at Moulin de Charlier, © 04 66 22 58 64 (*open daily 9–12 and 2–7; adm*), one man's amazing 30-year accumulation of period cars, motorcycles, gramophones, movie posters, locomotives, and more; the same Gaston Baron also built and runs the **Musée du Train et du Jouet**, dedicated to model trains and toys. Just west of Arpaillargues, the walled hilltop hamlet of **Aureilhac** has a superb view of Uzès' skyline. Nine km northwest of Uzès, off the road to Alès, **Aigalier,** with its medieval lanes, dungeons, Saracen wall, and Romanesque church all piled under a ruined castle, has long been a favourite subject of local painters.

The clay-rich soil north of Uzès has provided **St-Quentin-la-Poterie** with its vocation since the cows came home, and in some strange tangential way, inspired its most famous son, Joseph Monier (1823–1906) to invent reinforced concrete. After producing thousands of amphoras, roof tiles, all the glazed tiles for the floors of the Popes' Palace in Avignon, bricks and ceramic pipes, the last ceramic factory closed in 1974; in 1983, the kilns were fired up again as the village made a concerted effort to bring the potters back. Ten now live in the village year round; you can visit their workshops or get an overview of their work at the **Maison de la Terre,** © 04 66 22 74 38. Lovely **Lussan** is 18km north of Uzès, but well worth the detour: a nearly perfect, and unspoiled medieval *village perché* under a 13th-century château. Near Lussan, the sheer gorge of the river Aiguillon, **Les Concluses,** makes a magnificent and easy walk in the summer when the river is dry, with potholes (*marmites*) formed by the river, the eagle's nests and a remarkable steep and narrow **Portail** that closes in on top. Leave your car in one of the car parks along the D643; the walk to the Portail takes about 30 minutes.

Northeast, towards Bagnols-sur-Cèze, strange sandstone formations and quarzite quarries mark the environs of **St-Victor-des-Oules,** 'of the pots', another pottery village, this one specializing in stoneware (*grès*). Paths lead up the **Mont Aigu,** for scant ruins of a 5th-century BC *oppidum* and superb views of the Cévennes to the west. Further east, the 12th-century château in **La Capelle-Masmolène** was the summer palace of the Bishops of Uzès.

Where to Stay and Eating Out

Uzès ✉ 30700

Opposite the cathedral, the 15th-century ★★★**Hôtel d'Entraigues**, 8 Rue de la Calade, © 04 66 22 32 68, ✆ 04 66 22 57 01, is a fine old hotel with a pool and air conditioning, fit for a duke; try to get a room near the top for the view (*from 290F*). The same owners run the adjacent **Residence Blanche de Calafin**, Place de l'Eveché, spread in several 17th- and 18th-century houses; rooms equipped with kitchenettes, by the day or week. The elegant hotel restaurant, **Les Jardins de Castille,** © 04 66 22 32 68, has a classy 110F lunch menu (avocado salad with turkey gizzard confits (better than they sound), roast guinea hen on a bed of braised cabbage). A half mile from the centre, **★★Le Saint Genies**, Route de St-Ambroix, ℰ 04 66 22 29 99, ∰ 04 66 03 14 89, is an oasis of tranquillity, with a charming pool and three-star rooms. Back near the centre, **★★La Taverne**, 7 Rue Sigalon (just off Place Albert I), ℰ 04 66 22 13 10, ∰ 04 66 22 45 90, has renovated rooms, and the chance to dine out on a pretty garden terrace (*four good courses for 100F*). Little **Coté Jardin**, in central Place Dampmartin, ℰ 04 66 22 47 08, changes its menu every day, and has tables in the garden; in the evening there's pizza, too (*menus at 85 and 158F*). *Closed Sun and Mon out of season.*

Around Uzès ✉ 30700

Outside Uzès, you can sleep in an antique bed (or just dine) at the 18th-century **★★★Hôtel Marie d'Agoult**, 4km west of Uzès, ℰ 04 66 22 14 48, ∰ 04 66 22 56 10. Marie d'Agoult was Liszt's muse and Wagner's mother-in-law and a frequent guest at the château. There's a pool, tennis courts, and the garden restaurant serves a fine 130F menu and for a bit more, dishes with truffles. *Closed mid-Nov–mid-Mar.* Five km north, orchards and views encompass the **Ferme-Auberge de Cruviers**, Montée de Larnac, Route de St-Ambroix, ℰ 04 66 22 10 89, ∰ 04 66 22 06 76, a bed and breakfast (*290F for two*) and restaurant serving dishes based on homegrown asparagus, fruit, free-range chickens and ducks (*menus from 95F*). *Closed Tues.* Some of the best food around Uzès is served 6km south in St-Maximin, on the garden terrace of **L'Auberge de St-Maximin**, ℰ 04 66 22 26 41, where they do wonderful things with asparagus and other local products (*menus 99F and up*). *Closed Mon lunch, Tues lunch and mid-Nov–mid-Mar.* In La Capelle-Masmolène, hot air balloon pilot **Jean Donnet**'s bed and breakfast comes complete with a pool (ℰ 04 66 37 11 33, ∰ 04 66 37 15 21); also contact him about flights over Uzès in his *montgolfière*.

Bagnols-sur-Cèze

North of Uzès, where the river Cèze meets the Rhône, Bagnols-sur-Cèze is the traditional gateway—or exit—of Languedoc. The Romans named it for its sulphur baths, but these days Bagnols is more famous for its green beans (*les bagnolais*), and the nearby nuclear power plant at Marcoule, the construction of which saw Bagnols' population quadruple. In spite of all the new building, the narrow lanes of the old town have changed little; every now and then you'll see the city's quaint emblem of three golden pots.

Getting Around

Bagnols is on the main route between the north and Avignon, and takes nearly all **trains** except the TGV. **Buses** link the town with Uzès, Avignon, and Nîmes. **Bike hire** shop: La Roue Libre, Ave Léon Blum, ℰ 04 66 89 91 79.

Tourist Information

Bagnols-sur-Cèze ✉ 30200: Espace St-Gilles, Ave Léon Blum, ℰ 04 66 89 54 61, ∰ 04 66 89 83 38.

Pont St-Esprit ✉ 30130: 1 Rue Vauban, ℰ 04 66 39 44 45, ∰ 04 66 39 51 81.

Goudargues ✉ 30630: Maison de la Cèze, Route de Pont St-Esprit, ℰ 04 66 82 30 02, ∰ 04 66 82 29 63.

Bagnols: Wednesday and 2nd and 4th Friday of each month. **Pont St-Esprit**: Saturday. **Goudargues**: Wednesday.

Côtes du Rhône Gardoise: Bagnols is the centre of Languedoc's Côtes du Rhône production. Try the Cave des Vins Fins de Laudun at Les 4 Chemins, N86, near Laudun (✆ 04 66 82 00 22); Cave des Vignerons de Chusclan, at Chusclan (✆ 04 66 90 11 03, ✆ 04 66 90 16 52); or the Domaine Ste-Anne, at Les Cellettes in St-Gervais (✆ 04 66 82 77 41).

A Museum That Rose Out of the Flames

The prettiest square in Bagnols, central, arcaded **Place Mallet**, has a tower, the **Tour de l'Horloge** erected by Philip le Bel, and an 18th-century Hôtel de Ville housing the only real reason for visiting Bagnols: the **Musée de Peinture Albert André**, ✆ 04 66 50 56 56 (*open 10–12 and 2–6, summer 3–7, closed Tues, Feb, and holidays; adm*). In 1854, Léon Alègre, a local humanist and Sunday painter, set up a museum to instruct his fellow citizens, with everything from Roman pots to paintings to stuffed animals. In 1918, Albert André, a painter friend of Renoir's, was made volunteer-curator and gave the museum the first provincial collection of contemporary art in France—only to have the whole thing go up in smoke in 1924, when the local fireman set it alight during their annual ball. It proved to be a blessing in disguise when Albert André sent out a message to France's artists: 'I am the curator of a museum of naked walls. Help me fill them!' They did. The eight rooms blaze with colour: Fauvist Albert Marquet's famous *14 Juillet au Havre* (1906); Pierre Bonnard's *Bouquet des Fleurs des Champs*; Matisse's *La Fenêtre ouverte à Nice* (1919); and other works by Renoir, Van Dongen, Paul Signac, Gauguin, Jongkind, Picasso, and a room of Albert André's own works. Bagnols also has a small **Musée d'Archéologie**, 24 Rue Paul-Langevin (*open Thurs, Fri, and Sat 10–12 and 2–6, 3–7 in July and Aug, closed Feb*) with regional finds from the Iron Age to the Romans.

Around Bagnols, and the Valley of the Cèze

Many of the items in the archaeology museum were found at the lofty *oppidum* of **St-Vincent de Gaujac**, 13km south of Bagnols and a 2km walk up from the car park. Dating from the 5th-century BC–6th century AD, it became a holy site in Gallo-Roman times, and has the foundations of several temples as well as a bath complex from the 3rd century AD. If you're in the vicinity, don't miss medieval **St-Victor-la-Coste**, just east, a picturesque village gathered around its ruined castle, with a pair of 11th century chapels. **Laudun**, between St-Victor-la-Coste and Bagnols, is another handsome medieval village, with a 14th-century church, Renaissance château, and above, on a high plateau with superb views, the **Camp de César**, a 40-acre archaeological site. After its start as a Celtic *oppidum* in the 5th century BC, it grew into a Roman city and was abandoned in the 7th century: cycleopan walls, Roman towers, forum, houses and a basilica have so far been excavated (*guided tours possible, April–Nov, ✆ 04 66 79 34 93*). The Romans later built villas in the area: around **Tresques** just west, many were converted into Romanesque chapels. One, **St-Martin de Jussan**, on the north end of Tresques, is Lombard in inspiration—companies of builders from the banks of Lake Como roved far and wide in the Middle Ages—and has a carved portal. Another church, **St-Pierre de Castres**, 4km north east, is one of the oldest, with its archaic chapels.

Five km north of Bagnols, there are more views over the Rhône valley from **Vénejan**; 2km northeast the charming 11th-century **Chapelle de St-Pierre**, is decorated with Lombard-style bands of stone and a little square belltower. If you're lucky enough to find it open, the interior has curious, primitive sculptural decoration: six pointed stars, concentric circles, solar discs, birds, animals and two praying figures. Further north, **Pont Saint-Esprit** was named for its famous bridge over the Rhône, erected between 1265 and 1309 by a confraternity of builders called the brothers of the Holy Ghost. Nineteen of the 25 arches are original, but the mighty towers that once controlled access from either bank are long gone. There are fine views of the bridge from the terrace by the 15th-century parish church, once part of the influential Clunisien abbey of St-Saturnin-du-Port. Pilgrims to Compostela would cross the bridge, stop at the church, and head down Rue St-Jacques, a street that has preserved many of its medieval houses. Appropriately enough for a town named Holy Ghost Bridge, one of these (No.2) now contains a museum of religious art, the **Musée d'Art Sacré du Gard**, ✆ 04 66 39 17 61 (*open daily exc Mon, 10–12 and 2–6, mid-June–mid-Sept, 3–7; closed Feb; adm*). The house itself, the Maison des Chevaliers, was built in the 12th century by a prosperous family of merchants, who kept right on enlarging and improving their home until the 18th century. The museum displays a wide range of works from the 15th to 19th century, from paintings to *santons*. Just up the street, the **Musée Paul-Raymond**, Place de l'Ancienne Mairie, ✆ 04 66 39 09 98 (*same hours*), has a collection of prehistoric finds, ceramics, a reconstruction of an 18th-century hospital pharmacy, and more religious art.

Bagnols is also a good base for exploring the scenic lower valley of the Cèze, beginning with **St-Gervais**, a wine village set under the steep cliffs. Further upstream, **La Roque-sur-Cèze** is piled on a hill opposite a 13th-century bridge, with streets so narrow that cars are forbidden. La Roque overlooks the **Cascade du Sautadet**, where the Cèze flows through a mini-canyon that looks as if it were clawed out of the rock by a giant bear. Isolated in an oak forest to the north, the **Chartreuse de Valbonne** (✆ 04 66 90 41 00) dates from 1203, and was rebuilt in a grand Baroque style with a beautiful varnished tile roof after the Wars of Religion, only to be abandoned again in 1901. In the 1920s it found a new lease of life as a hospital for tropical diseases: you can visit the church, with its stuccoes and stone vaults, and the huge cloister, where one cell has been reconstructed as it was in the time of the Carthusians.

In the beginning of the 9th century, St Guilhem of Toulouse founded an abbey in **Goudargues**, which Louis the Pious gave to the abbey of Aniane: ruins of St Guilhem's original Chapelle St-Michelet still stand over the village, while the later abbey church, built in the 12th century and remodelled in the 18th and 19th centuries, is particularly grand and spacious. The Benedictines drained the marsh that once surrounded Goudargues into a canal, to water their crops and make Goudargues, with no little exaggeration, 'the Venice of the Gard'; in high summer it often has more water in it than the Cèze.

Across the Cèze from Goudargues, **Cornillon** is a 17th-century village with a ruined château and a grand view. Little **Montclus**, further up, is prettily set in a tight loop of the Cèze, guarded by a ruined castle keep.

Bagnols-sur-Cèze ✉ 30200

In a large park, with tennis courts and a pool, ★★★★**Le Château du Val de Cèze**, 69 Rte d'Avignon, ✆ 04 66 89 61 26, 📠 04 66 79 99 89, is Bagnols' most luxurious hotel, with rooms (*from 650F*) in individual bungalows around a 13th-century château, which houses a bar and restaurant (half-board mandatory in season). *Closed over Christmas.* Just west in **Sabran**, similar facilities along with a gym and hammam are offered at the Relais & Châteaux ★★★★**Château de Montcaud**, ✆ 04 66 89 60 60, 📠 04 66 89 45 04, in a park, with extremely comfortable, air-conditioned rooms (*from 690F*); equally exquisite and pricey restaurant. *Closed Jan and Feb.* In Bagnols proper, ★★**Le Saint-Georges**, 210 Ave Roger-Salengro, ✆ 04 66 89 53 65, 📠 04 66 79 98 01, is small and typical, all rooms with bath; the restaurant is the best in town, with local specialities at reasonable prices served on a garden terrace (*menus from 60F*). *Closed Sat lunch and Sun.*

Goudargues/Cornillon ✉ 30630

★★**Le Commerce**, 17 Quai du Canal, ✆ 04 66 82 20 68, 📠 04 66 82 31 22, is a pleasant country hotel in Goudargues, with a pool and restaurant. *Closed mid-Oct–Mar.* In the walls of the castle at Cornillon, charm reigns at ★★★**La Vieille Fontaine**, ✆ 04 66 82 20 56, 📠 04 66 82 33 64, with its eight rooms, each furnished with antiques and Provençal fabrics; the garden terraces descend to a pool, with views all around; the restaurant is just as delightful—and dear (*doubles from 550F, menus 195F*). *Closed Jan and Feb.*

Another elegant choice, the 17th-century **Mas Rodières**, is 7km north (take the D980 to the D141 towards Salazac), ✆ 04 66 82 32 32, 📠 04 66 82 26 34, and has been beautifully restored to house four elegant suites (*from 660F*) and one of the best restaurants in the area (*from 160F*). *Closed Mon, Tues and Feb.*

Between Nîmes and Montpellier: Nages and Sommières

There are three routes between the two rival cities to choose from: the *autoroute*, its southern parallel, the N113, or the longest, prettiest, and most interesting route, along the back roads through Sommières—the D40 from Nîmes to Sommières, then on the N110 to Montpellier.

Tourist Information

Sommières ✉ 30250: Ave du Général-Bruyère, ✆ 04 66 80 99 30, 📠 04 66 80 34 78.

market days

Sommières: Saturday. **Castries**: Tuesday and Friday.

A Celtic *Oppidum*

The D40 from Nîmes is a winding, pretty route that passes through lush, hilly country and slumberous villages like Caveirac and **St-Dionisy**. Above the latter, off the D737, is the 3rd-century BC *Oppidum* **of Nages**, one of the outstanding pre-Roman sites in the south (easy access by foot; signposted from the village of Nages-et-Solorgues, where the Mairie has the key, © 04 66 35 05 26). Like Nîmes, Nages was built around a spring, entirely of dry stone, with a temple, and walls punctuated by a round tower; on top of the tallest, the *tour monumentale*, a cache of stones for slings was discovered. The streets, with their rectangular houses, are laid out in a tidy grid—long before the Romans introduced their waffle-shaped city plans to Gaul. The first floor of Nages-et-Solorgues' Mairie has been converted into a small **archaeology museum**, with finds from the site.

Sommières

Hidden under the cliffs of the river Vidourle, Sommières only suffers moderately from the usual plagues besetting picturesque southern villages: the Parisians, the English, the trinket shops—it even has to do without a famous writer, since longtime resident Lawrence Durrell died in October 1990 (his Villa Saint Louis, opposite the Place des Aires car park, is up for sale at the time of writing, in case you're house hunting). Its streets and squares could be paintings by Maurice Utrillo: soft and pastel, well-worn and well-lived-in, with faded shop signs of a century ago and flowers under every window. Huge plane trees, a little bull ring, and an enormous *boulodrome* (for *pétanque*) line the river, and swans and mallards float calmly by, except, one imagines, during the *vidourlades*, the local name for the Vidourle's seasonal floods when it pours down from the Cevennes, hell bent for leather: recent measures have dampened some of its impetuosity.

Before Sommières, there was Sommières' **bridge**, built by Tiberius between AD 19 and 31. Its 17 arches have withstood centuries of *vidourlades*; they carry road traffic to this day, and still look in mint condition; the top was restored in 1715. Oddly, almost half of the bridge is now hidden inside the town; medieval Sommières expanded into the dry parts of the river-bed, and eventually an embankment was built. The **Tour de l'Horloge**, the entrance to the town, was built over the bridge's fifth arch in 1659.

The other arches of the bridge lie under Rue Marx Dormoy, the street leading from the bridge to **Place des Docteurs Dax** (natives of Sommières, who discovered the exact spot in the brain in charge of language), a lovely 12th-century market square that everyone in Sommières still calls by its old name, the **Marché-Bas**; it preserves the *pierre d'Inquant*, where slaves were once made to stand when they were being sold. The houses are all built on stone arcades: in the old days, the square would be underwater every spring, forcing the market up two streets to the **Marché-Haut** (now Place Jaurès). The web of lanes radiating from these squares have their share of handsome *hôtel particuliers*. Sommières was an enthusiastically Protestant town and was destroyed during the Wars of Religion after two terrible sieges, in 1573 and 1575, then again in 1622, so most of what you see is from the 17th-century rebuilding, and little has changed since then. Rue de la Taillade, cut into the cliffs by the Romans for the Nîmes–Lodève road, is one of the most attractive streets, with its well-preserved old shops; the former Ursuline convent here, now the **Espace Lawrence Durrell**, is used for temporary exhibits. From here the Montée des Régordanes lead up to the half-ruined **Château de Sommières** and the **Tour Bermond**, worth the climb for its views up and down the valley of the Vidourle, and as far away as Pic St-Loup and Aigues Mortes (*open 15 June–15 Sept, Mon–Fri 4–7, Sat and Sun 10–12 and 4–7; adm*).

Around Sommières

A mile away, on a hill above Sommières, the **Château de Villevieille**, ✆ 04 66 80 01 62 (*open April–Oct, 2.30–7, otherwise Sun only; adm*), was first built in the 11th century by the lords of Sommières, Bermond d'Anduze et Sauve, whose most famous scion was a Cathar and brother-in-law of Raymond VII of Toulouse—excuse enough for St Louis to confiscate their estate in 1243. He divided the vast property in two, leaving a bit for Bermond's daughter, and trading the remainder to the monks of Psalmody in exchange for Aigues-Mortes—which Louis built into France's first Mediterranean port. In 1527 the château was ceded to the Pavée family, who have owned it ever since. It escaped being sold off in the Revolution, thanks to the marquis de Villevieille's friendship with Mirabeau and Voltaire. You can count the châteaux in France that have preserved their original family furnishings on one hand—this is one of them.

Four km northwest of Sommières, along a Roman road, you can visit a pretty country chapel, **St-Julien-de-Montredon** at **Salinelles**, in a lovely setting among the vines, with an ancient cemetery (*ring the keyholder, René Peyrolle, ✆ 04 66 80 01 95 before setting out*). First mentioned in 813, the monks of Psalmody rebuilt it in the 11th century and decorated it with archaic carvings of animals and birds. Salinelles also has a **beach** along the Vidourle; others are nearby at Lecques and Villetelle.

Castries

Continuing towards Montpellier, there is only Castries to detain you, with a Renaissance-century **château** belonging to one of the 19 barons of Languedoc. Though wrecked in the Revolution, this castle came back into the possession of its original owners, the de Castries family, who restored it. Today it belongs to the Académie Française, which meets here once a year. The tour of the house and furnishings and kitchen is not compelling, but there are lovely gardens, designed in the style of Le Nôtre, watered by an 18th-century aqueduct (*open daily exc Mon 10–12 and 2–6, closed Jan; adm*).

Where to Stay and Eating Out

Sommières ✉ 30250

Close to the river in the centre of Sommières, the ★★★**Auberge du Pont Romain**, 2 Ave E. Jamais, ✆ 04 66 80 00 58, ✆ 04 66 80 31 52, has lovely, spacious rooms in a 19th-century herbal distillery, with a pool, and a gourmet restaurant serving the house foie gras and other delights on a peaceful garden terrace (*menus 165–245F*). *Closed mid-Jan–mid-Mar*. The other hotel is basic: **Le Commerce**, overlooking the river at 15 Quai Gaussorgues, ✆ 04 66 80 97 22, ✆ 04 66 80 32 64, has nine simple rooms. Alternatively Sommières has two fine (if pricey) guesthouses: the 17th-century **Hôtel d'Orange**, Chemin du Château Fort, ✆ 04 66 77 79 94, lovingly converted, with a pool and garage, but with only six rooms (*370F*) so book early in the summer; ask to see the *baume*, or cave. The second, in a 16th-century *mas*, the **Manoir du Cazalet**, Route de Junas, ✆ 04 66 80 87 60, ✆ 04 66 80 87 65, has three comfortable rooms (*from 300F*) and a good classic restaurant (*menus from 125F; if it's a special occasion, there's the 395F menu offering a six course feast, each course served with its own wine*). At lunchtime, watch the life of the Marché Bas pass by from an outdoor table at **L'Evasion**, 6 Rue

Paulin Capmal, ☎ 04 66 77 74 64; the menu is none too complicated: medallion of veal, frog legs and pizza, too (46–98F). *Closed Sun eve and lunch.*

Castries ✉ 34160

L'Art du Feu, in the centre at 13 Ave du 8 Mai 1945, ☎ 04 67 70 05 97, offers refined cooking on bargain menus of 95 and 105F; the house speciality is thin-sliced *aiguillettes* of beef or duck in delicate sauces. *Closed Tues eve and Wed.*

Nîmes to Montpellier: By Way of Perrier and Lunel

This faster, southern route along the N113 isn't as scenic as the Sommières route but has its own rewards, especially if you combine it with a detour to Aigues-Mortes on the edge of the Camargue (*see* p.337).

Tourist Information

Lunel ✉ 34400: Place des Martyrs, ☎ 04 67 71 01 37, 🖷 04 67 71 26 67.

market days

Lunel: food on Thursday and Sunday; flea market Sunday morning. **Marsillargues**: Tuesday and Thursday.

Fizzy Water and a Statue of Liberty

Bernis, 7km from Nîmes, offers the first potential stop for the sake of its 12th-century church, once a possession of the abbey of St-Gille; although mostly rebuilt after the Wars of Religion, its façade is intact, carved in a style archaic back in the 1100s, especially in the Carolingian-inspired decorations by the door. The capitals are carved with people, birds, animals, a dragon and mermaid. Just off the the N113 at **Vergèze**, trendies may make a pilgrimage to the **Source Perrier**. Surprisingly, the vast complex was begun by an Englishman in 1903, and looks less like a natural spring than an obsessively tidy aeroplane factory; ring ☎ 04 66 87 61 01 for the tour, to see the Indian-club-shaped green bottles come whizzing off the line in their billions, all guaranteed benzene-free.

The big town along this route is **Lunel**, and a peculiar place it is. Legend has it that Lunel was founded by Jews from Jericho under the reign of Vespasian—a story now dismissed as a play on words (Jericho was the city of the moon, the *ville de la lune*). Historians now say the first Jews probably settled in the 11th century, and until their expulsion in 1306, Lunel was their educational centre in France, with well-known schools of everything from medicine (predating even Montpellier's) to the Cabbala. Today, the town raises steers for bloodless *course libre* bullfights. Its landmark is a copy of the Statue of Liberty; its cops wear star-and-crescent badges just like those of New Orleans; one of its biggest businesses is dog food research and development.

Little remains of medieval Lunel: some bits of the Jewish schools on Rue Ménard, and a vaulted alley called the Passage des Caladons that once was part of a Templar commandery. In the 19th century the Lunel area was the holiday retreat of a man who hardly seemed the type to take a vacation in the South of France—Karl Marx. Marx suffered from asthma, and whenever he had a bad bout his wife Jenny sent him down to the **Château de la Tour de Fages**, owned by the husband of her best friend, opera diva Caroline Ungher. Just west of Lunel, recent excavation near the *école maternelle* **Lunel-Viel** have so far uncovered a Roman bath, houses, and three different cemeteries; in July and August you can watch the excavations in progress.

South of Lunel, the sweet and shady village of **Marsillargues** has an elegant Renaissance château. The rooms, with their marble and plaster relief decoration of the 1570s and later, are lovely, but empty; it's sad that this château, one of the few undamaged in the Revolution, should have lost most of its furnishings in a fire in 1936. Recently four of the rooms have been filled up with the contents of the villagers' attics to form a **Musée d'Arts et de Traditions Populaires** (*open afternoons in July and Aug, closed Sun; at other times contact the mairie to visit the château and museum, ✆ 04 67 83 52 06*). The **Château de Teillan**, on an unpaved road, just across the river Vidourle from Marsillargues, has a large park with some fragmentary Roman ruins, milestones, the largest *noria* in Languedoc and a gigantic *pigeon-nier*, once part of a 7th-century military depot (*open 15 June–15 Sept, 2–6; adm*). By the *autoroute* north of Lunel in **Villetelle,** a single arch of a Roman bridge stands in the middle of the Vidourle at **Ambrussum**, a Celtic *oppidum* from the same period as Nages (*see above*) and later way station on the Via Domitia. Archaeologists have recently uncovered 200 yards of paved Roman road (the deep grooves near the bridge mark the spot where the wagons and chariots stopped to pay their toll), as well as villas and public buildings.

Where to Stay and Eating Out

Lunel ✉ 34400

Lunel has several hotels, such as the moderately priced ★★★**Les Mimosas**, outside the centre on Ave du Vidourle, ✆ 04 67 71 25 40, 🖷 04 67 83 20 81, but you'll do better for the same price at the **Mas Saint-Félix**, 7km north of Lunel at St-Séries, ✆ 04 67 86 05 83, a bed and breakfast in an old posthouse of the Knights Hospitallers (*250F for a double, with breakfast and use of the kitchen*). You can dine very well on French classics at **Didier Chodoreille**, by the station 140 Rue Lakanal, ✆ 04 67 71 55 77, with a pretty garden terrace that makes Lunel's traffic seem far away (*menus from 125F*). *Closed Sun, Wed eve and the last half of Aug.*

Montpellier

If that town could suck as hard as it can blow, it could bring the ocean to it and become a seaport.

Although this old saying originally referred to the brash, booming, braggart Atlanta of the 1880s, it applies just as fairly to France's eighth city. The public relations geniuses in Montpellier have managed to outdo even Atlanta: their beloved Montpellier is cockadoodled as the 'Technopole', the *Surdoué* (the Specially Gifted), the 'Synergetic Euro-cité', the 'Capital of Southern Europe', rightful 'heir to the Florence of the Medicis', the 'French California', and indeed nothing less than 'the Rome of Tomorrow'. Unlike Atlanta, Montpellier has actually sucked hard enough to get a port of its own (for sailing boats at least) by widening a puny river called the Lez, a feat that has given it a new horn to toot: *Montpellier la Méditerranée!*

Until 1977 and the election of the irrepressible Socialist Mayor Georges Frêche (now in his fifth term), Montpellier was a pleasant, sleepy university backwater of fawn-coloured stone with a population of 100,000, one that could put forth the modest claim that Stendhal found it the 'only French city of the interior that doesn't look stupid' . Its population now approaches 300,000, including the large staff of IBM and 55,000 university students from around the world who come to study where Rabelais and Nostradamus learned medicine. With his huge development projects, notably the monumental new quarter called Antigone, Frêche has made Montpellier a European model for innovative and effective city government. And despite the noise it makes, this is one live-wire of a city, politically one of the most progressive in France, and fun and friendly.

History

Compared to its venerable Roman neighbours, Narbonne, Béziers and Nîmes, Montpellier is a relative newcomer, tracing its roots back a mere thousand years, to 985, when the count of Mauguio bestowed a large farm at *Monspestelarius* on a certain Master Guilhem. It was a fortunate site, near the old Via Domitia, and the newer *Cami Salinié* (salt route) and *Cami Roumieu* (the pilgrimage route between St-Gilles and Compostela), and it had access to the sea through the river Lez.

Guilhem's farm soon grew into a village of merchants, who made their fortunes by importing spices from the Levant, especially spices with medicinal uses taught them by their Arab and Jewish trading partners, and by graduates of the medical school of Salerno; by the year 1000 they were training pupils in Montpellier. By the late 1100s, the town was big enough to need a wall with 25 towers, shaped like an escutcheon, or *écusson* (as the old town is still known). It lost its independence when Guilhem VIII failed to produce a son, and gave his only daughter Marie to Pedro II of Aragon. Montpellier was her dowry, just in time to spare the town from the horrors of the Albigensian Crusade. And when Marie and Pedro's son, Jaime the Conqueror, divided Aragon between his two sons, Montpellier joined the kingdom of Majorca.

In 1220, the teachers of medicine formed a *Universitas Medicorum*, and began to attract students from all over Europe; in 1250 it was supplemented by a *studium* of law, both of which were given Pope Nicholas IV's seal of approval in 1289. Another impetus behind Montpellier's tremendous growth in the 13th and 14th centuries was dead bugs—dark red cochineal insects found on oaks in the surrounding *garrigues*, believed at the time to be grains, and used for dying cloth scarlet. The spice and gold-working trades thrived, especially after those mega-consumers, the popes, moved to Avignon.

In 1349 the Kings of Majorca sold Montpellier to France for 120,000 golden écus. A period of relative peace and prosperity continued until the 1560s, when the university academics and tradesmen embraced the Reformation. For the next 70 years much of what Montpellier had achieved was wiped out; churches and suburbs were destroyed, building and art came to a halt. In 1622 Louis XIII came in person to besiege the rebellious city and reassert royal authority; he built a citadel to keep an eye on the Montpellerains, then transferred the States-General of Languedoc here from Pézenas, with all its nobles, prelates and deputies, who then built themselves the patrician *hôtels* that still dominate the old city.

Putting its merchant republic days behind it, Montpellier settled down to the life of a university town and regional capital. The Revolution passed without kicking up much dust; a far bigger crisis for Montpellier occurred in the 1890s, when phylloxera knocked out the wine-making industry the city had come to depend on—an economic blow from which it only began to recover in the 1950s. With the French mania for categorizing, Montpellier now pigeon-holes its economy into five 'poles': *Euromédecine*, including its numerous labs and pharmaceutical industries, *Héliopolis* (tourism), *Informatique* (IBM has been here since 1965), *Agropolis* (it boasts the first European research centre of agronomy in hot climates, among other institutes), and *Pole Antenna* for its role as the telecommunications centre of Languedoc. Meanwhile, the city teasingly threatens to tax the balconies of its residents to pay for the ambitious 'follies' of Mayor Frêche, follies that are the envy of nearly every other city in France. The next one on the Mayor's schedule is a high-tech, ultramodern tramway, like those of Strasbourg and Nantes, due to be finished in time for the millennium.

Getting Around

By air: The city's airport, Montpellier-Méditerrannée, is 8km southeast of the centre on D21 (✆ 04 67 20 85 00); British Airways flies direct to London daily (✆ 04 67 65 88 88), and UTA to New York, once a week (✆ 04 67 58 56 56, ✆ 04 67 92 00 40). Air Littoral, ✆ 04 67 20 67 67 and ✆ 04 67 65 49 49, serves Nice, Marseille, Perpignan, and Barcelona. Other destinations are served by Air France, ✆ 04 67 92 48 28 and Air Inter, ✆ 04 67 22 66 67, ✆ 04 67 22 65 64. The regular airport shuttle leaves from the *gare routière*.

By train: The train station is in Place Auguste-Gilbert, just south of the *Ecusson*. You can race there from Paris in 4 hours and 40 mins on the TGV, or catch direct trains to Avignon, Nîmes, Marseille, Nice, Perpignan, Béziers, Narbonne, Agde, Lunel, Sète, and Carcassonne.

By bus: The train station is linked by an escalator with the coach station in nearby Rue du Grand St-Jean (✆ 04 67 92 01 43), which has buses to Nîmes, La Grande Motte, Béziers, Aigues-Mortes, etc.; every 20 mins bus no.17 trundles down to the sea at Palavas. In town, you may find useful the little vans called *Petibus*, which can take you around the pedestrian zones of the Ecusson and Antigone.

Car and bike hire: Brand name car hire firms are at the airport, or try **Budget** at 6 Rue J.-Ferry, ✆ 04 67 92 69 00; **City**, 25 Rue du Grand St-Jean, ✆ 04 67 58 34 78; or a less expensive used car from **A.D.A.**, 8 Blvd Berthelot, ✆ 04 67 58 10 15. Bike hire is available at the station, or outdoors in the Esplanade Charles de Gaulle, off Place de la Comédie—worth looking into, since the entire historic centre is a pedestrian zone.

Tourist Information

Allée du Tourisme, Le Triangle, just off the Place de la Comédie, ✆ 04 67 58 67 58. Also in the station, ✆ 04 67 22 08 80, and at Antigone, at the motorway exit, ✆ 04 67 22 06 16, ✆ 04 67 22 38 10. They have a hotel reservation service, and offer tours of the city centre, in English on Monday.

market days

At Espace Mosson, at La Paillade, there is a flower market on Tues and a flea-market on Sun morning, when free buses link it every 20 min with Square Planchon. Daily food markets take place in Place J. Jaurès, Halles Castellanes, Halles Laissac and Plan Cabannes; on Tues and Sat there's an organic market at Aux Arceaux, by Rue Marioge.

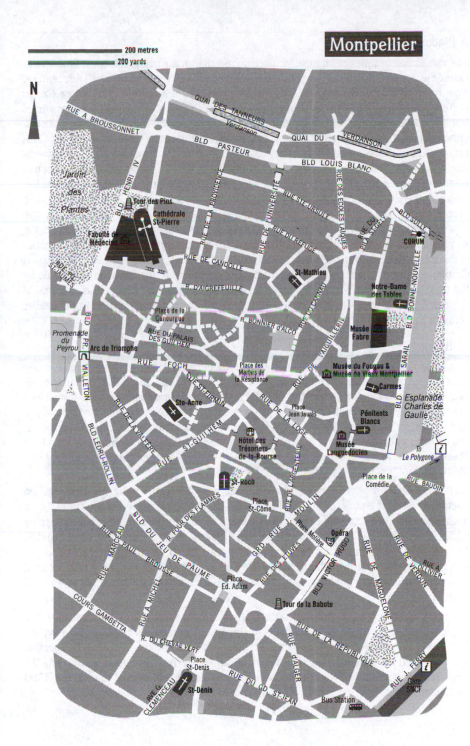

Montpellier

200 metres
200 yards

N

Jardin des Plantes

RUE A BROUSSONNET

QUAI DES TANNEURS
Verdanson
QUAI DU VERDANSON

BLD PASTEUR

BLD LOUIS BLANC

BLD HENRI IV

Tour des Pins
Cathédrale St-Pierre

Faculté de Médecine

BDE DE SJ JAUNES

RUE DE LA PROVIDENCE

RUE DE L'UNIVERSITÉ

RUE DU REFUGE

RUE STE-URSULE

RUE DES ECOLES LAIQUES

RUE DU PILA ST-GELY

BLD SULLY

CORUM

RUE DE CANDOLLE

R. D'AIGREFEUILLE

St-Mathieu

Notre-Dame des Tables

BLD BONNE-NOUVELLE

Place de la Canourgue

R. BONNIER d'ALCO

RUE DU PALAIS DES GUILHEM

RUE FOCH

RUE DE L'ARGENTERIE

RUE DU CARNOT

RUE DE L'AIGUILLERIE

Musée Fabre

BLD SARAIL

Promenade du Peyrou

PR. VIALLETON

Arc de Triomphe

Place des Martyrs de la Résistance

Musée du Fougau & Musée du Vieux Montpellier

Carmes

Esplanade Charles de Gaulle

RUE STE-FIRMIN

Ste-Anne

RUE DE LA LOGE

Place Jean Jaurès

Pénitents Blancs

BLD LEDRU-ROLLIN

RUE DE LAVALETTE

RUE ST-GUILHEM

Hôtel des Trésoriers-de-la-Bourse

Musée Languedocien

To Le Polygone

St-Roch

Place St-Côme

RUE J. MOULIN

Place Molière

Place de la Comédie

RUE BAUDIN

BLD DU JEU DE PAUME

R. FOUR DES FLAMMES

GRD. RUE J.

Opéra

RUE MARCEAU

RUE PAUL BROUSSE

RUE A. MICHEL

RUE DES ÉTUVES

BLD VICTOR HUGO

RUE DE MAGUELONE

RUE DE VERDUN

RUE A. OLLIVIER

Place Ed. Adam

Tour de la Babote

COURS GAMBETTA

RUE DE LA RÉPUBLIQUE

R. DU CHEVAL VERT

RUE D'ALGER

AVE G. CLEMENCEAU

Place St-Denis

St-Denis

RUE DU GD. ST-JEAN

Bus Station

RUE J. FERRI

Gare SNCF

A Place Named Comédie

The various personalities of Montpellier all come together in the lively, café-lined **Place de la Comédie**, locally known as *l'Oeuf*, or the Egg, due to the shape it had in the 18th century. Now flattened into an omelette, the centre is watered by the fountain of the *Three Graces* (1796), while along one side stretches the waist-level trough of a modern fountain, where three bronze stooges gesticulate frantically, presumably because they forgot their trousers. Other ornaments of the square include a *doppelgänger* of the Paris Opera, and various 19th-century larded bourgeois buildings with domes reminiscent of bathyspheres, while opposite looms a modern glass-and-steel semi-ziggurat, the **Polygone**, a shopping mall and town hall complex. To the north of Place de la Comédie extends the **Esplanade Charles de Gaulle**, replacing the city walls demolished by Louis XIII after the siege of 1622, the better to keep Montpellier at the mercy of the cannons of his new citadel. In the 18th century the Esplanade was planted with rows of trees and became Montpellier's chief promenade; among its monuments is a rare survival of 1908, the **Cinématographe Pathé**, a little cockerel-emblazoned palace from the magical early days of cinema (now renamed the Rabelais Cultural Centre; it often shows foreign films). The north end of the Esplanade is flanked by the mastodontic **CORUM**, 'the House of Innovation' designed by Claude Vasconi, one of Georges Frêche's Euro-Cité showcases, encompassing the Opéra Berlioz and two smaller congress halls.

Antigone

East of the Comédie lies another of the jewels in the Euro-Cité's crown: **Antigone**, a mostly moderate-income quarter with housing for 10,000 people, and shops and restaurants, all designed by Barcelona architect Ricardo Bofill in 1979 and spread along a huge formal axis down to the river Lez. Bofill understood just what a Rome of Tomorrow needs: 'a parody of Neo-Classicism' as Robert Hughes wrote, Mannerist neo-Roman arches, cornices, pilasters, and columns as big as California redwoods, built around the **Place du Nombre d'Or** and the **Place du Millenaire**, the squares of the 'Golden Number' and the 'Millennium' that link Montpellier to its newly dredged-out Tiber, the Lez.

Does Antigone work? Even though it stretches nearly to the centre of the city, there was no attempt to relate the project to the rest of town—as you'll discover when you try to find it (from Comédie, the only way to reach Antigone is to pass through the Polygone shopping mall, and walk out the back door of the Galéries Lafayette department store). On a bad day, Antigone looks like the surreal background to a De Chirico painting, as troubling as the Antigone of myth; on a good day, it seems like a delightful place to live, especially for kids, who can play football in the monumental Place du Millennium and still hear their parents call them in for lunch.

The newest parts of the project lie along the Lez: a gargantuan semicircle of apartments with a vaguely Stalinist air called the **Esplanade d'Europe**, decorated with a huge blue 'M' for Montpellier on the pavement. This part of the river has been blocked off by two bridges that hug the waterline, forming a space for paddling canoes; opposite Antigone, and closing the long axis, stands a sharp glass and stone castle housing the Hérault regional council, the **Hôtel de Région**.

Musée Fabre

Open 9–5.30, until 5 Sat and Sun, closed Mon; adm.

On Boulevard Bonne Nouvelle, between the Cinématographe and CORUM, in the fastness of a former Jesuit College, the Musée Fabre was long the main reason for visiting Montpellier, with one of the most important collections of art in provincial France. In the front courtyard, a large arch built into the wall is decorated with two mossy look-alikes of Michelangelo's *Day* and *Night*, although instead of moping in opposite directions, these two statues lean amorously towards each other—fittingly enough, for this museum was founded on a Florentine romance. François Xavier Fabre (1766–1837), a pupil of David, was in Florence at the outbreak of the French Revolution, where he became a close friend of the Countess of Albany, the merry widow of Bonnie Prince Charlie, and her lover the Italian dramatist Vittore Alfieri. When Alfieri died in 1805, he left the Countess his library and paintings. Fabre in turn inherited the Countess's affections, and when she died in 1824, she left everything to her young man from Montpellier. A year later, Fabre donated the lot to his native city; the valuable Alfieri and Albany libraries are now in the adjacent **Gutenburg Médiathèque**, in a building formerly (and more simply) known as the Hôtel de Massilian, where Molière played in the *Ballet des Incompatibles* in 1655.

The Musée Fabre has six levels. The penalty for touring it from the bottom up is to start with the compost of the 17th century, when sunlight was an abomination, and people who paid for paintings liked bloody hunting scenes of boars goring dogs, and only the hard-drinking Dutch seemed to have any fun (works by Ruysdael, Jan Steen, David Teniers, and a good Rubens portrait). The next floor up, formerly the Jesuits' kitchen, is devoted to ceramics: apothecary vases made in Montpellier in the 1600s, faïence portraits of the Caesars and, finest of all, a 16th-century plate by Orazio Fontana of Urbino.

The next floor up contains the bulk of Fabre's donation, and although much of it is overblown and unintentionally hilarious, there are some gems: a lush *Mystic Marriage of St Catherine* by Paolo Veronese, that explains why 'Veronese green' is such a popular colour in France; a self-portrait by Bernini; Magnasco's *Fondaco dei Turchi* set in Venice, where wraith-like creatures flit in the cavernous darkness; a Florentine *tondo* of the *Virgin and Child* by a talented follower of Botticelli. From Naples, there's an anonymous Caravaggiesque *Ecce Homo*; from Spain, a Ribera and a pair of Zurbaráns, *St Agatha* carrying her breasts on a plate and the *Angel Gabriel*, who looks as if he can't find the right address; and from England, landscapes by Richard Parkes Bonington and Joshua Reynolds' famous *Infant Samuel in Prayer*. Fabre himself (*St Sebastian* and *The Death of Narcissus*) proves to be a romantic in his art as in his life; more influential, though, was Jean-Baptiste Greuze, who seems to have invented the simpering genre of big-eyed kid pictures they sell in supermarkets. **Fabre's *cabinet*** on the fourth floor contains portraits of Alfieri, Canova, and of Fabre himself at the end of his life.

The Good Narcissist of Montpellier

The superb collection on **Floor 5** was donated by the museum's other great benefactor, Alfred Bruyas (1821–77). Born into a Montpellier banking family, Bruyas resolved the frustration of not being able to paint himself by befriending many of the artists of his day and asking them to paint him—there are 24 portraits of the red-bearded patron in this museum alone, lined up one after another, including examples by Delacroix and Alexandre Cabanel of Montpellier

(1823–89). Four are by Gustave Courbet (1819–77), who became Bruyas' friend, and whose works are the highlight of the museum. Two paintings were pivotal in Courbet's proto-Impressionist discovery of light: the *Baigneuses*, which caused such a scandal in the Salon of 1853 that Napoleon III ordered it removed, and the delightful, sundrenched *Bonjour, Monsieur Courbet* (1854), in which the jaunty Courbet, strutting down a country lane with easel and paints strapped to his back, meets who else but Alfred Bruyas.

Other paintings on this floor cover the artistic movements on either side of Courbet: the cold classicism of Ingres' *Stratonice* (1866) and David (the clean, unbloodied *Dead Hector*), paintings that stand as the antithesis of the warm exotic romanticism of Delacroix's *Mulatress* and *Algerian Odalisques* (1849) or the melting landscapes of Corot. From southern painters of the period there are big historical and exotic scenes and landscapes. The gloomy young romantic Théodore Géricault (1791–1824) is represented by an unidealized *Portrait of Lord Byron* and a surreal *Study of Arms and Legs*, cannibal leftovers painted in a medical school while students dissected the corpses.

Floor 6 is dedicated to painters from Montpellier. Eugène Castelnau (1827–94) painted bright landscapes around Languedoc, like the *Vue du Pic Saint-Loup* (1859). Alexandre Cabanel (1823–89), who studied in Rome, left his best work in Montpellier, including the pre-Raphaelesque *Albaydé, La Chiarruccia* and *Self-portrait at Age 29*. Best of all is the short-lived early Impressionist Frédéric Bazille (1841–70), a friend of Renoir and Monet, whose best works glow with the strong sun of Languedoc: *Les Remparts d'Aigues-Mortes* and *La Vue du Village* (Castelnau, now engulfed by Montpellier). Also here are the museum's more recent works, by Berthe Morisot's, jolly Fauvist Desnoyer, Robert Delaunay, Kees Van Dongen, and Nicolas de Staël's painting of *Ménerbes*, which if it really looked like that wouldn't attract so many tourists or disciples of Peter Mayle.

Into the Ecusson

There is nothing as compelling as the Musée Fabre in Montpellier's historic centre; much was lost in the Wars of Religion, and even the many 17th- and 18th-century *hôtels particuliers*, as stuccoed and ornate as many of them are inside, show mostly blank walls to the street. But few cities in the south of France manage to be as pleasant and lively. Instead of gaggles of tourists, Montpellier has students to keep the city on its toes; this is the biggest university town in the south. Mayor Frêche has made the entire Ecusson a pedestrian zone, and it's a delightful place for walking.

One of the major crossroads of the Ecusson is Place Notre-Dame, under the cool gaze of the neoclassical **Notre-Dames-des-Tables** (1748), originally the chapel connected to the Jesuit college (now the Musée Fabre). In front passes the old pilgrims' route, the *Cami Romieu*, now Rue du l'Aiguillerie, where St Roch was arrested as a spy (see the plaque by Rue de Pila-St-Gély), and where Montpellier merchants and innkeepers cashed in on passing pilgrims. Residential *hôtels* went up later; nearby **Rue du Cannau** has some of the flashiest 17th-century models, while in Place Pétrarque, the **Hôtel de Varennes'** façade (1758) conceals a pair of Gothic halls, one a depository for architectural fragments salvaged from medieval Montpellier. Upstairs, there's a pair of small museums devoted to the good old days. The **Musée du Fougau** ('the Foyer', *open Wed and Thurs 3–6.30*) was founded by the local Félibres to preserve the arts and traditions of old Montpellier. The **Musée de Vieux Montpellier** (*open daily exc Sun, 9.30–12 and 1.30–5; adm*), exhibits portraits of notables, and plans and views of the city from the 1500s on, along with some peculiar relics, such as the model of the Bastille carved from one of the fortresses's stones soon after it was demolished in 1789.

Around the corner, at 4 Rue Embouque-d'Or, the 1670 **Hôtel de Manse** is famous for its richly decorated openwork staircase, designed by Italian architects—a stair that became the prototype for a score of others in Montpellier, including the one in the gorgeous Renaissance courtyard of the nearby **Hôtel de Lunaret**, at 5 Rue des Trésoriers-de-France. This, combined with the adjoining **Hôtel des Trésoriers de France**, around the block on Rue Jacques Cœur, was the residence of the famous merchant and financier Jacques Cœur, whose motto was 'flies can't enter a closed mouth'. In 1441 he was appointed a treasurer of Charles VII, and charged with obtaining royal subsidies from Languedoc. Reasoning that the wealthier the land, the easier it is to tax, Cœur became one of Montpellier's greatest benefactors, among other things building a merchants' exchange and dredging the outlets of the Lez to make them navigable; this town-house originally had a tower so high that he could scan the sea and its traffic. His career ended abruptly in 1451, when he was accused of poisoning the king's mistress, Agnès Sorel; he escaped prison in 1454 and died in Chios, fighting the Ottomans for the Pope.

Although much renovated since Jacques Cœur's day, most of the *hôtel's* contents predate him, as it's now the **Musée Languedocien** (formerly the Musée de la Société Archéologique) with its entrance at 7 Rue Jacques Cœur. Although you may have to arrange your schedule to fit theirs (*open daily exc Sun 2–5, July and Aug until 6; guided tours Mon, Wed, Fri at 2.30; adm*), it has its rewards—Greek vases, dolmens, funeral steles and other prehistoric finds from the Hérault; an excellent collection of Romanesque sculpture salvaged from the 11th-century version of Notre-Dame-des-Tables and from surrounding abbeys; the rock-crystal seal of King Sancho of Aragon; and three 12th-century Islamic funeral steles discovered in Montpellier, a rare relic of the city's cosmopolitan spice trading days; from Jacques Cœur's day, two fine paintings, an anonymous Catalan *SS. Apolline and Guilhem* and, from the Clouets' workshop, *Gabrielle d'Estrées and her Sister in their Bath*. A major collection of 16th- to 18th-century faïence made in Montpellier rounds things off, together with a grand ceiling painting of 1660, *Justice discovering Truth with the help of Time* by Jean de Troy, the city's top interior decorator of the age.

A plaque nearby in Rue des Trésoriers-de-France recalls that another of the city's colourful cast of characters lived here: that great wanderer Rabelais, who enrolled at Montpellier's medical school in 1530, at the age of 40, and became a doctor as well as a priest, although he later wrote that 'the calling was far too tiresome and melancholy a one', and that 'physicians always smelled of enemas, like old devils' (*Pantagruel*, 1532).

To the south, Rue Jacques Cœur becomes Grand Rue Jean Moulin, one of Montpellier's most elegant streets. On weekdays you can drop in at the Chamber of Commerce and Industry to see the **Amphithéâtre Anatomique St-Côme**, built in 1757 with funds left by Louis XV's surgeon, François Gigot de Lapeyronie, and of a classical elegance that belies its function. Turn left at the foot of Grand Rue Jean Moulin for the **Tour de la Babote**, a recently restored medieval tower topped by an astronomical observatory in 1741.

Western Quarters: Rue Foch and the Promenade du Peyrou

Despite its Protestant leanings, Montpellier's fame in heaven's closed circle hinges on Roch, the pious son of a wealthy merchant, who was born around 1350 and abandoned all of his worldly goods to make the pilgrimage to Rome in 1367. On his way home, he came to an

Italian village decimated by plague; after curing a number of victims with the sign of the Cross, Roch went down with the disease himself, and retreated to the country where no one could hear his groans. Nourished by a friendly dog who stole food for him from its master's table, Roch recovered and returned to Montpellier, so ravaged and changed by his illness that he wasn't recognized, and was thrown into prison as a spy, where he died in 1379. Only then did his grandmother recognize him by a birthmark in the shape of a cross. News of Roch's reputation as an intermediary against the Black Death reached plague-torn Venice, and even though he had yet to be canonized, Venetians disguised as pilgrims stole his bones and built the magnificent Confraternity of San Rocco in his honour—one of the wonders of the lagoon city.

As patron saint of Montpellier, St Roch came through for his home town in the cholera epidemics of 1832 and 1849, and finally a church of **St-Roch** was built, in Viollet-le-Duc's Ideal Gothic, in the medieval quarter of the Ecusson. Rue Voltaire leads up to the socializing centre of the neighbourhood, Rue de l'Ancien Courrier and Place St-Ravy. Here, too, is the largest and one of the most handsome residences in old Montpellier, **Hôtel des Trésoriers-de-la-Bourse** (1631–93) on the street of the same name (No.4), with a fine interior garden courtyard.

From the centre of the Ecusson, **Rue Foch** was sliced out in the 18th century as a grand formal boulevard, just missing a rare Jewish ritual bath, or **Mikveh**, at 1 Rue Barralerie (*to visit contact the tourist office*). Dating from *c.* 1200, it was part of the synagogue in the midst of what was then a large, active Jewish quarter. Since the late 17th century, however, this loftiest edge of Montpellier has been devoted to tons of mouldy fol-de-rol glorifying Louis XIV, beginning with an **Arc de Triomphe** (the triumphs referred to include digging a canal, wrestling the English lion to the ground and conquering heresy—with the Revocation of the Edict of Nantes, a nasty piece of bigotry that went down like a lead balloon in Montpellier). Beyond stretches the **Promenade du Peyrou**, a nice park spoiled by an equestrian statue of his megalomaniac majesty as big as the Trojan Horse. It was brought down laboriously from Paris in 1718, fell into the Garonne en route, whence it was rescued and brought here, only to be smashed to bits in the Revolution—a fact that didn't prevent the erection of the present copy in 1838. At the edge of the promontory stands the far more elegant **Château d'Eau**, one of Montpellier's landmarks, a neoclassical temple designed by Jean Giral to disguise the reservoir of the **Aqueduc St-Clément** (1771) snaking below in curious perspective, a triple-tiered work inspired by the Pont du Gard that brings in water from the river Lez. The Promenade is about to undergo an upheaval: American architect Richard Meier has been charged with adding an 'Espace Pitot' to the area, whatever that might be. Looking south from the Promenade towards Place Giral, the huge **cross** was erected by a Catholic missionary society in the 1820s.

The Cathedral and the Jardin des Plantes

The waters feed the unicorn fountain in the nearby **Place de la Canourgue**, a charming 17th-century square shaded by nettle trees (*micocouliers*). It looks down on the medieval monastery college of St-Benoît, on Rue de l'Ecole de Médecine, built by papal architects from Avignon, currently (since 1795) the **Faculté de Médecine**, housing an enormous medical library, and a **Musée d'Anatomie** (*open Mon–Fri, 2.15–5*) with an important collection of mummies, bodily parts, ancient and modern medical instruments, and more. There's also the **Musée Atger** (*open weekdays, 1.30–4.30; adm*), with a hoard of drawings mostly by southern French artists like Rigaud, Fragonard and Mignard but also by Flemish, Dutch, German and Italian schools of the 15th–18th centuries. Adjacent, the former monastic chapel has been Montpellier's **Cathédrale de St-Pierre** ever since the see was transferred here from

Maguelone in 1563, although its status didn't spare it the usual depredations in the Wars of Religon and the Revolution. The cathedral's greatest distinction is its unusual porch, supported by two conical turrets.

Boulevard Henri IV, running alongside the Faculté, descends to the tree-topped **Tour des Pins**, a last vestige of the medieval walls. Beyond lies the lovely **Jardin des Plantes**, the oldest botanical garden in France, founded by a decree of Henri IV in 1593 to instruct students on native and exotic plants used for healing. It has several magnificent 400-year-old trees, exotic succulents, plants from the *garrigues*, and an *orangerie*; near the latter, in a spot celebrated for its exquisite melancholy, there's a marble plaque with the inscription *Placandis Narcissae Manibus*. The Narcissa in question is said to be the consumptive 18-year-old daughter of the poet Edward Young (best known for his *Night Thoughts*, illustrated by Blake). In 1734 he brought Narcissa to France, hoping the warm climate would cure her; instead the exertion of travelling killed her, and she was buried either in Lyon, or here 'in the garden she loved'—a story that made this a favourite rendezvous for romantic students like Paul Valéry and André Gide. At the highest point of the garden is the Tree of Secrets, its trunk pitted with niches where lovers would leave *billets d'amour* for one another (*open Mon–Fri, 8.30–12 and 2–5, until 7 in summer*).

The Montpellier Follies

Montpellier, one of the fastest growing cities in France, is spreading its tentacles to suck in all that surrounds it, and has already gobbled up a number of 18th-century châteaux and gardens that were the country retreats of its elite (before setting out, check hours at the tourist office; some places can only be visited on the office's *Les Folies* tour). One of the oldest is 3km east of Antigone on the D24, and can be reached by the no.12 city bus: the **Château de Flaugergues**, *©* 04 67 65 51 72 (*guided tours, July and Aug, Tues–Sun, 2.30–6.30, otherwise telephone ahead; adm*). Begun in the 1690s, the place is impressively filled with 17th- and 18th-century furnishings, tapestries, and a collection of optical instruments. A bit further east (take D172), **Château de la Mogère**, *©* 04 67 65 72 01, is a refined *folie* of 1716, with period furnishings, family portraits, and in the garden a delightful Baroque *buffet d'eau*, a fountain built into a wall (*guided tours, Pentecost–end of Sept, daily 2.30–6.30; other times Sat, Sun and holidays only; adm*).

North of Montpellier, on the road to Mende, the **Parc Zoologique de Lunaret** (*bus no.5, open daily 8–6, 7 in summer; adm*) has exotic and regional fauna, where you can wander amid woodlands and *garrigues*. The 1750 **Château d'O** (northwest, on the road to Grabels), now used for receptions and theatrical performances, is famous for its park, decorated with statues taken from the gardens of the **Château de la Mosson** (1729), which lies to the south, just off N109. La Mosson was the most opulent of all the follies until the Revolution and its conversion into a soap factory; after decades of neglect the city of Montpellier acquired it in 1982 and is restoring it. It has a lovely oval, Venetian-style music chamber and a poignant seashell and pebble *buffet d'eau* in the garden, now stripped of its ornaments.

From Mosson, take D27E/D5E and turn towards Pignan for the remarkable 1250 church of the Cistercian **Abbaye St-Martin-du-Vignogoul**, open by request to the custodian (*closed Wed am*). Believed to be the first attempt at Gothic in Languedoc, the church is small in size but grand in vision, a lofty, single-naved, pint-sized cathedral decorated with a trefoil arch, finely sculpted capitals, still more Romanesque than Gothic, and a unique polygonal choir, lit by a row of bull's-eye windows.

The city hosts four annual festivals: theatre in late June, during the **Printemps des Comédiens** at Château d'O, ✆ 04 67 61 06 30; dance performances of all kinds, including whirling dervishes, films, and workshops at the **Festival International Montpellier Danse**, also in June; all-star music to suit every taste from opera to jazz during late July through August at the **Festival de Radio France et de Montpellier**; and at the end of October, the **Festival International du Cinéma Méditerranéen** (info for the last three from 7 Blvd Henri IV, ✆ 04 67 61 11 20).

Shopping

The tourist office has a large display of wine, *confits* and other regional products; antique shops cluster around Place de la Canorque; or for something really special, pick up a bottle of 'Eau de Montpellier' (no kidding) for your sweetie-pie at G. de Guidais, 51 Rue de la Méditerranée. A good selection of reasonably priced English books and videos and the latest lowdown on Montpellier are available at Steve Davis' Bookshop, 4 Rue de l'Université, ✆ 04 67 66 09 08.

Montpellier ✉ *30400*   **Where to Stay**

Montpellier is well-endowed with hotels, especially two-star hotels for small business travellers that double well enough for pleasure travellers as well.

expensive

At the top of the line, there's the antique-furnished ★★★★**Alliance Métropole**, 2 Rue Clos-René, ✆ 04 67 58 11 22, ✆ 04 67 92 13 02, between the train station and Place de la Comédie, with a quiet garden courtyard and air conditioning. If you have a car, the most charming place to stay is ★★★**Demeure des Brousses** (a few minutes from either the city or the sea at Rte des Vauguières, 4km east of town on D24 and D127E, towards the Château de la Mogère, ✆ 04 67 65 77 66, ✆ 04 67 22 22 17), an 18th-century ivy-covered *mas*, surrounded by a vast park of shady trees, furnished with antiques and an excellent restaurant to boot. Another gem requiring your own transport, ★★★**La Maison Blanche**, 1796 Ave de la Pompignane (off the route to Carnon), ✆ 04 67 79 60 25, ✆ 04 67 79 53 39, has 38 rooms in a big, balconied house that escaped from the French quarter of New Orleans, here surrounded by a 5-hectare park.

moderate

The ★★**Parc**, 8 Rue Achille Bège, ✆ 04 67 41 16 49, ✆ 04 67 54 10 05, north of the Jardin des Plantes, is in an 18th-century *hôtel particulier*, fitted out with air conditioning, TVs, etc. More central (just off Rue Foch) the ★★**Palais**, 3 Rue du Palais, ✆ 04 67 60 47 38, ✆ 04 67 60 40 23, has comfortable rooms in a recently restored building. The ★★**Nice** manages to be very pretty and flowery on a dull street near the station (14 Rue Boussairolles, ✆ 04 67 58 42 54). ★**Les Arceaux**, 35 Blvd Arceaux, ✆ 04 67 92 03 03, ✆ 04 67 92 05 09, is clean and comfortable, with a small garden.

You'll find a choice of these on the side streets around Place de la Comédie. The ★**Etuves**, 25 Rue des Etuves, ✆ 04 67 60 78 19, and the ★**Majestic**, around the corner at 4 Rue du Cheval Blanc, ✆ 04 67 66 26 85, are both cheap and comfortable. On the other side of Comédie, there is the ★**Touristes**, 10 Rue Baudin, ✆ 04 67 58 42 37. Near the Jardin des Plantes, ★**Les Fauvettes**, 8 Rue Bonnard, ✆ 04 67 63 17 60, offers good value for money.

Eating Out

Montpellier isn't celebrated for its cuisine, but prosperity, as always, is encouraging newcomers to have a go, especially the three young men who opened **Le Jardin des Sens**, 11 Ave St-Lazare (off the N113 towards Nîmes; bus 4), ✆ 04 67 66 25 23, and have made their garden pavilion a bastion of imaginative cuisine, with a light, fresh touch—delicate courgette blossoms filled with scallops, fillet of *loup*, duck with pine-nuts, spinach and cream, superb desserts, and the best wines of Languedoc (*menus at 290 and 430F, 185F for weekday lunch*); book ahead as space is limited. Another established temple of fine cooking (complete with columns) is **Le Chandelier**, 3 Rue Leenhardt (off Rue du Grand St Jean, near the station, ✆ 04 67 92 61 62), featuring well-polished versions of the classic French repertoire (*lunch menus at 150F, dinner 250–360F*).

Lively Rue des Ecoles Laïques and Place de la Chapelle Neuve, with their reasonably priced restaurants, make up Montpellier's Latin Quarter, where the colours, smells and live music from the Turkish, Greek, Spanish and Tunisian restaurants collide in gleeful discord. At No.1 on the Place, **Le Vieil Ecu**, ✆ 04 67 66 39 44, 🖷 04 67 72 71 01, has good French food, served in the old chapel or on the terrace (*60F lunch menu, dinner 99 and 129F*).

Elsewhere in the centre, **Les Puits Ste-Anne**, near the church of Ste-Anne at 9 Rue de l'Amandier, ✆ 04 67 60 82 77, offers a vast choice for its 50F menu, or you can splurge and get an extra course from an equally long list for 80F, with wine. Near the Musée Languedocien at 20 Rue Jacques Cœur, **Tripti-Kulai** is a vegetarian restaurant and tea room that offers some exotic dishes: a good spot for an inexpensive light lunch. There's a place north of Rue Foch where you may safely break the Languedoc-Roussillon pizza rule (never order a pizza in Languedoc-Roussillon): the Italian-run **Pizzeria du Palais**, 22 Rue du Palais des Guilhem, ✆ 04 67 60 67 97, a wide choice of pizzas and other Italian dishes, always crowded (*about 70F*). For tapas and a down-to-earth ambience, try **La Bodega**, 27 Rue du Faubourg St-Jaumes by the Jardin des Plantes, ✆ 04 67 41 06 98. Come here to drink and nibble, or for the good value 75F menu with a Catalonian flavour. For lunch, cram into the small courtyard of **L'Epicurien**, at 24 Rue du Cardinal-de-Cabrières, ✆ 04 67 66 09 43, in the heart of the old city. Its proximity to university faculties means most of your fellow diners are professors or students, enjoying fertile salads and tantalizing *escalopes de veau* (*lunch 50F, otherwise 80–115F*).

To find out what's going on in the new Rome, pick up a copy of the city weekly *La Gazette*; or visit FNAC, in the Polygone, which has tickets for most events. For a babysitter, try AGEM, 5 Rue Croix-d'Or, ✆ 04 67 60 57 23, or CROUS, 2 Rue Monteil, ✆ 04 67 63 53 93.

During the year, there are performances at the CORUM, ✆ 04 67 67 67 61, home of **L'Orchestre Philharmonique de Montpellier** and **Montpellier Danse**, an internationally renowned company under its innovative choreographer/director Dominique Bagouet. The old **Opéra Comédie**, ✆ 04 67 66 00 92, still puts on opera and theatrical performances; popular singers and comedians often crop up at **Zénith**, Rte de Mauguio, ✆ 04 67 64 50 00. Montpellier is a great town for cinema, both recent releases and classics, some in English; complete listings for these, as well as clubs, theatre and music, can be found in *La Gazette*. *The* place to stop for a coffee: **Café Bibal**, 4 Rue Jacques-Cœur.

In a city where a quarter of the population are students, nightlife is never going to be dull. Most bars and clubs will not heat up until after 11pm, and the clubs rock until dawn. One of the most lively bars in Montpellier is **Le Fût**, out of the centre near Place Flandres-Dunkerque at 81 Avenue de Toulouse, ✆ 04 67 42 46 34; a new club just down the street at No.131, **Mimi la Sardine**, ✆ 04 67 69 27 90, offers music and dancing, pool and games. Otherwise head for the life-size red Cadillac implanted in the wall at **Le Rockstore** down from Place de la Comédie on Rue de Verdun, ✆ 04 67 58 70 10. Most dance-nights there is free entry and drinks are inexpensive. On weekends and often weekdays there's live jazz, blues or world music at **Le Cargo**, 5 Rue du Grand St Jean, ✆ 04 67 92 56 05; **Sax'Aphone**, 24 Rue Ernest-Michel, ✆ 04 67 58 80 90; **l'Antrouille**, 12 Rue Anatole-France; **La Jument Vert**, 16 Rue du Pila St-Gély, ✆ 04 67 66 20 67; rock and salsa at **Metal-Café Le Doyen**, 13 Rue du Grand St-Jean, ✆ 04 67 58 82 73; **Cotton Pub**, 9 Place Laissac, ✆ 04 67 92 21 60. For more harmonious entertainment, the **Centre Culturel Irlandais Your Bard**, 273 Rue Mas de Portaly, ✆ 04 67 92 95 98, is responsible for spreading Irish music in deepest, darkest Languedoc.

SAINT GUILHEM - LE - DÉSERT

The Hérault

France isn't the sort of country that allows itself to be neatly dissected for the benefit of geographers and travel writers. So it is only for convenience's sake that the rugged *garrigue* of the upper Hérault, the green hills of the Espinouse and the flat expanses of the Béziers coast are combined together in one chapter. In this *département*, some 150km across at the most, the diversity is tremendous: a microcosm of France, from mountain forests of oak and pine, limestone *cirques* and *causses*, to the endless beaches of the coast and the rolling hills around the Canal du Midi.

For devotees of rural France, this seemingly innocuous area may be the ultimate find. Just enough tourists come for there to be plenty of country inns and *fermes-auberges*, though in most villages foreigners are still a novelty. The food is good; and there's enough wine to make anyone happy—that's an understatement. The Hérault is the most prolific wine-producing region in France. It can be a perfect alternative to overcrowded and over-praised Provence: just as beautiful, more real and relaxed, full of things to see—and considerably less expensive.

Beaches

The sand of the Camargue continues around the elbow of the French coast. The Golfe d'Aigues-Mortes washes against immense swathes of sand, much of which is being eaten up by concrete development, such as the resort of La Grande Motte. Pavalas is Montpellier's summer cruising zone—trendy and overpopulated. For more space and less frills, head south past Sète, or north to the tranquil Plage des Aresquiers, accessible only by a dead-end road from Frontignan.

best beach

Palavas: wide sand, quite energetic.

Getting Around

Except along the coast, public transport is rudimentary at best; the **coastal SNCF line** runs from Montpellier through Frontignan, Sète, Agde and Béziers on its way to Narbonne and Perpignan, with as many as 22 trains a day. The only train service in the **interior** is from Béziers northwest to the Espinouse, taking a roundabout route through Bédarieux, Lamalou-les-Bains, Olargues and St-Pons on its way to Castres in the Tarn; a few trains daily at most.

St-Pons is also connected by bus to Béziers, via St-Chinian. **Coach** lines from the *gare routière* in Montpellier have regular services to Gignac, Clermont l'Hérault and Lodève, less regularly to other villages in the *département*; there are additional buses to some tourist attractions (like St-Guilhem-le-Désert) in the summer.

North of Montpellier: the *Garrigue*

On a map, you'll notice lots of blank space in this region, a *pays* without a name. It is a geographer's textbook example of *garrigue*, a dry limestone plateau with sparse vegetation, where

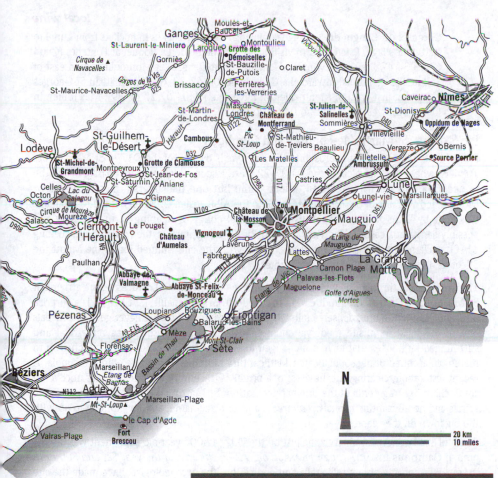

even sheep only just get by. *Garrigue* is an old Occitan word for the holly-oak, and these scrubby would-be trees grow everywhere, along with thyme and lavender-scented *maquis*, and increasingly vines, which not only thrive but are quickly changing the local economy. The windblown landscapes are as romantic as anything in Provence, although a shade more sombre. The few villages seem huddled, closed into themselves.

Tourist Information

Ganges ✉ 34190: Plan de l'Ormeau, ✆ 04 67 73 66 40, ✉ 04 67 73 63 24.

market days

Ganges: Tuesday and especially Friday morning, when the lively market takes over half the town.

Coteaux du Languedoc: A huge confusing region that takes in pockets from Lunel to Narbonne-Plage. Estates worth visiting are: Domaine de La Roque, at Fontanès (℡ 04 67 55 34 47); the prize-winning Domaine de la Devèze, at Montoulieu, 6km east of St-Bauzille-de-Putois, towards La Cadière (℡ 04 67 73 70 21); Château St-Georges d'Orques, just west of Montpellier, at Lavérune (℡ 04 67 27 60 89); Mas Jullien in Jonquières, west of Gignac (℡ 04 67 96 60 04).

Pic St-Loup, St-Martin-de-Londres and Cambous

From Montpellier, the best approach to the *garrigue* is by way of the D17 to St Mathieu-de-Tréviers, where you can pick up the D1/D122 west, a scenic high road that passes below the ruined **Château de Montferrand**, a long climb but one that offers a memorable view. Montferrand was one of the first castles to fall to the Albigensian Crusade, but the real damage was done by Louis XIV, as part of his general royal policy of cleaning up unnecessary and possibly dangerous castles. The view takes in **Pic St-Loup**, just up the road, a lone, striking 2110ft exclamation point of the *garrigue*. Along with the cliff rimmed lump, the Montagne d'Hortus, it is the remnant of a volcanic crater.

The D122 passes through the typical *garrigue* village of **Le Mas de Londres** before arriving at **St-Martin-de-Londres** (25km direct on the D986 from Montpellier). St-Martin is a surprise package. Passing the tiny, densely built village on the road, you would never guess it conceals one of the most exquisite medieval squares anywhere, picturesquely asymmetrical and surrounded by houses that have not changed for centuries. The ensemble has a **church** to match, an architecturally sophisticated 11th-century building with a rare elliptical cupola. A recent restoration, clearing out the dross of a brutal 19th-century remodelling, has uncovered some charming fragments of the original decoration: St Martin on horseback, carved Celtic spirals and neo-Byzantine capitals. *Londres* is a local place-name, and has nothing to do with the big town on the island.

South of St-Martin, in a military zone just off the D32, a 5000-year-old settlement was discovered at **Cambous** in 1967 (*open July–Aug daily 2–7, the rest of the year Sat and Sun only; adm*). With considerable intelligence and dedication, the archaeologists have made the site into a veritable recreation of ancient life for the benefit of visitors. They have reconstructed one of the communal houses of this 'Fontbouisse civilization' and gathered together enough artefacts to make you feel entirely at home among the Fontbouissians. These peaceful folk knew both farming and husbandry, and were just learning about copper tools. They also had a well-developed cultural life, as evidenced by their geometrically decorated pottery and stone statue steles.

From the 13th to the 18th century, the country north of the **Causse d'Hortus** was famous for its 'Gentlemen Glassblowers' who passed their secrets down through the generations. North of St-Martin, on the D107e, you can learn all about their art at the Renaissance **Verrerie de Couloubrines** in **Ferrières-les-Verreries,** restored in 1989 (*open daily in July and Aug, 4–7, other times Sun and hols only 2–5, closed Dec–Mar*); living glassmakers ply their trade to the west at the **Verrerie** in **Claret** where a centre dispenses information on the **Chemin des Verriers**, a route set up to explore the tiny villages once attached in some way to the trade. In Claret you can also visit Europe's only family-run cade oil mill; cade oil has been used for embalming since antiquity, and the mill offers a range of modern products made from the stuff.

Ganges, Caves and the Cirque de Navacelles

From St-Martin, the main D986 leads northwards towards the Cévennes. From the village of **St-Bauzille-de-Putois** (a *putois* is a skunk—St-Bauzille used to have more than its share) there is a steep side road to the **Grotte des Demoiselles**, © 04 67 73 70 02, an important Protestant hideout during the war of the Camisards (1702–04) that also has one of France's most spectacular displays of pipe-organ stalactites and stalagmites, in the staggeringly enormous 'Cathedral of the Abysses'. Visits take an hour by subterranean funicular; bring a sweater (*open daily summer 9–12 and 2–7, July and Aug continuously; winter 9.30–12 and 2–5; adm*).

Geologically, this is folded country; along the Hérault, you can clearly see the lines of stratification of limestone and schist in the cliffs. See them from river level, by floating down the Hérault in a canoe (hire one at Le Moulin, just under the cave, © 04 67 73 30 73) to **Brissac** which is guarded by a ruined castle perched on a pinnacle of rock.

Ganges is the only real town around, and quite a pleasant one, closed in between the river Hérault and *maquis*-carpeted hills. In the 18th century, it was France's capital of silk stockings. Like most of the Cévennes, Ganges was and remains a mostly Protestant area; the old part of town is crisscrossed by *chemins de traverse*, labyrinthine passes laid out to confuse Catholic troops, and it has an imposing, peculiar seven-sided Protestant 'temple', built in 1850. Just south, the village of **Laroque** is prettily set on the river and offers another stalactite cave to visit, the **Grotte des Laroque**, © 04 67 73 55 57, discovered in 1991 in the gorges of the Hérault; compared to the highly organized Grotte des Demoiselles, the tour, complete with a little toy train ride through the canyon, has an amateurish charm (*open April–June 2–5, July and Aug 10–6.30, Sept 2–6; adm*).

Ganges makes a good base for exploring the natural wonders of this pretty region, between the *garrigue* and the Causse du Larzac. The **Gorges de la Vis** can be followed on the D25 west of town, passing a waterfall and a 17th-century château (at St-Laurent-le-Minier). The route through the gorges is 34km long (one-way only); the best parts, after Madières, can only be reached on foot. If you go the whole route, there's a real curiosity at the end, the famous **Cirque de Navacelles**. A *cirque* looks like a deep lunar crater, though it is in fact a loop dug deep into the limestone of the *garrigue* by the meandering river Vis long ago. There are many in the *causses* and *garrigues* of the Midi, and this is the most striking, with steep, barren walls and a rocky 'island' in the centre; various points along the D713 offer views down into the *cirque*. You can spend a day walking through it by picking up the GR7 at **St-Martin-de-Navacelles**, or get a bird's eye view from a helicopter (Hélisud, ©/🖂 04 67 57 94 49).

A second popular excursion from Ganges is the 30km drive north to the **Observatoire Météorologique du Mont Aigoual** (1567m/5141ft) in the northern Gard (*open June–Sept, 10–7; free*). Set on the summit of the Cévennes, this has been the training ground for France's weather forecasters since 1887, and you can see why: on a clear day the view encompasses all the territory covered in this book, from Mont Blanc and the Alps to Canigou in the Pyrenees down to the Mediterranean. Inside, a museum has photos, and old and high-tech weather instruments.

Where to Stay and Eating Out

St-Martin-de-Londres 🖂 34380

Although St-Martin-de-Londres hardly seems big enough to support one restaurant, it has three. For years gourmets from Montpellier have driven up especially to feast at **Les Muscardins**, 19 Route des Cévennes, ℂ 04 67 55 75 90, which offers fancy *terrines* and pâté, game dishes, formidable desserts and a selection of the best regional wines on a choice of four menus (*from 170–390F*). *Closed Mon, Tues lunch*. A half km from St-Martin, the pretty **La Pastourelle**, 350 Chemin de la Prairie, ℂ 04 67 55 72 78, serves delicious dishes based on local *cèpes*, lamb, and seafood (*menus 100–260F*). *Closed Tues eve and Wed*. For inexpensive and tasty home-cooking, book a table at the **Bergerie du Bayle**, ℂ 04 67 55 72 16, in the *garrigue* just west at Frouzet. A bit further west, in Causse de la Selle, **★★Hostellerie le Vieux Chêne**, ℂ 04 67 73 11 00, 🖂 04 67 73 10 54, has three luxurious double rooms and a good restaurant serving French classics on a pretty terrace (*from 115F*). *Closed Mon*. For something extra special, attend a supper concert on the unique patios of 'Chapelle Musicale' at **La Ferme des Moreaux**, ℂ 04 67 73 12 11. Madame Moreaux prepares a tasty meal based on medieval recipes and seasonal ingredients (*around 120F*) while guests' ears are regaled with everything from Gregorian chant to jazz with an electronic touch; dress up, bring a sweater, don't smoke and be quiet (*June–Oct, nightly at 9pm, reservations mandatory; because of the delicate setting, no children or dogs are allowed*). For dinner, after a trip to the Grotte des Demoiselles, dine on farm fresh food at the **Ferme-Auberge du Mas Domergue**, 5km to the east on D108 at Montoulieu, ℂ 04 67 73 70 88 (*summer only, call ahead for the 90F menu*).

Ganges ✉ 34190

The **★★Hôtel de la Poste**, 8 Plan de l'Ormeau; ℂ 04 67 73 85 88, 🖂 04 67 73 83 79, has been prettily restored by its friendly new owners, Marie and Jean-Yves, who are mines of information about the area. Seven km east of Ganges on D999 at a place called **Moules et Baucels** (✉ 34190), the **Ferme-Auberge Domaine de Blancardy**, ℂ 04 67 73 94 94 or 04 67 73 13 13, has three rooms with bath in a distinctive old *mas* from the 12th century (*250F a double, with breakfast*) and offers homemade *confits* and pâté to accompany their fine wine; open all year. For solid good cooking and good grilled meats, try the large welcoming terrace at **Le Bon Coin**, Cours de la République, ℂ 04 67 73 80 47 (*menus from 60–125F*). *Closed Mon*. Or go to the more intimate **Joselyn Mélodie**, Place Fabre d'Olivet in the old town, ℂ 04 67 73 66 02, named after its two charming owners, who will fill you with good French cooking for less than 100F. *Closed Wed*. At Pont d'Hérault (famous for onions), 11km north of Ganges **Chez Maurice**, has the best *cuisine terroir* around, and excellent (*good value menus from 120–250F*). Book.

Gorniès ✉ 34190

If you're staying around the Cirque de Navacelles, a reasonable choice would be the **★Hôtel des Gorges de la Vis**, ℂ 04 67 73 85 05; at least stop for the restaurant, where river crayfish and game dishes are the specialities (*menus from 70–155F*). *Closed Nov–mid-Feb*. If you want to combine the austerity of the *garrigue* with style and creature comforts, **★★★★Château de Madières**, 7km west of Gorniès, ℂ 04 6773 84 03, 🖂 04 67 73 55 71, has ten luxurious rooms in a 14th-century fort; a park, pool, fitness centre, and beautiful vaulted dining room are some of the amenities (*from 585–1150F*). *Closed Nov–Mar*. At St-Maurice-de-Navacelles, **La Baume Auriol**, ℂ 04 67 44 62 67, serves good reasonably priced food to go with its match-less view over the cirque.

The Valley of the Hérault: the Haut Pays d'Oc

The Hérault slices dramatically through the *garrigue*, and the atmosphere is clear, luminous, otherworldly: the perfect landscape for saints and pilgrims, and wine.

Tourist Information

St-Guilhem-le-Désert ✉ 34150: At the Mairie, ✆ 04 67 57 44 33.
Gignac ✉ 34150: Pl Général Claparède, ✆ 04 67 57 58 83, 🖷 04 67 57 67 95.
Clermont-l'Hérault ✉ 34800: 9 Rue Doyen Réné Gosse, ✆ 04 67 96 23 86, 🖷 04 67 96 98 58.
Lodève ✉ 34700: 7 Pl de la République, ✆ 04 67 88 86 44, 🖷 04 67 88 86 44.

market days

Gignac: Saturday. **Clermont-l'Hérault**: Wednesday.

St-Guilhem-le-Désert

'Desert' might seem a little unfair to this rosemary-scented jumble of *garrigue* around St-Guilhem, northwest of Montpellier; there are plenty of green, shady spots for a picnic, and even forests of pines. But 'desert', in French or English, originally meant *deserted*, and this is still as lonely a region as it was when the hermit St Guilhem came here, in the reign of Charlemagne. Besides being a delightful place to visit, St-Guilhem is a living history lesson, evoking the time when the 'desert' was a troubled frontier between Frank and Saracen, and later, when it became a key cultural outpost in the process of making the Midi Christian and French.

Saint William Pug-nose

Guilhem Court-Nez, the powerful Frankish Count of Toulouse, Aquitaine and Orange, was a grandson of Charles Martel and a cousin, liegeman and friend to Charlemagne. For over thirty years, he campaigned from the Atlantic to the Alps, mostly against the Arabs, whose great wave of 8th-century expansion through Spain had washed up as far north as Poitou and Narbonne. Another of Guilhem's friends was Benedict, the monastic reformer from Aniane (*see* below); Benedict too had once been a warrior, and he convinced Guilhem to follow his example and renounce the world. Guilhem spent the last six years of his life in a humble cell here, at a place near the gorges of the Hérault, originally called Gellone, and was canonized soon after his death in 812.

And soon after that, pilgrims began to visit. As a vanquisher of the heathen, St-Guilhem was a popular saint with the Spaniards, and with northerners on their way to Compostela. The original community of hermit cells grew into a wealthy monastery; construction of the great abbey church began about 1050. Already in decline during the Wars of Religion, it was sacked by the Protestants in 1569—its celebrated library was burnt in the process. The final indignity came not during the Revolution, surprisingly, but a decade before, when clerics from Lodève and other towns succeeded in having the monastery suppressed, apportioning its treasures and holy relics among themselves.

The Abbaye de Gellone

The little village of St-Guilhem is stretched on the edge of a ravine. Its one street being too narrow for traffic, a parallel road and car park has been built on the other side; from here you'll have a good view of its rugged stone houses, their gardens and tiny bridges, little changed from medieval times. The abbey **church** is a remarkably grand and lovely specimen of Lombard architecture, with its blind arcading and trademark cross-shaped window. The best part, the broad, arcaded apse, recalls the contemporary churches of Milan or Pavia. The façade, facing an ancient, colossal plane tree in the village square, is somewhat blighted by an ungainly tower of cheap stone, built in the 1300s more for defence than for bell-ringing.

The interior, lofty and dark, has lost almost all of its original decoration. Some fragments of frescoes survive in the side chapels, and niches in the pillars around the choir once held the relics of St-Guilhem and a bit of the True Cross, a gift from Charlemagne. The organ, built in 1782, is the focus of a summer series of Baroque concerts. The cloister is ruined, and most of its capitals have ended up at the Cloisters Museum in New York.

On the village's main street, some modest Romanesque palaces survive from the 1200s, an especially picturesque one housing the *mairie*; at the opposite end, facing the D4 at the entrance to the village, the church of **St-Laurent** has another fine apse like that of St Guilhem. More medieval relics can be seen along the Hérault: medieval mills, for grain and for oak bark (used in tanning leather), set near the modern

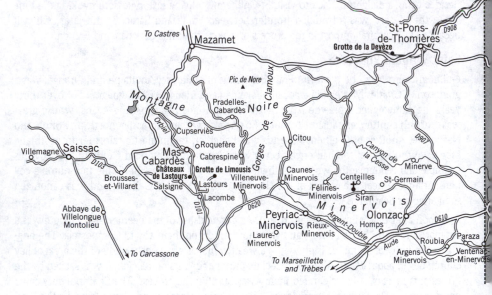

trout hatcheries by the river. The hills around St-Guilhem make interesting exploring on foot—a ruined castle and other fortifications, and the **Rue du Bout du Monde** that leads from the back end of the village to a lovely spot with a flowing spring. The steep **Gorges de l'Hérault** extend on both sides of the village, and can be followed on the D4.

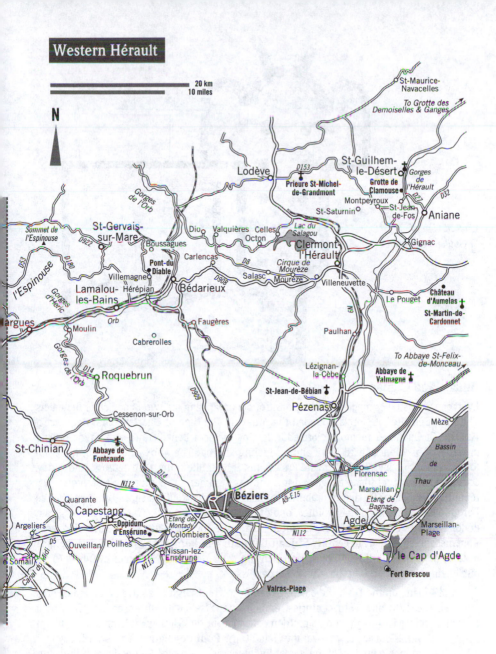

20 km
10 miles

N

St-Maurice-
Navacelles

*To Grotte des
Demoiselles & Ganges*

Lodève

D153

St-Guilhem-
le-Désert

Gorges
de
l'Hérault

Prieure St-Michel-
de-Grandmont

Grotte de
Clamouse

D32

Gorges
de l'Orb

Montpeyroux

St-Jean-
de-Fos

Aniane

St-Saturnin

Sommet de
l'Espinouse

St-Gervais-
sur-Mare

Dio

Valquières

Celles

Lac du
Salagou

D922

D180

Boussagues

Octon

Clermont-
l'Hérault

Gignac

Carlencas

D8

l'Espinouse

D53

Pont-du-
Diable

Villemagne

Hérépian

Bédarieux

Cirque de
Mourèze

Salasc

Mourèze

Villeneuvette

N9

Le Pouget

Château
d'Aumelas

Lamalou-
les-Bains

Gorges d'Héric

Orb

St-Martin-de-
Cardonnet

argues

Moulin

Faugères

Paulhan

Cabrerolles

Gorges de l'Orb

D14

Roquebrun

D908

Lézignan-
la-Cèbe

*To Abbaye St-Felix-
de-Monceau*

Abbaye de
Valmagne

St-Jean-de-Bébian

Cessenon-sur-Orb

Pézenas

Mèze

St-Chinian

Abbaye de
Fontcaude

D14

Florensac

Bassin

de

Thau

N112

Marseillan

Quarante

Capestang

Béziers

A9-E15

Etang de
Bagnas

Argeliers

Oppidum
d'Ensérune

Etang de
Montady

Colombiers

Agde

Marseillan-
Plage

D5

Ouveillan

Poilhes

N112

D113

Nissan-lez-
Ensérune

le Cap d'Agde

Somail

Canal du Midi

Fort Brescou

Valras-Plage

With all this eroded limestone about, you would expect caves, and there are several. The most impressive, 3km south, is the **Grotte de Clamouse**, ✆ 04 67 57 71 05, one of the big tourist attractions of the Hérault, with its lovely aragonite crystals (*open July and Aug 10–7; otherwise 10–5; Dec–Feb 12–5, guided tour; adm*). Some 500 yards to the south, don't miss the massive stone bridge of 1030, the **Pont du Diable**.

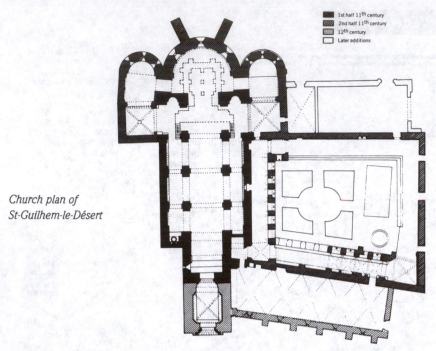

Church plan of
St-Guilhem-le-Désert

Aniane and Gignac

Everyone who studies medieval history has trouble untangling the two Benedictine Benedicts. The first, Benedict of Norcia, founded the order. In the time of Charlemagne, Benedict of **Aniane**, St Guilhem's mentor, reformed it, forcing the poor Benedictines back to the original precepts of obedience, hard work and no fooling around. The **abbey** he built in his home town was thoroughly wrecked by the Protestants and rebuilt in the 17th century, and is now occupied by a school (open for guided tours in the summer). The church, **St-Sauveur**, was rebuilt under Louis XIV, and in drab little Aniane it comes as quite a shock, with its glorious Baroque façade framed in big volutes, one of the best in the south. The interior is typically divided into two parts: one for the monks and one for the villagers. Nearby is a good Romanesque church, 12th-century **St-Jean-Baptiste des Penitents**. Aniane's astronomical observatory—seven little domes scattered in the trees—opens on summer evenings to the public; ring them on © 04 67 57 21 45 for details.

South of Aniane on the D32, the bustling market town of **Gignac** enjoyed a period of prosperity in the 17th and 18th centuries, embellishing itself with an ensemble of Baroque churches and palaces to go with its pretty medieval Tour de l'Horloge; its best-known monument, however, is outside town, over the Hérault: the **Pont de Gignac**. This bridge, begun in 1776, is every inch a product of the Age of Enlightenment, strong and functional architecture without a trace of Bourbon curlicues.

Mouldering Castles and a Rotten Borough

The monasteries of St-Guilhem and Aniane brought considerable prosperity to the surrounding areas. Villages like **St-Jean-de-Fos** and **St-Saturnin** have fine Romanesque churches and buildings. Near the latter, there are fine views from the ruined early 11th-century castle on the **Rocher des Vierges**. There are two other fascinating ruined castles in this region. **Montpeyroux**, a village between St-Jean and St-Saturnin, grew up around a mysterious abandoned pile called the Castel Viel, a long, impressive circuit of walls with nothing inside. Its history is utterly unknown; it may be from the 1000s, the 1500s or anywhere in between, and it was probably less a military post than a protection for livestock in times of war (*see* St-Pierre-des-Clars, p.426). Southeast of Gignac, off the main N109, the **Château d'Aumelas** occupies a romantically isolated hilltop. This castle, built sometime before 1036 by the Lords of Montpellier, is on a dirt track and difficult to reach, but it's a wonderful place to explore; parts of the noble residence, chapels and other buildings are still substantially intact.

The castle is located in one of the biggest completely blank spots on the French map. It is part of a real, old-fashioned rotten borough, a *commune* without a town and hardly any inhabitants; it does have a mayor, who has a say in deciding representatives to the French Senate—two centuries after the Revolution, such things are still common in rural France. Another attraction in this 'Commune d'Aumelas', south of the château on a rocky track, is a beautiful and austere Romanesque church, **St-Martin-de-Cardonnet**, set amidst the ruins of the monastery that once surrounded it. To the west, back towards civilization on the D139, the circular fortified village of **Le Pouget** is just north of the colossal **Dolmen Gallardet**.

Clermont-l'Hérault

Clermont is a peacefully bovine and prosperous town, living off the wine and table grapes of this more fertile part of the Hérault valley. Its medieval centre, on a hilltop, is large and well-preserved, including a tall and graceful Gothic church, **St-Paul**, begun in 1276. The 10th–11th-century **castle** around which the town grew up is also in good shape, including the gates, prisons and keep. Clermont has the big weekly market in this region, every Wednesday, and has done since the year 1000.

West of Clermont, you leave the green valley for more peculiar landscapes around the **Lac du Salagou**, a large man-made sheet of water surrounded by hills that is much more natural-looking and attractive than most artificial lakes. Circumnavigating it, you'll pass some singular cliffs and weirdly eroded rock formations, and also the village of **Celles** on the water's edge, now almost completely abandoned. The oddest formations lie to the south, in the **Cirque de Mourèze**, a long, stretched-out *cirque* with the dusty village of Mourèze and its ruined castle at the centre.

Between the Cirque and Clermont lies **Villeneuvette**, founded only in 1670. The 'little new town' was a manufacturing centre for *londrins*, printed linen cloth. Though the works are now closed (since 1954) Villeneuvette is still the very picture of an old French paternalistic company town. The manufactories remain—behind the gate with the big inscription *Honneur au Travail*—along with some of the workers' housing, school, church, warehouses and gardens. Lately, artists and artisans have been recolonizing the place, and there are art galleries and handicraft shops.

North of Clermont, the N9 heads into the *causses* of deepest France, passing **Lodève**, a comfortable, somewhat isolated town wedged between two rivers. Like Clermont-l'Hérault, Lodève has an impressive Gothic church with a lofty tower as its chief monument; **St-Fulcran**, named after a 9th-century bishop who became the city's patron, was begun in 1280, and turned into a fortress during the Hundred Years War. It is one of the few churches in

France with a chandelier—a present from Queen Victoria to Napoleon III. **Lodève's** textile-manufacturing past is recalled in a local workshop of the famous Parisian tapestry factory, the **Atelier National de Tissage de Tapis de Lodève**, ℘ 04 67 96 40 40 (*ring ahead to visit; open Tues, Wed, Thurs 2–5*). Lodève was a Roman town, and its **Musée Fleury**, in Rue de la République (*open 10–12 and 2–6, closed Mon*), has finds from that age, along with dinosaur bones and footprints, and fossil trilobites, paintings and sculptures.

East of Lodève, a narrow but very pretty country road, the D153, takes you 9km to the **Priory of St-Michel-de-Grandmont**, ℘ 04 67 44 09 31 (*open Easter–Aug, at 10.30, 3, and 5, otherwise Sun and hols only at 3; adm*). The Order of Grandmont, founded in the Limousin in the 1100s, was a monastic reform movement like that of Cluny or Cîteaux; it faded away five centuries ago and no one even remembers it today. This priory is its only surviving monument, gradually restored by private owners over the last century. The austere church and cloister, begun in the 12th century, are remarkably well preserved, but the real attraction here is a group of outlandish **dolmens** in the grounds, colossal works shaped like *cèpe* mushrooms, dating from about 2000 BC.

Where to Stay and Eating Out

St-Guilhem-le-Désert ✉ 34150

In St-Guilhem, rooms are scarce; if you're stuck in town try ***La Taverne de l'Escuelle** on Rue Val de Gellone, ℘ and ✆ 04 67 57 72 05 (*around 200F*); it has a good restaurant (*menus from 70F*) Closed Tues. The medieval **Auberge sur le Chemin**, 38 Rue Fond de Portal, ℘ 04 67 57 75 05, serves tasty regional treats (*menus 72–110F*), but only in season. Nearby at Aniane, ****Hostellerie St-Benoit**, ℘ 04 67 57 71 63, ✆ 04 67 57 47 10, is a comfortable motel,with a pool and a good restaurant specializing in trout and crayfish (*menus 95–200F*).

Gignac ✉ 34150

Try to be around Gignac at dinner-time; the **Ferme-Auberge Le Pélican**, Domaine du Pélican, ℘ 04 67 57 68 92, does a wonderful 98F menu–*pintade* (guinea-hen) stuffed with olives, duck in honey vinegar, homemade desserts and their own wines; booking essential. ****Capion**, Blvd de l'Esplanade, ℘ 04 67 57 50 8, ✆ 04 67 57 50 60. Run by the same family for almost a century, this popular hotel restaurant with an outdoor terrace eschews simple local cooking in favour of complex seafood fantasies like salmon *à trois façons* (prepared three different ways). (*Menus 190–300F.*) Closed Sun eve and Mon out of season.

Clermont-l'Hérault ✉ 34800

Clermont-l'Hérault will be the most likely place to find a room in this region if you haven't booked ahead: ****Sarac**, Rte de Nebian, ℘ 04 67 96 06 81, ✆ 04 67 88 07 30, is a pleasant Logis de France, with views over the vineyards. The best of the restaurants is **L'Arlequin**, in the medieval centre, on Place St-Paul, ℘ 04 67 96 37 47: smoked trout, *confits*, and good Faugères wine, in a refined candle-lit room (*good bargain, with 65 and 139F menus*). Closed Mon. Four km southwest in Villeneuvette, ****La Source,** ℘ 04 67 96 05 07 ✆ 04 67 96 90 09, makes a refreshing stopover, a charming rural retreat with a pool and tennis (*open Easter to 1 Oct, around 280F*) with an impressive restaurant, specializing in salmon and truffles (*menus from 149F*). *Closed Mon*. Near the Cirque de Mourèze, the **Ferme-Auberge de la Vallée du Salagou**, towards Salascon the D8, ✆ 04 67 96 15 62, is a comfortable bed and breakfast with lovely views; the restaurant serves a filling 90F menu, with grilled lamb or steaks and wine from nearby Octon. Another excellent choice in the area is the friendly ****Les Hauts de Mourèze**, 8km from Clermont overlooking the Cirque, ✆ 04 67 96 04 84, 🖷 04 67 96 25 85, with beautiful views. *Closed Dec–Feb*.

The Northern Fringes: Monts de l'Espinouse

If you continue along the northern fringes of the Hérault, you'll get an idea of what France is like for the next hundred miles northwards, through Aveyron and Lozère into the Auvergne—rough canyons and rough villages, an occasional dusting of snow, trout streams and chestnut groves. The natural beauty of the Espinouse did it little good in former times; even forty years ago, this was a poor area, losing its population to the cities. The creation of the Parc Régional du Haut Languedoc in the 1960s has made all the difference; *tourisme vert*, as the French call it—hiking and canoeing or just relaxing under the pines—increases every year. It's no strain on the kind and hospitable folk in the villages, and right now the Espinouse is as happy and content as a patch of mountains can be.

Tourist Information

Bédarieux ✉ 34600: Rue St-Alexandre, ✆ 04 67 95 08 79, 🖷 04 67 95 39 69.
Lamalou-les-Bains ✉ 34240: 2 Ave Dr. Ménard, ✆ 04 67 95 70 91, 🖷 04 67 95 64 52.
Olargues ✉ 34390: Rue Neuve, ✆ 04 67 97 71 26.
St-Pons-de-Thomières ✉ 34220: Place du Foirail, ✆ 04 67 97 06 65; for the Parc Régional, there is a Maison du Parc, 13 Rue du Cloître, ✆ 04 67 97 38 22.

market days

Lamalou-les-Bains: Tuesday. **La Salvetat**: Thursday and Sunday.

local wines

Faugères: Try Domaine Gilbert Alquier, Rte de Pézenas, in Faugères (✆ 04 67 78 06 09); Château des Estanilles, in Cabrerolles (call ahead, ✆ 04 67 90 29 25); and in Laurens, the Cave Coopérative de Laurens (✆ 04 67 90 11 12).

St-Chinian: Visit the Maison des Vins (✆ 04 67 38 11 69); Château Moulinier, Rue de la Digue in St-Chinian (✆ 04 67 38 14 21); Château Cazals in Cressenon (✆ 04 67 89 63 15).

Bédarieux and Lamalou-les-Bains: the Pays d'Orb

The only big road in this region, the D908, runs west from Clermont-l'Hérault across the base of the mountains, following the valleys of the Orb and the Jaur. The first town on the way is **Bédarieux**, a humble enough agricultural centre and market town. Humility stops, however, with Bédarieux's famous son, Pierre-Auguste Cot, one of the 19th-century kitsch-realist artists so popular with the academicians, the sort that made the Impressionist revolution necessary. They've named the main square after him, and you can see his work in the **Maison des Arts**, in the former poor house on Ave Abbé Tarroux (*open 3–6, closed Tues; adm*), along with some fossils, railroad memorabilia and exhibits recreating country life and costumes in the old days.

Lamalou-les-Bains, 10km further west, is a sort of museum in itself. A thermal spa since the 1600s, Lamalou made it big when the railroad came through in 1868. The prosperity of the next three decades—dukes and counts, famous actresses, even a Sultan of Morocco checked in for the cure—built it into a sweet little resort of *Belle Epoque* hotels and villas, cafés and a casino with a chocolate-box theatre. Today Lamalou is bidding to become fashionable once again. Its restored 19th-century centre makes a perfect setting for the big event on its calendar: an important festival of operettas (and opera) that lasts throughout the summer. Inside the cemetery, on the eastern edge of town, is an exceptional 11th-century Romanesque church with a sculpted portal and apse, **St-Pierre-de-Rhèdes**.

The Eastern Espinouse

Either of these towns is a good base for exploring the eastern half of the Espinouse. North of Bédarieux, the upper valley of the Orb starts out plagued by industry and power lines, but you can escape into the hills on either side, to **Dio** or to **Boussagues**, both delightful medieval villages with ruined castles; the latter's highly picturesque, stone-roofed Renaissance Maison du Bailli once belonged to Toulouse-Lautrec. Persevere northwards, and you'll come to the **Gorges de l'Orb**, ending in a big dam and artificial lake at Avène. East of Bédarieux, there's another pretty village, **Carlencas**, famous for chick-peas; to the south is **Faugères**, centre of a small wine region (*see* above).

Hérépian, between Bédarieux and Lamalou, has one of Europe's last bell foundries, the **Fonderie Bruneau-Garnier**, in business since 1605; it has recently created a **museum of bells**, ℂ 04 67 95 07 96 (*open July and Aug 10–12 and 2.30–6; adm includes a guided tour of the foundry*). Hérépian offers another medieval detour, north on the D922 to **Villemagne**. Villemagne-*l'Argentière* it was in the 1100s, when a Benedictine abbey here looked after a rich silver mine, owned by the Trencavels of Béziers and Carcassonne. Most of the abbey and its fortifications are in ruins, and the parts that are left are sadly neglected: two lovely churches, Romanesque **St-Grégoire** and Gothic **St-Majan**, along with a richly decorated 13th-century building believed to have been the mint, the **Hôtel des Monnaies**. Just to the north of Villemagne is a humpbacked medieval bridge called, like that of St-Guilhem and so many others, the **Pont du Diable**—it must have been hard for the medieval peasant imagination to see how such things could stand up without divine or infernal aid. Continuing west from Lamalou, at Moulin, the Orb turns south, away from the road; there's a choice of directions and of scenery: the **Gorges d'Heric** to the north, a hiker's paradise with no roads, and the **Gorges de l'Orb** to the south, leading towards **Roquebrun**. Sheltered by the mountains, this village grows mimosas and likes to call itself the 'Little Nice'. And south of Roquebrun, it's a clear shot along to Béziers and the sea, with nothing to detain you along the way.

The Parc Régional du Haut Languedoc

The loveliest village of the Espinouse, **Olargues**, is dominated by two medieval monuments, a striking 11th-century bell tower set up above on a hill and a humpbacked bridge. Next, **St-Pons-de-Thomières** is the little capital of the Espinouse, surrounded by forests. St-Pons probably gets more snow than anywhere in Languedoc east of the Pyrenees, giving it a decidedly Alpine air. Its landmarks are a **cathedral**, with a Romanesque portal and a tremendous 18th-century organ, and its **Musée Municpal de Préhistoire Régionale**, ℂ 04 67 97 22 61 (*open 15 June–15 Sept, daily 10–12, 3–6, otherwise daily exc Mon 10–12, Wed, Sat, and Sun also from 2.30–5.30; adm*). Never suspecting they were in a future Regional Park,

Neolithic people made St-Pons and the Espinouse one of their favourite haunts in France; archaeologists go so far as to speak of a *civilisation saintponienne.* This museum documents their career, but the star attractions are the **statue menhirs**, the true cultural totems of this part of the Mediterranean, similar to those found in the Gard, in Tuscany and in Corsica, from 3000 BC to Roman times.

St-Pons is the perfect base for visiting the **Parc Naturel du Haut Languedoc**, © 04 67 97 38 22, spread over a wide area of the Espinouse, on the borders of the Hérault, Tarn and Aveyron. It's an extremely well-organized park; all you need do is travel up the D907–D169 to the **Maison du Parc** at Prat-d'Alaric, a restored farm with exhibits and presentations on the park and the life and traditions of its inhabitants (*open July and Aug, 9–12 and 2–6, otherwise check first at the Maison du Parc in St-Pons*). There is a wide choice of hiking trails in the mountains through wild areas that have, among other things, what is said to be the largest population of *mouflons* in Europe.

From Prat-d'Alaric, the valley of the Agout spreads across the heart of the park; the roads that follow it, the D14 and D53, make a delightful tour, through beautiful villages like **La Salvetat-sur-Agout,** and **Fraisse-sur-Agout**, which has a curious statue-menhir in situ, carved with a serpent and egg, a universal symbol found as far afield as the prehistoric Indian mounds in Ohio. The D53 continues towards the summit of the Espinouse (1113m). A little further on— over the Lauze pass on the D180—there is a stone enclosure, a vestige of a Roman army camp, and beyond—on the D922—**St-Gervais-sur-Mare**, full of medieval and Renaissance buildings.

Much closer to St-Pons, there is the **Grotte de la Devèze**, another gorgeous cave of delicate stalactites and shining crystals (*open Mar–Sept, daily guided tours at 1pm, otherwise call* © *04 67 97 03 24*). To climb down from the Espinouse, there is the choice of the D907 out of St-Pons towards Minerve, or the N112 for Béziers and the Canal du Midi (*see* below). On this route, you'll pass through **St-Chinian** and its wine region; about 9km east of that village is the Romanesque **Abbey of Fontcaude**.

Where to Stay and Eating Out

Lamalou-les-Bains ✉ 34240

The simple ★★**Belleville**, 1 Ave Charnot, © 04 67 95 57 00, ✆ 04 67 95 64 18, is excellent value for relative luxury: some bathrooms come with jacuzzi and the restaurant's 85F menu is a good deal. The 100-year-old ★★**Hôtel de la Paix**, 18 Ave Daudet, © 04 67 95 63 11, ✆ 04 67 95 67 78, has been prettily renovated, and serves old French favourites in the restaurant (*menus from 80F*).

Villemagne-l'Argentière ✉ 34600

Combine a visit of the old abbey with lunch at the **Auberge de l'Abbaye**, next to the church, © 04 67 95 34 84, where duck marinated with cardamons and other delicacies are served in the garden or in the 12th-century dining room (*menus from 100–215F*). *Closed Sun eve and Mon.*

Olargues ✉ 34390

The 17th-century ★★★**Domaine de Rieumégé**, 3km out on the St-Pons road, © 04 67 97 73 99, ✆ 04 67 97 78 52, is an enchanting place to stay, and set in a 20-acre estate peace and quiet is guaranteed; 12 nice rooms (*from 320F*), pool and tennis—

and a separate farmhouse with its own pool for a big splurge. If you don't stay, at least eat in the superb restaurant in the beautifully restored grange: seafood, *boeuf en croûte* and a big wine list (*menus from 105F*).

St-Pons-de-Thomières ✉ 34220

In town, sleep at the simple **★★Le Somail**, 2 Ave de Castres, ✆ 04 67 97 00 12, and dine well at **La Route du Sel**, 15 Grand' Rue, ✆ 04 67 97 05 14, a new little restaurant, specializing in original, well-prepared dishes such as foie gras gilded with jerusalem artichokes (*topinambours*); good value, with menus from 95F. *Closed Sun eve and Mon*. Up in the heart of the mountains **★★Le Cabaretou**, 10km from St-Pons on the D907 towards La Salvetat, ✆ 04 67 97 02 31, 🖂 04 67 97 32 74, is a plain but comfortable motel with a surprisingly ambitious restaurant, with a cuisine entirely based on seasonal ingredients (*menus 95–215F*). *Closed Sun eve and Mon out of season*. The **Ferme-Auberge du Moulin**, 4km from La Salvetat, ✆ 04 67 97 05 62, has simple *chambre d'hôte* rooms and good farm cooking, with duck and mushrooms (*menus begin at 85F, book ahead*).

The Hérault Coast: La Grande Motte to Agde

West of the Camargue, the lagoons continue for another 80km, dotting the coast like beads on a string. Unlike the Camargue, almost all of this coast is easily accessible by car; there are beaches and resorts in abundance, and attractions like salty Sète and medieval Maguelone and Agde. Only a few kilometres from the walls of Aigues-Mortes, the Hérault coast begins with a bang, with an uncanny skyline of tall holiday ziggurats, a resort town straight from science fiction (*see* map p.379).

Tourist Information

La Grande Motte ✉ 34280: Ave J. Bene, ✆ 04 67 56 40 50, 🖂 04 67 56 78 30.

Palavas-les-Flots ✉ 34250: Blvd Joffre, ✆ 04 67 07 73 34, 🖂 04 67 07 73 58.

market days

Palavas-les-Flots: Sunday morning, and flea market on Saturday morning.

La Grande Motte

At the same time as the Fos complex was going up on the eastern edge of the Camargue, something even stranger was happening on the west. It almost seems as if France's planners wanted an appropriate book-end to Fos's weird mill furnaces and refinery towers. Making the Languedoc resort plan in 1963, they decided that one of the new holiday towns was to be boldly modernist, and they picked the 'big lump', an empty swathe of sand on the Gulf of Aigues-Mortes for the experiment.

Jean Balladur, the original architect, and his successors gave them more than they bargained for. La Grande Motte looks like no other resort in the world: its hotels and apartments rising in colourful triangles and roller-coaster curves, its public buildings in jarring, amoeboid shapes like a permanent 1960s World's Fair. The 'modernism' of the Motte is more surface than substance; there are no real innovations in architecture or design. The buildings themselves, like all the experiments of the kitschy '60s, already look a bit dated. But La Grande Motte is a great success as a resort, a proper city with room for almost 90,000 space-age holidaymakers.

The fun starts at **Point Zéro**, the name Balladur whimsically gave the central square on the waterfront. In season little 'train' tours around the town start from here. The first clutches of ziggurats (the Grande Mottois prefer to call them *pyramides*) rise to the west, around the marina; to the east are the outlandish buildings of the civic centre, including the Mairie and congress hall. Beyond that, the planners ensure you will be entertained to death, with broad beaches, thalassothérapie, 32 tennis courts, golf courses (three, designed by Robert Trent Jones), marinas, windsurfing, diving, scrabble clubs, a casino and all the rest. The complex has expanded to envelop the old fishing village of **Le Grau-du-Roi**, just to the east (*see* p.338).

For you fogies, a more old-fashioned beach holiday can be spent at **Carnon-Plage** or **Palavas-les-Flots**, 15km down the dune-lined coast. Built around a narrow canal full of boats, Palavas is an endearingly humble resort with some 8km of good beaches, where grocery clerks from Montpellier come to flash their polyester in the frowzy waterfront casino. The old centre has a wonderfully casual air about it, toured by a silly tourist train dedicated to French humorist Albert Dubout, whose works, if you are at all curious, are displayed in the **Musée Humoristique Albert Dubout**, in the 18th-century Redoute de Ballestras, built to defend Palavas' fishermen (*open afternoons, weekends only in the winter; adm*). Inland, towards Montpellier, in the village of **Lattes,** you can visit Roman necropolises and the **Musée Archéologique Henri-Prades**, 390 Rte de Pérols (*daily exc Tues 10–12 and 2–5.30*), with recent discoveries from the ongoing excavations at the adjacent Bronze Age site of Lattara.

Maguelone

To balance La Grande Motte, a town without a history, here we have a history without a town. Maguelone, 4km from Palavas, may have begun as a Phoenician or Etruscan trading post. It prospered under the Romans and Visigoths, becoming the seat of a bishop. After that the history is obscure. Old maps show the place as 'Port Sarrasin', suggesting Arab corsairs were using it as a base in the 700s, and there is a record of Charles Martel coming down from Paris to chase them out, destroying the town in the process.

Maguelone still had one attraction—salt—and the rights were owned by a powerful and progressive multinational, the Church. In the 1030s, when demand was high, a cleric named Arnaulf oversaw the town's rebuilding and added a monastery. The enterprise prospered; Urban II, the first of many popes to visit (1096), called Maguelone the 'second church of Rome', and gave its restored bishops special privileges. Later, Maguelone became a papal holding, a key base both politically and ideologically in the difficult 12th century. It gradually dwindled after that, and the see moved to Montpellier in 1536.

Though almost no trace of the town remains today (its very stones were hauled off by the canal builders), the impressive **Cathedral St-Pierre** was saved from ruin and restored in the 1870s (*open daily, 10–7*). Built, and built well, by Lombard masons in the 1170s, it is an austere building. The main decorative feature—reliefs around the main portal—show Christ in Majesty with the four Evangelists. Inside, there are fragments of the bishops' tombs, inscriptions and furnishings, and you may climb the surviving bell tower for views down the coast.

Except at the height of summer, Maguelone makes a peaceful place to escape to; there are plenty of beaches around it, a bit rocky but good for sea shells. The lagoons in this stretch of coast, from La Grande Motte to Frontignan, are rich in waterfowl, especially pink flamingos, but little else. Most are stagnant and lack oxygen; decomposing water plants in hot summers cause a phenomenon called the *malaïgue*, making the air smell like rotten eggs. The vineyards (*vin de sable* 'sand wine' and others, run by the Compagnons de Maguelone) don't mind the occasional pong; there's a *cave* for tasting next to the cathedral car park. From Maguelone, you'll need to backtrack to Palavas and continue around the landward side of the lagoons, rejoining the coast at **Frontignan**, an industrial town with a good 12th-century church, **St-Paul**, with a frieze of fish and boats over the door. Frontignan claims to be nothing less than the world capital of muscat, beloved by the ancient Romans and Thomas Jefferson; it comes in a screwy bottle, in honour of Hercules, who stopped here for a drink while performing his Twelve Labours. The big fellow liked the wine so much that he twisted the bottle to squeeze out the last drop.

Where to Stay and Eating Out

La Grande Motte ✉ 34280

The bad news about La Grande Motte is that you can't stay there; all the hotels in the centre are overpriced to the point of absurdity. ★★★**Mercure,** Rue du Port; ✆ 04 67 56 90 81, 🖷 04 67 56 92 29, is the splashy status address on the Big Lump, looming over the marina like a concrete refugee from Miami Beach; charmless and soberingly expensive, but a chance to meet that segment of the fast crowd who choose to avoid the Riviera. **Alexandre-Amirauté**, on the Esplanade Maurice-Justine, ✆ 04 67 56 63 63, is a splurge for refined regional specialities in an especially elegant setting (*menus from 195F*).

Palavas-les-Flots ✉ 34250

Palavas, on the other hand, has few pretensions, but some gratifying, no-nonsense seafood joints: right on the canal, **La Passerelle**, 04 67 68 55 80, Quai Paul-Cunq, couldn't be simpler, its menu limited to piles of fresh inexpensive shellfish; for something more swank, **L'Escale**, north of the canal on the seafront, 5 Blvd Sarrail, ✆ 04 67 68 24 17, has *sèche à la rouille* for starters, or extravaganzas like the mixed shellfish plate they call *panaché de coquillages*—the bill can go up to 300F before you recover your reason. Palavas has plenty of inexpensive, undistinguished hotels; for something special, go inland to **Lattes** (✉ 34970) and the ★★**Mas de Couran**, Route de Fréjorgues; ✆ 04 67 65 57 57, 🖷 04 67 65 37 56, set in a beautiful park, with swimming-pool and restaurant (*menus 110–240F*). *Closed Sun in the off season.*

Sète

After the glitzy candy-land of the Côte d'Azur, and the empty spaces that follow, you may have despaired by now of finding anything really *Mediterranean* on these shores; you can find it almost anywhere along the coast of Spain, Italy or Greece, but in southern France it is as rare as snowmen. Just in time, there's gritty, salty, workaday Sète, France's biggest Mediterranean fishing port. What could be more romantic? In Sète, you can stroll along the Canal Maritime and watch businesslike freighters carry French sunflower and rape-seed oil to every corner of the globe, along with dusty cement boats, gigantic tankers of Algerian natural gas (if one ever goes off, it will take the whole town with it) and Algerian wine (marginally less dangerous), and rusty trawlers jammed full of woebegone sardines or some of the 138 other fish caught by Sètois fishermen. After that, perhaps a leisurely tour of the city's historic monuments. Go ahead and try; in this infant city, younger even than Boston or New York, there isn't a single one.

For entertainment, there are the sailors' bars, or you might try one of the **boat tours** (along the Quai de la Résistance) through the Bassin de Thau, with a stop at an oyster farm. Or take in an American football match, and watch the Sète Praetorians joust with the dreaded Bastia Black Heads from Corsica. If you can stand a little modern madness, Sète will be great fun. It's an attractive town, laced with canals, and livelier and more colourful than any place on the coast, save only Marseille.

Tourist Information

60 Grand Rue Mario Roustan; ✆ 04 67 74 71 71, 🖃 04 67 46 17 54.

market days

Daily in Les Halles, Rue Jean-Jaurés; also Wednesday morning, in Place A. Briand, and Friday morning in Ave V. Hugo, opposite the SNCF station. Sunday morning flea market in Place de la République. In the summer the tourist office offers afternoon tours of the *Criée*, the extraordinary fish wholesale market on Quai Maximin-Licciardi.

Along the Grand Canal

The city's arms show a field of *fleurs-de-lis* with a whale—*cetus* in Latin—one of the possible explanations for the name, which is first mentioned in a Carolingian document of 814. In 1666, Louis XIV's minister, Colbert, began construction of the port, the terminus for the Canal du Midi (*see* p.403), which was begun in the same year. In 1673 the new town was declared a free port. The pesky English first came to visit in 1710, occupying the city during the War of the Spanish Succession; out in the harbour, you can see **Fort St-Pierre**, which failed to keep them out. Little has happened since. Despite its booming port, Sète never grew into a major city; hedged between Mont St-Clair, the lagoons and the sea, there simply isn't room.

Sète should be the twin city of Livorno (Leghorn) in Italy. Both grew up at the same time; both have canals (Sète likes to call itself the 'Venice of Languedoc') and a winsome architectural anonymity. And they have both made their offbeat contributions to modern culture; Livorno was the birthplace of Modigliani, Sète of the poet Paul Valéry, singer-composer Georges Brassens, and Jean Vilar, father of the Avignon festival.

The bustling centre of Sète is its 'Grand Canal', the **Canal de Sète**, lined with quays where the ambience ranges from boat-yards and ship chandlers to banks and boutiques. A block west, on Place Aristide Briand in front of the Mairie, Sète has what is undoubtedly the **world's biggest cast-bronze octopus**, writhing over a modern fountain. Just south of here, at 2 Rue Alsace Lorraine the old public baths have a fishy new occupant: the **Musée Imaginaire de la Sardine**, ✆ 04 67 74 91 75 (*open daily 10–1; adm*) the brain-child of 'sardinologist' Philippe Anginot dedicated to the secret world of Sète's cash crop, in the classic key-opened sardine can —invented by Frenchman Pierre-Joseph Colin (1785–1848). There's a thousand of these, including a model for visitors to crawl in to see what it feels like to be a sardine.

At the southern end of the canal, the **Vieux Port** handles most of the fishing fleet, as well as offering tourist fishing boats and excursions around the Thau lagoon. From the Vieux Port it's a bit of a climb up to the **Cimetière Marin**, celebrated in a famous poem by Paul Valéry, who was buried here in 1945, his family tomb (under the name Grassi—like Brassens, his mother was Italian) with an inscription from the poem (*Ô récompense après une pensée/Qu'on long regard sur le calme des dieux*). The adjacent **Musée Paul Valéry**, ✆ 04 67 46 20 98 (*open* *daily exc Tues, 10–12 and 2–6*), contains exhibits on the poet, and on the history of Sète, as well as a good collection of modern paintings, and older works by Courbet and even a minor Botticelli. Just below, the **Théâtre de la Mer** is dedicated to Jean Vilar; just above begin a network of paths up to **Mont St-Clair** (182m), once the Sunday promenade of the Sètois.

Sète's other contribution to French culture, Brassens (died 1981) is buried in the **Cimetière de Py**, under the Pierres Blanches, overlooking the Etang de Thau; fans or the merely curious can learn much, much more in the nearby **Espace Georges Brassens**, 67 Blvd Camille-Blanc, ✆ 04 67 53 32 77 (*open 10–12 and 2–6, closed Mon Oct–May, adm*), where you'll not only see photos and exhibits relating to Brassens' life, but you can hear it as well on the headphones, accompanied by his hit songs and words of wisdom.

Bassin de Thau

Sète's Bassin de Thau is one of the largest lagoons along the Mediterranean shore. There have always been salt-pans here, though today most of the lagoon has found a more lucrative employment as a huge oyster and mussel farm.

There are two roads south from Sète; taking the coastal route, passing quickly through the unhappy concrete piles of La Corniche, you'll pass 15km of unbroken, nearly perfect **beaches**. Since there is no room for development, this is your best chance on the entire coast to find some peacefully empty beach space, even in the height of summer. At the southern end, the beach piles up into an expanse of partly overgrown dunes, near the small resort of **Marseillan-Plage**. **Marseillan** itself, another fishing/oyster port, was founded in the 6th century BC by the Greeks and is made of the same black basalt as Agde. By the port you can find out the secret ingredients of Marseillan's own aperitif, **Noilly-Prat**. The other, longer route passes around the back of the lagoon. Along the way, it takes in the 11th–13th-century Benedictine (later Cistercian) **Abbaye St-Félix-de-Montceau**, ✆ 04 67 51 20 77 (*open Sat and Sun 2–5*), accessible on a white road from **Gigean**. Romantically ruined on its hilltop site, with a view over the lagoon, the abbey includes both a Romanesque and a Gothic church. Further south, the ancient lagoon port of **Mèze** still makes a go of it as a fishing village, though nowadays the money comes from the less romantic chores of oyster farming.

Abbaye de Valmagne

8km north of Mèze on the D161; guided tours; in summer open daily exc Tues, 3–6, the rest of the year Sun pm only; ✆ 04 67 78 06 09.

It might try the patience of some readers, dragging them on another detour to another ruined abbey—but this is the best one of all. Valmagne was an early Cistercian foundation, begun in 1138 and financed by Raymond Trencavel. Being one of the richest houses, it also gradually became one of the most decadent; the records mention a 16th-century Florentine abbot named Pietro da Bonzi, who built himself a palace on the site, plus a French garden with a statue of Neptune, and who threw the best dinner parties in Languedoc. Thoroughly trashed in the Revolution, the abbey has survived only by good luck; one owner proposed to dismantle it to provide building stone for a new church in Montpellier, but the canons there found the price too high. For the last century, the vast **church** has served as the biggest wine cellar in the Hérault, with some of the best fruity red AOC Coteaux de Languedoc and a traditional lemon-coloured white (*June–Sept, Wed–Mon 10–12 and 2.30–6.30, out of season, 2–6, or ring* ✆ *04 67 78 06 09*).

Valmagne is not your typical Cistercian church. St Bernard would have frowned on architectural vanities like the porch, the big bell towers and the sculpted decoration—grapevines, representing less the scriptural 'labourer in the vineyard' than the real vineyards that made Valmagne so rich. Its size is astonishing: a 370ft nave, and great pointed arches almost as high as Narbonne cathedral's. Most of the work is 14th-century, in a straightforward but sophisticated late Gothic; note how the nave columns grow slightly closer together towards the altar, a perspective trick that makes the church seem even longer (St Bernard wouldn't have fancied that either). The relatively few monks who lived here would hardly have needed such a church; here too, architectural vanity seems to have overcome Cistercian austerity.

Both the chapter house and the refectory are well preserved, around a pretty **cloister** that contains the loveliest thing in the abbey, an octagonal Gothic pavilion with a tall flowing fountain inside, a fantasy straight from a medieval manuscript or tapestry; an 18th-century poet, Lefranc de Pompignan, named it right: a *fontaine d'amour*. Other possible distractions around the Bassin de Thau are in nearby Mèze; in **Loupian**, a **Gallo-Roman villa** is being excavated and restored (*site open in the summer from 10–12 and 2–5*).

Sète ✉ *34200*   ### Where to Stay and Eating Out

For a night's flop in Sète, nothing less than the ★★★**Grand Hôtel** 17 Quai Lattre de Tassigny, ✆ 04 67 74 71 77, ✇ 04 67 74 29 27, will do. Right on Sète's 'Grand Canal', it almost deserves its name, with plenty of the original decor from the 1920s. If you can't swing the Danieli in Venice, this will do fine; nice people and very reasonable rates. The hotel's **Rotonde** restaurant is refined and serves rewarding menus at 95F and 145F. Otherwise no harm will come to you at the small and central ★★**Les Abysses**, 47 Grand' Rue Mario Roustan, ✆ 04 67 74 37 73, ✇ 04 67 74 24 82), or, for a bit more, at ★★**L'Orque Bleue**, 10 Quai Aspirant-Herber, ✆ 04 67 74 72 13, ✇ 04 67 74 72 13, where anyone who grew up in the '70s will feel at home.

Sète has lots of seafood but as part of the experience you should try a place called the 'Golden Spot', or 'Gold Rush', or some such American nonsense, located on the Canal de Sète, to watch harried cooks churn out mountains of *frites* while trading insults and banter with the Sètois (the sandwiches aren't bad, really). For lunch with the dockhands, try **La Péniche**, 1 Quai des Moulins, ✆ 04 67 48 64 13 (*55F and 80F menus*), simple stuff on an old barge in the harbour. For quality seafood, try **La Palangrotte**, on the lower end of the Canal de Sète, Rampe Paul Valéry, ✆ 04 67 74 80 35 (*menus 150–300F*): grilled fish, and several styles of fish stew, including the local *bourride sètoise*. *Closed Mon.* The row of restaurants along Quai Gérard Durand, on the Grand Canal, is another good place: the Baroque-o-cola **Le Chalut**, at No.38, ✆ 04 67 74 81 52 (*menus 90 and 140F*), where the seafood, including many sètois specialities, is as tasty as the decor. *Closed Wed and Jan.*

Agde, the 'Black Pearl of Languedoc'

If Sète is a brash young upstart, Agde has been watching the river Hérault flow down to the sea for some 2500 years. Founded by Greeks from Phocis, not long after Marseille, its name was originally *Agatha*, after *Agatha Tyche*, the 'good spirit' of popular Greek religion, usually portrayed carrying a cornucopia; the people of Agde are still called *Agathois*. In medieval times it was an important port, despite occasional visits by Arab sea-raiders. The last few centuries have left Agde behind, but it is still a good town, and a grey one—built almost entirely of volcanic basalt from nearby Mont St-Loup. With the massive new tourist development at nearby Cap d'Agde, this lovely town does not get much peace in the summer; in parts of the old quarter there are almost as many restaurants as houses.

Tourist Information

Agde ✉ 34300: Place Molière, ✆ 04 67 94 29 68.

Cap d'Agde ✉ 34300: 11 Impasse du Hourier, ✆ 04 67 01 04 04, 🖳 04 67 26 22 99.

market days

Agde: Thursday morning. **Cap d'Agde:** Sunday morning (May–Sept).

A Stroll around Town

The tiny old quarter is defined by its walls, now largely demolished for a promenade; a bit of the old ramparts remains, near the river, resting on Greek foundations (now below street level). Overlooking the Hérault, Agde's stern basalt **Cathédrale St-Etienne** was begun about 1150. Its fortress-like appearance—it looks like a baddie's castle in a Hollywood movie—is no accident; Agde's battling bishops used it as their citadel (the outworks have been demolished). Previous cathedrals had been wrecked in battles, once at the hands of Charles Martel himself. It's only open during mass; the only original feature is the 12th-century marble altar.

From the quay along the Hérault, Rue Chassefière leads into the *bourg*, or medieval addition to the city. On Rue de la Fraternité, the **Musée Agathois**, ✆ 04 67 94 82 51 (*open daily exc Tues, 10–12 and 2–6; adm*), is one of the best of the south's town museums, encapsulating nearly everything about Agde's history and traditions in a few well-arranged rooms: archaeological finds, religious art, costume exhibits, dances and festivals, an old-fashioned kitchen and fishermen's gear. Behind the museum, Agde's market shares Place Gambetta with the church of **St-André**, where important Church councils were held in the days of the Visigoths; of the present building, though, the oldest part is the 12th-century tower. Another church, **St-Sever** on Rue St-Sever, contains a fine Renaissance painting of Christ on wood, a little the worse for wear from having been thrown into the Hérault during the Revolution.

A Suspicious Saint and a Synthetic Resort

The road to Cap d'Agde, only 4km away, passes the ancient, extinct volcano **Mont St-Loup**, its top disfigured by communications pylons. Agde's black basalt comes from here. Whoever St Loup, or 'Holy Wolf', might have been is not clear (though there is a northern saint by that name, a 5th-century bishop of Troyes). *Loup* is also the name for sea-bass, the favourite fish in Agde's restaurants. **Cap d'Agde**, built around a small harbour and a lovely black basalt sand beach, is the biggest beach playground in all Languedoc and another triumph of French holiday efficiency. Like La Grande Motte, it began in the 1960s as a planned resort fostered by the government, and it looks it: a freshly built 'traditional' centre, with plenty of parking, broad boulevards, and everything in its place. The original plan even accommodated the *naturistes*; the camp called **Héliopolis** on the northern edge of town, at Port-Ambone, has become the biggest nudist colony in Europe, with a futuristic semicircular central building that includes shops, banks, even a *naturiste* supermarket, where German has become the second language.

Cap d'Agde may not be what you came to Languedoc for, but there's plenty to do: a first-rate golf course, championship tennis courts and matches, and other sports facilities (they hosted the Mediterranean Games in 1993); a wildlife sanctuary at the nearby **Etang de Bagnas**, with rare waterfowl (purple heron, grand bittern); boat trips to **Fort Brescou**, a 1586 fortress on a volcanic islet at the mouth of the Hérault, long used as a political prison by the French kings; a Casino, an **aquarium** (specializing in live coral) at 11 Rue des Deux Frères, a Luna Park, and the inevitable **Aqualand** with water-slides. One surprising attraction is a fine, small archaeological collection at the **Musée de l'Ephèbe**, © 04 67 26 81 00 (*open daily exc Tues and Sun am 9–12 and 3–6; summer 9.30–12.30 and 2.30–6.30; adm*), the star of which is the *Ephèbe d'Agde*, a Hellenistic bronze of a boy, discovered in 1964 in the bed of the Hérault.

Agde ✉ *34300*   ### Where to Stay and Eating Out

You won't regret stopping over at Agde if you're passing anywhere nearby. It's a sweet town, and the hotels and restaurants are as good as you'll find on the coast, although parking can be difficult. First choice is ★★**La Galiote**, in the old bishop's palace, at 5 Place Jean Jaurès, © 04 67 94 45 58, ✆ 04 67 94 41 33. Some of the rooms overlook the river; there's a bar full of English beer, and an excellent restaurant (*80–170F menus*): seafood or roast lamb with thyme, and alcoholic ices between courses. Second choice is across the square: ★★**Le Donjon**, © 04 67 94 12 32, ✆ 04 67 94 34 54, with old-fashioned, comfortable rooms. Four km down the Hérault, amid century-old parasol pines and roses, ★★★**La Tamarissière**, 21 Quai Théophile-Cornu (D32E) © 04 67 94 20 87, ✆ 04 67 21 38 40, is a real charmer, with quiet, stylish well equipped rooms, a pool, and the best restaurant in the area: fresh, colourful dishes such as saint-pierre baked with stuff baby courgettes and saffron (*menus from 149–360F*). For a lively atmosphere, good fish, and the 80F menu, try **Casa Pepe,** 29 Rue Jean Roger, © 04 67 21 17 67, in the centre of Agde.

Pézenas

The area inland from Agde, behind the Bassin de Thau, is one of the duller stretches of the Hérault, a rolling plain dotted with a score of agricultural villages—up-to-date and businesslike rather than picturesque and cosy. Right in the centre is Pézenas. If Carcassonne is Languedoc's medieval movie-set, this town has often been used for costume dramas (most famously, *Cartouche*) set in the time of Richelieu or Louis XIV. Few cities have a better ensemble of buildings from what the French (rather over-enthusiastically) used to call the 'Golden Age'. Even when the cameras aren't rolling, it is all too easy to imagine moustachioed musketeers and *grandes dames* with laced bodices and perfumed gloves strolling its elegant streets. In summer, the Piscénois live out a lingering *ancien régime* fantasy, with festivals, concerts and exhibitions called the *Mirondela dels Arts* that lasts from mid-June to September.

History

Roman *Piscenae* was known for wool, the best in Gaul. In the 1200s, it became a possession of the French crown and renewed its prosperity by royally chartered merchants' fairs. Later, the troubles of Béziers and Narbonne in the Albigensian Crusade and the Hundred Years War would prove lucky for Pézenas. Besides draining off trade and commerce from those cities, the royal town replaced Narbonne as seat of the Estates-General of Languedoc after 1456. The royal governors of the region followed in 1526, bringing in their wake a whole wave of wealthy nobles, clerics and jurists, who rebuilt Pézenas in their own image, with new churches, convents, government buildings and scores of refined *hôtels particuliers*. For the next two centuries they remained, preferring their little aristocratic town to decaying Narbonne or to Montpellier, full of untidy industry and Protestants. All this came to an end with the Revolution, but meanwhile Pézenas has done its best to keep up its monuments, while making a discreet living from agriculture and tourism.

Tourist Information

Place Gambetta, ℂ 04 67 98 35 45, ✉ 04 67 98 96 80.

market days

Saturday.

local wine

Coteaux du Languedoc: One of the best pockets of this AOC label is here. In Pézenas try the Prieuré de St-Jean de Bebian (ℂ 04 67 98 13 60), or Château St-André, Rte de Nizas (ℂ 04 67 98 12 58).

A Walk around Town

The tourist information office is the place to start. They offer a brochure with a detailed walking tour of the town and its 70-odd listed historical buildings. From the Renaissance through to the 1700s, Pézenas really did develop and maintain a distinctive architectural manner; this can best be seen in the *hôtels particuliers*, with their lovely arcaded courtyards and external staircases. It was an eclectic style, incorporating elements as diverse as Gothic vaulting and Italian Renaissance balustrades: tasteful, if not ambitious.

The tourist office was also once the shop of a barber named Gély. Molière spent some seasons in Pézenas in the 1650s, when his troupe was employed by the governor, the Prince de Conti. He liked passing the afternoons in Gély's salon, doing research for his comedies—watching the comings and goings and listening to the conversations. Across Place Gambetta, the former government palace, the **Maison Consulaire**, has been rebuilt so many times since the 1200s that it is a little museum of Pézenas architecture. Around the corner on Rue Alliès, the **Musée de Vulliod-St-Germain** contains memorabilia of Molière and his time in Pézenas, along with collections of tapestries, faience, paintings and the bric-à-brac of Pézenas' past (*open 10–12, 2–5, closed Sun am and Mon; adm*).

West of Place Gambetta are some of the best streets for peeking inside the courtyards of the *hôtels*: Rue Sabatini, Rue François-Oustrin (the **Hôtel de Lacoste**, with an elegant staircase, is at No.8); Rue de Montmorency, and especially **Rue de la Foire**, the status address of the old days, with a number of palaces including the Renaissance **Hôtel de Carrion-Nizas** at No.10. Just down the street, note the charming relief of child musicians at No.22. At the northern end of the street, a left takes you into Rue Emile-Zola, with the **Hôtel de Jacques Coeur** (the famous merchant of Montpellier; *see* p.371), at No.7, with an interesting allegorical sculpted façade. It faces the **Porte Faugères**, a 1597 remnant of the town walls, and the nearby entrance to the small **Jewish Ghetto**, a single poignant lane closed in by two gates in the 14th century.

The broad **Cours Jean-Jaurès**, site of the market, divides Pézenas in two. It too has its palaces: an especially good row of them at Nos. 14–22, including the **Hôtel de Grasset**. The

Cours leads into Place de la République, and the church of **St-Jean**, with profuse 17th- and 18th-century marble decoration that proves Pézenas' artistic instincts were much sounder in secular matters. South of the Cours, there are more palaces: the **Hôtel de Malibran** and **Hôtel de l'Epine**, with a lavish sculptural façade, both on Rue Victor Hugo; the **Hôtel Montmorency**, the Pézenas home of one of 16th-century France's most illustrious noble houses, on Rue Reboul; and best of all, the **Hôtel d'Alfonse** on Rue Conti, which has a delightful courtyard loggia on three levels, built in the 1630s.

Pézenas ✉ *34120*   **Where to Stay and Eating Out**

Pézenas could be a major tourist attraction if it really wanted, but places to stay and restaurants of any quality are both a bit lacking. ★★**Genieys**, 9 Ave Aristide Briand, © 04 67 98 13 99, ⊘ 04 67 98 04 80, is outside the historic centre, but it is the only good hotel in town; *demi-pension* obligatory in July and Aug. Just south of Pézenas in Nézignan l'Evêque, ★★★**Hostellerie de St-Alban**, 29 Rte d'Agde, © 04 67 98 11 38, ⊘ 04 67 98 91 63, is a quiet 19th-century villa in the vines, with a pool and tennis. For a shellfish feast, **Côté Sud**, Place 14 Juillet, © 04 67 09 41 74, comes up with the goods (*lunch 45F, other menus 70 and 99F*). **Le Castel**, Rue Anatole France, © 04 67 98 82 72, has a simple, yet filling 75F menu with wine. *Closed Mon.* Pézenas' claim to culinary fame, its spool-shaped *petits pâtés*, take French visitors by surprise ('what is this, half sweet and half mutton?'), but if you're British you may not find them too shocking: the recipe was introduced in 1770 by the Indian chef of Lord Clive, Governor of India, who spent a holiday in Pézenas. They still make them at **Maison Alary**, Rue St-Jean 9; eat them warm.

Béziers

This city's history is succinct: a rude interruption and a second chance. Béziers is older than the Romans; its site, a commanding, defensible hill on a key part of the Mediterranean coast, seems promising, but Béziers' long career has produced little distinction and only one famous anecdote. In 1209, at the beginning of the Albigensian Crusade, a large number of Cathars took refuge in the city and were besieged. When the besiegers offered the Cathars a chance to leave the city, they refused. The troops stormed the city, and found that the entire population had taken refuge in the churches. The Crusaders' ayatollah, the Abbot of Cîteaux, had ordered the massacre of all the Cathars. Asked how to distinguish them from the Catholics, he replied 'Kill them all, God will know his own.' From all accounts, that is exactly what happened; in his report to Rome, the papal legate bragged that some 20,000 people were put to death.

Not surprisingly, Béziers languished for centuries. The second chance came in the 1660s, with the building of the Canal du Midi (*see* below). A new Béziers has grown up since then, a busy port and industrial town of some 90,000, known best for its crack rugby squad. Approaching it from the surrounding plains, you'll see its heroic hilltop skyline from miles away, crowned by its impressive cathedral; seen from inside, unfortunately, Béziers will not sustain your initial expectations, a pigeon-grey city with plenty of traffic, but with three good museums.

Getting Around

Béziers is on the **main coastal rail line**, and it's easy to get to Narbonne, Sète, Montpellier or points beyond, with trains never more than two hours apart. The other line from the city heads north for Castres, passing through Bédarieux and St-Pons. The *gare routière* is on Place Jean Jaurès, with regular connections to Pézenas (and to everywhere the trains go), and less regular ones to villages of the eastern Hérault. City buses run from here to nearby Valras, the popular lido of the Biterrois.

Tourist Information

Palais des Congrès, 29 Ave Saint-Saëns, © 04 67 76 47 00, ✆ 04 67 76 50 80.

market days

Daily exc Monday in the beautiful 19th-century Halles. Friday flowers, antiques, food and clothes in Allées Paul Riquet, Place David-d'Angers, and around.

Allées Paul-Riquet and the Cathedral

Life in Béziers centres along the the the **Allées Paul Riquet**, a broad promenade of plane trees named after the city's great benefactor, the builder of the Canal du Midi. Besides a statue of Riquet, there is a handsome 19th-century theatre, and a monument to Resistance hero Jean Moulin (another Bitérois) at the top of the **Plateau des Poètes,** a romantic garden with ponds and swans and statues by local sculptor Jean-Antoine Injalbert that descends gracefully down to the train station. From the other end of the Allées Paul Riquet, any of the streets to the west will take you up to the top of the hill and the medieval centre.

Someone must have been left in Béziers after 1209, for the city spent the next two centuries working on its grandiose **cathedral**, replacing the original that was wrecked in the sack. Its grim, fortress-like exterior, similar to Narbonne's, seems a foreign presence, the citadel of an occupying force. The inside is more graceful, in clean, warm ashlar masonry with plenty of stained glass; it creates a light and airy effect, especially in the apse, where large windows of blue and white decorative glass (behind a dreadful Baroque altar) are the prettiest feature in the church. In two chapels (2nd right and 2nd left) there are fragments of Giottoesque frescoes, and at the west front, a magnificent organ almost as good as the one in Narbonne, carved in walnut in 1623 by Giulhaume Martois, who is buried next to it. Architectural fragments from the earlier church can be seen in the beautiful vaulted **cloister**, a work of the late 1300s.

Behind the cathedral, the **Musée Fabregat** in Place de la Révolution, © 04 67 28 38 78, houses Béziers' fine arts museum, founded in 1859 (*open Tues–Sat 9–12 and 2–6, Sun 2–6, adm*), with something for every taste: a 16th-century Virgin and child by Martin Schaffner of Ulm, a portrait by Hans Holbein the Younger, 17th-century Italian works (including a Domenichino), a Richard Bonington *Storm*, and 18th- and 19th-century French paintings, by the likes of Géricault, Corot, Delacroix, and Rousseau. Many of the fine modern works (de Chirico, Soutine, Friesz) were purchased by Jean Moulin; the great Resistance leader posed as a designer and art dealer under the name of Romanin. Just north, the **Musée Fayet**, in a delightful 17th-century *hôtel particulier* at 9 Rue du Capus, © 04 67 49 04 66 (*open Tues–Fri 9–12 and 2–6; same adm*), contains several rooms of 18th- and 19th-century paintings and decorative arts, and several rooms dedicated to the sculptures of Injalbert.

If you have time for more churches, the Romanesque **Madeleine** (*closed for restoration at the time of writing*), north of the cathedral and market on Place de la Madeleine, was one of the sites of the massacre of 1209, when the population sought to take refuge in its walls. **St-Aphrodise**, further north, hidden behind newer buildings in Place St-Aphrodise, was Béziers' cathedral in the 8th century. 'St-Aphrodise', if it isn't Aphrodite herself, would be the legendary first bishop, who rode into Béziers one day on a camel (now the city's symbol). The Romans naturally chopped off his head and threw it into a well—but the water rose miraculously to the surface, floating the head with it. Aphrodise fished it out and carried it under his arm to the site of this church, and then disappeared into the ground. It's more likely that pagan Aphrodite had a temple on or near this site. Almost nothing remains of the original building, but a 4th-century sarcophagus has been recycled for use as a baptismal font.

A third Romanesque church, simple **St-Jacques**, is on a belvedere on the south side of Béziers, by a third museum, the **Musée du Biterrois** (or de St-Jacques), ✆ 04 67 36 71 01 (*open daily summer 10–6, winter 9–12 and 2–6, closed Mon; adm*), newly housed in an 18th-century barracks, on Rampe du 96ème (from the top of Ave Gambetta, turn down Ave de La Marine). The museum divides its space between regional archaeological finds, medieval capitals and other bits (including St Aphrodise with his head), ethnography (especially wine making), science and ceramics.

Béziers ✉ *34500*   **Where to Stay and Eating Out**

Béziers is not necessarily a convenient place to stay; getting in and out of it is a problem, and parking is murder. But if you want to do it in relative style, without much expense, the ★★★**Imperator** has the best location in town, 28 Allées Paul Riquet, ✆ 04 67 49 02 25, 🖂 04 67 28 92 30, and there's a garage. Down the street, the ★**Paul Riquet**, 46 Allées Paul Riquet, ✆ 04 67 76 44 37, 🖂 04 67 49 00 37, is small, pleasant and considerably cheaper. Several of the rooms in the ★★★**Hôtel du Nord**, 15 Place Jean Jaurès, ✆ 04 67 28 34 09, 🖂 04 67 49 00 37, have a romantic view over the rooftops up to the towers of St-Jacques.

You can dine well and elegantly while watching the progress of your meal (the kitchen has a large window in the wall) at **L'Ambassade**, 22 Blvd de Verdun, ✆ 04 67 76 06 24, with good value menus (*from 115F*). *Closed Sun eve and Mon.* The finest local ingredients go into the wide-awake cuisine at **Le Jardin**, 37 Ave Jean Moulin, near Place 14 Juillet, ✆ 04 67 36 41 31 (*menus from 115–295F*). *Closed Sun eve and Mon.* An old favourite, **La Cigale**, 60 Allées Paul Riquet, ✆ 04 67 28 21 56, offers a good mix of meat and fish dishes (*menus 90–120F*). *Closed Mon eve and Tues.* **Le Bistrot des Halles**, Place de la Madeleine, ✆ 04 67 28 30 46 has 71–119F menus often including smoked salmon, and homemade desserts. *Closed Sun eve and Mon.* **Brasserie Le Mondial**, 2 Rue Solférino, ✆ 04 67 28 22 15, is packed most evenings, not so much for its food but its free concerts usually on Wednesday–Saturday nights.

The Canal du Midi

The best thing to do in Béziers is go west for one of Languedoc's best-kept secrets. The waterways of other parts of France are well-enough known; this one, one of very few in the south, remains serene and relatively unburdened by tourism, planted its entire length with parallel rows of great plane trees (not just for decoration; they hold the soil, and help keep the canal from silting up). However shady and idyllic, Paul Riquet's canal is also an early monument of economic planning, from the days of Louis XIV's great minister Colbert, when everything in France was being reformed and modernized (and Louis was blowing all the profits on Versailles and his endless wars). Riquet was a local baron, the state's Tax Farmer (*fermier-*

général) for Languedoc (a wonderful system: *ancien régime* tax farmers bought rights to collect taxes in a region, and got to keep any amounts above the sum expected by the government). He conceived the idea for the canal and sold it to Colbert, then saw through its construction with remarkable single-mindedness, inventing ingenious tricks to get the canal over the highest stretches, paying a third of the expenses himself, and even sacrificing his daughters' dowries to the cause. From 1666, as many as 12,000 men worked on the project, which required over 100 locks, and runs for 235km. It was completed 39 years later; Riquet died a few months before the opening.

No one has shipped any freight on the Canal du Midi for years, but it is still kept up for the benefit of holiday-makers. Some of the locks are tended; at others you'll have to figure out the mechanism yourself. You can take a slow cruise from Béziers all the way to Toulouse, or just rent a rowing-boat or canoe in one of the villages and spend a drowsy day under the plane trees.

Getting Around

Forget about buses and trains; you'll need a **car** to get around here, or better a **mountain bike** (*VTT* in French); the shady tow paths are lovely for cycling. Best of all, hire a small **boat** (ask at any of the villages), or spend a week on a canal barge (the canal is open to navigation March–November). Reputed firms include **Rive du Sud** in Colombiers, southwest of Béziers along the canal, ✆ 04 67 37 14 60, ✉ 04 67 37 60 03. Also try **Crown Blue Line**, in Castelnaudary, ✆ 04 68 94 52 72, ✉ 04 68 94 52 73; **Connoisseur Cruisers**, 7 Quai d'Alsace, Narbonne, ✆ 04 68 65 14 55, ✉ 04 68 90 66 72, or **Locaboat Plaisance**, in Argens-Minervois, ✆ 04 68 27 03 33, ✉ 04 68 27 71 96. For 4 to 6 people for a week, prices in July and Aug range from 7500–9200F; off season they can go as low as 5200F. Add 500 to 800F a week for fuel. No previous experience is required: maximum speed is 6km an hour, and most people bring bikes along for outings along the way. Other firms offer day trips: *La Belle Isaure* is the only horse-drawn boat still in use on the canal; it cruises regularly between Béziers and Poilhes in the summer. Most luxurious of all are the barge hotels (*péniches hôtels*): one of the biggest firms is **Loueurs de Péniche La Tortue**, 8 Ave de la Gare, Capestang, ✆ 04 67 93 43 20, ✉ 04 67 93 31 65. For more information, write to Comité Regional du Tourisme, 20 Rue de la République, 34000 Montpellier, ✆ 04 67 22 81 00, ✉ 04 67 58 06 10, e-mail address: contact@crtlrcnusc.fr or website details http://www.cr-languedocroussillon.fr/tourisme/ or get the *Canal du Midi Tourisme Fluvial* brochure from the tourist office in Carcassonne.

Nissan-lez-Ensérune ✉ 34440: ✆ 04 67 37 14 12, ✆ 04 67 37 63 00.

market days

Capestang: Wednesday and Sunday mornings.

The Canal West of Béziers

The canal connects Sète on the Mediterranean with Toulouse—where it still flows right past the central railway station—and thence to the Atlantic, by way of the river Garonne. The best parts of it are west of Béziers, where it passes through a score of lovely old villages, fitting so well into the landscape that it seems to have been there all the time. Pick it up just outside Béziers, at the **Ecluses de Fonséranes**, just off the N113 for Narbonne. This is a series of seven original locks, a watery stair that facilitated the biggest drop in altitude along the canal's length. If you have kids in tow and it's a Wednesday, Saturday or Sunday, don't miss the wonderful, homemade automated *crèche* (Christmas crib) in the **Monastère de Fonsérannes**, a short walk away from the Ecluses.

No one road follows the canal for long; with a good map and some careful navigation you can stay close to it, on the back roads through **Colombiers**, first of the canal villages, then to **Nissan-lez-Ensérune**, a busy place with a 14th-century Gothic church. You will already have noticed this landmark in the flat countryside; signs from Nissan will lead you up to it, and to the remains of one of the most important pre-Roman towns of southern Gaul, the Oppidum d'Ensérune. The Canal du Midi passes right under it by way of the 567ft **Malpas tunnel** (1679), the first canal tunnel, ever, dug by Riquet, who knew best, in spite of considerable controversy at the time.

Oppidum d'Ensérune

Open April–Oct 9–12 and 2–6, July and Aug 9.30–7, otherwise 10–12 and 2–4; guided tours; adm; ✆ 04 67 37 01 23.

The site is a relic of the time when these coasts were first coming into the mainstream of Mediterranean civilization. Initially settled in the 6th century BC, it began as a fortified trading village under Greek influence, closely connected to Marseille. By 250 BC it may have had as many as 10,000 people, though later in that century it was wrecked, possibly by Hannibal, on his way to Italy during the Punic Wars. Under Roman rule it revived again, refounded as a Roman colony, but in peaceful, settled times it could not survive. The cramped, difficult site was good for defence; when this was no longer necessary, people and trade gradually moved down to the plains and the coast, and Ensérune was largely abandoned by the 1st century AD.

Not much remains of the town: the foundations of the wall, cisterns and traces of habitations can be seen. The excellent **museum** in the centre of the excavations has a collection of ceramics, including some fine Greek and Etruscan works, along with local pieces that show the strong influence of the foreigners. Just outside the town, where an ancient column with an unusual, trapezoidal capital has been re-erected, you can take in one of the oddest panoramas in France, a gigantic surveyor's pie, neatly sliced. This was the **Etang de Montady**, a roughly circular swamp reclaimed in the 13th century, when the new fields were precisely divided by drainage ditches radiating from the centre.

Canal Villages

Most of these have at least one restaurant, some have guest houses and boat rentals; all of them are agreeable spots to while away an afternoon. From Nissan, the D37 takes you to **Poilhes**, a sleepy, lovely village built around one of Paul Riquet's graceful brick canal bridges. **Capestang**, the next one, has a landmark visible for miles around: the tall, unfinished Gothic **Collégiale St-Etienne**, a monument to unfulfilled ambition, like Narbonne Cathedral, which indeed may have been the work of the same architect. A detour south of Capestang, and just west of the village of Ouveillan, will take you to an unusual and almost completely forgotten medieval monument, the **Grange de Fontcalvy**. A testament to the wealth of the Cistercian order, this was a key stronghold of Fontfroide Abbey (*see* p.426), a fortified barn of considerable architectural sophistication, 66ft square, with ogival vaulting.

Quarante

All along, the lands around the canal have been packed full with vineyards. Further west, this continues, but the countryside becomes greener and lusher, with some of the cosiest landscapes in the Languedoc. **Quarante** isn't on the canal (although there's an impressive aqueduct nearby, one of Vauban's last works (1693) over the river Quarante), but it is worth a 4km side trip, north on D36/D37E, for its severe and dignified Romanesque church, the **Abbatiale Ste-Marie**, built between 982 and 1053. The *Trésor* contains a marble sarcophagus of the 3rd century, decorated with angels and portraits of the deceased, and a remarkable example of Montpellier silversmithing from the 1440s, a very leonine bust of *St John the Baptist* with almond eyes and a Gallic nose. Quarante also has a pretty picnic-ground and park (with a pool), in the grounds of the Château de Rouière.

Back on the canal, the string of villages continues: **Argeliers** and **Le Somail**, a sweet hamlet where the bargemen traditionally stop to take their afternoon naps. It has a great second-hand bookshop, an ice house, chapel, and a quirky **Musée des Chapeaux**, housing thousands of hats (*open 9–12 and 2–7, closed Sun; adm*). Further west are **Ventenac-en-Minervois, Paraza**, **Roubia** and **Argens-Minervois**, a once-fortified village with a ruined castle. The canal at this point runs parallel to the River Aude, and in places the two are only a few hundred feet apart. Near Roubia, the canal passes over a small stream on the **Pont-Canal de Répudre**. Paul Riquet designed this too; it is the oldest canal bridge in France. Further west comes **Homps**, with another ruined castle, built by the Knights Hospitallers, and then a long, empty, very scenic stretch leading towards Marseillette in the Minervois, and then **Trèbes**, a fortified village with a triple set of locks and an impressive canal bridge over the Orb built by Vauban in 1686.

Where to Stay and Eating Out

Can you dine well under the *platanes* of the Canal? Indeed; most of the villages have at least one place with a garden terrace overlooking it. And as you get closer to Minervois, there will also be some chances for wine-tasting on the banks, as at the **Château de Ventenac** at Ventenac, and the **Domaine de Sérame**, a lovely *mas* outside Argens-Minervois.

Poilhes ✉ 34310

Poilhes is the place to stop along the Canal, a village relaxed to the point of coma. Imaginative *haute cuisine* is represented here with **La Tour Sarrasine** on Blvd Paul

Riquet, © 04 67 93 41 31; pigeon stuffed with foie gras, steaks in a sauce of wine and marrow—a memorable dinner (*menus at 130–295F*). *Closed Sun eve and Mon.* Less expensively, **La Romaine,** © 04 67 93 42 84, is located right on the canal, with good if somewhat fussy cooking (a *casselote d'escargots* or an *entrecôte* with Roquefort sauce) (*100F menu*). *Closed Wed and Sat eve, and Nov–Mar.* They also rent boats.

Nissan-lez-Ensérune and around ✉ 34440

The peaceful ★★**Résidence**, 35 Ave de la Cave, © 04 67 37 00 63, ✆ 04 67 37 68 63, has an antiquated charm and a more modern annex at the bottom of the garden. In the centre, ★**Du Commerce,** 13 Place du Marché, © 04 67 37 63 38, is old-fashioned and inexpensive. In **Colombiers**, you can stop over at the ★★**Via Domitia**, © 04 67 35 62 63, ✆ 04 67 35 62 00, which offers more creature comforts, with colour TV and air conditioning.

Homps and Le Somail ✉ 11120

By the port in Homps, the terrace at **Les Tonnaliers**, © 04 68 91 14 04, is a favourite stop for lunch or dinner; try the marinated salmon (*menus from 78–180F*). At Le Somail, there's a charming **bed and breakfast** in a 17th-century house, © 04 68 46 16 02 . *Open April–Oct.*

Trèbes ✉ 11800

Just east of Trèbes in Floure, the ivy-covered **Château de Floure**, 1 Allée Gaston Bonheur, © 04 68 79 11 29, ✆ 04 68 79 04 61, was a Romanesque abbey converted into a home by writer Gaston Bonheur; now a *Relais de Silence* hotel, it has an elegant French garden, with pool and tennis, comfortable air-conditioned rooms (*500–790F*) and a good restaurant. *Closed Nov–Easter.*

The Minervois

This is a *pays* with plenty of character, though not many people. With typical French irony, the Minervois suffered grievously from poverty and rural depopulation throughout this century—then, just when everyone was gone, vintners improved the quality of their Minervois wines. They have become increasingly popular across France, and the region's prosperity has returned. The Corbières, just across the Aude (*see* below), tells much the same story. And in other ways, too, the Minervois is a prelude to the Corbières: the sharp contrast of tidy, lovingly cared for vineyards with ragged, wild country and outcrops of weird, eroded limestone, the sense of strangeness and isolation—in a region of France that has been inhabited for more or less 200,000 years.

Tourist Information

Olonzac ✉ 34210: Mairie, © 04 68 91 20 11.

Minerve ✉ 34210: © 04 68 91 81 43.

Rieux-Minervois ✉ 11160: Place de l'Eglise, © 04 68 78 13 98.

The Minervois do love their region, and truly welcome visitors from faraway places. A women's association called **Les Capelles du Minervois** conducts individual tours of the region's sights, coupled with dinner and visits to wine cellars; call Mme Vidal on © 04 68 91 17 17 for details. In Olonzac, **Evasion-balades** (mornings), © 04 68 91 15 47, arrange nature walks on the back trails.

Laure-Minervois: Sunday. **Rieux-Minervois**: Tuesday, Thursday, and Saturday.

Minervois: Worth a visit are Château Fabas, at Laure-Minervois on the Rieux road (℗ 04 68 78 17 82), and Cave Coopérative de Peyriac-Minervois at Peyriac (℗ 04 68 78 11 20). By the Canal du Midi, try the Domaine de Sérame, an old *mas* outside Argens, or the Château de Ventenac, at Ventenac (℗ 04 68 43 25 10). Château de Paraza is high above the canal (Paraza, 11200 Lézignan, ℗ 04 68 43 20 76); for white wines try Château La Grave at Badens (℗ 04 68 79 14 47), and Château de Paraza (*see* above).

From the Canal to Minerve

Olonzac, just north of the Canal, is the centre of the wine district and the closest thing the eastern Minervois has to a town. To the northwest, some of the most civilized landscapes in the Minervois lie around the village of **Siran**, with three little-known attractions: to the east, an impressive dolmen called the **Mourel des Fades** ('fairy dolmen') and the 12th-century country church of **St-Germain-de-Cesseras**, with a beautifully sculpted apse. Both are signposted off the D168. Another country church, the **Chapelle de Centeilles** north of Siran, is a unique survival, entirely covered inside with frescoes from the 13th to the 15th centuries; there is also a fragment of Roman mosaic, found nearby.

From Olonzac, the narrow D10 will take you up into the heights of the Minervois, to **Minerve**, a town as old as any in Languedoc. Minerve is a natural place for a defensible settlement, on a steep rock between two rivers, but that does not explain why the area around it should have been so popular for so long. Traces of habitation dating back 170,000 years have been found in its caves; Neolithic dolmens abound. The Celts and the Romans built the town itself, and in the Middle Ages it was a feudal stronghold with a Cathar slant. Minerve accepted refugees from the sack of Béziers in 1209; Simon de Montfort followed them, and took the town after a two-month siege, followed by the usual butchery and burning of 140 Cathars at the stake.

Minerve today counts little over a hundred inhabitants; nothing has been done or built since Unspeakable Simon's visit, and the medieval relic on its dramatic site has become a peaceful and unambitious tourist attraction, with potters, artists and souvenir stands filling the spaces left by all the folks who moved to the cities in the last 80 years. Parts of the walls are still in good nick, but all that is left of the château is a single, slender, octagonal tower; the Minervois call it the 'candela'. There are narrow medieval alleys, gates and cisterns, a simple 12th-century church with a white marble altar from 456, said to be the oldest in Europe, and a small **Musée Municipal** across from a *caveau de dégustation* of Minervois wines (*open May–Nov, 10–6, weekends only the rest of the year*).

The real attractions are out in the country. A short walk from town, there are **'natural bridges'**—really more like tunnels, eroded through the limestone by streams. To the west extends the narrow, blushing pink **Canyon de la Cesse**, and determined hikers can seek out a collection of caves and dolmens north of this, at Bois Bas, off the D147.

The Seven-Sided Church of Rieux-Minervois

West of Siran, the Minervois flattens out into the valley of the Argent-Double ('silver water'; *dubron* was a Celtic word for water, and the Romans made it *Argentodubrum*). A handsome

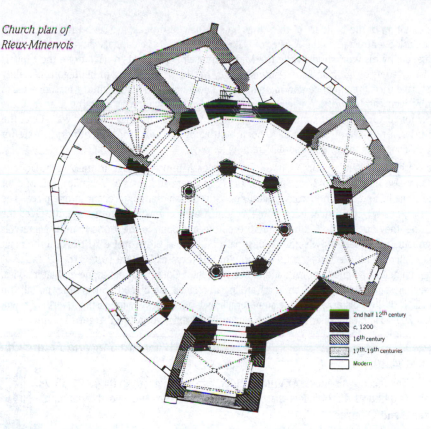

2nd half 12ᵗʰ century
c, 1200
16ᵗʰ century
17ᵗʰ-19ᵗʰ centuries
Modern

old bridge spans it for the village of Rieux, built around one of the most uncanny medieval monuments in France.

The seven-pointed star is the recurring mystic symbol of the Midi. The Cathar castle at Montségur, in Ariège, was laid out subtly to fit inside its angles; the Félibres of Provence used it as part of their emblem and it has been a recurring theme in folk art. Just what it means has never been adequately explained; neither has anyone ventured an explanation for the presence in this unremarkable Minervois village of what may be the only seven-sided church anywhere. Dedicated to the Virgin, the church was built sometime in the late 12th century, exactly when, why and by whom no one knows. A medieval scholar would have cited Scripture: *Wisdom has built her house; she has set up her seven pillars* (Proverbs 1:9), also recalling that the Divine Wisdom was identified (at the time) with the Virgin Mary. Clearly, this temple opens a deep vein of intellectual medieval mysticism, full of geometry and allegory and not entirely recoverable by our minds. Its builders, pressed to explain why the central heptagon around the altar has four squat pilasters and three columns, might have mumbled something about the 'Marriage of Heaven and Earth'—the foursquare world and the spiritual triangle. Modern investigators have also discovered various series of ley lines based on this site; according to them the line of the midsummer sunrise passes from an altar inside the church, through a (now closed up) window and begins an alignment that goes as far as Minerve and St-Guilhem-le-Désert, passing several chapels dedicated to St John along the way.

The ambition of the builders of this church, and their resources, are seen in the sculptural detail inside, entrusted to the Master of Cabestany. Most of the capitals carved with fanciful foliage are by his workshop, while the Master himself is believed to have done the capitals with the reliefs of *lions* and the *Assumption of the Virgin*. Building in heptagons certainly must have tried the patience and mathematical know-how of a 12th-century mason; we can admire their careful work, especially the seven-sided belfry, directly over the altar, and the tricky toroid vaulting that connects the heptagon with the 14-sided exterior wall. Over the centuries, a number of chapels have been built along the edges of the church; its exterior aspect, along with the original portal, are now lost.

The marble for Rieux's church came from **Caunes-Minervois**, just up the Argent-Double, which is also the source of the marble for the Paris Opera and parts of Versailles. It is rare for good stone in so many tints, from green to pink to reddish-orange, to occur in one place. The quarries, neatly geometrical excavations around Caunes, make an unusual sight. Over the centuries they have made Caunes more prosperous and open to the world than its Minervois neighbours. Its streets show some modest palaces, such as the **Hôtel d'Alibert** on the main square, along with the former abbey church of **St-Pierre-et-St-Paul** (*open 10–12 and 2–7; adm*), founded by Benedict of Aniane, a hotchpotch of Gothic, Romanesque and later styles, conserving some odd capitals from the Carolingian original and a good 13th-century portal; you can also visit the cloister, and in the summer admission includes a wine tasting. North of town, the D620 leads past the quarries into the narrow and scenic **Gorge de l'Argent-Double**.

Where to Stay and Eating Out

Siran ✉ 34210

The recently opened ★★★**Villa d'Eléis**, Ave du Château, ✆ 04 68 91 55 98, ✉ 04 68 91 48 34, offers charming comfortable rooms and a good restaurant.

Minerve and Olonzac ✉ 34210

The only hotel is the ★**Relais Chantovent**, 17 Grande Rue, ✆ 04 68 91 14 18, ✉ 04 68 91 81 88, with just seven rooms; also a fine restaurant with a terrace overlooking the gorges, serving truffles and *cèpes*, and some seafood (*menus 100–225F*). South in Olonzac, a typical Minervois lunch waits at the **St-Louis**, on Place de la Citadelle, ✆ 04 68 91 21 90: stewed chicken, half the village for company, and a slowly ticking clock *chez grand-mère* (75F). If you'd rather forgo the clock for lasagne with foie gras and smoked salmon, try the **Du Minervois**, 2 Rue Ecoles, ✆ 04 68 91 20 73 (*menus from 105F*). *Closed Sat and Sun eve in winter*.

Rieux-Minervois ✉ 11160

★★**Logis de Merinville** Ave Georges Clemenceau, ✆ 04 68 78 12 49, is an atmospheric 19th-century stone inn in the village centre, with lovely rooms, 1930s furniture and a good restaurant. *Closed Jan*. Just west, in a restored farm complex outside Peyriac-Minervois, the ★★★**Château de Violet** is the Minervois' luxury resort; elegant, sumptuously furnished, with pool and gardens (Route de Pepieux, ✆ 04 68 78 10 42, ✉ 04 68 78 30 01, a bit expensive for its rating, it also has a restaurant with 180–260F menus). Up in Caunes-Minervois, the ★★**Hôtel d'Alibert**, Place de la Mairie, ✆ 04 68 78 00 54, is a sweet little place to stay or eat, with good regional food in the restaurant (*menu 120F*) . *Closed Jan, Feb*.

The Montagne Noire

Even wilder than the Minervois, if not as unusual, the bleak, brooding Black Mountain is a 30km-wide stretch of peaks, taller than their neighbours and difficult to access until modern times. The long ridge in fact divides two climates: its north face, looking towards the Massif Central (the Montagne Noire is the southernmost point of the range) has an Atlantic climate, while the south is Mediterranean. Its slate-roofed villages have a solemn air, and their people are bent to serious mountain pursuits—mining and quarrying, logging and paper-making. In the old days they scratched iron and copper out of the mountain; this still continues, along with a bit of silver and gold—the deposits at Salsigne, discovered a century ago, yield a ton of gold each year. The trees are even more important; you'll see plenty of chestnut groves, some planted in the Middle Ages when chestnuts were a mountain staple, and also stands of foreign intruders—Scots pine and Douglas fir, important to the lumber business.

All the routes into the mountains follow narrow parallel valleys leading up from the river Aude; the first is the Argent-Double, from Caunes (*see* above). Next comes the Clamoux (on the D112), with equally impressive **gorges**, north of Villeneuve-Minervois; six km up the Clamoux is **Cabrespine** with its lofty castle (Simon de Montfort slept here) and deep abyss, the **Gouffre Géant de Cabrespine**, part of it accessible to all, including wheel chairs (*open Mar–Nov, 10–12 and 2–6, continuously in July and Aug, ✆ 04 68 26 14 22*), and part of it left as it was, explored in four- to five-hour excursions guided by Les Safaris Souterrains (to book, call ✆ 04 67 66 11 11, ✉ 04 67 66 27 27). Further up is the Gorge de Clamoux in **Pradelles-Cabardès**, where the people used to make a living by shipping ice down to the cities of the valley. Their sunken ice chambers are still a feature of the landscape. Above Pradelles looms **Pic de Nore**, at 1200m the highest point of the Montagne Noire.

Châteaux de Lastours

The next valley, that of the Orbiel (D101), is the most populous of the region, and perhaps the most beautiful. It also contains the region's landmark, the **Châteaux de Lastours**, ✆ 04 68 77 56 02 (*open daily April–Oct 10–5, May, June, Sept 10–6, July and Aug 9–8, Feb, Mar, Nov, Dec, weekends only 10–5; adm*)—not one, but four castles, in various states of picturesque ruin, all on the same hilltop to defend the Montagne Noire's mineral richness. The Lords of Cabardès, bosses of the Montagne Noire before the arrival of de Montfort in 1211, built the first of them, the castles of Cabaret and Quertinheux; the two between these, Surdespine and Tour Régine, were added by the French kings in the 13th century. Remember the Drac, in Beaucaire? Apparently after his embarrassment there he took refuge in the Hérault. The legendary knight Roland himself was on his trail near Lastours, and his horse left a hoof-print in a great boulder near the Châteaux, a place still called the *Saut de Roland*.

Salsigne, with its gold mine, lies just to the west of Lastours. To the east is a remarkable cave, the **Grotte de Limousis**, ✆ 04 68 77 50 26, with unique formations of gleaming white aragonite crystals, one of which, called the *Lustre* (chandelier) is over 30ft across (*open daily April–Sept, 2–6; adm*). Further up the valley are two of the most beautiful and unspoiled villages of the region: **Roquefère** and **Mas-Cabardès**; north of Roquefère a 5km detour will take you up to a high, lovely **waterfall** at a place called Cupserviès. Mas-Cabardès has some half-timbered houses and a 16th-century church with a rugged octagonal belfry. In the village centre, note the pretty, carefully carved stone **cross**, a typical decoration of Montagne Noire villages. This one was a 16th-century gift of the weavers' guild; with its abundance of water, this region had a thriving textile trade before the black-hearted English Industrial Revolutionaries started underselling them in the 1700s. Another water powered trade was paper; in **Brousses-et-Villlaret**, west of Mas-Cabardès, you can visit an 18th-century paper mill and learn how to make paper by hand at the **Musée du Moulin à Papier** (*open 10–12 and 2.30–6; adm*).

Further west, the crown of the Montagne Noire is dotted with artificial lakes, part of a big hydroelectric scheme. In the valley furthest west, that of the Vernassonne, **Saissac** is another lovely village, built over a ravine and surrounded by forests. Saissac too has its romantically ruined, overgrown fortress, and a 10ft **menhir**, just to the north off the D4. To the south, **Montolieu**, balanced over the gorges of the the Alzeau and Dure, has become the 'Village du Livre' a centre of the local bookmaking trade: in the centre, the **Montolieu, Village du Livre,** ✆ 04 68 24 80 04 (*open Mar–Oct 2–6, July and Aug 10–12.30 and 2–6.30; adm*), traces the history of bookbinding and printing, and there are a number of bookshops (including Colophon, with second-hand books in English, Rue de la Mairie, ✆ 04 68 24 87 43), and summer book fairs. West, on the D64, the 13th-century **Abbaye de Villelongue**, has little artistic interest, but is one of the best preserved monastic complexes in Languedoc (*guided tours—English spoken; open May–Oct 10–12 and 2–6.30; adm*).

For regions to the west and south, *see* Carcassonne and Castelnaudary, p.427. North of Pic de Nore, the Montagne Noire descends to rolling hills, in a vast forested area that is part of the Parc Régional du Haut Languedoc. Beyond the boundaries of this book, in the Tarn, there are two towns worth a detour if you are interested in the Cathars or Spanish art. **Mazamet** has the **Cathar Museum**, with a full exposition of the cult and its demise (*open Tues–Sat 10–12 and 3–6*); **Castres** offers its **Musée Goya** (*open 9–12 and 2–6, Sun 10–12 and 2–6, closed Mon; adm*), a small collection of paintings by the Spanish magician, and other minor works by Velazquez, Murillo, Valdes Leal and Alonso Cana.

Where to Stay and Eating Out

Accommodation up here is rudimentary, partly because Carcassonne (*see* next chapter) is close enough for the Montagne Noire to be an easy day trip. But you'll always eat well.

Brousses et Villaret ✉ 11390

La Cascade, in an old stone *bastide* by the little Lac des Rochers, ✆ 04 68 26 66 71, offers trout, and a wide selection of seafood (*80F or more*) and eight inexpensive rooms. Closest to Lastours, at **Lacombe-du-Sault**, **La Galaube**, ✆ 04 68 26 51 23, is a simple but welcoming restaurant.

Saissac ✉ 11310

In Saissac, the **Montagne Noire** on Ave Maurice Sarrault, ✆ 04 68 24 46 36, @ 04 68 24 46 20, has inexpensive rooms and serves tasty dishes with *cèpes* and freshwater crayfish under its century-old trees (*menus from 70F, with wine*). To the south on the Montolieu road, at the **Lac Saint-Pierre,** ✆ 04 68 24 40 97, you can fish for trout and then eat them forthwith.

Montolieu ✉ 11170

Sit under the trees and feast on *cassoulet* (after all, this is near Castelnaudary, bean central) at **Le Floréal** by the church. *Menus from 75F, closed eve out of season.* West of Montolieu, the **Abbaye de Villelongue**, ✆ 04 68 76 92 58, has simple *chambres d'hôte* rooms to rent.

CORBIÈRES COUNTRY.

Narbonne, Carcassonne and the Corbières

This southern corner of Languedoc, mostly in the *département* of the Aude, is famous for two things—wine and castles—and it has more of them than any other part of France. Western Languedoc traditionally fills an ample bay of the European Union's wine lake, and provides the raw materials for much of the *vin ordinaire* on French tables. After centuries of complacency, it is also beginning to produce some really good wine. The castles, on the other hand, are strictly AOC.

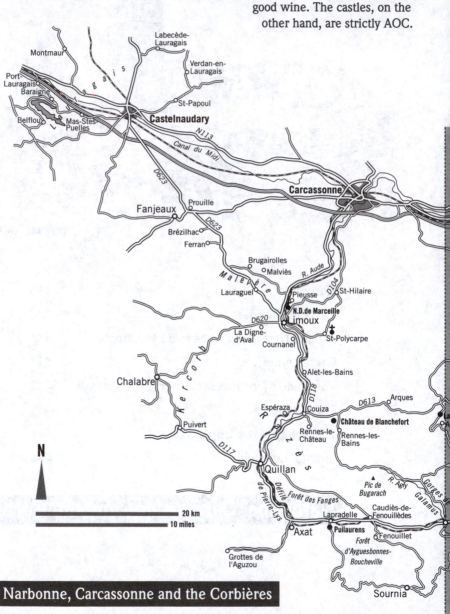

Montmaur
Labecède-Lauragais
Verdan-en-Lauragais
Port Lauragais
Baraigne
St-Papoul
Belflou
Mas-Stes-Puelles
Castelnaudary
N113
Canal du Midi
D623
Carcassonne
Prouille
Fanjeaux
Brézilhac
D623
Ferran
Brugairolles
Malviès
R. Aude
Malepère
D104
St-Hilaire
Lauraguel
Pieusse
N.D.de Marceille
Limoux
D620
La Digne-d'Aval
Cournanel
St-Polycarpe
Kercorb
Chalabre
Alet-les-Bains
D613
Arques
Espéraza
Couiza
Puivert
Rennes-le-Château
Château de Blanchefort
La Au
Rennes-les-Bains
D117
Nèzes
Quillan
Défilé de Pierre-Lys
Forêt des Fanges
Pic de Bugarach
R. Agly
Gorges de Galamus
Caudiès-de-Fenouillèdes
Lapradelle
Axat
Puilaurens
Fenouillet
Forêt d'Ayguesbonnes-Boucheville
Grottes de l'Aguzou
Sournia

N

20 km
10 miles

Narbonne, Carcassonne and the Corbières

Before the border with Spain was definitively drawn in 1659, this was a hotly contested region for a thousand years, disputed first by Visigoths and Saracens, and finally by Madrid and Paris. The French determination to hold it has left us Carcassonne, queen of all medieval castles, cloud-top Cathar redoubts like Aguilar and Quéribus, and over a hundred others, in every shape, colour and style known to military science.

Seldom does the Midi offer a greater jumble of landscapes, with wild mountain gorges just an hour's ride from sandy coastal lagoons where the tramontane blows your hat off in the spring; in greenness the region ranges from the lush Aude valley to the scrubby plateau of Opoul, where the French Army enjoys its desert training.

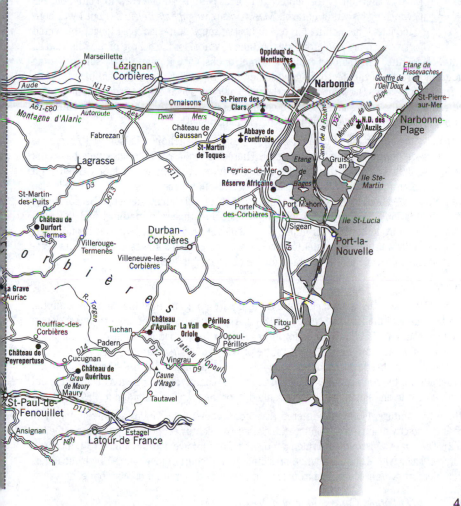

Beaches

From Narbonne south into Spain is really just one long beach. The sand is perfect and lagoons often give you the feeling of being isolated on a desert island, amongst sand dunes and flocks of summer flamingos.

best beaches

Gruissan Plage: setting for the cult film *Betty Blue*; a wide expanse of sand populated by curious raised houses on stilts.

Port-la-Nouvelle: un-chic, watching the tankers roll by.

Narbonne

Narbonne gave birth to the last of the troubadours, Guiraut Riquier (d. 1292). A melancholy soul, like many men of his time, Riquier never seemed to earn his lady's affection, or the appreciation of his patrons, and he grew to a bitter old age watching his world unravel. *Mas trop suy vingutz als derriers*—'but I was born too late'—he mourned in one of his last songs. If he had lived longer, he would have seen his own proud city become a symbol for the eclipse of the Midi and its culture. Narbonne, Languedoc's capital and metropolis since Roman times, suffered some outrageous fortune in the decades after Riquier's death, enough trouble to plunge it into a centuries-long decline. The symbol for Narbonne's own particular eclipse is its majestic, unfinished cathedral, the arches and truncated columns of its skeletal nave haunting the square in front of the plain brick façade thrown up when ambition died.

Fortunately, the Narbonne of today has no interest in melancholy whatsoever ('*J'aime ma ville—il y a de punch!*' is its current slogan). Thanks to roads and railroads, trade has come back for the first time since the Middle Ages. The local economy is still largely fuelled on plonk—the bountiful vineyards of the Corbières and other nearby regions. The city is also finding a new vocation as an industrial centre, and its outskirts have developed accordingly. With a population of only 45,000, Narbonne can nonetheless sometimes fool you into thinking it a metropolis. With its impressive medieval monuments, boulevards and lively streets, it is quite a happy and contented town—one of the Midi's most agreeable urban destinations—with an excellent museum, and the best cathedral in the south.

History

Colonia Narbo Martius, a good site for a trading port along the recently built Via Domitia, began by decree of the Roman Senate in 118 BC. The colony rapidly became the most important city of southern Gaul, renowned for its beauty and wealth. Under Augustus, it was made the capital of what came to be known as the province of *Gallia Narbonensis*. After 410, it briefly became the headquarters of the Visigoths, and continued as their northernmost provincial capital until the Arab conquest of Spain in the 8th century; the Arabs took Narbonne, but could not hold it, and Pépin the Short reclaimed it for the Frankish Kingdom in 759.

In the 12th century, Narbonne entered its second golden age. Under a native dynasty of viscounts, the city maintained its independence for two centuries and began its great cathedral (1272). The famous Viscountess Ermengarde, who ruled for five decades after 1134, managed the ship of state with distinction while presiding over a 'court of love' graced by troubadours such as Bernart de Ventadorn. The troubled 14th century was murder on Narbonne, however.

As if wars and plagues were not enough, the harbour began to silt up; finally even the river Aude decided to change its course and desert the city, ruining its trade. By the end of the century, the city had shrunk to a mere market town, albeit one with an archbishop and a very impressive cathedral.

Stagnation continued until the present century, despite the efforts of the indefatigable Paul Riquet in the 1680s; though his Canal du Midi met the sea further north, Riquet began a branch canal, the Robine, that followed the old course of the river through Narbonne. Powerful interests in Béziers and Sète, however, kept it from being completed until 1786; the man who finally saw it through was Narbonne's last archbishop, an Irishman named Arthur Dillon, who played an important role in the city's history. Only in the last hundred years has Narbonne started to revive, thanks to industry and the wine trade; since the Second World War it has overtaken Carcassonne as the largest city of the Aude *département*.

Getting Around

By rail: Narbonne is an important rail junction, in the middle of the main Bordeaux–Toulouse–Nice route across the Midi; there are frequent connections (about 12 a day) to Perpignan, Toulouse, and Béziers and the other coastal cities to the east. The station is just north of the centre on Boulevard Frédéric Mistral.

By bus: The *gare routière*, on Quai Victor Hugo, across the canal from the market, offers coach services that largely duplicate the trains; there will also be a bus or two a day to Gruissan, Leucate and other points along the coast.

By boat: If you haven't any particular destination in mind, take a trip on the canal boat (*coche d'eau*) that traverses the Canal de la Robine and the coastal lagoons; in season it leaves every morning except Monday from the Pont des Marchands, and goes as far as Port-la-Nouvelle on the coast (✆ 04 68 90 63 38 for details). Otherwise rent a boat for yourself, on the Quai d'Alsace north of the railway bridge.

Tourist Information

Place Roger-Salengro, ✆ 04 68 65 15 60, ✉ 04 68 65 59 12. The **post office** is on 25 Blvd Gambetta.

market days

Outdoor market on Thursday.

The City Centre

Narbonne is a city of surprises. If you come by train or bus, the first thing you're likely to see is the gargantuan, horrific **Palais du Travail** on Blvd Frédéric Mistral, a full-blown piece of 1930s Stalinist architecture with statuary to match. Turn the corner on Rue Jean Jaurès, though, and you'll be following the **Canal de la Robine** into the centre of the city, lined with a delightful park called the **Jardin Entre Deux Villes**. Behind the Hôtel de Ville, the **Pont des Marchands** is covered with shops, a charming miniature version of Florence's Ponte Vecchio.

Palais des Archevêques

Narbonne's centre is the busy **Place de l'Hôtel de Ville**; in the middle of the square a recently discovered section of the Via Domitia is cleverly displayed in its original bed and alignment. Standing over this countersunk exhibit and looking at the entrance to the Rue Droite on the northeast side of the square and the Pont des Marchands opposite, you see a pair of steel strips, set in the ground, tracing the edge of the old highway to the two streets. This gives the rather eerie feeling that only a dust-cover has been thrown over ancient Narbo Martius. Facing the square, the twin façades of the **Palais des Archevêques** were blessed with a romantic Gothic restoration by the master himself, Viollet-le-Duc, in the 1840s; opinion has been divided ever since over whether this 19th-century fancy was an improvement on the austere 13th-century original it replaced. The passage between the two buildings (the *Palais Neuf* on the left, and the *Palais Vieux* on the right) leads to a small courtyard, and the entrances to Narbonne's two excellent museums, the **Musée d'Art et d'Histoire** and the **Musée Archéologique**.

To Carcassonne

AVENUE DE TOULOUSE

To Perpignan

BLD DR LEON AUGE

Palais du Travail

Pont de l'Escoute

BOULEVARD

L'ANCIENNE

AVENUE DES PYRÉNÉES

RUE DE CHENNEBIER

R. DU 1er MAI

Chapelle des Pénitents Bleus

MARÉCHAL JOFFRE

Pont Voltaire

RUE VOLTAIRE

QUAI

RUE JEAN

R. GUSTINE FABRE

R. DE L'ARCHEVÊCHE

Jardin de l'Archevêché

BOULEVARD ARAGO

Place Voltaire

RUE DE LA PARERIE

RUE TURGOT

DILLON

Palais des Archevêques

Cloître

Place des Pyrénées

RUE

RUE

R. D. L'ÉTOILE

JAURÈS

Hôtel de Ville

Place de l'Hôtel de Ville

Cimetière Paléo-Chrétien

St-Paul-Serge

RABELAIS

Pont des Marchands

RUE DE L'HÔTEL-DIEU

RUE DES 3 NOURRICES

RUE

Place d. 4 Fontaines

Canal de la Robine

Jardin des Martyrs de la Résistance

BOULEVARD DU DOCTEUR LACROIX

Centre Hospitalier Général

Maison des Trois Nourrices

RUE CABIROL

Place de Belfort

Place des Jacobins

COURS MIRABEAU

R. DES

PL. EMILE DIGEON

Place Vincent Hyspa

Notre-Dame de Grâce

Place de Lamourguier

RUE MARAUSSAN

Musée Lapidaire

Marché

BOULEVARD DU DR. FERROUL

RUE MAZZINI

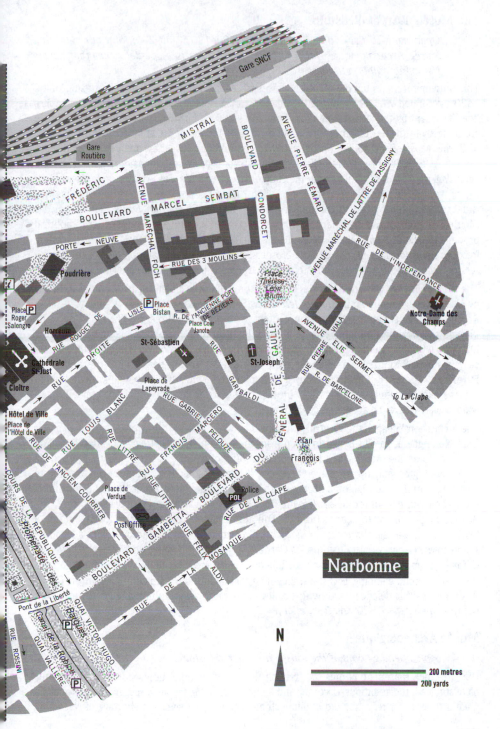

Gare SNCF

Gare
Routière

MISTRAL

BOULEVARD

AVENUE PIERRE SÉMARD

AVENUE MARÉCHAL DE LATTRE DE TASSIGNY

FRÉDÉRIC

AVENUE MARÉCHAL FOCH

BOULEVARD MARCEL SEMBAT

CONDORCET

RUE DE L'INDÉPENDANCE

PORTE ← NEUVE

Poudrière

RUE DES 3 MOULINS ←

Place
Thérèse
Léon
Blum

AVENUE MARÉCHAL DE LATTRE DE TASSIGNY

Notre-Dame des
Champs

Place
Roger
Salengro

Place
Bistan

RUE DE LISLE

R. DE L'ANCIENNE PORT
DE BÉZIERS

Place Cour
Janote

AVENUE VIALA

Horreum

RUE ROUGET DE LISLE

DROITE

St-Sébastien

RUE GARIBALDI

St-Joseph

DE GAULLE

RUE PIERRE ELIE SERMET

Cathédrale
St-Just

Place de
Lapeyrade

R. DE BARCELONE

To La Clape

Cloître

RUE LOUIS BLANC

RUE GABRIEL

RUE LITTRE

RUE FRANCIS

RUE MARCERO

PELOUZE

DU GÉNÉRAL

Plan
St-
François

Hôtel de Ville
Place de
l'Hôtel de Ville

RUE DE L'ANCIEN COURRIER

RUE LITTRE

Place de
Verdun

BOULEVARD

Police

POL

RUE DE LA CLAPE

COURS DE LA RÉPUBLIQUE

Post Office

BOULEVARD GAMBETTA

RUE FÉLIX

MOSAIQUE

Promenade des

Pont de la Liberté

QUAI VICTOR HUGO

RUE DE LA ALDY

RUE

Narbonne

Canal de la Robine

QUAI VALLÈRE

QUAI VAUBAN

RUE ROSSINI

N

200 metres
200 yards

419

The Musée d'Art et d'Histoire

Open daily 10–12 and 2–5, May–Sept, 9.30–12.15 and 2–6; joint adm with the Musée Archéologique—for a little bit more there is a special ticket that covers Narbonne's other museums.

This museum occupies the old archbishops' apartments; it is reached by an elegant stair of the 1620s, decorated with a bust of the Venetian historian Andrea Morosini, and a bronze capitoline Wolf, sent by the city of Rome for Narbonne's 2000th birthday. These reminders of Italy are perfectly fitting, for this museum could easily pass for one of the great aristocratic galleries of Rome. Most of the collection belonged to the archbishops; they must have acquired a Roman taste on sojourns there. The sumptuous rooms of these princes of the Church have been well-preserved, beginning with the chapter house or **Salle des Audiences**, where there is a portrait of the redoutable Archbishop Dillon (the last of the line—his period of office was rudely interrupted by the Revolution in 1792), and an *Equestrian Louis XIV* by van der Meulen—a pompous, quite offensive portrait, typical of the Sun King's use of art as political propaganda. Louis slept here in 1642, in the adjacent **Chambre du Roi**. The 1632 ceiling frescoes are by local talent, the Rodière brothers: harmless *Muses* that look more like nursery-school teachers. Note the floor, a restored Roman mosaic in a labyrinth pattern.

The third room, the **Grande Galerie**, contains some of the best paintings: a gloomy landscape by Gaspard Dughet and an intense *St Jerome* by Salvator Rosa (both artists were favourites in Rome), a Canaletto and, among many Dutch and Flemish pictures, a *Wedding Dance*, by Pieter Breughel the Younger. The 16th- and 17th-century enamelled plaques come from Limoges, with portraits of French kings. Opposite these, a collection of lovely faience apothecary jars from Montpellier makes a proper introduction to the next room, the **Salle des Faïences**. These 18th-century painted ceramics come mostly from well-known French centres like Moustiers and Varange, though many are from cities such as Marseille and Montpellier, where the art has since died out.

The archbishops' chapel, the **Oratoire**, harbours a few surprises: 14th-century carved alabaster from Nottingham, an odd Byzantine icon from the Aegean, and a perfect, incandescent 15th-century Florentine *Madonna*; though anonymous (once falsely attributed to Piero della Francesca) it gracefully upstages everything else in the museum. The rest of the apartments are a grab bag: Archbishop Dillon's library, with his well-thumbed St Augustine, and his dining room. You will encounter an *azulejo* tile floor from Portugal, King François I's vinegar pot, Beauvais tapestries with scenes from La Fontaine's fairy-tales, and more good painting: a luscious Veronese (the *Anointing of King David*), portraits by Nattier and by Venice's favourite 18th-century celebrity portraitist Rosalba Carriera, a sprinkling of native and foreign followers of Caravaggio, and a tortured *St Andrew* by Ribera. The last room contains 19th-century works.

If you don't mind climbing 162 steps, they'll let you up into the 13th-century **Donjon Gilles Aycelin**, a Gothic defence tower with a collection of medieval sculpture, and good views from the top (*open daily 10–12 and 2–5; adm*).

Musée Archéologique

Same opening hours as the Musée d'Art and d'Histoire.

It is only luck that made Nîmes the 'French Rome', while none of Narbonne's monuments have survived; the ambitious viscounts and archbishops of medieval Narbonne obviously had a greater appetite for recycling old building stone. There is, however, no shortage of remaining bits and pieces, and the best of them have been assembled here: reliefs from Narbonne's three triumphal arches and the gates of its walls, milestones from the Via Domitia, funeral monuments, and a model of a Roman house. The **Chapelle de la Madeleine**, where Greek and pre-Greek ceramics are displayed, retains some fragments of its original 14th-century frescoes; it also offers the best view of the apse and buttresses of the adjacent cathedral, which is almost completely surrounded by buildings.

Christianity seems to have come late to Narbonne; the first bishop, Paul, is recorded in the 3rd century; nevertheless there are some Christian sarcophagi, and an unusual reliquary in the form of the Church of the Holy Sepulchre in Jerusalem. The products of other faiths here are more interesting: a Greek statue of a *drunken silenus*, altars dedicated to Cybele and Attis, and an *image of Priapus*, that mythological embarrassment, this time at least keeping it decently covered.

The parts of the Archbishops' Palace not used for museums house Narbonne's city hall. In the Palais Neuf, the 1628 Hall of the Synods has original Aubusson tapestries. Now a reception room for the city, it was once the political centre of the region; Narbonne's archbishop had the right of presiding over the *Etats-Généraux*, or parliament, of Languedoc, though that body moved to Pézenas in 1456.

Cathédrale St-Just

This can be entered through the fine 14th-century **Cloister**, near the entrance to the museums, a Gothic quadrangle with leering gargoyles. A better way, though, is to circumnavigate the huge bulk of the cathedral and palace complex towards the west front, and the **Cour St-Eutrope**, a spacious square that occupies the unfinished two-thirds of the cathedral itself. On every side rise truncated pilasters, walls and bases of arches, witness to medieval Narbonne's ambition and the 14th-century disasters that stopped it cold.

This is the third church to occupy the site; the first was a basilica from the reign of Emperor Constantine, the second a Carolingian rebuilding of AD 890. The present church was begun in 1272, at the height of the city's fortunes. Funds were hardly lacking; the cornerstone was sent by Pope Clement IV, a former Archbishop of Narbonne, and he probably contributed a little more besides. To extend the new cathedral to its planned length, it would have been necessary to rebuild a section of the city wall; in 1340 a lawsuit over this broke out between the city and the Church, a good, old-fashioned French lawsuit—just what was needed in those bad times to put an end to construction forever.

Just the same, this one-third of a cathedral is by any measure the finest in the Midi, the only one comparable to the magnificent Gothic structures of the Ile-de-France. The short nave, in fact, heightens the exuberant verticality of the 40m apse and choir, exceeded in height only by those of Amiens and Beauvais. Throughout, the structural lines are accented with ribbing or with protruding stone courses, as if the builders wanted to leave a gentle reminder of the extraordinary technical skill that made such a building possible. The whole is done in a clean and elegant stone, grey perhaps, but a grey that here bids to be included among the colours of the spectrum.

Inside, most of the best features are in the ambulatory and its chapels. Near the altar, facing the chapels, are two remarkable archepiscopal tombs: the **Tomb of Cardinal Briçonnet** (1514), with a decorative mix of Renaissance refinement and ghoulish, grinning skeletons, typical of that age. The other, the **Tomb of Cardinal Pierre de Jugie**, is an exquisite Gothic work of 1376; though much damaged, some of the original paint remains. The ambulatory chapels are illuminated by lovely 14th-century glass: the *Creation* (left chapel), the *Infancy of Christ* in the centre, and *SS Michael, Peter and Paul* (right chapels). Some faded original frescoes can be seen in the far right chapel, and also around the main altar. The central **Chapelle de la Vierge**, has something really special, unique polychrome reliefs of the late 1300s. Ruined and covered in a Baroque remodelling of 1732, these were rediscovered in the last century, and currently they are being restored and replaced. On the upper band (left to right): an *Annunciation* and *Kings of France*, the *Presentation at the Temple*, *Palm Sunday* and *Crucifixion*. Lower band: *Purgatory*, *Hell* and *Limbo*.

The side chapels have little to see but tapestries; in the first right is a 16th-century polychrome *Entombment of Christ* from Bavaria. Almost the entire west wall is covered by a spectacular **organ**, a mountain of carved wood and statuary that took over a hundred years to complete (1741–1856).

Cathedral Treasury

Long ignored by many visitors, who miss the entrance in a tiny door in the right ambulatory chapel, the treasury has recently extended its hours in a bid for recognition (*theoretically, open daily in summer, otherwise daily exc Mon and Wed 2.15–4, but if no one is around phone © 04 68 32 09 52; adm*). Arranged in a domed chamber with odd acoustics, formerly housing the cathedral archives, the collection includes medieval reliquaries, books and a 10th-century carved ivory plaque. Also the most outlandish of all Narbonne's surprises, two early 16th-century Flemish tapestries, unlike any others you're ever likely to see. Originally a set of ten, belonging to Archbishop François Fouquet, eight-and-a-half have disappeared, probably ending up as insulation, mattress-stuffing and a bed for the dog. The half-tapestry depicts Adversity, from an *Allegory of Prosperity and Adversity*. Amidst a landscape of shipwrecks and earthquakes you will notice Cleopatra, Antiochus Seleucis and other celebrities of antiquity who met bad ends (all conveniently labelled), while Vulcan grinds out strife on his forge and a grinning Penury exults over the unfortunates. Part of the centrepiece also survived (on the left), dominated by an uncanny Goddess of Fortune on horseback, her face veiled.

The other tapestry, much better preserved, is a strange account of the *Creation*. The seven days of Genesis are arranged in tableaux, each with figures of the Holy Trinity, represented as three crowned, bearded old men. The iconography is unorthodox in the extreme; the symbolism throughout seems to hint at some concealed vein of medieval mysticism. In any case, the artists who created it produced a true *tour de force*, filling every corner with delightful naturalistic detail—a forest, the firmament, spring flowers, the Kingdom of the Sea. Bring the children, and see if they can spot the elephant.

Roman Narbonne

There isn't much of it. The centre of the ancient city, north of the Cathedral, is a dowdy, blank-faced quarter, with a newly-formed neighbourhood development group trying to interest people in fixing up the many abandoned houses. Small signs on the street corners direct you to the only Roman monument left—a warehouse or **Horreum**, on Rue Rouget de Lisle (*same hours as the art and archaeology museums; adm*). Typical of the state-run warehouses of any Roman city, this is the only complete one anywhere. Just a small part has been excavated, a maze of tiny chambers; the original structure was over 500ft long. Among the ancient fragments displayed in the various rooms is a charming relief of bear-trainers and their bears, bathing together. To the west, on Rue de l'Ancienne Porte Neuve, the **Maison Vigneronne** is a 17th-century powder-house converted into a museum of wine and its cultivation.

From the Place de l'Hôtel de Ville, Rue Droite runs northwards, roughly following the route of the Roman main street; it ends at **Place Bistan**—the former Forum, though nothing remains but some re-erected columns and a modern mural painting. One block east is the 15th-century Flamboyant church of **St-Sébastien**, built over the (apocryphal) birthplace of the saint himself. A favourite of artists across southern Europe (usually depicted stuck full of arrows), Sebastian was always a popular saint for the belief that he could intercede against the plague.

The Bourg

This is Narbonne's medieval extension across the river (now across the canal). Cross over by the bridge in the **Promenade des Barques**, the elegant park along the canal. On the other side, the city's covered **market** is a rare sensory experience even by French market standards. The Narbonnais take great pride in it, and it recently won an annual award as the best in France. Behind it, the deconsecrated 13th-century church of Notre-Dame-de-Lamourguier now houses the **Musée Lapidaire**, a large collection of architectural fragments from ancient Narbonne, displayed more or less at random (*open July and Aug 9.30–12.15, otherwise ring ℂ 04 68 65 53 58; adm*). The fragments are here thanks to François I; on a visit, he recommended to the Narbonnais that they incorporate the vast heaps of antique rubble lying about into the new walls they were building. The walls themselves thus became an open-air museum, much commented on by travellers, until they were demolished in the last century and the old bits assembled here.

Follow the boulevards west, along the course of the demolished medieval walls; the modern city hospital on Boulevard Dr Lacroix incorporates the old one, the **Hôtel-Dieu**, with a grand Baroque chapel decorated by Narbonnais painters of the 1780s. Behind this, the **Maison des Trois Nourrices** on the street of the same name is the best surviving example of a Renaissance palace in the city; the 'three nurses' are the three classical caryatids holding up the main window.

Narbonne's other ancient church, the **Basilique St-Paul-Serge**, was first built in the 5th century, and dedicated to the first bishop of Narbonne. The present building was begun in 1229, an imposing monument that was one of the first in the south to adopt the new Gothic architecture. Three early Christian sarcophagi remain from the first church, an introduction to the catacomb-like **cemetery-crypt** beneath (*open daily exc Mon 10–12 and 2–6; adm*). This subterranean necropolis was begun in the time of Constantine. Such burials were not peculiar to the Christians. In Rome, pagan and Christian catacombs exist side by side; parts of this one are decorated with pagan symbols, raising the intriguing possibility that this cemetery was for a time non-denominational.

Narbonne ✉ *11100*   ***Where to Stay***

 But for the lack of parking and a bit of street noise, ****La Dorade**, 44 Rue Jean Jaurès, ℂ 04 68 32 65 95, 🖷 04 68 65 81 62, would be perfect. Narbonne's old 'Grand Hôtel', with marble telamones holding up the balcony, this establishment is still well kept, centrally located overlooking the canal, and a good bargain. Another gracious old establishment, a bit fancier and more expensive, the *****Languedoc**, is now part of the

Mapotel chain, at 22 Blvd Gambetta, ℗ 04 68 65 14 74, ✉ 04 68 65 81 48. Near the Cathedral, an old *hôtel particulier* contains ★★★**La Residence**, 6 Rue du 1er Mai, ℗ 04 68 32 19 41, ✉ 04 68 65 51 82 (*from 300F*), with calm, well equipped rooms and a useful garage.

Most of the inexpensive places are around the station, especially on or around Ave Pierre Semard. ★★**Will's Hôtel**, 23 Ave Pierre Semard, ℗ 04 68 90 44 50, is not run by a Will, and the present owners can't imagine who Will might have been, but it is still a comfortable and extremely friendly place. Otherwise try the ★★**Hôtel du Lion d'Or** at No.39, ℗ 04 68 32 06 92, ✉ 04 68 65 51 13, with a good restaurant (*menus from 90F*). Closer to the centre, the ★★**France**, 6 Rue Rossini, ℗ 04 68 32 09 75, ✉ 04 60 65 50 30, is on a quiet side street near the covered market. The cheapest places are on Ave Pierre Semard, and there are quite a few, including the very nice ★**de la Gare**, 7 Ave Pierre Semard, ℗ 04 68 32 10 54.

Eating Out

As you might expect after a tour of their wonderful market, the Narbonnais are a gastronomically fastidious lot; their restaurants reflect this, with a minimum of pretension. Try the restaurant of the Lion d'Or (*see* above) and its *terroir* menu, or for more adventurous dishes, **Le Petit Comptoir**, 4 Blvd du Maréchal Joffre, ℗ 04 68 42 30 35 (*menus from 98F*). East of the centre, near a delightful park called the Place Thérèse et Léon Blum, **L'Eglefin**, 22 Rue de l'Ancienne Porte de Béziers, specializes in seafood as its name implies; an *eglefin* is a haddock, and he appears on the menu cooked in cider, along with grilled *loup* and other delights; *60, 100 and 120F menus*. Another place for seafood is the **Restaurant de la Gare**, 5 Ave Pierre Semard: grilled fish, oysters and seafood *brochettes* on menus of 80 and 130F.

For Chinese-Vietnamese cooking, very correct and tasty too, the best in town is still **La Baie d'Along**, on Place Bistan in old Narbonne; 98F menu, though you may want to splurge for the elaborate starters, ℗ 04 68 65 58 83. **Le Castel**, with a wide choice of pizzas, also has steaks and chops with good salads, 26 Blvd du Dr Lacroix, ℗ 04 68 41 35 07 (*150F at most, much less for pizza*).

Entertainment

On a wet day in Narbonne you could do worse than head out of town on the N9 towards Perpignan to **L'Espace de Liberté**, a giant aquatic park with three huge swimming pools, ten-pin bowling and ice-skating: a life-saver if you have children (℗ 04 68 42 17 89, open daily).

Narbonne's Coast

The coastal road, more or less following the path of the Roman Via Domitia, cannot follow this complicated shoreline, a miasma of marshes and lagoons; some detours on the backroads will be necessary to see it. One big obstacle is the mouth of the Aude, northeast of Narbonne; this pretty and amiable river comes all the way from the high Pyrenees to meet an inglorious end in a boggy landscape called (literally) 'Piss-cow Swamp'.

Gruissan ✉ 11430: 1 Blvd Pech-Maynaud, ℂ 04 68 49 03 25, 🖶 04 68 49 33 12.

Sigean ✉ 11130: Place de la Libération (attached to a little museum with stuffed birds and archaeological titbits), ℂ 04 68 48 14 81.

local wines

Coteaux de Languedoc-La Clape: Château Rouquette-sur-Mer, off the D168 south-west of Narbonne-Plage in Gruissan (ℂ 04 68 49 90 41); Château de Pech Redon, Rte de Gruissan in Narbonne (ℂ 04 68 90 41 22); and for whites, Domaine du Fraisse, at Autignac (ℂ 04 67 90 23 40).

Quatourze: A noble variation on Corbières made along the back roads around Bages and Peyriac-de-Mer.

Fitou: Coopérative de Fitou, on the N9 (ℂ 04 68 45 71 41).

Narbonne-Plage to Port-la-Nouvelle

South of Etang de Pissevaches, one of the rare fishing villages in these parts, St-Pierre-sur-Mer, has been swallowed up by the bright modern characterless resort of **Narbonne-Plage**, with plenty of sand and its full whack of seaside amusements. Just to the north is Languedoc's answer to the Fontaine de Vaucluse, a 'bottomless' pool called the **Gouffre de l'Oeil Doux**— the 'sweet eye', always full of pure, fresh water, though only a mile from the sea. Beyond Narbonne-Plage, the landscape rises into the **Montagne de la Clape,** once an island and still a world in itself. Parts are lush and pine-clad, others rugged and desolate, reminiscent of a Greek island; on the lower slopes are vineyards that produce small quantities of a very good wine (*see* above). Near the top, the chapel of **Notre-Dame-des-Auzils** has a fascinating collection of sailors' ex votos—ship models, paintings and the like, many over a century old (*open Sun pm, and daily in summer, 3–6*).

Most of those sailors came from **Gruissan**, south of La Clape. One of Narbonne's ports in the Middle Ages, Gruissan today is surrounded by lagoons and salt-pans; the charming village is set in concentric rings around a ruined 13th-century castle, built to defend the approaches to Narbonne. Its tower, the 'Tour de Barbarousse', possibly takes its name from a visit by the famous Turkish pirate-admiral Barbarossa; in the 1540s the Ottoman sultan's fleet was briefly based in Toulon, helping the French against the Holy Roman Emperor Charles V. To Gruissan's fine beaches the government has added a pleasure marina, resulting in one of the more agreeable resorts on these coasts. Gruissan's other landmark is the *Plage des Pilotis*, where neat rows of beach cottages hang in the air. The sea regularly covers the sand here, and over a century ago people began the habit of building their holiday retreats on stilts. The houses and beach gained romantic notoriety as the setting for Jean-Jacques Beineix' cult film of love, lust and bowls of chilli—*Betty Blue*.

To go further south, you'll have to return to Narbonne, and circle around the **Etang de Bages et de Sigean**. This broad lagoon, with its many islands and forgotten, half-abandoned hamlets, is especially rich in waterfowl, including a few flamingos, as well as cormorants, egrets and herons. **Boat trips** can be arranged through the Cercle Nautique des Corbières, starting from the dock of a vanished medieval village, Port-Mahon, near **Sigean**, a pleasant if rather forgotten village that began as a station on the Via Domitia. Wildlife of an entirely different sort coexists peacefully nearby at the **Réserve Africaine** north of Sigean, ℂ 04 68 48 20 20, a big zoo and drive-through safari park with the only white rhinoceroses, most likely, in all Languedoc (*open daily year round, 9–7; adm*).

When the builders of the Canal de la Robine laid out their coastal port in 1820, they gave it the strikingly original name of **Port-la-Nouvelle**. Now France's third-largest Mediterranean port, it is a gritty, no-nonsense town of Communist stevedores, where the most prominent restaurant is called 'Le Chicken Shack', and where the waterfront promenade takes in a panorama of shiny oil tanks. It has good beaches, and for a long time it was also a resort; there are, incredibly, still some holiday motels in town. If you didn't fancy the palms and ice-cream of La Grande Motte or Cap d' Agde, a day on the beach here, watching cement barges and tankers sail past, might be just the thing. If you're sticking around, don't miss **La Baleine et le Vigneron**: a skeleton of a dead whale that washed up on the beach which has been carefully reconstructed in a wine warehouse (*open daily Mar–Oct, free*). If you know your plants, cross the Canal de la Robine to the **Ile Ste-Lucie**, abandoned and overgrown with 100 rare specimens.

Where to Stay and Eating Out

Narbonne-Plage ✉ 11100

Narbonne-Plage is hardly upmarket but ★★**Hôtel de la Clape,** Rue des Flots Bleus, ✆ 04 68 49 80 15, ✆ 04 68 75 05 05, is a wonderful address from which to write home. *Closed Nov–Easter.* Slightly better is ★★**La Caravelle**, Ave Front de Mer, ✆ 04 68 49 80 38 ✆ 04 68 49 85 22. *Closed Oct–Easter.* Good seafood can be had at **Restaurant L'Oasis** on Ave Front de Mer, ✆ 04 68 49 82 12 (*menus 80–200F*).

Gruissan ✉ 11430

Gruissan, still a real fishing port, is obviously a good place for seafood. The popular **L'Estagnol**, a converted fishermen's cottage at the entrance to the village, ✆ 04 68 49 01 26, offers sumptuous sea-food and fish menus from 98–210F. The ★★**Hôtel Corail** on Quai Ponant in Gruissan Port ✆ 04 68 49 04 43, ✆ 04 68 49 62 89, is perfectly acceptable and has a fine restaurant, specializing in *bouillabaisse*. Several menus from 100F. *Closed Nov through Jan.*

Around Narbonne: Abbaye de Fontfroide

Some attractions within a short drive of the city: 11km to the north, the **Oppidum de Montlaurès**, the site of a pre-Roman town, similar to the Oppidum d'Ensérune (*see* p.405) and set on the same sort of hilltop. Better, take the N113 west from the city, and turn south on the D613. The first sight, to the left, is the derelict, frequently overlooked castle of **St-Pierre-des-Clars**. In its grounds, Roman coins with the images of Pompey and Brutus have been found, but the present building probably dates from the late 12th or 13th century. The purpose of this ineffably romantic ruin was probably to protect sheep in wartime. This is not as daft as it may sound; after iron, sheep were the most valuable commodity of the Middle Ages, the wool-on-the-hoof that made the banking fortunes of so many medieval cities.

Three km further down the D613, you'll see another ruined castle in the distance, madly perched on a perpendicular cliff. A perfect introduction to the fortified wilderness of the Corbières (*see* below), **St-Martin-de-Toques** was gradually built between the 10th and 13th centuries, and occupied until the 1600s. Someone, somehow, has got a crane up to it, and restorations are underway.

A little further along, a marked side road leads to the **Abbaye de Fontfroide**, ✆ 04 68 45 11 08 (*open daily July and Aug 9.30–6.30; other times 10–12 and 2–5; adm; mandatory guided tours, generally on the hour*). When the tour reaches the monks' refectory, the guide will take pains to point out that the fireplace is a recent addition; heating of any kind was a little too posh for medieval Cistercians. On the other hand, after inspecting the lavish church and grounds it is hard to believe the monks were giving much away to the poor—a typical medieval enigma: power and wealth, without the enjoyment of them. One of the most important Cistercian abbeys in the south, Fontfroide was founded in 1145 on the site of an earlier Benedictine house. Until its suppression in 1791, it was one of the richest and most influential of all Cistercian houses. It was largely in ruins when a local family, the Fayets, bought it early in this century; they have been fixing it up a little at a time ever since—an example of the kind of shoe-string private restoration that has saved so many French monuments, neglected by a traditionally stingy national government.

The best part of the tour is Fontfroide's lovely 13th-century **cloister**; its style of broad arches, inset with smaller ones, was much copied in later cloisters in Languedoc. The 12th-century **church** impresses with its proportions and Romanesque austerity; following Cistercian custom simple floral patterns constitute the only decoration. The art of making stained glass, once one of France's proudest achievements, had nearly died out by the 19th century. There has been a modest revival in our own century; one of its first productions was the excellent set of windows here, a *Last Judgement* and *signs of the zodiac* done in the '20s. More glass can be seen in the **dormitory**—fascinating abstract collages of old fragments, brought here from northern French churches wrecked during the First World War. Behind the cloister is a nursery of roses where medieval varieties are grown by a local firm.

To protect the produce of its vast estates, the Abbey maintained a network of fortified farms and storehouses all over the region. The most impressive one is near Capestang (*see* p.406); the closest, 8km west of Fontfroide, is the **Château de Gaussan**. Followers of Viollet-le-Duc restored it in the last century, with plenty of neo-Gothic ornament and frescoes inside.

From Narbonne to Carcassonne

The *Autoroute des Deux Mers* and the N113 follow this corridor inland, across the coastal plain and the valley of the Aude. There is nothing especially interesting along the way, unless you make some detours, or take the back roads following the Aude and the Canal du Midi (for areas to the north, *see* 'Canal du Midi', p.403, and 'Minervois', p.407; for south, *see* 'Corbières', p.435.

Carcassonne

Standing before the great eastern gate of the walled city, the writer had his notebook out and was scribbling furiously. It was market day, and rustic villeins in coarse wool tunics were offering hung pheasants and great round cheeses from their wooden carts. Geese honked from cages made of twigs and rushes, while pigs and hounds poked about in the cobbled gutters. 'This is medieval indeed,' the writer mused—just then the director and his entourage appeared over the drawbridge. 'Lovely, everyone, but we'll want more sheep; lots more sheep!'

Plenty of obscure costume dramas have been shot here, drawn by Viollet-le-Duc's romantic restoration. Even without pigs in the gutters, Carcassonne is the Middle Ages come to life. The people of the city do their best to heighten the medieval atmosphere every August for the two-

week festival called the *Médiévales*, with artisans in costume, music and even jousts under the walls. Reality intrudes in the history of the place. Today a dour manufacturing town, Carcassonne was once the strategic key to the Midi; the castle built here by St Louis was a barrier greater than the Pyrenees to invaders.

History

After running north down from the Pyrenees, the river Aude makes a sharp right turn for the sea, thus conveniently providing not only an easy natural route into the mountains, but also one across the 'French isthmus', between the Mediterranean and the Atlantic. The river's angle, one of the crossroads of France since prehistoric times, is an obvious site for a fortress; there seems to have been one nearby since the 8th century BC. The Tectosage Gauls occupied the site of the present *cité* in the 3rd century; a century later the Romans established a fortified veterans' colony on it called *Carcaso*, which gradually grew into a town. With the coming of the Visigoths, in the Germanic invasions of the 5th century, Carcassonne began to assume its present role, as a border stronghold between France and Spain—the Frankish and Visigothic kingdoms. The action started as early as AD 506, when the Frankish King Clovis unsuccessfully besieged the town.

Arabs from Spain arrived about 725, one of the high-water marks of the Muslim tide in Europe. Pépin the Short chased them out 30 years later. Not that the Franks could hold it either. With the collapse of the Carolingian Empire, local viscounts attained a *de facto* independence. From 1084 to 1209 Carcassonne enjoyed a glorious period of wealth and culture under the Trencavels, a family who were also viscounts of Béziers and Nîmes. Under them the cathedral and the Château Comtal were begun. Simon de Montfort, realizing the importance of the town, made it one of his first stops in the Crusade of 1209. The last viscount, Raymond-Roger Trencavel, was no Cathar, but a gentleman and a patriot, determined to oppose the planned rape of Languedoc by the northerners. His famous declaration is still remembered today: 'I offer a town, a roof, a shelter, bread and my sword to all the persecuted people who will soon be wandering in Provence.'

Unfortunately, Trencavel allowed himself to be tricked outside the *cité* walls on pretence of negotiation; he was put in chains, and the leaderless town surrendered soon after. Raymond-Roger died in prison three months later, probably poisoned by Montfort, who declared himself viscount and used Carcassonne as his base of operations until his death in 1218. His son, Amauri, ceded the town and the rest of Montfort's conquests to King Louis IX. The last of the

Trencavels, Raymond-Roger's son and heir, also named Raymond, fought to reclaim his lands until 1240, without success despite popular revolts. Under Louis and his son, Philip III, the outer walls were built, making the entire town into the greatest fortress in Europe, the impregnable base of French power in the south. No attempts were ever made on it; even the Black Prince, passing through in 1355, declined to undertake a siege.

When France gobbled up the province of Roussillon in 1659, this mighty bastion no longer had any military purpose, and it was allowed to fall into disrepair. While the lower town, with its large textile industries, prospered until English competition ruined the trade in the 1800s, the *cité* gradually decayed into a half-abandoned slum. It was the writer Prosper Mérimée, France's Inspector-General of Historic Monuments in the 1830s, who called attention to this sad state of affairs. Viollet-le-Duc, fresh from sprucing up Narbonne, got the huge job of restoring the *cité* in 1844; work continued, according to his plans, for the rest of the century.

Today's Carcassonne has a split personality: up on its hill, the pink towers of the lovingly restored *cité* glitter like a dream. No longer impregnable, its 750 inhabitants (all of whom, it seems, have opened Ye Olde tourist shops or snack bars) are invaded by over 200,000 visitors each year, while down below, the workaday *Ville Basse* gets on with the job.

Getting Around

By train: From the SNCF station, on Ave du Maréchal Joffre at the northern edge of the Ville Basse, there are regular connections to Narbonne (11 a day), and from there to all the coastal cities; also a few trains down the Aude valley to Limoux, Quillan and from there to Perpignan.

By bus: The *gare routière* is a few streets south of the rail station, on Boulevard de Varsovie (℃ 04 68 25 12 74). There are several buses a day to Narbonne and Castelnaudary, three to Toulouse, and a rare few to outlying towns like Limoux or Foix; also a daily coach to Barcelona. Some buses to villages in the Montagne Noire and Minervois leave from the Café Bristol in front of the rail station. To get up to the *cité* from the lower town, take the no.4 city bus (every 30 minutes) from the rail station or from Place Gambetta near the tourist office.

Bike and boat hire: You can rent bicycles and scooters opposite the station—and also boats; the station is right on the Canal du Midi (**Midi-Croisières**, ℃ 04 68 47 57 58).

Tourist Information

15 Blvd Camille Pelletan, opposite Place Gambetta, in the centre of the Ville Basse; ℃ 04 68 10 24 30, @ 04 68 10 24 38. Also in the *cité* (summer only), just inside the Porte Narbonnaise, ℃ 04 68 25 68 81. The **post office** is on Rue Jean Bringer in the Ville Basse, and Rue Trencavel in the *cité*.

market days

Tuesday, Thursday and Saturday in Place Carnot.

The Walls of the Cité

Most visitors come in through the back door, by the car parks and the bus stop, at the **Porte Narbonnaise**. This is not the best introduction to the impressive military sophistication of Carcassonne's defences. It's probably the weakest point along the walls, though there may have been outworks that have since disappeared. Still, it looks strong enough, with two stout rounded bastions on the inner wall from which to mow down any attackers so fortunate as to have got through the outer wall.

Between the two walls, you can circumnavigate Carcassonne through the open space called **les Lices**, the 'lists', where knights trained, and where tournaments were held. The **outer wall** is the work of Louis IX; note how it is completely open on the inside, so that attackers who stormed it would have no protection from the defenders on the **inner wall**. Parts of this date back to the Romans—wherever you see large, irregular blocks without mortar, or layers of smaller stones interspersed with courses of thin brick; the ground level within the lists was slightly lowered by the French, so that you will often see their rectangular stones, either smooth or rusticated, beneath Roman work, where they had to underpin the towers.

To the right of the Porte Narbonnaise, the first large tower is the mighty **Tour du Trésau**. Beyond it, the northern side of the inner wall is almost completely Roman, begun in the 1st century and rebuilt in the imperial decline of the 4th century, like the walls of Rome itself, with the characteristic rounded bastions used all over the Empire. Near the second-last of them is a Roman postern gate. The walls to the left of the Porte Narbonnaise were almost completely rebuilt under Philip III, a long stretch of impressive bastions culminating in the great **Tour St-Nazaire**.

Atop both the inner and outer walls, almost everything you see today—the crenellations, wooden galleries (*hourds*) and pointed turrets that make up Carcassonne's memorable skyline—is the work of Viollet-le-Duc. As in all his other works, the pioneer of architectural restoration has been faulted for not adhering literally to original appearances. This is true, especially concerning the pointed turrets and northern slate roofs, but Viollet-le-Duc worked in a time before anyone could have imagined our own rigorous, antiseptic approach to recreating the old. His romantic, 19th-century appreciation of the Middle Ages made possible a restoration that was not only essentially correct, but creative and beautiful.

Château Comtal

Approaching the *cité* from the western side, above the river, you pass the Gothic church of **St-Gimer**, ascending to the **Porte d'Aude**. In the old days, you couldn't come empty-handed; the *cité* has no natural source of water, and commoners from the Ville Basse had to bring up two buckets each time to get in. The Porte d'Aude was the ultimate discouragement for an attacker, employing every trick in the medieval bag. Note, for example, how the approach comes from the right; to protect themselves, soldiers on the way up would have to keep their shields in their right hand, making it difficult to do anything else. The winding path made it impossible to use a battering ram on the gate, and attackers would be under fire from the walls the entire way; there is another gate inside, and if anyone got through the first they would find themselves trapped in a box, under fire from all sides.

The defences are strongest on the western side because here, the *cité's* three lines of defence—the outer and inner walls and the citadel, the **Château Comtal**—are closely compressed. Probably the site of the Roman governors' palace, it was rebuilt by the Trencavels for their own palace, and expanded by King Louis IX (✆ 04 68 25 01 66, *open daily exc Sun and hols, June–Sept 9–7, other times 9.30–12.30 and 2–5; adm*). You have a choice of **guided tours** of the walls and towers (40 or 90 minutes, usually on the hour, schedule posted at the entrance) which begin with a room-sized model and continue, in fascinating, excruciating detail, through an advanced course in medieval military architecture. Louis' builders laid as many traps for invaders inside the walls as without—for example the stairways where each riser is a different height. Be careful.

Your ticket also includes the **Musée Lapidaire**, which fills much of the palace. The collection includes ancient and medieval fragments: from Roman inscriptions and milestones to Merovingian sarcophagi, and country roadside crosses (in local folklore, erroneously believed to be tombstones of the Cathars). Old prints and paintings give an idea of the half-ruined state of the *cité* before Viollet-le-Duc went to work on it, with houses half-filling les Lices and windmills along the walls. Two medieval works saved from the town's churches are especially worth a look: an unusual 15th-century English alabaster of the *Transfiguration*, and an excellent sculpted altarpiece, with a host of expressive faces in attendance.

Basilique St-Nazaire

In 1096 (the year after he declared the First Crusade), Pope Urban V visited here, giving his blessing to the beginning of the works. The building took shape as an austere, typically southern Romanesque cathedral, and stayed that way until 1270. The French conquerors had more ambitious plans, and rebuilt the transepts and choir in glorious, perpendicular Gothic. The best features can be seen from outside: two tremendous rose windows and a tall apse with more acres of windows and gargoyles projecting like cannons, although these are now wrapped up tight like fish in nets, awaiting restoration.

The windows illuminate the interior (*open summer 9–12 and 2–7, winter 9–12 and 2–5.30*) with beautiful 16th- and 17th-century stained glass, depicting the *Tree of Jesse* and *Life of Christ*. In the right aisle, you can pay your respects to the devil himself, at the **Tomb of Simon de Montfort**, marked by a small plaque. Understandably, Montfort is no longer present; six years after his death, his descendants took him back up north where there would be in less danger of desecration.

The Ville Basse

Before Louis IX, the *cité* was surrounded by long-established suburbs. In 1240, these were occupied by Raymond Trencavel, son of the last viscount. With the help of the townspeople, he besieged the *cité* and nearly took it back. Louis pardoned the rebels, but did find it necessary to knock their houses down, to deprive any future attackers of cover. To replace the old *bourg*, he laid out a new town across the river, in the strict (and here, rather drab) grid pattern of a *bastide*. Don't confuse this with the *bastides*, or old farmhouses, in Provence and Languedoc; as you approach the former English possessions of Aquitaine, *bastide* takes on the meaning of a medieval new town, one of hundreds constructed by the French and English rulers during the Hundred Years' War; this *Ville Basse* (or Bastide St-Louis, as it's sometimes called, especially by the tourist office) has gradually replaced the *Cité* as the centre of modern Carcassonne.

Descending the cité from the Porte d'Aude, you'll pass some streets of houses that managed to creep back despite the royal decree. Rue Trivalle, with a pair of elegant Renaissance *hôtels*, leads down to the long, 14th-century **Pont Vieux**. At the far end, there once was a sort of triumphal arch, as can be seen in the old prints in the Château Comtal. Now there remains only the chapel of **Notre-Dame-de-la-Santé**, built in 1538.

The Ville Basse proper begins two streets further down, with a circle of boulevards that replaced the old walls. In 1355, during the Hundred Years' War, the walls failed to keep out the Black Prince, who burned the *bastide* to the ground. Only the street plan survived, and at the north and south ends, two huge, mouldering Gothic churches: **St-Vincent** and **St-Michel**, both begun under Louis IX, and both on Rue Dr Tomey. St-Michel was restored by Viollet-le-Duc, and serves as co-cathedral along with St-Nazaire. A *bastide* was always built around a central market square (here, Place Carnot), while one street over, off Rue Verdun, you can see the handsome 18th-century **Halles aux Graines**. You can learn all about the famous heretics at the Centre for Cathar Studies in the **Maison des Mémoires**, 53 Rue de Verdun, ✆ 04 68 47 24 66; this was the home of Carcassonne's contribution to Surrealism, Joë Bousquet, and there's a display about him, and another organization dedicated to the study of folk traditions in the Aude. At 1 Rue du Verdun, the 17th-century Presidial houses the **Musée des Beaux Arts** (*open 10–12 and 2–6, closed Mon and Tues and hols from 15 June–15 Sept, closed Sun and Mon other times; free*) with paintings and decorative arts from the 16th century to the present.

Lastly, between Easter and 1 November, you can watch an exhibition of falconry, **Les Aigles de la Cité**, at Colline Pech Mary (1km from the Cité, signposted off the road to Narbonne), ✆ 04 68 47 88 99 (*open 1 April–2 Nov, demonstrations at 3, with an additional demonstration at 4.30 on Sun; in July and Aug continuous demonstrations 3–7; adm*).

Carcassonne ✉ *11000* **Where to Stay**

Stay in the *cité* if you can, though it won't be cheap. ★★★★**Hôtel de la Cité**, Place St-Nazaire, ✆ 04 68 25 03 34, ✆ 04 68 71 50 15, in a pretty garden right under the walls, occupies the former episcopal palace, grandly restored in 1909: marble baths, a pool, the works. *Closed Jan.* Another charming old mansion of the *cité* houses the ★★★**Hôtel du Donjon**, Rue du Comte Roger, ✆ 04 68 71 08 80, ✆ 04 68 25 06 60, with a small garden and a fine restaurant. For anything cheaper, you'll be outside the walls; one of the closest to the *cité*, and one of the best is the ★★**Hôtel du Pont Vieux**, 32 Rue Trivalle, ✆ 04 68 25 24 99, ✆ 04 68 47 62 71. The **Auberge de Jeunesse** is in the centre at Rue Vicomte-Trencavel, ✆ 04 68 25 23 16, ✆ 04 68 71 14 84 (fax or write to reserve in summer). *Closed Jan–Feb.*

All of the rest are down in the Ville Basse, near the train station or around Blvd Jean Jaurès. Some are real dives, as in any industrial town, but most are respectable enough; for a touch of class at economy prices, try the Art Deco ★★**Terminus**, 2 Ave Maréchal Joffre, ✆ 04 68 25 25 06, ✆ 04 68 71 39 09, used as a set in a number of French films; try to get one of the rooms that have not been 'renovated'. The ★★**Central**, 27 Blvd Jean Jaurès, ✆ 04 68 25 03 84, ✆ 04 68 72 46 41, is one of the cheapest, but quite nice. Otherwise try the incongruously named ★★**Hotel Royal**, 22 Blvd Jean-Jaurès, ✆ 04 68 25 19 12, ✆ 04 68 47 33 01, or the friendly family-run ★**Astoria**, 18 Rue Tourtel, ✆ 04 68 25 31 38, ✆ 04 68 71 34 14, with a comfy decor *à l'anglaise*.

A luxury alternative to staying in the *cité* is the Relais & Châteaux ★★★★**Domaine d'Auriac**, south of town on the Rte St-Hilaire, ✆ 04 68 25 72 22, ✆ 04 68 47 35 54, a stately, ivy-covered 18th-century mansion set in a large, immaculately kept park. There's a pool, tennis, and even a golf course close by. Also an elegant and highly-rated restaurant, featuring some seafood but mostly traditional dishes of the Aude, such as pigeon, which you can get here with truffles (*dinner 220–400F, rooms 550F and up for a double*). *Closed mid-Nov–Feb*. Another fine choice in the surrounding countryside, the ★★★**Auberge du Château de Cavanac**, in Cavanac, 4km south on the Rte St-Hilaire, ☏ 04 68 79 61 04, 🖷 04 68 79 79 67, is a big old farmhouse in a quiet garden, with an excellent restaurant in the former stables, serving a unique five-course 195F menu with wine and all the works, starting with a kir and a choice of starters—foie gras, smoked salmon or lobster. *Closed Jan, and Sun eve and Mon out of season.*

Eating Out

In the *cité*, the restaurant of the **Brasserie le Donjon** (*see* above), ☏ 04 68 71 08 70, dedicates itself to the best of Languedoc cooking—even the humble *cassoulet* reaches new heights (*120F menu*). More ambitiously, and expensively, **Le Pont-Levis** has an outdoor terrace near the Porte Narbonnaise, ☏ 04 68 25 55 23 (*135–280F menu*), and specializes in *langoustines* in various guises. *Closed Sun eve and Mon.* In the midst of the tourist haunts, don't miss **Dame Carcas**, 3 Place du Château, ☏ 04 68 71 23 23 (*menus from 195F*), and its delicious wood-fired food. *Closed Mon.* There are less expensive places, but as you might expect in such an intense tourist zone, none are anything special.

Down in the Ville Basse, you can feast on smoked duck magret and other southwest fare at **L'Oeil**, 32 Rue de Lorraine, ☏ 04 68 25 64 81 (*menus from 80F*). *Closed Sat lunch and Sun, and Aug.* The informal **Escalier**, 23 Blvd Omer Sarraut, ☏ 04 68 25 65 66 (*around 80F*) is something of an institution in Carcassonne, where Tex Mex, pizza and moussaka share the menu. If you have a car, besides the aforementioned Domaine d'Auriac and Auberge du Château, there's the **Château Saint-Martin Trencavel**, at Montredon (follow Blvd Jean-Jaurès, to Rue A. Marty and follow the signs), ☏ 04 68 71 09 53, situated in a handsome *gentilhommerie* with a huge terrace over a park, offering a choice of traditional dishes and fresh market cuisine; delicious seafood salad (*menus from 160F*). *Closed Wed.* And in most of Carcassonne's *pâtisseries* you can satisfy your sweet tooth on the local favourite, *boulets de Carcassonne*, which are made with peanuts and honey.

The Aude's Northwest Corner: the Lauragais

West of Carcassonne and the Montagne Noire lies a region called the Lauragais, a mostly flat expanse of serious farming of the humbler sort: beans, of course, barley and pigs, and in some villages a substantial chicken-plucking trade. Windmills are a chief landmark, as is the shady blue and nearly straight ribbon of the Canal du Midi on route to Toulouse. Rugby makes the juices flow in these parts, but in the old days it was religion: St-Felix-de-Caraman, where the doctrines of the Catharism were formulated is here (*see* **Topics**, pp.54–5).

Tourist Information

Castelnaudary ✉ 11400: Place de la République, ☏ 04 68 23 05 73, 🖷 04 68 23 61 40.

Castelnaudary: Monday.

Castelnaudary, Famous for Beans

To be right, a *cassoulet* requires four things: 'white beans from Lavelanet, cooked in the pure water of Castelnaudary, in a casserole made of clay from the Issel, over a fire of furze from the Black Mountain'. Every French book ever written on the area mentions this, so we felt obliged to pass it on. The clay pot of *cassoulet* in Castelnaudary's kitchen is the town's Eiffel Tower, its Acropolis, its very identity. Having finally penetrated to deepest France, what you find is not always what you might expect. Here, the precious insight into the folk soul is a cherished mess of beans, lard, goose grease and miscellaneous pork parts. Back in the 1570s, Castelnaudary's *cassoulet* was prescribed to Queen Margot as a cure for sterility, unfortunately without success. Today, all over central France, housewives are torn between making their own, which takes hours, or succumbing to the allure of canned *cassoulet*; any good supermarket will stock at least six brands.

With *cassoulet*, the charms of Castelnaudary are nearly exhausted. There is the 14th-century church of **St-Michel**, with a tall steeple that dominates the city; the **Moulin de Cugarel**, a restored 17th-century windmill, one of over 30 that once spun in the vicinity (*open summer 10–12 and 3–7*) and the port and turning basin of the Canal du Midi.

The Medieval Lauragais

In the Middle Ages, **St-Papoul**, 8km east of Castelnaudary on the D103, was the centre of the Lauragais and the home of its bishop. An **abbey** (*guided tours, Easter–Oct, contact the mairie, © 04 68 94 90 93*) has been here since the time of Charlemagne; in 1317 Pope John XXII turned the abbot into a bishop and the monks into canons—the better to keep an eye on local heretics. In decline for centuries, this forgotten town still has some of its walls and half-timbered houses, as well as a fine Romanesque **cathedral**—from the 14th century, a typically archaic building in a region that disdained the imported Gothic of the hated northerners. Though remodelled in trashy Baroque inside, the exterior has remained largely unchanged, including a beautiful apse with carved capitals attributed to the Master of Cabestany. Other good Romanesque churches with carvings are west of Castelnaudary at **Mas-Stes-Puelles** and **Baraigne** (take the D33 and D218 from Castelnaudary) and at **Montmaur**, north of the D113 on the D58; the latter two preserve examples of small circular roadside crosses, like those in the Carcassonne museum. In medieval times this region had hundreds of them; almost all have been destroyed or moved.

West of Castelnaudary, the Canal du Midi loses most of its tranquillity, as both the *Autoroute des Deux Mers* and the N113 move in to keep it company on the way to Toulouse. On the borders of the *département*, at **Port-Lauragais** the canal passes its highest point. Figuring out how to cross it was Paul Riquet's biggest challenge; he solved it by an elaborate system of smaller canals and reservoirs, carrying water to the locks from as far as 50km away, in the Montagne Noire. Near Port-Lauragais there is a large obelisk in Riquet's honour (erected by his descendants in 1825, the year the canal finally turned in a profit!) and a small museum-cum-information centre about the canal, accessible from the autoroute. The same Port-Lauragais rest area also has the French rugby hall of fame, **L'Ovalie** (*open mid-May–mid-Sept 9–8, otherwise 10–6; adm*) in a curiously designed building representing a scrum, a pass and a pair of goal posts: there's the history of rugger, its spread in France (in the southwest, it's more popular than football), its heroes, posters, and films of France's greatest tries.

South of Castelnaudary are more reminders of the Cathars and their oppressors. **Fanjeaux**, on the D119, began its career as *Fanum Jovis*, from an ancient temple of Jupiter; from that you can guess that the town, like almost all the sites dedicated to the god of thunder and storms, is on a commanding height, with a wide view over the Lauragais plains. Fanjeaux was a hotbed of Catharism and gained its fame in 1206, when St Dominic himself came from Spain to live here as a missionary to the heretics—quite peacefully and sincerely, though his Dominican followers would be the Church's chief inquisitors and torture-masters for centuries to come. They bequeathed Fanjeaux a 14th-century Gothic church, in the former Dominican monastery; a better work, the parish church of 1278, has a *trésor* full of unusual old reliquaries. St Dominic founded a monastery in nearby **Prouille**, after a vision from Fanjeaux, and it became a pilgrimage site. Unfortunately it was wrecked in the Revolution, and charmlessly rebuilt in the 19th century. South of Fanjeaux, on the way to Limoux, the villages are often laid out on a circular or even elliptical plan: Ferran, Brézilhac and La Digne, among others. They are medieval new towns or *bastides* (*see* Carcassonne); no one knows exactly why the medieval planners decided here to depart from their accustomed strict rectangularity, but there are clusters of them in Languedoc. They even have their own association, so if you want to know more, contact Association des Villages Circulaires, Maire de Paulan ✉ 34230 ✆ 04 67 25 00 08, 🖷 04 67 25 28 91.

Castelnaudary ✉ *11400*   ***Where to Stay and Eating Out***

The family-run, remodelled but still a bit old-fashioned ★**Grand Hôtel Fourcade**, 14 Rue des Carmes, ✆ 04 68 23 02 08, 🖷 04 68 94 10 67, is the classic place to sleep in bean town (apologies to Boston!). Even if you're not staying, its restaurant is the best in town, the place to experience gourmet *cassoulet* with goose *confits* or many less folkloric treats (*menus 80–130F*). *Closed Sun eve and Mon out of season*. Another highly respected pot of beans is dished up 11km southeast in Villepinte, at **Aux Deux Acacias**, D113, ✆ 04 68 94 24 67, 🖷 04 68 94 21 28, on menus of 69 or 165F; they also have inexpensive rooms.

West of Castelnaudary, **Auberge Le Cathare** at the Château de la Barthe in **Belflou** (✉ 11410), on an artificial lake off the D217, ✆ 04 68 60 32 49, 🖷 04 68 60 37 90, offers home cooking, peace and quiet, and pleasant rooms at bargain rates. Five km from St-Papoul, in **Verdun-en-Lauragais** (✉ 11400), the **Hôtel Sanègre**, ✆ 04 68 94 33 59, occupies a restored farmhouse, with a garden and a good, simple restaurant.

The Corbières

Thanks to wine, the Corbières has finally found its vocation. This scrubby, mountainous area, where landscapes range from classic Mediterranean to rugged Wild West, has been the odd region out since ancient times. As a refuge for disaffected Gauls, it was a headache to the Romans. In the Middle Ages, sitting astride the boundaries of France and Aragon, it was a permanent zone of combat. Local *seigneurs* littered the landscape with castles in incredible, impregnable mountain-top sites. Some of these became the last redoubts of the persecuted Cathars; nearly all of them are ruined today. For anyone with clear lungs and a little spirit, exploring them will be a challenge and a delight. Amidst the lonely landscapes of limestone crags and hills carpeted in *maquis*, the vineyards advance tenaciously across every dusty, sun-bleached hectare of arable ground.

Getting Around

SNCF rail-lines make a neat square around the Corbières—they define its boundaries almost exactly, but none of them ventures inside the region. The only useful one is from Carcassonne, following the Aude and then turning east through the Fenouillèdes, stopping at Limoux, Alet-les-Bains, Couiza, Quillan and St-Paul-de-Fenouillet on its way to Perpignan. Don't count on buses either. There are some regular services from Perpignan's *gare routière* up the Agly valley to Maury, St-Paul and Quillan, and one a day through the heart of the Fenouillèdes to Sournia.

If you're **driving** keep the tank full. The Corbières is the badlands of France, and its unique fascination comes from traversing spaces as empty as central Anatolia with all the specific charms of France close at hand. There are few good roads.

Here are two possibilities for a quick tour: from Narbonne, the D613/D3 passing Fontfroide and Lagrasse, then south on the scenic D212, rejoining the D613 and ending up in Couiza. Alternatively, the N9/D611A/D611/D14/D10/ D7 from south of Narbonne passes the best of the wine country, the castles of Aguilar, Peyrepertuse and Quéribus, and the Gorges de Galamus, ending up on the main D117 route for Perpignan.

Tourist Information

Lagrasse ✉ 11220: 6 Blvd de la Promenade, ✆ 04 68 43 11 56, 📠 04 68 43 16 34.

Lézignan-Corbières ✉ 11200: Cours de la République, ✆ 04 68 27 05 42, 📠 04 68 27 62 47.

St-Paul-de-Fenouillet ✉ 66220: ✆ 04 68 59 07 57.

market days

Lagrasse: Monday. **Lézignan-Corbières**: Wednesday. **Tuchan**: Thursday.

local wines

Corbières: Along the D611A, you can visit Château Gléon, west of Portel (✆ 04 68 48 28 25); or nearby, the vast Château Lastours, Portel-des-Corbières (✆ 04 68 48 29 17). The new superstar of Corbières has to be Domaine de Cascadais, but the domaine is not open to visitors. Good rosé (as well as red) comes from Château La Baronne near Fontcouverte (✆ 04 68 43 90 20).

Fitou: Try the Cave Pilot, or Cave de Villeneuve-les-Corbières (✆ 04 68 45 91 59); Château de Nouvelles (✆ 04 68 45 40 03), on a side-road north of Tuchan; or Château L'Espigne, the very best of the bunch, at Villeneuve-les-Corbières (✆ 04 68 45 91 26).

Maury: Visit the village cooperative, Ave Jean Jaurès, Maury (✆ 04 68 59 00 95).

Lézignan-Corbières and Lagrasse

The Corbières' 'capital', **Lézignan-Corbières**, lies half way between Carcassonne and Narbonne, and offers, besides a few places to flop, an introduction to what the *pays* does best:

the **Musée de la Vigne et du Vin**, 1 Rue Necker (*open daily 9–7; adm*). Just south of Lézignan, on the other side of the autoroute, **Fabrezan** remembers the Corbières' most famous son in the **Salle du Souvenir Charles Cros** (© 04 68 43 61 11, in the Mairie). Cros (1842–88) was a poet and would certainly be better known had he not also been the unluckiest inventor ever. In 1869 he invented a process of colour photography at exactly the same time as Ducos de Hauron, who got the credit for it, and in 1877 he invented the phonograph and discovered how to record sounds at the same time as Edison, who beat him to the patent office.

This northern part of the Corbières has more monasteries than castles. The greatest of these was the Abbey of Fontfroide, just west of Narbonne (*see* p.426). Continuing in that direction on the D613/D3 takes you to **Lagrasse**, a walled medieval village that grew up around a Benedictine abbey founded in the 8th century and chartered by Charlemagne himself. Some of the houses date back to the 14th century, while the walls and the graceful arched **Pont Neuf** are from the 12th. The bridge leads to the **Abbey**, partly in ruins and partly the restored home of a Byzantine Catholic monastic community, © 04 68 43 13 97 (*open daily 10–12 and 2–6, 2–7 in summer, guided tours*).

Southwest of Lagrasse, in one of the remotest corners of the Corbières, there is a remarkable country church at **St-Martin-des-Puits**. The oldest part, the choir, was built in the 900s, and the nave has some still older capitals, recycled Merovingian pieces. The fanciful frescoes all around are 12th-century (ask at the mayor's house for the key).

Aguilar and Quéribus

The humble, two-lane D611 and D14 were the medieval main routes through the Corbières, connecting with the passes over the Pyrenees to Spain. Castles occur with the frequency of petrol stations on a motorway; before the kings of France asserted their authority, one wonders how many times the poor merchants had to pay tolls. Even the landscape is suggestive of castles, with limestone outcrops resembling ruined walls and bastions.

All of the real strongholds are in ruins today; the first, one of the smaller models, is at **Durban-Corbières**, in the centre of the wine-growing region; it was built by the kings of Aragon. **Tuchan**, another typically stark and dusty Corbières village, has no fewer than three ruined castles; the best of them, the impressive **Château d'Aguilar** (one of the 'five sons of Carcassonne'—along with Puilaurens, Quéribus, Peyrepertuse, and Termes) saw plenty of action: Simon de Montfort stormed it in 1210, but the French had to take it again from rebellious barons 30 years later; over the next 200 years the Spaniards knocked at the gate with regularity (it was always open; just a short climb from the end of the signposted road).

West of Tuchan the landscapes become higher and wilder. **Padern** has another castle, ruined despite rebuilding work in the 18th century, so does **Cucugnan**, a colourful little village. Both these towns offer scenic detours—from Padern, north through the **Gorges du Torgan**, and from Cucugnan, south through the spectacular **Grau de Maury**, the Corbières' back door.

Cucugnan's landmark is obvious from a distance, the picture-postcard **Château de Quéribus**, (*open daily 10–6, July and Aug til 8pm, in Feb, Mar, Nov, and Dec weekends only 10–5, closed Jan; adm*), balancing nonchalantly on a slender peak, a half-mile in the air over the gorge. Quéribus was the last redoubt of the Cathars; a small band of bitter-enders held out against the French for months here in 1255. Probably the best maintained of the Corbières castles, it's also the most difficult to reach—a 30-minute vertical climb. Admission includes an optional stop at the Achille Mir theatre to hear the famous speech of the parish priest of

Cucugnan, from the story in Alphonse Daudet's *Lettres de Mon Moulin*. And who was Achille Mir? The local scribe who wrote the story that Daudet shamelessly plagiarized for his own.

Château de Peyrepertuse

Open April–Sept 10–7, July and Aug 9–9; adm; at other times, free—there's no gate.

Castles atop mountains will be nothing new by now, but nowhere else, perhaps, is there a bigger castle atop a taller, steeper mountain. If the air is clear, and you know where to look for it, you can see Peyrepertuse from any bit of high ground as far as the coast. From Cucugnan, it is an unforgettable sight, a white, limestone cliff rising vertically up to the clouds, crowned by a stretch of walls and towers over 777ft long. Close up, from the bottom of the cliff, you can't see it at all.

Probably begun in the 10th century, Peyrepertuse was expanded to its present dimensions by St Louis in the 1240s. As important to the defence of France's new southern border as Carcassonne, Peyrepertuse was intended as an unconquerable base, big enough to hold a large force that could come down and attack the rear of any Aragonese invader. As you will see when you climb up to it, attacking the place would be madness; no one ever tried. The vertiginous road to the castle starts from the village of Duilhac; from the car park it's an exhausting 20-minute struggle up to the walls. The entrance leads into the **Château Vieux**, the original castle, rebuilt by St Louis. Here you'll discover one of Peyrepertuse's secrets; the castle may indeed be long, but conforming to its narrow site, it is in places only a few yards across. Nearly everything is in ruins; the keep is still in good shape, and a large cistern and the ruined chapel can be seen directly behind it. Further up is a vast open space that held most of the barracks and stores; and above this, Louis added yet another citadel, the **Château St-Georges**, with another keep and chapel.

Do you need more castles? North of Peyrepertuse, in the wildest, least-travelled part of the Corbières, there are at least four more, starting with one at **Auriac**, an old copper-mining village; nearby, at La Grave is an unusual 9th- to 12th-century country church, the **Chapelle de St-André**. A bit further north, castles at **Termes** (*open 9–7.30 in July and Aug, other times 10–5, weekends only Nov, Dec, Feb and Mar, closed Jan; adm*) and **Durfort** are less than 5km apart. Both the strongholds of local barons, both were besieged and taken by Simon de Montfort under the pretext of the Albigensian Crusade: Termes held out for four months, until a lack of water drove the defenders to surrender. Montfort also conquered the much better-preserved **Château de Villerouge-Termenès**, 14km to the east, ✆ 04 68 70 09 11 (*same hours as Termes*), the venue for a festival in August—all in honour of Guillaume Bélibaste, the last Cathar *parfait*, who was burned here at the stake in 1321.

There are no easy roads in any other direction from Peyrepertuse, but if you're heading west, rejoin the main route by way of the D7 and the white cliffs of the **Gorges de Galamus**, the most impressive natural wonder of the Corbières.

The Plateau d'Opoul

The southern border of the Corbières is a long rocky wall, crossed by the Gorges de Galamus and the Grau de Maury. Near the sea it spreads into a petite plateau, one of the most barren and isolated places in France. Don't be surprised to find tanks and suchlike growling across your path. The western half of the Plateau d'Opoul is one of the French army's zones for manoeuvres, the closest France can get to desert conditions. Most of the time, however, you won't see anyone at all, save old farmers half-heartedly trying to keep their ancient Citroëns on the road, on their weekly trip to the village to get a goose or a haircut. The village is **Opoul-Périllos**, a cosy place that shuts itself off from the surrounding void. It is a relatively new settlement; its predecessor, **Périllos**, is an eerie ruined village higher up on the plateau, now inhabited only by praying-mantises, with another castle nearby. Both castle and village have enormous stone cisterns. Water was always a problem here—indeed, everything was a problem, and the 14th-century Aragonese kings who built both village and castle had to bribe people with special privileges to live on Opoul. Today there are vineyards, but until very recently the only real occupation was smuggling. Near the castle, a rocky side-road leads west into the most desolate part of the plateau; at a spot called La Vall Oriole, you'll see a massive, lonely limestone outcrop with a door at the bottom (locked). Sometime in the early Middle Ages, this rock seems to have been hollowed out by a community of cave-dwelling monks, like the famous ones of Cappadocia in Turkey.

Tautavel and the Fenouillèdes

Descending from Opoul to the southwest, the D9 passes through some romantically empty scenery towards **Tautavel**, a pretty village under a rocky escarpment. Throughout Europe, prehistoric man picked the unlikeliest places to park his carcass. Around Tautavel, human bones have been found from as far back as 450–680,000 BC, making 'Tautavel Man' a contender for the honour of First European; the only older finds come from Isernia, an equally unpromising spot in southern Italy. Back then, the climate was quite different, and Tautavel Man had elephants, bison and even rhinos to keep him company. Palaeolithic bones have become a cottage industry—over 430,000 have been found, especially in a cave called the **Caune de l'Arago** (north of the village, *open June–Aug for guided tours*)—the best being displayed in the village's **archaeological museum**, © 04 68 29 07 76, which shares a car park with the wine cooperative and a stand selling honey perfumed by the Opoul *maquis* (*open 10–12 and 2–6, July and Aug 9–9; adm*).

From Tautavel, the D9 continues south into the valley of the Agly, joining the D611 and finally the D117 west, the main route inland from the coast to Foix and the Ariège. This road passes **Maury**, a village famous for its dessert wines and its pottery of deep blues and greens, and St-Paul-de-Fenouillet, better known for almond cookies. The next village, **Caudiès-de-Fenouillèdes**, has become something of an art centre, especially in the summer. To the north, you will see the Pic de Bugarach, the highest crag in the Corbières. Three km to the south, the hamlet of Fenouillet is guarded by three more ruined castles, all within a few hundred yards of each other (for the crow, anyhow). Beneath them, the simple medieval chapel of **Notre-Dame-de-Laval** has a wonderful polychrome wooden altarpiece, dated 1428. Higher into the mountains, there's yet another mountain-top castle to climb (about 20min): **Puilaurens** (*open Easter—mid-Nov, 9–7; adm*) Even Simon de Montfort couldn't get into this one; its fortifications were the most complete and sophisticated of any in the region. The Cathars who took refuge here only surrendered in 1256, after the fall of Monségur.

The Agly valley and the mountains around it make up the **Fenouillèdes**—or *Fenouillet*, in Catalan, the northernmost region of medieval Catalunya. Though equally mountainous, its scenery makes a remarkable contrast to the dry and windswept Corbières. Here, limestone gradually gives way to granite, the true beginning of the Pyrenees. Much of it is covered by ancient virgin forest, broken by quick-flowing streams and scenic ravines. The best parts are the **Forêt d'Ayguesbonnes-Boucheville** southwest of Fenouillet, and the **Forêt des Fanges**, in the steep mountains behind Puilaurens Castle.

The D619 south from St-Paul-de-Fenouillet is the only good road through the Fenouillèdes, passing through **Sournia** on the Desix river, the only real town. Along the way, be sure to stop at **Ansignan** to see its **Roman aqueduct**, a rustic, seldom-visited version of the famous Pont du Gard. An arcade of 551ft, with 29 arches, carries it over the Agly; it is still in use, carrying water to the vineyards, and you can walk over it, or follow the channel towards the village. The question is why the Romans built it, with no nearby towns for it to serve. It is unlikely that agriculture on the coastal plains was ever so intensive as to merit such a work. One possibility is an important patrician villa—such things were often cities in themselves—but no traces of one have been discovered. Signs in Ansignan point the way up to a **dolmen** and to **Felluns**; there are wide-ranging views over the mountains just beyond, along the D7 south to Sournia.

Where to Stay and Eating Out

For tourism, the Corbières is virgin territory. Not only will you have trouble finding a petrol station, but accommodation is scarce—the price you pay for experiencing the least-touristed corner of the Midi. Most people make daytrips, hopping between Carcassonne, Narbonne, Perpignan and Quillan. But if you want to spend some time exploring, here are most of the possibilities:

Lézignan-Corbières ✉ 11200

Lézignan-Corbières has three inexpensive hotels, among them ★★**Le Tassigny**, Place de Tassigny, ✆ 04 68 27 11 51, 🖂 04 68 27 67 31. The town has a good restaurant, **Le Patio**, on the outskirts, on Blvd Général Sarrail, ✆ 04 68 27 42 23 (*best for seafood, menus 60–200F, closed Mon eve, Tues eve*), and a popular, better-than-average pizzeria, **Stromboli**, 43 Cours Lapeyrouse, ✆ 04 68 27 00 81.

Lagrasse ✉ 11220

Lagrasse gets a few visitors for the abbey, and there are simple hotels; try the **L'Auberge St Hubert**, 9 Blvd de la Promenade, ✆ 04 68 43 15 22, 🖂 04 68 43 16 56 (*decent restaurant with menus from 68–180F*). *Closed Jan–Mar.*

Ornaisons ✉ 11200

For a luxury base on the northern edge of the Corbières, there is the ★★★**Relais du Val d'Orbieu**, on the D24, ✆ 04 68 27 10 27, 🖂 04 68 27 52 44, north of Fontfroide Abbey. A modernized *mas* among the fields north of the village, it has tennis and a pool and all the amenities, including an excellent restaurant serving fish baked with rosemary and other delicacies (*menus from 175–375F*). Southwest of Frontfroide, lost in the middle of nowhere at **Fontjoncousse** (off the D611, south of Thézan-des-Corbières), join the Narbonnais who make a special trip to dine at the **Vieux Puits**, Ave de Ripaud, ✆ 04 68 44 07 37, to feast on the gorgeous cuisine of Gilles Goujon, who learned a trick or two at the Moulin de Mougins (*menus at 148, 220 and 315F*). *Closed Sun eve and Mon out of season.*

Maury ✉ 66460

Well worth the 20min drive from Maury, **L'Auberge du Grand Rocher**, Rue Eloi Tresserres, in **Caramany**, ✆ 04 68 84 51 58, is a simply furnished restaurant in a pretty hill town; the terrace has lovely views over the valley. The husband-and-wife team prepare perfectly cooked local specialities at moderate prices: *confit de canard* with potatoes roasted in duck fat (the best in the region), or roast lamb with thyme. Leave room for *crème catalan* and a glass of Banyuls. *Closed Nov; always call ahead to check they're open.* If you're passing by **Estagel** near Tautavel on the D117, you can eat and/or sleep well and economically at the ★★**Hôtel des Graves**, owned by the local wine barons (9 Blvd Jean-Jaurès, ✆ 04 68 29 47 04, 🖂 04 68 29 47 04); Catalan specialties served with wine from you know where, from 65F.

Cucugnan ✉ 11350

There's one choice but it's a good one: the ★★**Auberge du Vigneron**, 1 Rue Achille-Mir, ✆ 04 68 45 03 00, 🖂 04 68 45 03 08, with cosy rustic rooms and a restaurant in a former wine cellar, serving simple but fragrant dishes (*menus from 80F*). *Closed Sun eve and Mon in the off season, and mid-Dec–mid-Feb.*

St-Paul-de-Fenouillet ✉ 66220

St-Paul has two comfortable Logis de France hotels: ★★**Le Chatelet**, Rte de Caudies, ✆ 04 68 59 01 20, 🖂 04 68 59 01 29, with a pool, and the cheaper, smaller, central ★**Relais des Corbières**, 10 Ave Jean Moulin, ✆ 04 68 59 23 89.

Gincla (near Puilaurens) ✉ 11140

★★**Hostellerie du Grand Duc**, 2 Rue de Boucheville, ✆ 04 68 20 55 02, 🖂 04 68 20 61 22, occupies a handsome old mansion with a shady garden; the restaurant serves tasty French classics from 120F with wine. *Closed Wed in the off season; hotel closed mid-Nov–mid-Mar.*

The Valley of the Upper Aude

Near the castle of Puilaurens, the D117 joins the course of the Aude, passing northwards through a spectacular canyon, the **Défilé de Pierre-Lys**. The *pays* that begins here is called the **Razès**, a sparse, scrubby, somewhat haunted region, the back door to the Corbières. As *Rhedae*, it has been known to history since the time of the Visigoths; according to author Henry Lincoln, the uncanniness begins with the Razès' sacred geometry: its five most prominent peaks, including the perch of Languedoc's conspiracy headquarters, Rennes-le-Château, describe a unique, perfect, natural pentangle. The precise measurements were repeated in the Middle Ages, in the geomantic placing of churches around Espéraza. Even in the off season, you'll see cars with number plates from far-away countries, cruising about, looking for goodness knows what.

Tourist Information

Quillan ✉ 11500: Place de la Gare, ✆ 04 68 20 07 78, 🖂 04 68 20 04 91.
Chalabre ✉ 11230: Cours Colbert, ✆ 04 68 69 26 28, 🖂 04 68 69 29 29

market days

Quillan: Wednesday. **Espéraza**: Thursday and especially Sunday. **Couiza**: Tuesday and Saturday. **Chalabre**: Saturday.

Quillan, Espéraza and Couiza

Quillan, the first town after the Pierre-Lys canyon, makes its living from manufacturing shoes; it has an odd, perfectly square castle from the 1280s, a ball and three *quilles* (bowling pins) on its coat of arms, and does its bit to cash in on the Cathars with models of the castles and exhibits at the **Espace Cathare,** by the tourist office in Place de la Gare (*open daily 10–12 and 2–6; adm*). Dinosaurs were fond of the Aude valley and especially **Espéraza,** just north, where they left a nest of eggs, now displayed with fossils, skeletons, dioramas and more Jurassic era souvenirs at **Dinosauria,** Ave de la Gare (*open Mon–Sat 10–7, 10–12 Sun; adm*). In later years the village was nothing less than 'the world's second greatest maker of hats in the first half of the 20th century' and, like many a hat manufacturer, curses the day JFK set the fashion for going without. The village's glory days are recalled in the **Musée de la Chapellerie** (*open daily 10–12 and 2–6; adm*).

The Razès' biggest town, gritty and peculiar **Couiza,** makes even more shoes, and plastic panelling too. Its landmark is the imposing Renaissance château of the Ducs de Joyeuse, who made nuisances of themselves on the Catholic side during the Wars of Religion; their descendants have just turned the old homestead into a hotel (*see* below). To the east of Couiza are **Rennes-les-Bains,** a small spa in business since the time of the Romans (finds from the ancient baths are in the **Villa Marie**) and **Arques,** where a few Cathars still go about their business. Arques has a tall, elegant, Gothic 13th-century **château**—or just the keep of one, framed in turrets as Simon de Montfort took it from the Termes family in 1231 and gave it to one of his lieutenants (*open April–Oct, 10–5, til 8pm in July and Aug, other times weekends only, closed Jan; adm*). The same ticket admits you to the **Maison de Déodat Roché** (1877–1978); a famous Cathar historian, Roché was born in Arques, and his house in the centre of the village has a permanent exhibition on Catharism in the 19th and 20th centuries.

Rennes-le-Château

This is a terrible place.

Abbé Saunière's inscription over the door of Ste-Marie-Madeleine

Whatever is haunting the Razès, it resides here, in a woebegone mountain-top village above Couiza that is possibly familiar to more people in Britain and America than Carcassonne. The fun began in the 1890s, when the young parish priest, Berenger Saunière, began spending huge sums of money on himself and on embellishing his church. The story, and the speculation, hasn't stopped unfolding since. In a nation addicted to secret conspiracies, preferably with a medieval pedigree, every sort of shadowy religious cult and fantastico-political faction has got its oar in, from neo-fascists to neo-Jews, along with monarchists, satanists, dilettante Cathars and dressed-up Templars.

With its few dusty streets, spectacular views over the Aude valley, and a super-abundance of mangy dogs, Rennes-le-Château is an unsurpassed vortex of weirdness. Its one permanent business is an occult bookshop, where you can pick up a copy of the 1970s bestseller *Holy Blood, Holy Grail,* the first and best account in English that attracted international attention to Rennes, describing Jesus' problematical but well-publicized western European tour, an escape from Israel after a faked crucifixion. It has been a recurring theme in French and English legend from the beginning ('And did those feet in ancient time,' etc.). Here, the idea is that Jesus came to Gaul with his wife Mary Magdalene (*see* p.331); both may have been buried in

Rennes, and their descendants were the Merovingian kings of France, deposed in the 8th century by a shady deal between the popes and Carolingians. Supposedly, the blood line has survived to this day.

Did Saunière discover proof of Jesus' tomb in Rennes and make his fortune by blackmailing the Vatican to keep his mouth shut? Or did he find the Holy Grail, or the treasure of the Visigoths, the Merovingians, or the Templars? The most fashionable theory these days leans towards the fabulous treasure of the Jews, stolen from Jerusalem by Titus in AD 10, and pillaged in turn by the Visigoths, who carted it off from Rome to Carcassonne in the 5th century. When Clovis, king of the Franks, took the Visigoths' capital of Toulouse, the treasure was secretly removed further away for safekeeping in the impregnable fortress at Rennes. Rennes became the capital of the region when Amairic, a Visigothic prince, married a Frankish princess, and is claimed to have eventually had a population of 30,000 (3000 would be closer to reality) before it was definitively sacked by the Aragonese in 1170, only to be destroyed again for good measure in Simon de Montfort's blitzkrieg.

When Berenger Saunière was appointed parish priest of Rennes-le-Château, the village was in a sorry state; even the 12th-century church was falling over. During the repairs on the church in 1891, Saunière found, under a statue of the Virgin (she stands on a stone carved with a cross set upside down—perhaps a Visigothic altar?), a parchment in a glass phial. Not long after, Saunière was spotted by the villagers, digging furtively most evenings in the local cemetery. One of his activities was the systematic defacement of the inscription on the tomb of the last Lady of Rennes, Hautpoul de Blanchefort (d. 1781), not knowing that someone had already copied it out in the early 1820s (it had Greek letters reading 'Et in Arcadia ego', i.e. death is present, even in Arcadia). Hautpoul, who died without heirs, had in her last hours of life confided some great secret to the parish priest, who left the enigmatic epitaph on her tomb. The same inscription, by apparently no coincidence at all, appears on the tomb in one of Nicolas Poussin's best known paintings. The background of his painting shows—surprise!—the distinctive profile of Rennes-le-Château.

After his nocturnal digs, Saunière began spending money like nobody's business, paving the road up to Rennes, and redoing the **church** dedicated (naturally) to Mary Magdalene (*open by the caretaker at 10.45, 11.45, 2.45, 3.45, 4.45 and 5.45, in summer till 7.45*), in a style the French have labelled 'Saint-Sulpicien', or the 'last reaction against the separation of Church and state'. This hardly seems to have been Saunière's main concern in his decorative schemes; rather, the somewhat unorthodox imagery of his bevy of plaster statues apparently distills a secret message to the initiated (note, for instance, that in the Holy Family both Mary and Joseph hold babies). Even Saunière got into hot water with the Church over the demonic figure that supports the font by the door, representing not Satan, but Asmodeus, the guardian of the treasure of Solomon. Outside the church, the statue of the Virgin still stands on her mysterious stone.

An adjacent **museum** (*open 10–12 and 2–6; adm*) relates some of this to the Cathars, who had a mysterious treasure of their own that they slipped out of Montségur and hid in parts unknown before the bitter end (*see* p.54).

You can visit the **Domaine du l'Abbé Saunière** (*open daily, 10–5; adm*), the genteely dilapidated bourgeois villa and garden that Saunère built for himself with his secret loot. A video by Henry Lincoln shown in the parlour tells the amazing tale (translated into French, though); under the abbé's peculiar library-belvedere, the **Tour Magdala**, you'll find documents and photos relating to his doings and the whole history of Rennes. Saunière died in 1917, leaving everything to his housekeeper Marie Dénaraud, who took the secret with her to the grave in 1953. From the top of the belvedere you can see a number of towers, fortresses and other ruins, their origin and purpose a matter of conjecture; the largest of them, the **Château de Blanchefort**, was probably wrecked by Simon de Montfort.

Further up the Aude, and Down into the Earth

The tourist office in Quillan can arrange visits of the **Grotte L'Agouzou**, 27km up the Aude on the D188. This is a spectacular stalactite cave, full of lovely delicate formations and crystals, but unlike others open to visitors. It hasn't been fitted out with walkways and lights; rather, small groups from eight to ten (children must be at least 10 years old) are taken in with lighted helmets, overalls, belts and lights to explore. Diehard couch potatoes should abstain. Visits begin at 9am and end at 5pm; bring a packed lunch.

Where to Stay and Eating Out

Quillan ✉ 11500

Quillan, the only town of any size for a long way in any direction, is a comfortable base for the eastern Corbières. On the north end of town, the modern ★★**Pierre Lys**, Ave de Carcassonne, ✆ 04 68 20 08 65, offers comfort, quiet, and the best meals in the town (*sea perch, confits and so on, from 65–230F*). Four other hotels and restaurants are on Blvd Charles de Gaulle by the train station and Quillan's indoor pool: ★★**Hôtel Cartier** at No.31, ✆ 04 68 20 05 14, 🖂 04 68 20 22 57 (*closed mid-Dec–mid-March*); rotund ★★★**La Chaumière**, at No.25, ✆ 04 68 20 17 90, 🖂 04 68 20 13 55, has cosy rooms and gratifying mountain cooking featuring trout and salmon (*menus 80–190F*); or least expensively, ★**Terminus**, at No.40 Rue Foix, ✆ /🖂 04 68 20 05 72.

Couiza ✉ 11190

Off the main road, set amid playing fields, the handsome 16th-century **Château des Ducs Joyeuse** ✆ 04 68 74 02 80, 🖂 04 68 74 14 65, has attractive rooms from 180–320F; the elegant restaurant serves the best meals around (*menus from 90–190F, closed Sun night and Mon in winter; hotel closes in Jan and Feb*).

Into the Limouxin

Before its right turn at Carcassonne, the Aude traverses a lovely, modest stretch of open rolling country, the Limouxin. Most of the roads here are still graced with their long arcades of plane trees—there isn't enough traffic yet to threaten them.

Tourist Information

Alet-les-Bains ✉ 11580: Ave Nicolas Pavillon, ✆ 04 68 69 93 56, 🖂 04 68 69 94 07.

Limoux ✉ 11300: Promenade du Tivoli, ✆ 04 68 31 11 82, 🖂 04 68 31 87 14.

market days

Limoux: Friday.

Blanquette de Limoux: The big firm Aimery-Les Arques, north on the D118, welcomes visitors (© 04 68 31 14 59). Best of the smaller producers are Domaine de Fourn, north on the D104 at Pieusse (© 04 68 31 15 03), and the Maison Antech, at Domaine de Flaissan on the D118 towards Carcassonne (© 04 68 31 15 88).

Côtes de la Malepère: around Malepère, Brugairolles, Malviès and Lauraguel. Try Château de Malviès (© 04 68 31 14 41).

Alet-les-Bains

Continuing down the Aude, **Alet-les-Bains** is one of the most beautiful and best-preserved medieval villages of Languedoc. A small spa since Roman times, Alet owes its prominence to the popes, who made it a bishopric in 1318. Its two jewels are the 14th-century church of **St-André** with frescoes and a fine west portal, and the nearby impressive Benedictine **Abbey**, founded in the 9th century and wrecked in the Wars of Religion. The tourist office next door has the key to the gate if you want to inspect the ruins (*open 9–2 and 3–5; adm*). The narrow streets of the village itself are an equal attraction, with a score of 13th- and 14th-century buildings such as the colonnaded house called the **Maison Romane**. Alet is still a thriving spa; it bottles its water to clean out your digestive tract and runs a casino to clean out your pockets.

Limoux

Even before you notice the vineyards, the civilized landscapes suggest wine. **Limoux**, the capital, is an attractive town, with a medieval bridge across the Aude, the **Pont Neuf**; this meets the apse and steeple of **St-Martin**, a good piece of Gothic, if anachronistic—though the church was begun in the 1300s, most of the work is from three centuries later. The centre is the arcaded **Place de la République**. Like Carcassonne's Ville Basse, Limoux was a *bastide*, and this was its market square; the streets of the old town around it make a pleasant stroll. Rue Blanquerie, named for the tanneries that once were Limoux's main business, is one of the streets with 15th- and 16th-century houses, like the 1549 **Hôtel de Clercy**, with a lovely and unusual courtyard of interlocking arches.

On the Promenade du Tivoli, a broad boulevard that replaced the town walls, the tourist office shares the home of the Petiet family with the **Musée Petiet** (*open daily 9–12 and 2–6; adm*), containing a collection of 19th-century paintings, and canvases by the museum's founder, Marie Petiet, a talented, neglected artist of the 1880s. A woman painter, and a woman's painter, her work brings a touch of magic to very domestic subjects, nowhere better than in the serene, luminous composition called *Les Blanchisseuses* (the washerwomen). Limoux's other attraction sounds like something P. T. Barnum would think up: **Catha-rama**, 47 Ave F. d'Egaltine, a 30-minute audiovisual spectacular on the history of the Cathars, in a choice of languages from Catalan to Japanese (*open Easter–1 Nov 10.30–12 and 2–6, July–Aug continuously 10.30–7; adm*).

In the sculptured countryside around Limoux, you can combine picnics and piety with a tour of three sites. The chapel of **Notre-Dame-de-Marceille**, just to the northeast, houses a 'Black Virgin', an icon from the 11th century. To the east, an exceptionally pretty side road (the D104) takes you to **St-Hilaire d'Aude** (*open July and Aug, 10–12 and 3–7, otherwise ring ahead, © 04 68 69 43 36*), an abbey founded in the 8th century; its Benedictine monks invented the bubbly *blanquette de Limoux* (*see* above). A graceful, double-columned Gothic cloister survives, along with the Romanesque abbey church, containing the white marble sarcophagus of St Sernin (d. 250), the patron of Toulouse, sculpted by the vigorous hand of the Master of Cabestany—one of his masterpieces. South of St-Hilaire, the monastery of **St-Polycarpe** is just as old, though not as well preserved. Its Romanesque church retains some bits of early frescoes and Carolingian carved altars.

Southwest of Limoux, you may venture into one of the most obscure *pays* in all France. Very few French people, even, have heard of the **Kercorb** (or Quercorb), a sleepy region that has plenty of sheep and plenty of trees. **Kercorb** is known for its apple cider, and little else. **Chalabre**, an attractive village of old stone houses with overhanging windows, is its capital.

At **Puivert**, 8km south, the **Musée du Quercorb**, ✆ 04 68 20 80 98 (*open 15 April–Sept, daily 10–1 and 2.30–6.30; adm*), will tell you everything there is to know (a reconstructed kitchen, cow bell manufacturing, and other crafts); it also includes eight reconstructions of 14th-century musical instruments, based on the sculptures of musicians found in the donjon of the **Château de Puivert**; its lords were famous as patrons and protectors of the troubadours (*open April–Oct, 8–8; adm*).

Where to Stay and Eating Out

Alet-les-Bains ✉ 11580

There are two choices: the riverside bishop's mansion, now the **★★Hostellerie de l'Evêché**, ✆ 04 68 69 90 25; plain and inexpensive, it nevertheless has a huge garden with century-old cypresses. *Closed Oct–Mar.* An alternative outside town is the **Domaine de Coursilhac**, ✆ 04 68 69 91 09, a simple and very inexpensive country inn, with a restaurant.

Limoux ✉ 11300

In town, the **★★★Grand Hôtel Moderne et Pigeon**, Place Général Leclerc, ✆ 04 68 31 00 25, ✉ 04 68 31 12 43, is the most luxurious choice. It has a history as strange as its name, having served as a convent, a *hôtel particulier* and a bank in the past. The restaurant is good, appropriately serving *magret de pigeon* on its 185F menu. *Closed Mon.* Just off Place de la République, **★★Des Arcades**, 96 Rue St-Martin, ✆ 04 68 31 02 57, ✉ 04 68 31 66 42, has seven comfortable rooms. The Aimery company runs the **Maison de la Blanquette**, 46 Promenade du Tivoli, ✆ 04 68 31 01 63, offering wine sampling and home cooking, with an emphasis on the local specialities, from Limoux's *charcuterie* to *confits* to the people's choice, a variation on *cassoulet* called *fricassée* (the Limouxins are very proud of it; Limoux even has an 'Association pour la Promotion de la Fricassée'). *Menus range from 75–210F. Closed Wed.* South of Limoux, just off the D118 at Cournanel, the **★Auberge de la Corneilla**, ✆ 04 68 31 17 84, is an inexpensive find; an unpretentious, restored farmhouse with nice rooms, and a lovely garden and pool.

ILLE-SUR-TÊT - LES ORGUES

Roussillon

Crossing the Agly river, bound for the southernmost angle of the French hexagon, you'll begin to notice a certain non-Gallic whimsy in the names of the towns. The further south you go in Roussillon the stranger they become: Llivia, Llous and Llupia, Eus and Oms, Molitg, Politg and Py. You'll also notice that some malcontents have decorated the yellow diamond 'priority road' signs with four red stripes, making them into little escutcheons of the long-ago Kingdom of Aragon. Streets signs appear in two languages. On your restaurant table, impossibly sweet wines and peculiar desserts will appear, and you may begin to suspect that you are not entirely in France any more.

You are in fact among the Catalans, in the corner of Catalunya that, for military considerations in the 17th century, was destined to become part of France. Like the other captive nations of the Hexagon—the Bretons and Corsicans, for example—most of Roussillon's people have rationally decided that being French isn't such a terrible fate after all. Catalan is spoken by relatively few (though numbers are growing), and this culturally passionate people stays in close touch with the rest of Catalunya, over in Spain, and in the squares of many villages they still do a weekly *sardana,* the national dance and symbol of Catalan solidarity.

Perpignan is the capital; around it stretches the broad Roussillon plain, crowded with the dusty, introverted villages that make all that sweet wine.

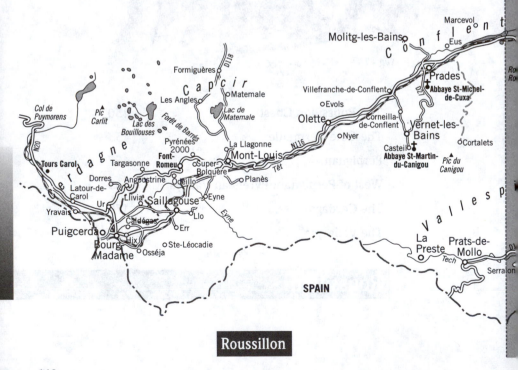

Roussillon

The real attractions are on the periphery: Collioure and the delectable Côte Vermeille on one side, and on the other valleys that climb up into the Pyrenees. The scenery is tremendous, even an hour's drive from the coast; among the pine forests and glacial lakes you can visit Vauban fortresses, ride the famous Little Yellow Train, and get an introduction to the surprising architectural and sculptural monuments of Catalunya's brilliant Middle Ages.

Leucate
Leucate-Plage
Fitou
Etang
Opoul-Périllos
de
Leucate
ou de
Port-Leucate
Salses
le-Château
Fort de Salses
Sales
Port-Barcarès
Espira-
de-l'Agly
Rivesaltes
Toreilles-Plage
Perpignan
Ste-Marie-Plage
Canet-en-Roussillon
Bélesta
Canet-Plage
Régleille
Tét
Cabestany
Les Orgues
Ille-sur-Têt
N116
St-Michel-
St-Cyprien-Plage
Bouleternère
de-Llotes
Thuir
La Catalane
St-Cyprien
Roque
Bages
Rouge
Castelnou
Elne
Prieure de
Forques
Serrabonne
Tech
Chapelle
Prunet et-
St-Génis-des-
Argelès-Plage
de la Trinité
Belpuig
Fontaines
D618
Argelès-sur-Mer
Llauro
Sorède
Collioure
Le Boulou
Cap Béar
Montesquieu
Laroque-des-
Notre-Dame
St-Martin-de-
Albères
de Consolation
Port-Vendres
Fenollar
Abbaye de
Banyuls-
Céret
Valbonne
Tour
sur-Mer
Gorges
Col du
Madeloc
Cap
de la Fou
Amélie-les-Bains
Perthus
Rederis
Arles-sur-Tech
Le Perthus
Cerbère
Cap
Portbou
Cerbère
La Jonquera

N

20 km
10 miles

449

The sand continues into Roussillon, to beaches once favoured by expert beach bum, Pablo Picasso. From Port-Barcarès southwards beach follows beach, some less accessible than others (these tend to be haunted by overweight nudists). Picasso's favourite was Collioure, with its three small stretches of sand.

best beaches

South of Port-Barcarès: empty miles of sand.

Collioure: because Picasso can't be wrong, but be prepared to share the space.

The Roussillon Coast

A geographical oddity, this run of coastline is nearly perfectly straight, and runs due north–south for 40km, from Port-Barcarès to Argelès. It isn't the most compelling landscape, but it is almost solid beach, and has been greatly developed since the 1940s.

Getting Around

The **coastal railway** from Narbonne to Spain passes through Leucate, Salses and Rivesaltes, dipping inland for Perpignan before returning to the coast; there are frequent services to Elne, and then Collioure and Cerbère. There are **buses** from the station in Perpignan to resorts where the train doesn't go, such as Canet and Port-Barcarès, as well as frequent services to Collioure and the Côte Vermeille. In the summer the tourist offices operate a **Bus Inter-Plages**, which stops at all ten resorts, from Barcarès and Cerbère.

Tourist Information

Port-Barcarès ✉ 66420: Place de la République, ✆ 04 68 86 16 56, 🖷 04 68 86 34 20.

Salses ✉ 66600: Place de la République, ✆ 04 68 38 66 13, 🖷 04 68 39 60 83.

St-Cyprien ✉ 66750: Quai Arthur Rimbaud, ✆ 04 68 21 01 33, 🖷 04 68 21 98 33.

Elne ✉ 66201: 2 Rue Docteur-Bolte, ✆ 04 68 22 05 07, 🖷 04 68 39 95 05.

market days

Salses: Wednesday. **Elne**: Monday, Wednesday and Friday.

local wines

Rivesaltes: Try some at Rivesaltes itself at the Domaine Cazes, 4 Rue Francisco-Ferrer (✆ 04 68 64 08 26).

Côtes du Roussillon: Made all over the *département*, but there are a few good estates to visit. In the hot corner around Perpignan, try Domaine Sarda-Malet (Chemin de Ste-Barbe, ✆ 04 68 56 72 38); or visit the Château de Jau on the D117 in Cases-de-Pène (✆ 04 68 38 90 10). The finest red and white wines can be found at Domaine Gaby in Calce (✆ 04 68 64 35 19).

Port-Barcarès and Around

South of Port-la-Nouvelle, the hill of **Cap Leucate** anchors the northern end of this coast, with new government-planned resorts at Leucate-Plage and Port-Leucate. These initiate perhaps the most animated but least attractive of Languedoc's resorts, beginning with Port-Leucate and continuing for 8km down to **Port-Barcarès**. You might like it; there's minigolf, shopping centres, 'thalasso-therapy', horse-riding, model airplanes, folkloric spectacles and windsurfing. Port-Leucate is mostly holiday bungalows, built around man-made canals so that everyone can park their boat at the front door. Further south, the beaches are less cluttered but harder to reach; back roads lead off the D81 to **Torreilles-Plage** and **Ste-Marie-Plage**.

Forteresse de Salses

The alternative to traversing this inferno means a voyage through the back end of the lagoon, the **Etang de Salses** (also called Etang de Leucate). The divorce of land and sea here is startlingly complete. Until the last few decades the malarial coast was utterly deserted, and no one in the region gave it a second thought; from the landward side of the lagoon in a few minutes you can be up in the rugged, dusty hills of the Corbières and Opoul (*see* previous chapter) where it is hard to believe any sea could be within a hundred miles. The only village on this side of the lagoon is **Fitou**, justifiably famous for one of the finest wines of Languedoc-Roussillon (though most Fitou wine comes from a nearby area of the Corbières).

After another 7km of total emptiness appears the last, lowest, and least spectacular of all this region's many castles—but the **Forteresse de Salses** was the most important of them all, *✆ 04 68 38 60 13 (guided tours on the hour daily exc Tues, open summer 9.30–7, June–Aug 9.30–6.30, winter 10–12 and 2–5; adm).* Built in 1497 by Ferdinand the Catholic, first king of united Spain, Salses was the last word in castles for its time, the masterpiece of a great military architect named Ramiro Lopez. Set squarely on the French-Spanish border, Salses was meant to guard Perpignan and the coastal road. It did not have a chance to do so until 1639, and sadly it was not up to the task. The Spaniards, caught by surprise, had only a small garrison at Salses; nevertheless, it required 18,000 Frenchmen and a month's siege to take it. The same year, a Spanish army spent three months winning it back. Both sieges were serious operations; the locals still go out cannonball-hunting for fun in the surrounding hills. When France acquired Roussillon in 1659, Salses no longer had a role to play.

At first glance, Salses looks strikingly streamlined and modern. It is a product of a transitional age, when defenders were coming to terms with the powerful new artillery that had made medieval castles obsolete. Salses is all curves and slopes, designed to deflect the cannonballs; its walls are not only incredibly thick (28ft on average, 50ft thick at the base), but also covered with heavy stone barrel-vaulting to protect the walkway at the top. Besides the fortress, Salses has a **Musée Catalan d'Histoire**, 14 Ave de Gaulle (*open daily, 2.30–7*), with weapons and relics from the wars between France and Spain—sorry, Catalunya.

The region around Salses and **Rivesaltes**, to the south, is famous for its inexpensive sweet wines, sold throughout France. Rivesaltes was the home of Marshal Joffre, now the small Musée du Maréchal Joffre, dedicated to the Battle of the Marne (*open Mon–Thurs 8–12 and 2–6, Fri till 5; adm*). In nearby **Espira-de-l'Agly** stands the impressive fortified Romanesque church of **Ste-Marie**, built in 1136 as part of a monastery by the bishops of Urgel in Spain (powerful Catalan clerics whose successors, along with the presidents of France, are still the joint tributary lords of Andorra). The businesslike exterior has one fine carved portal, but the lavish interior still comes as a surprise, with polychromed marbles and elaborate altarpieces from the 16th century.

Canet-en-Roussillon to Argelès

Back on the coast, **Canet-en-Roussillon** has long been the favourite resort of the Perpignanais. After taking a beating in the last war, it has been rebuilt without much distinction. It does have three **museums** to amuse the bathers on rainy days (*all open daily exc Tues 2–6, July and Aug 2–8pm; adm*): one of antique cars, one of ship models, and one of toys (the **Musée du Jouet**, a fun collection with exhibits from as far back as ancient Mesopotamia). There is also an **Aquarium** by the port, © 04 68 80 49 64, where the star attraction is that impossibly unlovely living fossil from the depths of the Indian Ocean, the coelacanth (*open daily exc Tues, 10–12, 2–6, July and Aug daily 10–8; adm*). South, past a long stretch of wild beach, good for windsurfing and kite flying, you'll find **St-Cyprien-Plage**, which looks just like Canet, only more so, with fancier restaurants, a 27-hole hole golf course, 33 tennis courts and a summer chamber music festival. It has two museums of its own, set back in St-Cyprien proper, 3km from the beach: the **Musée des Arts Catalan**, Rue J. Romains, dedicated to Catalan artists such as Maillol, Delfau and Bonel (*open daily exc Tues 2–6; adm*), and the **Musée Desnoyer,** Rue Emile-Zola, © 04 68 21 06 96 (*same hours*), with a small collection of lesser works by Picasso, Dufy, Chagall, Miró and especially François Desnoyer, who spent time here. South of St-Cyprien, **Argelès-Plage** makes some claim as the European Capital of Camping with 84 sites and a capacity for 100,000 happy campers. You've been warned.

Elne and Its Cloister

Between these last two resorts, set a little way inland atop a steep hill, the citadel of Elne has guarded the Roussillon plain for at least 2700 years. Its ancient name, *Illiberis*, is said to come from the Iberians. Hannibal sojourned here on his way to Italy, waiting to negotiate an alliance with the Celts to guard his rear; the locals, apparently unimpressed even with the elephants, made him pay a toll to pass through. The name-change came in the time of Constantine, to *Castrum Helenae*, after the Emperor's mother, St Helen, legendary discoverer of the True Cross. Through the Middle Ages, and until the 1500s, Elne remained the most important city in Roussillon and seat of the archbishops. The town is now reduced to some 6000 souls, having lost all its honours and status to Perpignan.

But they couldn't take away its **Cathedral**, a fortified church begun in 1069 with a wonderful stage presence, with its crenellated roof-line and stout, arcaded tower. Inside, in a chapel on the right is an Italianate 14th-century altarpiece of St Michael and there are some fine tombs, especially that of Ramon de Costa (1310). The **cloister**, © 04 68 22 70 90 (*open daily exc Sun, summer 9.30–6.45, winter 9.30–11.45 and 2–4.45; adm*), is perhaps the best in the Midi, and also the best-preserved. Capitals and pillars are decorated with imaginative, exquisitely carved arabesques and floral patterns. The four sides were completed in different periods, in roughly 50-year intervals; that closest to the cathedral is the earliest, from the 1100s, and its capitals show the influence of the sculptors of St-Michel-de-Cuxa (*see* below). Oddly, each generation of sculptors chose to repeat the subjects of their predecessors: all but the **north** gallery have central pillars carved with serpentine dragons and mermaids, spreading their forked tails; others capitals repeat scenes from the Old Testament. The little history **museum** tells the sad tale of the cloister's lost upper gallery, dismantled in 1827 and sold off at an auction in 1960. Elne, sadly, couldn't bid high enough; to see the other capitals you have to go to the Château Villeveque in Angers. Admission to the cloister includes the chance to climb the steps up to the tower and admission to the new **Musée Terras** across the square; the painter Terras was a friend of Matisse and Derain and the museum contains mainly his works.

There is more art, much of it sweet and bright and winsome, in **Bages**, 7km west of Elne, the **Musée International d'Art Naïf**, 9 Ave de la Méditerranée, ℰ 04 68 21 71 33 (*open daily exc Tues 10–12 and 2–7, continuously in summer, Sundays 2–7; adm*).

Where to Stay and Eating Out

Port-Barcarès and its homogenous fellows to the south are a little too young and raw and too commercial to have produced many places of distinction. Two of the class resort hotels in the area are in **St-Cyprien** ✉ 66750: the ★★★**Mas d'Huston**, ℰ 04 68 21 65 63, ✆ 04 68 21 64 64, adjacent to the golf course, also with a pool and tennis, and an excellent restaurant (*menus 160–270F*); and modern and comfortable lagoon-side. *Closed Feb*. ★★★**Ile de la Lagune L'Almandin**, Blvd de l'Almadin, ℰ 04 68 21 24 24, ✆ 04 68 21 00 00, has air-conditioned rooms, tennis, pool and the finest restaurant on the Catalan coast, where even the humble anchovy becomes an epiphany (*menus 160–360F*). *Closed Sun eve and Mon exc summer, Jan and Feb*. In **Elne** ✉ 66201, the delightful ★★**Le Weekend**, 29 Ave Paul Roig, ℰ 04 68 22 06 68, ✆ 04 68 22 17 16, has only 8 rooms and a garden terrace far from the crowds; good home cooking, too (*menu 80F*). *Closed Nov–mid-Feb*.

The Côte Vermeille

For anyone with the determination to follow France's long Mediterranean coast all the way to the end, there is a lovely surprise. After Argelès, the shoreline changes dramatically, climbing into the Pyrenees and a delicious southern world of crystalline rock, olive trees and uncanny sunlight, a 30km prelude to Spain's famous Costa Brava. Forgive yourself for cynically thinking that the name 'Vermilion Coast' might have been cooked up by tourist promoters—of course it was, just like the 'Côte d'Azur', 'Costa Smeralda' and all the rest. The red clay soil of the ubiquitous olive groves does lend the area a vermilion tint, but as far as colours go that is only the beginning. Every point or bend in the Mediterranean coast is a sort of meteorological vortex, given to strange behaviour: the Fata Morgana at the southern tip of Italy, the winds of the Mani in the Peloponnese or the glowing, subdued light of Venice. The Côte Vermeille gets a particularly strong dose of the tramontane wind, but also a remarkable mix of light and air, inciting the coast's naturally strong colours into an unreasonably heady and sensual Mediterranean spectrum. Henri Matisse spent one summer here, at Collioure, and the result was a milestone in the artistic revolution called Fauvism.

Tourist Information

Collioure ✉ 66190: Place du 18 Juin, ℰ 04 68 82 15 47, ✆ 04 68 82 46 29.

Port-Vendres ✉ 66660: Quai Forgas, ℰ 04 68 82 07 54, ✆ 04 68 82 53 48.

Banyuls-sur-Mer ✉ 66650: Ave de la République, ℰ 04 68 88 31 58, ✆ 04 68 88 36 84.

market days

Collioure: Thursday. **Port-Vendres:** Tuesday and Saturday .

Banyuls: 80 per cent of this wine passes through the Cellier des Templiers cooperative, Route de Mas-Reig (© 04 68 88 06 74), who receive visitors for tastings at their
magnificently vaulted 13th-century Cellier des Templiers. The Cave de l'Etoile, 26
Ave de Puig-del-Mas in Banyuls (© 04 68 88 00 06), is a cooperative where everything is done lovingly in the old-fashioned way; up the same street try the private
Domaine de la Rectoire (© 04 68 88 07 78).

Collioure

If the tourists would only leave it in peace, Collioure would be quite happy to make its living
in the old way, filling up barrels with anchovies. As it is, the town bears their presence as
gracefully as possible. In a way, Collioure is unspoiled—if it has 16 hotels for its 2500 inhabitants, it does not have a casino, a miniature golf course, or a water slide, or all the hype
projected on St-Tropez, that other unaffectedly beautiful resort discovered at the beginning of
the 20th century by the Fauves. Instead, you'll find every other requisite for a civilized
Mediterranean resort: a castle, a pretty church by the sea, three small beaches, a shady market
square with cafés—and warehouses full of anchovies.

History

It's hard to believe, looking at the map, but in the Middle Ages this village was the port for
Perpignan; with no good harbours on the dismal and (then) unhealthy coast to the north,
Perpignan's fabrics and other goods had to come to the Pyrenees to go to sea. In the 14th
century Collioure was one of the biggest trading centres of Aragon, but nearly the whole town
was demolished by the French after they took possession in 1659. They weren't angry with
the Colliourencs; the town was merely in the way of modernizing its castle's fortifications.
Our own century has no monopoly on twisted military logic. Collioure had to be razed in
order that it could be better defended.

The population moved into the part that survived, the steep hillside quarter called the Mouré,
where they have made the best of it ever since. Collioure was discovered in 1905 by Matisse
and Derain. Many other artists followed, including Picasso, but these two were the most
inspired by the place, and who put a little of Collioure's vermilion tint into the deep colours of
their first Fauvist experiments. A couple of Matisses are in nearby Céret, but the best are in
private collections, or in the Hermitage in St Petersburg. None are in Collioure. To rectify the
lack, the village has created the *Chemin du fauvisme*, placing copies of Matisse and Derain's
works on the spots where the two set up their easels.

Castle and Church

Collioure (or as the locals call it, Cotllures) is a thoroughly Catalan town, and the red and
yellow striped Catalan flag waves proudly over the **Château Royal**, © 04 68 82 06 43, dominating the harbour (*open daily Easter–mid-Nov 9–5; adm*). With its outworks it is nearly as big
as the town itself. First built by the Templars in the 13th century, it was expanded by various
Aragonese kings. The outer fortifications, low walls and broad banks of earth, were state-of-the-
art in 1669. The great Vauban, Louis XIV's military genius, oversaw the works and the
demolition of the old town. Collioure's fate could have been even worse; Vauban had wanted
to level it completely, and force everyone to move to Port-Vendres. The older parts of the castle
have been restored, and are open for visits, along with a small collection of modern art.

From the castle, cross the small stream called the Douy (usually dry and used as a car park) into the Mouré, the old quarter that is now the centre of Collioure. There is an amiable shorefront, with a small beach from which a few anchovy fishermen still ply their trade, and several brightly painted fishing smacks are usually pulled up to complete the effect. At the far end you'll see Collioure's landmark, painted by Matisse and many others: the church of **Notre-Dame-des-Anges**. The Colliourencs built it in the 1680s to succeed the original church destroyed by Vauban; they chose the beach site to use the old cylindrical lighthouse as a bell tower. On entering, you'll pass a neatly handwritten, hysterical missive from the parish priest, who must be hard beset in summer: 'No Dogs! Not even in the Corridor! They do not know where they are.'

The best thing about the church (under restoration at the time of writing) is that you can hear the waves of the sea from inside, a profound *basso continuo* that makes the celebration of mass here a unique experience. The next best are the retables, five of them, done between 1699 and 1720 by Joseph Sunyer and others. Catalan Baroque at its eccentric best, influenced by the Spanish Churrigueresque, often concentrated its finest efforts on these towering constructions of carved wooden figures, dioramas of scriptural scenes with intricately painted stage-drop backgrounds. Sunyer's are especially lifelike.

The second of Collioure's beaches lies right behind the church; really an old sand-bar that has become part of dry land, it connects the town with a former islet, the **Ilôt St-Vincent**, crowned with a tiny medieval chapel. A scenic footpath called the Sentier de la Moulade leads from near the church along the rocky shore north of Collioure. High above, you'll see **Fort Miradoux**, the Spanish King Philip II's addition to Collioure's defences, and still in military use.

Port-Vendres and Banyuls-sur-Mer

Few of us, probably, give any thought to anchovies and how they are apprehended in the open sea. It isn't, in fact, a terribly difficult operation. The diabolical Catalans have boats called *lámparos*, with big searchlights. They sneak out on warm summer nights, when the normally shy anchovies are making their promenade, and nab the lot. After spending a few months in barrels of brine, the unfortunate fish reappear, only to be stuffed into olives, a Catalan favourite. Much of this doubtful business goes on in Port-Vendres. This is a real port, modern-style, with none of the charm of Collioure. Louis XVI's government had big plans for developing Port-Vendres, all of which were scuppered with the Revolution; some grandiose neoclassical buildings remain from this programme, around the central **Place de l'Obélisque**, along with a 98ft obelisk, decorated with propaganda reliefs celebrating poor Louis' glorious reign.

From here, the coast juts out eastwards, with a picturesque small promontory called **Cap Béar**, topped by another of this area's many Baroque-era fortresses. Its monument to Sidi-Ferruch was originally erected in Algiers in 1930 to celebrate the centenary of French colonization; after 1962, when the Algerians didn't want the thing anymore, it was set up here. There are many isolated **beaches** in the vicinity, though they are hard to reach; most are south of the cape, including the one at Paulilles, near an abandoned dynamite factory (a mildly historic one, because it belonged to Alfred Nobel, inventor of dynamite and plywood, who used the profits to finance his Prizes).

Banyuls-sur-Mer (Banyuls de la Marenda in Catalan) is the next town along the picturesque coastal N114, a sleepy resort with a beach and mini-golf right at the centre. The heart of the Banyuls wine region, it is also the home of the **Fondation Arago**, an oceanographic laboratory affiliated to the University of Paris. Their excellent Aquarium of Mediterranean species, © 04 68 88 00 40, was built in 1883; don't miss the granddaddy lobster and sea anenomes and 250 kinds of birds (*open daily 9–12 and 2–6.30, till 10 in July and Aug; adm*). As for art, Banyuls has a good 11th-century Romanesque church, **La Rectorie**, on Ave du Puig-del-Mas (*open July and Aug, Tues and Fri at 3.30–4.45*) and takes credit for Aristide Maillol, perhaps the best-known French sculptor of the last century after Rodin, born here in 1861. He contributed the town's War Memorial, on the waterfront promontory, as well as many other monuments along the Côte Vermeille and in Perpignan; his tomb, documents tracing his life, and a few copies of works are in his old farm house, La Métairie, now the **Musée Aristide Maillol**, 4km up the Col de Banyuls road, © 04 68 88 57 11 (*open 10.30–12.30 and 2–5, May–Sept 10–12 and 4–7, closed Tues and hols; adm*).

If you don't care to go to Cerbère, or to Spain, there is an alternative to retracing your steps along the coast—an extremely scenic route through the mountains back to Collioure, along the steep and narrow D86. It begins from the back of Banyuls, beyond the railway overpass, and climbs through ancient olive groves on the lower slopes of the Monts-Albères. Several abandoned fortresses come into view, though none is especially easy to reach. This border region rivals even the Corbières for quantity of castles. There is also a ruined monastery, the Abbaye de Valbonne, on the heights to the west; the track to it begins at the pilgrimage chapel of Notre-Dame-de-Consolation. A little before this, the **Tour Madeloc** is the climax of the trip; it was a signal tower, part of the sophisticated communications network that kept the medieval Kings of Aragon in close contact with their borders.

Cerbère, and Beyond

You may well have already been here, but Cerbère won't bring back any pleasant memories—being herded from one train to another in the middle of the night (because Spanish railways still use a different track gauge) under the gaze of soldiers with submachine-guns and impossible customs men who do their best to make this seem like an old Hitchcock spy film instead of one of the busiest, most unexciting border rail-crossings in the EU. No one has ever seen Cerbère in daylight, but you might give it a try. The coast here is at its most spectacular (it's especially good for diving) and there are a few pebble beaches, never crowded. With its three small hotels, Cerbère is a miniscule resort, with a World's End air about it.

There is a lot to be said for pressing on even further, into Unoccupied Catalunya (the signs at the border still say 'Spain' for courtesy's sake). Barcelona, one of the most vibrant and creative cities in Europe today, is only two hours by train from Cerbère. Girona, with its exquisite medieval centre and unique cathedral, is half the distance. If you liked the Côte Vermeille, continue south for more of the same in the Costa Brava, often overcrowded though still nice (especially the northern parts). And if you can manage only one unambitious day trip into Spain, try Figueras, a short hop by train or a pleasant 50km drive along the C252; the Salvador Dalí Museum here, in the artist's home town, is an unforgettable attraction, the 'temple of surrealism', where you may water the plants in the garden by feeding pesetas into a Cadillac.

Where to Stay and Eating Out

Collioure ✉ 66190

In the centre, ★★★**Casa Païral Impasse des Palmiers,** © 04 68 82 05 81, ✆ 04 68 82 52 10, is the place for an agreeable stay; a dignified, Mansard-roofed palace a few streets from the shore. There is a wide choice of rooms, from the simple to the luxurious and expensive; also a pool and enclosed garden. *Closed Nov–April.* The pink and jolly ★★★**La Frégate**, Ave Camille Pelletan, ✆ 04 68 82 06 05, ▦ 04 68 82 55 00, is on the busiest corner of Collioure, but has been sound-proofed and air-conditioned; it has a good restaurant, decorated with *azulejos* (*mostly seafood; menus from 110–195F*). Picasso, Matisse, Dufy and Dalí all stayed at ★★**Les Templiers**, Ave Camille Pelletan, ✆ 04 68 98 31 10, ▦ 04 68 98 31 50, and owner Réné Pous was friend to them all. Original works cover the walls of this unique hotel, although the Picassos have been locked away since several were stolen by a 'guest' a few years ago. Each room has its own charm; reservations are imperative. **Boramar**, 19 Rue Jean-Bart on the Plage du Faubourg, ✆ 04 68 82 07 06, is a simple budget choice overlooking the busiest beach. *Closed Nov–Mar.* Another alternative is the **Ermitage** Notre-Dame-de-Consolation, above Colliour on the D86, ✆ 04 68 82 17 66, converted into a pleasant B&B (*doubles 180F*).

Dinner in Collioure need not necessarily include anchovies, but the rest of the local catch merits your attention. **La Marinade** on Place 18 Juin, ✆ 04 68 82 32 78, serves delectable seafood from simple sardines en papillote to an elaborate Catalan *bouill-abaisse; menus from 78 to 156F. Closed Jan.* Small and Spanish, **L'Andalou** just back from the port at 10 Rue de la République, ✆ 04 68 82 32 78, offers a long list of tasty seafood cooked *a la planxa*, in tapas, portions, or full courses.

Banyuls-sur-Mer ✉ 66650

Banyuls lacks Collioure's glamour, but also its high prices. The seaside ★★**Les Elmes**, Plages des Elmes, ✆ 04 68 88 03 12, ▦ 04 68 88 53 03, has pleasant rooms and an excellent restaurant, serving Catalan dishes with savoir faire; half *pension* is excellent value. By the port, ★★**La Pergola**, 5 Ave Fontaulé, ✆ 04 68 88 02 10, ▦ 04 68 88 55 45, has immaculate rooms and good fish. *Closed Dec and Jan.* ★**La Plage**, at the centre of the beach strip, ✆ 04 68 88 34 90, serves satisfying seafood dinners; various set menus at 130F including sole meunière, grilled salmon, or *parillade*, a Catalan mixed grill. For lunch, the lace-curtained neighbourhood favourite is **Chez Rosa**, Rue St-Pierre, ✆ 04 68 88 31 89; not much seafood, but tasty roast pork, couscous, chicken, and mushrooms (*85F menu*).

Cerbère ✉ 66290

The choice spot in Cerbère is ★★**La Vigie**, on the N114, ✆ 04 68 88 41 84, ▦ 04 68 88 48 87, built on the sea cliffs, with a fine view; it also has a restaurant. *Closed Dec and Jan.*

Perpignan

PERPIGNAN DEAD CITY is the slogan the local anarchists write on the walls, and if that's slightly premature, you can't help wondering about a town named after a reactionary murderer, one that has let its most beautiful Gothic monument become a hamburger franchise, and which highlights its tourist brochure with a photo of its trucking terminal. And how can any self-respecting city of 114,000 support 23 foxtrot academies?

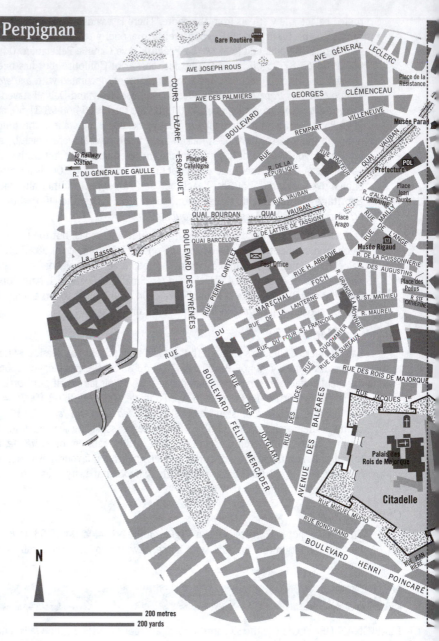

Perpignan

Gare Routière

AVE GÉNÉRAL LECLERC

AVE JOSEPH ROUS

Place de la Resistance

AVE DES PALMIERS

GEORGES CLÉMENCEAU

VILLENEUVE

BOULEVARD

REMPART

Musée Parad

COURS LAZARE ESCARQUET

RUE

R. DE LA RÉPUBLIQUE

RUE PASTEUR

QUAI VAUBAN

POL

Préfecture

To Railway Station

Place de Catalogne

Place Jean Jaurès

R. d'ALSACE LORRAINE

R. DU GÉNÉRAL DE GAULLE

RUE VAUBAN

QUAI BOURDAN

QUAI VAUBAN

Q. DE LATTRE DE TASSIGNY

Place Arago

RUE DE L'ANGE

RUE DE MAILLY

QUAI BARCELONE

Musée Rigaud

M

La Basse

BOULEVARD DES PYRÉNÉES

RUE PIERRE CARTELET

Post Office

R. DE LA POISSONNERIE

R. DES AUGUSTINS

RUE H. ABBADIE

Place des Poilus

MARECHAL

FOCH

R. GRANDE LA MONNAIE

R. ST. MATHIEU

R. STE CATHERINE

RUE

DU

RUE DE LA LANTERNE

R. MAUREIL

RUE DU FOUR ST-FRANÇOIS

DUGOMMIER

RUE DES SUREAUX

RUE DES ROIS DE MAJORQUE

BOULEVARD

RUE

DES

RUE JACQUES I

DES

LICES

BALÉARES

RUE

JDIGLIARS

FÉLIX

AVENUE

Palais des Rois de Majorque

MERCADER

DES

Citadelle

RUE MIGUEL MUCIO

RUE BONDURAND

RUE JEAN RIÈRE

BOULEVARD HENRI POINCARÉ

N

200 metres
200 yards

There's a little craziness in every Catalan soul. In *Perpínyà* (as its residents call it), this natural exuberance is rather suppressed by French centralization. While grateful for the croissants, this former capital of the Kings of Majorca and the Counts of Roussillon is obviously a bit bored, and not a few Perpignanais hope that as Europe's frontiers melt away, the electricity of Barcelona may once again galvanize it along with the rest of greater Catalunya—note the

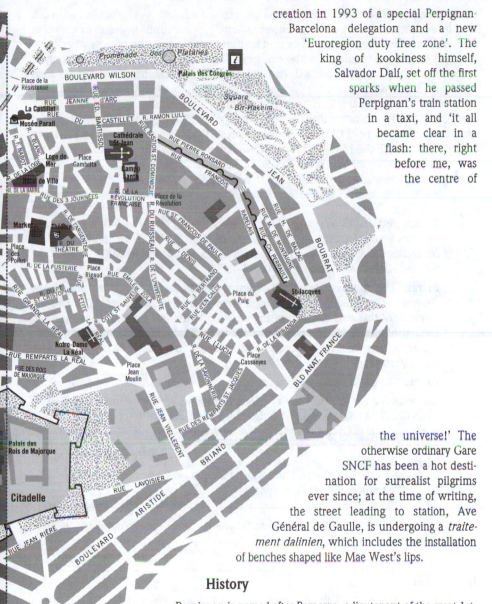

creation in 1993 of a special Perpignan-Barcelona delegation and a new 'Euroregion duty free zone'. The king of kookiness himself, Salvador Dalí, set off the first sparks when he passed Perpignan's train station in a taxi, and 'it all became clear in a flash: there, right before me, was the centre of the universe!' The otherwise ordinary Gare SNCF has been a hot destination for surrealist pilgrims ever since; at the time of writing, the street leading to station, Ave Général de Gaulle, is undergoing a *traitement dalinien*, which includes the installation of benches shaped like Mae West's lips.

History

Perpignan is named after Perperna, a lieutenant of the great 1st-century BC populist general, Quintus Sertorius. While Rome was suffering under the dictatorship of Pompey, Sertorius governed most of Spain in accordance with his astonishing principle that one should treat Rome's provinces decently. The enraged Senate sent out five legions to destroy him, but his army, who all swore to die if he were killed, defeated each one until the villainous Perperna invited his boss to a banquet in the Pyrenees and murdered him.

In 1197, Perpignan became the first Catalan city granted a municipal charter, and governed itself by a council elected by the three estates or 'arms'. Its merchants traded as far abroad as Constantinople, and the city enjoyed its most brilliant period in the 13th century when Jaime I, king of Aragon and conqueror of Majorca, created the Kingdom of Majorca and County of Roussillon for his younger son Jaime II. This little kingdom was absorbed by the Catalan kings of Aragon in the 14th century, but continued to prosper until 1463, when Louis XI's army came to claim Perpignan and Roussillon as payment for mercenaries sent to Aragon. Besieged, the Perpignanais ate rats rather than become French, until the King of Aragon himself ordered them to surrender. In 1493 Charles VIII, more interested in Italian conquests, gave Perpignan back to Spain. But in the 1640s Richelieu pounced on the first available chance to grab back this corner of the mystic Hexagon, and French possession of Roussillon and the Haute Cerdagne was cemented in the 1659 Treaty of the Pyrenees.

Getting Around

By air: Perpignan's airport is 7km northwest of the city, and linked by aerobus *navettes* from the station an hour before each flight (℅ 04 68 55 68 00); there are connections with Paris Orly on TAT (℅ 08 00 05 50 05) and AOM (℅ 04 68 50 59 59); and Nice on Air Littoral (℅ 08 03 83 48 34).

By rail: The railway station, Dalí's 'centre of the universe', is at the end of Ave Général de Gaulle and has frequent trains down to the Spanish border at Port Bou and a new TGV that cuts the journey to Paris to 6 hours. An early morning bus from Perpignan's station links up with the **Le Petit Train Jaune** into the Cerdagne, departing from Villefranche-Vernet-les-Bains (*see* p.465); call ℅ 04 68 96 56 62 for more information.

By bus: The coach station is to the north, on Ave Général Leclerc, ℅ 04 68 35 29 02.

Car and bike hire: You can hire a car from **Europcar**, 28 Avenue de Gaulle, ℅ 04 68 34 65 03, ✉ 04 68 34 02 60, and **Avis**, 13 Blvd du Conflent, ℅ 04 68 34 26 71. Bike hire is available at **Cycles Mercier**, 1 Rue du Président Doumer, ℅ 04 68 85 02 71.

Tourist Information

Inside the Palais des Congrès, Place Armand-Lanoux, ℅ 04 68 66 30 30, ✉ 04 68 66 30 26. **Post office**: Rue Dr Zamenhof.

market days

Daily in Place de la République, and Saturday and Sunday mornings in Place Cassanyes.

Le Castillet

When most of Perpignan's walls were destroyed in 1904, its easy-going river-cum-moat, La Basse, was planted with lawns, flower-beds, mimosas and Art Nouveau cafés. The fat brick towers and crenellated gate of **Le Castillet** in Place Verdun were left upright, for memories' sake; built in 1368 by Aragon to keep out the French, it became a prison once the French got in, especially during the Revolution. In 1946, a mason broke through a sealed wall in Le Castillet and found the body of a child, which on contact with the air dissolved into dust; from the surviving clothing fragments the corpse was dated to the end of the 18th century. And ever since, people have wondered: could it have been Marie-Antoinette's son, the dauphin Louis XVII? After all, the child buried in the Temple in Paris was known to be a substitute, and there have always been rumours that the Revolutionaries used the Dauphin as a secret bargaining chip in dealing with his Bourbon relatives in Spain.

Along with this mysterious ghost, Le Castillet houses a cosy museum of Catalan art and traditions, the **Musée Pairal**, ℗ 04 68 35 42 05 (*open daily exc Tues 9–6, summer 9.30–7; adm*), with items ranging from casts of Pau (Pablo) Casals' hands to a kitchen from a Catalan *mas*, complete with a hole in the door for the Catalan cat. Place du Verdun, by Le Castillet, is one of Perpignan's liveliest squares, while just outside the gate, the **Promenade des Platanes** is lovely place to walk, lined with rows of magnificent plane trees.

Loge de Mer to the Musée Rigaud

From Le Castillet, Rue Louis Blanc leads back to Place de la Loge, where the cafés provide a grandstand for contemplating Aristide Maillol's voluptuous bronze *Venus* and Perpignan's most beautiful building, the Gothic **Loge de Mer**, or Llotja, built in 1397 by the king of Aragon to house the exchange and the *Consolat de Mar*, a branch of the Barcelona council founded by Jaime I to resolve trade and maritime disputes. This proud and noble building of ochre stone, with its Venetian arches and loggia and ship-shaped weathercock, fell on hard times—but Perpignan takes good care of its monuments. The city rented the Llotja to a fast food chain, and now it looks very much the beggared pasha, flipping out Quick Burgers.

The neighbouring 13th-century **Hôtel de Ville** has been spared the Llotja's humiliation, probably because it still serves its original purpose: on Saturday mornings, its courtyard fills with blushing brides posing for photos by Maillol's allegory of the Mediterranean (as a naked woman, of course). The Hôtel is built of rounded river pebbles and bricks in the curious layer-cake style of medieval Perpignan; three bronze arms sticking out of the façade are said to symbolize Perpignan's three estates, or *bras*. To the right, the **Palais de la Députation Provinciale** (1447) is a masterpiece of Catalan Renaissance, formerly the seat of Roussillon's parliament and now housing dismal municipal offices. Rue Fabrique d'en Nabot, opposite the palace, was once the street of drapers: note the **Hôtel Julia** (No.2), a rare survival of a 1400s town house, with a Gothic courtyard.

South of the Députation, in Rue de l'Ange the **Musée Rigaud**, ℗ 04 68 35 43 40, is named after Perpignan native Hyacinthe Rigaud (1659–1743), portrait painter to Louis XIV (*open daily exc Tues 9.30–12 and 2.30–6, till 7 in the summer; adm*). Hyacinthe, master of raising the mediocre and unworthy to virtuoso heights of rosy cheeked, debonair charm and sophistication, is well represented, most famously in his portrait of the Cardinal de Bouillon, who beams with self satisfaction as chubby *putti* wallow in his worldly loot. All the hyper-sensitive alarms, however, are around the *Retable de la Trinité* (1489) by the Master of Canapost, painted for the 100th anniversary of the Consolat de Mar and showing, underneath, a fanciful scene of the sea lapping at the base of the pre-Quick Burger Llotja. Works by Picasso, Dufy, Maillol, Miró and a score of others, are upstairs.

Cathédrale de St-Jean and the Dévôt Christ

Just east of Place de la Loge unfolds Place de Gambetta, site of Perpignan's pebble-and-brick cathedral, topped by a lacy 19th-century wrought-iron campanile. Begun in 1324 but not ready for use until 1509, the interior is a success because the builders stuck to the design provided in the 1400s by Guillem Sagrera, architect of the great cathedral of Palma de Majorca. Typical of Catalan Gothic, it has a single nave, 157ft long, striking for its spacious width rather than its soaring height.

The chapels, wedged between the huge piers, hold some unique treasures, the oldest of which is a mysterious marble **baptismal font** (first chapel on the left). Pre-Romanesque, perhaps even Visigothic in origin, and carved from the drum of a Roman column to look like a tub bound with a cable, it bears a primitive face of Christ over an open book. Further up the left aisle, the massive organ was decorated in the 15th century with painted shutters and sumptuous carvings. On the pendentive under the organ note the Moor's head—a common Catalan conceit symbolizing wisdom, taken from the Templars, who exerted a powerful influence over the kings of Aragon. The jaw was originally articulated, to vomit sweetmeats on holidays; now it's stuck, gaping open. Beyond the Moor's head, in an 11th-century chapel from the original cathedral, is a pawn-shop window of dingy reliquaries, and the effigy of the cathedral's founder, Jaime's son Sancho, his feet resting on a Chinese lion.

The cathedral is proudest of its exquisite retables: on the high altar, the marble *Retable de St-Jean*, carved in a late Renaissance style in 1621 by Claude Perret; at the end of the left crossing, the **Retable des Stes Eulalie et Julie** (1670s); in the apsidal chapels, the painted wood *Retable de St-Pierre* (mid-1500s) and to the right, the lovely, luminous *Notre-Dame de la Mangrana* (1500)—its name 'of the pomegranate' comes from an earlier statue of the Virgin, which held a pomegranate, symbolic of fertility.

A door in the right aisle leads out to a 16th-century chapel constructed especially to house an extraordinary wooden sculpture known as the **Dévôt Christ**. Carved in the Cologne region in 1307, this wasted Christ, whose contorted bones, sinews and torn flesh are carved with a rare anatomical realism, is stretched to the limits of agony on the Cross. Almost too painful to behold, it comes straight from the gloomy age when Christendom believed that pain, contemplated or self-inflicted, brought one closer to God. It is an object of great veneration, and the Perpignanais claim that when the Christ's bowed head sags another quarter inch to touch His chest, the world will end.

Nearby in Place Gambetta is the entrance to the cathedral's **Campo Santo** (1302) (*open 10–12 and 2–5, 3–7 summer, closed Tues; also closed Sun in winter*), the only cloister-cemetery of its kind of France, the tombs decorated with fine bas reliefs; this being Perpignan, until the late 1980s it was used as offices by the local Gendarmerie. A door from the cloister leads into the striking 15th-century **Salle Capitulaire**, its complex ogival vaulting attributed to Guillem Sagrera. To the left of the cathedral's façade is Perpignan's oldest church, **St-Jean-le-Vieux** (1025), converted into an electrical generating station in 1890. Its Romanesque portal offers a very different view of Jesus from the German Dévôt Christ: the imperious and typically Catalan *Majestat* (Christ in Majesty).

Quartier St-Jacques

The piquant neighbourhood south of the cathedral, built on the slopes of Puig des Lépreux (Lepers' Hill) was once the *aljama*, or Jewish quarter of Perpignan. In its happiest days, in the

13th century, it produced a remarkable body of literature—especially from the pen of the mathematician and Talmudic scholar Gerson ben Salomon (author of the philosophical *Gate of Heaven*), as well as rare manuscripts and calligraphy, all now in Paris. After the Jews were exiled, the quarter was renamed St-Jacques, and inhabited by workingmen's families and gypsies, and most recently by Algerians. The 12th–14th-century church of **St-Jacques** is opulent and rich inside: there's a 'Cross of Insults' as in Elne, a statue of St James in Compostela pilgrimage gear (1450) and more fine retables, especially the 15th-century *Notre-Dame de l'Espérance*, featuring a rare view of the pregnant Virgin. In the early 1400s, while the fire-eating Dominican preacher St Vincent Ferrer was in Perpignan to advise in the dispute between Antipope Benedict XIII and Rome, he founded in this church the confraternity of the Holy Blood (*de la Sanch*) to bring religious comfort to prisoners condemned to death. As in Seville, the confraternity reaches a wider audience during Holy Week, when it dons spooky Klu Klux Klan-like hoods and bears a procession of holy floats (the *misteri*) while singers wail dirges from the crowd.

The Palace of the Kings of Majorca

Enclosed in a vast extent of walls, originally medieval and later enlarged by Vauban, the Palais des Rois de Majorque (*entrance in Rue des Archers, © 04 68 34 48 29, open daily May–Sept 10–6, winter 9–5; adm*) is the oldest royal palace in France, begun in the 1270s by Jaime the Conqueror and occupied by his son Jaime II after 1283. Yet for all its grandeur, only three kings of Majorca were to reign here before Roussillon, Montpellier, the Cerdagne and the Balearic islands were reabsorbed by Aragon in 1349. The scale of magnificence that they intended to become accustomed to survives, but not much else.

A rectangle built around a mastodonic but elegant Romanesque-Gothic courtyard, the palace is now a favourite venue for events, exhibitions and dancing the *sardana*, the Catalan national dance. The **Salle de Majorque**, or throne room, with its three vast fireplaces, and the double-decker chapels in the **donjon**, with the queen's chapel on the bottom and the king's on top, both offer hints at the exotic splendour of the Majorcan court. The sacristy was the entrance to a network of underground passageways that connected the palace to its enormous 147ft-deep wells, which also afforded Jaime II an escape from his fierce and unwelcome older brother, Pedro III of Aragon. The palace once stood in the midst of what the archives call 'Paradise'— partly enclosed terraced gardens, inspired by Moorish gardens on Majorca. A few traces remain to the right of the mightiest tower, the **Tour de Homage**. The narrow grid of streets under the palace, around the church of **St-Mathieu**, were designed by the Templar tutors of Jaime the Conqueror, although most of the buildings date from the 18th century.

Lastly, on the northwest side of town, the **Musée Josep Puig**, 42 Ave de Grande-Bretagne (*open 8.15–12 and 2–6, closed Sun and Mon; adm*), has an excellent collection of coins and medals from antiquity to modern times, with a special section on Catalan money.

Cabestany

Of all the villages ingested by Greater Perpignan, none is as celebrated as Cabestany (*Cabestanh*), 4km to the southeast. It produced a highly original Romanesque sculptor known as the Master of Cabestany who worked as far afield as Tuscany, and left his hometown church a **tympanum** of the *Dormition and Assumption of the Virgin*, and a scene of the Virgin in heaven, handing her girdle (definitely not Playtex) down to St Thomas.

Cabestany was also the home of the troubadour Guilhem de Cabestanh, who wrote some of the most popular love poems of the Middle Ages. He is most famous for a legend that reached even Boccaccio (*Decameron*, Day 4: 9). Guilhem loved and was loved by the wife of a knight, one Raymond of Castel-Rossello. When Raymond learned of their affair, he ambushed Guilhem, murdered him, and cut out his heart, which he gave to his cook to prepare with plenty of pepper. His wife ate it all, and praised the dish. 'I am not surprised,' said her husband, 'As you loved it so well when it was alive.' And he told her what she had eaten. But the lady kept her sang-froid. 'Sir,' she said, 'You have given me such an excellent thing to eat that God forbid any other food should again pass my lips.' And she leapt out of the window to her death.

Perpignan ✉ 66000 — *Where to Stay*

The ★★★★**La Villa Duflot**, Perpignan's only luxury hotel is at 109 Ave Victor Dalbiez, ✆ 04 68 56 67 67, ✆ 04 68 56 54 05—near the Perpignan–Sud–Argelès motorway exit, in the middle of an industrial zone! You can pretend to be elsewhere in the comfortable air-conditioned rooms, garden, or in the popular restaurant overlooking the pool (*meals around 250F*).

Near the tourist office, ★★★**Le Park**, 18 Blvd Jean-Bourrat, ✆ 04 68 35 14 14, ✆ 04 68 35 48 18, offers plush, air-conditioned, sound-proofed rooms with an old Spanish flair. Nicest in the centre, in a 16th-century building, the ★★★**Hôtel de la Loge**, 1 Rue Fabrique d'en Nabot, ✆ 04 68 34 41 02, ✆ 04 68 34 25 13, has pretty rooms, some with TV and air conditioning and a lovely inner courtyard. ★★**Le Maillol**, 14 Impasse des Cardeurs, ✆ 04 68 51 10 20, ✆ 04 68 51 20 29, occupies a 17th-century building: not too noisy, and convenient for the sights. The charming ★★**La Poste et Perdix**, 6 Rue Fabrique d'en Nabot, ✆ 04 68 34 42 53, ✆ 04 68 34 58 20, has kept much of its original 1832 décor and reasonable prices. *Closed Feb.*

Less expensive choices are near the 'Centre of the Universe' station: ★★**Le Helder**, Ave Général de Gaulle, ✆ 04 68 34 38 05; ★**Le Berry**, 6 Ave Général de Gaulle, ✆ 04 68 34 59 02; and the little **Auberge de la Jeunesse**, Ave de Grande-Bretagne, ✆ 04 68 34 63 32; bed and breakfast 70F (book in summer).

Eating Out

In the Park Hôtel (*see* above) **Le Chapon Fin** has been Perpignan's finest restaurant for years, as well as one of the prettiest with its Catalan ceramics. But it's the *tartare de saumon* and ravioli stuffed with scallops that keep its clients coming back for more, even all the way from Spain (*menus 180, 250 and 350F*). *Closed Sun and last two weeks in Aug.* But in Perpignan you can easily eat well for less: Art Deco **Le Vauban**, 29 Quai Vauban, ✆ 04 68 51 05 10, is another sure bet, with well-prepared *plats du jour* and menus from 100–135F. *Closed Sun.* **L'Echanson**, Quai Sadi Carnot, ✆ 04 68 34 92 81 also comes highly recommended (*excellent 100 and 170F menus*). *Closed Sun, July.*

Brasserie l'Arago, in pretty Place Arago, ✆ 04 68 51 81 96, is packed day and night; good food and pizza—not always a strong point with the Catalans; *menus from 78F.* Near Le Castillet, lively **Casa Sansa**, 3 Rue Fabriques Couvertes, ✆ 04 68 34 21 84, has average food but more than its share of Catalan flair: occasional live music and wine tasting in a 14th-century cellar (*around 150F, book Fri and Sat nights*). *Closed*

Sun and Mon lunch. The classic 68F lunch with wine is served at **Les Expéditeurs**, 19 Ave Général Leclerc, ✆ 04 68 35 15 80; Catalan cooking and paella on Wed.

Entertainment and Nightlife

On evenings from June to September in Place de la Castellet, the Perpignanais come to dance *sardanas,* the national Catalan circle dance. Nightlife is mostly concentrated on students; there's heavy metal every Friday and Saturday night till 2am at **Le Goya** bar, Rue Talrich, ✆ 04 68 51 80 84, and live rock on Thursdays at **Le Kilt Pub**, 18 P. Ramell, ✆ 04 68 34 80 52. It's worth checking the listings at the **Cinema Castillet**, 19 Quai Vauban, ✆ 04 68 51 25 47, or drive out to Mas Sabole, 11km south, for first run films at **Le Drive-In-Ciné**, an American-style drive-in cinema (first show at 9.45).

West of Perpignan: Pyrenean Valleys

There are two important valleys: the **Conflent** (the valley of the river Têt) and the **Vallespir** (of the river Tech), sloping in parallel lines toward the Spanish border. Don't think that this butt end of the Pyrenees consists of mere foothills; in between the two valleys stands snow-capped **Canigou**, not the highest (a mere 9134ft) but certainly one of the most imposing peaks of the chain, jauntily wearing a Phrygian cap of snow until late spring. The *muntanya regalada,* 'fortunate mountain' of the Catalans, is one of the symbols of the nation, the subject of one of the best-known Catalan folksongs. Every summer solstice Catalans from both sides of the frontier ceremoniously light a huge bonfire on its summit, the signal for surrounding villages to light their own, all at the exact moment. Legends and apparitions abound on Canigou. Fairies and 'ladies of the waters' are said to frequent its forested slopes, and King Pedro of Aragon climbed it in 1285, and met a dragon near the top.

Getting Around

The coach and train service is probably better here than in any other rural region in this book—only it won't help you see rural monuments like St-Michel or Serrabone. Using Perpignan as a base, it's possible to see quite a bit of the Conflent and Vallespir; from the *gare routière* there are 10 or 12 buses a day to Prades and Villefranche-de-Conflent, and a few of these continue on to Font-Romeu and Latour-de-Carol. At Villefranche you can pick up **Le Petit Train Jaune**, a scenic narrow-gauge train that runs twice a day into the Cerdagne, practically unchanged since 1910. One of the most unlikely railways in France, it was entirely a political project, meant to bring some new life into the impoverished mountain valleys. It has kept puffing ever since—only tourism has saved it from closing: while checking the schedule make sure you don't choose one of the departures taken over by buses. The scenery is striking, even more so in summer when viewed from topless carriages. The last station is Latour-de-Carol, where you can pick up a bus to Andorra and Spain, or a train to Toulouse or Barcelona. For the Vallespir, there are frequent, convenient daily buses to Arles-sur-Tech and Amélie-les-Bains-Palada, with a few pressing on further up the valley to Prats-de-Mollo.

Tourist Information

Ille-sur-Têt ✉ 66130: Ave Pasteur, ✆ 04 68 84 02 62, 🖷 04 68 84 02 62.

Prades ✉ 66500: 4 Rue Victor Hugo, ✆ 04 68 05 41 02, 🖷 04 68 05 21 79.

Vernet-les-Bains ✉ 66820: 6 Pl de la Mairie ✆ 04 68 05 55 35, 🖷 04 68 05 60 33.

Villefranche-de-Conflent ✉ 66500: Place de l'Eglise, ✆ 04 68 92 22 96, 🖂 04 68 96 23 93.

market days

Ille-sur-Têt: Wednesday and Friday; flea market Sunday. **Prades**: Tuesday.

From Perpignan to Ille-sur-Têt

The fish-filled Têt, before passing through Perpignan, washes a wide plain packed full of vine-yards and fat villages. The fattest, **Thuir**, puts up signs all over Roussillon inviting us over to see the **World's Biggest Barrel**, in the cellars of the famous aperitifs Byrrh and Dubonnet—wine mixed with quinine, invented here a little over a century ago (*tours April–Oct 9–11.45 and 2.30–5.45, July and Aug 10–11.45 and 2–6.45*). After a few aperitifs, head 6km west for golden-hued **Castelnou**, a perfectly preserved medieval village on winding, pebble paved lanes and steps under the 10th-century **castle** of the Counts of Cerdagne (*open Feb–May 11–7, June–Sept 10–8, Oct–Dec 12–5, closed Tues; adm*). Restored after the roof caught fire in 1981, this castle, unlike most military castles in France, never graduated into a lordly residence, and the rooms are empty today.

The narrow D48 wiggling west of Castelnou is unabashedly beautiful: if you have a couple of hours to spare, you can circle around to the Prieuré de Serrabonne (*see* below) by way of the D2 to Caixas, Fourques, then on to the D13 for Llauro, and **Prunet-et-Belpuig**, where the ruins of the **Château de Belpuig** offer a superb view and the 11th-century **Chapelle de la Trinité** has sculpture by the same school as Serrabonne; in **Boule d'Amont** just up the road, there's another charming church from the same century. A shorter alternative, but on even more dubious roads, is to take the D2 north to St-Michel-de-Llotes (site of the **Dolmen de la Creu de la Llosa**) and turn back to Serrabonne by way of Casefabre, with its tremendous views.

At **Ille-sur-Têt**, an attractive old village at the gateway to the mountains, neglected art from the 11th to 19th centuries from churches all over Roussillon has been assembled in a 16th-century hospital, the **Centre d'Art Sacré**, with exhibitions on various themes and periods, changing every six months or so (*open 10–12 and 3–6, closed Tues and Sat and Sun morning; daily 10–12 and 3–7 in July and Aug; adm*).

The D2 northwest of Ille to Montalba-le-Château takes you very quickly to some surprising scenery: orange eroded 'fairy chimneys' called the **Orgues**, with a forgotten ruin of the 12th century tower perched on top, with the Pyrenees forming a magnificent backdrop. The fortified church of **Régleille** (from Ille, take the D2 over the river, and after a kilometre turn right on a little road) looks like a castle at first sight—a typical example of a monastic church, in an area without any castles, that grew into a fortress to protect not only the monks, but the population of the village; Ille was located here before its population drifted to the present site.

Six km north on the D21, in little **Bélesta**, the **Château-Musée**, ✆ 04 68 84 56 56, holds the treasure found in a Neolithic tomb in 1983; the castle itself is a 13th-century work built by St Louis (*open mid Mar–mid-Nov, daily 10–12.30 and 2–6.30, July and Aug 10–7; adm*).

Prieuré de Serrabonne

Seeing the finest medieval sculpture in Roussillon requires dedication: the most direct route (for others, *see* above) requires 13km of hairpin turns on a road where you dread oncoming traffic, starting from the D618 at Bouleternère, just west of Ille, and ending in a lofty, remote, barren spot on the slopes of a mountain called Roque Rouge. The solemn, spare shape and dark schist of Serrabonne's church (© *04 68 84 09 30; open daily 10–6; adm*) are not promising, making the surprise inside that much the greater. The best efforts of the 12th-century Catalan sculptors were concentrated in the single gallery of the cloister and especially in the **tribune**, in rose marble from Canigou. Perfectly preserved in its isolated setting, this includes a fantastical bestiary, centaurs, a grimacing St Michael, reliefs of the four evangelists and more. The style of these capitals will become familiar if you spend much time in the Conflent; like most of the works in the region, Serrabonne's was done by the school of artists that grew up at St-Michel-de-Cuxa. Note the small figure of the Virgin; a narrow window allows a ray of sunlight to illuminate it only one day each year—the Feast of the Assumption on 15 August.

Prades, St-Michel-de-Cuxa, and Canigou

Prades is known around the world in connection with the music festival founded in 1951 by Pablo Casals, but few people could place it on a map. Casals, in exile after the Spanish Civil War, spent much of the 1940s and '50s here, in the one safe corner of his beloved Catalunya. From the beginning his **festival** (late July–early August) attracted many of the world's greatest musicians. Otherwise Prades is a rather typical, stolid Catalan town. There are a couple of things to see: at 4 Ave Victor Hugo, the **Musée Municipal** (*open 9–12 and 2–5*) has an archaeological collection, paintings by native son Martin Vives, and a section dedicated to Casals—photos, his piano and pipes, records, letters, etc. In the heart of Prades, the church of **St-Pierre** has a fine Romanesque bell tower with a pyramid crown and inside, an operatic Baroque retable in full 17th-century fig by Catalan chisel virtuoso Joseph Sunyer.

Best of all, it's only a few kilometres from Prades up through orchards to **St-Michel-de-Cuxa**, one of the most important monasteries of medieval Catalunya (*open daily exc Sun morning, 9.30–11.50 and 2–6, winter 2–5pm; adm*). Even in its reduced, semi-ruined state, the scale is impressive; this was one of the great monastic centres from which medieval Europe was planned and built.

The coming of the French Revolution found St-Michel already in a state of serious decay. Looted and abandoned, the abbey suffered greatly in the last century. One of the two bell-towers collapsed, and much of the best sculptural work went 'in exile' as the Catalans put it, carted off to the Cloisters Museum in New York; when restoration began the rest of the cloister was in a public bathhouse in Prades, while the altar top was found holding up a balcony in Vinça. Now restored, St-Michel is occupied once again by a small community of Benedictine monks from Montserrat, the centre of Catalan spiritualism and nationalism.

While much of the inspiration for early medieval architecture in Languedoc came from north Italy or France, Roussillon was heavily influenced by nearby Spain. Here the obvious Spanish feature is the more-than-semicircular 'Visigothic' arches in the nave. This style, which goes back almost to Roman times, never became too popular in Christian Europe, though the Muslims of Spain adopted it to create the architectural fantasies of Seville and Granada. Other notable features of St-Michel include the massive and extremely elegant bell tower, and an unusual circular crypt, built in the 11th century under a building that was later demolished. The crypt is covered by toroid barrel-vaulting, with a mushroom-like central column almost unique in medieval architecture. Antonio Gaudí used similar columns in his work in Barcelona—a fascinating piece of Catalan cultural continuity; Gaudí could not have got the idea here, since the crypt was discovered and excavated only in 1937. In the cloister, you can see the galleries and capitals that didn't go to Manhattan: monsters from the medieval bestiary in the corners, intertwined with men on the four faces. There is an obsession with lions, almost Chinese in their stylization, biting and licking each other.

If **Canigou's** magnetism is working its juju on you, don't resist the call. You can make two thirds of the climb—7053ft—by car, on a forest road that begins on the east end of Prades. This leaves you at the **Chalet-Hôtel des Cortalets** refuge (*open May–Sept; call © 04 68 96 36 19 to book a bed*). From here it's a fairly easy three- to four-hour walk to the summit, requiring only a decent pair of walking shoes and windbreaker. There's a second, even more hair-raising forest road up to the refuge from the D27, practical only in a four-wheel drive. The Prades tourist office has a list of operators; leave the driving to them.

Vernet-les-Bains and St-Martin-du-Canigou

The D27, the narrow road that snakes around the lower slopes of Canigou, is an exceptional drive through the mountain forests, with grand views of the big mountain itself; after St-Michel-de-Cuxa, it meets **Vernet-les-Bains**, a bustling modern spa with most of the accommodation in the area, and hot sulphuric waters that are good for your rheumatism and respiratory problems. Three kilometres further up, **Casteil**, a little wooded resort with a small museum of mountain life and plenty of picnic grounds, is the base for visiting Canigou's other great medieval monument, the abbey of **St-Martin-du-Canigou**, © 04 68 05 50 03—a taxing though lovely 40-minute walk up from the town (*open daily exc Tues, tours at 10, 11.45 (12 on Sun), 2, 3, 4, 5, on the half-hour in winter; adm*).

A monkish architect named Sclua designed this complex, begun in the early 11th century by a count of the Cerdagne named Guifred Cabreta. Sclua was a designer ahead of his time; he made his monastery a rustic acropolis, spectacularly sited with views around Canigou and the surrounding peaks, and arranged as a series of courtyards and terraces on different levels. The church, with its immense, fortress-like bell tower, has two levels, an upper church dedicated to St-Martin and a lower crypt for a certain obscure subterranean Virgin Mary: *Notre-Dame-sous-Terre*. Some good white marble capitals can be seen in the cloister, heavily restored in the early 1900s, and medieval tombs, including Count Guifred's, survive in the upper church. But on the whole St-Martin, damaged by an earthquake in 1428, abandoned after the Revolution, restored between 1952–71 and reinhabited, retains relatively few of its former glories.

To complete the tour of Romanesque Canigou, there is another 11th- to 12th-century **church** in the village of **Corneilla-de-Conflent**, a former Benedictine priory full of good sculpture. Side-roads to the west, in the valley of the Rotja, can take you to several more, including rare 10th-century churches in the tiny villages of **Fuilla** and **Sahorre**. Not all the area's attractions are on Canigou. Five km northeast of Prades, in the empty, largely forested Pyrenean foothills, **Eus**, 'One of the most beautiful villages in France' is an ambitious place; it also claims to have 'the most sunshine of any *commune* in France'. Spilling down its steep hillside, as you see it from the Têt valley, it makes an elegant composition. The parish church has some elaborate 17th-century polychrome retables. Closer to Prades, on the D14, **Molitg-les-Bains** on a hill in the forest, has been a spa (specializing in skin disorders) since the Belle Epoque with a suitably grand hotel.

Villefranche-de-Conflent

Some villages have their own ideas for welcoming visitors. This one casually points cannons down at you as you pass along the N116, by way of an invitation to drop in. Villefranche, the most logical place from which to defend the Têt valley, has had a castle at least since 1092. In the 17th century it took its present form, as a model Baroque fortress-town, rebuilt and re-fortified by Vauban. Almost nothing has changed since, and Villefranche remains as a fascinating historical record, a sort of stage set of that era. Tours of Vauban's **ramparts** with their walkway built through in the wall are offered (*daily June–Sept 10–6.30, Oct–May 2–5; adm*) and if you have sufficient puff and military curiosity, there's a steep climb up the remarkable 1000 subterranean rock hewn steps (at the end of Rue St-Pierre) to **Fort Liberia**, © 04 68 96 34 01 (*open daily exc Mon, 9–6; adm*), another Vauban opus, further fortified by Napoleon III, dominating the valley and long used as a prison where you can 'meet the villainous female prisoners' (don't be alarmed—they're made of wax). There's a bus up from Villefranche's Café Canigou if you're feeling lazy.

A survivor from the pre-Vauban Villefranche, the church of **St-Jacques** is a fine 12th-century building with the familiar capitals from the workshop of St-Michel-de-Cuxa; inside there's another retable by Sunyer and, by the door, note the measures engraved in the stone, used by drapers who had market stalls in the square. Vauban built its walls and tower into his wall to help with the defence. For all its grim purpose, Villefranche is a lovely town, lately attracting a number of crafty types, woodcarvers and potters. One km up the Vernet road, some of the Pyrenees' most peculiar stalactites await your inspection at the **Grotte des Canalettes** (*open 10–6, summer 9–7; adm*) and the **Grotte des Grandes Canalettes** (*open Easter–Oct 10–12 and 2–6.30, then Sun only 2–5; adm*).

Where to Stay and Eating Out

As with Venice or Malta, total indifference in the kitchen is part of the Catalans' charm. Near the coasts they will occasionally excel with seafood, but up here visitors are on their own.

Prades ✉ 66500

Tucked in a quiet courtyard, **Les Glycines**, 12 Rue Général De Gaulle, © 04 68 96 51 65, has comfortable rooms and a decent restaurant (*rooms from 210F*). Down the street at No.156, a big neon sign makes it easy to find the ***Hostalrich**, © 04 68 96 05 38, where all rooms have TV and showers and some have balconies from which to observe the throbbing street life below (but avoid the restaurant). In the centre, dine at the intimate **El Patio**, which faces the church, © 04 68 05 35 60 (*menus 90 and 135F*), and serves well prepared Catalan treats, pizzas, and a good house wine to wash them down. *Closed Wed.* Above St-Michel-de-Cuxa, in Taurinya, the **Auberge des Deux Abbayes**, © 04 68 96 49 53, serves reliable French classics; spit-roasted lamb is the speciality in the summer (*menus from 98F*).

Molitg-les-Bains ✉ 66500

Molitg may have only 180 inhabitants, but it can claim Roussillon's top luxury hotel, the sumptuous Relais & Châteaux ******Château de Riell**, © 04 68 05 04 40, ☏ 04 68 05 04 37, a Baroque folly from the turn of the century, in a theatrically Baroque setting, perched on a rock with exquisite views of Canigou; elegant, luxurious Hollywoodian rooms—a contrast with the medieval oubliettes, which you can visit—two pools, including one on top of the tower, perhaps the best place in the world to watch the Catalan bonfires go up on the equinox. Lots of extras, and a restaurant worthy of the decor (*menus from185F*). *Closed Nov–Mar.*

Vernet-les-Bains ✉ 66820

Plenty of choice here, with the century-old ★★★**Le Mas Fleuri**, 25 Blvd Clemenceau (the road up to St Martin), ✆ 04 68 05 51 94, 🖷 04 68 05 50 77, at the top of the list, set in a pretty park, with a pool; rooms are air-conditioned. *Closed Sept–May.* In the centre, the modern★★★**Comte Guilifred**, ✆ 04 68 05 51 37, 🖷 04 68 05 64 11, is the training ground for the local hotel school; ask for a room in the back overlooking the garden. For something cheaper, the ★★**Princess**, Rue Lavandières, ✆ 04 68 05 56 22, 🖷 04 68 05 62 45, is a pleasant Logis de France, with a better-than-average restaurant.

Villefranche-de-Confluent ✉ 66500

Outside the walls, on the river near the train station, the ★★**Auberge du Cèdre**, Domaine Ste-Eulalie, ✆ 04 68 96 37 37, has nine comfortable rooms, an adequate restaurant and two fat, friendly ginger cats in the garden. *Open all year.* Within the walls, the lovely **Auberge St-Paul**, Place de l'Eglise, ✆ 04 68 96 30 95, fetches from Canigou the basic ingredients for mountain surprises like *filet mignon de sanglier* (boar) and beef with morel mushrooms (*menus at 130–340F*). *Closed Mon in summer, Mon and Tues in winter.* For something more modest, try **Au Grill**, 81 Rue St-Jean, ✆ 04 68 96 17 65 (*90F menu*): solid traditional cuisine. *Closed Tues and Wed eve.*

The Cerdagne

This is as close as we get, in this book, to the heart of the Pyrenees, but it's far enough for the real thing: mountain rhododendrons and blue gentians, hordes of skiers, herds of horses, and snow on top until May or June. The lofty plateau of the Cerdagne (*Cerdanya* in Catalan) was an isolated and effectively independent county in the Middle Ages; from the 10th century its counts gradually extended their power, becoming eventually Counts of Barcelona—the founders of the Catalan nation. In spite of this heritage, the Cerdagne was split between Spain and France in the 1659 Treaty of the Pyrenees. The building of the Little Yellow Train, in 1911, brought the French Cerdagne into the modern world (*see* p.465); skiing has made it rather opulent today. And besides skiing, you can see some good Romanesque churches, warm up at the world's largest solar furnace, visit the highest railway station in France—and circumnavigate Spain in less than an hour.

Tourist Information

Mont-Louis ✉ 66210: Rue du Marché, ✆ 04 68 04 21 97 (summer only).
Les Angles ✉ 66210: 2 Avenue de l'Aude, ✆ 04 68 04 32 76, 🖷 04 68 30 93 09.
Font-Romeu ✉ 66120: 33 Ave E.-Brousse, ✆ 04 68 30 68 30, 🖷 04 68 30 29 70.
Bourg-Madame ✉ 66760: Pl de la Mairie, ✆ 04 68 04 55 35, 🖷 04 68 04 66 55.

market day

The best market in the area is the Sunday morning spread in Puigcerdà.

To Mont-Louis and the Capcir

After Villefranche, the main N116 climbs dramatically into the mountains. There are a few possible stop-offs on the way: at **Olette**, you can turn off to explore nearly abandoned old mountain villages like **Nyer** and **Evols.** A bit further up, at **Thuès-entre-Valls**, you can stretch your legs in the beautiful Gorges de la Carança, then soak your weary bones in the natural hot-springs jacuzzi at **St-Thomas-les-Bains** at Fontpedrouse, where no matter the weather you can take a dip outside (*open daily 10–7, till 9 in the summer; adm*).

Climb, climb, climb and at last you'll reach the gateway to the Cerdagne, **Mont-Louis**, another work of Vauban's and the highest fortress in France (5250ft), named after Louis XIV. The army still resides here, though only to look after a pioneer **solar furnace** (*open 10–12.30 and 2–6; adm*), built in 1953 and used, not for generating power, but for melting substances for scientific experiments; the huge mirror generates temperatures up to 6000 degrees. It shares the small space inside the walls with some 200 residents and a few cafés and shops. A 7km detour up into the mountains will take you to tiny **Planès** and its equally tiny and unique triangular 11th-century church. Like the seven-sided model at Rieux-Minervois, this one has occasioned much speculation; some have claimed it as the centre of a network of ley-lines.

The road to Planès is a dead end, but there are better choices from the big crossroads at Mont-Louis. To the north, D118 carries you to the isolated plateau of the **Capcir**. It's a perfect place to get away from it all—after a road was built into the Capcir in the last century, almost the entire population deserted it, tired of scratching a living from land that would only support a few cows. They left behind beautiful pine forests, and a score of little lakes carved out long ago by Pyrenean glaciers. Skiing has brought the Capcir back to life since the '60s, and the government has transformed the landscape with a number of dams and artificial lakes.

On your way into the Capcir, don't miss the church of St-Vincent in **La Llagonne**, only 3km from Mont-Louis. The centuries have left it in peace, with a remarkable collection of medieval art, including an altarpiece and painted baldachin (12th- and 13th-century) and an excellent polychrome *Majestat*. Further north, **Les Angles**, **Matemale** and **Formiguères** are the main ski centres. Les Angles has, as well as some 30 ski pistes, a **Parc Animalier** (*summer 8–7, winter 9–5; adm*), a free-range zoo with native fauna of the Pyrenees, both current and past residents, including bears, reindeer, wolves and bison. Formiguères (not the ski station, but the village, 4km away) is one of the prettiest and best preserved in the region, hardly changed since the days when the Kings of Majorca sojourned here to relieve their asthma. This region is great for hiking. The best parts lie to the west, on the slopes of the 2921m **Pic Carlit**; there you will find the sources of both the Têt and the Aude (above the D60, in the Forêt de Barrès).

Font-Romeu

The western road (D618) will take you through more pine forests to **Font-Romeu**; along with its new satellite towns, Super-Bolquère and Pyrénées 2000, this is one of the biggest ski resorts in France. Font-Romeu grew up after 1910, around a now-closed 'Grand Hôtel'; it prospers today partly by its excellent sports facilities, often used for training France's Olympic teams. Stamped from the same mould as every other continental ski resort, it has plenty of fake Alpine chalets, innumerable pizzerias, and 260 snow machines to help out when the weather isn't cooperating. But no other resort has the World's Largest **Solar Furnace**, 'stronger than 10,000 suns!' the successor to the one in Mont-Louis. With its curved mirror, covering an entire side of the nine-storey laboratory building, it reflects the Pyrenees beautifully while helping scientists work out all sorts of high-temperature puzzles (*open daily 10–12.30 and 1.30–5.30; adm*). Above the town, the pilgrimage chapel of **Notre-Dame-de-Font-Romeu** has an exuberant altarpiece by Joseph Sunyer and a 12th-century statue of the Virgin.

Another solar experiment can be seen at **Targasonne** west of Font-Romeu on the D618; this big mirror was built to generate electricity, but hasn't quite worked as well as intended. The glaciers that reshaped the Capcir were busy here too, leaving a strange expanse of granite boulders called the **Chaos**. The Cerdagne is famous for its Romanesque churches and chapels, testimony to the mountain Catalans' prosperity and level of culture even in the very early Middle Ages. One of the best of the churches is St-André, at **Angoustrine**, west of Targasonne, with fragments of 13th-century frescoes representing the months of the year. To the west, **Dorres** is a lofty *village perché* with another church, this one from the 11th century, with another Romanesque Virgin inside and a chance to soak in a granite hot tub with a sulphurous pong (*daily 8am–9pm*).

The Vallée du Carol

From the village of **Ur** (with yet another richly decorated Romanesque church), you can make a northern detour into the Vallée du Carol, the western edge of Roussillon. **Latour-de-Carol** is a romantic name for another great border rail-crossing most of us have blinked at in the dark; the name does not come from Charlemagne, as most people think, but the Carol river. Latour's church has more work by Joseph Sunyer. The best church in the area, however, is the Chapelle St-Fructueux in the miniscule village of **Yravals**, above Latour-de-Carol—with a wealth of medieval art inside, and a magnificent mid 14th-century altarpiece of St Martha, by a Catalan named Ramon Destorrents.

Further up this scenic valley, you'll pass the tower of the ruined 14th-century castle that gives Latour its name. The trees give out as the tortuous road climbs to the pass of Puymorens. From here, if you have a sudden hankering for some tax-free Havanas, or a new phonograph, it's only 40km to the Pyrenean Ruritania, the Principality of **Andorra**.

Llivia, Llo and Eyne

Bourg-Madame 'the same latitude as Rome, but sunnier' as its brochure claims, is the crossing point for Spain; just across the border lies Puigcerdà, with a 14th-century church and the best ice-hockey squad on the Iberian peninsula. The N116 will take you northeast from here, back to Mont-Louis, completing your circumnavigation of Spain—or at least the tiny Spanish enclave of **Llivia**, left marooned by accident in the Treaty of 1659. The treaty stipulated that Spain must give up the *villages* of the Cerdagne, and everyone had forgotten that Llivia had the legal status of a *ville*; it had been a Roman *municipium*, the capital of the Cerdagne in ancient times. Llivia's historic centre is clustered around a 15th-century fortified church, housing a superb 13th-century sculpture of Christ; opposite, in the **Musée Municipal** (*open daily exc Mon 10–1 and 3–6*), the unlikely attraction is a 16th-century **pharmacy**, one of the most beautiful, oldest and best-preserved in Europe.

East of Bourg-Madame, more Catalan Romanesque churches can be visited: at **Hix**, an impressive edifice of 1177, built when the town was the residence of the counts of the Cerdagne, and containing a majestic Romanesque Virgin, with a little kingly Christ child on her lap, and at **Caldégas**, where the frescoes include a hunting scene with falcons. Further east, along the N116, road signs will startle you with town names like Llo and Err; linguists say they're Basque, evidence that the Basques lived here in remote times. **Llo** has a church with a lovely sculptured portal and an exceptionally sweet cemetery in nearby **Sainte-Léocadie** (home of the highest vineyard in Europe). You can visit the **Musée de Cerdagne** (*open summer 10–7, winter 10–12 and 2–6; closed Tues*) in a 17th-century farm, dedicated to the pre-ski trades of the great plateau—shepherding and farming. There are opportunities for hiking, southwards into the narrow **Gorges du Sègre**. Even better, come to nearby **Eyne** in May, late enough to avoid the skiers from the resort called Eyne 2600, and just in time for a spectacular display of wildflowers and medicinal herbs in the Vallée d'Eyne, climbing up to the Spanish border. The aforementioned Musée de Cerdagne offers day or half-day guided tours in July and August through the **Réserve Naturelle d'Eyne** (✆ 04 68 04 77 07) as well and a three-hour **Balade Archéologique** to the village's menhirs and dolmens (*the last two weeks of July–Aug Wed–Sat, departing from the village at 2.30; ✆ 04 68 04 08 05 for more information*).

Where to Stay and Eating Out

Mont-Louis ✉ 66210

Get a room with a view at the grey stone ★★**Le Clos Cerdan**, on a cliff overlooking the valley, ✆ 04 68 04 23 29, ✉ 04 68 04 23 79; modern but comfortable. *Closed Nov.* In the village, by the ramparts, the family-run **Lou Rouballou**, Rue des Ecoles-Laïques, ✆ 04 68 04 23 26, ✉ 04 68 04 14 09, is pleasant (*rooms150–220F*) and serves delicious food specializing in mushrooms (including one called the *rouballou*) in various guises (*menus 100–240F*). *Closed May, Nov, and Dec.*

Font-Romeu ✉ 66120

Font-Romeu has any number of modern places that cater to the ski crowd, like the ★★**Clair Soleil**, Ave Arago, ✆ 04 68 30 13 65, ✉ 04 68 30 08 27, also with a view, and a swimming pool. *Closed May and Nov–Dec.* For something completely different, go another 8km to Angoustrine, to **Cal Xandera**, ✆ 04 68 04 61 67, a beautifully restored 18th-century farmhouse serving flavour-packed traditional mountain cuisine, with four *chambres d'hôte* (*book for rooms and meals, menus at 85 and 120F*).

Llo and Saillagouse ✉ 66800

Country inns unconcerned with the skiing business are somewhat rare. Llo, above Saillagouse, has the ivy-covered ★★★**Auberge l'Atalaya**, ✆ 04 68 04 70 04, ✉ 04 68 04 01 29; tranquillity is assured in this setting, close to the wildflowers of the Vallée d'Eyne and infinitely far from anything else, with a pool and an excellent restaurant (*rooms from 480 F, menus 160–380F*). In the centre of Saillagouse, in a former post house, the ★★**Planes**, Place des Comtes-de-Cerdagne, ✆ 04 68 04 72 08, ✉ 04 68 04 75 93, has been hosting guests since 1895; the dining room with its huge fireplace is a great place to settle down to a plate of Catalan anchovies and red peppers (*menus from 60–160F*). The same family runs the modern **Planotel**, Rue de la Poste (same phone), with a heated pool.

The Vallespir

The valley of the Tech, the southernmost valley of Roussillon, and of France, winds a lonesome trail around the southern slopes of Canigou. Known for its mineral waters since Roman times, it traditionally made its living from these and from ironworking, the basis of Catalan prosperity in the Middle Ages. When the iron gave out, there was smuggling. Today, as smugglers have become superfluous, the Vallespir lives by tourism, with some francs on the side from cherries and cork oak—the *primeurs*, the first cherries in the French market each year, and the *grand cru* corks that have kept the best champagne bubbly for centuries.

Céret ✉ 66400: Ave Clemenceau (opposite Funetech, a pseudo-Egyptian funeral parlour), ✆ 04 68 87 00 53, 🖅 04 68 87 32 43.

Arles-sur-Tech ✉ 66150: Rue Barjau, ✆ 04 68 39 11 99, 🖅 04 68 39 11 99.

Prats-de-Mollo ✉ 66230: Place le Foiral, ✆ 04 68 39 70 83, 🖅 04 68 39 74 51.

market days

Céret: Saturday. **Arles-sur-Tech**: Wednesday.

Le Boulou and St-Martin-de-Fenollar

From Perpignan, you reach the Vallespir by the A9, getting off at **Le Boulou**, a truck-stop known to every European TIR jockey. The ancient Roman teamsters knew it too. Le Boulou has been fated by geography as an eternal transit point; just coincidentally it has a fine Romanesque church with a superb white marble tympanum sculpted by the Master of Cabestany, portraying the *Resurrection of the Virgin*. The cornice shows scenes of the Nativity, the Christ Child's first bath (also rarely depicted in art), the Shepherds, Magi, and Flight into Egypt. East of Le Boulou, **St-Génis-des-Fontaines** was one of the important early medieval monasteries of Roussillon. Its church has a remarkable carved lintel dated 1020, with a *Majestat* and stylized apostles shaped like bowling-pins; the cloister was dismantled and sold off in 1924, one of the final scandals of France's traditional lack of concern for its medieval heritage. In 1988 it was rebuilt as it was, with originals and copies.

The A9 and N9 continue south into Spain, passing **St-Martin-de-Fenollar** and its 9th-century church, with some of the most unusual and best-preserved 12th-century frescoes in the Midi (*open mid-June–mid-Sept, 10.30–12 and 3.30–7, winter daily exc Tues 2–5; adm*). Nine-tenths of all early medieval painting is lost to us, and this is a rare example of the best of what is left: brilliant colours and a confident stylization, with an imagery untroubled by the dogma of later religious painting, as in the *Nativity*, where Mary lies not in a stable, but in a comfortable bed under a chequered baldachin. The scene from the Apocalypse, of Christ in Majesty with the four symbols of the Evangelists and the 24 elders, was a favourite 12th-century theme on both sides of the Pyrenees.

Hannibal entered Gaul through **Le Perthus**, the last, or first stop in France. As a fitting bookend to this long volume, archaeologists have recently uncovered, at Panisars, a monumental pedestal, identified as belonging to the **Trophée de Pompée**. Similar to La Turbie near the Italian border, this trophy was erected by a victorious Pompey in 71 BC on the Gallo-Hispanic frontier. Part of the stone was used to built a priory in 1011 (the ruins are nearby); the rest was quarried by Vauban in the 17th century to build the **Fort de Bellegarde** (*open end June–end Sept 10.30–12.50 and 2.30–6.30; adm*).

Céret: the 'Mecca of Cubism'

Back in the valley of the Tech, the D115 streaks from Le Boulou to Céret, centre of the optimal cherry-growing region suspended between the Pyrenees and the sea. Amid the orchards, Céret is a laid-back town under enormous plane trees, with perfect little squares (especially the **Plaça dels Nou Raigs**), medieval gates, the biggest Baroque church in Roussillon, **St-Pierre**, a war memorial by Maillol, and an elegant 14th-century **bridge** over the Tech.

Visit Céret before visiting the **Musée d'Art Moderne**, 8 Blvd du Maréchal Joffre, © 04 68 87 27 76; (*open Oct–June 10–6, closed Tues, July–Sept daily 10–7; adm*), and you'll be surprised at how many scenes you'll recognize. Céret found its artistic destiny at the turn of the century, thanks to Picasso, Braque, Gris, Manolo, Matisse, Soutine, Kisling, Masson, Tzara, Lhote, Marquet and others who spent time here up until 1940, and whose works fill the rooms. Best of all are the works donated by Picasso in 1953, among them 28 little plates painted in a five-day spurt of energy, all with variations on the *corrida* under a blasting sun. Although not as dazzling, the **Maison de l'Archéologie in** the Tour Port d'Espagne (*open July–Sept 10–12 and 2.30–6, closed Sun am; other times ring © 04 68 87 31 59*) has well-arranged Neolithic, classical and medieval finds from the Vallespir.

Amélie-les-Bains and Arles-sur-Tech

Sulphurous waters, good for your rheumatism, have been the fortune of **Amélie-les-Bains** since ancient times; a Roman swimming-pool with a vaulted roof has been uncovered, and the spa, rising on either side of the river Tech, still does a grandstand business. Amélie's pretty medieval ancestor, **Paulada**, is piled on a nearby hill, and offers a small **Musée de la Poste** for snail-mail nostalgia from the days of Louis XI to 1900; there's a collection of stamps, and telephones, too (*open Mon–Thurs 10–12 and 2–7, Fri–Sun 3–7, closed Tues; adm*).

Just west, **Arles-sur-Tech**, the ancient capital of the Vallespir, is a curious old village built on a narrow maze of lanes and offers some even curiouser hagiography in its 11th- and 12th-century church of **Ste-Marie**, originally the centre of an important monastery. Dark Age Arles-sur-Tech got by with an anonymous saint—an empty 4th-century sarcophagus known as *Sainte-Tombe*—until the dreaded *simiots* came to town, ape-like monsters that trampled the crops and violated the women. In despair, the abbot of Ste-Marie went to the pope asking for some holy relics. This was in 957, when demand for saints' bones was at its historic high, and the best pope could offer was a pair of Persian martyrs named Abdon and Sennen. The abbot brought them back in a false-bottomed water-barrel, to fool the Venetians and Germans and any other relic thieves, and they dealt with the *simiots* as efficiently as if they had been the bones of St Peter himself. The story is portrayed in a 17th-century retable, in the chapel where Abdon and Sennen's relics are kept. The *Sainte-Tombe* itself, once a major pilgrimage attraction, is kept in a little enclosure outside the front door. It fills continually with perfectly pure water—some 500 to 600 litres a year, ceremoniously pumped every 30 July.

Arles-sur-Tech is the home of **Tissages Catalans**, where they've been making cloth since 1900 (there's a little museum on Rue du 14 Juillet, *open Mon–Fri 10–12 and 2.30–5.30*) and it was the last redoubt of the valley's famous medieval iron industry; the last working mine in Roussillon up at Batère closed down in the early 1990s. Two km northwest along the D44 you can go through the World's Narrowest Gorge, the **Gorges de la Fou** (*open April–Oct, 10–6; adm*), a giant crack in the rock with sides towering 650 feet, with waterfalls and caves along the mile-long walkway. Legend made it the lair of witches, bogeymen, and *traboucayres*, robbers who pounced on passing diligences.

Continuing up the valley, just south of the D115, the hilltop village of **Serralongue** has a church dating from 1018, with a fine portal and one of the only surviving examples of a Catalan *conjurador*; this is a small, square pavilion with a slate roof, and statues of the four Evangelists facing the four cardinal directions. When a storm threatened, the priest would go up to the *conjurador* and perform certain rites facing the direction of the storm, to avert its wrath. A detour further south, on the D3, will uncover **St-Laurent-de-Cerdans**, famous for making espadrilles, and **Coustouges**, which has a lovely early 12th-century fortified church with a slate roof and two carved portals, one inside the other.

Some towns just ask for it. As if having a name like **Prats-de-Mollo** weren't enough, this tiny spa advertises itself as the 'European Capital of Urinary Infections'. Prats-de-Mollo's other claim to fame is a European record for rainfall, 33 inches in 16 hours on 15 October 1940. The baths are really at **La Preste**, 8km up in the mountains; Prats-de-Mollo itself is an attractive old village, with remains of its walls and medieval buildings that recall the days when it was a textile centre, specializing in Catalan bonnets. Don't miss the whale bone stuck in the church wall. This is as far as we go; the Spanish border is 14km away.

Where to Stay and Eating Out

Céret ✉ 66400

On a hill overlooking Céret, ★★★★**Terrasse au Soleil**, Route Fontfrède, ✆ 04 68 87 01 94, ✉ 04 68 87 39 24, a restored and modernized *mas*, has a view, a heated pool and tennis court (a bit dear, especially on full board). *Closed Jan–Feb.* Then there is **Le Mas Trilles** at le Pont de Reynes on the Céret–Amélie-les-Bains road, ✆ 04 68 87 38 37, ✉ 04 68 87 42 62, also a tastefully renovated *mas* with a heated pool, and a charming garden overlooking a trout stream. Otherwise head to the ★**Vidal**, 4 Place du 4 Septembre, ✆ 04 68 87 00 85, ✉ 04 68 87 62 63, in a charming if quirky listed building. *Closed mid-Oct–mid-Nov.* For food to match Céret's art you can't beat **Les Feuillants**, 1 Blvd Lafayette, ✆ 04 68 87 37 88, Catalan cooking with *haute cuisine* ambitions, amidst startling 1930s decor (*menus 250–450F*). *Closed Sun eve and Mon.* For something a tad simpler, try **Le Pied dans le Plat**, with tables out in pretty Plaça dels Nou Raigs, ✆ 04 68 87 17 65 (*65 and 100F menus and crêpes*). *Closed Sun.*

Amélie-les-Bains ✉ 66110

Amélie-les-Bains has dozens of budget hotels; one good one that does not require full board is ★★**La Pergola** at 60 Ave du Vallespir, ✆ 04 68 39 05 71, ✉ 04 68 39 81 15. *Closed Jan.* The place to get away from it all is ★★**Castel Emeraude**, Route de la Corniche, ✆ 04 68 39 02 83, ✉ 04 68 39 03 09, a big white manor on the banks of the river, with a good restaurant. *Closed Dec and Jan.*

Arles-sur-Tech ✉ 66150

Named for the ancient wisteria that shades the garden terrace, ★★**Les Glycines**, Rue Joc de Paume, ✆ 04 68 39 10 09, ✉ 04 68 39 83 02, has modernized rooms all with bath and a wonderful restaurant, where chef Thierry Pineda defies every snide remark we've made about Catalan cuisine with the best 105F menu for miles around: try his aubergine *tian* and delectable *panaché* of Mediterranean fish; there are even cheaper lunch menus. *Closed Dec and Jan.* The **Auberge du Vallespir**, 4km from Arles on the D115, ✆ 04 68 39 12 73, is a peaceful retreat in a rustic setting by some woods, with comfortably attired rooms and serving good food and an enormous choice of wines from 68–260F. *Closed Sun eve and Mon.*

Abbaye:	abbey.
Anse:	cove.
Arrondissement:	a city district.
Auberge:	inn.
Aven:	a sink-hole (a pre-Gallic word).
Bastide:	a taller, more elaborate version of a *mas*, with balconies, wrought-iron work, reliefs, etc; also a medieval new town, fortified and laid out in a grid.
Beffroi:	tower with a town's bell.
Borie:	dry-stone shepherd's hut with a corbelled roof.
Buffet d'eau:	in French gardens, a fountain built into a wall with water falling through levels of urns or basins.
Cabane:	a simple weekend or holiday retreat, usually near the sea; a *cabane de gardian* is a thatched cowboy's abode in the Camargue.
Calanque:	a narrow coastal creek, like a miniature fjord.
Capitelles:	the name for *bories* in Languedoc.
Caryatid:	column or pillar carved in the figure of a woman.
Causse:	rocky, arid limestone plateaus, north of Hérault and in the Bas Languedoc.
Cave:	cellar.
Château:	mansion, manor house or castle.
Chemin:	path.
Chevet:	eastern end of a church, including the apse.
Cirque:	a round natural depression created by erosion at the loop of a river.
Cloître:	cloister.
Clue:	a rocky cleft or transverse valley.
Col:	mountain pass.
Côte:	coast; on wine labels, *côtes, coteaux* and *costières* mean 'hills' or 'slopes'.
Cours:	wide main street, like an elongated main square.
Couvent:	convent or monastery.
Crèche:	a Christmas crib with *santons*.
Donjon:	castle keep.
Ecluse:	canal lock.
Eglise:	church.
Etang:	lagoon or swamp.

Geographical and Architectural Terms

Félibre:	member of the movement to bring back the use of the Provençal language.
Ferrade:	cattle branding.
Gardian:	a cowboy of the Camargue.
Gare:	train station (SNCF).
Gare routière:	coach station.
Garrigues:	irregular limestone hills pitted with caves, especially those north of Nîmes and Montpellier.
Gisant:	a sculpted prone effigy on a tomb.
Gîte:	shelter.
Gîte d'etape:	basic shelter for walkers.
Grande Randonnée (GR):	long-distance hiking path.
Grau:	a narrowing, either of canyon or a river.
Halles:	covered market.
Hôtel:	any large building or palace; a Hôtel de Ville is the city hall.
Mairie:	town hall.
Manade:	a *gardian*'s farm in the Camargue.
Maquis:	Mediterranean scrub. Also used as a term for the French Resistance during the Second World War.
Marché:	market.
Mas:	a farmhouse and its outbuildings.
Motte:	a hammock, or a raised area in a swamp.
Oppidum:	pre-Roman fortified settlement.
Pays:	region.
Pont:	bridge.
Porte:	gateway.
Predella:	small paintings beneath the main subject of a retable.
Presqu'île:	peninsula.
Restanques:	vine or olive terraces.
Retable:	a carved or painted altarpiece, often consisting of a number of scenes.
Rez-de-chaussée (RC):	ground floor.
Santon:	a figure in a Christmas nativity scene, usually made of terracotta and dressed in 18th-century Provençal costume.
Source:	spring.
Tour:	tower.
Transi:	in a tomb, a relief of the decomposing cadaver.
Tympanum:	sculpted semicircular panel over a church door.
Vieille ville:	historic, old quarter of town.
Village perché:	hilltop village.

BC

c. 1,000,000	First human presence, near Menton; use of bone as a tool
c. 450,000	Tautavel Man in northern Roussillon
c. 400,000	Discovery of fire, as at Terra Amata in Nice
c. 60,000	Neanderthal hunters on the Riviera and around Ganges
c. 40,000	Advent of *Homo sapiens*; invention of art
c. 3500	Development of Neolithic culture; first villages built
c. 2000	First metallurgy; copper and tin at Vence and Caussols
c. 1800–1000	Worship at Mont Bégo, at Tende, and Vallée des Merveilles incisions
c. 800	Celts begin to occupy Languedoc
c. 600	Greek traders found Marseille
c. 380	Celtic invasions in Provence
218	Hannibal and elephants pass through region on the way to Italy
125	Roman legions attack Celto-Ligurian tribes that threaten Marseille
122	Founding of *Aquae Sextiae* (Aix)
118	Founding of Narbonne and *Provincia*, the first Roman province in Gaul
102	Marius and his legionaries defeat the Teutones
49	Marius' nephew, Julius Caesar, punishes Marseille for supporting Pompey
14	Augustus defeats Ligurian tribes in the Alpes Maritimes

AD

46	Arrival of the Boat of Bethany at Stes-Maries-de-la-Mer (traditional)
310	Emperor Maximilian captured at Marseille by son-in-law Constantine
314	Constantine calls Church Council at Arles
410	Honorat founds Lérins monastery
413	Visigoths conquer Languedoc
476	Formal end of Western Roman Empire
535	Provence and Languedoc ceded to the Franks
719	Arab invasions in Languedoc
737	Charles Martel defeats Arabs and crushes anti-Frank rebellions in Arles, Avignon and Marseille
759	Pépin the Short adds region to his Frankish empire
812	Canonization of St-Guilhem, Languedoc's warrior saint
855	Creation of the kingdom of Provence for Charles the Bald
879	Duke Viennois Boson proclaims himself king of Provence
c. 890	More Arab raids and invasions
924	Magyars (Hungarians) sack Nîmes
946	Lords of Cerdagne become Counts of Barcelona; beginning of Catalan nation
949	Conrad of Burgundy inherits Provence and divides it into four feudal counties
979	Count William defeats Saracens at La Garde-Freinet, proclaims himself Marquis of Provence

Chronology

985	Montpellier founded
1002	First written text in Occitan
1032	Death of Rudolph II, king of Burgundy and Provence; lands bequeathed to Holy Roman Emperor Conrad II
1084	Trencavels rule Carcassonne and Béziers
1095	Occitans join First Crusade under Raymond of St-Gilles, Count of Toulouse and Marquis of Provence; William of Aquitaine writes first troubadour poetry
1112	Marriage of Douce, duchess of Provence, with Raymond-Berenger III, Count of Barcelona
1125	Provence divided between the houses of Barcelona and Toulouse
1137	Catalunya unified as Kingdom of Aragon
1176	Pierre Valdo of Lyon founds Waldensian (Vaudois) sect
1186	Counts of Provence make Aix their capital
1187	Discovery of relics of St Martha at Tarascon
1208	Albigensian Crusade begins
1209	Sack and massacre at Béziers by Simon de Montfort
1213	Battle of Muret; Montfort defeats Count of Toulouse and King of Aragon
1229	French annex Carcassonne and eastern Languedoc
1246	Charles I of Anjou weds Béatrice, heiress of Provence, beginning the Angevin dynasty
1248	St Louis embarks on Seventh Crusade from Aigues-Mortes
1255	Fall of Quéribus, the last Cathar stronghold
1266	Battle of Benevento gives Charles of Anjou the Kingdom of Naples
1272	Narbonne Cathedral begun
1274	Papacy acquired Comtat Venaissin
1276	Division of Aragon; Kingdom of Majorca founded with capital at Perpignan
1280	Relics of Mary Magdalene 'discovered' at St-Maximin-la-Ste-Baume
1286	First meeting of the Etats de Provence
1289	The school of medicine in Montpellier becomes a university
1295	The death of the 'last troubadour', Guiraut Riquier
1297	Francesco Grimaldi the Spiteful, merchant-prince of Genoa, conquers Monaco (but is forced to abandon it in 1301)
1303	Boniface VIII founds University of Avignon
1309	Papacy moves to Avignon
1327	Petrarch first sees Laura
1340s	Siennese painters bring International Gothic style to Avignon
1344	Kingdom of Aragon reunited
1348	Jeanne of Naples and Provence sells Avignon to the Pope; the Black Death strikes the South
1349	Jews expelled from France and take refuge in Comtat Venaissin
c. 1350	First paper mills in the Comtat Venaissin
1362	Election of abbot of St-Victor as Pope Urban V
1360s	The *Grandes Compagnies* ravage the countryside
1363	The Grimaldis recover Monaco and hold it still
1377	Papacy returns to Rome

1380	Louis I d'Anjou adopted by Jeanne of Naples
1388	Regions of Nice, Barcelonnette and Puget-Théniers secede from Provence, join County of Savoy
1464	Founding of the Fair of Beaucaire
1481	Count of Provence leaves Provence to the King of France
1492	Union of Aragon and Castile (Ferdinand and Isabella); end of Catalan independence
1496	Military port founded in Toulon
1501	French create Parlement of Aix to oversee Provence
1524	Provence invaded by the imperial troops of Charles V
1525	Jews in the Comtat Venaissin compelled to wear yellow hats
1539	Edict of Villars-Cotterêts forces use of French as official language
1540	Parlement of Aix orders massacre of Waldensians in the Lubéron
1559	Completion of the canal between the Durance and Salon
1560	First Protestant synod in Languedoc
1562	Beginning of Wars of Religion: Protestant assembly at Mérindol
1577	First soap factory (Prunemoyr) founded in Marseille
1590–92	Carlo Emanuele of Savoy invades Provence
1598	Edict of Nantes ends the Wars of Religion
1603	Royal college founded at Aix
1639	Last meeting of the Etats de Provence before the Revolution
1646	Jews confined to ghettos
1650	Molière moves to Pézenas
1659	Treaty of the Pyrenees; French annex Roussillon
1666	Digging begins on the Canal du Midi; founding of Sète
1680	Louis XIV enters rebellious Marseille
1685	Louis XIV revokes Edict of Nantes
1702–4	The War of the Camisards
1707	Toulon unsuccessfully besieged by the English and Duke of Savoy
1720–21	100,000 die of plague, mostly in Marseille
1731	Principality of Orange incorporated into France
1752	Last Protestant persecutions
1766	Tobias Smollett publishes his *Travels*, enticing the British to Nice
1779	Roman mausoleum and palace of the counts demolished, at Aix
1784	Hot air balloon goes up in Marseille
1787	The Edict of Tolerance
1790	France divided into *départements*
1791	France annexes Comtat Venaissin
1792	Volunteers from Marseille sing *La Marseillaise* to Paris
1793	Revolutionary tribunal in Marseille; Siege of Toulon makes Bonaparte famous
1795	Massacres in Marseille and Tarascon
1800	Marseille population around 100,000
1815	Napoleon escapes Elba and pops up again near Juan-les-Pins
1820	First signs of tourist industry at Hyères
1830	Revolution brings Louis Philippe to power
1831	Lord Brougham begins the vogue for wintering in Cannes

1839	Inauguration of Marseille–Sète railroad; birth of Cézanne
1840–8	Prime Ministry of Guizot, Protestant liberal from Nîmes
1844	Viollet-le-Duc begins restoration of Carcassonne
1851	Louis Napoleon's coup ends Second Republic; armed resistance in the south
1854	Founding of the Félibrige at the Château de Fontségugne
1859	Mistral publishes *Miréio*
1860	Plebiscite in County of Nice votes for union with France
1861	The prince of Monaco sells Roquebrune and Menton to France
1865	Silkworm industry destroyed by disease
1868–90	Phylloxera epidemic devastates vines
1869	Opening of Suez Canal brings boom times to Marseille
1888	Stephen Liégeard gives the Côte d'Azur its name
1888–90	Van Gogh in Provence
1900	Population reaches 500,000 in Marseille, 20% of which is Italian
1904	Frédéric Mistral wins the Nobel Prize for Literature
1906	Colonial *Exposition* at Marseille
1907	Climax of farm protests; Languedoc occupied by the army
1911	Diaghilev signs contract to bring the Ballets Russes to Monte Carlo
1924–5	Scott and Zelda Fitzgerald raise hell on the Riviera
1928	Creation of the Camargue Regional Park
1930	D.H. Lawrence dies in Vence
1930s	Marcel Pagnol films his *Marius, Fanny* and *César* trilogy in Marseille
1939	Founding of the Cannes Film Festival
1942	Sinking of the fleet at Toulon
1943	Formation of the Maquis resistance cells
1944	American and French landings around St-Tropez; Provence liberated in two weeks
1945	Creation of the Institut d'Etudes Occitanes
1947	Val de Roya incorporated into France
1956	Bardot and Vadim make *And God Created Woman* in St-Tropez
1962	Independence of Algeria: tens of thousands of French North Africans (*pieds-noirs*) settle in the south
1965	Last silk weaving company closed
1966	Steelworks founded at Fos
1968	Big resort development plan begins in Languedoc
1970	Completion of Paris–Lyon–Marseille autoroute
1982	Regional governments created
1988	Floods in Nîmes
1992	30 die in Vaison-la-Romaine floods

A working knowledge of French will make your holiday more enjoyable, but is hardly essential in the most visited parts of the south—the Côte d'Azur and resorts of Languedoc, the cities, and heartland of Provence where you can always find someone working in travel offices, banks, shops, hotels, and restaurants who speaks at least rudimentary English. Venturing into the less-travelled hinterlands may well require an effort to recall your school French: a small travel phrase book and English-French dictionary can come in handy. On either end of the coast you can try out your Italian or Catalan.

Even if your French is brilliant, the soupy southern twang may throw you a curve. Any word with a nasal *in* or *en* becomes something like *aing* (*vaing* for *vin*). The last vowel on many words that are silent in the north get to express themselves in the south as well (*encore* becomes something like *engcora*). What stays the same is the level of politeness: use *monsieur*, *madame* or *mademoiselle* when speaking to anyone, from your first *bonjour* (and never *garçon* in restaurants!) to your last *au revoir*.

Many of the restaurants in this book don't translate their menus, so we've included the decoder below; try the section on regional specialities (pp.20–2) if an item isn't listed.

Deciphering French Menus

Hors d'œuvre et Soupes — Starters and Soups

Assiette assortie	Mixed cold hors d'oeuvres
Bisque	Shellfish soup
Bouchées	Mini vol-au-vents
Bouillon	Broth
Consommé	Clear soup
Crudités	Raw vegetable platter
Potage	Thick vegetable soup
Velouté	Thick smooth soup, often fish or chicken
Vol-au-Vent	Puff pastry case with savoury filling

Poissons et Coquillages (Crustacés) — Fish and Shellfish

Aiglefin	Little haddock
Anchois	Anchovies
Anguille	Eel
Barbue	Brill
Baudroie	Anglerfish
Belons	Rock oysters
Bigourneau	Winkle
Blanchailles	Whitebait
Brème	Bream
Brochet	Pike
Bulot	Whelk
Cabillaud	Fresh cod
Calmar	Squid
Carrelet	Plaice
Colin	Hake
Congre	Conger eel
Coques	Cockles
Coquilles St-Jacques	Scallops
Crabe	Crab
Crevettes grises	Shrimps
Crevettes roses	Prawns
Cuisses de grenouilles	Frogs' legs
Darne	Thin slice of fish
Daurade	Sea bream
Ecrevisse	Freshwater crayfish
Eperlans	Smelt
Escabèche	Fish fried, marinated, and served cold
Escargots	Snails

Espadon	Swordfish	Biftek	Beefsteak
Flétan	Halibut	Blanc	Breast or white meat
Friture	Deep fried fish	Blanquette	Stew of white meat, thickened with egg yolk
Fruits de mer	Seafood		
Gambas	Giant prawns	Boeuf	Beef
Gigot de mer	A large fish cooked whole	Boudin blanc	Sausage of white meat
Grondin	Red gurnard	Boudin noir	Black pudding
Hareng	Herring	Brochette	Meat (or fish) on a skewer
Homard	Lobster	Caille	Quail
Huîtres	Oysters	Canard, caneton	Duck, duckling
Langouste	Spiny Mediterranean lobster	Carré	The best end of a cutlet or chop
Langoustines	Dublin Bay Prawns		
Limande	Lemon sole	Cervelles	Brains
Lotte	Monkfish	Châteaubriand	Porterhouse steak
Loup (de mer)	Sea bass	Cheval	Horsemeat
Maquereau	Mackerel	Chevreau	Kid
Merlan	Whiting	Civet	Stew of rabbit (usually), marinated in wine
Morue	Salt cod		
Moules	Mussels	Confit	Meat cooked and preserved in its own fat
Oursin	Sea urchin		
Pageot	Sea bream	Contre-filet	Sirloin steak
Palourdes	Clams	Côte, côtelette	Chop, cutlet
Poulpe	Octopus	Cuisse	Thigh or leg
Praires	Small clams	Dinde, dindon	Turkey
Raie	Skate	Entrecôte	Ribsteak
Rascasse	Scorpion fish	Epaule	Shoulder
Rouget	Red mullet	Estouffade	A meat stew marinated, fried, and then braised
Saumon	Salmon		
Saint-Pierre	John Dory	Faisan	Pheasant
Sole (à la meunière)	Sole (with butter, lemon and parsley)	Faux filet	Sirloin
		Foie	Liver
Stockfisch	Stockfish (wind-dried cod)	Foie gras	Goose liver
Telline	Tiny clam	Frais de veau	Veal testicles
Thon	Tuna	Fricadelle	Meatball
Truite	Trout	Gésier	Gizzard
Truite saumonée	Salmon trout	Gibier	Game
		Gigot	Leg of lamb

Viandes et Volailles Meat and Poultry

		Graisse	Fat
Agneau (de pré salé)	Lamb (grazed in fields by the sea)	Grillade	Grilled meat
		Grive	Thrush
Ailerons	Chicken wings	Jambon	Ham
Andouillette	Chitterling (tripe) sausage	Jarret	Knuckle
		Langue	Tongue

Lapereau	Young rabbit
Lapin	Rabbit
Lard (lardons)	Bacon (diced bacon)
Lièvre	Hare
Maigret (de canard)	Breast (of duck)
Marcassin	Young wild boar
Merguez	Spicy red sausage
Museau	Muzzle
Navarin	Lamb stew with root vegetables
Noix de veau	Topside of veal
Oie	Goose
Os	Bone
Perdreau (perdrix)	Partridge
Petit salé	Salt pork
Pieds	Trotters
Pintade	Guinea fowl
Porc	Pork
Poularde	Capon
Poulet	Chicken
Poussin	Baby chicken
Queue de boeuf	Oxtail
Ris (de veau)	Sweetbreads (veal)
Rognons	Kidneys
Rôti	Roast
Sanglier	Wild boar
Saucisses	Sausages
Saucisson	Dry sausage, like salami
Selle (d'agneau)	Saddle (of lamb)
Steak tartare	Raw minced beef, often topped with a raw egg yolk
Suprême de volaille	Fillet of chicken breast and wing
Tête (de veau)	Head (calf's)
Toro	Bull's meat
Tortue	Turtle
Tournedos	Thick round slices of beef fillet
Travers de porc	Spare ribs
Tripes	Tripe
Veau	Veal
Venaison	Venison

Légumes, herbes, etc.	**Vegetables, herbs, etc.**
Ail	Garlic
Algue	Seaweed
Aneth	Dill
Artichaut	Artichoke
Asperges	Asparagus
Aubergine	Aubergine (eggplant)
Avocat	Avocado
Basilic	Basil
Betterave	Beetroot
Cannelle	Cinnamon
Céleri (-rave)	Celery (celeriac)
Cèpes	Wild dark brown mushrooms
Champignons	Mushrooms
Chanterelles	Wild yellow mushrooms
Chicorée	Curly endive
Chou	Cabbage
Choufleur	Cauliflower
Choucroute	Sauerkraut
Ciboulettes	Chives
Citrouille	Pumpkin
Coeur de palmier	Heart of palm
Concombre	Cucumber
Cornichons	Gherkins
Courgettes	Courgettes (zucchini)
Cresson	Watercress
Echalote	Shallot
Endive	Chicory
Epinards	Spinach
Estragon	Tarragon
Fenouil	Fennel
Fèves	Broad beans
Flageolets	White beans
Fleurs de courgette	Courgette blossoms
Frites	Chips (French fries)
Genièvre	Juniper
Gingembre	Ginger
Girofle	Clove
Haricots (rouges, blancs)	Beans (kidney, white)
Haricots verts	Green (French) beans

Jardinière	With diced garden vegetables	*Acajou*	Cashew
Laitue	Lettuce	*Amandes*	Almonds
Laurier	Bay leaf	*Ananas*	Pineapple
Lentilles	Lentils	*Banane*	Banana
Maïs (épis de)	Sweet corn (on the cob)	*Bavarois*	Mousse or custard in a mould
Marjolaine	Marjoram	*Biscuit*	Cake
Menthe	Mint	*Bombe*	Ice-cream dessert
Mesclum	Salad of various leaves		in round mould
Morilles	Morel mushrooms	*Bonbons*	Sweets, candy
Moutarde	Mustard	*Brebis*	Sheep cheese
Navet	Turnip	*Brioche*	Light sweet yeast bread
Oignons	Onions	*Brugnon*	Nectarine
Oseille	Sorrel	*Cacahouète*	Peanut
Panais	Parsnip	*Cassis*	Blackcurrant
Persil	Parsley	*Cérise*	Cherry
Petits pois	Peas	*Charlotte*	Custard and fruit
Piment	Pimento		in almond biscuits
Pissenlits	Dandelion greens	*Chausson*	Turnover
Poireaux	Leeks	*Chèvre*	Goat cheese
Pois chiches	Chick-peas	*Citron*	Lemon
Pois mange-tout	Sugar-peas	*Citron vert*	Lime
Poivron	Bell pepper	*Clafoutis*	Berry tart
Pomme de terre	Potato	*Coing*	Quince
Primeurs	Young vegetables	*Compôte*	Stewed fruit
Radis	Radishes	*Corbeille de fruits*	Basket of fruit
Raifort	Horseradish	*Coupe*	Ice cream
Riz	Rice	*Crème anglaise*	Custard
Romarin	Rosemary	*Crème Chantilly*	Sweet whipped cream
Safran	Saffron	*Crème fraîche*	Sour cream
Salade verte	Green salad	*Crème pâtissière*	Thick cream pastry
Salsafi	Salsify		filling made with eggs
Sarnette	Savory	*Dattes*	Dates
Sarrasin	Buckwheat	*Figues (de Barbarie)*	Figs (prickly pear)
Sauge	Sage	*Fraises (de bois)*	Strawberries (wild)
Seigle	Rye	*Framboises*	Raspberries
Serpolet	Wild thyme	*Fromage (plateau de)*	Cheese (board)
Thym	Thyme	*Fromage blanc*	Yoghurty cream cheese
Truffes	Truffles	*Fromage frais*	Similar to sour cream
		Fruit de la passion	Passion fruit

Fruits, Desserts, Noix — Fruits, Desserts, Nuts

		Gâteau	Cake
		Génoise	Rich sponge cake
Abricot	Apricot	*Glace*	Ice cream

Grenade	Pomegranate	A l'anglais	Boiled
Groseilles	Red currants, gooseberries	A l'arlésienne	With aubergines, potatoes, tomatoes, onions, rice
Lavande	Lavender		
Macarons	Macaroons	A la châtelaine	With chestnut purée and artichoke hearts
Madeleines	Small sponge cakes		
Mandarine	Tangerine	A la grecque	Cooked in olive oil and lemon
Mangue	Mango		
Marrons	Chestnuts	A la périgordine	In a truffle and foie gras sauce
Merise	Wild cherry		
Miel	Honey	A la provençale	Cooked with tomatoes, garlic, olive oil
Mirabelle	Mirabelle plum		
Mûres	Mulberry, blackberry	Allumettes	Strips of puff pastry
Myrtilles	Bilberries	A point	Medium steak
Noisette	Hazelnut	Au feu de bois	Cooked over a wood fire
Noix	Walnuts	Au four	Baked
Oeufs à la neige	Meringue	Auvergnat	With sausage, bacon, cabbage
Pamplemousse	Grapefruit	Baguette	Long loaf of bread
Parfait	Frozen mousse	Barquette	Pastry boat
Pastèque	Water melon	Beignets	Fritters
Pêche (blanche)	Peach (white)	Béarnaise	Sauce of egg yolks, shallots and white wine
Petits fours	Tiny cakes and pastries		
Pignons	Pine-nuts	Beurre	Butter
Pistache	Pistachio	Bien cuit	Well done steak
Poire	Pear	Bleu	Very rare steak
Pomme	Apple	Bordelaise	Red wine, bone marrow and shallot sauce
Prune	Plum		
Pruneau	Prune	Broche	Roast on a spit
Raisins (sec)	Grapes (raisins)	Chasseur	Mushrooms and shallots in white wine
Reine-clande	Greengage		
Sablé	Shortbread	Chaud	Hot
Savarin	A filled cake, shaped like a ring	Chou	Puff pastry
Tarte, tartelette	Tart, little tart	Confiture	Jam
Tarte Tropézienne	Sponge cake filled with custard and topped with nuts	Coulis	Strong clear broth
		Couteau	Knife
		Crème	Cream
Truffes	Chocolate truffles	Crêpe	Thin pancake
		Croque-monsieur	Toasted ham and cheese sandwich

Cooking terms, miscellaneous, snacks

		Croustade	Small savoury pastry
Addition	Bill	Cru	Raw
Aigre-doux	Sweet and sour	Cuillère	Spoon
Aiguillette	Thin slice	Cuit	Cooked
		Diable	Spicy mustard sauce

Emincé	Thinly sliced	*Poché*	Poached
En croûte	Cooked in a pastry crust	*A point*	Medium-done steak
En papillote	Baked in buttered paper	*Poivre*	Pepper
Epices	Spices	*Quenelles*	Dumplings of fish or poultry
Farci	Stuffed	*Raclette*	Toasted cheese with
Feuilleté	Flaky pastry		potatoes, onions and pickles
Flambé	Set aflame with alcohol	*Salé*	Salted, spicy
Forestière	With bacon and mushrooms	*Sanglant*	Rare steak
Fourchette	Fork	*Sel*	Salt
Fourré	Stuffed	*Sucré*	Sweet
Frais, fraîche	Fresh	*Timbale*	Pie cooked in dome-shaped mould
Frappé	With crushed ice	*Tranche*	Slice
Frit	Fried	*Vapeur*	Steamed
Froid	Cold	*Véronique*	Green grapes, wine,
Fromage	Cheese		and cream sauce
Fumé	Smoked	*Vinaigre*	Vinegar
Galantine	Cooked food served	*Vinaigrette*	Oil and vinegar dressing
	in cold jelly		

Boissons	**Drinks**
Galette	Flaky pastry case or pancake

Garni	With vegetables	*Bière (pression)*	Beer (draught)
(au) Gratin	Topped with crisp browned	*Bouteille (demi)*	Bottle (half)
	cheese and breadcrumbs	*Café*	Coffee
Grillé	Grilled	*Chocolat (chaud)*	Chocolate (hot)
Hachis	Minced	*Demi*	A third of a litre (beer)
Hollandaise	A sauce of butter and vinegar	*Doux*	Sweet (wine)
Huile (d'olive)	Oil (olive)	*Eau (minérale)*	Water (mineral, spring)
Marmite	Casserole	*Eau de vie*	Brandy
Médaillon	Round piece	*Eau gazeuse/*	Sparkling/still
Mijoté	Simmered	*non gazeuse, plate*	water
Mornay	Cheese sauce	*Glaçons*	Ice cubes
Nouilles	Noodles	*Infusion (or tisane)*	Herbal tea
Oeufs	Eggs	*Lait*	Milk
Pain	Bread	*Moelleux*	Semi-dry
Pané	Breaded	*Pichet*	Pitcher
Parmentier	With potatoes	*Pressé*	Fresh fruit juice
Pâte	Pastry, pasta	*Sec*	Dry
Paupiette	Rolled and filled thin	*Sirop d'orange/de citron*	Orange/lemon
	slices of fish or meat		squash
Pavé	Slab	*Thé*	Tea
Piquante	Vinegar sauce with	*Verre*	Glass
	shallots and capers	*Vin blanc/rosé/rouge*	White/rosé/red wine
Pissaladière	A kind of pizza with		
	onions, anchovies, etc.		

Ardagh, John, *France Today* (Penguin, 1987). One in Penguin's informative paperback series on contemporary Europe.

Barr, Alfred, *Henri Matisse: his Art and his Public* (Museum of Modern Art, New York, 1951).

Bishop, Morris, *Petrarch and His World* (Chatto & Windus, 1964).

Bonner, Anthony, *Songs of the Troubadours* (Allen & Unwin, 1973). An introduction to the life and times of the troubadours, with translations of best-known verses.

Cézanne, Paul, *Letters* (London, 1941).

Cook, Theodore A., *Old Provence* (London, 1905). A classic traveller's account of the region, out of print and hard to find.

Daudet, Alphonse, *Letters from my Windmill* (Penguin, 1982). Bittersweet 19th-century tales of Midi nostalgia by Van Gogh's favourite novelist.

Dumas, Alexandre, *The Count of Monte Cristo*, many editions; romantic fantastical tale of revenge, much of it set in Marseille and the Château d'If.

Durrell, Lawrence, *The Avignon Quintet* (Faber, 1974–85); lush wartime sagas that take place in Avignon and around.

Fitzgerald, F. Scott, *Tender is the Night*, many editions. 1920s Riviera decadence based on personal research.

Ford, Ford Madox, *Provence: From Minstrels to the Machine* (Allen & Unwin, 1935). A lyrical pre-war view of the region.

Fortescue, Winifred, *Perfume from Provence* (1935). Poor, intolerable Lady Fortescue's misadventures with the garlicky peasants near Nice.

Giono, Jean, *To the Slaughterhouse, Two Riders of the Storm* (Peter Owen, 1988). Giono is a major 20th-century novelist of Provence, whose deep pessimism contrasts with the sunnier views of his contemporary Pagnol.

Goldring, Douglas, *The South of France* (Macdonald, 1952). Travels and comments by another English resident.

Gramont, Sanche de, *The French: Portrait of a People* (Putnam, New York, 1969). One of the funnier attempts at the favourite French pastime: national self-analysis.

Greene, Graham, *J'Accuse: The Dark Side of Nice* (Bodley Head, 1982). The late Graham Greene, resident of Antibes, discovers the mafia connections and graft in the government of discredited mayor Jacques Médecin.

Hugo, Victor, *Les Misérables*, many editions. Injustice among the galley-slaves and basis for the hit musical.

Ladurie, Emmanuel Leroi, *Love, Death and Money in the Pays d'Oc* (Scolar, 1982).

de Larrabeiti, Michael, *The Provençal Tales* (Pavilion, 1988). Troubadours' tales, legends and stories told by shepherds around the camp fire.

Lugand, Jacques, Robert St-Jean and Jean Nougaret, *Languedoc Roman* (Zodiaque, 1975). The best of Languedoc's Romanesque architecture, with plans, lots of photos and an English translation.

Further Reading

Lyall, Archibald, *Companion Guide to the South of France* (Collins, 1978). Personal, well-written but dated guide of the entire Mediterranean coast.

Mayle, Peter, *A Year in Provence* and *Toujours Provence* (Sinclair Stevenson/Pan, 1989 and 1991). The entertaining bestsellers on ex-pat life in the Lubéron.

Mistral, Frédéric, *Miréio* and *Poème de la Rhône*, epic poems by the Nobel prize-winning Félibre, widely available in French or Provençal.

More, Carey and Julian, *A Taste of Provence* (Pavilion, 1987). Father and daughter team up to evoke the countryside and gastronomy of Provence in words and photographs.

Morris, Edwin T., *Fragrance: The Story of Perfume from Cleopatra to Chanel* (Charles Scribner & Sons, 1984).

Pagnol, Marcel, *Jean de Florette* and *Manon of the Springs*, *The Days were too Short* (Picador, 1960). Autobiography by Provence's most beloved writer.

Petrarch, Francesco, *Songs and Sonnets from Laura's Lifetime* (Anvil Press, 1985).

Pope Hennessy, James, *Aspects of Provence* (Penguin, 1952). A fussy but lyrical view of the region in the '40s and '50s.

Smollett, Tobias, *Travels through France and Italy* (London, 1776). The irrepressible, grouchy Tobias 'Smellfungus' makes modern travel writing look like advertising copy.

Stendhal, *Travels through the South of France* (London, 1971).

Süskind, Patrick, *Perfume* (Penguin, 1989). Thrilling and fragrant murder in the 18th-century perfume industry in Grasse.

Van Gogh, Vincent, *Collected Letters of Vincent Van Gogh* (New York, 1978).

Vergé, Roger, *Cuisine of the Sun* (London, 1979). The owner of the Moulin de Mougins tells some of his secrets of nouvelle Provençal cooking.

Whitfield, Sarah, *Fauvism* (Thames and Hudson, 1991). A good introduction to the movement that changed art history.

Worwood, Valerie, *Aromantics* (Pan, 1987). An amusing look at aromatherapy.

Wylie, L., *Village in the Vaucluse* (Harvard University Press, 1971). The third edition of a very readable sociologist's classic based on the village of Roussillon.

Zeldin, Theodore, *France 1845–1945* (Oxford University Press, 1980). Five well-written volumes on all aspects of the period.

Main page references are in **bold**; page references to maps are in *italic*

Index

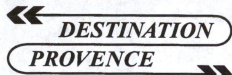